Windows NT™
Resource
Guide

Microsoft® **WINDOWS NT**

RESOURCE KIT

Volume 1 of the 3 volume set

PUBLISHED BY
Microsoft Press
A Division of Microsoft Corporation
One Microsoft Way
Redmond, Washington 98052-6399

Library of Congress Cataloging-in-Publication Data
Microsoft Windows NT resource kit / Microsoft Corporation.
     p.   cm.
    Includes indexes.
    Contents: v. 1. Resource guide -- v. 2. Messages -- v.
3. Optimizing Windows NT.
    ISBN 1-55615-598-0 (v. 1) -- ISBN 1-55615-600-6 (v. 2)
-- 1-55615-619-7 (v. 3)
    1. Operating systems (Computers) 2. Windows NT. I. Microsoft
Corporation.
QA76.76.O63M5238   1993
005.4'469--dc20   93-4950
                                CIP

Printed and bound in the United States of America.

2 3 4 5 6 7 8 9 FFG 9 8 7 6 5 4

Distributed to the book trade in Canada by Macmillan of Canada, a division of Canada Publishing Corporation.

British Cataloging-in-Publication Data available from Penguin Books Ltd., Harmondsworth, Middlesex, England

Apple, AppleTalk, and Macintosh are registered trademarks of Apple Computer, Inc. CompuServe is a registered trademark of CompuServe Inc. Corel is a registered trademark of Corel Systems Corporation. Alpha AXP is a trademark of Digital Equipment Corporation. Hitachi is a registered trademark of Hitachi, Ltd. IBM and OS/2 are registered trademarks of International Business Machines Corporation. Intel is a registered trademark of Intel Corporation. Lotus is a registered trademark of Lotus Development Corporation. CodeView, Microsoft, Microsoft Access, MS, MS-DOS, QuickC, and XENIX are registered trademarks and Win32, Windows, and Windows NT are trademarks of Microsoft Corporation in the U.S.A. and other countries. MIPS is a registered trademark and R4000 is a trademark of MIPS Computer Systems, Inc. NEC is a registered trademark of NEC Corporation. Denon is a registered trademark of Nippon Columbis Co., Inc. NT is a trademark of Northern Telecom Limited in the U.S.A. and other countries. Pioneer is a registered trademark of Pioneer Kabushiki Kaisha. Tandy is a registered trademark of Tandy Corporation.

Technical Writers: Sharon Carroll, Mark Williams, and Stephen Wood
Database Designer and System Administrator: Cary E. Reinstein
Team Manager: Peggy Etchevers
Technical Editor: Sharon Tighe
Production Team: Donalee Edwards, Wendy Boyd, Risa P. Suzuki, and Yong Ok Chung
Graphic Designer: Sue Wyble
Interface Design Consultant: Bill O'Daly
Technical Consultants: Donald Funk and Chris St. Valentine

U.S. Patent No. 4955066

Contents

PART II   Setting Up Windows NT

PART III   Using Windows NT

PART IV   Windows NT Registry

PART V   Networking

PART VI Migrating and Compatibility

PART VIII   Appendixes

Introduction

Welcome to the *Windows NT Resource Kit*, Volume 1: *Windows NT Resource Guide.*

This manual is designed for people who are, or who want to become, expert users of Microsoft® Windows NT™ and Microsoft Windows NT Advanced Server. The *Windows NT Resource Guide* presents detailed, easy-to-read technical information to help you better manage how Windows NT is used at your site. It contains specific information for system administrators who are responsible for installing, managing, and integrating Windows NT in a network or multiuser environment.

The *Windows NT Resource Guide* is a technical supplement to the documentation included as part of the Windows NT product and does not replace that information as the source for learning how to use Windows NT features and utilities.

This introduction includes three kinds of information you can use to get started:

- The first section outlines the contents of this book, so that you can quickly find technical details about specific elements of Windows NT.

- The second section introduces the Resource Guide disks.

- The third section describes the conventions used to present information in this book.

About the Resource Guide

This guide includes the following chapters. Additional tables of contents are included in each part to help you find the information you want quickly.

Part I, About Windows NT

Chapter 1, "Windows NT Architecture," describes the architecture of Windows NT and discusses the components of its modular design.

Chapter 2, "Windows NT Security Model," describes in detail the security architecture for Windows NT. This security architecture is pervasive throughout the entire operating system, from logon security to access control for files, directories, printers and other resources on the system.

Part II, Setting Up Windows NT

Chapter 3, "Customizing Windows NT Setup," contains a technical discussion of the Windows NT Setup program, details about setting up Windows NT on a network, and instructions for creating a custom installation routine for automated setup.

Chapter 4, "Windows NT Files," describes the purpose of each file in the Windows NT directory structure.

Part III, Using Windows NT

Chapter 5, "File Systems and Advanced Disk Management," describes the three main file systems supported by Windows NT—the file allocation table (FAT), the high-performance file system (HPFS), and the Windows NT file system (NTFS). This chapter also describes how to organize and safeguard data on disk using the Windows NT disk management techniques.

Chapter 6, "Printing," presents the components of the Windows NT printing model and describes some advanced printing features you can use.

Chapter 7, "Fonts," examines technical issues related to fonts in Windows NT, focusing on the new TrueType® font technology.

Chapter 8, "Microsoft Mail," presents information about the Microsoft Mail application provided with Windows NT. This chapter describes the architecture of Mail and tips for customizing Mail.

Chapter 9, "Microsoft Schedule+," presents information about the Microsoft Schedule+ application provided with Windows NT, including architecture and key features of interest to system administrators.

Part IV, Windows NT Registry

Chapter 10, "Overview of the Windows NT Registry," describes the Windows NT Registry, which replaces the configuration files used with MS-DOS and the .INI files used with Microsoft Windows™ for MS-DOS®.

Chapter 11, "Registry Editor and Registry Administration," describes what Registry Editor is and how to use it, with an emphasis on protecting the Registry contents and using Registry Editor to monitor and maintain the system configuration on remote computers.

Chapter 12, "Configuration Management and the Registry," provides some examples of problem-solving tasks that involve changes made to the Registry using Registry Editor.

Chapter 13, "Initialization Files and the Registry," describes how .INI files and other configuration files are used under Windows NT and how these values are stored in the Registry.

Chapter 14, "Registry Value Entries," identifies the Registry entries that you can add or change using the Registry Editor to configure system startup, network adapter cards, device drivers, services, Mail and Schedule+, user preferences, fonts and printing, and the Windows NT subsystems.

Part V, Networking

Chapter 15, "Windows NT Networking Architecture," contains information for the support professional who may not have a local area network background. This chapter provides a technical discussion of networking concepts and discusses the networking components included with Windows NT.

Chapter 16, "Network Interoperability," describes how Windows NT works together with your existing Novell networks, IBM mainframe systems, and UNIX systems.

Chapter 17, "Network Security and Administration," describes how security is implemented for workgroups and domains under Windows NT, including local logon and pass-through validation for trusted domains and network browsing.

Chapter 18, "Using NBF with Windows NT," describes the implementation of the NetBIOS Extended User Interface (NetBEUI) protocol under Windows NT, including how network traffic and sessions are managed.

Chapter 19, "Using TCP/IP with Windows NT," describes how TCP/IP on Windows NT works and provides specific details for administering and tuning Transmission Control Protocol/Interface Protocol (TCP/IP) and Simple Network Management Protocol (SNMP).

Chapter 20, "Using NWLink with Windows NT," shows how to integrate Windows NT into Novell NetWare environments using two software components, the NetWare Redirector and Microsoft NWLink.

Chapter 21, "Using DLC with Windows NT," presents details about the Data Link Control (DLC) protocol device driver in Windows NT, which provides connectivity to IBM mainframes and to local area network printers attached directly to the network.

Chapter 22, "Client-Server Connectivity on Windows NT," discusses how MS-DOS, Windows, Windows NT, and OS/2 client workstations communicate with Windows NT databases, focusing on Ingres™ and Microsoft SQL Server as examples of distributed applications.

Part VI, Migration and Compatibility

Chapter 23, "Windows 3.x Compatibility and Migration," presents issues for running versions of Microsoft Windows for MS-DOS under Windows NT and describes how that subsystem is implemented.

Chapter 24, "OS/2 Compatibility," describes how to run Microsoft OS/2 1.*x* applications under Windows NT and also presents the related application programming interface (API) and implementation of the OS/2 subsystem.

Chapter 25, "POSIX Compatibility," describes how to run POSIX applications and also presents information about POSIX conformance and the implementation of this subsystem under Windows NT.

Part VII, Troubleshooting

Chapter 26, "Troubleshooting," provides specific information for troubleshooting problems, showing the key steps for isolating and solving common problems with software and hardware under Windows NT.

Part VIII, Appendixes

Appendix A, "Windows NT Resource Directory," provides a list of resources for product support, training, and consulting for Windows NT, plus information about related Microsoft Press books and the Windows NT driver library.

Appendix B, "Remote Access Server Administration," provides administrators with implementation details for the remote access service, including configuring modems, troubleshooting hardware and software, and using MODEM.INF.

Appendix C, "Windows NT User Rights," describes the advanced user rights defined by Windows NT.

Appendix D, "International Considerations," describes Unicode™ support in Windows NT, plus information about supported locales, code pages, and national language support (NLS) information for the subsystems.

Appendix E, "Hardware Compatibility List," presents a complete list of the tested hardware that is compatible with Windows NT, including microprocessors, small computer system interface (SCSI) adapters and drives, disk controllers, video displays, network adapters, audio adapters, modems, pointing devices, uninterruptible power supplies, keyboards, and printers.

The **Glossary** presents a rich set of definitions for the technical terms that appear in the *Windows NT Resource Guide.*

Resource Guide Disks

The disks that accompany the *Windows NT Resource Guide* include a collection of information resources, tools, and utilities that can make working with Windows NT even easier. These include the following kinds of tools:

Administrative Tools

- Net Watcher shows who is connected to shared directories.
- PERMS.EXE displays a user's access permissions to a specified file or set of files.
- POSIX Utilities, including CAT.EXE, CHMOD.EXE, GREP.EXE, VI.EXE, and others.
- Server Manager for Remote Computers provides for remote administration of replication, services, shared and open resources, and so on.
- User Manager for Remote Computers provides for remote administration of security.

- Command Scheduler allows you to easily schedule commands and programs to run at a specified time and date.

- REMOTE.EXE lets you start and control command line programs remotely.

- NET2COM.EXE allows MS-DOS, Microsoft Windows 3.*x*, and Windows NT clients to use modems attached to a Windows NT server for outbound modem services.

Desktop Tools

- Animated Cursor Editor creates animated cursors.

- TopDesk provides a powerful way to switch between and organize applications while conserving screen space.

- Image Editor allows you to edit or create cursor and icon images.

File System Tools

- DIRUSE.EXE shows disk space usage.

- SCOPY.EXE copies files and directories with their security intact.

- WinDiff graphically shows the difference between two files or directories.

Performance and System Monitoring Tools

- Browser Monitor monitors the status of browsers on selected domains.

- Domain Monitor monitors the status of servers in a domain.

- Process Viewer displays everything you want to know about running processes.

- QuickSlice shows the total CPU used by each process in the system.

- SMBTRACE.EXE, a network diagnostic tool that traces Server Message Blocks (SMBs) sent and received by the server and redirector.

Registry Tools

- REGBACK.EXE and REGREST.EXE, used to back up and restore Registry hives without the use of a tape drive.

- REGENTRY.HLP, a database of Registry entries. Use this Help file while working in Registry Editor to find ranges, minimum-maximum values, and instructions for setting specific values in the Registry.

Setup and Troubleshooting Tools

- Computer Profile Setup for easy installation of Windows NT on multiple computers.

- NTCARD.HLP assists you in the Setup of adapter cards for Windows NT.

- REPAIR.EXE updates the Emergency Repair Disk.

- TROUBLE.HLP provides the same information as the Troubleshooting flowcharts (Chapter 26) in online form.

- OEMNSVKT.INF installs the AppleTalk Protocol and Services for Macintosh administrative tools.

▶ **To see a list of the files and installation instructions**

- See README.WRI on the first disk.

▶ **To find out how to use a tool or utility**

- See RKTOOLS.HLP on the first disk.

Conventions in This Manual

This document assumes that you have read the Windows NT documentation set and that you are familiar with using menus, dialog boxes, and other features of the Windows family of products. It also assumes that you have installed Windows NT on your system and that you are using a mouse. For keyboard equivalents to menu and mouse actions, see the Microsoft Windows NT online Help.

This document uses several conventions to help you identify information. The following table describes the typographical conventions used in the *Windows NT Resource Guide*.

Convention	Used for
bold	MS-DOS–style command and utility names such as **copy** or **ping** and switches such as **/?** or **-h**. Also used for Registry value names, such as **IniFileMapping**.
italic	Parameters for which you can supply specific values. For example, the Windows NT root directory appears in a path name as *SystemRoot*\SYSTEM32, where *SystemRoot* can be C:\WINNT or some other value.
ALL CAPITALS	Directory names, filenames, and acronyms. For example, DLC stands for Data Link Control; C:\PAGEFILE.SYS is a file in the boot sector.
Monospace	Sample text from batch and .INI files, Registry paths, and screen text in non-Windows–based applications.

Other conventions in this document include the following:

- "MS-DOS" refers to Microsoft MS-DOS version 3.3 or later.

- "Windows-based application" is used as a shorthand term to refer to an application that is designed to run with 16-bit Windows and does not run without Windows. All 16-bit and 32-bit Windows applications follow similar conventions for the arrangement of menus, dialog box styles, and keyboard and mouse use.

- "MS-DOS–based application" is used as a shorthand term to refer to an application that is designed to run with MS-DOS but not specifically with Windows or Windows NT and is not able to take full advantage of their graphical or memory management features.

- "Command prompt" refers to the command line where you type MS-DOS–style commands. Typically, you see characters such as C:\> to show the location of the command prompt on your screen. In Windows NT, you can double-click the MS-DOS Prompt icon in Program Manager to use the command prompt.

- An instruction to "type" any information means to press a key or a sequence of keys, and then press the ENTER key.

- Mouse instructions in this document, such as "Click the OK button" or "Drag an icon in File Manager," use the same meanings as the descriptions of mouse actions in the *Windows NT System Guide* and the Windows online tutorial.

PART I

About Windows NT

Part One provides an overview of the software components that make up Windows NT and its security subsystem. This part contains more theory and less practice but provides a foundation that will help you understand the technical details you'll find while reading this *Resource Guide* and while working with Windows NT.

C H A P T E R   1

Windows NT Architecture

When users first look at Microsoft® Windows NT, they notice the familiar Windows 3.*x* interface and appreciate the fact that they can continue to run their favorite applications for Microsoft Windows 3.*x*, MS-DOS, and Microsoft OS/2 1.*x*. But what is visible to users is only a small part of Windows NT—a host of powerful features lie beneath the surface.

Windows NT is a preemptive, multitasking operating system based on a 32-bit design. It includes security and networking services as fundamental components of the base operating system. Windows NT also provides compatibility with many other operating systems, file systems, and networks. This operating system runs on both complex instruction set computing (CISC) and reduced instruction set computing (RISC) processors. Windows NT also supports high-performance computing by providing Kernel support for computers that have symmetric multiprocessor configurations.

Windows NT only looks familiar. This chapter describes the powerful features under the graphical user interface. It provides an overview by introducing the Windows NT components and showing how they interrelate. Other chapters in this book provide the details, explaining more about particular components such as the Windows NT security model, integrated networking features and connectivity options, Windows NT file systems, the printing system, and the Registry.

Windows NT Design Goals

Windows NT was not designed as a reworked version of an earlier product. Its architects began with a clean sheet of paper and this list of goals for a new operating system:

- Compatibility. In making this operating system *compatible*, the designers included the well-received Windows interface and provided support for existing file systems (including FAT and HPFS) and applications (including those written for MS-DOS, OS/2 1.*x*, Windows 3.*x*, and POSIX). The designers also provided network connectivity to several existing networking environments.

- Portability. *Portability* means that Windows NT runs on both CISC and RISC processors. CISC includes computers running with Intel® 80386® or higher processors. RISC includes computers with MIPS® R4000™ or Digital Alpha AXP™ processors.

- Scalability. *Scalability* means that Windows NT is not bound to single-processor architectures but takes full advantage of symmetric multiprocessing hardware. Today, Windows NT can run on computers with from 1 to 32 processors. Windows NT allows you to add bigger and faster workstations and servers to your corporate network as your business requirements grow. And it gives you the advantage of having the same development environment for both workstations and servers.

- Security. Windows NT includes a uniform *security* architecture that meets the requirements for a U.S. government rating. For the corporate environment, it provides a safe environment to run critical applications.

- Distributed processing. *Distributed processing* means that Windows NT is designed with networking built into the base operating system. Windows NT also allows for connectivity to a variety of host environments through its support of multiple transport protocols and high-level client-server facilities including named pipes, remote procedure calls (RPCs), and Windows Sockets.

- Reliability and robustness. *Reliability and robustness* refer to an architecture that protects applications from damaging each other and the operating system. Windows NT employs the robustness of structured exception handling throughout its entire architecture. It includes a recoverable file system and provides protection through its built-in security and advanced memory management techniques.

- *Internationalization* means that Windows NT will be offered in many countries around the world, in local languages, and that it supports the International Organization for Standardization (ISO) Unicode standard.

- Extensibility. *Extensibility* points to the modular design of Windows NT, which, as described in the next section, provides for the flexibility of adding future modules at several levels within the operating system.

Windows NT Architectural Modules

As Figure 1.1 shows, Windows NT is a modular (rather than monolithic) operating system composed of several relatively simple modules. From the lowest level to the top of the architecture, the Windows NT modules are the Hardware Abstraction Layer (HAL), the Kernel, the Executive, the protected subsystems (included as part of the security model), and the environment subsystems.

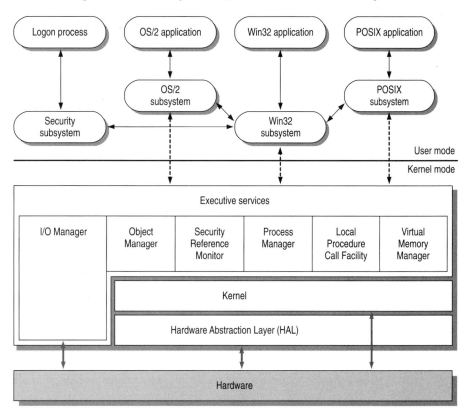

Figure 1.1   Windows NT Modular Architecture

Briefly, these layers perform the following functions.

The *Hardware Abstraction Layer* (HAL) virtualizes hardware interfaces, making the hardware dependencies transparent to the rest of the operating system. This allows Windows NT to be portable from one hardware platform to another.

The *Kernel* is at the core of this layered architecture and manages the most basic operations of Windows NT. This component is designed to be small and efficient. The Kernel is responsible for thread dispatching, multiprocessor synchronization, hardware exception handling, and the implementation of low-level, hardware-dependent functions.

The *Executive* is the Kernel-mode module that provides basic operating system services to the environment subsystems. It includes several components; each manages a particular set of system services. One component, the Security Reference Monitor, works together with the protected subsystems to provide a pervasive security model for the system.

Environment subsystems are user-mode protected servers that run and support programs from different operating systems environments. Examples of these subsystems are the Win32™ subsystem and the OS/2 subsystem.

The remainder of this chapter describes in detail these architectural components of Windows NT, beginning with the Hardware Abstraction Layer, the layer seated between the computer's hardware and the rest of the operating system.

Hardware Abstraction Layer

The Hardware Abstraction Layer (HAL) is a thin layer of software provided by the hardware manufacturer that hides, or *abstracts*, hardware differences from higher layers of the operating system. Thus, through the filter provided by HAL, different types of hardware all look alike to the operating system, removing the need to specifically tailor the operating system to the hardware with which it communicates.

The goal for HAL was to provide routines that allow a single device driver to support the same device on all platforms. HAL allows a large number of variations in hardware platforms for a single processor architecture without requiring a separate version of the operating system for each one.

HAL routines are called from both the base operating system and from device drivers. For drivers, HAL provides the ability to support a wide variety of input/output (I/O) architectures, instead of either being restricted to a single hardware model or needing extensive adaptation for each new hardware device.

HAL is also responsible for hiding the details of symmetric multiprocessing hardware from the rest of the operating system.

Kernel

Working very closely with the HAL is the Kernel, the heart of Windows NT. It schedules activities for the computer processor to perform. If the computer has multiple processors, the Kernel synchronizes activity among the processors to optimize performance.

The activities the Kernel schedules are called *threads*, the most basic entity in the system that can be scheduled. Threads are defined in the context of a process, (described more fully later in "Process Manager") which represents an address space, a set of *objects* visible to the process, and a set of threads that runs in the context of the process. Objects are resources that can be manipulated by the operating system. (These are discussed more fully in the "Object Manager" section.)

The Kernel dispatches threads in a way that ensures that the system's processor is always as busy as possible, processing the highest-priority threads first. (There are 32 priorities distributed across two priority classes—Real-time and Variable.) This helps make the operating system as efficient as possible.

The Kernel also handles hardware exceptions, provides power-failure recovery, and implements low-level, hardware-dependent functions.

Subcomponents at the Executive level, such as the I/O Manager and the Process Manager, use the Kernel to synchronize activities. They also rely on the Kernel for higher levels of abstraction, called Kernel objects, which are exported within user-level application programming interface (API) calls.

The Kernel manages two types of objects, called *Kernel objects*, because they are used only by the Kernel.

- Dispatcher objects. This includes events, mutants, mutexes, semaphores, threads, and timers. Dispatcher objects have a signal state (signaled or nonsignaled) and control the dispatching and synchronization of system operations.

- Control objects. This includes asynchronous procedure calls, interrupts, power notifies, power statuses, processes, and profiles. Control objects are used to control the operation of the Kernel but do not affect dispatching or synchronization.

Table 1.1 describes how the Executive uses each type of dispatcher object.

Table 1.1   Dispatcher Objects

Object type	Description
Event	Used to record the occurrence of an event and synchronize it with some action that is to be performed.
Mutant	One of two objects that the Kernel provides for controlling mutually exclusive access to a resource. This type of object is intended for use in providing a user-mode mutual exclusion mechanism that has ownership semantics. It can also be used in Kernel mode.
Mutex	The other of two objects that the Kernel provides for controlling mutually exclusive access to a resource. This type of object can only be used in Kernel mode and is intended to provide a deadlock-free mutual exclusion mechanism with ownership and other special system semantics.
Semaphore	Used to control access to a resource, but not necessarily in a mutually exclusive fashion. A semaphore object acts as a gate through which a variable number of threads may pass concurrently, up to a specified limit. The gate is open (signaled state) as long as there are resources available. When the number of resources specified by the limit are concurrently in use, the gate is closed (nonsignaled state).
Thread	The agent that runs program code and is dispatched to be run by the Kernel. Each thread is associated with a process object, which specifies the virtual address space mapping for the thread and accumulates thread run time. Several thread objects can be associated with a single process object, which enables the concurrent execution of multiple threads in a single address space (possibly simultaneous execution in a multiprocessor system).
Timer	Used to record the passage of time.

Table 1.2 describes how the Executive uses each type of control object.

Table 1.2   Control Objects

Object type	Description
Asynchronous Procedure Call	Used to break into the execution of a specified thread and cause a procedure to be called in a specified processor mode.
Interrupt	Used to connect an interrupt source to an interrupt service routine via an entry in an Interrupt Dispatch Table (IDT). Each processor has an IDT that is used to dispatch interrupts that occur on that processor.
Power notify	Used to automatically have a specified function called when power is restored after a power failure.
Power status	Used to check whether the power has already failed.
Process	Used to represent the virtual address space and control information necessary for the execution of a set of thread objects. A process object contains a pointer to an address map, a list of ready threads containing thread objects while the process is not in the balance set, a list of threads that belong to the process, the total accumulated time for all threads executing within the process, a base priority, and a default thread affinity. A process object must be initialized before any thread objects that specify the process as their parent can be initialized.
Profile	Used to measure the distribution of run time within a block of code. Both user and system code may be profiled.

Generally, the Kernel does not implement any policy since this is the responsibility of the Executive. However, the Kernel does make policy decisions about when it is appropriate to remove processes from memory.

The Kernel runs entirely in Kernel mode and is nonpageable. Software within the Kernel is not preemptible and therefore cannot be context-switched, whereas all software outside the Kernel is almost always preemptible and can be context-switched.

The Kernel can run simultaneously on all processors in a multiprocessor configuration, synchronizing access to critical regions as appropriate.

The third and most intricate module that runs in Kernel mode is the Executive. The next several pages describe the functions of the Executive and its components.

Windows NT Executive

The Executive manages the interface between the Kernel and the environment subsystems by providing a set of common services that all environment subsystems can use. Each group of services is managed by one of these separate components of the Executive:

- Object Manager
- Virtual Memory Manager
- Process Manager
- Local Procedure Call Facility
- I/O Manager
- Security Reference Monitor which, with the Logon and Security protected subsystems, makes up the Windows NT security model

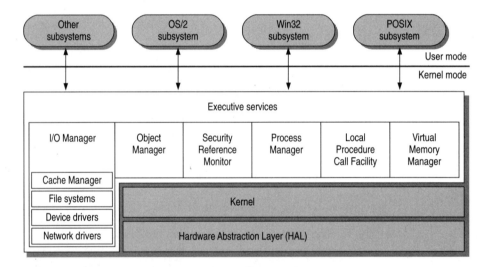

Figure 1.2   Windows NT Executive and Its Components

A thin top layer of the Executive is called the Executive Services. The Executive Services shown in Figure 1.2 route messages from one Windows NT component to another. The following sections describe the role of each Executive component.

Object Manager

Objects are run-time instances of a particular object type that can be manipulated by an operating system process. An *object type* includes a system-defined data type, a list of operations that can be performed upon it (such as wait, create, or cancel), and a set of object attributes. Object Manager is the part of the Windows NT Executive that provides uniform rules for retention, naming, and security of objects.

Before a process can manipulate a Windows NT object, it must first acquire a handle to the object. An *object handle* includes access control information and a pointer to the object itself. All object handles are created through Object Manager.

Note The Executive does not distinguish between a file handle and an object handle. Thus, the same routines that are used to create a file handle can be used to create an object handle.

Like other Windows NT components, Object Manager is extensible so that new object types can be defined as technology grows and changes.

In addition, Object Manager manages the global name space for Windows NT and tracks the creation and use of objects by any process. This name space is used to access all named objects that are contained in the local computer environment. Some of the objects that can have names include the following:

- Directory objects
- Object type objects
- Symbolic link objects
- Semaphore and event objects
- Process and thread objects

- Section and segment objects
- Port objects
- Device objects
- File system objects
- File objects

The object name space is modeled after a hierarchical file system, where directory names in a path are separated by a backslash (\). You can see object names in this form, for example, when you double-click entries in the Event Viewer log, as shown in the following illustration.

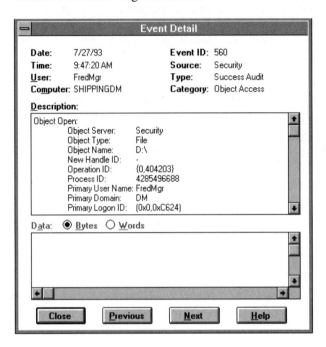

Process Manager

Process Manager is the component that tracks two types of objects—process objects and thread objects. A process is defined as an address space, a set of objects (resources) visible to the process, and a set of threads that run in the context of the process. A thread is most the basic schedulable entity in the system. It contains its own set of registers, its own Kernel stack, a thread environment block, and user stack in the address space of its process.

Process Manager is the Windows NT component that manages the creation and deletion of processes. It provides a standard set of services for creating and using threads and processes in the context of a particular operating system environment. Beyond that, Process Manager does little to dictate rules about threads and processes. Instead, the Windows NT design allows for robust environment subsystems that can define specific rules about threads and processes.

Process Manager does not impose any hierarchy or grouping rules for processes, nor does it enforce any parent/child relationships.

The Windows NT process structure works in conjunction with the security model and the Virtual Memory Manager to provide to provide interprocess protection. Each process is assigned a security access token, called the primary token of the process. This token is used by the Windows NT access-validation routines when threads in the process reference protected objects. For more information about how Windows NT uses security access tokens, see Chapter 2, "Windows NT Security Model."

Virtual Memory Manager

The memory architecture for Windows NT is a demand-paged virtual memory system. It is based on a flat, linear address space accessed via 32-bit addresses.

Virtual memory refers to the fact that the operating system can actually allocate more memory than the computer physically has. Each process is allocated a unique virtual address space, which is a set of addresses available for the process's threads to use. This virtual address space is divided into equal blocks, or *pages*. Every process is allocated its own virtual address space, which appears to be 4 gigabytes (GB) in size—2 GB reserved for program storage and 2 GB reserved for system storage.

Demand paging refers to a method by which data is moved in pages from physical memory to a temporary paging file on disk. As the data is needed by a process, it is paged back into physical memory.

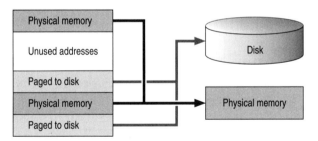

Figure 1.3   Conceptual View of Virtual Memory

The Virtual Memory Manager maps virtual addresses in the process's address space to physical pages in the computer's memory. In doing so, it hides the physical organization of memory from the process's threads. This ensures that the thread can access its process's memory as needed, but not the memory of other processes. Therefore, as illustrated by Figure 1.4, a thread's view of its process's virtual memory is much simpler than the real arrangement of pages in physical memory.

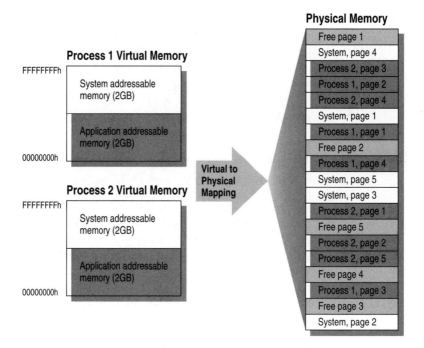

Figure 1.4   Protecting Processes' Memory

Because each process has a separate address space, a thread in one process cannot view or modify the memory of another process without authorization.

Local Procedure Call Facility

Applications and environment subsystems have a client-server relationship. That is, the client (an application) makes calls to the environment server (a subsystem) to satisfy a request for some type of system services. To allow for a client-server relationship between applications and environment subsystems, Windows NT provides a communication mechanism between them. The Executive implements a message-passing facility called a Local Procedure Call (LPC) facility. It works very much like the Remote Procedure Call (RPC) facility used for networked processing (described in Chapter 15, "Windows NT Networking Architecture"). However, the LPC facility is optimized for two processes running on the same computer.

Applications communicate with environment subsystems by passing messages via the LPC Facility. The message-passing process is hidden from the client applications by function *stubs* (nonexecutable placeholders used by calls from the server environment) provided in the form of special dynamic link libraries (DLLs), as illustrated by Figure 1.5.

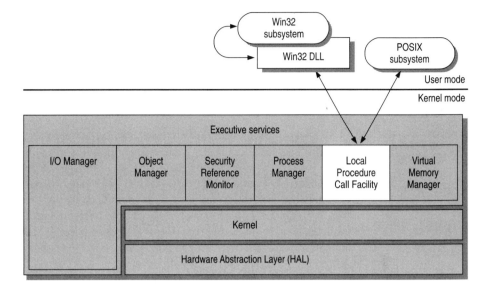

Figure 1.5   Interaction with the Local Procedure Call Facility

When an application makes an application program interface (API) call to an environment subsystem, the stub in the client (application) process packages the parameters for the call and sends them to a server (subsystem) process that implements the call. It is the LPC facility that allows the stub procedure to pass the data to the server process and wait for a response.

For example, consider how this process works in the Win32 subsystem. When a Win32 application is loaded to run, it is linked to a DLL that contains stubs for all of the functions in Win32 API. When the application calls a Win32 function, the call is processed as follows [where **CreateWindow()** is a sample Win32 function]:

1. The **CreateWindow()** stub function in the DLL is called by the client Win32 application.

2. The stub function constructs a message that contains all of the data needed to create a window and sends the message to the Win32 server process (that is, the Win32 subsystem).

3. The Win32 subsystem receives the message and calls the real **CreateWindow()** function. The window is created.

4. The Win32 subsystem sends a message containing the results of the **CreateWindow()** function back the stub function in the DLL.

5. The stub function unpacks the server message from the subsystem and returns the results to the client Win32 application.

From the application's perspective, the **CreateWindow()** function in the DLL created the window. The application does not know that the work was actually performed by the Win32 server process (the Win32 subsystem), that a message was sent to make it happen, or even that the Win32 server process exists.

I/O Manager

I/O Manager is the part of the Windows NT Executive that manages all input and output for the operating system. A large part of the I/O Manager's role is to manage communications between drivers. I/O Manager supports all file system drivers, hardware device drivers, and network device drivers and provides a heterogeneous environment for them. It provides a formal interface that all drivers can call. This uniform interface allows I/O Manager to communicate with all drivers in the same way, without any knowledge of how the devices they control actually work. I/O Manager also includes device driver helper routines specifically designed for file system drivers, for hardware device drivers, and for network device drivers.

The Windows NT I/O model uses a layered architecture that allows separate drivers to implement each logically distinct layer of I/O processing. For example, drivers in the lowest layer manipulate the computer's physical devices (called *device drivers*). Other drivers are then layered on top of the device drivers, as in Figure 1.6. These higher-level drivers do not know any details about the physical devices. With the help of I/O Manager, higher-level drivers simply pass logical I/O requests down to the device drivers, which access the physical devices on their behalf. The Windows NT installable file systems and network redirectors are examples of high-level drivers that work in this way.

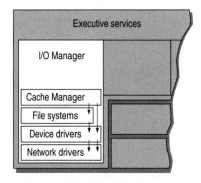

Figure 1.6   Layered Device Drivers

This scheme allows easy replacement of file system drivers and device drivers. It even allows multiple file systems and devices to be active at the same time while being addressed through a formal interface.

Drivers communicate with each other using data structures called *I/O request packets*. The drivers pass I/O request packets to each other via I/O Manager, which delivers the packets to the appropriate destination drivers using the drivers' standard services. Drivers can exchange I/O request packets synchronously or asynchronously. The simplest way to perform I/O is to synchronize the execution of applications with completion of the I/O operations that they request. (This is known as *synchronous I/O*.) When an application performs an I/O operation, the application's processing is blocked. When the I/O operation is complete, the application is allowed to continue processing.

One way that applications can optimize their performance is to perform *asynchronous I/O*, a method employed by many of the processes in Windows NT. When an application initiates an I/O operation, the I/O Manager accepts the request but doesn't block the application's execution while the I/O operation is being performed. Instead, the application is allowed to continue doing work. Most I/O devices are very slow in comparison to a computer's processor, so an application can do a lot of work while waiting for an I/O operation to complete.

When an environment subsystem issues an asynchronous I/O request, the I/O Manager returns to the environment subsystem immediately after putting the request in a queue, without waiting for the device driver to complete its operations. Meanwhile, a separate thread from the I/O Manager runs requests from the queue in the most efficient order (not necessarily the order received).

When each I/O request is finished, the I/O Manager notifies the process that requested the I/O.

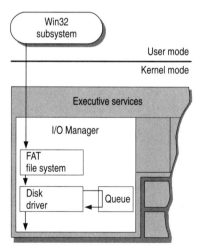

Figure 1.7   Queued I/O Requests

While asynchronous I/O permits an application to use the computer's processor during I/O operations, it also makes it harder for the application to determine when I/O operations have completed. Some applications provide a callback function that is called when the asynchronous I/O operation is completed. Other applications use synchronization objects that the I/O system sets to the signaled state when the I/O operation is complete.

Cache Manager

The I/O architecture includes a single Cache Manager that handles disk caching for the entire I/O system. *Disk caching* is a method used by a file system to improve performance. Instead of reading and writing directly to the disk, frequently used files are temporarily stored in a cache in memory, and reads and writes to those files are performed in memory. Reading and writing to memory is much faster than reading and writing to disk.

The Cache Manager uses a file-mapping model that is closely integrated with the Windows NT virtual memory management. Cache Manager provides caching services to all file systems and network components under the control of the I/O Manager. Cache Manager can dynamically grow and shrink the size of the cache as the amount of available RAM varies. When a process opens a file that already resides in the cache, Cache Manager simply copies data from the cache to the process's virtual address space, and vice versa, as reads and writes are performed.

Cache Manager offers services such as lazy write and lazy commit, which can improve overall file system performance. *Lazy write* is the ability to record changes in the file structure cache, which is quicker than recording them on disk, and then later, when demand on the computer's central processing unit (CPU) is low, the Cache Manager writes the changes to the disk. *Lazy commit* is similar to lazy write. Instead of immediately marking a transaction as successfully completed, the committed information is cached and later written to the file system log as a background process.

For more information about how file systems interact with Cache Manager, see Chapter 5, "Windows NT File Systems and Advanced Disk Management."

File System Drivers

In the Windows NT I/O architecture, file system drivers are managed by I/O Manager. Windows NT supports multiple active file systems, including existing file systems such as FAT and HPFS. Windows NT supports FAT and HPFS file systems for backward compatibility with MS-DOS, Windows 3.*x*, and OS/2 1.*x* operating systems.

Windows NT also supports NTFS—a new file system designed for use with Windows NT. NTFS offers the simple design features of FAT and the speed of HPFS. It also provides many other features including file system security, Unicode support, recoverability, long filename support, and support for POSIX.

The Windows NT I/O architecture not only supports traditional file systems but has implemented its network redirector and server as file system drivers. From the perspective of I/O Manager, there is no difference between accessing files stored on a remote networked computer and accessing those stored locally on a hard disk. In addition, redirectors and servers can be loaded and unloaded dynamically, just like any other driver, and multiple redirectors and servers can coexist on the same computer.

For more information about supported file systems, see Chapter 5 "Windows NT File Systems and Advanced Disk Management." For more information about supported redirectors and servers, see Chapter 15, "Windows NT Networking Architecture."

Hardware Device Drivers

Hardware device drivers are also components of the I/O architecture. All hardware device drivers (such as printer drivers, mouse drivers, and disk drivers) are written in the C programming language, are 32-bit addressable, and are able to address and use multiprocessors. Device drivers are isolated from operating system code that directly accesses the hardware registers of the peripheral devices. Conveniently, device drivers for Windows NT are portable across different processor types.

The I/O Manager's design includes a *simple elegance*, which insists upon clear separation between device drivers. For example, the Intel 8042 processor is an interface device through which the keyboard and mouse communicate. I/O Manager requires three separate drivers—i8042, keyboard, and mouse—rather than one large monolithic driver. This allows more flexibility to customize device configurations on the computer and to layer device drivers and other drivers.

Network Device Drivers

A third type of driver implemented as a component in the I/O architecture is network device drivers. Windows NT includes integrated networking capabilities and support for distributed applications. As shown in Figure 1.8, networking is supported by a series of network drivers.

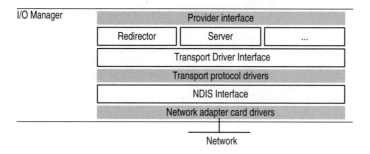

Figure 1.8   Networking Components in Windows NT

Redirectors and servers are implemented as file system drivers and run at or below a provider interface layer where NetBIOS and Windows Sockets reside.

Transport protocol drivers communicate with redirectors and servers through a layer called the Transport Driver Interface (TDI). Windows NT ships with a number of transports, including NBF, Transmission Control Protocol/Internet Protocol (TCP/IP), Data Link Control (DLC), and NWLink. NBF [a descendant of NetBIOS extended user interface (NetBEUI)] provides compatibility with existing LAN Manager, LAN Server, and MS-Net installations. TCP/IP provides a popular routable protocol for wide-area networks. DLC provides an interface for access to mainframes and network-attached printers. NWLink (an implementation of IPX/SPX) provides connectivity with Novell NetWare®.

At the bottom of the networking architecture is the network adapter card device driver. Windows NT currently supports device drivers written to the NDIS (Network Device Interface Specification) version 3.0. NDIS allows for a flexible environment of data exchange between transport protocols and network adapters. NDIS 3.0 allows a single computer to have several network adapter cards installed in it. In turn, each network adapter card can support multiple transport protocols for access to multiple types of network servers.

For more information about network device drivers, see Chapter 15, "Windows NT Networking Architecture."

Windows NT Security Model

The Security Reference Monitor component plus two others—the Logon Process and Security protected subsystems—form the Windows NT security model. In a multitasking operating system such as Windows NT, applications share a variety of system resources including the computer's memory, I/O devices, files, and system processor(s). Windows NT includes a set of security components (shown in Figure 1.9) that ensure that applications cannot access these resources without authorization.

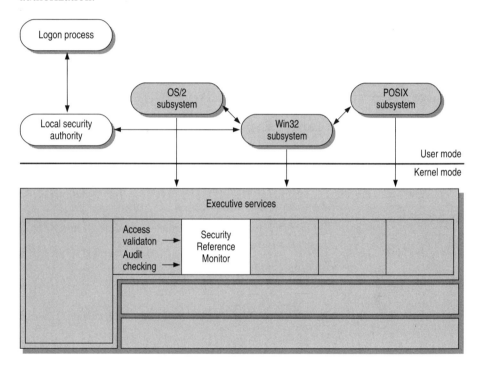

Figure 1.9   Windows NT Security Components

The Security Reference Monitor is responsible for enforcing the access-validation and audit-generation policy defined by the local Security subsystem. The Reference Monitor provides services to both Kernel and user mode for validating access to objects, checking user privileges, and generating audit messages. The Reference Monitor, like other parts of the Executive, runs in Kernel mode.

The user-mode Logon Process and Security protected subsystems are the other two components of the Windows NT security model. The Security subsystem is known as an *integral subsystem* rather than an environment subsystem because it affects the entire Windows NT operating system. (Environment subsystems are discussed later in this chapter.)

The Windows NT Kernel and Executive are based on an object-oriented model that allows for a consistent and uniform view of security, right down to the fundamental entities that make up the base operating system. This means that Windows NT uses the same routines for access validation and audit checks for all protected objects. That is, whether someone is trying to access a file on the disk or a process in memory, there is one component in the system that is required to perform access checks, regardless of the object type.

Windows NT is designed to meet very stringent security requirements. For the first release of Windows NT, Microsoft is in the process of having Windows NT evaluated for the U.S. Department of Defense for a C2 rating. This rating provides for the following:

- Discretionary access control. This means monitoring access to protected objects based on the identity of a user, or group of users, or both.
- Object reuse protection. For example, if someone deletes data from a file, no other user is allowed access to any of the deleted data.
- Mandatory logon. All users must be identified and authenticated before they can access the system.
- Auditing. Once a user is authenticated, any security-related event (for example, access to a protected file) can be audited.

Together these features offer a complete set of security safeguards.

The Windows NT Logon Process provides for mandatory logon to identify users. Each user must have an account and must supply a password to access that account. Figure 1.10 illustrates the interaction among Windows NT components during logon:

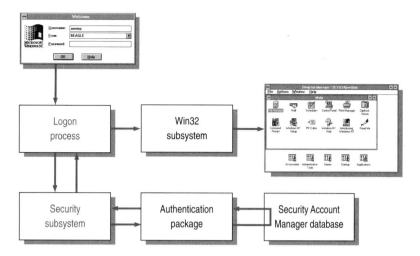

Figure 1.10   Logon Security Process

Logon authentication and validation works this way: Before a user can access any resource on a Windows NT computer, he or she must logon through the Logon Process so that the Security subsystem can authenticate the person's username and password. After successful authentication, whenever the user tries to access a protected object, the Security Reference Monitor runs an access-validation routine against the user's security information to ensure the user has permission to access the object.

The security model also provides for discretionary access control so that the owner of a resource can specify which users or groups can access resources and what types of access they're allowed (such as read, write, and delete).

Resource protection is another feature provided by the security model. This means that tasks can't access each others' resources, such as memory, except through specific sharing mechanisms. This feature helps enforce object hiding.

Windows NT also provides for auditing so that administrators can keep an audit trail of which users perform what actions.

By providing these features, the Windows NT security model prevents applications from gaining unauthorized access to the resources of other applications or the operating system either intentionally or unintentionally.

For a complete description of how the security model works, see Chapter 2, "Windows NT Security Model."

In addition to the protected subsystems—Logon Process and Security— Windows NT includes a number of other user-mode components called environment subsystems. The next section describes each of the Windows NT environment subsystems.

Environment Subsystems

Windows NT was designed to allow many different types of applications to run seamlessly on the same graphical desktop. It runs applications written for existing operating systems such as MS-DOS, OS/2 1.*x*, and Windows 3.*x*. It also runs applications written for newer APIs such as POSIX and Win32.

Windows NT supports a variety of applications through the use of environment subsystems. *Environment subsystems* are Windows NT processes that emulate different operating system environments.

This chapter has discussed how the Windows NT Executive provides generic services that all environment subsystems can call to perform basic operating system functions. The subsystems build on the Executive's services to produce environments that meet the specific needs of their client applications. Figure 1.11 shows a simplified view of the Windows NT environmental subsystem design.

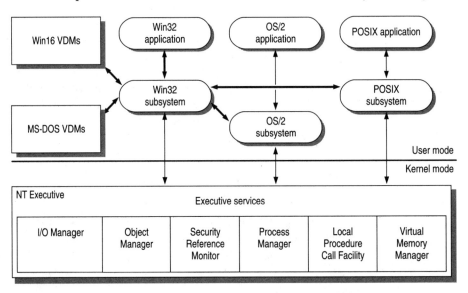

Figure 1.11   Conceptual View of Windows NT Environment Subsystems

As shown in this figure, each subsystem runs as a separate user-mode process. Failure in one won't cause another subsystem or the Executive to be disabled. Each subsystem is protected from errors in the others. (An exception to this is if the Win32 subsystem crashes, since it handles keyboard and mouse input and screen output for all subsystems.) Applications are also user-mode processes, so they can't hinder the subsystems or Executive.

Windows NT provides these protected environments subsystems and multiple Virtual DOS Machines (VDMs):

- MS-DOS VDM
- Win16 VDMs
- OS/2 subsystem
- POSIX subsystem
- Win32 subsystem

With the exception of the Win32 subsystem, each environment is optional and is loaded only when its services are needed by a client application.

MS-DOS Environment

When run on Windows NT, MS-DOS applications run within the context of a process called a Virtual DOS Machine (VDM). A *VDM* is a Win32 application that establishes a complete virtual *x*86 (that is, 80386 or higher) computer running MS-DOS. There is no limit on the number of VDMs that can be run. Each VDM runs in its own address space, which protects the applications from each other and the rest of the operating system from the VDMs.

When Windows NT is running on an *x*86 processor, a processor mode called Virtual-86 mode is available. This mode allows direct execution of most instructions in an MS-DOS–based application. A few instructions, such as I/O instructions, must be emulated in order to virtualize the hardware. When Windows NT is running on a RISC processor, hardware support for executing *x*86 instructions is not available. In such an environment it is necessary to emulate all of the *x*86 instructions in addition to providing a virtual hardware environment.

To run MS-DOS–based applications, the VDM creates a virtual computer that provides the following:

- Support for processing *x*86 instructions, provided by the Instruction Execution Unit
- Support for read-only memory basic input and output (ROM BIOS) interrupt services, provided by the MS-DOS emulation module
- Support for MS-DOS Interrupt 21 services, provided by the MS-DOS emulation module
- Virtual hardware for devices such as the screen and keyboard, provided by Virtual Device Drivers (VDDs)

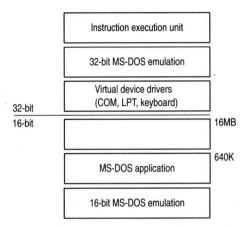

Figure 1.12   Structure of an MS-DOS VDM

On *x*86-based computers, character-based applications can run either in a window or in a full screen. Graphical applications can run only in full screen. If an application is in a window and then changes the video mode, it is automatically switched to full screen. On RISC-based computers, character-based and graphical applications run only in a window.

Windows 16-Bit Environment

Windows NT uses a single multithreaded VDM support to run 16-bit Windows-based (Win16) applications. One of the main goals for Win16 support is to provide a seamless interface for running Win16 applications in the Windows NT environment.

The Win16 VDM (sometimes called *WOW* for Win16 on Win32) is preemptively multitasked with respect to other processes running on the system. However, each Win16 application is nonpreemptively multitasked with respect to each other. That is, only one Win16 application can run at a time while the others are blocked. If the Win16 VDM is preempted when the system returns, it always unblocks the Win16 application that was running before the Win16 VDM was preempted.

Additionally, the Win16 VDM provides stubs for Windows 3.1 Kernel, User, graphical device interface dynamic-link libraries (GDI DLLs), and it automatically handles translation of 16-bit Windows APIs and messages.

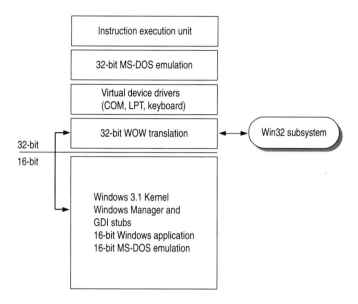

Figure 1.13   Structure of the Win16 VDM

For more information about using Windows 3.*x* applications on Windows NT, see Chapter 23, "Windows 3.*x* Compatibility."

OS/2 Subsystem

The OS/2 subsystem supports OS/2 1.*x* character-based applications on *x*86-based computers. This subsystem isn't supported on RISC-based computers; however, OS/2 real-mode applications can run on a RISC-based computer in the MS-DOS environment.

Bound applications, which are applications designed to run under either OS/2 or MS-DOS, will always run in the OS/2 subsystem if it is available.

For more information about using OS/2 1.*x* applications on Windows NT, see Chapter 24, "OS/2 Compatibility."

POSIX Subsystem

The Windows NT POSIX subsystem is designed to run POSIX applications and meets the requirements of POSIX.1.

POSIX (Portable Operating System Interface for Computing Environments) is a set of standards being drafted by the Institute of Electrical and Electronic Engineers (IEEE) that define various aspects of an operating system, including topics such as programming interface, security, networking, and graphical interface. So far, only one of these standards, POSIX.1 (also called IEEE Standard 1003.1-1990), has made the transition from draft to final form and gained a base of customer acceptance.

POSIX.1 defines C-language API calls between applications and the operating system. It is an API based on ideas drawn from the UNIX® file system and process model. Because POSIX.1 addresses only API-level issues, most applications written to the POSIX.1 API must rely on non-POSIX operating system extensions to provide services such as security and networking.

POSIX applications need certain file-system functionality, such as support for case-sensitive filenames and support for files with multiple names (or *hard links*). The new file system, NTFS, supports these POSIX requirements. Any POSIX application requiring access to file system resources must have access to an NTFS partition. POSIX applications that do not access file system resources can run on any of the supported file systems.

For more information about using POSIX applications on Windows NT, see Chapter 25, "POSIX Compatibility."

Win32 Subsystem

The main environment subsystem is the Win32 subsystem. In addition to being able to run Win32 applications, this subsystem manages keyboard and mouse input and screen output for all subsystems.

The Win32 subsystem is responsible for collecting all user input (or messages, in this message-driven environment) and delivering it to the appropriate applications. The Win32 input model is optimized to take advantage of the Windows NT preemptive multitasking capabilities. Figure 1.14 shows how the Win32 subsystem handles input for Win32 and 16-bit Windows-based applications.

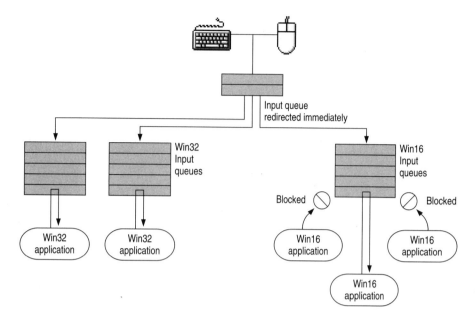

Figure 1.14   Win16 (Synchronized) and Win32 (Desynchronized) Input

Win32 uses a desynchronized input model for Win32 applications and the synchronized input for 16-bit Windows-based applications.

For example, when the Win32 subsystem receives a message for a Win32 application, it stores the message in a single raw input queue. As soon as it can, the Win32 subsystem transfers the message to the input queue thread for the appropriate Win32 application. If the input queue thread stops retrieving its messages, no other Win32 applications are affected.

By contrast, all input messages for 16-bit Windows-based applications sit in a common queue. At any point in time, all applications except the one retrieving messages from the input queue are blocked. However, as with Windows 3.1, if the executing application has some problem with retrieving messages from the queue, or it does it very slowly, the remaining applications stay blocked.

Application Types on Various Hardware Platforms

Windows NT runs on computers with Intel 80386 or higher processors, MIPS, or Digital Alpha AXP processors. The following table shows how Windows NT supports applications of various types on these different hardware platforms.

Table 1.3   Application Compatibility

Processor	Win32	MS-DOS and Windows 3.x	POSIX	OS/2 1.x
Intel x86	Source-compatible	Runs application in a VDM	Source-compatible	16-bit character-based only
Digital Alpha AXP	Source-compatible	Runs application in 286 emulation	Source-compatible	Not available; can run real-mode applications in MS-DOS subsystem
MIPS R4000	Source-compatible	Runs application in 286 emulation	Source-compatible	Not available; can run real-mode applications in MS-DOS subsystem

CHAPTER 2

Windows NT Security Model

Security in Windows NT was included as part of the initial design specifications for Windows NT and is pervasive throughout the operating system. The security model includes components to control who accesses which objects (such as files and shared printers), which actions an individual can take on an object, and which events are audited.

This chapter provides an overview of the security model and describes the components that make up the model. It also explains how Windows NT tracks each user and each securable object. This overview helps you understand system messages and information found in the Event Viewer. This chapter also provides examples of Windows NT security, showing how Windows NT validates access requests and how it audits activities performed on protected objects.

The Security Model

Chapter 1, "Windows NT Architecture," describes the overall architecture of Windows NT. As shown in Figure 2.1, the Windows NT security model includes these components:

- Logon Processes, which accept logon request from users. These include the initial interactive logon, which displays the initial logon dialog box to the user, and remote logon processes, which allow access by remote users to a Windows NT server process.

- Local Security Authority, which ensures that the user has permission to access the system.

  This component is the center of the Windows NT security subsystem. It generates access tokens (described later in this chapter), manages the local security policy, and provides interactive user authentication services. The Local Security Authority also controls audit policy and logs the audit messages generated by the Security Reference Monitor.

- Security Account Manager (SAM), which maintains the user accounts database. This database contains information for all user and group accounts. SAM provides user validation services, which are used by the Local Security Authority.

- Security Reference Monitor, which checks to see if the user has permission to access an object and perform whatever action the user is attempting. This component enforces the access validation and audit generation policy defined by the Local Security Authority. It provides services to both kernel and user mode to ensure the users and processes attempting access to an object have the necessary permissions. This component also generates audit messages when appropriate.

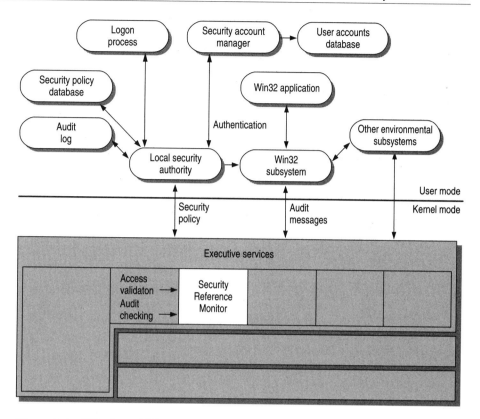

Figure 2.1   Windows NT Security Components

Together, these components are known as the security subsystem. This subsystem is known as an *integral subsystem* rather than an *environmental subsystem* because it affects the entire Windows NT operating system.

The Windows NT security model is designed for C2-level security as defined by the U.S. Department of Defense. Some of the most important requirements of C2-level security are the following:

- The owner of a resource (such as a file) must be able to control access to the resource.

- The operating system must protect objects so that they are not randomly reused by other processes. For example, the system protects memory so that its contents cannot be read after it is freed by a process. In addition, when a file is deleted, users must not be able to access the file's data.

- Each user must identify himself or herself by typing a unique logon name and password before being allowed access to the system. The system must be able to use this unique identification to track the activities of the user.

- System administrators must be able to audit security-related events. Access to this audit data must be limited to authorized administrators.

- The system must protect itself from external interference or tampering, such as modification of the running system or of system files stored on disk.

Users, Objects, and Permissions

The key objective of the Windows NT security model is to monitor and control who accesses which objects. The security model keeps security information for each user, group, and object. It can identify access attempts that are made directly by a user or indirectly by a program or other process running on the user's behalf. Windows NT also tracks and controls access to both objects that users can see in the user interface (such as files and printers) and objects that users can't see (such as processes and named pipes).

As mentioned before, the security model controls not only which users can access which objects; it also controls how they may be accessed. An administrator can assign *permissions* to users and groups to grant or deny access to particular objects.

For example, these permissions may be assigned to a user for a particular file:

Read	Execute
Delete	Take Ownership
Write	No access
Change Permission	

The ability to assign permissions at the discretion of the owner (or other person authorized to change permissions) is called *discretionary access control*. Administrators can assign permissions to individual users or groups. (For maintenance purposes, it's best to assign permissions to groups.) For example, an administrator can control access to the REPORTS directory by giving GROUP1 read permission and GROUP2 read, write, and execute permissions. (To do this, in File Manager, choose Permissions from the Security menu.)

Auditing Security Events in the Security Log

Windows NT auditing features can record events to show which users access which objects, what type of access is being attempted, and whether or not the access attempt was successful. You can view audited security events through Event Viewer by selecting Security from the Log menu. (For complete information about how to use Event Viewer, see the chapter on Event Viewer in either the *Microsoft Windows NT System Guide* or the *Microsoft Windows NT Advanced Server System Guide*.)

You can see detailed information, as shown in Figure 2.2, about a particular audited event in the security log by double-clicking on that event.

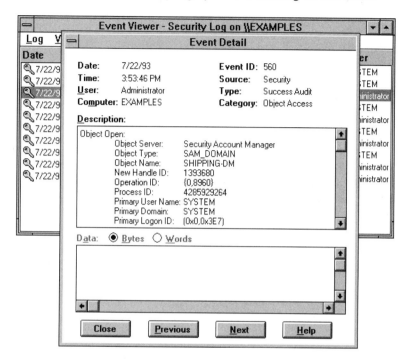

Figure 2.2   Event Detail Dialog Box

To set up auditing on your computer, use the Auditing and Security options in the User Manager, File Manager, Print Manager, and other tools. From these tools, you can specify the types of auditing events you want to include in the security log. For more information about setting auditing options within these tools, see the Windows NT documentation.

Note   While Event Viewer is adequate for most requirements, the security model is defined so that developers can write their own custom security event viewer/monitor. For details on Windows NT security-related APIs, see the *Microsoft Win32 Software Development Kit.*

Security Information for Users

Users are identified to the system by a unique *security ID* (SID). Security IDs are unique across time and space, meaning that there is no possibility of having two identical security IDs. For example, suppose Sally, who has a Windows NT account, leaves her job at a company but later returns to a different job at the same company. When Sally leaves, the administrator deletes her account, and Windows NT no longer accepts her security ID as valid. When Sally returns, the administrator creates a new account, and Windows NT generates a new security ID for that account. The new security ID does not match the old one, so nothing from the old account is transferred to the new account.

When a user logs on, Windows NT creates a *security access token*. This includes a security ID for the user, other security IDs for the groups to which the user belongs, plus other information such as the user's name and the groups to which that user belongs. In addition, every process that runs on behalf of this user will have a copy of his or her access token. For example, when Sally start Notepad, the Notepad process receives a copy of Sally's access token.

Figure 2.3 illustrates the contents of an access token.

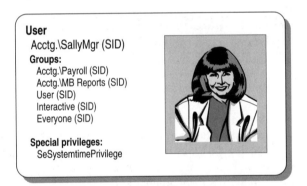

Figure 2.3   Access Token Contents

Windows NT refers to the security IDs within a user's access token when he or she tries to access an object. The security IDs are compared with the list of access permissions for the object to ensure that the user has sufficient permission to access the object.

How Windows NT Creates an Access Token

Before a user can do anything on a Windows NT system, he or she must log on to the system by supplying a username and password. Windows NT uses the username for identification and password for validation. The following procedure illustrates the interactive logon process for Windows NT.

The initial logon process for Windows NT is *interactive*, meaning that the user must type information at the keyboard in response to a dialog box the operating system displays on the screen. Windows NT grants or denies access based upon the information provided by the user.

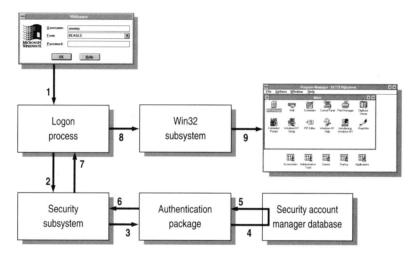

Figure 2.4   Windows NT Validation Process

The following list details the steps included in the interactive logon and validation process, as illustrated in Figure 2.4:

1. The user presses CTRL+ALT+DEL to gain the attention of Windows NT. This key combination before logon protects against Trojan Horse-type programs that impersonate the operating system and trick users into disclosing their username and password.

2. When the user provides a username and a password, the Logon Process calls the Local Security Authority.

3. The Local Security Authority runs the appropriate authentication package.

Note Windows NT has the ability to support multiple authentication
packages that are implemented as DLLs. This flexibility allows third-party
software vendors the opportunity to integrate their own custom authentication
packages with Windows NT. For example, a network vendor might augment
the standard Windows NT authentication package by adding one that allows
users to log onto Windows NT and the vendor's network simultaneously.

---

4. The authentication package checks the user accounts database to see if the
account is local. If it is, the username and password are verified against those
held in the user accounts database. If not, the requested logon is forwarded to
an alternate authentication package.

5. When the account is validated, the SAM (which owns the user accounts
database) returns the user's security ID and the security IDs of any global
groups to which the user belongs.

6. The authentication package creates a logon session and then passes the logon
session and the security IDs associated with the user to the Local Security
Authority.

7. If the logon is rejected, the logon session is deleted, and an error is returned to
the Logon Process.

   Otherwise, an access token is created, containing the user's security ID and
   the security IDs of Everyone and other groups. It also contains user rights
   (described in the next section) assigned to the collected security IDs. This
   access token is returned to the Logon Process with a Success status.

8. The logon session calls the Win32 subsystem to create a process and attach
the access token to the process, thus creating a *subject* for the user account.
(Subjects are described in the section called "Subjects and Impersonation,"
later in this chapter.)

9. For an interactive Windows NT session, the Win32 subsystem starts Program
Manager for the user.

After the validation process, a user's shell process (that is, the process in
which Program Manager is started for the user) is given an access token. The
information in this access token is reflected by anything the user does, or any
process that runs on the user's behalf.

User Rights

Typically, access to an object is determined by comparing the user and group memberships in the user's access token with permissions for the object. However, some activities performed by users are not associated with a particular object.

For example, you may want certain individuals to be able to create regular backups for the server. These people should be able to do their job without regard to permissions that have been set on those files. In cases like this, an administrator could assign specific *user rights* (sometimes called privileges) to give users or groups access to services that normal discretionary access control does not provide. (You can use the dialog box shown below from the User Manager tool to assign user rights.)

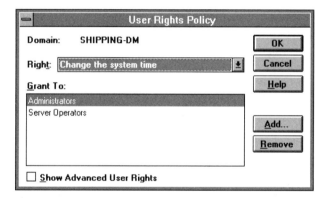

Backing up files and directories, shutting down the computer, logging on interactively, and changing the system times are all examples of user rights defined by Windows NT.

Note   In the first release of Windows NT, the set of user rights is defined by the system and cannot be changed. Future versions of Windows NT may allow software developers to define new user rights appropriate to their application.

For more information about permissions and user rights, see the *Windows NT System Guide*. Details for administrators are also included in the *Windows NT Advanced Server Concepts and Planning Guide* and the *Windows NT Advanced Server System Guide*.

Subjects and Impersonation

One objective of the Windows NT security model is to ensure that the programs that a user runs have no more access to objects than the user does. That is, if a user is granted only read access to a file, then when he or she runs a program, that program cannot write to the file. The program, like the user, is granted only read permission.

A *subject* is the combination of the user's access token plus the program acting on the user's behalf. Windows NT uses subjects to track and manage permissions for the programs each user runs.

When a program or process runs on the user's behalf, it is said to be running in the s*ecurity context* of that user. The security context controls what access the subject has to objects or system services.

To accommodate Windows NT's client-server model, there are two classes of subjects within the Windows NT security architecture:

- A *simple subject* is a process that was assigned a security context when the corresponding user logged on. It is not acting in the capacity of a protected server, which may have other subjects as clients.
- A *server subject* is a process implemented as a protected server (such as the Win32 subsystem), and it does have other subjects as clients. In this role, a server subject typically has the security context of those clients available for use when acting on their behalf.

In general, when a subject calls an object service through a protected subsystem, the subject's token is used within the service to determine who made the call and to decide whether the caller has sufficient access authority to perform the requested action.

Windows NT allows one process to take on the security attributes of another through a technique called *impersonation*. For example, a server process typically impersonates a client process to complete a task involving objects to which the server does not normally have access.

In the scenario shown in Figure 2.5, a client is accessing an object on a Windows NT server.

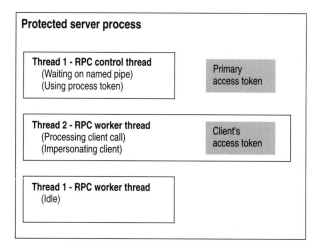

Figure 2.5   Server Subject Security Context

The first thread in the process is a control thread. It is waiting to receive RPC calls via a named pipe. This thread is not impersonating anyone, so any access validation to which Thread 1 is subjected will be carried out against the process's primary token.

The second thread in the process is currently handling a call from a client. This thread handles the client's call by temporarily using the client's access token to run with that client's access permissions (that is, the client's security context). While impersonating the client, any access validation to which Thread 2 is subjected is carried out in the security context of the client.

The third thread in this scenario is an idle worker thread that is not impersonating any other process.

The following illustration shows an audited event in which impersonation was used. (Use the Event Viewer to see this type of information for your system.) Here, information for both the primary user and client user is recorded in the security log.

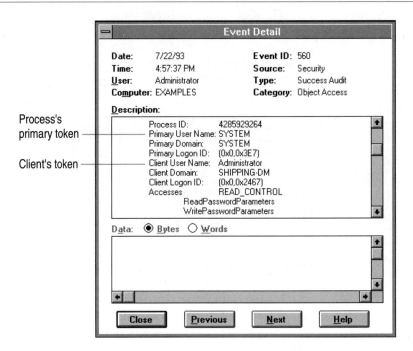

Process's
primary token —

Client's token —

Security Information for Objects

All named objects in Windows NT, and some unnamed objects, can be secured. The security attributes for an object are described by a *security descriptor.* An object's security descriptor includes four parts (see Figure 2.6):

- An owner security ID, which indicates the user or group who owns the object. The owner of an object can change the access permissions for the object.

- A group security ID, which is used only by the POSIX subsystem and ignored by the rest of Windows NT.

- A discretionary *access control list* (ACL), which identifies which users and groups are granted or denied which access permissions. Discretionary ACLs are controlled by the owner of the object. (These are described later, in "Access Control Lists and Access Control Entries.")

- A system ACL, which controls which auditing messages the system will generate. (For more information about auditing objects, see "Auditing Security Events," later in this chapter.) System ACLs are controlled by the security administrators.

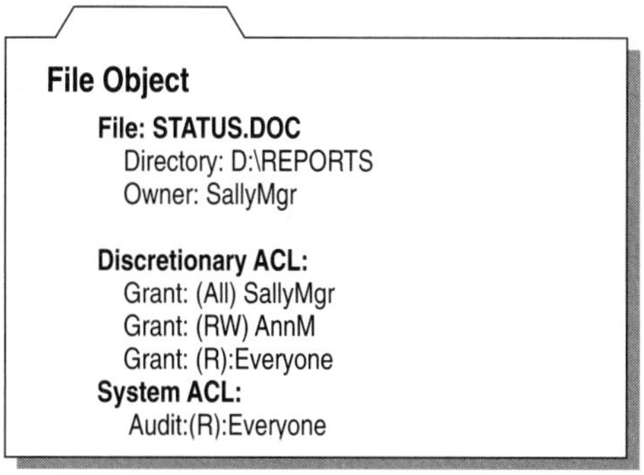

Figure 2.6   Security Descriptor for a File Object

Types of Objects

The type of permissions that can be granted or denied for an object depends on the object's type. For example, you can specify permissions like Manage Documents and Print for a printer queue, while for a directory you can specify Read, Write, Execute, and so on.

Another quality that affects the permissions of an object is whether that object is a container object or a noncontainer object. A *container object* is one that logically contains other objects; *noncontainer* objects do not contain other objects. For example, a directory is a container object that logically contains files and other directories. Files are noncontainer objects. This distinction between container and noncontainer objects is important because objects within a container object can inherit certain permissions from the parent container. For more information, see "Access Control Inheritance," later in this chapter.

Note NTFS (described in Chapter 5, "Windows NT File Systems and Advanced Disk Management") supports the inheritance of ACLs from directory objects to file objects that are created within the directory.

Access Control Lists and Access Control Entries

Each ACL is made up of *access control entries* (ACEs), which specify access or auditing permissions to that object for one user or group. There are three ACE types—two for discretionary access control and one for system security.

The discretionary ACEs are AccessAllowed and AccessDenied. Respectively, these explicitly grant and deny access to a user or group of users.

Note There is an important distinction between a discretionary ACL that is empty (one that has no ACEs in it) and an object without any discretionary ACL. In the case of an empty discretionary ACL, no accesses are explicitly granted, so access is implicitly denied. For an object that has no ACL at all, there is no protection assigned to the object, so any access request is granted.

SystemAudit is a system security ACE uses to keep a log of security events (such as who accesses which files) and to generate and log security audit messages.

Access Masks

Each ACE includes an *access mask*, which defines all possible actions for a particular object type. Permissions are granted or denied based on this access mask.

One way to think of an access mask is as a sort of menu from which granted and denied permissions are selected:

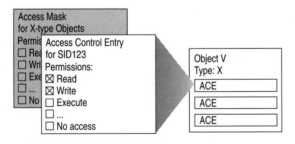

Figure 2.7   Access Control Mask

Specific types include access options that apply specifically to this object type. Each object type can have up to 16 specific access types. Collectively, the specific access types for a particular object type are called the *specific access mask*. (These are defined when the object type is defined.) For example, Windows NT files have the following specific access types:

ReadData	WriteEA (Extended Attribute)
WriteData	Execute
AppendData	ReadAttributes
ReadEA (Extended Attribute)	WriteAttributes

Standard types apply to all objects and consist of these access permissions:

- SYNCHRONIZE, used to synchronize access and to allow a process to wait for an object to enter the signaled state
- WRITE_OWNER, used to assign write owner
- WRITE_DAC, used to grant or deny write access to the discretionary ACL
- READ_CONTROL, used to grant or deny read access to the security descriptor and owner
- DELETE, used to grant or deny delete access

The following table shows the·generic types that are mapped from specific and standard types.

Generic type	Mapped from these specific and standard types
FILE_GENERIC_READ	STANDARD_RIGHTS_READ FILE_READ_DATA FILE_READ_ATTRIBUTES FILE_READ_EA SYNCHRONIZE
FILE_GENERIC_WRITE	STANDARD_RIGHTS_WRITE FILE_WRITE_DATA FILE_WRITE_ATTRIBUTES FILE_WRITE_EA FILE_APPEND_DATA SYNCHRONIZE
FILE_GENERIC_EXECUTE	STANDARD_RIGHTS_EXECUTE FILE_READ_ATTRIBUTES FILE_EXECUTE SYNCHRONIZE

Specific and standard types appear in the details of the security log, as in the following display. Here, Administrator is accessing D:\ . The access types used are SYNCHRONIZE (a standard type) and ReadData/ListDirectory (a specific type for files and directories).

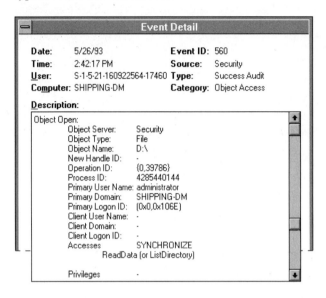

Note Generic types do not appear in the security log. Instead, the corresponding specific and standard types are listed.

Access Control Inheritance

Objects can be classified as either container objects or noncontainer objects: Container objects (such as a directory) can logically contain other objects; noncontainer objects (such as a file) can't.

By default, when you create new objects within a container object, the new objects inherit permissions from the *parent* object. For example, in Figure 2.8, D:\REPORTS\ANNM inherited permissions from its parent directory, D:\REPORTS.

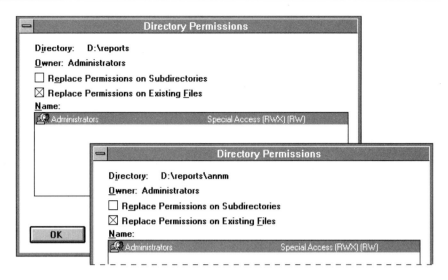

Figure 2.8   Directory Permissions Dialog Boxes for Parent and Subdirectory

In the case of files and directories, when you change permissions on a directory, those changes affect that directory and its files but do not automatically apply to existing subdirectories and their contents. (They do, however, if you check the Replace Permissions On Existing Files check box.) You can apply the changed permissions to existing subdirectories and their files by selecting the Replace Permissions On Subdirectories check box shown in Figure 2.8.

Figure 2.9 shows the file permissions that are inherited from the parent directory by a file within that directory.

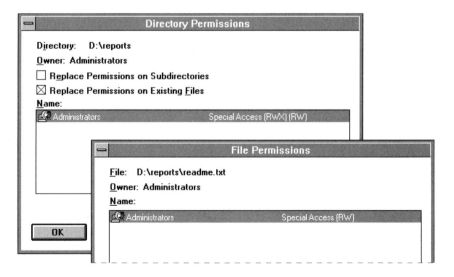

Figure 2.9   Permissions Dialog Boxes for Parent Directory and Files

Access Validation

When a user tries to access an object, Windows NT compares security
information in the user's access token with the security information in the
object's security descriptor, as shown in Figure 2.10:

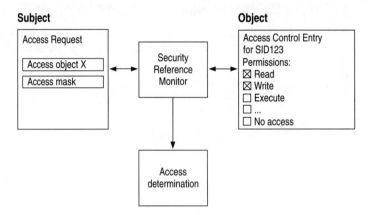

Figure 2.10   Access Validation

A *desired access mask* for the subject is created based on what type of access the
user is attempting. This desired access mask, usually created by a program that the
user is running, is compared with the object's ACL. (All generic access types in
the ACL are mapped to standard and specific access types.)

Each ACE in the ACL is evaluated in this way:

1. The security ID in the ACE is compared with the set of security IDs in the
   user's access token. If a match is not found, the ACE is skipped.

   Further processing is based upon the type of the ACE. AccessDenied ACEs
   are ordered (and therefore processed) before AccessAllowed ACEs.

2. If access is denied, the system checks to see if the original desired access
   mask contained only a ReadControl and/or WRITE_DAC. If so, the system
   also checks to see if the requester is the owner of the object. In this case,
   access is granted.

3. For an AccessDenied ACE, the accesses in the ACE access mask are
   compared with the desired access mask. If there are any accesses in both
   masks, further processing is not necessary, and access is denied. Otherwise,
   processing continues with the next requested ACE.

4. For an AccessAllowed ACE, the accesses in the ACE are compared with those
   listed in the desired access mask. If all accesses in the desired access mask are
   matched by the ACE, no further processing is necessary, and access is granted.
   Otherwise, processing continues with the next ACE.

5. At the end of the ACL, if the contents of desired access mask are still not completely matched, access is implicitly denied.

Four examples of this access validation process are described next.

Example 1: Requesting Read and Write Access

A user whose user ID is FredMgr tries to gain Read and Write access to G:\FILE1.TXT, which has the discretionary ACL as shown in the next figure. The FredMgr access token indicates that he is a member of the groups Users, Mgrs, and Everyone.

Note The order in which permissions are listed by the File Permissions dialog box doesn't necessarily reflect the order in which ACEs are processed by Windows NT. It is important to note, however, that the Permissions Editor (controlled by means of this dialog box) orders all AccessDenied ACEs first so that they are the first to be processed within each ACL.

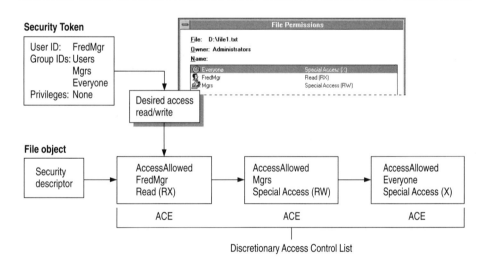

In this example, Windows NT evaluates the ACL by comparing the desired access mask with each ACE and processes the desired mask as follows:

1. Windows NT reads FredMgr's desired access mask to see that he is trying to gain Read and Write access.

2. Windows NT reads the AccessAllowed ACE for FredMgr and finds a match to the Read permission requested in the desired access mask.

3. Windows NT reads the AccessAllowed ACE for Mgrs and finds a match to the Write permission requested in desired access mask.

At this point, processing of the ACL stops even though there is another ACE in the ACL. Processing stops, and access is granted because Windows NT found matches for everything in the desired access mask.

Example 2: When Access Is Denied

In this example, FredMgr wants Read and Write access to the file whose discretionary ACL is shown next. FredMgr is a member of the Users and Mgrs groups.

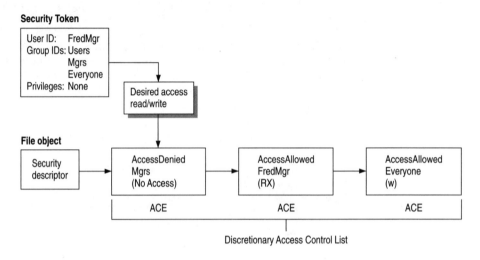

Note The File Manager Permissions Editor always orders AccessDenied ACEs first in the ACL.

In Example 2, the ACL is evaluated as follows:

1. Windows NT reads FredMgr's desired access mask to see that he is trying to gain Read and Write access.

2. Windows NT reads the AccessDenied ACE, which denies all access (No Access) to Mgrs.

At this point, processing of the ACL stops even though there are other ACEs in the ACL that grant permissions to FredMgr.

Example 3: Requesting Read and Write Access as Object Owner

In the example shown next, Windows NT knows by reading FredMgr's access token that he is a member of the Mgrs group. Processing of the ACL will stop as soon as Windows NT sees that NoAccess (None) is assigned to the Mgrs group, even though the other two ACEs allow Read, Write, and Execute access for FredMgr.

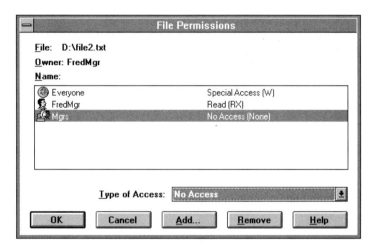

However, after failing to gain access via the discretionary ACL, Windows NT notices that FredMgr is the owner of the object. Because of this, he is granted ReadControl and WRITE_DAC automatically. Since this is all the access he is asking for, his request is granted.

If FredMgr had asked for any other access in addition to ReadControl and WRITE_DAC, the request would be denied even though Fred is the object's owner. In this case, FredMgr receives the following message:

```
G:\FILE2.TXT
You do not have permission to open this file.
See the owner of the file or an administrator to obtain permission.
```

In this case, because FredMgr is the owner, he can change his own permissions to grant himself appropriate access to the file.

Example 4: When a Custom Application Assigns Permissions

> **Important** The three preceding examples demonstrate discretionary access control for file and directory permissions that are applied through the Windows NT Permissions Editor (found in File Manager) either directly or by inheritance. If you use a custom application that sets and changes permissions on files and directories, the Windows NT Permissions Editor may not be able to handle the ACL that the custom application creates or modifies.
>
> Even though the logic above still applies, there is no way of precisely determining the access to the object. The following example illustrates this point.

The user BobMgr wants Read and Write access to the file object that has the discretionary ACL shown next. The access token for BobMgr indicates that he is a member of the groups Users, JnrMgrs, and Everyone.

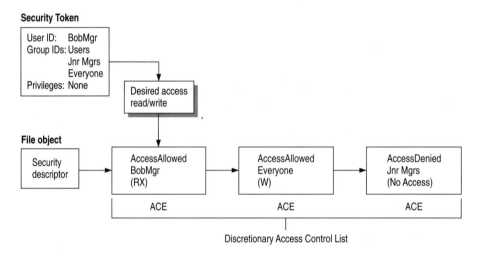

In this example, a custom application has been used to update the ACL for a file, thus confusing the usual order in which the ACEs for this file are processed. Normally, all AccessDenied ACEs are processed first.

Windows NT evaluates this ACL as follows:

1. Windows NT reads BobMgr's desired access mask to see that he is trying to gain Read and Write access.

2. Windows NT reads the AccessAllowed ACE for BobMgr and finds a match to the Read permission requested in the desired access mask.

3. Windows NT reads the AccessAllowed ACE for Everyone and finds a match to the Write permission requested in the desired access mask.

BobMgr is granted Read and Write access to the file object, even though the third ACE explicitly denies JnrMgrs access to the file object.

If the Windows NT Permissions Editor had been used to apply the same permissions to the file object, the AccessDenied ACE for JnrMgrs would have been ordered first in the ACL, and BobMgr would have been denied access to the file.

Auditing Security Events

Windows NT includes auditing features you can use to collect information about how your system is being used. These features also allow you to monitor events related to system security, to identify any security breaches, and to determine the extent and location of any damage. The level of audited events is adjustable to suit the needs of your organization. Some organizations need little auditing information, while others would be willing to trade some performance and disk space for detailed information they can use to analyze their system.

Note Remember that when you enable auditing, there is some small performance overhead for each audit check the system performs.

Windows NT can track events related to the operating system itself and to individual applications. Each application can define its own auditable events. Definitions of these events are added to the Registry when the application is installed on your Windows NT computer.

Audit events are identified to the system by the event source module name (which corresponds to a specific event type in the Registry) and an event ID.

In addition to listing events by event ID, the security log in Event Viewer lists them by category. The following categories of events are displayed in the Security Log. (Those in parentheses are found in the Audit Policy dialog box of User Manager.)

Category	Meaning
Account Management (User and Group Management)	These events describe high-level changes to the user accounts database, such as User Created or Group Membership Change. Potentially, a more detailed, object-level audit is also performed (see Object Access events).
Detailed Tracking (Process Tracking)	These events provide detailed subject-tracking information. This includes information such as program activation, handle duplication, and indirect object access.
Logon/Logoff (Logon and Logoff)	These events describe a single logon or logoff attempt, whether successful or unsuccessful. Included in each logon description is an indication of what type of logon was requested or performed (that is, interactive, network, or service).
Object Access (File and Object Access)	These events describe both successful and unsuccessful accesses to protected objects.
Policy Change (Security Policy Changes)	These events describe high-level changes to the security policy database, such as assignment of privileges or logon capabilities. Potentially, a more detailed, object-level audit is also performed (see Object Access events).
Privilege Use (Use of User Rights)	These events describe both successful and unsuccessful attempts to use privileges. It also includes information about when some special privileges are assigned. These special privileges are audited only at assignment time, not at time of use.
System Event (System)	These events indicate something affecting the security of the entire system or audit log occurred.

(Examples of most of these event categories are included later in this chapter.)

Process IDs and Handle IDs of Audit Events

One of the most important aspects of security is determining who is actually behind operations of security interest, such as file writes or security policy change. With the client-server model of Windows, user account identification can be rather tricky. Although a thread that requests access to a resource is identified by the user ID, the thread may be impersonating someone else. In this case, it would be misleading to log events by user ID and may not be very useful in finding the perpetrator in the case of a security breach.

To prevent this problem, there are two levels of subject identification used in Windows NT auditing and the security log—the user ID (also called the primary ID) and the impersonation ID (also called the client ID), as applicable. These two IDs show security administrators who is performing auditable actions.

In some cases, a security administrator wants to see what is happening with each process, however. To meet this need, auditing information also includes a subject's process ID where possible.

When process tracking is enabled (through the Audit Policy dialog box of User Manager), audit messages are generated each time a new process is created. This information can be correlated with specific audit messages to see not only which user account is being used to perform auditable actions, but also which program was run.

Many audit events also include a handle ID, enabling the event to be associated with future events. For example, when a file is opened, the audit information indicates the handle ID assigned. When the handle is closed, another audit event with the same handle ID is generated. With this information, you can determine exactly how long the file remained open. This could be useful, for example, when you want to assess damage following a security breach.

The following list shows some of the information that Windows NT tracks within a process's access token. This information also is used for auditing.

- The security ID of the user account used to log on
- The group security IDs and corresponding attributes of groups to which the user is assigned membership
- The names of the privileges assigned to and used by the user, and their corresponding attributes
- Authentication ID, assigned when the user logs on

Security Event Examples

As described earlier, you can track several categories of security events. This section provides examples for most of these categories. This set of examples does not constitute a strategy for using the auditing capabilities of Windows NT; they merely serve as an introduction to help you interpret these events when you enable auditing for your Windows NT system.

Example 1: Tracking File and Object Access

In this example, auditing is enabled as follows (assuming you are logged on as an administrator):

- From File Manager, select the .TXT file, and then choose Auditing from the Security menu. Assign Full Control permission to the user accessing the .TXT file and enable auditing for Success and Failure of Read and Write events.

- From User Manager, choose Audit from the Policies menu. Then enable auditing for Success and Failure of File and Object Access and Process Tracking.

From File Manager, the user double-clicks the .TXT file (which is associated with Notepad) and then writes some data to the file, saves it, and closes the file.

This results in 11 audit events, as shown in Figure 2.11:

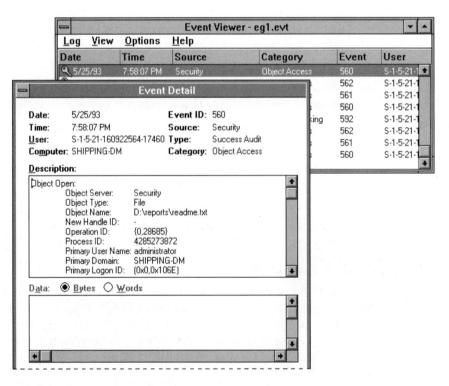

Figure 2.11   Security Events Posted After Updating a File

From this view of the security log, you get a quick summary of security-related events that occurred. Double-click the first event to examine the details. (For example, details of this first event are shown in the Event Detail box.)

The data that needs to be interpreted is listed in the Description list box. The following table summarizes the audited events for this example, in the order they occurred.

Table 2.1   Security Events for File Access Example

Event ID and description	Analysis
Event 560: Object Open Event 561: Handle Allocated Event 562: Handle Closed	In this sequence of events, Windows NT is doing some internal checks, such as checking to see if the file exists and checking to see that there is no sharing violation.
Event 592: A New Process Has Been Created Event 560: Object Open Event 561: Handle Allocated Event 562: Handle Closed	In this series of events, a new process is created for NOTEPAD.EXE. This process opens the .TXT file for reading. Next, the process allocates, then closes, a handle to the file. Note that from the security log it is clear that Notepad does not keep an open handle to the file; it simply keeps a copy of the file in memory.
Event 560: Object Open Event 561: Handle Allocated Event 562: Handle Closed	The process opens the file for reading and writing, and since the event is a successful audit, new data is written to the file. Next, the handle is allocated for the open file, then closed.
Event 593: A Process Has Exited	This event indicates that the process, whose process ID relates to NOTEPAD.EXE, has ended.

Example 2: Use of User Rights

In this example, auditing is enabled by using User Manager to enable auditing for Success and Failure of Use of User Rights.

When the user tries to change the system time, only one event is generated, as shown in Figure 2.12.

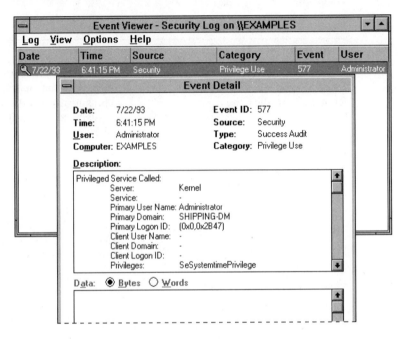

Figure 2.12   Security Event Posted After Changing the System Time

This event indicates that a privileged service was called and that a server component named Kernel has called an audit check on the primary username of the user. The audit type is a Success Audit, meaning that the user successfully exercised the right to use the SeSystemtimePrivilege (that is, the right to change the system time).

Example 3: User and Group Management

In this example, a new user account is added to the user accounts database. Auditing is enabled in User Manager by specifying both Success and Failure of User and Group Management. This generates four audit events, as shown below:

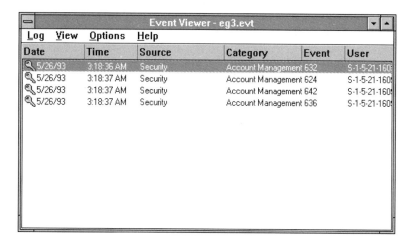

Figure 2.13   Security Events Posted After Adding a User Account

Table 2.2   Security Events for Added User Account

Event ID and description	Analysis
Event 632: Global Group Member Added Event 624: User Account Created	A new security ID (member) is created and added to the group represented by the target account ID. This is a default global group Domain Users. At this point, the security ID does not have a username allocated to it.
Event 642: User Account Changed	This event indicates that the account name of the security ID represented by the Target Account ID has been changed to the new user's.
Event 636: Local Group Member Added	This event indicates that the account represented by the new user's security ID is created. The new user is added to the local group represented the security ID under Target Account ID (Users).

Example 4: Restart, Shutdown and System

In this example, auditing is enabled in User Manager for both Success and Failure of Restart, Shutdown and System.

In this example, seven events were generated. Note, however, that the number of events generated is related to the number of trusted systems that you start when the system is restarted. This number may vary if you replicate this scenario on your own Windows NT computer.

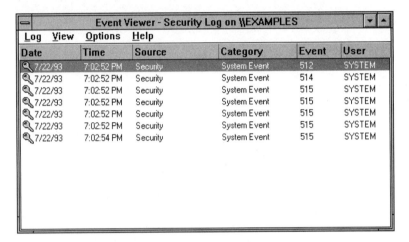

Table 2.3   Security Events for System Startup

Event ID and description	Analysis
Event 512: Windows NT is starting up.	Identifies the date and time the system started.
Event 514: Authentication package loaded	The description of this event says: An authentication package has been loaded by the Local Security Authority. This authentication package will be used to authenticate logon attempts. Authentication Package Name: msv 1_0 This is the standard authentication package shipped with Windows NT.

Table 2.3   Security Events for System Startup *(continued)*

Event ID and description	Analysis
Events 515: Trusted logon process	The description for each of these events says: `A trusted logon process has registered with the Local Security Authority. This logon process will be trusted to submit logon requests.` The logon process name is listed for each of these events, as follows: Winlogon Service Control Manager LAN Manager Workstation Service LAN Manager Server LAN Manager Redirector Each of these events is a successful audit in the category of system event. These events indicate that the respective logon processes have registered themselves with the Local Security Authority and are now trusted to submit logon requests.

Audit Determination

Windows NT has an audit determination process similar to its access determination process, described earlier in this chapter. Following access determination, Windows NT evaluates the following information for possible auditing:

- The subject attempting the access (that is, the set of identifiers representing the subject)
- The desired accesses with all generic access types mapped to standard and specific access types
- The final determination of whether access is granted or denied
- The audit ACL associated with the target object

Each ACE in the audit ACL is evaluated as follows:

1. Windows NT checks to see if the type is SystemAudit. If not, the ACE is skipped.

2. Windows NT compares the identifier in the ACE to the set of identifiers representing the subject. If no match is found, the ACE is skipped.

3. The desired accesses are compared to the access mask specified in the ACE.

4. If none of the accesses specified in the ACE's mask were requested, the ACE is skipped. The SUCCESSFUL_ACCESS_ACE_FLAG and FAILED_ACCESS_ACE_FLAG flags of the ACE are compared to the final determination of whether access was granted or denied.

5. If access was granted but the SUCCESSFUL_ACCESS_ACE_FLAG flag is not set, or if access was denied but the FAILED_ACCESS_ACE_FLAG flag is not set, the ACE is skipped.

If Windows NT performs all of these steps successfully, an audit message is generated.

The scenario shown in Figure 2.14 illustrates this process. In this scenario, a system access ACL is being evaluated. Here, Write access to the file object is granted, and the SUCCESSFUL_ACCESS_ACE_FLAG is set in each ACE.

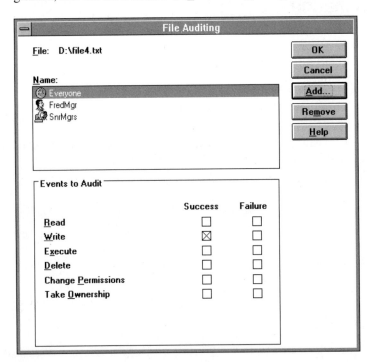

Figure 2.14   Auditing Determination

In this example, Windows NT evaluates the ACL by comparing the desired access mask with each ACE and processes the desired mask as follows:

1. Windows NT evaluates an ACE for SnrMgrs (of which FredMgr is a member). However, when the desired access is compared to the access mask of the ACE, no match is found, and the ACE is skipped.

2. Windows NT evaluates the ACE for FredMgr and finds a match.

3. Windows NT checks access flags and finds the SUCCESSFUL_ACCESS_ACE_FLAG is set. Processing stops, and an audit message is generated.

PART II

Setting Up Windows NT

Part Two discusses issues related to installing and starting Windows NT on your computer, including how to use computer profiles to set up multiple Windows NT computers. Chapter 4 also describes each of the files included on the Windows NT Setup disks.

CHAPTER 3

Customizing Windows NT Setup

This chapter describes how an administrator can customize the Windows NT Setup program to meet the specific needs of an organization. Administrators can customize Setup, for example, by adding files and applications to Windows NT, or by removing certain unused features, such as POSIX or OS/2 support, to reduce the amount of disk space needed to install Windows NT.

This chapter also explains how to use Computer Profile Setup, a utility program which makes it easy to install Windows NT on multiple computers with identical configurations within your organization.

This chapter assumes that you are very familiar with Windows NT Setup procedures presented in the *Windows NT System Guide*.

Note To ensure that you have sufficient permissions to complete all steps needed to customize Setup and modify information (.INF) files, you should log on as a member of the Administrator group.

About Windows NT Information Files

The first thing you need when you want to customize Windows NT Setup is a clear understanding of the Windows NT information (.INF) files. This is because .INF control the Setup program. These files are what you must modify when you want to customize Windows NT Setup for your organization.

As with MS-DOS versions of Windows, .INF files are used by Windows NT Setup uses to install the operating system. However, the structure of Windows NT .INF files is somewhat different than those used Windows 3.*x* and Windows for Workgroups. One main difference is that Windows NT .INF files contain a rich scripting language that allows the Setup program to perform various tasks.

The .INF files also contain lists of files that need to be copied to the target computer, plus the disk numbers for each to indicate where Setup can find the source of each file. The location of the source file depends on the *source media* used—3.5-inch floppy disks, 5.25-inch floppy disks, or CD-ROM. (If you are setting up from a shared network directory, Setup ignores any source disk numbers it finds, assuming instead that all files are on that shared directory.) The .INF files also list destinations for the files it copies.

Key Information Files Used by Setup

There are over 70 .INF files which are used by Setup, and each .INF file controls a different aspect of Setup. For a complete list of the .INF files and what they do, see Chapter 4, "Windows NT Files."

To customize Setup for your organization, you don't need a thorough understanding of all 70 .INF files. Instead, you need to be familiar with five key files, described in the table below.

Filename	Controls this part of Setup
TXTSETUP.INF	Text-mode installation of core Windows NT components. Used by Setup from CD-ROM or floppy disks, or via **winnt** command (discussed later).
INITIAL.INF	Graphical-mode installation of additional Windows NT components. Used by Setup via CD-ROM, floppy disks, or **winnt**.
PARTIAL.INF	Graphical-mode installation of optional Windows NT components and creation of Program Manager groups. Used by Setup via CD-ROM, floppy disks, or **winnt**.
DOSNET.INF	Contains the list of files copied to your local hard disk during **winnt** Setup. Used by the MS-DOS portion of **winnt** Setup only.
FILELIST.INF	Contains the list of files copied from the source media (CD or floppy disks) to create a network distribution share. Only used to create a network distribution share (discussed later).

While these five .INF files call other supporting .INF files, these five control the main flow for Setup. This section explains how each these files is used by Setup and how you might use them to customize your installation.

TXTSETUP.INF

When you begin the Setup program from CD-ROM or floppy disks, Setup first asks you where you want to install Windows NT and lets you reformat and repartition you hard disk. This all occurs in text mode (rather than Windows graphics mode). After the questions are answered, Setup copies the minimum set of files necessary for running Windows NT.

During this text-mode phase of Setup, drivers for your keyboard, mouse, video, SCSI adapter, and so on are installed. Setup also copies files (such as SETUP.EXE and all the .INF files) required to complete the setup process, then continue Setup in the graphical Windows environment.

TXTSETUP.INF is the file that lists all the files which need to be copied in this stage. TXTSETUP.INF also provides the lists of choices for video, mouse, and keyboard drivers.

INITIAL.INF

After all the files listed in TXTSETUP.INF are copied to your hard disk, Setup prompts you to restart your computer. The computer boots into graphical Windows Setup and INITIAL.INF guides this next part of Setup.

INITIAL.INF installs all the files needed to run a completely functional version of Windows NT. That is, INITIAL.INF causes Setup to install key components, including File Manager, Program Manager, fonts, and compatibility files for MS-DOS, Windows 16-bit, OS/2, and POSIX environments. INITIAL.INF does not install optional components such as CD Player.

INITIAL.INF initiates other parts of Setup, such as asking the user to choose optional components and install a printer.

If you are going to add to or subtract from the list of files to Setup that always installs, you will most likely make changes to this file. To change the fonts that are installed, you will need to change this file as well.

PARTIAL.INF

PARTIAL.INF contains the list of optional components, including screen savers, wallpapers, README files, and games. When someone installs Windows NT, he or she can selectively install only those files wanted on the local computer. All optional components are automatically installed with Windows NT if you selected Express Setup.

PARTIAL.INF is also responsible for creating Program Manager groups and adding programs to those groups.

If you want to add new optional components to Setup, or you want to restrict the set of optional components from which a user can choose, modify PARTIAL.INF. If you want to add new program groups for installation, modify this file.

FILELIST.INF

FILELIST.INF is only used to create a network distribution share. A *distribution share* is simply a shared network directory that contains all the files from the Windows NT CD-ROM or the Windows NT Setup floppy set. From this shared directory, a user can run the **winnt** command to install Windows NT from MS-DOS.

FILELIST.INF controls the process of creating a distribution share. This file contains a complete list of every file on the Setup floppy disk set or CD-ROM. When an administrator runs the following command to create a distribution share, Setup copies every file listed in FILELIST.INF to the destination directory:

```
Setup -n -d <destination> -i initial.inf -s <source>
```

For more information about the **Setup** command, see the *Windows NT System Guide*.

DOSNET.INF

DOSNET.INF is only used when setting up Windows NT across the network via the **winnt** command. To understand about DOSNET.INF, you must understand how the Setup process with **winnt** works.

Winnt copies files from a distribution share (rather than from a CD-ROM or set of floppies) to the target computer. The distribution share includes the complete set of files from the Windows NT Setup CD-ROM or floppy set.

When you run **winnt**, all the files on the distribution share are copied to the hard drive of the target computer. There, they are placed in a temporary directory called WIN_NT.~LS. DOSNET.INF defines which files get copied to this temporary directory.

Once the files are copied to the temporary directory, Winnt prompts you to restart the computer. At this point, Setup continues proceeds as though you were running Setup from a CD-ROM, except that Setup copies files from the WIN_NT.~LS directory rather than from CD-ROM.

As Setup progresses, TXTSETUP.INF, INITIAL.INF, and PARTIAL.INF specify which files are copied from the WIN_NT.~LS directory to the target directory you specify. At the end of Setup, the WIN_NT.~LS directory is deleted.

If several people within your company use the **winnt** command to install Windows NT and you want to customize the set of files that are installed, you must add or remove files from DOSNET.INF.

Important   Whenever you alter DOSNET.INF, you must alter at least one other .INF file (INITIAL.INF, PARTIAL.INF, or TXTSETUP.INF).

For example, if you add a file to INITIAL.INF, PARTIAL.INF or TXTSETUP.INF, you must also add it to DOSNET.INF. Otherwise Setup will not be able to find the file in the WIN_NT.~LS directory and will generate an error when it tries to copy the file. Conversely, if you add a file to DOSNET.INF but not add it to one of the other .INF files, then when you run winnt the file will be copied to the WIN_NT.~LS directory but will not be installed on your computer.

When making a custom floppy Setup set, FILELIST.INF also needs to be modified when files are added or deleted from the other .INF files.
(See "Creating a Custom Setup Floppy Disk Set" for details.)

Format of the INF Files

This chapter details several different scenarios for customizing Setup by altering the Windows NT .INF files. To best understand these scenarios, you need to understand how each of these five key .INF files are formatted.

INITIAL.INF, PARTIAL.INF, and FILELIST.INF

INITIAL.INF, PARTIAL.INF, and FILELIST.INF all have similar structure. They are text files that contain one or more sections. Each section begins with a section title, set off by brackets (for example, "[Files-I386-nt-system32]"). Most often, sections contain lists of files to be installed by Setup. Sections can also contain Setup scripting language.

Files are listed in the following format, where *disk number* is the number of the Setup floppy disk or CD on which the file exists:

disk number, *filename*, SIZE=*file size*

The following is an example of a section typical of INITIAL.INF, PARTIAL.INF, and FILELIST.INF files:

```
[Files-I386-nt-system32]
2,NETAPI.DLL , SIZE=23434
4,OS2SS.EXE , SIZE=47676
```

Each .INF file also contains a [Source Media Descriptions] section, which lists the Setup media. The number in the first column is related to the *disk number* in the file list above.

```
[Source Media Descriptions]
    1  = "Windows NT Setup Disk #1"  , TAGFILE = disk1
    2  = "Windows NT Setup Disk #2"  , TAGFILE = disk2
    3  = "Windows NT Setup Disk #3"  , TAGFILE = disk3
    ...
    29 = "Windows NT Setup Disk #29" , TAGFILE = disk29
```

Note Lines in these files in which the first character is a semicolon (;) are considered to be comments and are not used by Setup. Including comments in these files is helpful, for example, when you want to document changes you are making to them.

TXTSETUP.INF and DOSNET.INF use a pound sign, #, instead of a semicolon for commenting out lines.

Remember that you must use the correct symbol for the file you are modifying, otherwise Setup will fail.

TXTSETUP.INF

TXTSETUP.INF has a different format than INITIAL.INF, PARTIAL.INF, and FILELIST.INF. It too contains sections with section titles set off by brackets, but contains no scripting language.

TXTSETUP.INF includes lists of files, where each file is listed in the following format:

disk id,filename,install directory

Disk id is defined in the [SourceDisks] section. This section is similar to the [Source Media Descriptions] section but with a slightly different format.

Install directory is the directory the file will be copied to, as defined in the [WinntDirectories] section.

The following section is typical of TXTSETUP.INF:

```
[WinntFiles]
d10,DEFAULT,3
d3,SOFTWARE,3
d2,SYSTEM,3
```

Note   Lines in TXTSETUP.INF in which the first character is a pound sign (#) are considered to be comments and are not used by Setup. Remember that you must use the correct symbol for the file you are modifying, otherwise Setup will fail.

DOSNET.INF

DOSNET.INF is composed of section which contain no scripting language. Files are listed in the following format:

d1,*filename*

Note "d1," is not a disk number. This value, as defined in the [Directories] section, indicates where the file exists relative to the root of the distribution share.

Unlike the other .INF files, DOSNET.INF does not have a [Source Media Descriptions] section. In fact, no disk numbers are listed in it. The following section is a typical of DOSNET.INF:

```
[Files]
d1,256COLOR.BMP
d1,40291730.PPD
d1,40293930.PPD
d1,4MMDAT.SYS
d1,_DEFAULT.PIF
```

Note Lines in DOSNET.INF in which the first character is a pound sign (#) are considered to be comments and are not used by Setup.

Creating a Distribution Share

In most cases, people who customize Windows NT Setup are doing so for a corporation whose users want to run Setup from a distribution share. (Most of the scenarios described in this chapter assume this is the case.) Therefore, the first step—after installing Windows NT on at least one computer—is to set up a distribution share for your corporation.

As mentioned before, a distribution share is a directory which is shared on a network that contains all the files from either the Windows NT CD-ROM or the Windows NT floppy disks. Eventually you will be modifying the files on the distribution share, rather than trying to modify the files on a set of 23 floppy disks.

This section explains some of the caveats to creating Setup shares which you should be aware of, along with a few preparatory steps you will need to take before modifying the .INF files.

▶   **To create a distribution share**

1. Install Windows NT or Windows NT Advanced Server on any computer.

2. Run the following command:

```
Setup -n -d <destination> -i initial.inf -s <source>
```

<destination> is the name of the directory where you want all the Setup files to be copied to.

<source> is the location of the Windows NT Setup floppy disks (either A: or B:), or the path to the \i386 directory on the Windows NT Setup CD-ROM.

3. Setup will now copy the files from the source to the destination. When source is a floppy drive, Setup will keep prompting for new floppy disks until all of the appropriate files are copied.

4. Share the destination directory, making it read-only.

From target computers, users can connect to the distribution share and run the **winnt** command to start the installation process.

For more information, see the *Windows NT System Guide*.

Need for Multiple Distribution Shares

One problem exists when you create only a single distribution share. Because the .INF files were originally copied from either the Setup CD-ROM or the Setup floppy disk set, each copy of Windows NT installed via **winnt** also assumes it was installed by the same media (that is, CD-ROM or floppy disks). When a user at a workstation Setup via **winnt** wants to add a driver or otherwise adjust Windows NT via Setup, the Setup program will prompt the user for a disk from the original floppy disk set or for the CD-ROM. This is particularly inconvenient if the user's workstation does not include the correct drive type to use the original disk set.

(By the way, simply exchanging one media type for another will not work because Windows NT is reading a particular .INF file which lists the file it is seeking as being on a particular disk within the set. Disk 2 for the 3.5-inch Setup disks does not contain the same files as Disk 2 of the 5.25-inch Setup disks.)

Even more importantly, this problem prevents the user from using the Emergency Disk to replace damaged or deleted files.

To avoid problems like these, it is highly recommended that you create multiple distribution shares for the different types of computers in your organization, as in the following table.

Distribution share	Content
WINNT.144	Windows NT 1.44 MB layout for computers whose drive A is for 3.5-inch, 1.44 MB disks.
WINNT.12	Windows NT 1.2 MB layout for computers that do not have a drive for 3.5-inch, 1.2 MB disks. (Note that the 5.25-inch disk set is available by contacting Microsoft.)
WINNT.CD	Windows NT CD layout for computers with a CD-ROM drive.
WINNTAS.144	Windows NT Advanced Server 1.44 MB layout for computers whose drive A is for 3.5-inch, 1.44 MB disks.
WINNTAS.12	Windows NT Advanced Server 1.2 MB layout for computers that do not have a drive for 3.5-inch, 1.2 MB disks. (Note that the 5.25-inch disk set is available by contacting Microsoft.)
WINNTAS.CD	Windows NT Advanced Server CD layout for computers with a CD-ROM drive.

The simplest, though most time-consuming, way to create all these distribution shares is to go through the steps outlined in the previous section for each different type of computer in your organization. That is, perform all the steps using the 3.5-inch Setup disk set, then repeat the process using the 5.25-inch disk set, then using the Setup CD-ROM.

A less time-consuming way around this problem is to replace the file FILELIST.INF in the *SystemRoot*\SYSTEM32 directory with a version of the file from the CD, 3.5-inch, or 5.25-inch product sets before performing step 2 in the previous section. This method works because when you run **setup -n**, Setup looks at the file FILELIST.INF to determine which type of media (floppy disk or CD-ROM) the files are to be copied from.

Note FILELIST.INF is located on Disk 4 for both the 3.5-inch and 5.25-inch Windows NT and Advanced Server floppy sets, and is in the \I386 directory of the Windows NT and Windows NT Advanced Server CD-ROM.

Remember that the file is compressed on the distribution media (with the name FILELIST.IN_) and must be uncompressed using the **expand** command when you put it in the *SystemRoot*\SYSTEM32 directory. For more information, type **expand /?** to see online help about the **expand** command.

For example, suppose you have installed Windows NT via CD-ROM and you want to create a Setup share for computers with a 3.5-inch drive A. Follow these steps before running the **setup -n** option.

1. Log on with an account that has administrative privileges.
2. From the *SystemRoot*\SYSTEM32 directory, rename FILELIST.INF to FILELIST.OLD (or some other name).
3. Insert Setup Disk 4 in drive A (or drive B, as appropriate).
4. Assuming the disk is in drive A, type the following command (replace *SystemRoot* with the actual drive letter and directory of the Windows NT root directory):

```
expand -r a:\filelist.in_ %SystemRoot%\system32
```

The main use for the distribution shares you create is for installing Windows NT with the **winnt** command. These shares can also be used after a user has installed Windows NT wants to install additional files. For instance, suppose you want to install a printer driver. When Setup prompts you for the location of the printer driver, you can type in the path to the network distribution share.

Important Before modifying the .INF files you will need to decompress INITIAL.INF, FILELIST.INF, and PARTIAL.INF using the **expand -r** command. For example, you can type **expand -r initial.in_** to decompress INITIAL.IN_ from the distribution share. After using the Expand program to decompress these files, delete INITIAL.IN_, PARTIAL.IN_, and FILELIST.IN_ so Setup will not be confused about which file to use and so you will have a backup copy of these files. DOSNET.INF and TXTSETUP.INF are not, and should never be, compressed.

Customizing Setup

Caution   Setup is very unforgiving about bad syntax in its instructions, so please be very careful about modifications made to the .INF files. Never modify the original file (always make a copy). When you get part of your changes working, save a copy of the working file. Troubleshooting changes to the Setup .INF files is quite difficult!

Making changes to the Windows NT Setup .INF script files is not supported. This information is provided for your reference, but is not supported by Microsoft, or Microsoft Product Support Services.

Adding a File to the Windows NT Installation

If you simply want to add files during the installation of Windows NT, but don't need the file added to a Program Manager group, you will need to put the file on the distribution share and modify DOSNET.INF and INITIAL.INF.

For example, suppose an administrator at Terra Flora, Inc. wants to add an online help file that employees can reference to help resolve common problems for Terra Flora's business. The administrator adds TERRA.HLP to the distribution share, then makes changes to DOSNET.INF and INITIAL.INF as described in the next two sections.

Note   When you add files to Setup, be sure to change the minimum required disk space needed for installation. For more information, see "Changing Minimum Disk Space Requirements" later in this chapter.

DOSNET.INF

All files that need to be copied down from the Setup share when a user runs **winnt** are listed in the [Files] section of DOSNET.INF, preceded by "d1,".

The Terra Flora administrator adds the following line (in boldface type) to DOSNET.INF:

```
[Files]
d1,256COLOR.BMP
d1,40291730.PPD
d1,40293930.PPD
d1,terra.hlp
```

INITIAL.INF

Next, the administrator modifies the INITIAL.INF file, where entries are in the following format:

source disk number, filename, SIZE=*file size*

Since this and other Setup customization examples in this chapter assume you are modifying a distribution share, the *source disk number* is not important. This is because no floppy disks are used when running **winnt**. By default, set the disk number to 2. If you are creating a custom floppy Setup set, the *source disk number* is significant. See "Creating a Custom Floppy Setup" at the end of this chapter for more information.

The administrator adds the following line (in boldface type) to INITIAL.INF. In this case TERRA.HLP will be installed in the *SystemRoot*\SYSTEM32 directory.

```
[Files-I386-nt-system]
2,APPSTART.ANI , SIZE=999
2,BANANA.ANI , SIZE=999
2,BARBER.ANI , SIZE=999
2,COIN.ANI , SIZE=999
2,terra.hlp , SIZE=234
```

It makes a difference where you add a new filename in INITIAL.INF. This is because the section title determines the target directory in which the file will be installed. The following table shows the mapping of sections to the directory.

Section of INITIAL.INF	Installation directory
[Files-I386-nt]	*SystemRoot*
[Files-I386-nt-system]	*SystemRoot*\SYSTEM32
[Files-I386-nt-system-drivers]	*SystemRoot*\SYSTEM32\DRIVERS
[Files-I386-nt-system16]	*SystemRoot*\SYSTEM[1]
[Files-I386-nt-system16always]	*SystemRoot*\SYSTEM
[Files-I386-nt-compatibility]	*SystemRoot*[1]
[Files-I386-nt-system-os2]	*SystemRoot*\SYSTEM32\OS2
[Files-I386-nt-system-os2-dll]	*SystemRoot*\SYSTEM32\OS2\DLL

[1] Files are installed only if the user does not install Windows NT onto an existing Windows 3.*x* or Windows for Workgroups directory

Adding a New Program Manager Group

Windows NT Setup automatically creates the Main, Accessories, Administrative Tools, Games, and Startup Program Manager groups. To have Windows NT create a new Program Manager group you will need to modify PARTIAL.INF.

For example, the Terra Flora administrator creates a new program group called TerraFlora in which the help file, Terra Flora Help, will be included. To do this, the administrator added the following lines (boldface) to PARTIAL.INF:

```
[ProgmanGroups]
    Main
    Accessories
    AdminTools
    Games
    Startup
    TerraFlora

[ProgmanGroupsDescriptionENG]
    Main          = "Main"
    Accessories   = "Accessories"
    Games         = "Games"
    Startup       = "Startup"
    AdminTools    = "Administrative Tools"
    TerraFlora    = "Terra Flora Help"
```

Adding File Manager and Other Programs to the Startup Group

You may want to add frequently-used programs to the Startup group so they will be run automatically after logon. To add a program to the Startup group, you will need to modify PARTIAL.INF.

For example, the following changes to PARTIAL.INF start File Manager after the user logs on:

```
[InstallProgramGroups]
    set Groups                = ^(ProgmanGroups, 1)
    set MainToInstall         =
^(MainItems$(!STF_PRODUCT)$(!STF_PLATFORM), 1)
    set AdminToolsToInstall        = ^(AdminToolsItems$(!STF_PRODUCT),
1)
    set StartupToInstall          = ^(StartupItems,1)
; NOTE: Comment out the following line by prepending a semicolon.
;    set StartupToInstall = {}

[PartialDestinationVars]
    AdminToolsDest    = $(!STF_WINDOWSSYSPATH)
    StartupDest       = $(!STF_WINDOWSSYSPATH)
```

```
[StartupItems]
    FileManager

[StartupItemsENG]
    FileManager = "File Manager", WINFILE.EXE , WINFILE.EXE , "" , 0
```

You can install other standard Windows NT programs in the Startup group by just adding to the items in the [StartupItems] section and the [StartupItemsENG] section. The following table shows what to put in these sections. The last item, MiniUserManager, is part of Windows NT only. UserManager and ServerManager are part of Windows NT Advanced Server only.

[StartupItems]	[StartupItemsENG]
FileManager	FileManager = "File Manager", WINFILE.EXE , WINFILE.EXE , ""
Mail	Mail = "Mail", MSMAIL32.EXE , MSMAIL32.EXE , ""
SchedulePlus	SchedulePlus = "Schedule+", SCHDPL32.EXE , SCHDPL32.EXE , ""
ControlPanel	ControlPanel = "Control Panel", CONTROL.EXE , CONTROL.EXE , ""
PrintManager	PrintManager = "Print Manager", PRINTMAN.EXE , PRINTMAN.EXE , ""
Clipboard	Clipboard = "ClipBook Viewer", CLIPBRD.EXE , CLIPBRD.EXE , ""
Command	Command = "Command Prompt", CMD.EXE , CMD.EXE , "progman.exe",10
PerformanceMon	PerformanceMon = "Performance Monitor", PERFMON.EXE , PERFMON.EXE , "" , 0
Backup	Backup = "Backup", NTBACKUP.EXE , NTBACKUP.EXE , "" , 0
DiskManager	DiskManager = "Disk Administrator", WINDISK.EXE , WINDISK.EXE , "" , 0
EventViewer	EventViewer = "Event Viewer", EVENTVWR.EXE , EVENTVWR.EXE , "" , 0
UserManager	UserManager = "User Manager for Domains", USRMGR.EXE , USRMGR.EXE , "" , 0
ServerManager	ServerManager = "Server Manager", SRVMGR.EXE , SRVMGR.EXE , "" , 0
MiniUserManager	MiniUserManager = "User Manager", MUSRMGR.EXE , MUSRMGR.EXE , "" , 0

Adding Any Program to Any Program Manager Group

You are not restricted to adding programs to the Startup group only. This example shows how the Terra Flora administrator added the file TERRA.HLP (with the TERRA.ICO icon) to the Terra Flora Help Program group. The steps shown here can be used to add any program to any Program Manager group.

The first step in this process is to make sure the files are installed. In this case, the Terra Flora administrator adds the files TERRA.HLP and TERRA.ICO to Setup as described earlier in "Adding a File to the Windows NT Installation."

Next, if you are adding programs to a new program group, you must create that group, as described earlier in "Adding a New Program Manager Group."

Finally, you will need to modify PARTIAL.INF. For example, the Terra Flora administrator makes a number of changes to PARTIAL.INF to ensure that TERRA.HLP will be added to the Terra Flora Help program group.

The first change that the administrator makes is to the [PartialDestinationVars] section:

```
[PartialDestinationVars]
    ReadmeDest          = $(!STF_WINDOWSPATH)
    AccessoriesDest     = $(!STF_WINDOWSSYSPATH)
    GamesDest           = $(!STF_WINDOWSSYSPATH)
    SaversDest          = $(!STF_WINDOWSSYSPATH)
    WallpapersDest      = $(!STF_WINDOWSPATH)
    MainDest            = $(!STF_WINDOWSSYSPATH)
    AdminToolsDest  = $(!STF_WINDOWSSYSPATH)
    StartupDest = $(!STF_WINDOWSSYSPATH)
    TerraFloraDest  = $(!STF_WINDOWSSYSPATH)
```

The [PartialDestinationVars] section indicates where the files for the specific components will be installed in the system. $(!STF_WINDOWSPATH) means the *SystemRoot* directory. $(!STF_WINDOWSSYSPATH) means the *SystemRoot*\SYSTEM32 directory. The name in the left column matches the name of the group listed in the [ProgmanGroups] section (followed in the [ProgmanGroups] section by the text "Dest").

Next, the Terra Flora administrator adds a line to the [InstallProgramGroups] section:

```
[InstallProgramGroups]
    set Groups          = ^(ProgmanGroups, 1)
    set MainToInstall            =
^(MainItems$(!STF_PRODUCT)$(!STF_PLATFORM), 1)
    set AdminToolsToInstall          = ^(AdminToolsItems$(!STF_PRODUCT),
1)
    set TerraFloraToInstall   = ^(TerraFloraItems,1)
```

The [InstallProgramGroups] section specifies which group items will need to be installed in their respective groups. The item in the left column is the name of the group as mentioned in the [ProgmanGroups] section (followed in the [ProgmanGroups] section by the text "ToInstall"). The text in the right column is the name of the section where the program items are listed.

The administrator adds a new section to PARTIAL.INF to list the new program group and file:

```
[MainItemsWinntI386]
    FileManager
    ControlPanel
    ...
    readme

[TerraFloraItems]
    TerraFloraHelp
```

The [TerraFloraItems] section lists the key names of the items which will be installed in the TerraFlora group.

Finally, the administrator specifies the actual name of the file which is represented by the name TerraFloraHelp, using this format:

keyname = item description, command line, command line parameters, icon resource file, icon offset

```
[GamesItemsENG]
    Solitaire = "Solitaire",SOL.EXE,SOL.EXE,"",0
    Minesweeper = "Minesweeper",WINMINE.EXE,WINMINE.EXE, "",0
    Freecell = "Freecell",FREECELL.EXE,FREECELL.EXE, "",0

[TerraFloraItemsENG]
    TerraFloraHelp = "Terra Flora Help",WINHLP32.EXE,"WINHLP32.EXE
"$(!STF_WINDOWSSYSPATH)"\TERAFLOR.HLP","TERAFLOR.ICO",0
```

Adding a New Optional Accessory

Setup gives the user the opportunity to choose what optional accessories he or she wants to install and then creates a new program item for them in the Accessories Program Manager group. To add a new accessory, you must make the following modifications to PARTIAL.INF and DOSNET.INF.

For example, the Terra Flora administrator is adding a program called ORGCHART.EXE to the Accessories program group. To do this, the administrator first modifies PARTIAL.INF as follows:

```
[Files-I386-WindowsOptions]
Calculator = 2,CALC.EXE , SIZE=999
Cardfile = 2,CARDFILE.EXE , SIZE=999
TerraFloraOrgChart = 2,ORGCHART.EXE , SIZE=999
CDPlayer = 2,CDPLAYER.EXE , SIZE=999

[OptionalAccessoriesENG]
    Calculator              = "Calculator"
    Cardfile                = "Cardfile"
    TerraFloraOrgChart = "Terra Flora Organizational Chart"
    Clock                   = "Clock"

[AccessoriesItemsENG]
    Paintbrush      = "Paintbrush",      PBRUSH.EXE  , PBRUSH.EXE   ,
"" , 0
    Chat            = "Chat",            WINCHAT.EXE , WINCHAT.EXE  ,
"" , 0
    TerraFloraOrgChart = "Organizational Chart" , ORGCHART.EXE ,
ORGCHART.EXE , "" , 0
    Terminal        = "Terminal",        TERMINAL.EXE , TERMINAL.EXE ,
"" , 0
```

Next, the administrator adds a line (boldface) to DOSNET.INF:

```
[Files]
d1,256COLOR.BMP
d1,40291730.PPD
d1,40293930.PPD
d1,ORGCHART.EXE

...
```

Adding TrueType Fonts to Setup

If you have a license for the Microsoft Font Pack for Windows, you may want to have those fonts installed automatically by Setup. A TrueType font consists of a .TTF file and a .FOT file. The extension .TTF is given to the actual TrueType font file. The .FOT extension is used for the font header that points to the .TTF file.

Typically, during installation of the Font Pack, or by installing a TrueType font from the Control Panel, the .FOT file will be created, and appropriate entries made in the Windows NT Registry. To create the .FOT files to be locally installed on the Windows NT workstation, you will first need to install the Font Pack on any computer. Then copy the .TTF and .FOT files to the Windows NT distribution share.

There are 44 files in the Microsoft TrueType Font Pack for Windows. However, for the purpose of demonstration, we will install four files—Arial Narrow, Arial Narrow Bold, , Arial Narrow Bold Italic, and Arial Narrow Italic. The files are as follows in order:

True Type File	True Type Font Header
ARIALN.TTF	ARIALN.FOT
ARIALNB.TTF	ARIALNB.FOT
ARIALNBI.TTF	ARIALNBI.FOT
ARIALNI.TTF	ARIALNI.FOT

Add these files to Setup, as described earlier in "Adding a File to the Windows NT Installation." Make sure to install the files into the *SystemRoot*\SYSTEM directory by including them in the [Files-I386-nt-system16always] section.

Then make the following modification to INITIAL.INF. These modifications (boldface) will cause the fonts to be added to the Windows NT Registry:

```
INITIAL.INF

[FontList]
"Arial (TrueType)"                        = ARIAL.FOT
....
"Times New Roman Italic (TrueType)"       = TIMESI.FOT
"WingDings (TrueType)"                     = WINGDING.FOT
"Arial Narrow (TrueType)"                  = ARIALN.FOT
"Arial Narrow Bold (TrueType)"             = ARIALNB.FOT
"Arial Narrow Bold Italic (TrueType)"      = ARIALNBI.FOT
"Arial Narrow Italic (TrueType)"           = ARIALNI.FOT
```

Removing Files from Windows NT

If you do not need to have all of the functionality that Windows NT provides, and want to reduce the amount of disk space required by Windows NT, you may want to modify the Setup script files to not install the necessary supporting files. It is possible, for example, to save several megabytes of disk space by removing help files, NTBACKUP.EXE (tape backup), Windows NT Sequence Files, and infrequently-used programs. However, it is very important that you do not remove files which are required for the functioning of Windows NT. Refer to Chapter 4, "Windows NT Files" for information on the files you are thinking about removing. Chapter 4 describes the function of each file and helps to identify which ones you can safely remove, and which .INF file each is installed by.

To remove a file you must first comment out the filename in DOSNET.INF as in the following example. Prepend the appropriate line in the [Files] section with a #.

```
[Files]
...
d1,EXEBYTE2.SYS
# d1,EXE2BIN.EXE
d1,EXPAND.EXE
```

Next, if the file is listed in INITIAL.INF, comment out all occurrences of the file by prepending the line(s) with a semicolon.

Note Some files are listed more than once in INITIAL.INF. To remove these files you must make sure comment out both occurrences. If you comment out only one of them Setup will display an error message. Use the searching capability of your text editor to verify that you have commented out all occurrences of any file you want to remove.

The following example shows a line that is commented out in the INITIAL.INF file:

```
[Files-I386-nt-system]
...
2,EVENTVWR.EXE , SIZE=204676
;2,EXE2BIN.EXE , SIZE=8424
2,EXPAND.EXE , SIZE=39284
```

If the file is listed in TXTSETUP.INF, comment out the file by prepending the appropriate line in the [WinntFiles] section with a #, as in the following example:

```
[WinntFiles]
...
d2,MSMAIL32.HLP,2
d2,PERFMON.HLP,2
#d2,PIFEDIT.HLP,2
#d2,PRINTMAN.HLP,2
#d2,PROGMAN.HLP,2
d2,RASSETUP.HLP,2
#d2,REGEDT32.HLP,2
d2,SCHDPL32.HLP,2
```

Warning   Take extra care when removing files from TXSETUP.INF as most files listed here are required for running Windows NT.

The **findstr** command can help you find out which .INF files contain a certain file you want to remove.

Removing the OS/2 Subsystem

If you do not need support for OS/2 applications you can remove the files needed for OS/2 support by commenting the OS/2 support files. When users try to start an OS/2 application, they receive a message saying the executable file could not be located or that the subsystem is not available.

Modify INITIAL.INF as follows:

```
[Files-I386-nt-system-os2-dll]
;2,DOSCALLS.DLL , SIZE=12341
[Files-I386-nt-system]
;2,NETAPI.DLL , SIZE=119808
;2,OS2.EXE , SIZE=53552
;2,OS2SRV.EXE , SIZE=206848
;2,OS2SS.EXE , SIZE=15360
```

Comment out the same files in DOSNET.INF by prepending each file name with a "# ":

```
# d1,DOSCALLS.DLL
# d1,NETAPI.DLL
# d1,OS2.EXE
# d1,OS2SRV.EXE
# d1,OS2SS.EXE
```

Removing the POSIX Subsystem

To remove the POSIX subsystem, comment out the following files in INITIAL.INF and DOSNET.INF:

- PSXDLL.DLL
- PAX.EXE
- POSIX.EXE
- PXSSS.EXE

Removing Support for MS-DOS and Windows 16-Bit Applications

To remove the files needed to support for MS-DOS and Windows 16-bit applications, you must modify the INITIAL.INF file. There, you must comment out the routine that modifies the Registry key for MS-DOS and Windows 16-bit support as follows, otherwise Setup will report an error:

```
;vdmconfig =+
;    shell "subroutn.inf" PushBillboard STATUSDLG $(Billboard5)
;    Debug-Output "SETUP.INF: Configuring the DOS Subsystem."
;    ifstr(i) $(!STF_WIN31UPGRADE) == NO
;        shell "registry.inf" AppendToSystemPath "%SystemRoot%"
;    endif
;    read-syms ConfigSysAppend
;    read-syms AutoexecBatAppend
;    LibraryProcedure STATUS,$(!LIBHANDLE),VdmFixup $(AddOnConfig)
$(AddOnBatch)
;    ifstr(i) $(STATUS) == ERROR
;        shell "subroutn.inf" PopBillboard
;        EndWait
;        read-syms NonFatalError2$(!STF_LANGUAGE)
;        shell "subroutn.inf" SetupMessage $(!STF_LANGUAGE) NONFATAL
$(NonFatal)
;        StartWait
;    endif
;    ifstr(i) $(!STF_PLATFORM) == $(!PlatformID_Mips)
;        set wowfile = krnl286
;    else
;        set wowfile = krnl386
;    endif
;    shell "registry.inf" MakeWOWEntry $(wowfile)
```

Then comment out the following files from INITIAL.INF and DOSNET.INF so the files that support MS-DOS and Windows 16-bit applications will not be installed.

_DEFAULT.PIF	ANSI.SYS	APP850.FON
APPEND.EXE	ATTRIB.EXE	AUTOEXEC.NT
BIOS1.ROM	BIOS2.ROM	BLACK16.SCR
CGA40850.FON	CGA40WOA.FON	CGA80850.FON
CGA80WOA.FON	CHCP.COM	CHKDSK.EXE
CMOS.RAM	COMM.DRV	COMMAND.COM
COMMDLG.DLL[1]	COMP.EXE	CONFIG.NT
COUNTRY.SYS	DDEML.DLL	DEBUG.EXE
DISKCOMP.COM	DISKCOPY.COM	DOSAPP.FON
DOSKEY.EXE	DOSX.EXE	DRWATSON.EXE
EDIT.COM	EDIT.HLP	EDLIN.EXE
EGA.CPI	EGA40850.FON	EGA40WOA.FON
EGA80850.FON	EGA80WOA.FON	EXE2BIN.EXE
EXPAND.EXE	FASTOPEN.EXE	FC.EXE
FIND.EXE	FINDSTR.EXE	FORCEDOS.EXE
FORMAT.COM	GDI.EXE	GRAFTABL.COM
GRAPHICS.COM	GRAPHICS.PRO	HELP.EXE
HIMEM.SYS	KB16.COM	KEYB.COM
KEYBOARD.DRV	KEYBOARD.SYS	KRNL386.EXE
LABEL.EXE	LANMAN.DRV	LOADFIX.COM
MAPI.DLL	MCIOLE16.DLL	MEM.EXE
MMSYSTEM.DLL[1]	MMTASK.TSK[1]	MODE.COM
MORE.COM	MOUSE.DRV	NTCMDS.HLP
NTCMDS.IND	NTDOS.SYS	NTIO.SYS
NTVDM.DLL	NTVDM.EXE	OLECLI.DLL
OLESVR.DLL[1]	PIFEDIT.EXE	QBASIC.EXE
RECOVER.EXE	REDIR.EXE	REGEDIT.EXE
REGEDIT.HLP	REMLINE.BAS	REPLACE.EXE
RESTORE.EXE	SETUP16.INF	SETVER.EXE
SHARE.EXE	SHELL.DLL[1]	SORT.EXE
SOUND.DRV	SUBST.EXE	SYSEDIT.EXE
SYSTEM.DRV	SYSTEM.INI	TOOLHELP.DLL
TREE.COM	V7VGA.ROM	VDMDBG.DLL
VDMREDIR.DLL	VER.DLL[1]	VGA.DRV

WFWNET.DRV	WIN.COM	WIN.INI
WIN87EM.DLL	WINFILE.INI	WINHELP.EXE
WOW32.DLL	WOWDEB.EXE	WOWEXEC.EXE
WRITE.EXE	XCOPY.EXE	

[1] These files are listed twice in INITIAL.INF. Be sure to remove both occurrences of each to avoid receiving an error message from Setup.

Bypassing Printer and Application Setup on Express Installation

To skip printer and application Setup when Express Setup is chosen, add the following two lines (boldfaced) to INITIAL.INF.

```
[DoOptions]
    set Status = STATUS_FAILED
options = +
    ifstr(i) $(!STF_PRODUCT) == Winnt
        set OptionsGreyed = {}
    else
        set OptionsGreyed = {3}
    endif
    ifstr(i) $(!STF_WIN31UPGRADE) == "YES"
        set !DoAppSetup = $(!NotChosen)
        set OptionsGreyed = >($(OptionsGreyed), 4)
    endif
    ifstr(i) $(!STF_INSTALL_MODE) == EXPRESS
        set !DoPrinter   = $(!NotChosen)
        set !DoAppSetup  = $(!NotChosen)
        set Status = STATUS_SUCCESSFUL
```

Skipping Installation of All Optional Components

In Express Setup, the Setup program automatically installs all optional components. To not install any optional components in Express installation, you can explicitly comment out all the optional components (games, accessories, wallpapers, screen savers, and so on). This is rather time-consuming. A quicker process is to simply modify PARTIAL.INF as shown below, commenting out the instructions that tell Windows NT Setup to install the components:

```
set_partial_components = +
    StartWait
    ForListDo $(ComponentList)
        set $($)ToInstall = $($($)Install)
        set $($)ToRemove  = {}
    EndForListDo
    set SrcDir = $(!STF_SRCDIR)
;   install Install-PartialFileCopy
....
```

```
[ConfigureProgman]
    set Status = STATUS_FAILED
    read-syms PartialDestinationVars
    set AccessoriesToInstall = {}
    set ReadmeToInstall      = {}
    set GamesToInstall       = {}
    set WallpapersToInstall  = {}
    set SaversToInstall      = {}
;   ForListDo $($0)
;       set *($($), 1)ToInstall = *($($), 2)
;   EndForListDo
```

Changing Minimum Disk Space Requirements

If you remove or add files to Setup, it is a good idea to change the minimum disk space requirement as well. If the disk space requirement is too large, Setup will request more free disk space than necessary, and you may not be able to install on computers that really do have enough disk space. If the disk space requirement is too small, Setup may fail when trying to copy files to a full hard disk. Note that there is no way to change the disk space requirements for a CD-ROM or floppy disk based installation. The instructions here affect Setup via **winnt** only.

First modify DOSNET.INF as follows:

```
[SpaceRequirements]
BootDrive = 1048576
# NtDrive   = 89128960 NOTE: Commented out original disk space
requirement.
NtDrive   = 76000000
```

NtDrive is the number of bytes required on the drive where Windows NT is to be installed. Change this number as appropriate. For example, if you remove 3 megabytes of files from the original Windows NT installation, subtract 3 megabytes from the *NtDrive* number. If you add 3 megabytes of files to the Windows NT installation, add 3 megabytes to the *NtDrive* number. Do not change *BootDrive*.

Creating a Custom Setup Floppy Disk Set

Caution Do not modify the original Setup floppies. Make a copy of each floppy and modify the copy. It is very important for you to use DISKCOPY.EXE or the Copy Disk option in File Manager to do this.

Creating a custom floppy disk set is much more complicated than modifying a distribution share. One reason is because you may need to create additional Setup floppy disks to hold new files. In addition, if you modify an .INF file, it's possible that the file will no longer fit on the floppy where Setup expects to find it, so a custom floppy disk set may require shuffling files around from one floppy disk to another with more space. You will also need to modify FILELIST.INF, an .INF file you didn't need to change for modifying a distribution share.

Although the examples provided earlier in this chapter were written to assume that you were using a distribution share, all of them can be applied to creating a custom set of Setup floppy disks. One difference is that you will need to modify the .INF files on the Setup disks. In addition, while it made no difference which disk numbers you used for .INF files used by **winnt**, it is important that you are careful about specifying the correct disk numbers for the floppy disk set.

When creating a custom floppy disk set, be sure to remember these general guidelines:

- When you want to add new files to Setup, and hence need to add a new floppy disk to the disk set, modify the [Source Media Descriptions] sections in FILELIST.INF, INITIAL.INF, and PARTIAL.INF and/or [SourceDisks] section in TXTSETUP.INF.

- When you add or remove files from Setup, or move files from one floppy disk to another, change FILELIST.INF so that each file you added, deleted, or moved is recorded with the correct disk number.

- Change INITIAL.INF, PARTIAL.INF, or TXTSETUP.INF to accurately point to each file you add or move. (Although disk numbers are not important for distribution shares, they are critical for floppy disk sets.)

Hint If you are having trouble locating a particular file in the floppy disk set, look in the FILELIST.INF file on Disk 4. This file lists the disk on which each file is located. Remember that if an .INF file is compressed, you will first have to decompress it using **expand**, and then compress it with the **compress** utility when you are done back onto the same floppy disk.

Modifying .INF Files for a Custom Disk Set

If you are adding new files to Setup, you will need to create a new Setup disk to hold those files. If you modify an .INF file and it no longer fits on the original floppy disk, you may also need to create a new Setup disk to hold it.

To create a new Setup disk, first add the following line to the [Source Media Descriptions] section of FILELIST.INF, INITIAL.INF, and PARTIAL.INF.

```
[Source Media Descriptions]
    1  = "Windows NT Setup Disk #1"  , TAGFILE = disk1
    2  = "Windows NT Setup Disk #2"  , TAGFILE = disk2
    3  = "Windows NT Setup Disk #3"  , TAGFILE = disk3
    ...
   29 = "Windows NT Setup Disk #29" , TAGFILE = disk29
   30 = "Terra Flora Setup Floppy" , TAGFILE = disk30
```

The [Source Media Descriptions] section lists all the floppy disks in the Setup set. The format for the entries is as follows:

disk number = disk title, TAGFILE = *tagfile*

Disk title is the name of the disk; the user will be prompted for this text when Setup tries to copy files from that disk.

Tagfile is the name of a file on the floppy that Setup uses to verify that the correct disk is in the drive.

Next, add a similar line as follows to TXTSETUP.INF for each new floppy disk you are adding to the set:

```
[SourceDisks]
d0 = "Windows NT Setup Disk #1",\disk1
d1 = "Windows NT Setup Disk #1",\disk1,\,TopLevelSource
d2 = "Windows NT Setup Disk #2",\disk2,\,TopLevelSource
d3 = "Windows NT Setup Disk #3",\disk3,\,TopLevelSource
...
d29 = "Windows NT Setup Disk #29",\disk29,\,TopLevelSource
d30 = "Terra Flora Setup Floppy",\disk30,\,TopLevelSource
```

Now that Setup knows there is a new floppy disk in the set, create that disk. For example, the Terra Flora administrator copies the custom files onto a blank floppy disk labeled "Terra Flora Setup Floppy." To conserve disk space, you can compress the files you add with the Compress utility (included on the disks that come with this Resource Guide).

Next, create a file with the name disk30, or whatever name you specified for *tagfile*, on the disk. (The content of *tagfile* can be anything.)

The next step is to make sure that FILELIST.INF correctly reflects the contents of your disk set. For any file you add or move from one floppy disk to another, make sure that is reflected in FILELIST.INF. Be sure to specify the proper disk number for the file. The following is an example of a new entry in FILELIST.INF for a file added to Disk 30:

```
10, TELNET.TRM, SIZE=4096
9, TERMINAL.EXE, SIZE=216576
9, TERMINAL.HLP, SIZE=53248
30, TERRA.HLP , SIZE=23543
16, TFTP.EXE, SIZE=23040
```

Be sure that any file you add to PARTIAL.INF, INITIAL.INF, or TXTSETUP.INF is listed with the correct disk number as well. The following is an example from TXTSETUP.INF showing how the files are referenced:

```
d4,FILELIST.INF,2
d11,HARDWARE.INF,2
d9,INITIAL.INF,2
d11,KEYBOARD.INF,2
d4,LANGUAGE.INF,2
d11,LAYOUT.INF,2
```

Importance of the SETUP.LOG File

Setup creates a hidden, system, read-only file called SETUP.LOG in your *SystemRoot* directory. This file becomes very important if you need to reinstall Windows NT.

Caution Do not delete the SETUP.LOG file.

To reinstall Windows NT, the Setup program must be started again. As it did in the initial installation, Setup inspects your system's configuration and determines whether your computer has the required free disk space to install Windows NT. It also detects existing versions of Windows NT.

If your computer does not have the required free disk space, Setup gives you the option to delete the previous versions. If you select Yes, Setup uses the SETUP.LOG file to determine which files it can delete to make space on your hard disk. If SETUP.LOG is missing, no files can be deleted and you may be forced to reformat your hard disk to reinstall.

Using Windows NT Computer Profile Setup

The Windows NT Computer Profile Setup (CPS) utilities simplifies the distribution process for preinstalling and configuring Windows NT and Windows NT Advanced Server systems. The CPS utilities make a profile of a fully installed Windows NT or Windows NT Advanced Server system, then load the profile onto identical target computers streamlining subsequent installations. The CPS utility is only used with Intel-based processors.

The CPS uses *master* and *target* systems. The master system is the Windows NT or Windows NT Advanced Server computer that the prototype system is installed and configured on. The target systems are the computers onto which the master system profile is duplicated.

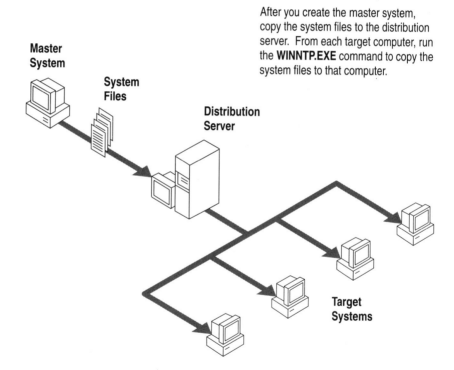

After you create the master system, copy the system files to the distribution server. From each target computer, run the **WINNTP.EXE** command to copy the system files to that computer.

Master System

System Files

Distribution Server

Target Systems

Loading CPS on the Master System

Windows NT or Windows NT Advanced Server must be fully installed on the master system before you can load the CPS utilities. See your *Windows NT Systems Guide* for more installation information.

▶ **To load the CPS**

1. Create the directory MASTER to store your master system. This directory should be in a location from which you can distribute it later. For example, create the share and directory X:\MASTER

2. From the Windows NT Resource Kit directory, type

   uplodprf -s:*x:\master* **-i:profile.ini** *[\additional software \additional software \..]*

   Where *x:\master* is the share where your master system is stored and *additional software* is the optional software you can configure to be installed on a computer.

   The **uplodprf** command copies the Registry files from the master system and removes user specific information. It also copies the WINNT directory and any additional applications or files that you specify.

Copying the Master-System Profile to Target Systems

The target computers must have the same hardware options as the master system such as video cards and bus types. However, target systems can have more memory and a larger disk than the master system. You can choose from several duplication options according to your requirements. Some of the methods used for duplicating the master disk include:

- Serial or Parallel Port File Transfer using a parallel connector--for example Xircom® Pocket Ethernet Adapter™
- Network Adapter or Interface

▶ **To copy the master-system profile to target systems**

1. Create a bootable disk that can access the network and/or a SCSI disk.
2. On the target system, type the WINNTP command from the Windows NT Resource Kit directory:

   winntp /s :*x:\master* /r

   Where *x:\master* is the directory storing your master computer profiles. The **/r** switch indicates that a profiled directory is being downloaded instead of a normal CD-ROM distribution.

   The **winntp** command downloads profiled files and installs them on the target systems.

C H A P T E R   4

Windows NT Files

This chapter describes the files included with Windows NT, including associated files that may be required or that work together with a specific file. Before deleting files from your system, you should check this chapter to determine whether the file is required to run Windows NT or any of its components.

Not all of these files may appear in your system, depending on your system hardware and the applications and accessories you choose to install.

The following list identifies the table to which you can refer for more information on files with a particular filename extension.

Extensions	See table	Extensions	See table
.ANI	4.16: Animated Cursors	.INF	4.4: Setup Script (.INF) Files
.BAS	4.19: Quick Basic Sample Files	.LEX	4.13: Spelling Lexicon Files
.BMP	4.18: Bitmapped Wallpaper Files	.NLS	4.14: National Language Support Files
.COM	4.1: Executable Files	.PPD	4.11: Adobe PostScript Printer Description Files
.CPI	4.9: Font Files	.SCR	4.17: Screen Saver Files
.DLL	4.3: Dynamic Link Library Files	.SEP	4.12: Printer Separator Page Definition Files
.DRV	4.2: Driver Files	.SEQ	4.7: Introduction to Windows NT Sequence Files
.EXE	4.1: Executable Files	.SYS	4.2: Driver Files
.FON	4.9: Font Files	.TTF	4.10: TrueType Font and Font Header Files
.FOT	4.10: TrueType Font and Font Header Files	.TXT	4.8: Text Files
.HLP	4.5: Online Help Files	.WAV	4.15: Sound Wave Files
.IND	4.6: Full Text Search Index for Online Helps	Other	4.20: Miscellaneous Files

Executable Files

The following table lists all of the executable (.EXE and .COM) files included with the Windows NT. The right column lists files that the executable file needs to run. That is, both the executable and associated library files must be installed in order to run the executable file. If you remove an associated library file from your system, the executable file will not run.

For a description of the DLLs listed in this table, see Table 4.3.

Table 4.1   Executable (.EXE and .COM) Files

Filename	File description and associated supported/supporting files
ACLCONV.EXE[2]	ACL conversion utility; converts OS/2 LAN Manager Server ACLs. Files: ULIB.DLL[4]
APPEND.EXE[2]	MS-DOS 5.0 utility.
ARCINST.EXE	Setup utility for RISC-based systems.
ARP.EXE	TCP/IP network utility to manipulate the ARP cache. Files: CRTDLL.DLL[4], WINSTRM.DLL[4], WSOCK32.DLL[4]
AT.EXE	Windows NT scheduling utility; schedules commands and programs to run on a computer. Files: NETAPI32.DLL[4]
ATSVC.EXE[2]	Windows NT Scheduling service. Files: CRTDLL.DLL[4], NETAPI32.DLL[4], RPCRT4.DLL[4]
ATTRIB.EXE[2]	File Attribute utility; displays or changes file attributes. Files: ULIB.DLL[4]
AUTOCHK.EXE[1]	Autocheck utility run during boot sequence.
AUTOCONV.EXE[2]	Startup file conversion utility.
AUTOSETP.EXE[2]	Component of Setup program.
BACKUP.EXE[2]	MS-DOS 5.0 backup utility.
BOOTOK.EXE[2]	Boot OK; part of the Service Controller; used for LastKnownGood control set functionality.
BOOTVRFY.EXE[2]	Boot Verify; LastKnownGood startup support component.
CALC.EXE[3]	Calculator tool. Files: SHELL32.DLL[4]
CARDFILE.EXE[3]	Cardfile tool. Files: COMDLG32.DLL[4], OLECLI32.DLL[4], SHELL32.DLL[4]
CDPLAYER.EXE[3]	CD-ROM Audio player support. Files: CRTDLL.DLL[4], SHELL32.DLL[4]
CHARMAP.EXE[3]	Character Map tool.
CHCP.COM[2]	MS-DOS utility (Change Code Page); displays or sets the active code page number.
CHKDSK.EXE[2]	Check Disk utility; checks a disk and displays a status report. Files: IFSUTIL.DLL[4], ULIB.DLL[4]
CLIPBRD.EXE[2]	Clipbook Viewer tool. Files: COMCTL32.DLL[4], NDDEAPI.DLL[4]
CLIPSRV.EXE[2]	Network DDE Clipbook service. Files: NDDEAPI.DLL[4]
CLOCK.EXE[3]	Clock tool. Files: COMDLG32.DLL[4], SHELL32.DLL[4]

Table 4.1   Executable (.EXE and .COM) Files *(continued)*

Filename	File description and associated supported/supporting files
CMD.EXE[2]	Windows NT single command shell interpreter.
COMMAND.COM[2]	Command interpreter for MS-DOS and Windows 16-bit VDMs.
COMP.EXE[2]	MS-DOS Compare utility; compares the contents of two files or sets of files. Files: ULIB.DLL[4]
CONTROL.EXE[2]	Control Panel.
CONVERT.EXE[2]	FAT to NTFS and HPFS to NTFS file system conversion utility. Files: IFSUTIL.DLL[4], ULIB.DLL[4]
CSRSS.EXE[1]	Client-server run-time server subsystem; Win32 API support. Files: CSRSRV.DLL[4]
DDESHARE.EXE[2]	Network dynamic data exchange share support. Files: CRTDLL.DLL[4], NDDEAPI.DLL[4]
DEBUG.EXE[2]	MS-DOS 5.0 Debug utility.
DISKCOMP.COM[2]	MS-DOS Disk Compare utility; compares the contents of two floppy disks.
DISKCOPY.COM[2]	MS-DOS Disk Copy utility; copies the contents of one floppy disk to another.
DISKPERF.EXE[2]	Performance Monitor command-line interface to enable and disable the disk counters.
DOSKEY.EXE[2]	MS-DOS 5.0 utility. Files: ULIB.DLL[4]
DOSX.EXE[2]	VDM DOS extender.
DRWATSON.EXE[2]	Win16 version of Dr. Watson; records faults in Win16 subsystem.
DRWTSN32.EXE[2]	Win32 version of Dr. Watson; records fault in native Windows NT. Files: COMDLG32.DLL[4], CRTDLL.DLL[4], WINMM.DLL[4]
EDIT.COM[2]	MS-DOS Editor.
EDLIN.EXE[2]	MS-DOS line editor.
EVENTLOG.EXE[2]	EventLog service. Files: RPCRT4.DLL[4]
EVENTVWR.EXE[2]	Event Viewer. Files: LMUICMN0.DLL[4], LMUICMN1.DLL[4]
EXE2BIN.EXE[2]	MS-DOS Exe2Bin utility.
EXPAND.EXE[2]	Expand utility to decompress files.
FASTOPEN.EXE[2]	MS-DOS utility.
FC.EXE[2]	File Comparison command utility; compares two files or sets of files, and displays the differences between them. Files: ULIB.DLL[4]
FIND.EXE[2]	Find command utility; searches for a text string in a file or files. Files: ULIB.DLL[4]
FINDSTR.EXE[2]	Find String command utility; searches for strings in files.
FINGER.EXE	TCP/IP utility; displays information about a user on a specified system running the Finger service. Output varies based on the remote system. Files: CRTDLL.DLL[4], WINSTRM.DLL[4], WSOCK32.DLL[4]
FORCEDOS.EXE[2]	Forces Windows NT to run the specified program as an MS-DOS application when the application executable file contains both the OS/2 and MS-DOS version in a bound executable file.
FORMAT.COM[2]	Windows NT command utility; formats a disk for use with Windows NT.
FREECELL.EXE[3]	Freecell solitaire game. Files: CARDS.DLL[4], SHELL32.DLL[4]

Table 4.1   Executable (.EXE and .COM) Files *(continued)*

Filename	File description and associated supported/supporting files
FTP.EXE	File Transfer Program; TCP/IP utility. Files: CRTDLL.DLL[4], WINSTRM.DLL[4], WSOCK32.DLL[4]
FTPSVC.EXE	FTP Server service . Files: CRTDLL.DLL[4], RPCRT4.DLL[4], WSOCK32.DLL[4]
GDI.EXE[2]	Win16 Graphics Device Interface API library; core Windows component.
GRAFTABL.COM[2]	Utility to enable Windows NT to display an extended character set in graphics mode.
GRAPHICS.COM[2]	Utility to allow MS-DOS to print screen contents when using CGA, EGA, or VGA display mode.
HELP.EXE[2]	Provides Help information for Windows NT. Files: ULIB.DLL[4], all online help (.HLP) files listed in Table 4.5
HOSTNAME.EXE	TCP/IP network utility to determine the system's local hostname. Files: CRTDLL.DLL[4], WINSTRM.DLL[4], WSOCK32.DLL[4]
INTRO.EXE[2]	Introduction to Windows NT executable. Files: All sequence (.SEQ) files; listed in Table 4.7; NT.DOC
IPXROUTE.EXE	Network IPX. Files: CRTDLL.DLL[4], WINSTRM.DLL[4]
KB16.COM[2]	Command-line keyboard program for specific language keyboard layouts[7]. Files: KEYBOARD.SYS[4]
KEYB.COM[2]	MS-DOS keyboard program for specific language keyboard layouts[7].
KRNL286.EXE	Win16 Standard-mode kernel routines.
KRNL386.EXE[2]	Win16 Enhanced-mode kernel routines.
LABEL.EXE[2]	Command-line utility to create, change, or delete the volume label of a disk. Files: IFSUTIL.DLL[4], ULIB.DLL[4]
LMREPL.EXE	LAN Manager Replicator service. Files: CRTDLL.DLL[4], NETAPI32.DLL[4], RPCRT4.DLL[4]
LMSVCS.EXE[2]	LAN Manager services including Workstation, Server, Alerter, Xactsrv. Files: RPCRT4.DLL[4]
LOADFIX.COM[2]	Windows command-line utility to load MS-DOS programs above the first 64K of memory.
LOCATOR.EXE	Supports Remote Procedure Calls (RPC). Files: NETAPI32.DLL[4], RPCRT4.DLL[4]
LSASS.EXE[1]	Local Security Authority server process. Files: CRTDLL.DLL[4], LSASRV.DLL[4], SAMSRV.DLL[4]
MAILSP32.EXE[2]	Microsoft Mail Spooler (32-bit). Files: CRTDLL.DLL[4], DEMIL32.DLL[4], MAILM32.DLL[4], STORE32.DLL[4]
MAPISRV.EXE	Microsoft Message API (MAPI) Server for Microsoft Mail and Microsoft Schedule+; processes internal service requests from other applications using MAPI. FILES: DEMIL32.DLL, MAPIXX.DLL
MEM.EXE[2]	Command-line utility; displays the amount of used and free memory in the system.
MODE.COM[2]	Command-line command utility.
MORE.COM[2]	Command-line command utility; displays output one screen at a time; similar to the MS-DOS MORE utility, but with added functionality.
MPLAY32.EXE[3]	Media Player multimedia application. Files: COMDLG32.DLL[4], MPR.DLL[4], OLESVR32.DLL[4], SHELL32.DLL[4], WINMM.DLL[4]

Table 4.1   Executable (.EXE and .COM) Files *(continued)*

Filename	File description and associated supported/supporting files
MPNOTIFY.EXE[2]	Run by Winlogon to notify multiple providers (such as Banyan®, Novell, and so on) of security events (such as change password and logon). Files: MPR.DLL[4]
MSCDEXNT.EXE[2]	Microsoft CD-ROM extensions.
MSGSVC.EXE[2]	Messenger Service. Files: CRTDLL.DLL[4], NETAPI32.DLL[4], RPCRT4.DLL[4]
MSMAIL32.EXE[2]	Microsoft Mail (32-bit). Files: COMDLG32.DLL[4], CRTDLL.DLL[4], AB32.DLL[4], DEMIL32.DLL[4], FRAME32.DLL[4], MAILM32.DLL[4], STORE32.DLL[4], VFORM32.DLL[4], SHELL32.DLL[4], WINMM.DLL[4]
MSRMND32.EXE[2]	Microsoft Schedule+ Reminder utility. Files: CRTDLL.DLL[4], DEMIL32.DLL[4], MAILM32.DLL[4], MSSCHD32.DLL[4], WINMM.DLL[4]
MUSRMGR.EXE[2]	User Manager (Windows NT base product). Files: LMUICMN0.DLL[4], LMUICMN1.DLL[4]
NBTSTAT.EXE	NetBIOS over TCP/IP networking statistics application. Files: CRTDLL.DLL[4], WINSTRM.DLL[4], WSOCK32.DLL[4]
NDDEAGNT.EXE[2]	Network DDE . Files: CRTDLL.DLL[4], NDDEAPI.DLL[4]
NDDEAPIR.EXE[2]	Network DDE. Files: CRTDLL.DLL[4]
NET.EXE[2]	Network command-line utility supporting commands such as **net use** and **net print**. Files: NETRAP.DLL[4], CRTDLL.DLL[4], NETAPI32.DLL[4], RPCRT4.DLL[4], SAMLIB.DLL[4]
NETDDE.EXE[2]	Network DDE background application. Files: CRTDLL.DLL[4], NDDEAPI.DLL[4], RPCRT4.DLL[4]
NETSTAT.EXE	TCP/IP utility for gathering network statistics information. Files: CRTDLL.DLL[4], WINSTRM.DLL[4], WSOCK32.DLL[4]
NLSFUNC.EXE[2]	Command-line utility to load country-specific information.
NOTEPAD.EXE[3]	Notepad tool. Files: COMDLG32.DLL[4], SHELL32.DLL[4]
NTBACKUP.EXE[2]	Windows NT Tape Backup application. Files: COMDLG32.DLL[4], MPR.DLL[4]
NTDETECT.COM[1]	Windows NT hardware detection code.
NTKRNLMP.EXE[1]	Windows NT Multiprocessor kernel. Files: HAL.DLL[4]
NTOSKRNL.EXE[1]	Windows NT operating system kernel. Files: HAL.DLL[4], HAL.DLL[5], HAL486C.DLL[5], HALAST.DLL[5], HALCBUS.DLL[5], HALMCA.DLL[5], HALNCR.DLL[5], HALOLI.DLL[5], HALSM2.DLL[5], HALSP.DLL[5], HALWYSE7.DLL[5],
NTVDM.EXE[2]	MS-DOS and Win16 application support. Files: VCDEX.DLL[5], VDMREDIR.DLL[5], WOW32.DLL[5],
NWLNKSVC.EXE	NWLink service. Files: CRTDLL.DLL[4], WINSTRM.DLL[4], WSHNWLNK.DLL[4]
NWNBLINK.EXE	NetWare NetBIOS Link (NWNBLink) service. Files: CRTDLL.DLL[4], WINSTRM.DLL[4]
OS2.EXE[2]	OS/2 command shell. Files: MPR.DLL[4], NETAPI32.DLL[4]
OS2SRV.EXE[2]	OS/2 subsystem server.
OS2SS.EXE[2]	OS/2 subsystem.
OSLOADER.EXE[1]	Loader for RISC-based systems. Files: SETUPAPP.EXE

Table 4.1   Executable (.EXE and .COM) Files *(continued)*

Filename	File description and associated supported/supporting files
PACKAGER.EXE[3]	Win16 Object Packager application. Files: COMDLG32.DLL[4], OLECLI32.DLL[4], OLESVR32.DLL[4], SHELL32.DLL[4]
PACKGR32.EXE[3]	Win32 Object Packager.
PAX.EXE[2]	POSIX tape archive program. Files: PSXDLL.DLL[4]
PBRUSH.EXE[3]	Paintbrush tool. Files: COMDLG32.DLL[4], OLESVR32.DLL[4], SHELL32.DLL[4]
PERFMON.EXE[2]	Performance Monitor application. Files: COMCTL32.DLL[4], COMDLG32.DLL[4], CRTDLL.DLL[4], SHELL32.DLL[4]
PIFEDIT.EXE[2]	Program Information File Editor; configures MS-DOS program execution attributes. Files: COMDLG32.DLL[4], SHELL32.DLL[4]
PING.EXE	TCP/IP Ping utility. Files: ICMP.DLL[4], CRTDLL.DLL[4], WINSTRM.DLL[4], WSOCK32.DLL[4]
PORTUAS.EXE[2]	Utility to Port the OS/2 LAN Manager User Account service to Windows N. Files: CRTDLL.DLL[4], NETAPI32.DLL[4], RPCRT4.DLL[4], SAMLIB.DLL[4]
POSIX.EXE[2]	POSIX console session manager.
PRINT.EXE[2]	Command-line utility to print a text file. Files: ULIB.DLL[4]
PRINTMAN.EXE[2]	Print Manager facility. Files: COMCTL32.DLL[4], COMDLG32.DLL[4], MPR.DLL[4], SHELL32.DLL[4]
PROGMAN.EXE[1]	Program Manager. Files: SHELL32.DLL[4]
PSXSS.EXE[2]	POSIX subsystem server. Files: NETAPI32.DLL[4], SAMLIB.DLL[4]
QBASIC.EXE[2]	Command-line Quick Basic application.
RASADMIN.EXE[1]	Remote Access Server Administrator. Files: LMUICMN0.DLL[4], LMUICMN1.DLL[4], NETAPI32.DLL[4], SAMLIB.DLL[4]
RASDIAL.EXE	Remote Access Server Dial tool. Files: RASAPI32.DLL[4]
RASMAN.EXE	Remote Access Server Manager. Files: RASMAN.DLL[4]
RASPHONE.EXE[1]	Remote Access user tool. Files: LMUICMN0.DLL[4], RASAPI32.DLL[4], RASFIL32.DLL[4], RASMAN.DLL[4]
RASSRV.EXE	Remote Access Server. Files: NETAPI32.DLL[4], RASADMIN.DLL[4], RASMAN.DLL[4], RASSAUTH.DLL[4]
RCP.EXE	Remote copy command (TCP/IP utility). Files: CRTDLL.DLL[4], WINSTRM.DLL[4], WSOCK32.DLL[4]
RECOVER.EXE[2]	Command-line utility to recover readable information from a bad or defective disk. Files: IFSUTIL.DLL[4], ULIB.DLL[4]
REDIR.EXE[2]	Network redirector for Win16 support; not required for startup.
REGEDIT.EXE[2]	Win16 Registry Editor.
REGEDT32.EXE[2]	Windows NT Registry Editor. Files: ACLEDIT.DLL[4], COMDLG32.DLL[4], NTLANMAN.DLL[4], SHELL32.DLL[4], ULIB.DLL[4], UREG.DLL[4]
REPLACE.EXE[2]	Command-line utility to replace files. Files: ULIB.DLL[4]

Table 4.1   Executable (.EXE and .COM) Files *(continued)*

Filename	File description and associated supported/supporting files
RESTORE.EXE[2]	Command-line utility for restoring files backed up using the MS-DOS Backup command.
REXEC.EXE	Remote shell with password authentication (TCP/IP tool). Files: CRTDLL.DLL[4], WINSTRM.DLL[4], WSOCK32.DLL[4]
ROUTE.EXE	TCP/IP network tool to modify or view IP routing tables. Files: CRTDLL.DLL[4], WINSTRM.DLL[4], WSOCK32.DLL[4]
RPCSS.EXE	Remote Procedure Call subsystem. Files: NETAPI32.DLL[4], RPCRT4.DLL[4]
RSH.EXE	TCP/IP network remote shell utility. Files: CRTDLL.DLL[4], WINSTRM.DLL[4], WSOCK32.DLL[4]
SCHDPL32.EXE[2]	Microsoft Schedule+. Files: COMDLG32.DLL[4], CRTDLL.DLL[4], AB32.DLL[4], DEMIL32.DLL[4], FRAME32.DLL[4], MAILM32.DLL[4], MSSCHD32.DLL[4], STORE32.DLL[4], SHELL32.DLL[4]
SCREG.EXE[1]	Services Control Registry and Service Control API; required for startup. Files: CRTDLL.DLL[4], RPCRT4.DLL[4]
SETACL.EXE[2]	Assigns ACLs during Setup.
SETUP.EXE[1]	Windows NT Setup program. Files: LZ32.DLL[4], SHELL32.DLL[4], VERSION.DLL[4]
SETUPAPP.EXE	Application setup portion of Windows NT Setup. Files: OSLOADER.EXE[4], USPIFS.DLL[5],
SETVER.EXE[2]	Command-line utility; sets the version number that Command-line reports to a program.
SFMPRINT.EXE	Services for Macintosh® Print Service. Files: SFMPSFNT.DLL[4]
SFMPSEXE.EXE	Services for Macintosh PostScript® Raster Image Processor program. Files: SFMPSDIB.DLL[4]
SFMSVC.EXE	Services for Macintosh file service. Files: NETAPI32.DLL[4], RPCRT4.DLL[4], SAMLIB.DLL[4]
SHARE.EXE[2]	Command-line utility to enable file sharing facilities.
SMSS.EXE[1]	Session Manager subsystem.
SNDREC32.EXE[3]	Sound Recorder application. Files: COMDLG32.DLL[4], OLESVR32.DLL[4], SHELL32.DLL[4], WINMM.DLL[4]
SNDVOL32.EXE[3]	Sound volume setting tool. Files: SHELL32.DLL[4], VERSION.DLL[4], WINMM.DLL[4]
SNMP.EXE	SNMP Service; proxy agent that listens for requests and hands them off to the appropriate network provider. Files: CRTDLL.DLL[4], WSOCK32.DLL[4]
SNMPTRAP.EXE	SNMP Trap Service; works with SNMP.EXE to receive Trap Packets. Files: CRTDLL.DLL[4], MGMTAPI.DLL[4]
SOL.EXE[3]	Solitaire game. Files: SHELL32.DLL[4]
SORT.EXE[2]	Command-line utility; sorts input and writes results to the screen, a file, or another device. Files: ULIB.DLL[4]
SPOOLSS.EXE[2]	Spooling subsystem for printing support. Files: RPCRT4.DLL[4], SPOOLSS.DLL[4]
SRVMGR.EXE[2]	Server Manager application. Files: LMUICMN0.DLL[4], LMUICMN1.DLL[4]
SUBST.EXE[2]	Command-line utility; associates a path with a drive letter. Files: ULIB.DLL[4]
SYSEDIT.EXE[2]	Win16 System Editor (for reading and editing CONFIG.SYS, AUTOEXEC.BAT, WIN.INI, and SYSTEM.INI files).

Table 4.1   Executable (.EXE and .COM) Files *(continued)*

Filename	File description and associated supported/supporting files
TASKMAN.EXE[2]	Task Manager program. Files: SHELL32.DLL[4]
TELNET.EXE	Starts the Telnet service (if not started already) and Windows Terminal.
TERMINAL.EXE[3]	Terminal application. Files: COMDLG32.DLL[4], SHELL32.DLL[4]
TFTP.EXE	Trivial File Transfer Protocol (TFTP) client over UDP (TCP/IP utility). Files: CRTDLL.DLL[4], WINSTRM.DLL[4], WSOCK32.DLL[4]
TREE.COM[2]	Command-line command utility; graphically display the directory structure of a drive or path.
UPEDIT.EXE[2]	User Profile Editor Application. Files: COMDLG32.DLL[4], LMUICMN0.DLL[4], SHELL32.DLL[4]
UPS.EXE[2]	Uninterruptible Power Supply Service. Files: CRTDLL.DLL[4], NETAPI32.DLL[4]
USER.EXE[2]	Win16 User for Win16 application compatibility.
USERINIT.EXE[2]	Windows NT logon user interface. Files: MPR.DLL[4]
USRMGR.EXE[2]	Windows NT User Manager for Domains. Files: LMUICMN0.DLL[4], LMUICMN1.DLL[4]
WIN.COM[2]	Win16 loader (for compatibility).
WINCHAT.EXE[3]	Windows NT Chat tool. Files: COMCTL32.DLL[4], COMDLG32.DLL[4], MPR.DLL[4], NTLANMAN.DLL[4], SHELL32.DLL[4], WINMM.DLL[4]
WINDISK.EXE[2]	Disk Administrator tool. Files: SHELL32.DLL[4]
WINFILE.EXE[2]	File Manager tool. Files: COMCTL32.DLL[4], SHELL32.DLL[4]
WINHELP.EXE[2]	Win16 help application.
WINHLP32.EXE[1]	Windows NT help application.
WINLOGON.EXE[1]	Windows NT logon utility. Files: NETAPI32.DLL[4]
WINMINE.EXE[3]	Minesweeper game. Files: SHELL32.DLL[4]
WINMSD.EXE[2]	Windows NT Microsoft Diagnostics. Files: CLB.DLL[4], COMCTL32.DLL[4], COMDLG32.DLL[4], CRTDLL.DLL[4], MPR.DLL[4], SHELL32.DLL[4], VERSION.DLL[4], WINMSD.DLL[4]
WINNT.EXE	Network-based Windows NT installation utility.
WINSPOOL.EXE[2]	Win16 print spooler/stub.
WINVER.EXE[2]	Windows NT version reporting utility.
WOWDEB.EXE[2]	Win16 debugger.
WOWEXEC.EXE[2]	Win16 shell; used to run 16-bit applications on behalf of Win32 applications.
WRITE.EXE[2]	Windows Write application (16-bit).
XCOPY.EXE[2]	Command-line command utility; copies files and directory trees. Files: IFSUTIL.DLL[4], ULIB.DLL[4]

[1] Installed during text-mode Setup by TXTSETUP.INF.

[2] Installed during graphical Setup by INITIAL.INF.

[3] Optional Windows NT component installed during graphical Setup by PARTIAL.INF.

[4] Supporting file. To use this file, the file listed in the "Filename" column must be installed.

[5] Supported file. This file must be installed to use the file listed in the "Filename" column.

[7] For information about using alternate keyboard layouts, see Appendix D, "International Considerations."

Driver Files

Drivers make device independence possible for Windows NT applications, providing the hardware-specific interface between physical devices and Windows NT. Setup can install several kinds of drivers for Windows NT, including the following:

Comm drivers	Display drivers	Keyboard drivers
Mouse drivers	Multimedia drivers	Network drivers
Printer drivers	Sound drivers	System drivers

(Multimedia and printer drivers are optional.)

Table 4.2 lists all of the driver (.DRV and .SYS) files included with Windows NT. The right column lists files that the driver file needs to run. Both the driver and associated files must be installed for the driver to function properly.

For a description of .EXE files listed in this table, see Table 4.1. For a description of .DLL files listed here, see Table 4.3.

Table 4.2   Driver (.DRV and .SYS) Files

Filename	File description and associated supported/supporting files
4MMDAT.SYS	4 mm DAT drive support; Archive® 4x20, WangDAT, HP 35470a, HP 35480a, COMPAQ®. Files: NTOSKRNL.EXE[4]
ABIOSDSK.SYS[1]	MCA non-SCSI (WD1003 compatible controller); *x86* only. Files: HAL.DLL[4],, NTOSKRNL.EXE[4]
AFD.SYS[2]	Ancillary Function Driver; provides kernel-mode support for Windows Sockets transport interface by extending the functionality of TDI. Files: HAL.DLL[4], NTOSKRNL.EXE[4], TDI.SYS[4]
AHA154X.SYS[1]	SCSIAdaptec 154x SCSI driver. Files: SCSIPORT.SYS[4]
AHA174X.SYS[1]	Adaptec 174x SCSI driver. Files: SCSIPORT.SYS[4]
ALWAYS.SYS[1]	Always SCSI miniport. Files: SCSIPORT.SYS[4]
AM1500T.SYS	AMD AM2100, AM1500T, and PCnet driver support. Files: HAL.DLL[4], NDIS.SYS[4], NTOSKRNL.EXE[4]
ANSI.SYS[2]	MS-DOS utility.
ARCHQIC.SYS	Tape driver support for Archive 2150s, 2525s, 2750. Files: NTOSKRNL.EXE[4]
ARROW.SYS[1]	SCSI miniport disk driver for Adaptec™ 2740/AIC 777x. Files: SCSIPORT.SYS[4]
ASYNCMAC.SYS	Remote Access Server Serial network driver. Files: HAL.DLL[4], NDIS.SYS[4], NTOSKRNL.EXE[4]
ATDISK.SYS[1]	ISA/EISA non-SCSI (WD1003 compatible controller). Files: HAL.DLL[4], NTOSKRNL.EXE[4]
ATI.SYS[1]	ATI video display driver (640 x 480 x 16 colors up to 1280 x 1024 x 16,777,216 colors). Files: NTOSKRNL.EXE[4], VIDEOPRT.SYS[4]

Table 4.2   Driver (.DRV and .SYS) Files *(continued)*

Filename	File description and associated supported/supporting files
BEEP.SYS[1]	Speaker port driver (ISA, MCA, EISA). Files: HAL.DLL[4], NTOSKRNL.EXE[4]
BRHJ770.DLL[4]	Network browser kernel component; redirector.
BUSLOGIC.SYS[1]	BusLogic family SCSI miniport. Files: SCSIPORT.SYS[4]
BUSMOUSE.SYS[1]	Microsoft or Logitech™ bus mouse driver. Files: HAL.DLL[4], NTOSKRNL.EXE[4]
CDAUDIO.SYS[2]	CD Audio support, only for specific non-SCSI-2 CD-ROM drives. Files: NTOSKRNL.EXE[4]
CDFS.SYS[1]	CD-ROM file system driver. Files: HAL.DLL[4], NTOSKRNL.EXE[4]
CDFS_REC.SYS[1]	CD-ROM file system recognizer. Files: NTOSKRNL.EXE[4]
CIRRUS.SYS[1]	Cirrus Logic display driver (640 x 480 x 16 colors to 1024 x 768 x 256 colors). Files: VIDEOPRT.SYS[4]
COMM.DRV[2]	Win16 communications driver.
COUNTRY.SYS[2]	MS-DOS utility; supports international time, dates, currency, case conversions, and decimal separators.
CPQARRAY.SYS[1]	COMPAQ disk array driver. Files: HAL.DLL[4], NTOSKRNL.EXE[4]
DELL_DGX.SYS[1]	Dell® DGX video display driver (640 x 480 x 256 colors to 1280 x 1024 x 256 colors; note: 1152 x 900 x 65536 color mode). Files: VIDEOPRT.SYS[4]
DELLDSA.SYS[1]	Driver for Dell intelligent disk array controller (available on high-end server systems from Dell). Files: HAL.DLL[4], NTOSKRNL.EXE[4]
DIGIFEP5.SYS	Digiboard FEP 5 adapter driver. Files: HAL.DLL[4], NTOSKRNL.EXE[4]
DISKPERF.SYS[2]	Disk performance statistics gatherer, collects simple statistics on the system disk performance; used in conjunction with the Performance Monitor. Files: HAL.DLL[4], NTOSKRNL.EXE[4]
DLC.SYS	Data Link Control driver. Files: HAL.DLL[4], NDIS.SYS[4], NTOSKRNL.EXE[4]
DPTSCSI.SYS[1]	EISA DPT controller. Files: SCSIPORT.SYS[4]
DTC329X.SYS[1]	DTC329x SCSI miniport driver. Files: SCSIPORT.SYS[4]
EE16.SYS	Network NDIS driver: Intel Ether Express card. Files: HAL.DLL[4], NDIS.SYS[4], NTOSKRNL.EXE[4]
ELNK16.SYS	Network NDIS driver: 3Com® Etherlink®-16 card. Files: HAL.DLL[4], NDIS.SYS[4], NTOSKRNL.EXE[4]
ELNK3.SYS	Network NDIS driver: 3Com Etherlink-III card. Files: HAL.DLL[4], NDIS.SYS[4], NTOSKRNL.EXE[4]
ELNKII.SYS	Network NDIS driver: 3Com Etherlink-II® card. Files: HAL.DLL[4], NDIS.SYS[4], NTOSKRNL.EXE[4]
ELNKMC.SYS	Network NDIS driver: 3Com Etherlink-MC card, 3Com Etherlink MCA driver. Files: HAL.DLL[4], NDIS.SYS[4], NTOSKRNL.EXE[4]
ET4000.SYS[1]	Video driver for Tseng Labs ET-4000 video chipset. Files: VIDEOPRT.SYS[4]
EXABYTE1.SYS	Tape driver for Exabyte 8200 series (SCSI-1). Files: NTOSKRNL.EXE[4]
EXABYTE2.SYS	Tape driver for Exabyte 8500 series (SCSI-2). Files: NTOSKRNL.EXE[4]
FASTFAT.SYS[1]	File Allocation Table (FAT) file system driver. Files: HAL.DLL[4], NTOSKRNL.EXE[4]
FAT_REC.SYS[1]	FAT file system recognizer. Files: NTOSKRNL.EXE[4]

Table 4.2   Driver (.DRV and .SYS) Files *(continued)*

Filename	File description and associated supported/supporting files
FD16_700.SYS[1]	SCSI miniport driver for Future Domain 16*xx* series cards. Files: SCSIPORT.SYS[4]
FD7000EX.SYS[1]	SCSI disk driver for Future Domain/Western Digital™ 7000EX controller (EISA). Files: SCSIPORT.SYS[4]
FD8XX.SYS[1]	SCSI disk driver for Future Domain 8*xx* controller. Files: SCSIPORT.SYS[4]
FLOPPY.SYS[1]	Floppy disk driver (non-SCSI). Files: HAL.DLL[4], NTOSKRNL.EXE[4]
FTDISK.SYS[1]	Fault Tolerant volume management driver. Files: HAL.DLL[4], NTOSKRNL.EXE[4]
HIMEM.SYS[2]	XMS driver for VDMs.
HPFS_REC.SYS[1]	High-performance file system recognizer driver. Files: NTOSKRNL.EXE[4]
I8042PRT.SYS[1]	Keyboard and i8042 mouse port driver. Files: HAL.DLL[4], NTOSKRNL.EXE[4]
IBMTOK.SYS	Network NDIS driver for IBM® Token Ring adapter and IBM Token Ring adapter/A. Files: HAL.DLL[4], NDIS.SYS[4], NTOSKRNL.EXE[4]
INPORT.SYS[1]	Microsoft InPort mouse port driver. Files: HAL.DLL[4], NTOSKRNL.EXE[4]
JAZZG300.SYS[1]	Jazz display driver.
JAZZG364.SYS[1]	Jazz display.
JAZZSND.SYS[1]	Acer ARC1 sound.
JZVXL484.SYS[1]	Video driver.
KBDCLASS.SYS[1]	Keyboard class driver. Files: HAL.DLL[4], NTOSKRNL.EXE[4]
KEYBOARD.DRV[2]	Win16 keyboard driver.
KEYBOARD.SYS[2]	Command-line keyboard driver.
LANCE.SYS	Network NDIS driver: DEC Lance adapter driver. Files: HAL.DLL[4], NDIS.SYS[4], NTOSKRNL.EXE[4]
LANMAN.DRV[2]	Win16 LAN Manager network driver.
LOOP.SYS	Microsoft loop-back network NDIS driver. Files: HAL.DLL[4], NDIS.SYS[4], NTOSKRNL.EXE[4]
LT200.SYS	Software for Macintosh, Apple LocalTalk® driver. Files: HAL.DLL[4], NDIS.SYS[4], NTOSKRNL.EXE[4]
MIPSSND.SYS	MIPS ARCSystem 100/150 sound.
MOUCLASS.SYS[1]	Mouse Class driver. Files: HAL.DLL[4], NTOSKRNL.EXE[4]
MOUSE.DRV[2]	Win16 mouse stub driver.
MSACM32.DRV[2]	Microsoft Audio Compression Manager driver.
MSFS.SYS[1]	Mailslot file system driver. Files: NTOSKRNL.EXE[4]
MUP.SYS[2]	Network Multiple UNC Provider (required). Files: NTOSKRNL.EXE[4]
MVAUDIO.SYS	Media Vision™ ProAudio Spectrum 16 driver. Files: HAL.DLL[4], NTOSKRNL.EXE[4]
MVOPL3.SYS	Media Vision OPL3 FM Synthesizer driver. Files: HAL.DLL[4], NTOSKRNL.EXE[4]
NBF.SYS	NetBEUI Frame (NBF) driver. Files: HAL.DLL[4], NDIS.SYS[4], NTOSKRNL.EXE[4], TDI.SYS[4]

Table 4.2   Driver (.DRV and .SYS) Files *(continued)*

Filename	File description and associated supported/supporting files
NBT.SYS	NetBIOS for TCP/IP driver, used for Windows Networking (RFC1001/1002). Files: HAL.DLL[4], NTOSKRNL.EXE[4], STREAMS.SYS[4]
NCR53C9X.SYS[1]	NCR SCSI disk driver for MIPS-based computers. Files: SCSIPORT.SYS[4]
NCR77C22.SYS[1]	Video driver for NCR 77C22 SVGA adapters. Files: VIDEOPRT.SYS[4]
NCRC700.SYS[1]	SCSI disk driver for NCR 53c700 controller. Files: SCSIPORT.SYS[4]
NCRC710.SYS[1]	SCSI disk driver for NCR 53c710 controller. Files: SCSIPORT.SYS[4]
NDIS.SYS[2]	NDIS wrapper driver; required for NDIS drivers. Files: HAL.DLL[4], NTOSKRNL.EXE[4]
NE1000.SYS, NE2000.SYS, NE3200.SYS	Network NDIS drivers for Novell NE1000, NE2000, and NE3200 adapters. Files: HAL.DLL[4], NDIS.SYS[4], NTOSKRNL.EXE[4]
NETBIOS.SYS	NetBIOS API driver; Microsoft NetBIOS Transport Interface. Files: HAL.DLL[4], NTOSKRNL.EXE[4]
NETDTECT.SYS[1]	Network card detection driver. Files: HAL.DLL[4], NTOSKRNL.EXE[4]
NETFLX.SYS	Network NDIS driver for COMPAQ NetFlex/DualSpeed Token Ring adapter card. Files: HAL.DLL[4], NDIS.SYS[4], NTOSKRNL.EXE[4]
NPEISA.SYS	Network peripherals FDDI, EISA NDIS driver. Files: HAL.DLL[4], NDIS.SYS[4], NTOSKRNL.EXE[4]
NPFS.SYS[1]	Named pipes file system driver. Files: HAL.DLL[4], NTOSKRNL.EXE[4]
NPMCA.SYS	Network peripherals FDDI, MCA NDIS driver. Files: HAL.DLL[4], NDIS.SYS[4], NTOSKRNL.EXE[4]
NTCX.SYS	Network NDIS driver for Digiboard C/X adapter. Files: HAL.DLL[4], NTOSKRNL.EXE[4]
NTDOS.SYS[2]	Command-line emulation driver.
NTFS.SYS[1]	Windows NT file system driver. Files: HAL.DLL[4], NTOSKRNL.EXE[4]
NTFS_REC.SYS[1]	Windows NT file system recognizer driver. Files: NTOSKRNL.EXE[4]
NTIO.SYS[2]	MS-DOS emulation BIOS driver.
NTXALL.SYS	Network NDIS driver for Digiboard PC/Xi, PC/2e, PC/4e, PC/8e. Files: HAL.DLL[4], NTOSKRNL.EXE[4]
NTXEM.SYS	Network NDIS driver for Digiboard PC/Xem. Files: HAL.DLL[4], NTOSKRNL.EXE[4]
NULL.SYS[1]	NULL device driver. Files: NTOSKRNL.EXE[4]
NWLINK.SYS	NWLink library. Files: HAL.DLL[4], NTOSKRNL.EXE[4], STREAMS.SYS[4]
NWNBLINK.SYS	NetWare NetBIOS Link (NWNBLink) network transport driver. Files: HAL.DLL[4], NTOSKRNL.EXE[4], STREAMS.SYS[4]
OLISCSI.SYS[1]	SCSI disk driver for Olivetti® ESC-1/ESC-2. Files: SCSIPORT.SYS[4]
PARALLEL.SYS[2]	Parallel port driver. Files: HAL.DLL[4], NTOSKRNL.EXE[4]
PCIMAC.SYS	Network NDIS driver for DigiBoard ISDN adapter. Files: HAL.DLL[4], NDIS.SYS[4], NTOSKRNL.EXE[4]
PINBALL.SYS[1]	HPFS driver. Files: HAL.DLL[4], NTOSKRNL.EXE[4]
PROTEON.SYS	Network driver for Proteon Token Ring adapter. Files: HAL.DLL[4], NDIS.SYS[4], NTOSKRNL.EXE[4]

Table 4.2   Driver (.DRV and .SYS) Files *(continued)*

Filename	File description and associated supported/supporting files
QIC117.SYS	Tape driver for QIC 117 floppy/tape drive. Files: HAL.DLL[4], NTOSKRNL.EXE[4]
QV.SYS[1]	Video miniport driver for COMPAQ Vision. Files: VIDEOPRT.SYS[4]
RASHUB.SYS	RAS Hub driver. Files: HAL.DLL[4], NDIS.SYS[4], NTOSKRNL.EXE[4]
RDR.SYS	Network redirector driver. Files: HAL.DLL[4], NTOSKRNL.EXE[4], SMBTRSUP.SYS[4]
S3.SYS[1]	Video driver library for S3 video chipsets (640 x 480 x 256 colors up to 1280 x 1024 x 256 colors). Files: VIDEOPRT.SYS[4]
SCSICDRM.SYS[1]	SCSI CD-ROM class driver. Files: NTOSKRNL.EXE[4]
SCSIDISK.SYS[1]	SCSI disk class driver. Files: HAL.DLL[4], NTOSKRNL.EXE[4]
SCSIFLOP.SYS[1]	SCSI class floppy driver; not required for startup. Files: HAL.DLL[4], NTOSKRNL.EXE[4]
SCSIPORT.SYS[1]	SCSI port driver. Files: HAL.DLL[4], NTOSKRNL.EXE[4]
SCSIPRNT.SYS[2]	SCSI print class driver. Files: NTOSKRNL.EXE[4]
SCSISCAN.SYS[2]	SCSI scanner class driver. Files: NTOSKRNL.EXE[4]
SERIAL.SYS[1]	Serial port driver. Files: HAL.DLL[4], NTOSKRNL.EXE[4]
SERMOUSE.SYS[1]	Serial mouse driver. Files: HAL.DLL[4], NTOSKRNL.EXE[4]
SFMATALK.SYS	Services for Macintosh AppleTalk® protocol driver. Files: HAL.DLL[4], NDIS.SYS[4], NTOSKRNL.EXE[4], TDI.SYS[4]
SFMSRV.SYS	Services for Macintosh file server driver. Files: HAL.DLL[4], NTOSKRNL.EXE[4]
SMBTRSUP.SYS	SMB trace support; required for RDR.SYS and SRV.SYS. Files: HAL.DLL[4], NTOSKRNL.EXE[4]
SMC8000N.SYS	Network NDIS driver for SMC (Western Digital) network adapter cards.
SNDBLST.SYS	Audio driver for Creative Labs SoundBlaster, also the Media Vision Thunder Board. Files: HAL.DLL[4], NTOSKRNL.EXE[4]
SNDSYS.SYS	Multimedia kernel driver. Files: HAL.DLL[4], NTOSKRNL.EXE[4]
SONIC.SYS	Network NDIS driver for MIPS (built-in on Jazz computers). Files: HAL.DLL[4], NDIS.SYS[4], NTOSKRNL.EXE[4]
SOUND.DRV[2]	Win16 Sound driver.
SPARROW.SYS[1]	Adaptec 151*x* and 152*x* SCSI miniport driver. Files: SCSIPORT.SYS[4]
SPOCK.SYS[1]	SCSI MCA SCSI driver. Files: SCSIPORT.SYS[4]
SRV.SYS	Network Server driver. Files: HAL.DLL[4], NTOSKRNL.EXE[4], SMBTRSUP.SYS[4], TDI.SYS[4]
STREAMS.SYS[2]	Streams driver; used by Streams-based protocols including TCP/IP and NWLink. Files: HAL.DLL[4], NDIS.SYS[4], NTOSKRNL.EXE[4], TDI.SYS[4]
SYNTH.SYS	Synthesizer driver. Files: HAL.DLL[4], NTOSKRNL.EXE[4]
SYSTEM.DRV[2]	Win16 system driver.
T128.SYS[1]	Trantor 128 SCSI miniport driver. Files: SCSIPORT.SYS[4]
T13B.SYS[1]	Trantor 130b SCSI miniport driver. Files: SCSIPORT.SYS[4]

Table 4.2   Driver (.DRV and .SYS) Files *(continued)*

Filename	File description and associated supported/supporting files
TANDQIC.SYS	Tape driver for Tandberg 3660, 3820, 4120, and 4220. Files: NTOSKRNL.EXE[4]
TCPIP.SYS	TCP/IP driver; includes TCP/IP modules such as IP, UDP, TCP, and ARP. Files: HAL.DLL[4], NTOSKRNL.EXE[4], STREAMS.SYS[4]
TDI.SYS[2]	Network TDI wrapper (required). Files: NTOSKRNL.EXE[4]
TELNET.SYS	Telnet driver. Files: HAL.DLL[4], NTOSKRNL.EXE[4]
TMV1.SYS[1]	SCSI miniport driver for Trantor MediaVision. Files: SCSIPORT.SYS[4]
TRIDENT.SYS[1]	Video driver for Trident display adapters (640 x 480 x 16 colors to 1024 x 768 x 256 colors). Files: VIDEOPRT.SYS[4]
UBNEI.SYS	Ungermann-Bass® network adapter driver. Files: HAL.DLL[4], NDIS.SYS[4], NTOSKRNL.EXE[4]
ULTRA124.SYS[1]	SCSI disk driver for UltraStor 124f controller. Files: SCSIPORT.SYS[4]
ULTRA14F.SYS[1]	SCSI disk driver for UltraStor 14f, 34f controller. Files: SCSIPORT.SYS[4]
ULTRA24F.SYS[1]	SCSI disk driver for UltraStor 24f controller. Files: SCSIPORT.SYS[4]
V7VRAM.SYS[1]	Video Seven VRAM driver. Files: VIDEOPRT.SYS[4]
VGA.DRV[2]	Windows-16 VGA stub driver.
VGA.SYS[1]	VGA class driver. Files: VIDEOPRT.SYS[4]
VGA_ALT.SYS[2]	VGA alternate video driver. Files: VIDEOPRT.SYS[4]
VIDEOPRT.SYS[1]	VGA video port driver. Files: HAL.DLL[4], NTOSKRNL.EXE[4]
WANGQIC.SYS	Tape driver for Wangtek 525, 250 tape drives. Files: NTOSKRNL.EXE[4]
WD33C93.SYS	SCSI disk driver for Maynard/Western Digital 33c93 controller (ISA). Files: SCSIPORT.SYS[4]
WDVGA.SYS[1]	Video driver for Western Digital/Paradise display adapters (604 x 480 x 16 colors to 1024 x 768 x 256 colors). Files: VIDEOPRT.SYS[4]
WFWNET.DRV[2]	Windows for Workgroups 16-bit network stub driver.
WINSPOOL.DRV[1]	Win32 print spooler interface that contains the print spooler API calls.
XGA.SYS[1]	XGA video driver. Files: VIDEOPRT.SYS[4]

[1] Installed during text-mode Setup by TXTSETUP.INF.

[2] Installed during graphical Setup by INITIAL.INF.

[3] Optional Windows NT component installed during graphical Setup by PARTIAL.INF.

[4] Supporting file. To use this file, the file listed in the "Filename" column must be installed.

[5] Supported file. This file must be installed to use the file listed in the "Filename" column.

Dynamic Link Library Files

The following table lists all of the dynamic link library (.DLL) files included with Windows NT. Certain files in the left column (those with a superscript 5) must have supporting files present on your system; if you remove the associated file from your system, the DLL will not function properly.

For a description of .EXE files listed in this table, see Table 4.1.

Table 4.3   Dynamic Link Library (.DLL) Files

Filename	File description and associated supported/supporting files
AB32.DLL[2]	Microsoft Mail and Microsoft Schedule+ Address Book (32-bit) library. Files: CRTDLL.DLL[4], DEMIL32.DLL[4], FRAME32.DLL[4], MAILM32.DLL[4], MSMAIL32.EXE[5], SCHDPL32.EXE[5], MAPIXX.DLL[5], SCHMSG32.DLL[5], VFORM32.DLL[5]
ACLEDIT.DLL[2]	Access control list editor library. Files: CRTDLL.DLL[4], LMUICMN0.DLL[4], LMUICMN1.DLL[4], NETAPI32.DLL[4], RPCRT4.DLL[4], REGEDT32.EXE[5]
ADVAPI32.DLL[1]	Advanced API Services library supporting numerous APIs including many security and Registry calls.
ALRSVC.DLL[2]	Alerter service library. Files: CRTDLL.DLL[4], NETAPI32.DLL[4], RPCRT4.DLL[4]
AMDNCDET.DLL[1]	Network Control Panel Tool detection library for AM1500T card. Files: NETDTECT.DLL[4]
ATI.DLL[1]	Driver support library for ATI video display driver. Files: WINSRV.DLL[4]
BASESRV.DLL[1]	Windows NT base services support. Files: CSRSRV.DLL[4], WINSRV.DLL[5]
BRHJ770.DLL	Brother® HJ-770 printer driver library.
BROTHER9.DLL	Brother 9-pin dot-matrix driver (Brother M-1309, M-1809, M-1818, M-1909, M-1918).
BROTHR24.DLL	Brother 24-pin dot-matrix driver (Brother M-1324, M-1824L, M-1924L).
BROWSER.DLL	Network browser service. Files: CRTDLL.DLL[4], NETAPI32.DLL[4], RPCRT4.DLL[4]
CANON330.DLL	Canon® Bubble-Jet driver (supports BJ models 10e, 10ex, 10sx, 130, 130e, 20, 200, 230, 300, 330); also supports Mannesmann Tally MT 93, 94. Files: —
CANON800.DLL	Canon Bubble-Jet BJC-800 driver.
CARDS.DLL[2]	Playing cards library used by FREECELL.EXE. Files: FREECELL.EXE[5]
CIT24US.DLL	Citizen 24-pin dot-matrix printer driver; supports Citizen models 124D, 224, GSX models 130, 140, 140+, 145, 230, PN48, Prodot24, Swift models 200, 24, 24e, 24x. Files: —
CIT9US.DLL	Citizen 9-pin dot-matrix printer driver, supports Citizen models 120D, 120D+, 180D, 200GX, 200GX/15 and HSP models 500, 550, Prodot 9, Prodot 9x, Swift 9 and Swift 9x.
CITOH.DLL	C. Itoh® printer driver supports AT&T 470, 475 and C-Itoh 8510.
CLB.DLL[2]	Microsoft Diagnostics support library. Files: COMCTL32.DLL[4], CRTDLL.DLL[4], WINMSD.EXE[5]
COMCTL32.DLL[1]	Windows NT common internal controls library. Files: CLIPBRD.EXE[5], PERFMON.EXE[5], PRINTMAN.EXE[5], WINCHAT.EXE[5], WINFILE.EXE[5], WINMSD.EXE[5], CLB.DLL[5]

Table 4.3   Dynamic Link Library (.DLL) Files *(continued)*

Filename	File description and associated supported/supporting files
COMDLG32.DLL[1]	Windows NT common dialog API library. Files: SHELL32.DLL[4], CARDFILE.EXE[5], CLOCK.EXE[5], DRWTSN32.EXE[5], MPLAY32.EXE[5], MSMAIL32.EXE[5], NOTEPAD.EXE[5], NTBACKUP.EXE[5], PACKAGER.EXE[5], PBRUSH.EXE[5], PERFMON.EXE[5], PIFEDIT.EXE[5], PRINTMAN.EXE[5], REGEDT32.EXE[5], SCHDPL32.EXE[5], SNDREC32.EXE[5], TERMINAL.EXE[5], UPEDIT.EXE[5], WIN3270.EXE[5], WINCHAT.EXE[5], WINMSD.EXE[5], DRIVERS.DLL[5], HTUI.DLL[5], MSSFS32.DLL[5], VFORM32.DLL[5], WGPOMG32.DLL[5], WOW32.DLL[5]
COMMDLG.DLL[2]	Win16 common dialog API library.
CRTDLL.DLL[1]	C Run-time support library (not recommended to remove this file). Files: ARP.EXE[5], ATSVC.EXE[5], CDPLAYER.EXE[5], DDESHARE.EXE[5], DRWTSN32.EXE[5], FINGER.EXE[5], FTP.EXE[5], FTPSVC.EXE[5], HOSTNAME.EXE[5], IPXROUTE.EXE[5], LMREPL.EXE[5], LSASS.EXE[5], MAILSP32.EXE[5], MCSXNSVC.EXE[5], MSGSVC.EXE[5], MSMAIL32.EXE[5], MSRMND32.EXE[5], NBTSTAT.EXE[5], NDDEAGNT.EXE[5], NDDEAPIR.EXE[5], NET.EXE[5], NETDDE.EXE[5], NETSTAT.EXE[5], NWLNKSVC.EXE[5], NWNBLINK.EXE[5], PERFMON.EXE[5], PING.EXE[5], PORTUAS.EXE[5], RCP.EXE[5], REXEC.EXE[5], ROUTE.EXE[5], RSH.EXE[5], SCHDPL32.EXE[5], SCREG.EXE[5], SNMP.EXE[5], SNMPTRAP.EXE[5], SYMEDIT.EXE[5], TFTP.EXE[5], TOOLKIT.EXE[5], UBNBSVC.EXE[5], UPS.EXE[5], WINMSD.EXE[5], AB32.DLL[5], ACLEDIT.DLL[5], ALRSVC.DLL[5], BOWSVC.DLL[5], CFG3270.DLL[5], CLB.DLL[5], CUFAT.DLL[5], CUHPFS.DLL[5], DEMIL32.DLL[5], DGCONFIG.DLL[5], DIGIINST.DLL[5], DLC3270.DLL[5], FRAME32.DLL[5], FTPSVC.DLL[5], HPMON.DLL[5], ICMP.DLL[5], IFSUTIL.DLL[5], IMPEXP32.DLL[5], INETMIB1.DLL[5], ISDN.DLL[5], LMHSVC.DLL[5], LMMIB2.DLL[5], LMUICMN0.DLL[5], LMUICMN1.DLL[5], LOCALMON.DLL[5], LSASRV.DLL[5], MAILM32.DLL[5], MAPI32.DLL[5], MAPIXX.DLL[5], MGMTAPI.DLL[5], MSSCHD32.DLL[5], MSSFS32.DLL[5], NBTSVC.DLL[5], NDDEAPI.DLL[5], NETAPI32.DLL[5], NETBIOS.DLL[5], NETLOGON.DLL[5], NTLANMAN.DLL[5], NWLNKCFG.DLL[5], PABNSP32.DLL[5], PERFCTRS.DLL[5], PHONE32.DLL[5], RASAPI32.DLL[5], RASCFG.DLL[5], RASFIL32.DLL[5], RASGTWY.DLL[5], RASMXS.DLL[5], RASSAUTH.DLL[5], RASSER.DLL[5], SCHMSG32.DLL[5], SENDFL32.DLL[5], SETUPDLL[5].DLL[5], SFMATCFG.DLL[5], SFMPSDIB.DLL[5], SFMUTIL.DLL[5], SFMWSHAT.DLL[5], SNA3270.DLL[5], SRVSVC.DLL[5], STORE32.DLL[5], TCPIPSVC.DLL[5], TELNET.DLL[5], TRC3270.DLL[5], TRNSCH32.DLL[5], UFAT.DLL[5], UHPFS.DLL[5], ULIB.DLL[5], UNTFS.DLL[5], UREG.DLL[5], VCDEX.DLL[5], VDMREDIR.DLL[5], VFORM32.DLL[5], WGPOMG32.DLL[5], WIN32SPL.DLL[5], WINSTRM.DLL[5], WKSSVC.DLL[5], WOW32.DLL[5], WSHTCPIP.DLL[5], WSOCK32.DLL[5], XACTSRV.DLL[5], XNSCFG.DLL[5]
CSRRTL.DLL[1]	Client-server run-time library.
CSRSRV.DLL[1]	Client-server run-time server. Files: CSRSS.EXE[5], BASESRV.DLL[5], MMSNDSRV.DLL[5], WINSRV.DLL[5]
CUFAT.DLL[2]	FAT to NTFS file system conversion library. Files: IFSUTIL.DLL[4], CRTDLL.DLL[4], UFAT.DLL[4], ULIB.DLL[4], UNTFS.DLL[4]
CUHPFS.DLL[2]	HPFS to NTFS file system conversion library. Files: IFSUTIL.DLL[4], CRTDLL.DLL[4], UHPFS.DLL[4], ULIB.DLL[4], UNTFS.DLL[4]
DDEML.DLL[2]	DDE Manager library API library.
DEC24PIN.DLL	Digital printer driver; supports the DECwriter 95, Digital LA models 324, 424, 75 Plus.
DEC3200.DLL	Digital printer driver; supports the DEClaser 1100, 2100, 2200, 3200.
DEC9PIN.DLL	Digital printer driver; supports the LA models 310, 70, 75.

Table 4.3   Dynamic Link Library (.DLL) Files *(continued)*

Filename	File description and associated supported/supporting files
DEMIL32.DLL[2]	Microsoft Workgroup Applications System Services layer. Files: CRTDLL.DLL[4], MPR.DLL[4], MAILSP32.EXE[5], MAPISRV.EXE[5], MSMAIL32.EXE[5], MSRMND32.EXE[5], SCHDPL32.EXE[5], AB32.DLL[5], FRAME32.DLL[5], IMPEXP32.DLL[5], MAILM32.DLL[5], MAPIXX.DLL[5], MSSCHD32.DLL[5], MSSFS32.DLL[5], OOF32.DLL[5], PABNSP32.DLL[5], SCHMSG32.DLL[5], STORE32.DLL[5], TRNSCH32.DLL[5], VFORM32.DLL[5], WGPOMG32.DLL[5]
DGCONFIG.DLL	Network NDIS driver for Digiboard serial driver. Files: CRTDLL.DLL
DICONIX.DLL	Diconix 150 Plus.
DIGIINST.DLL	Network NDIS driver for Digiboard ISDN. Files: CRTDLL.DLL[4]
DLCAPI.DLL[2]	Data Link Control API library. Files: HPMON.DLL[5]
DOSCALLS.DLL[2]	OS/2 subsystem thunk DLLs.
DRIVERS.DLL[2]	Control Panel tool for installing drivers. Files: COMDLG32.DLL[4], VERSION.DLL[4], WINMM.DLL[4]
Epson24.DLL	Printer driver for Epson® compatible 24-pin dot-matrix printers.
Epson9.DLL	Printer driver for Epson compatible 9-pin dot-matrix printers.
ESCP2E.DLL	Printer drive for Epson compatible scalable printers, Citizen GSX 240, Citizen Swift 240, and Epson AP models 3250, 5000, 5500, and Epson models LQ-100, LQ-1070, LQ-570, LQ-870, SQ-1170.
FMIFS.DLL[2]	Mediator between the Installable File System utilities and File Manager. Files: IFSUTIL.DLL[4], ULIB.DLL[4]
FRAME32.DLL[2]	Microsoft Workgroup Applications Framework layer. Files: CRTDLL.DLL[4], DEMIL32.DLL[4], SHELL32.DLL[4], MSMAIL32.EXE[5], SCHDPL32.EXE[5], AB32.DLL[5], IMPEXP32.DLL[5], MAPIXX.DLL[5], SCHMSG32.DLL[5], VFORM32.DLL[5], WGPOMG32.DLL[5]
FRAMEBUF.DLL[1]	Display library to support the DELL DGX display driver. Files: WINSRV.DLL[4]
FTENG32.DLL[1]	Full-text search engine library. Files: FTUI32.DLL[4], FTUI32.DLL[5]
FTPSMX.DLL	File Transfer Program (FTP) Server management extensions for Server Manager . Files: FTPSVC.DLL[4], LMUICMN0.DLL[4], LMUICMN1.DLL[4], NETAPI32.DLL[4], WSOCK32.DLL[4]
FTPSVC.DLL	FTP Server management API support for Control Panel . Files: CRTDLL.DLL[4], NETAPI32.DLL[4], RPCRT4.DLL[4], FTPSMX.DLL[5]
FTUI32.DLL[1]	Full text search user interface library. Files: FTENG32.DLL[4], FTUI32.DLL[5]
FUJI24.DLL	Printer driver for Fujitsu® DL series of printers, including the 900, 1100, 1100 color, 1150, 1200, 1250, 2400, 2600, 3300, 3350, 3400, 3450, 3600, 4400, 4600, and 5600.
FUJI9.DLL	Printer driver for Fujitsu DX series of printers, including the 2100, 2200, 2300, 2400.
GDI32.DLL[1]	Windows NT 32-bit Graphics Device Interface API library; core Windows NT component.
HAL.DLL[1]	Hardware Abstraction Layer (HAL) for Industry Standard Architecture (ISA) computers. Files: NTOSKRNL.EXE[4], NTKRNLMP.EXE[5], NTOSKRNL.EXE[5]
HAL486C.DLL[1]	HAL for COMPAQ 486C computers. Files: NTOSKRNL.EXE[4]
HALACR.DLL[1]	HAL for pica-61 (Acer) computers.
HALAST.DLL[1]	HAL for AST® computers. Files: NTOSKRNL.EXE[4]

Table 4.3   Dynamic Link Library (.DLL) Files *(continued)*

Filename	File description and associated supported/supporting files
HALCBUS.DLL[1]	HAL for Corollary Extended C-bus. Files: NTOSKRNL.EXE[4]
HALDTI.DLL[1]	HAL for Deskstation Arcstation I.
HALDUOMP.DLL[1]	HAL for duo MP computers.
HALFXS.DLL[1]	HAL for jazz computers.
HALMCA.DLL[1]	HAL for MCA. Files: NTOSKRNL.EXE[4]
HALNCR.DLL[1]	HAL for NCR. Files: NTOSKRNL.EXE[4]
HALOLI.DLL[1]	HAL for Olivetti. Files: NTOSKRNL.EXE[4]
HALSP.DLL[1]	SystemPro version of HAL. Files: NTOSKRNL.EXE[4]
HALWYSE7.DLL[1]	HAL for Wyse. Files: NTOSKRNL.EXE[4]
HPDSKJET.DLL	Printer driver for HP DeskJet and DeskJet models 500, 500C, 510, 550C, Plus, and Portable.
HPMON.DLL	HP Monitor; HP LaserJet IIIsi support library. Files: DLCAPI.DLL[4], CRTDLL.DLL[4], SPOOLSS.DLL[4]
HPPCL.DLL	HP Printer Control Language driver; used by many HPPCL compatible printers.
HPPCL5MS.DLL	Microsoft implementation of the HPPCL 5.0 driver; used by various HPPCL5-compatible printers.
HTUI.DLL[2]	User interface library provided for display or printer driver's halftone color adjustments . Files: COMDLG32.DLL[4], PSCRPTUI.DLL[5], RASDDUI.DLL[5]
IBM238X.DLL	Printer driver for IBM 4216-020 version 47.0.
IBM239X.DLL	Printer driver for IBM Personal Printer II models 2390, and 2391.
IBM5204.DLL	Printer driver for IBM QuickWriter 5204.
IBMPORT.DLL	Printer driver for IBM Portable 5183.
ICMP.DLL	ICMP helper DLL used by Ping . Files: CRTDLL.DLL[4], WINSTRM.DLL[4], PING.EXE[5]
IFSUTIL.DLL[2]	Startup **chkdsk** utility; can be omitted from a bare-bones startup system if all volumes used to startup are guaranteed not to be corrupt. Files: CRTDLL.DLL[4], ULIB.DLL[4], CHKDSK.EXE[5], CONVERT.EXE[5], LABEL.EXE[5], RECOVER.EXE[5], XCOPY.EXE[5], CUFAT.DLL[5], CUHPFS.DLL[5], FMIFS.DLL[5], UFAT.DLL[5], UHPFS.DLL[5], UNTFS.DLL[5]
IMAGEHLP.DLL[2]	An API set for manipulating images. Files: CHECKFIX.EXE[5], NTSD.EXE[5], SYMEDIT.EXE[5]
IMPEXP32.DLL[2]	Microsoft Mail file import utility. Files: CRTDLL.DLL[4], DEMIL32.DLL[4], FRAME32.DLL[4], STORE32.DLL[4], VFORM32.DLL[4]
INETMIB1.DLL	TCP/IP Management Information Base. Files: CRTDLL.DLL[4], WINSTRM.DLL[4], WSOCK32.DLL[4]
IOLOGMSG.DLL[2]	Contains message file for error log status codes.
ISDN.DLL	Network NDIS driver for Digiboard ISDN. Files: CRTDLL.DLL[4]
JP350.DLL	Printer driver used by the Universal Printer Driver (RASDD.DLL) to support Olivetti JP 350, Olivetti JP 350S, Digital DECmultiJET 2000, Bull Compuprint PM 201, Fujitsu Breeze 200, Citizen PROjet, Olivetti JP 150, Digital DECmultiJET 1000, Fujitsu Breeze 100, Royal CJP 450, NEC Jetmate 400, NEC Jetmate 800. Files: RASDD.DLL

Table 4.3   Dynamic Link Library (.DLL) Files *(continued)*

Filename	File description and associated supported/supporting files
JZVXL484.DLL	Video driver.
KBDBE.DLL[1]	Belgian keyboard layout[7].
KBDCA.DLL[1]	Canadian multilingual keyboard layout[7].
KBDDA.DLL[1]	Danish keyboard layout[7].
KBDDV.DLL[1]	U.S. English Dvorak keyboard layout[7].
KBDES.DLL[1]	Español (Spanish alternate) keyboard layout[7].
KBDFC.DLL[1]	French Canadian keyboard layout[7].
KBDFI.DLL[1]	Finnish keyboard layout[7].
KBDFR.DLL[1]	French keyboard layout[7].
KBDGR.DLL[1]	German keyboard layout[7].
KBDIC.DLL[1]	Icelandic keyboard layout[7].
KBDIT.DLL[1]	Italian keyboard layout[7].
KBDLA.DLL[1]	Latin (Latin American Spanish) keyboard layout[7].
KBDNE.DLL[1]	Netherlands (Dutch) keyboard layout[7].
KBDNO.DLL[1]	Norwegian keyboard layout[7].
KBDPO.DLL[1]	Polish keyboard layout[7].
KBDRU.DLL[1]	Russian keyboard layout[7].
KBDSF.DLL[1]	Swiss-French keyboard layout[7].
KBDSG.DLL[1]	Swiss-German keyboard layout[7].
KBDSP.DLL[1]	Spanish keyboard layout[7].
KBDSW.DLL[1]	Swedish keyboard layout[7].
KBDUK.DLL[1]	UK-English keyboard layout[7].
KBDUS.DLL[1]	U.S. keyboard layout[7].
KBDUSX.DLL[1]	U.S. English keyboard layout[7].
KERNEL32.DLL[1]	Windows NT 32-bit base API support; core Windows NT component.
KYOCERA.DLL	Printer driver for Apricot Laser and Kyocera F series printers.
LMHSVC.DLL	NetBIOS over TCP/IP (NBT) LMHOSTS parsing support. Files: CRTDLL.DLL[4], WINSTRM.DLL[4]
LMMIB2.DLL	LAN Manager management information base. Files: CRTDLL.DLL[4], NETAPI32.DLL[4]
LMUICMN0.DLL[1]	Network user interface DLLs. Files: CRTDLL.DLL[4], LMUICMN1.DLL[4], SAMLIB.DLL[4], EVENTVWR.EXE[5], MUSRMGR.EXE[5], RASADMIN.EXE[5], RASPHONE.EXE[5], SRVMGR.EXE[5], UPEDIT.EXE[5], USRMGR.EXE[5], ACLEDIT.DLL[5], FTPSMX.DLL[5], LMUICMN1.DLL[5], MPRUI.DLL[5], NTLANMAN.DLL[5], RASCFG.DLL[5], SFMATCFG.DLL[5]
LMUICMN1.DLL[1]	LAN Manager Common User Interface library. Files: NETRAP.DLL[4], CRTDLL.DLL[4], LMUICMN0.DLL[4], NETAPI32.DLL[4], SAMLIB.DLL[4], EVENTVWR.EXE[5], MUSRMGR.EXE[5], RASADMIN.EXE[5], SRVMGR.EXE[5], USRMGR.EXE[5], ACLEDIT.DLL[5], FTPSMX.DLL[5], LMUICMN0.DLL[5], MPRUI.DLL[5], NTLANMAN.DLL[5], RASCFG.DLL[5], SFMATCFG.DLL[5]

Table 4.3   Dynamic Link Library (.DLL) Files *(continued)*

Filename	File description and associated supported/supporting files
LOCALMON.DLL[2]	Local Monitor; used to send a print job to a port. Files: CRTDLL.DLL[4], SPOOLSS.DLL[4]
LOCALSPL.DLL[2]	Local Spooling support for printing. Files: SPOOLSS.DLL[4]
LSASRV.DLL[1]	Local Security Authority server process. Files: CRTDLL.DLL[4], RPCRT4.DLL[4], SAMSRV.DLL[4], LSASS.EXE[5], MSV1_0.DLL[5], NETLOGON.DLL[5], SAMSRV.DLL[5]
LZ32.DLL[1]	Windows NT 32-bit compression routines. Files: SETUP.EXE[5], VERSION.DLL[5]
LZEXPAND.DLL[2]	Windows NT 32-bit expansion routines.
MAILM32.DLL[2]	Microsoft Mail Manager and support functions (32-bit). Files: CRTDLL.DLL[4], DEMIL32.DLL[4], STORE32.DLL[4], MAILSP32.EXE[5], MSMAIL32.EXE[5], MSRMND32.EXE[5], SCHDPL32.EXE[5], AB32.DLL[5], MAPIXX.DLL[5], MSFT32.DLL[5], MSSCHD32.DLL[5], MSSFS32.DLL[5], PABNSP32.DLL[5], PHONE32.DLL[5], SCHMSG32.DLL[5], STORE32.DLL[5]
MANTAL24.DLL	Printer driver for Mannesmann Tally® 24-pin dot-matrix printers; supports MT series 82, 130/24, 131/24, 150/24, 230/24, 330, 350, 360.
MANTAL90.DLL	Printer driver for Mannesmann Tally MT 90.
MANTALBJ.DLL	Printer driver for Mannesmann Tally MT 92, 92C.
MAPI.DLL[2]	Microsoft Messaging API library (16-bit).
MAPI32.DLL[2]	Microsoft Messaging API library (32-bit). Files: CRTDLL.DLL[4]
MAPIXX.DLL[2]	Microsoft MAPI support routines for Microsoft Mail and Microsoft Schedule+; used by the MAPSRV.EXE process to service MAPI calls. Files: CRTDLL.DLL[4], AB32.DLL[4], DEMIL32.DLL[4], FRAME32.DLL[4], MAILM32.DLL[4], STORE32.DLL[4], VFORM32.DLL[4], MAPISRV.EXE[5]
MCIAVI32.DLL[2]	Media Contol Interface Audio Video Interleave API support library. Files: MSVFW32.DLL[4], WINMM.DLL[4]
MCICDA.DLL[2]	Compact Disk Audio MCI library. Files: WINMM.DLL[4]
MCIOLE16.DLL[2]	MCI Object Linking and Embedding (OLE) library, 16-bit.
MCIOLE32.DLL[2]	MCI OLE library, 32-bit. Files: OLECLI32.DLL[4]
MCISEQ.DLL[2]	Music Instrument Digital Interface Sequencer MCI layer. Files: WINMM.DLL[4]
MCIWAVE.DLL[2]	MCI Wave output library. Files: WINMM.DLL[4]
MF3216.DLL[1]	Converts Win32 metafiles to Win16 metafiles.
MGMTAPI.DLL	SNMP component; Management API library. Files: CRTDLL.DLL[4], WSOCK32.DLL[4], SNMPTRAP.EXE[5]
MIDIMAP.DLL[2]	Control Panel tool library. Files: WINMM.DLL[4],
MMDRV.DLL[2]	Multimedia API library. Files: WINMM.DLL[4]
MMSNDSRV.DLL[1]	Multimedia sound server library. Files: CSRSRV.DLL[4]

Table 4.3   Dynamic Link Library (.DLL) Files *(continued)*

Filename	File description and associated supported/supporting files
MMSYSTEM.DLL[2]	16-bit entry point to multimedia applications.
MORICONS.DLL[2]	More Icons, a resource library of icons.
MPR.DLL[1]	Multiple Provider Router library; takes Win32 networking APIs and passes the call to the correct network provider (should not be required for startup, except that Program Manager calls restore connections). Files: MPLAY32.EXE[5], MPNOTIFY.EXE[5], NTBACKUP.EXE[5], OS2.EXE[5], PRINTMAN.EXE[5], USERINIT.EXE[5], WINCHAT.EXE[5], WINMSD.EXE[5], DEMIL32.DLL[5], MPRUI.DLL[5], MSSFS32.DLL[5], OLECLI32.DLL[5], TRNSCH32.DLL[5], WGPOMG32.DLL[5], WOW32.DLL[5]
MPRUI.DLL[2]	Multiple Provider user interface, helper library for MPR.DLL. Files: LMUICMN0.DLL[4], LMUICMN1.DLL[4], MPR.DLL[4], LMMON.DLL[5]
MSAUDITE.DLL[2]	Message library used by the Audit Event Viewer.
MSNCDET.DLL[1]	Network card detection library. Files: NETDTECT.DLL[4]
MSOBJS.DLL[2]	Auditing support.
MSPELF32.DLL	Finnish language spell checker help.
MSPELL32.DLL[2]	Spell checker help for all languages except Finnish.
MSPRIVS.DLL[2]	Microsoft privilege name strings library.
MSSCHD32.DLL[2]	Microsoft Schedule+. Files: CRTDLL.DLL[4], DEMIL32.DLL[4], MAILM32.DLL[4], STORE32.DLL[4], MSRMND32.EXE[5], SCHDPL32.EXE[5], TRNSCH32.DLL[5]
MSSFS32.DLL[2]	Microsoft Shared File System Transport library (32-bit). Files: COMDLG32.DLL[4], CRTDLL.DLL[4], MPR.DLL[4], DEMIL32.DLL[4], MAILM32.DLL[4], NETAPI32.DLL[4], STORE32.DLL[4]
MSV1_0.DLL[1]	LAN Manager logon library. Files: LSASRV.DLL[4], SAMLIB.DLL[4], SAMSRV.DLL[4], NETLOGON.DLL[5]
MSVFW32.DLL[2]	Microsoft Video for Windows 32-bit driver. Files: WINMM.DLL[4], MCIAVI32.DLL[5]
MSVIDC32.DLL[2]	Supporting library for Microsoft Video for Windows driver. Files: WINMM.DLL[4]
MT735.DLL	Printer driver for Mannesmann Tally MT 730/735.
MT99.DLL	Printer driver for Mannesmann Tally MT 98/99.
MVAPI32.DLL[2]	Full text search.
MVAUDIO.DLL	Media Vision ProAudio Spectrum 16 driver library. Files: WINMM.DLL[4]
MVFS32.DLL[2]	Microsoft Viewer File System; Microsoft multimedia-specific installable file system support for Windows multimedia applications. Files: WINMM.DLL[4]
MVOPL3.DLL	Media Vision OPL3 FM Synthesizer driver library. Files: WINMM.DLL[4]
NBTSVC.DLL	NetBIOS over TCP/IP (NBT) service. Files: CRTDLL.DLL[4], WINSTRM.DLL[4], WSOCK32.DLL[4]

Table 4.3   Dynamic Link Library (.DLL) Files *(continued)*

Filename	File description and associated supported/supporting files
NDDEAPI.DLL[2]	Network DDE API library. Files: CRTDLL.DLL[4], RPCRT4.DLL[4], CLIPBRD.EXE[5], CLIPSRV.EXE[5], DDESHARE.EXE[5], NDDEAGNT.EXE[5], NETDDE.EXE[5]
NEC24PIN.DLL	Printer driver for NEC® Pinwriter models CP6, CP7, P20, P2200, P2plus, P30, P3200, P3300, P5200, P5300, P5XL, P6, P60, P6200, P6300, P6plus, P7, P70, P7plus, P90, P9300, and P9XL. Files: —
NETAPI.DLL[2]	OS/2 subsystem thunk DLLs.
NETAPI32.DLL[1]	Windows NT 32-bit Network API library. Files: NETRAP.DLL[4], CRTDLL.DLL[4], RPCRT4.DLL[4], SAMLIB.DLL[4], AT.EXE[5], ATSVC.EXE[5], LMREPL.EXE[5], LOCATOR.EXE[5], MSGSVC.EXE[5], NET.EXE[5], NTWRAP.EXE[5], OS2.EXE[5], PORTUAS.EXE[5], PSXSS.EXE[5], RASADMIN.EXE[5], RASSRV.EXE[5], RPCSS.EXE[5], SFMSVC.EXE[5], UPS.EXE[5], WINLOGON.EXE[5], ACLEDIT.DLL[5], ALRSVC.DLL[5], BOWSVC.DLL[5], FTPSMX.DLL[5], FTPSVC.DLL[5], LMMIB2.DLL[5], LMUICMN1.DLL[5], MSSFS32.DLL[5], NETBIOS.DLL[5], NETLOGON.DLL[5], NETRAP.DLL[5], NTLANMAN.DLL[5], RASCAUTH.DLL[5], RASGTWY.DLL[5], RASSAUTH.DLL[5], RPCLTC5.DLL[5], RPCLTS5.DLL[5], SRVSVC.DLL[5], VDMREDIR.DLL[5], WIN32SPL.DLL[5], WKSSVC.DLL[5], XACTSRV.DLL[5]
NETBIOS.DLL[2]	Network DDE. Files: CRTDLL.DLL[4], NETAPI32.DLL[4]
NETDTECT.DLL[1]	Network card auto-detection library. Files: AMDNCDET.DLL[5], MSNCDET.DLL[5]
NETEVENT.DLL[2]	Network components error messages library.
NETH.DLL[2]	Help messages for NETCMD (network command-line interface) and network services; needed even without a network adapter card to start and stop services and to add users to groups at the command line. Files: —
NETLOGON.DLL[1]	Network logon library. Files: CRTDLL.DLL[4], LSASRV.DLL[4], MSV1_0.DLL[4], NETAPI32.DLL[4], RPCRT4.DLL[4], SAMSRV.DLL[4]
NETMSG.DLL[1]	LAN Manager network error messages library.
NETRAP.DLL[1]	Routines library used for talking to or from downlevel systems; support routines for Rpcxlate and Xactsrv. Files: NETAPI32.DLL[4], NET.EXE[5], LMUICMN1.DLL[5], NETAPI32.DLL[5], WIN32SPL.DLL[5], XACTSRV.DLL[5]
NPINCDET.DLL[1]	Network peripherals detection driver (EISA).
NTDLL.DLL[1]	Windows NT API library; core Windows NT component.
NTLANMAN.DLL[2]	Windows NT LAN Manager provider for MPR. Files: CRTDLL.DLL[4], LMUICMN0.DLL[4], LMUICMN1.DLL[4], NETAPI32.DLL[4], REGEDT32.EXE[5], WINCHAT.EXE[5]
NTVDM.DLL[2]	Windows NT Virtual DOS Machine (VDM) support library.
NWLNKCFG.DLL	NWLink configuration library. Files: CRTDLL.DLL[4]
NWLNKMSG.DLL	NWLink message library.
NWNBLINK.DLL	NetWare NetBIOS Link (NWNBLink); Novell NetWare NetBIOS compatible network transport library. Files: —

Table 4.3   Dynamic Link Library (.DLL) Files *(continued)*

Filename	File description and associated supported/supporting files
OKI24.DLL	Printer driver for Okidata® ML Plus and Elite models 380, 390, 391, 393, 393C, 590, and 591.
OKI9.DLL	Printer driver for Okidata ML models 192, 192 Plus, 193, 193 Plus, 320, and 321 .
OKI9IBM.DLL	Printer driver for Okidata ML (Elite and IBM) models 92, 93, 182, 192, 193, 280, 320, 321, 3410, also the AT&T 473/478, and the Generic IBM 9-pin graphics printers.
OLECLI.DLL[2]	OLE client API library (16-bit).
OLECLI32.DLL[2]	OLE client API library (32-bit). Files: MPR.DLL[4], CARDFILE.EXE[5], PACKAGER.EXE[5], MCIOLE32.DLL[5], VFORM32.DLL[5]
OLESVR.DLL[2]	OLE server API library (16-bit).
OLESVR32.DLL[2]	OLE server API library (32-bit). Files: MPLAY32.EXE[5], PACKAGER.EXE[5], PBRUSH.EXE[5], SNDREC32.EXE[5]
OLIDM24.DLL	Printer driver for Olivetti DM series 124 C, 124L, 124, 324, 324L, 324S, 324SL, 600, 600S, and 624.
OLIDM9.DLL	Printer driver for Olivetti DM series 109,309, 309 L, 309 S, and 309 SL.
PABNSP32.DLL[2]	Library used by Microsoft Mail. Files: CRTDLL.DLL[4], DEMIL32.DLL[4], MAILM32.DLL[4], STORE32.DLL[4]
PAINTJET.DLL	Printer driver for HP® Paintjet® and HP PaintJet XL.
PANSON24.DLL	Printer driver for Panasonic KX series models P1123, P1124, P1124i, P1624, P2123, P2124, and P2624.
PANSON9.DLL	Printer driver for Panasonic KX series models P1081, P1180, P1695, and P2180.
PERFCTRS.DLL[2]	Performance Monitor counter library. Files: CRTDLL.DLL[4], WINSTRM.DLL[4]
PMSPL.DLL[2]	Print Manger spooler library.
PROPRINT.DLL	Printer driver for IBM Proprinter® II, Proprinter III, Proprinter XL, Proprinter XL II, Proprinter XL III and the IBM Proprinter.
PROPRN24.DLL	Printer driver for IBM Proprinter X24, X24e, XL24, and XL24e.
PS1.DLL	Printer driver for IBM PS/1 2205.
PSCRIPT.DLL	PostScript printer driver. Files: WINSRV.DLL[4]
PSCRPTUI.DLL	PostScript print driver user interface. Files: HTUI.DLL[4], SHELL32.DLL[4],
PSXDLL.DLL[2]	Provides core POSIX API support. Files: PAX.EXE[5]
QUIETJET.DLL	Printer driver for HP QuietJet® and QuietJet Plus.
QWIII.DLL	Printer driver for IBM QuietWriter III.
RASADMIN.DLL	Remote Access Server Administrator library. Files: RASMAN.DLL[4], RASSRV.EXE[5]
RASAPI32.DLL	Remote Access Server API library. Files: CRTDLL.DLL[4], RASCAUTH.DLL[4], RASFIL32.DLL[4], RASMAN.DLL[4], RASDIAL.EXE[5], RASPHONE.EXE[5]
RASCAUTH.DLL	Remote Access Server Client authority library. Files: NETAPI32.DLL[4], RASMAN.DLL[4], RASAPI32.DLL[5]

Table 4.3   Dynamic Link Library (.DLL) Files *(continued)*

Filename	File description and associated supported/supporting files
RASCFG.DLL[1]	Remote Access Server configuration library. Files: CRTDLL.DLL[4], LMUICMN0.DLL[4], LMUICMN1.DLL[4], RASFIL32.DLL[4]
RASDD.DLL	Raster printer device driver library. Files: WINSRV.DLL[4],
RASDDUI.DLL	Raster printer device driver user interface library. Files: HTUI.DLL[4], SHELL32.DLL[4]
RASFIL32.DLL[1]	Remote Access Server filter library. Files: CRTDLL.DLL[4], RASPHONE.EXE[5], RASAPI32.DLL[5], RASCFG.DLL[5], RASMXS.DLL[5], RASSER.DLL[5]
RASGTWY.DLL	Remote Access Server gateway library. Files: CRTDLL.DLL[4], NETAPI32.DLL[4], RASMAN.DLL[4],
RASMAN.DLL	Remote Access Server Manager library. Files: RASMAN.EXE[5], RASPHONE.EXE[5], RASSRV.EXE[5], RASADMIN.DLL[5], RASAPI32.DLL[5], RASCAUTH.DLL[5], RASGTWY.DLL[5], RASSAUTH.DLL[5]
RASMSG.DLL	Remote Access Server message library.
RASMXS.DLL	Library used by Remote Access. Files: CRTDLL.DLL[4], RASFIL32.DLL[4],
RASPHONE.EXE	Remote Access Server Phone application. Files: LMUICMN0.DLL, RASAPI32.DLL, RASFIL32.DLL, RASMAN.DLL
RASRES.DLL[1]	Remote Access Server resource library.
RASSAUTH.DLL	Remote Access Server authentication library. Files: CRTDLL.DLL[4], NETAPI32.DLL[4], RASMAN.DLL[4], SAMLIB.DLL[4], RASSRV.EXE[5]
RASSER.DLL	Remote Access Server serial library. Files: CRTDLL.DLL[4], RASFIL32.DLL[4]
RPCLTC1.DLL[1]	Remote Procedure Call client support for Named Pipes (if using LPC for local communication, these won't be needed for minimal startup). Files: RPCRT4.DLL[4]
RPCLTC3.DLL[2]	RPC transport drivers that allow RPC to talk to TCP/IP and NetBIOS. Files: RPCRT4.DLL[4], WSOCK32.DLL[4]
RPCLTC5.DLL[2]	RPC transport driver. Files: NETAPI32.DLL[4], RPCRT4.DLL[4], RPCLTS5.DLL[5]
RPCLTC6.DLL[2]	RPC transport driver. Files: RPCRT4.DLL[4], WSOCK32.DLL[4]
RPCLTS1.DLL[1]	Remote Procedure Call server support for Named Pipes (if using LPC for local communication, these won't be needed for minimal startup). Files: RPCRT4.DLL[4]
RPCLTS3.DLL[2]	RPC transport driver. Files: RPCRT4.DLL[4], WSOCK32.DLL[4]
RPCLTS5.DLL[2]	RPC transport driver. Files: NETAPI32.DLL[4], RPCLTC5.DLL[4], RPCRT4.DLL[4]
RPCLTS6.DLL[2]	RPC transport driver . Files: RPCRT4.DLL[4], WSOCK32.DLL[4]
RPCNS4.DLL[2]	RPC Name Service support (should not be needed for starting the system). Files: RPCRT4.DLL[4]
RPCRT4.DLL[1]	RPC run time (if go to LPC for local communication these won't be needed for minimal startup). Files: ATSVC.EXE[5], EVENTLOG.EXE[5], FTPSVC.EXE[5], LMREPL.EXE[5], LMSVCS.EXE[5], LOCATOR.EXE[5], MSGSVC.EXE[5], NET.EXE[5], NETDDE.EXE[5], PORTUAS.EXE[5], RPCSS.EXE[5], SCREG.EXE[5], SFMSVC.EXE[5], SPOOLSS.EXE[5], ACLEDIT.DLL[5], ALRSVC.DLL[5], BOWSVC.DLL[5], FTPSVC.DLL[5], LSASRV.DLL[5], NDDEAPI.DLL[5], NETAPI32.DLL[5], NETLOGON.DLL[5], RPCLTC1.DLL[5], RPCLTC3.DLL[5], RPCLTC5.DLL[5], RPCLTC6.DLL[5], RPCLTS1.DLL[5], RPCLTS3.DLL[5], RPCLTS5.DLL[5], RPCLTS6.DLL[5], RPCNS4.DLL[5], SAMLIB.DLL[5], SAMSRV.DLL[5], SFMAPI.DLL[5], SRVSVC.DLL[5], VDMREDIR.DLL[5], WIN32SPL.DLL[5], WKSSVC.DLL[5]

Table 4.3   Dynamic Link Library (.DLL) Files *(continued)*

Filename	File description and associated supported/supporting files
S3.DLL[1]	Video driver library for S3 video chipsets. Files: WINSRV.DLL[4]
SAMLIB.DLL[1]	Security Authority Manager API library. Files: RPCRT4.DLL[4], NET.EXE[5], PORTUAS.EXE[5], PSXSS.EXE[5], RASADMIN.EXE[5], SFMSVC.EXE[5], LMUICMN0.DLL[5], LMUICMN1.DLL[5], MSV1_0.DLL[5], NETAPI32.DLL[5], RASSAUTH.DLL[5], SETUPDLL[5].DLL[5], XACTSRV.DLL[5]
SAMSRV.DLL[1]	Security Authority Manager server library. Files: LSASRV.DLL[4], RPCRT4.DLL[4], LSASS.EXE[5], LSASRV.DLL[5], MSV1_0.DLL[5], NETLOGON.DLL[5]
SCHMSG32.DLL[2]	Microsoft Schedule+ message library. Files: CRTDLL.DLL[4], AB32.DLL[4], DEMIL32.DLL[4], FRAME32.DLL[4], MAILM32.DLL[4], STORE32.DLL[4], VFORM32.DLL[4]
SEIKO.DLL	Printer driver for Seiko Professional ColorPoint 8BPP.
SEIKO24E.DLL	Printer driver for Seikosha LT-20, SL-80 IP, SL-92, and SL 92 Plus.
SEIKOSH9.DLL	Printer driver for Seikosha SP models 1900, 1900+, 2000, 2400, and 2415.
SENDFL32.DLL[2]	Microsoft Mail Send File utility to send attached files. Files: CRTDLL.DLL[4]
SETUPDLL.DLL[1]	Setup library. Files: CRTDLL.DLL[4], SAMLIB.DLL[4]
SFMAPI.DLL	Services for Macintosh API library. Files: RPCRT4.DLL[4],
SFMATCFG.DLL	Services for Macintosh AppleTalk protocol configuration library. Files: CRTDLL.DLL[4], LMUICMN0.DLL[4], LMUICMN1.DLL[4]
SFMATMSG.DLL	Services for Macintosh AppleTalk protocol message library.
SFMMON.DLL	Services for Macintosh Print Monitor library. Files: SPOOLSS.DLL[4]
SFMMSG.DLL	Services for Macintosh Message library.
SFMPSDIB.DLL	Services for Macintosh PostScript Raster Image Processor library. Files: CRTDLL.DLL[4], SFMPSFNT.DLL[4], SFMPSEXE.EXE[5]
SFMPSFNT.DLL	Services for Macintosh PostScript font library. Files: SFMPRINT.EXE[5], SFMPSDIB.DLL[5]
SFMPSPRT.DLL	Services for Macintosh PostScript print processor library.
SFMRES.DLL	Services for Macintosh Setup dialog resources library.
SFMUTIL.DLL	Services for Macintosh Setup Utilities library. Files: CRTDLL.DLL[4]
SFMWSHAT.DLL	Services for Macintosh Windows Sockets Helper AppleTalk protocol library. Files: CRTDLL.DLL[4]
SHELL.DLL[2]	Win16 Shell library for Win16 application compatibilty.
SHELL32.DLL[1]	Windows NT 32-bit Shell API library. Files: CALC.EXE[5], CARDFILE.EXE[5], CDPLAYER.EXE[5], CLOCK.EXE[5], CONVGRP.EXE[5], FREECELL.EXE[5], MPLAY32.EXE[5], MSMAIL32.EXE[5], NOTEPAD.EXE[5], PACKAGER.EXE[5], PBRUSH.EXE[5], PERFMON.EXE[5], PIFEDIT.EXE[5], PRINTMAN.EXE[5], PROGMAN.EXE[5], REGEDT32.EXE[5], SCHDPL32.EXE[5], SETUP.EXE[5], SNDREC32.EXE[5], SNDVOL32.EXE[5], SOL.EXE[5], TASKMAN.EXE[5], TERMINAL.EXE[5], UPEDIT.EXE[5], WIN3270.EXE[5], WINCHAT.EXE[5], WINDISK.EXE[5], WINFILE.EXE[5], WINMINE.EXE[5], WINMSD.EXE[5], COMDLG32.DLL[5], FRAME32.DLL[5], PSCRPTUI.DLL[5], RASDDUI.DLL[5], STORE32.DLL[5], VFORM32.DLL[5], WOW32.DLL[5]
SNDBLST.DLL	Audio driver library for Creative Labs SoundBlaster, also the Media Vision Thunder Board. Files: WINMM.DLL[4]

Table 4.3   Dynamic Link Library (.DLL) Files *(continued)*

Filename	File description and associated supported/supporting files
SNDSYS32.DLL	Configuration and MIDI patch code. Files: WINMM.DLL[4]
SOCKUTIL.DLL	Berkeley-style UNIX sockets interface support .
SOUND.DLL[2]	Control Panel Sound library. Files: WINMM.DLL[4]
SPOOLSS.DLL[2]	Spooling subsystem library support. Files: SPOOLSS.EXE[5], HPMON.DLL[5], LMMON.DLL[5], LOCALMON.DLL[5], LOCALSPL.DLL[5], SFMMON.DLL[5], WIN32SPL.DLL[5], WINPRINT.DLL[5]
SRVSVC.DLL[2]	Server service library. Files: CRTDLL.DLL[4], NETAPI32.DLL[4], RPCRT4.DLL[4], XACTSRV.DLL[4]
STAR24E.DLL	Printer driver for Star LC24-*xxx*, NB24-*xx*, NX-24*xx*, XB-24*xx*, and XB24-*xxx* models of printers.
STAR9E.DLL	Printer driver for Star models of printers: LC-*xxx*, NL-10, NX-1*xxx*, XR-1*xxx*, ZA-200, ZA-250.
STARJET.DLL	Printer driver for Star SJ-48 printer.
STORE32.DLL[2]	Microsoft Mail store support functions. Files: CRTDLL.DLL[4], DEMIL32.DLL[4], MAILM32.DLL[4], SHELL32.DLL[4], MAILSP32.EXE[5], MSMAIL32.EXE[5], SCHDPL32.EXE[5], IMPEXP32.DLL[5], MAILM32.DLL[5], MAPIXX.DLL[5], MSSCHD32.DLL[5], MSSFS32.DLL[5], PABNSP32.DLL[5], SCHMSG32.DLL[5], VFORM32.DLL[5], WGPOMG32.DLL[5]
SYNTH.DLL	Synthesizer library. Files: WINMM.DLL[4]
TCPIPSVC.DLL	TCP/IP service library. Files: CRTDLL.DLL[4], WINSTRM.DLL[4], WSHTCPIP.DLL[4], WSOCK32.DLL[4]
TELNET.DLL	Telnet driver library. Files: CRTDLL.DLL[4], WSOCK32.DLL[4]
THINKJET.DLL	Printer driver for HP ThinkJet® (2225 C-D). Files: —
TI850.DLL	Printer driver for TI 850 and 855. Files: —
TOOLHELP.DLL[2]	Windows-16 Tool Helper library. Files: —
TOSHIBA.DLL	Printer driver for Toshiba® P351 and P1351. Files: —
TRNSCH32.DLL[2]	Microsoft Schedule+ shared file system transport library. Files: CRTDLL.DLL[4], MPR.DLL[4], DEMIL32.DLL[4], MSSCHD32.DLL[4]
UFAT.DLL[2]	Unicode FAT file system library. Files: IFSUTIL.DLL[4], CRTDLL.DLL[4], ULIB.DLL[4], CUFAT.DLL[5]
UHPFS.DLL[2]	Unicode HPFS library. Files: IFSUTIL.DLL[4], CRTDLL.DLL[4], ULIB.DLL[4], CUHPFS.DLL[5]
ULIB.DLL[2]	Windows NT Utilities library. Files: CRTDLL.DLL[4], ACLCONV.EXE[5], ATTRIB.EXE[5], CHKDSK.EXE[5], COMP.EXE[5], CONVERT.EXE[5], DOSKEY.EXE[5], FC.EXE[5], FIND.EXE[5], HELP.EXE[5], LABEL.EXE[5], PRINT.EXE[5], RECOVER.EXE[5], REGEDT32.EXE[5], REPLACE.EXE[5], SORT.EXE[5], SUBST.EXE[5], XCOPY.EXE[5], CUFAT.DLL[5], CUHPFS.DLL[5], FMIFS.DLL[5], IFSUTIL.DLL[5], UFAT.DLL[5], UHPFS.DLL[5], UNTFS.DLL[5], UREG.DLL[5]

Table 4.3   Dynamic Link Library (.DLL) Files *(continued)*

Filename	File description and associated supported/supporting files
UNTFS.DLL[2]	Unicode NTFS library. Files: IFSUTIL.DLL[4], CRTDLL.DLL[4], ULIB.DLL[4], CUFAT.DLL[5], CUHPFS.DLL[5]
UREG.DLL[2]	Used by the Registry. Files: CRTDLL.DLL[4], ULIB.DLL[4], REGEDT32.EXE[5]
USER32.DLL[1]	Windows NT User library to provide support for user interface routines.
USPIFS.DLL[1]	Setup utility that contains Chkdsk and file system code for FAT, HPFS, and NTFS. Files: SETUPAPP.EXE[4]
VCDEX.DLL[2]	Virtual MSCDEX driver; supports MS-DOS-based and Windows-based applications using the Microsoft CD ROM extensions (MSCDEX). Files: CRTDLL.DLL[4], NTVDM.EXE[4]
VDMDBG.DLL[2]	Virtual DOS Machine (VDM) debugging library.
VDMREDIR.DLL[2]	Multiple VDM network support (named pipes, mailslots, network APIs, NetBIOS, DLC). Files: CRTDLL.DLL[4], NTVDM.EXE, NETAPI32.DLL[4], RPCRT4.DLL[4], XACTSRV.DLL[4]
VER.DLL[2]	Win16 Windows version library. Files: KERNEL.EXE[4], USER.EXE[4]
VERSION.DLL[1]	Windows NT version library. Files: LZ32.DLL[4], SETUP.EXE[5], SNDVOL32.EXE[5], WINMSD.EXE[5], DRIVERS.DLL[5]
VFORM32.DLL[2]	Microsoft Mail Viewer Forms library. Files: COMDLG32.DLL[4], CRTDLL.DLL[4], AB32.DLL[4], DEMIL32.DLL[4], FRAME32.DLL[4], STORE32.DLL[4], OLECLI32.DLL[4], SHELL32.DLL[4], MSMAIL32.EXE[5], IMPEXP32.DLL[5], MAPIXX.DLL[5], SCHMSG32.DLL[5]
VGA.DLL[1]	VGA video driver library. Files: WINSRV.DLL[4]
VGA256.DLL[1]	VGA 256-color library. Files: WINSRV.DLL[4]
WGPOMG32.DLL[2]	Windows NT workgroup postoffice manager functions. Files: COMDLG32.DLL[4], CRTDLL.DLL[4], MPR.DLL[4], DEMIL32.DLL[4], FRAME32.DLL[4], STORE32.DLL[4]
WIN32SPL.DLL[2]	Windows NT Spooler library. Files: NETRAP.DLL[4], CRTDLL.DLL[4], NETAPI32.DLL[4], RPCRT4.DLL[4], SPOOLSS.DLL[4]
WIN87EM.DLL[2]	Win16 *x*87 math coprocessor emulation.
WINMM.DLL[1]	Windows NT Multimedia DLL. Files: DRWTSN32.EXE[5], MPLAY32.EXE[5], MSMAIL32.EXE[5], MSRMND32.EXE[5], SNDREC32.EXE[5], SNDVOL32.EXE[5], WINCHAT.EXE[5], DRIVERS.DLL[5], MCIAVI32.DLL[5], MCICDA.DLL[5], MCISEQ.DLL[5], MCIWAVE.DLL[5], MIDIMAP.DLL[5], MMDRV.DLL[5], MSVFW32.DLL[5], MSVIDC32.DLL[5], MVAUDIO.DLL[5], MVFS32.DLL[5], MVOPL3.DLL[5], SNDBLST.DLL[5], SNDSYS32.DLL[5], SOUND.DLL[5], SYNTH.DLL[5]
WINMSD.DLL[2]	Windows NT Microsoft Diagnostics. Files: WINMSD.EXE[5]
WINPRINT.DLL[2]	Windows NT Print API library. Files: SPOOLSS.DLL[4],
WINSOCK.DLL[1]	16-bit Windows Sockets interface support (thunks through to WSOCK32.DLL) for TCP/IP. Files: WSOCK32.DLL

Table 4.3   Dynamic Link Library (.DLL) Files *(continued)*

Filename	File description and associated supported/supporting files
WINSRV.DLL	Contains the server side of the 32-bit User and GDI routines (graphics engine). Files: BASESRV.DLL[4], CSRSRV.DLL[4], ATI.DLL[5], FRAMEBUF.DLL[5], PSCRIPT.DLL[5], RASDD.DLL[5], S3.DLL[5], VGA.DLL[5], VGA256.DLL[5], XGA.DLL[5]
WINSTRM.DLL	Windows NT TCP/IP interface for the Route utility . Files: CRTDLL.DLL[4], ARP.EXE[5], FINGER.EXE[5], FTP.EXE[5], HOSTNAME.EXE[5], IPXROUTE.EXE[5], MCSXNSVC.EXE[5], NBTSTAT.EXE[5], NETSTAT.EXE[5], NWLNKSVC.EXE[5], NWNBLINK.EXE[5], PING.EXE[5], RCP.EXE[5], REXEC.EXE[5], ROUTE.EXE[5], RSH.EXE[5], TFTP.EXE[5], UBNBSVC.EXE[5], ICMP.DLL[5], INETMIB1.DLL[5], LMHSVC.DLL[5], NBTSVC.DLL[5], PERFCTRS.DLL[5], TCPIPSVC.DLL[5], WSOCK32.DLL[5]
WKSSVC.DLL	Network Workstation service library. Files: CRTDLL.DLL[4], NETAPI32.DLL[4], RPCRT4.DLL[4]
WOW32.DLL[2]	32-bit code for Win16 support. Files: COMDLG32.DLL[4], CRTDLL.DLL[4], MPR.DLL[4], NTVDM.EXE, SHELL32.DLL[4], WSOCK32.DLL[4]
WSHNWLNK.DLL	Windows NT Windows Sockets helper for NWLink. Files: WSOCK32.DLL[4], NWLNKSVC.EXE[5]
WSHTCPIP.DLL	Windows NT Windows Sockets helper for TCP/IP. Files: CRTDLL.DLL[4], WSOCK32.DLL[4], TCPIPSVC.DLL[5]
WSOCK32.DLL	32-bit Windows Sockets API library. Files: CRTDLL.DLL[4], WINSTRM.DLL[4], ARP.EXE[5], FINGER.EXE[5], FTP.EXE[5], FTPSVC.EXE[5], HOSTNAME.EXE[5], NBTSTAT.EXE[5], NETSTAT.EXE[5], PING.EXE[5], RCP.EXE[5], REXEC.EXE[5], ROUTE.EXE[5], RSH.EXE[5], SNMP.EXE[5], TFTP.EXE[5], FTPSMX.DLL[5], INETMIB1.DLL[5], MGMTAPI.DLL[5], NBTSVC.DLL[5], RPCLTC3.DLL[5], RPCLTC6.DLL[5], RPCLTS3.DLL[5], RPCLTS6.DLL[5], TCPIPSVC.DLL[5], TELNET.DLL[5], WOW32.DLL[5], WSHNWLNK.DLL[5], WSHTCPIP.DLL[5], WSHXNS.DLL[5]
XACTSRV.DLL[2]	Transaction Server, supports remote API calls from downlevel systems. Files: NETRAP.DLL[4], CRTDLL.DLL[4], NETAPI32.DLL[4], SAMLIB.DLL[4], SRVSVC.DLL[5], VDMREDIR.DLL[5]
XGA.DLL[1]	XGA video driver library. Files: WINSRV.DLL[4]

[1] Installed during text-mode Setup by TXTSETUP.INF.

[2] Installed during graphical Setup by INITIAL.INF.

[3] Optional Windows NT component installed during graphical Setup by PARTIAL.INF.

[4] Supporting file. To use this file, the file listed in the "Filename" column must be installed.

[5] Supported file. This file must be installed to use the file listed in the "Filename" column.

Setup Script Files

The following table lists all of the setup script information (.INF) files included with the Windows NT. For more information about .INF files, see Chapter 3, "Customizing Windows NT Setup."

Table 4.4   Setup Script (.INF) Files

Filename	File description
APP.INF[1]	Used when searching the hard drive for existing applications and for automatically configuring MS-DOS application Program Information Files (PIFs)
DOSNET.INF	Used by WINNT.EXE Setup
FILELIST.INF[1]	Used to create a network sharepoint for WINNT.EXE Setup.
HARDWARE.INF[1]	Hardware configuration file used by Windows NT Setup
INITIAL.INF[1]	Windows NT Setup script file
IPINFOR.INF	TCP/IP default IP address
KEYBOARD.INF[1]	Setup information for keyboards
LANGUAGE.INF[1]	Setup information for installing language-specific support files
LAYOUT.INF[1]	Setup information to install specific keyboard layout support
MMDRIVER.INF[2]	Setup information for multimedia drivers
MODEM.INF[1]	Remote Access Server modem setup script file
NBINFO.INF[1]	Setup information for NetBIOS
NCPARAM.INF[1]	Network card parameters setup information file
NCPASHEL.INF[1]	Network Control Panel tool shell Setup information file
NETDTECT.INF[1]	Network card autodetection Setup information file
NTLANMAN.INF[1]	Windows NT LAN Manager setup information file
NTLMINST.INF[2]	Network installation setup information file
OEMNADAM.INF[1]	Network adapter setup information for AMD AM2100, AM1500T, and PCnet adapters, also Novell/Anthem NE1500T, and NE2100 adapters
OEMNADD1.INF[1]	Network driver setup script for DEC EtherWORKS LC adapter and Turbo/LC adapter cards
OEMNADD2.INF[1]	Network driver setup script for DEC EtherWORKS Turbo adapter
OEMNADD4.INF[1]	Network driver setup script for DEC EtherWORKS Turbo EISA adapter
OEMNADDE.INF[1]	Network driver setup script for DEC Turbo Channel Ethernet adapter
OEMNADDI.INF[1]	Network driver setup script for DigiBoard PCIMAC (ISA, PCIMAC) MC, and PCIMAC/4 adapters (DigiBoard ISDN adapters)
OEMNADDP.INF[1]	Network driver setup script for DEC Etherworks DEPCA adapter

Table 4.4   Setup Script (.INF) Files *(continued)*

Filename	File description
OEMNADDS.INF[1]	Digiboard C/X, PC/Xem, PC/8i, PC/2e, PC/4e, PC/8e adapter setup script
OEMNADE1.INF[1]	Network driver setup script for 3Com Etherlink 16 TP adapter
OEMNADE2.INF[1]	Network driver setup script for 3Com Etherlink II adapter
OEMNADE3.INF[1]	Network driver setup script for 3Com Etherlink III adapter
OEMNADEE.INF[1]	Network driver setup script for 3Com Etherlink III EISA adapter
OEMNADEM.INF[1]	Network driver setup script for 3Com 3C523 Etherlink/MC adapter
OEMNADEN.INF[1]	Network driver setup script for 3Com Etherlink III MCA adapter
OEMNADFD.INF[1]	Network Peripherals FDDI, MCA network adapter setup script
OEMNADIN.INF[1]	Network driver setup script for Intel EtherExpress® 16 LAN adapter
OEMNADLB.INF[1]	Network driver setup script for MS Loopback adapter
OEMNADLM.INF[1]	Network driver setup script for DayStar Digital LocalTalk adapter (MCA)
OEMNADLT.INF[1]	Network driver setup script for DayStar Digital LocalTalk adapter
OEMNADN1.INF[1]	Network driver setup script for Novell NE1000 adapter
OEMNADN2.INF[1]	Network driver setup script for Novell NE2000 adapter
OEMNADNE.INF[1]	Network driver setup script for Novell NE3200 EISA adapter
OEMNADNF.INF[1]	Network driver setup script for COMPAQ NetFlex/DualSpeed Token Ring adapter
OEMNADNP.INF[1]	Network driver setup script for Network Peripherals FDDI EISA adapter
OEMNADP3.INF[1]	Network driver setup script for Proteon P1390 adapter
OEMNADP9.INF[1]	Network driver setup script for Proteon P1990 adapter
OEMNADS1.INF[1]	Network driver setup script for Sonic EISA adapter
OEMNADTK.INF[1]	Network driver setup script for IBM Token Ring adapter
OEMNADTM.INF[1]	Network driver setup script for IBM Token Ring adapter/A
OEMNADUB.INF[1]	Network driver setup script for Ungermann-Bass Ethernet NIUpc, NIUpc/EOTP, NIUps adapters
OEMNADUM.INF[1]	Network driver setup script for Ungermann-Bass Ethernet NIUps adapter
OEMNADWD.INF[1]	Network driver setup script for SMC (Western Digital) ISA adapter
OEMNADWM.INF[1]	Network driver setup script for SMC (Western Digital) adapters: 8003E /A, 8003W /A, 8013WP /A, 8013EP /A
OEMNSVFT.INF[1]	Network service setup script for FTP Server
OEMNSVNB.INF[1]	Network service setup script for NetBIOS Transport Interface
OEMNSVRA.INF[1]	Network service setup script for Remote Access Server, NetBIOS Gateway, API Layer, RAS Hub, and AsyMAC driver
OEMNSVRP.INF[1]	Network service setup script for Remote Procedure Call Locator service
OEMNSVSV.INF[1]	Network service setup script for Windows NT LAN Manager Server

Table 4.4   Setup Script (.INF) Files *(continued)*

Filename	File description
OEMNSVWK.INF[1]	Network service setup script for Windows NT LAN Manager Workstation
OEMNXPDL.INF[1]	Network transport setup script for DLC protocol
OEMNXPIP.INF[1]	Network transport setup script for NWLink Transport driver and NWLink NetBIOS driver
OEMNXPNB.INF[1]	Network transport setup script for NetBEUI 3.0 Transport
OEMNXPSM.INF[1]	Network transport setup script for Service for Macintosh, including the AppleTalk protocol, File Server for Macintosh, Kernel driver, and Print Server for Macintosh
OEMNXPSN.INF[1]	Network transport setup script for SNMP Network Management Service
OEMNXPST.INF[1]	Network transport setup script for Streams environment
OEMNXPTC.INF[1]	Network transport setup script for TCP/IP protocol, including TCP/IP NetBIOS, Telnet, Loop Support Environment, and TCP/IP NetBIOS helper
OTHER.INF[1]	Setup script for "Other Driver" selections
PAD.INF[1]	PAD script information for Remote Access Server configuration (X.25)
PARTIAL.INF[1]	Windows NT Setup script to configure Windows NT partial installation
POINTER.INF[1]	Pointing devices setup script (including mouse)
PRINTER.INF[1]	Printer setup script file; specific printer driver information
PRNSETUP.INF[1]	Printer setup script file
REGISTRY.INF[1]	Registry setup script file
REPAIR.INF[1]	Repair disk setup script file
SCSI.INF[1]	SCSI installation setup script
SETUP.INF[1]	Windows NT Setup script file
SETUP16.INF[2]	Win16 SETUP.INF file
SFMICONS.INF	Services for Macintosh icon information
SFMMAP.INF	Services for Macintosh Type Creator mappings information file
SUBROUTN.INF[1]	Windows NT Setup common subroutines script file
SWITCH.INF[1]	Remote Access Server switch configuration information file
TAPE.INF[1]	Setup script for tape devices
TXTSETUP.INF	Text mode Setup script file
UTILITY.INF[1]	Utility script used for network setup
VIDEO.INF[1]	Video driver setup script
VIRTUAL.INF[1]	Setup information for configuring the Windows NT paging file

[1] Installed during text-mode Setup by TXTSETUP.INF.

[2] Installed during graphical Setup by INITIAL.INF.

Your system might also include other information files. Many of these files are for specific hardware devices provided by original equipment manufacturers (OEMs). Filenames for these files are in the form OEM*xxxyy*.INF, where *xxx* refers to the type of information file in the list below and *yy* represents the specific device(s).

Filename	Type	Filename	Type
OEMCPT*yy*.INF	Computer	OEMSND*yy*.INF	Sound
OEMVIO*yy*.INF	Video	OEMDRV*yy*.INF	Driver
OEMPTR*yy*.INF	Pointer	OEMNAD*yy*.INF	NetAdapter
OEMKBD*yy*.INF	Keyboard	OEMNDR*yy*.INF	NetDriver
OEMLA*yy*Y.INF	Layout	OEMNXP*yy*.INF	NetTransport
OEMLNG*yy*.INF	Language	OEMNSV*yy*.INF	NetService
OEMPRN*yy*.INF	Printer	OEMNWK*yy*.INF	Network
OEMSCS*yy*.INF	Scsi	OEMNPR*yy*.INF	NetProvider
OEMTAP*yy*.INF	Tape		

Online Help Files

The following table lists all of the online help (.HLP) files included with
Windows NT. To see online Help, select an item from the Help menu of the
application or tool you are using, or press F1. For a description of how to use
online Help, choose How To Use Help from the Help menu in Program Manager.

Table 4.5   Online Help Files

Filename	File description
BACKUP.HLP[1]	Windows NT Backup utility help
CALC.HLP[3]	Calculator tool help
CARDFILE.HLP[3]	Cardfile tool help
CDPLAYER.HLP[3]	CD Player help
CHARMAP.HLP[3]	Character Map tool help
CLIPBRD.HLP[1]	Clipbook Viewer help
CONTROL.HLP[1]	Control Panel help
DRWTSN32.HLP[2]	Dr. Watson help
EDIT.HLP[2]	MS-DOS Editor help
EVENTVWR.HLP[1]	Event Viewer help
FREECELL.HLP[3]	Freecell game help
FTPSMX.HLP[2]	File Transfer Program Manager Extensions help
GLOSSARY.HLP[1]	Windows NT Glossary help
HALFTONE.HLP[2]	Halftone printing option help
HELP.HLP[2]	Help file for Help utility
HPMON.HLP	HP Monitor Help file
ISDNHELP.HLP	Digiboard ISDN help
MPLAYER.HLP[3]	Media Player help
MSMAIL32.HLP[1]	Microsoft Mail help
MUSRMGR.HLP	Mini User Manager help
NET.HLP[2]	Network command-line help
NETWORK.HLP[2]	Network help (Windows help format)
NOTEPAD.HLP[3]	Notepad help
NTCMDS.HLP[2]	Windows NT command-line help
PACKAGER.HLP[3]	Win16 Object Packager help

Table 4.5   Online Help Files *(continued)*

Filename	File description
PBRUSH.HLP[3]	Paintbrush help
PERFMON.HLP[1]	Performance Monitor help
PIFEDIT.HLP[1]	PIF Editor help
PRINTMAN.HLP[1]	Print Manager help
PROGMAN.HLP[1]	Program Manager help
PSCRIPT.HLP	PostScript miniport help
QBASIC.HLP[3]	Command-line Quick Basic help
RASADMIN.HLP	Remote Access Server Administrator help
RASDDUI.HLP	Raster Printer Device Driver User Interface help
RASPHONE.HLP	Remote Access Server Phone help
RASSETUP.HLP[1]	Remote Access Server Setup help
REGEDIT.HLP[2]	Win16 Registry Editor help
REGEDT32.HLP[1]	Windows NT Registry Editor help
SCHDPL32.HLP[1]	Microsoft Schedule+ help
SETUPNT.HLP[1]	Setup help
SFMMGR.HLP	Services for Macintosh Manager help
SNDVOL32.HLP	Sound Volume tool help
SOL.HLP[3]	Solitaire game help
SOUNDREC.HLP[3]	Sound Recorder help
SRVMGR.HLP[2]	Server Manager help
TERMINAL.HLP[3]	Terminal application help
UPEDIT.HLP[2]	User Profile Editor help
USRMGR.HLP	Windows NT User Manager for Domains help
WINCHAT.HLP[3]	Windows NT Chat help
WINDISK.HLP[2]	Windows NT Disk Administrator help
WINDISKA.HLP[2]	Windows NT Advanced Server Disk Administrator help
WINFILE.HLP[1]	File Manager application help
WINHELP.HLP[2]	Win16 Help application help
WINMINE.HLP[3]	Minesweeper help
WINNT.HLP[1]	Network-based Windows NT installation utility help
WRITE.HLP[3]	Windows Write help

[1] Installed during text-mode Setup by TXTSETUP.INF.

[2] Installed during graphical Setup by INITIAL.INF.

[3] Optional Windows NT component installed during graphical Setup by PARTIAL.INF.

Because most of the Help files for Windows NT have full-text search functionality, deleting one or more Help files has other than the typical "Cannot open Help file" message seen in Windows 3.1. With Windows NT, if you remove a Help file that is part of a full-text search index, you will still see the full-text search dialog box and its list of all the Help files to search (whether or not the file is available). From there, you can type a search request and get a list of all topics containing the search string. However, if the Help file is not available, you will see the message, "Cannot open Help file."

Table 4.6 shows which files are part of each full-text search index (.IND) file. If you remove the index file and then try to use full-text search from a corresponding online Help file, Windows NT displays the message "Old or Missing Index File."

For a description of the .HLP files listed in this table, see Table 4.5.

Table 4.6   Full-Text Search Index (.IND) Files for Online Help

Index file	Corresponding Help files	
CALC.IND[2]	Calculator	CALC.HLP
	Cardfile	CARDFILE.HLP
	CD Player	CDPLAYER.HLP
	Character Map	CHARMAP.HLP
	Freecell	FREECELL.HLP
	Media Player	MPLAYER.HLP
	Notepad	NOTEPAD.HLP
	Paintbrush	PBRUSH.HLP
	Solitaire	SOL.HLP
	Sound Recorder	SOUNDREC.HLP
	Sound Volume Control	SNDVOL32.HLP
	Terminal	TERMINAL.HLP
	Win 3270 Emulator	WIN3270.HLP
	Chat	WINCHAT.HLP
	Minesweeper	WINMINE.HLP
MUSRMGR.IND[2]	Disk Administrator for NT	WINDISK.HLP
	User Manager for NT	MUSRMGR.HLP
NTCMDS.IND[2]	Command Reference	NTCMDS.HLP
USRMGR.IND[6]	Disk Administrator[6]	WINDISKA.HLP
	User Manager[6]	USRMGR.HLP
	User Profile Editor	UPEDIT.HLP
	Server Manager	SRVRMGR.HLP

Table 4.6   Full-Text Search Index (.IND) Files for Online Help *(continued)*

Index file	Corresponding Help files,	
WINNT.IND[1]	Backup	BACKUP.HLP
	Control Panel	CONTROL.HLP
	ClipBrd Viewer	CLIPBRD.HLP
	Event Viewer	EVENTVWR.HLP
	File Manager	WINFILE.HLP
	Microsoft Mail	MSMAIL32.HLP
	Performance Monitor	PERFMON.HLP
	PIF Editor	PIFEDIT.HLP
	Program Manager	PROGMAN.HLP
	Print Manager	PRINTMAN.HLP
	Registry Editor	REGEDT32.HLP
	Schedule+	SCHDPL32.HLP
	Setup	SETUPNT.HLP
	Windows NT Help	WINNT.HLP
(None) Not indexed for full-text search	Postscript driver	PSCRIPT.HLP
	"Generic" print driver	RASDDUI.HLP
	Halftone	HALFTONE.HLP
	Network Connect	NETWORK.HLP
	Glossary	GLOSSARY.HLP
	Object Packager	PACKAGER.HLP
	Help on Help	WINHELP.HLP
	Write	WRITE.HLP

[1] Installed during text-mode Setup by TXTSETUP.INF.

[2] Installed during graphical Setup by INITIAL.INF.

[3] Optional Windows NT component installed during graphical Setup by PARTIAL.INF.

[6] Windows NT Advanced Server only

Other relationships of the various Help and Index files follow:

- If WINHELP.HLP is removed, errors occur when the user chooses the Help menu item How To Use Help.

- If NTCMDS.HLP is removed, an error occurs when the user chooses the Command Reference button from the Windows NT Help file located in the Main program group.

- If GLOSSARY.HLP is removed, the definition popups in nearly every Help file will give an error.

Introducing Windows NT Sequence Files

Windows NT includes an online introduction to Windows NT. The following table lists the sequence (.SEQ) files used by Introducing Windows NT.

To run Introducing Windows NT, choose its icon from the Main program group.

Table 4.7   Introduction to Windows NT Sequence Files

CLIP01.SEQ[2]	CONN02.SEQ[2]	NTMENU.SEQ[2]	SETT02.SEQ[2]
CLIP02.SEQ[2]	CREAT01.SEQ[2]	PANEL.SEQ[2]	SETT03.SEQ[2]
CLIP03.SEQ[2]	CREAT02.SEQ[2]	PAUSE.SEQ[2]	SETT04.SEQ[2]
COMM01.SEQ[2]	INTRO1.SEQ[2]	PRINT01.SEQ[2]	SHARE01.SEQ[2]
COMM02.SEQ[2]	INTRO2.SEQ[2]	REVIEW.SEQ[2]	SHARE02.SEQ[2]
CONN01.SEQ[2]	LOG01.SEQ[2]	SETT01.SEQ[2]	

[2] Installed during graphical Setup by INITIAL.INF.

Introducing Windows NT also uses a file called NT.DOC.

Text Files

Windows NT also includes online information in the form of text files. The following table lists the text files included with Windows NT. Text files are in ASCII format and can be viewed by using Notepad, Write, or any text editor or word processing package.

Table 4.8   Text Files

Filename	File description
BUGREP.TXT[2]	Bug reporting template
RASREAD.TXT[1]	Remote Access Server README
README.TXT	Windows NT README
SAMPBUG.TXT[2]	Sample bug report
SFMUAM.TXT	Services for Macintosh User Authentication Module README
WINPERMS.TXT[2]	Windows NT permission list

[1] Installed during text-mode Setup by TXTSETUP.INF.

[2] Installed during graphical Setup by INITIAL.INF.

Font and Printer Files

Windows NT has several fonts for use with various types of applications, display monitors, and code pages. For details about Windows NT fonts, see Chapter 7, "Fonts." For more information about code pages, see Appendix D, "International Considerations."

Table 4.9 lists the raster and vector fonts that are shipped with Windows NT.

Table 4.9   Font Files

Filename	File description
APP850.FON[2]	MS-DOS application font; uses code page 850
CGA40850.FON[2]	CGA font; uses code page 850
CGA40WOA.FON[2]	CGA font; uses code page 437 (WOA is an acronym for Windows Old Application)
CGA80850.FON[2]	CGA font; uses code page 850 (80 column display)
CGA80WOA.FON[2]	CGA font; uses code page 437 (80 column display)
COURE.FON[1]	Windows 3.0 Courier system font, VGA display compatible; aspect ratio 1:1, 96 ppi x 96 ppi (pixels per inch)
COURF.FON[1]	Windows 3.0 Courier system font, 8514 display compatible; aspect ratio 1:1, 120 ppi x 120 ppi
DOSAPP.FON[2]	MS-DOS application font; uses code page 437
EGA.CPI	EGA ROM international fonts; used for displaying full-screen MS-DOS applications
EGA40850.FON[2]	EGA font; uses code page 850
EGA40WOA.FON[2]	CGA font; uses code page 437
EGA80850.FON[2]	EGA font; uses code page 850 (80 columns)
EGA80WOA.FON[2]	CGA font; uses code page 437 (80 columns)
MODERN.FON[2]	Windows 3.1 vector font
NT.FNT[2], NT2.FNT[2]	Introduction to Windows NT font files
ROMAN.FON[2]	Vector font
SCRIPT.FON[2]	Vector font
SERIFE.FON[1]	Windows 3.0 serif system font, VGA display compatible; aspect ratio 1:1, 96 ppi x 96 ppi

Table 4.9   Font Files *(continued)*

Filename	File description
SERIFF.FON[1]	Windows 3.0 serif system font, 8514 display compatible; aspect ratio 1:1, 120 ppi x 120 ppi
SMALLE.FON[2]	Windows 3.0 small system font, VGA display compatible; aspect ratio 1:1, 96 ppi x 96 ppi
SMALLF.FON[2]	Windows 3.0 small system font, 8514 display compatible ; aspect ratio 1:1, 120 ppi x 120 ppi
SSERIFE.FON[1]	Windows 3.0 sans serif system font, VGA display compatible; aspect ratio 1:1, 96 ppi x 96 ppi
SSERIFF.FON[1]	Windows 3.0 sans serif system font, 8514 display compatible; aspect ratio 1:1, 120 ppi x 120 ppi
SYMBOLE.FON[2]	Windows 3.0 Symbol system font, VGA display compatible; aspect ratio 1:1, 96 ppi x 96 ppi
SYMBOLF.FON[2]	Windows 3.0 Symbol system font, 8514 display compatible; aspect ratio 1:1, 120 ppi x 120 ppi
VGA850.FON[1]	VGA font support for code page 850 (International)
VGA860.FON[2]	VGA font support for code page 860 (Portuguese)
VGA861.FON[2]	VGA font support for code page 861 (Icelandic)
VGA863.FON[2]	VGA font support for code page 863 (French Canadian)
VGA865.FON[2]	VGA font support for code page 865 (Norwegian/Danish)
VGAFIX.FON[1]	VGA fixed font (typically used as a monospace system font)
VGAOEM.FON[1]	VGA OEM font; used to display Clipboard objects in the Clipboard Viewer
VGASYS.FON[1]	VGA System font (proportional)

[1] Installed during text-mode Setup by TXTSETUP.INF.

[2] Installed during graphical Setup by INITIAL.INF.

The TrueType downloadable fonts shipped with Windows NT support the Arial®, Courier New, Times New Roman®, Symbol, and Wingdings™ font families. Each family requires two files, a font header (.FOT) file, and a TrueType font (.TTF) file.

Caution   Setup installs TrueType font and font header files in *%systemroot%*\SYSTEM. Be careful not to delete the TrueType files from this directory. These files are used by Windows NT 32-bit applications as well as 16-bit applications.

Table 4.10 lists the TrueType font and font header files included with Windows NT.

Table 4.10   TrueType Font and Font Header Files

Filename	File description
ARIAL.FOT[2]	Arial TrueType font header
ARIAL.TTF[2]	Arial
ARIALBD.FOT[2]	Arial Bold TrueType font header
ARIALBD.TTF[2]	Arial Bold
ARIALBI.FOT[2]	Arial Bold Italic TrueType font header
ARIALBI.TTF[2]	Arial Bold Italic
ARIALI.FOT[2]	Arial Italic TrueType font header
ARIALI.TTF[2]	Arial Italic
COUR.FOT[2]	Courier TrueType font header
COUR.TTF[2]	Courier
COURBD.FOT[2]	Courier Bold TrueType font header
COURBD.TTF[2]	Courier Bold
COURBI.FOT[2]	Courier Bold Italic font header
COURBI.TTF[2]	Courier Bold Italic
COURI.FOT[2]	Courier Italic TrueType font header
COURI.TTF[2]	Courier Italic
SYMBOL.FOT[2]	Symbol TrueType font header
SYMBOL.TTF[2]	Symbol
TIMES.FOT[2]	Times New Roman TrueType font header
TIMES.TTF[2]	Times New Roman
TIMESBD.FOT[2]	Times New Roman Bold TrueType font header
TIMESBD.TTF[2]	Times New Roman Bold
TIMESBI.FOT[2]	Times New Roman Bold Italic font header
TIMESBI.TTF[2]	Times New Roman Bold Italic
TIMESI.FOT[2]	Times New Roman Italic font header
TIMESI.TTF[2]	Times New Roman Italic
UCLUCIDA.TTF[2]	Unicode Lucida® TrueType
WINGDING.FOT[2]	WingDings TrueType font header
WINGDING.TTF[2]	WingDings

[1] Installed during text-mode Setup by TXTSETUP.INF.

[2] Installed during graphical Setup by INITIAL.INF.

PostScript Printer Description Files

The following files provide additional PostScript description information for specific printers. For more information about printing with PostScript printers, see Chapter 6, "Printing."

Table 4.11   Adobe PostScript Printer Description Files

Filename	File description
40291730.PPD	IBM LaserPrinter 4029 PostScript version 52.3; also known as the IBM LaserPrinter 4029 PS17
40293930.PPD	IBM LaserPrinter 4029 PostScript version 52.3; also known as the IBM LaserPrinter 4029 PS39
AMCHR518.PPD	Agfa Matrix ChromaScript version 51.8
EPL3KF21.PPD	Epson LP-3000PS F2 version 52.3
LWNT_470.PPD	Apple LaserWriter® II NT version 47.0
LWNTX470.PPD	Apple LaserWriter II NTX version 47.0
LWNTX518.PPD	Apple LaserWriter II NTX version 51.8
CNLBP4_1.PPD	Canon LBP-4PS-2 version 51.4
CNLBP8_1.PPD	Canon LBP-8IIIPS-1 version 51.4
CNLBP8R1.PPD	Canon LBP-8IIIRPS-1 version 51.4
CNLBP8T1.PPD	Canon LBP-8IIITPS-1 version 51.4
CN_500_1.PPD	Canon PS-IPU Color Laser Copier version 52.3
CN_500J1.PPD	Canon PS-IPU Kanji Color Laser Copier version 52.3
NCOL_519.PPD	Colormate PS version 51.9
CPPMQ151.PPD	COMPAQ PAGEMARQ 15 version 2012.015
CPPMQ201.PPD	COMPAQ PAGEMARQ 20 version 2012.015
DATAP462.PPD	Dataproducts LZR-2665 version 46.2
DP_US470.PPD	DataproductsLZR1260version 47.0
DPL15601.PPD	DataproductsLZR1560version 2010.127
DPLZ9601.PPD	DataproductsLZR960version 2010.106
DC1152_1.PPD	Digital DEClaser 1152 (17fonts) version 2011.113
DC1152F1.PPD	Digital DEClaser 1152 (43fonts) version 2011.113
DC2150P1.PPD	Digital DEClaser 2150 plus version 51.4
DC2250P1.PPD	Digital DEClaser 2250 plus version 51.4
DCD11501.PPD	Digital DEClaser 1150 version 51.4
DCD21501.PPD	Digital DEClaser 2150 version 51.4
DCD22501.PPD	Digital DEClaser 2250 version 51.4
DCLN03R1.PPD	Digital LN03R ScriptPrinter version 47.2

Table 4.11   Adobe PostScript Printer Description Files *(continued)*

Filename	File description,
DCLPS171.PPD	Digital PrintServer 17 version 48.3
DCLPS201.PPD	Digital PrintServer 20 version 48.3
DCLPS321.PPD	Digital PrintServer 32 version 48.3
DCLPS401.PPD	Digital PrintServer 40 Plus version 48.3
DCTPS201.PPD	Digital turbo PrintServer 20 version 48.3
DEC3250.PPD	Digital DEClaser 3250 version 47.0
DECCOLOR.PPD	Digital Colormate PS version 51.9
EPL75523.PPD	Epson EPL-7500 version 52.3
EPL3KF51.PPD	Epson LP-3000 PS F5 version 52.3
EP826051.PPD	Epson PostScript CARD version 52.5
F71RX503.PPD	Fujitsu RX7100PS version 50.3
GCBLP2_1.PPD	GCC BLP II version 52.3
GCBLP2S1.PPD	GCC BLP IIS version 52.3
GCBLPEL1.PPD	GCC BLP Elite version 52.3
GCBL4921.PPD	GCC Business LaserPrinter version 49.2
GCBL5141.PPD	GCC Business LaserPrinter version 51.4
GDGL8001.PPD	Gestetner GLP800-Scout version 52.3
HERMES_1.PPD	Hermes H 606 PS (13Fonts)
HERMES_2.PPD	Hermes H 606 PS (35fonts)
HP_3D522.PPD	HP LaserJet IIID PostScript Cartridge version 52.2
HP_3P522.PPD	HP LaserJet IIIP PostScript Cartridge version 52.2
HP3SI523.PPD	HP LaserJet IIISi PostScript version 52.3
HP4SI6_1.PPD	HP LaserJet 4Si or 4SiMXAPS 600dpi
HPELI522.PPD	HP LaserJet ELI PostScript version 52.3
HPIID522.PPD	HP LaserJet IID PostScript Cartridge version 52.2
HPIII522.PPD	HP LaserJet III PostScript Cartridge version 52.2
HPIIP522.PPD	HP LaserJet IIP PostScript Cartridge version 52.2
HPLJ_31.PPD	HP LaserJet III PostScript Plus version 2010.118
HPLJ_3D1.PPD	HP LaserJet IIID PostScript Plus version 2010.118
HPLJ_3P1.PPD	HP LaserJet IIIP PostScript Plus version 2010.118
HPLJ_4M.PPD	HP LaserJet 4 PostScript version 2011.110
HPPJXL31.PPD	HP PaintJet XL300 version 2011.112
IBM17523.PPD	IBM 4019 17fonts version 52.3 or 52.1
IBM39523.PPD	IBM 4019 39 fonts version 52.3 or 52.1

Table 4.11   Adobe PostScript Printer Description Files *(continued)*

Filename	File description
IBM4039.PPD	IBM 4039 LaserPrinter PS
IBM20470.PPD	IBM 4216-020 version 47.0
IBM30505.PPD	IBM 4216-030 version 50.5
IBM4079.PPD	IBM Color Jetprinter PS 4079
L100_425.PPD	Linotronic® 100 version 42.5
L200_471.PPD	Linotronic 200 version 47.1
L200_493.PPD	Linotronic 200 version 49.3
L200230.PPD	Linotronic 200 and 230
L300_471.PPD	Linotronic 300 version 47.1
L300_493.PPD	Linotronic 300 version 49.3
L330_523.PPD	Linotronic 330 version 52.3
L3330523.PPD	Linotronic 330-RIP30 version 52.3
L500_493.PPD	Linotronic 500 version 49.3
L530_523.PPD	Linotronic 530 version 52.3
L5330523.PPD	Linotronic 530-RIP30 version 52.3
LH_630_1.PPD	Linotronic 630 version 52.3
MT_TI101.PPD	Microtek TrueLaser
MOIM1201.PPD	Monotype ImageMaster 1200 version 52.3
MONO_522.PPD	Monotype Imagesetter version 52.2
NCCPS401.PPD	NEC Colormate PS/40 version 51.9
NCCPS801.PPD	NEC Colormate PS/80 version 51.9
N2090522.PPD	NEC Silentwriter2 90 version 52.2
N2290520.PPD	NEC Silentwriter2 290 version 52.0
N890_470.PPD	NEC Silentwriter LC890 version 47.0
N890X505.PPD	NEC Silentwriter LC890XL version 50.5
NC95FAX1.PPD	NEC Silentwriter 95 version 2011.111
NC97FAX1.PPD	NEC Silentwriter 97 version 2011.111
NCS29901.PPD	NEC Silentwriter2 990 version 52.3
NCSW_951.PPD	NEC SilentWriter 95 version 2010.119
NX_NLP_1.PPD	NeXT 400 dpi LaserPrinter version 2000.6
O5241503.PPD	OceColor G5241 PS
O5242503.PPD	OceColor G5242 PostScript Printer version 50.3
OK801PF1.PPD	Oki Microline 801PS+F version 52.3
OL830525.PPD	Oki OL830-PS version 52.5

Table 4.11 Adobe PostScript Printer Description Files *(continued)*

Filename	File description
OL840518.PPD	Oki OL840-PS version 51.8
OLIVETI1.PPD	Olivetti PG 306 PS (13 fonts)
OLIVETI2.PPD	Olivetti PG 306 PS (35 fonts)
P4455514.PPD	Panasonic KX-P4455 version 51.4
QMS1725.PPD	QMS® 1725 Print System
QMS2025.PPD	QMS 2025 Print System
QMS3225.PPD	QMS 3225 Print System
QMS420.PPD	QMS 420 Print System version 2011.22 r15
QMS4525.PPD	QMS 4525 Print System
Q30SI503.PPD	QMS ColorScript 100 Mod 30si
QCS10503.PPD	QMS ColorScript 100 Model 10 version 50.3
QCS20503.PPD	QMS ColorScript 100 Model 20 version 50.3
QCS30503.PPD	QMS ColorScript 100 Model 30 version 50.3
QMSCS210.PPD	QMS ColorScript 210 version 2011.22
QMSCS230.PPD	QMS ColorScript 230 version 2011.22
QMSCS494.PPD	QMS ColorScript 100 version 49.4
QMSJ_461.PPD	QMS PS Jet version 46.1
QMSJP461.PPD	QMS PS Jet Plus version 46.1
Q2200523.PPD	QMS-PS 2200 version 51.0 or 52.3
Q2210523.PPD	QMS-PS 2210 version 51.0 or 52.3
Q2220523.PPD	QMS-PS 2220 version 51.0 or 52.3
Q810T517.PPD	QMS-PS 810 Turbo version 51.7
Q820_517.PPD	QMS-PS 820 version 51.7
Q820T517.PPD	QMS-PS 820 Turbo version 51.7
QM1700_1.PPD	QMS-PS 1700 version 52.4
QM2000_1.PPD	QMS-PS 2000 version 52.4
QM815MR1.PPD	QMS-PS 815 MR version 52.4
QM825MR1.PPD	QMS-PS 825 MR version 52.4
QMPS4101.PPD	QMS-PS 410 version 52.4
QMPS8151.PPD	QMS-PS 815 version 52.4
QMPS8251.PPD	QMS-PS 825 version 52.4
QMS8_461.PPD	QMS-PS 800 version 46.1
QMS81470.PPD	QMS-PS 810 version 47.0
QMS8P461.PPD	QMS-PS 800 Plus version 46.1

Table 4.11   Adobe PostScript Printer Description Files *(continued)*

Filename	File description
QUME_470.PPD	Qume ScripTEN version 47.0
R6000505.PPD	Ricoh PC Laser 6000-PS version 50.5
SCG20522.PPD	Scantext 2030-51 version 49.3 or 52.2
S5232503.PPD	Schlumberger 5232 Color PostScript Printer version 50.3
SEIKO_04.PPD	Seiko ColorPoint PS Model 04
SEIKO_14.PPD	Seiko ColorPoint PS Model 14
S746J522.PPD	Shinko Color CHC-746PSJ PostScript Printer version 52.2
PHIIPX.PPD	Tektronix Phaser II PX
PX.PPD	Tektronix Phaser PX
TK200172.PPD	Tektronix Phaser 200e with 17 fonts version 2011.108(3)
TK200392.PPD	Tektronix Phaser 200e with 39 fonts version 2011.108(3)
TKP200I2.PPD	Tektronix Phaser 200i version 2011.108(3)
TKPH2SD1.PPD	Tektronix Phaser IISD version 2011.108
TKPHZ2J1.PPD	Tektronix Phaser II PXiJ version 2011.108
TKPHZ3J1.PPD	Tektronix Phaser III PXiJ version 2011.108
TKPHZR21.PPD	Tektronix Phaser IIPXi version 2010.116
TKPHZR22.PPD	Tektronix Phaser II PXi version 2011.108
TKPHZR31.PPD	Tektronix Phaser III PXi version 2010.116
TKPHZR32.PPD	Tektronix Phaser III PXi version 2011.108
TKPXE171.PPD	Tektronix Phaser II PXe version 2010.128 with 17 fonts
TKPXE391.PPD	Tektronix Phaser II PXe version 2010.128 with 39 fonts
ALJII523.PPD	Adobe® LaserJet II Cartridge version 52.3
AC500503.PPD	Agfa TabScript C500 PostScript Printer version 50.3
A_PNT518.PPD	Apple LaserWriter Personal NT version 51.8
AP_NTXJ1.PPD	Apple LaserWriter II NTX-J version 50.5
APLWIIF1.PPD	Apple LaserWriter IIf version 2010.113
APLWIIG1.PPD	Apple LaserWriter IIg version 2010.113
APLWNTR1.PPD	Apple Personal LaserWriter NTR version 2010.129
APPLE230.PPD	Apple LaserWriter version 23.0
APPLE380.PPD	Apple LaserWriter Plus version 38.0
APPLE422.PPD	Apple LaserWriter Plus version 42.2
APS08522.PPD	APS-PS PIP with APS-6-108 version 49.3 or 52.2
APS12522.PPD	APS-PS PIP with LZR1200 version 49.3 or 52.2

Table 4.11   Adobe PostScript Printer Description Files *(continued)*

Filename	File description
APS26522.PPD	APS-PSP IP with LZR2600 version 49.3 or 52.2
APS80522.PPD	APS-PSP IP with APS-6-80 version 49.3 or 52.2
AST__470.PPD	AST TurboLaser-PS version 47.0
CG94_493.PPD	Agfa-Compugraphic 9400P version 49.3
OLIV5000.PPD	Olivetti PG 308 HS PostScript printer
QMS860.PPD	QMS 860 Print System version 2011.22 r15
T1513470.PPD	TI 2115 13 fonts version 47.0
T1535470.PPD	TI 2115 35 fonts version 47.0
TIM17521.PPD	TI microLaser PS17 version .52.1
TIM35521.PPD	TI microLaser PS35 version .52.1
TITRB161.PPD	TI microLaser16 Turbo version 2010.119
TITRBO61.PPD	TI microLaser6 Turbo version 2010.119
TITRBO91.PPD	TI microLaser9 Turbo version 2010.119
TIX17521.PPD	TI microLaser XL PS17 version .52.1
TIX35521.PPD	TI microLaser XL PS35 version .52.1
TI08_450.PPD	TI OmniLaser 2108 version 45.0
TI15_470.PPD	TI OmniLaser 2115 version 47.0
TRIUMPH1.PPD	Triumph Adler SDR 7706 PS13
TRIUMPH2.PPD	Triumph Adler SDR 7706 PS35
UNI17521.PPD	Unisys® AP9210 17 Fonts version 52.1
UNI39521.PPD	Unisys AP9210 39 Fonts version 52.1
U9415470.PPD	Unisys AP9415 version 47.0
V5334522.PPD	Varityper Series 4000-5330 version 49.3 or 52.2
VT42P522.PPD	Varityper 4200B-P version 49.3 or 52.2
VT43P522.PPD	Varityper 4300P version 49.3 or 52.2
VT4510A1.PPD	Varityper VT4_510A version 52.3
VT49901.PPD	Varityper VT4990 version 52.3
VT4L3001.PPD	Varityper 4000-L300 version 52.3
VT4L3301.PPD	Varityper 4000-L330 version 52.3
VT4L5001.PPD	Varityper 4000-L500 version 52.3
VT4L5301.PPD	Varityper 4000-L530 version 52.3
VT530522.PPD	Varityper Series 4000-5300 version 49.3 or 52.2
VT550522.PPD	Varityper Series 4000-5500 version 52.2
VT600P1.PPD	Varityper VT-600P

Table 4.11 Adobe PostScript Printer Description Files (continued)

Filename	File description
VT600W1.PPD	Varityper VT-600W version 48.0
VT60P480.PPD	Varityper VT-600P version 48.0
VT60W480.PPD	Varityper VT-600W version 48.0
WANG15FP.PPD	Varityper VT-600P version 48.0
VT4530A1.PPD	VT4_530A version 52.3
VT4530B1.PPD	VT4_530B version 52.3
VT4530C1.PPD	VT4_530C version 52.3
VT4533B1.PPD	VT4_533B version 52.3
VT4533C1.PPD	VT4_533C version 52.3
VT453EA1.PPD	VT4_53EA version 52.3
VT453EB1.PPD	VT4_53EB version 52.3
VT4550A1.PPD	VT4_550A version 52.3
VT4550B1.PPD	VT4_550B version 52.3
VT4550C1.PPD	VT4_550C version 52.3
VT4551A1.PPD	VT4_551A version 52.3
VT4563A1.PPD	VT4_563A version 52.3
VT4563B1.PPD	VT4_563B version 52.3
WANG15.PPD	Wang LCS15
XRDT1351.PPD	Xerox® DocuTech 135 version 2010.130
XRDT0851.PPD	Xerox DocuTech 85 version 2010.130
XRDT0901.PPD	Xerox DocuTech 90 version 2010.130
AGFAP400.PPD	PostScript Printer Description file for Agfa Compugraphic 400PS
IBM31514.PPD	Printer driver for IBM Personal Page Printer II-31

Windows NT includes the following separator page files. For more information about separator pages, see Chapter 6, "Printing."

Table 4.12 Printer Separator Page Definition Files

Filename	File description
PCL.SEP[2]	HPPCL
PSLANMAN.SEP[2]	LAN Manager PostScript file
PSCRIPT.SEP[2]	PostScript
SYSPRINT.SEP[2]	PostScript devices with error handling

[2] Installed during graphical Setup by INITIAL.INF.

Spelling Lexicon and National Language Support Files

Windows NT includes the following lexicon files. For related information, see Appendix D, "International Considerations."

Table 4.13   Spelling Lexicon Files

Filename	File description
MSP32_AM.LEX[2]	U.S. English spelling
MSP32_BR.LEX	International English spelling
MSP32_DA.LEX	Danish spelling
MSP32_ES.LEX	Spanish spelling
MSP32_FI.LEX	Finnish spelling
MSP32_FR.LEX	French spelling
MSP32_GE.LEX	German spelling
MSP32_IT.LEX	Italian spelling
MSP32_NB.LEX	Norwegian spelling
MSP32_NL.LEX	Dutch spelling
MSP32_PB.LEX	Portuguese spelling
MSP32_SW.LEX	Swedish spelling

[2] Installed during graphical Setup by INITIAL.INF.

Windows NT includes the following national language support files. These files convert code page information to Unicode. For more information about national language support, code pages, and Unicode, see Appendix D, "International Considerations."

Table 4.14   National Language Support Files

Filename	File description
C_037.NLS[1]	EBCDIC Latin1
C_10000.NLS	Macintosh Roman
C_10006.NLS	Macintosh Greek 1
C_10007.NLS	Macintosh Cyrillic
C_10029.NLS	Macintosh Slavic
C_1026.NLS	EBCDIC Latin 1/Turkish
C_1250.NLS	Win 3.1 Eastern European
C_1251.NLS	Win 3.1 Cyrillic
C_1252.NLS	Win 3.1 US (ANSI)

Table 4.14 National Language Support Files (*continued*)

Filename	File description
C_1253.NLS	Win 3.1 Greek
C_1254.NLS	Win 3.1 Turkish
C_437.NLS[1]	MS-DOS U.S.
C_500.NLS	EBCDIC Latin 1
C_850.NLS[1]	MS-DOS Latin I
C_852.NLS	MS-DOS Latin II
C_855.NLS	IBM Russian
C_857.NLS	IBM Turkish
C_860.NLS	MS-DOS Portuguese
C_861.NLS	MS-DOS Icelandic
C_863.NLS	MS-DOS French Canadian
C_865.NLS	MS-DOS Nordic
C_866.NLS	MS-DOS "Russian" (former USSR)
C_869.NLS	IBM Modern Greek
C_875.NLS	EBCDIC Greek
CTYPE1.NLS[1]	Character type 1 Unicode translation data file, always installed
CTYPE2.NLS[1]	Character type 2 Unicode translation file, always installed
CTYPE3.NLS[1]	Character type 3 Unicode translation data file, always installed
L_ELL.NLS	Greek casing table (upper and lowercase character tables)
L_INTL.NLS	International casing table (upper and lowercase character tables)
L_TRK.NLS	Turkish casing table (upper and lowercase character tables)
LOCALE.NLS[1]	Locale information for all locales; required for startup
SORTKEY.NLS[1]	National Language Support sort keys
SORTTBLS.NLS[1]	National Language Support sort tables
UNICODE.NLS[1]	Unicode translation data file; required for startup

[1] Installed during text-mode Setup by TXTSETUP.INF.

Sound Wave Files

Windows NT includes the following sound wave files. To associate sound waves with certain system events, choose the Sound icon from Control Panel. (You must have a sound card installed to use sound waves.)

Table 4.15   Sound Wave Files

Filename	File description
CHIMES.WAV[3]	Chimes
CHORD.WAV[3]	Chord
DING.WAV[3]	Ding
RINGIN.WAV[2]	Chat tool sound file for incoming call
RINGOUT.WAV[2]	Chat tool sound file for outgoing call
TADA.WAV[3]	Windows NT Startup sound

[2] Installed during graphical Setup by INITIAL.INF.

[3] Optional Windows NT component installed during graphical Setup by PARTIAL.INF.

Animated Cursors, Screen Savers, Wallpaper

Windows NT includes the following animated cursor files. To use animated cursors, choose the Cursors icon from Control Panel.

Table 4.16   Animated Cursors

Filename	File description
APPSTART.ANI[2]	Rotating hourglass with falling sand
BANANA.ANI[2]	Peeling banana
BARBER.ANI[2]	Rotating barber pole
COIN.ANI[2]	Rotating coin
COUNTER.ANI[2]	Stopwatch with incrementing counter
DRUM.ANI[2]	Drummer
FILLITUP.ANI[2]	Pointer that fills with color
HAND.ANI[2]	Fingers tapping on desktop
HORSE.ANI[2]	Running horse
HOURGLAS.ANI[2]	Rotating hourglass with falling sand
METRONOM.ANI[2]	Metronome
PIANO.ANI[2]	Cycling piano keys

Table 4.16 Animated Cursors *(continued)*

Filename	File description
RAINBOW.ANI[2]	Pointer filled with multicolors
RAINDROP.ANI[2]	Pointer with animated ripplets
SIZENESW.ANI[2]	Expanding NE-SW double-arrow
SIZENS.ANI[2]	Expanding N-S double-arrow
SIZENWSE.ANI[2]	Expanding NW-SW double-arrow
SIZEWE.ANI[2]	Expanding W-E double-arrow
STOPWTCH.ANI[2]	Stopwatch
VANISHER.ANI[2]	Vanishing animated cursor
WAGTAIL.ANI[2]	Point with wagging tail animated cursor

[2] Installed during graphical Setup by INITIAL.INF.

Windows NT includes the following screen saver files. To use screen savers, choose the Desktop icon from Control Panel.

Table 4.17 Screen Saver Files

Filename	File description
BLACK16.SCR[2]	Black screen (16-bit)
LOGON.SCR[3]	Randomly-positioned Windows NT Logon dialog box
SCRNSAVE.SCR[3]	32-bit black screen
SSBEZIER.SCR[3]	Bezier curves
SSMARQUE.SCR[3]	Marquee
SSMYST.SCR[3]	Mystify
SSSTARS.SCR[3]	Stars

[2] Installed during graphical Setup by INITIAL.INF.

[3] Optional Windows NT component installed during graphical Setup by PARTIAL.INF.

Windows NT includes the following wallpaper files. Use the Desktop icon from Control Panel to specify the wallpaper you want to use.

Table 4.18 Bitmapped Wallpaper Files

Filename	File description
256COLOR.BMP[3]	256-color design
ARCADE.BMP[3]	Gray textured diamond against light green background
ARCHES.BMP[3]	Roman coliseum effect or aqueduct effect
ARGYLE.BMP[3]	Argyle pattern
BALL.BMP[3]	Three-dimensional ball against checked background
CARS.BMP[3]	Car on street pointing to upper-right corner
CASTLE.BMP[3]	Castle wall
CHITZ.BMP[3]	Random squares-and-squiggles pattern
EGYPT.BMP[3]	Egyptian-style pattern
HONEY.BMP[3]	Honeycomb pattern
LANMANNT.BMP[2]	Windows NT Advanced Server bitmap (for Windows NT Advanced Server only)
LEAVES.BMP[3]	Leaves
MARBLE.BMP[3]	Marble pattern
REDBRICK.BMP[3]	Red brick pattern
RIVETS.BMP[3]	Rivets
SQUARES.BMP[3]	Squares
TARTAN.BMP[3]	Tartan
THATCH.BMP[3]	Thatch
WINLOGO.BMP[3]	Windows logo
WINNT.BMP[2]	Windows NT logo (for the base Windows NT product only)
ZIGZAG.BMP[3]	Zig-zag pattern

[2] Installed during graphical Setup by INITIAL.INF.

[3] Optional Windows NT component installed during graphical Setup by PARTIAL.INF.

Quick Basic Sample and Miscellaneous Files

Windows NT includes the following sample files for Quick Basic.

Table 4.19   Quick Basic Sample Files

Filename	File description
GORILLA.BAS[3]	MS-DOS Quick Basic sample file
MONEY.BAS[3]	MS-DOS Quick Basic sample file
NIBBLES.BAS[3]	MS-DOS Quick Basic sample file
REMLINE.BAS[2]	Windows command line

[2] Installed during graphical Setup by INITIAL.INF.

[3] Optional Windows NT component installed during graphical Setup by PARTIAL.INF.

Windows NT also includes these files.

Table 4.20   Miscellaneous Files

Filename	File description
_DEFAULT.PIF[2]	Default PIF for MS-DOS applications
AUTOEXEC.NT[2]	Default AUTOEXEC.BAT file for Windows NT
BIOS1.ROM[2], BIOS2.ROM[2]	Required for VDM emulation
CANYON.MID[3]	Multimedia sample file
CMOS.RAM[2]	Required for VDM emulation
CONFIG.NT[2]	Default CONFIG.SYS for Windows NT
CURSORS.CPL[2]	Animated cursor Control Panel tool
DEFAULT[1]	Registry hive
FATBOOT.BIN[1]	FAT boot sector
FTPMGR.CPL	FTP Server (Control Panel tool)
GRAPHICS.PRO[2]	Graphics Profile file; used by the Graphics utility to load printer profile information
HOSTS	Windows Sockets database file; provides hostname and IP address name resolution for Windows Sockets
HPFSBOOT.BIN[1]	HPFS boot sector
IDP_XFS.BIN	Network NDIS driver: Digiboard ISDN

Table 4.20   Miscellaneous Files *(continued)*

Filename	File description
INTRO.ICO[2]	Introduction to Windows NT icon
LMHOSTS	Windows Sockets database file; provides computername and IP address name resolution for Windows Networking
MAIN.CPL[2]	Control Panel's Main icons: color, fonts, ports, mouse, desktop, keyboard, printer, international, system, date/time
MIB.BIN	SNMP component; SNMP service
MIDIMAP.CFG[2]	MIDI configuration file; controls the mapping of MIDI sound channels onto instruments
MULTIMED.CPL[2]	Control Panel module for multimedia Control Panel tools: Sound, MIDI Mapper, Drivers
MUSRMGR.IND	User Manager help index
MVOPL3.PAT	Media Vision OPL3 FM Synthesizer patches for OPL3 Synthesizer driver
NCPA.CPL[1]	Network Control Panel tool
NETFLX.BIN	Network NDIS driver for COMPAQ NetFlex/DualSpeed Token Ring adapter card
NETWORKS	Sockets database file; provides network name and net ID resolution for TCP/IP management utilities
NT.DOC[2]	Introduction to Windows NT documentation
NTLDR[1]	Windows NT loader
OSO001.007	OS/2 message file in German
OSO001.009[2]	OS/2 message file in English
OSO001.010	OS/2 message file in Spanish
OSO001.012	OS/2 message file in French
OSO001.016	OS/2 message file in Italian
OSO001.029	OS/2 message file in Swedish
PASSPORT.MID[2]	MIDI sound file
PROFILE.SPC	Needed for MS-DOS and Win16 VDMs
PROTOCOL	Sockets database file; provides protocol name and protocol ID resolution for Windows Sockets applications
SERVICES	Sockets database file; provides service name and port ID resolution for Windows Sockets applications
SETUPLDR	Setup loader
SFMMGR.CPL	Services for Macintosh Control Panel tool

Table 4.20   Miscellaneous Files *(continued)*

Filename	File description
SFMUAM.IFO	Services for Macintosh user authentication manager volume information file
SFMUAM.RSC	Services for Macintosh user authentication module volume resource file
SOFTWARE[1]	Software hive; default Registry configuration
SRVMGR.CPL	Control Panel tool; includes Server, Services, and Devices tools
SYNTH.PAT	Synthesizer patch codes
SYSTEM[1]	Windows NT System hive
SYSTEM.INI[2]	Win16 system initialization file, for Win16 compatibility
TAGFILE.TAG	Windows NT Setup uses this file
TELNET.TRM	Windows NT Terminal configuration file for the Telnet driver (used by TELNET.EXE)
UPS.CPL[2]	Uninterruptible Power Supply control panel tool
V7VGA.ROM[2]	Emulation of Video 7 BIOS code required for VDM emulation
WIN.INI[2]	Win16 Windows initialization file (for compatibility)
WINFILE.INI[2]	File Manager initialization file

[1] Installed during text-mode Setup by TXTSETUP.INF.

[2] Installed during graphical Setup by INITIAL.INF.

[3] Optional Windows NT component installed during graphical Setup by PARTIAL.INF.

Using Windows NT

Part Three describes some of the most basic features of the Windows NT product, including its file systems and printing. This part also examines technical issues related to using fonts, Microsoft Mail, and Microsoft Schedule+ under Windows NT.

C H A P T E R 5

Windows NT File Systems and Advanced Disk Management

Windows NT supports multiple active file systems including the existing FAT and HPFS file systems. It also includes a new file system called NTFS, designed to take advantage of the very large disks and very fast processors on current and future computers.

As noted in Chapter 1, "Windows NT Architecture," Windows NT also implements redirectors and servers as file systems. In addition, Windows NT supports the CD file system for use on CD-ROM drives. It also supports the Named Piles File System (NPFS) and the Mailslot File System (MSFS), both used for communication between processes.

These nontraditional file systems are not included in the discussion of this chapter. Instead, this chapter focuses on FAT, HPFS, and NTFS, the three file systems that can be used on read/write hard drives.

This chapter describes FAT and HPFS both as progenitors to NTFS and as file systems that can be used with Windows NT. It also details the features of NTFS and compares features of NTFS, FAT, and HPFS.

This chapter also describes the disk management techniques offered by Windows NT that you can use to organize and safeguard data on your disks.

File System History

In 1981, IBM introduced its first personal computer, which ran a new operating system designed by Microsoft, MS-DOS. The computer contained a 16-bit 8088 processor chip and two drives for low-density floppy disks. The MS-DOS file system, FAT (named for its file allocation table), provided more than enough power to format these small disk volumes and to manage hierarchical directory structures and files. The FAT file system continued to meet the needs of personal computer users even as hardware and software power increased year after year. However, file searches and data retrieval took significantly longer on large hard disks than on the original low-density floppies of the first IBM PC.

By the end of the 1980s, the prediction of "a computer on every desk and in every home" was less a dream and more a reality. Personal computers now had 16-bit processors and hard disks of 40 MB and more—so big that users had to partition their disks into two or more volumes because the file allocation table's limit was 32 MB per volume. (Later versions of MS-DOS allowed for larger disk volumes.)

In 1990, a high-performance file system (HPFS) was introduced as a part of the OS/2 operating system version 1.x. This file system was designed specifically for large hard disks on 16-bit processor computers. On the heels of HPFS came HPFS386. It was introduced as part of Microsoft LAN Manager and was designed to take advantage of the 32-bit 80386 processor chip.

Today's personal computers include a variety of very fast processor chips and can accommodate multiple, huge hard disks. The new Windows NT file system, NTFS, is designed for optimal performance on these computers.

Because of features such as speed and universality, FAT or HPFS are now popular and widely used file systems. NTFS offers consistency with these two file systems, plus advanced functionality needed by corporations interested in greater flexibility and in data security.

Before discussing how each file system organizes data on the disk, the next section briefly reviews how a disk is organized.

About Disks and Disk Organization

Each disk is divided into top and bottom sides, rings on each side called *tracks*, and sections within each track called *sectors*. A *sector* is the smallest physical storage unit on a disk, typically 512 bytes in size. The **format** command organizes the disk into tracks and sectors for use by a particular file system. Unless you specify a particular sector size, **format** evaluates your disk and determines an appropriate sector size for you.

As a file is written to the disk, the file system allocates the appropriate number of sectors to store the file's data. For example, if each sector is 512 bytes and the file is 800 bytes, two sectors are allocated for the file. Later, if the file is appended, for example, to twice its size (1600 bytes), another two sectors are allocated. If *contiguous* sectors (sectors that are next to each other on the disk) are not available, the data is written elsewhere on the disk, and the file is considered to be *fragmented*. Fragmentation only becomes an issue when the file system must search several different locations to find all the pieces of the file you want to read. The search causes a delay before the file is retrieved. Allocating larger sectors reduces the potential for fragmentation but increases the likelihood that sectors would have unused space.

The way data is retrieved depends on the indexing methods used by the file system. The following sections provide details about FAT, HPFS, and NTFS, including how each stores, indexes, and retrieves data on the disk.

FAT File System

As mentioned earlier, the FAT file system is named for its method of organization—the file allocation table. This table of values provides links from one allocation unit (one or more sectors) to another, as shown in Figure 5.1.

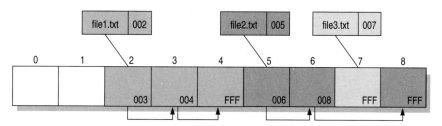

Figure 5.1   File Allocation Table

This illustration includes three files. The file named FILE1.TXT is a file that is large enough to take the space of three allocation units. A small file, FILE3.TXT, takes space in only one allocation unit. The third file, FILE2.TXT, is a large, fragmented file. In each case, the directory entry points to the first allocation unit containing the file. If the file contents go beyond one allocation unit, the first allocation unit points to the next in the chain. FFF indicates the end of the chain.

The FAT file system is a simple file system originally designed for small disks and simple directory structures. Its design has been improved over the years to work more effectively with larger disks and more powerful personal computers. With MS-DOS version 4.0, the FAT entries grew from 12 bits to 16 bits in size, thus allowing for partitions larger than 32 MB.

The FAT file system organizes the disk in this way:

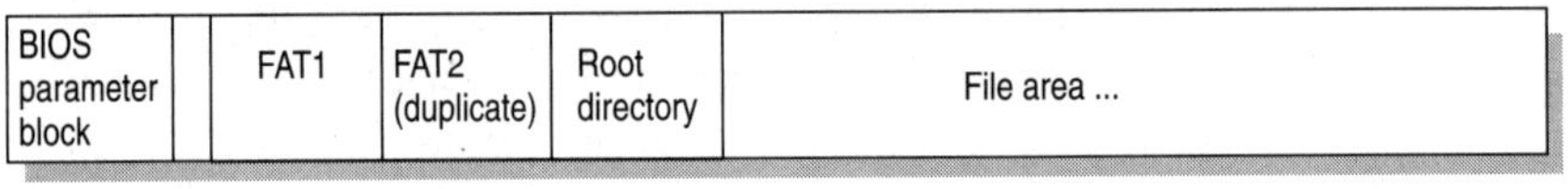

BIOS parameter block		FAT1	FAT2 (duplicate)	Root directory	File area ...

Figure 5.2   FAT Disk Partition (Volume)

The root directory has a fixed size and location on the disk. Directories are special files with 32-byte entries for each file contained in that directory. The entry for each file includes the following information:

- Filename (eight-plus-three characters)
- Attribute byte (8 bits worth of information, described below)
- Modification time (16 bits)
- Modification date (16 bits)
- Starting allocation unit (16 bits)
- File size (32 bits)

FAT file attributes include the file's subdirectory, the volume label, and four special attributes that can be turned on or off—archive file, system file, hidden file, and read-only.

A key feature of the FAT file system is simplicity. This file system has very little overhead. It is FAT's simplicity that yields performance.

However, FAT's performance slows noticeably on large disk volumes. In addition, it lacks more sophisticated features such as recoverability and security. And its eight-plus-three naming convention is commonly regarded as restrictive. These were some of the main reasons why HPFS was developed.

Using the FAT File System with Windows NT

The Windows NT FAT file system works the same as it does with MS-DOS and Windows. In fact, you can install Windows NT on your existing FAT partition.

Note Remember that you cannot use Windows NT with any compression or partitioning software that requires drivers to be loaded by MS-DOS. Rather, you must have Windows NT-specific versions of the drivers to enable Windows NT to read the disk.

You can move or copy files between FAT and NTFS volumes. When you move or copy a file from NTFS to FAT, any NTFS-style long filename, permissions, and alternate streams are lost. In addition, the short name for the file is case-insensitive, and at the command line, is displayed as uppercase.

HPFS

The high-performance file system (HPFS) includes features that make it a fast and powerful manager of large hard-disk volumes. HPFS also supports long filenames (up to 255 characters), which allows users to give files descriptive names.

While the FAT file system organizes the disk into partitions and logical drives, HPFS organizes the disk into *volumes*. When HPFS formats a volume, it reserves the first 18 sectors for the boot block, the super block, and the spare block. These three structures are used to boot the operating system, maintain the file system, and recover from possible errors.

HPFS also reserves space for a pair of 2K bitmaps at 16 MB intervals throughout the volume. Each bitmap contains one bit for each allocation unit (equal to one sector) in the 8 MB band, showing which allocation units are in use.

Figure 5.3 illustrates how HPFS organizes a volume:

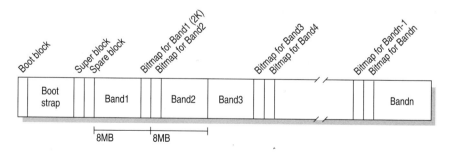

Figure 5.3   An HPFS Volume

The bitmaps are alternately located at the end and beginning of each band to allow a maximum amount of contiguous space for data (almost 16 MB instead of almost 8 MB). In addition, HPFS plans where it writes new files, leaving room between new and existing files so that each has room to expand into contiguous space on the disk. This feature helps HPFS to allow fast data retrieval and to minimize file fragmentation.

Another feature that accounts for fast data access is HPFS's use of B-trees. A *B-tree* is a tree structure with a root and several nodes. It contains data organized in some logical way so that the whole structure can be quickly traversed. The root contains a small amount of administrative information, a map to the rest of the structure, and possibly a small amount of data. The nodes contain most of the data. On large, relatively full disks, B-trees perform much better than the linear lists used by the FAT file system.

HPFS uses B-trees to structure each of its directories and each of its files. Each directory points to Fnodes for files contained in that directory. An *Fnode* is 512 bytes in length and contains a header, the filename (truncated to 15 characters), the file length, extended attributes (EA) and access control list (ACL) information, and the location of the file's data.

Note   HPFS ACLs are supported by the OS/2 operating system but not by Windows NT. If you want access control list support, use NTFS.

Figure 5.4 shows the Fnode for a file whose data is contained in Extent1, Extent2, and Extent3 (where an *extent* is a range of contiguous sectors).

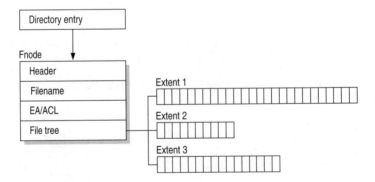

Figure 5.4   An HPFS File

Because of the arrangement of bitmaps on the volume shown in Figure 5.3, a file extent can be nearly 16 MB in length. Depending on the size of the file, the Fnode can point to as many as eight extents. If the file is so large that it cannot be contained within eight extents, the Fnode includes up to 12 pointers to allocation nodes that have space for more file extents.

If the extended attribute and ACL information cannot be contained in the Fnode, the Fnode includes a pointer to that information.

Disk caching and *lazy writing* are two more features that speed operations in HPFS. In most cases, when a program needs to write information to the hard disk, it is not necessary that the information be written immediately. With HPFS on an OS/2 system, information that a program sends to be written to disk is temporarily stored in a cache in memory. This is called *disk caching*. Later, when the disk would otherwise be idle, HPFS writes the information to the disk as a background task. This is called *lazy writing*.

Note   With Windows NT, disk caching and lazy writing are managed by Cache Manager and not the file system. Cache Manager offers these features to all file systems.

Because HPFS uses lazy writes, it is conceivable that a write error could occur long after an application is in a position to do anything about it. With OS/2, HPFS uses a technique called *hot-fixing* to handle write errors. When an error is detected, the file system takes a free block out of a reserved hot-fix pool, writes the data to that block, and updates the hot-fix map. HPFS also replaces any bad sector numbers with the corresponding number of the good sector holding the data. A copy of this map is written to disk. If more than a specified number of hot-fixes occur, the file system displays a message to encourage the user to run **chkdsk /f** to check and possibly repair the volume.

In short, HPFS includes powerful features, such as extended attributes, not offered by FAT, and it works relatively quickly and efficiently on disks of up to 2 GB. The HPFS design does have some weaknesses. For example, if something damages the first portion of the volume, which contains boot information and a pointer to the root directory, use of the volume is lost. HPFS's use of **chkdsk** at each system boot and to repair disk errors can be time-consuming. In addition, its design requiring 512-byte sectors is not well-suited for larger volumes.

Using HPFS with Windows NT

Some HPFS features are implemented differently for Windows NT than for OS/2. For example, Windows NT does not support HPFS access control list information or HPFS hot-fixing. (However, these features are available with NTFS.) Also, disk caching and lazy writing are managed by the Windows NT Cache Manager and not the file system.

When you move or copy a file from NTFS to HPFS, any extended attributes not supported by HPFS, permissions, and alternate streams are lost. In addition, the filename becomes case-insensitive.

NTFS

NTFS provides a combination of performance, reliability, and compatibility not found in either FAT or HPFS. It is designed to quickly perform standard file operations such as read, write, and search—and even advanced operations such as file-system recovery—on very large hard disks.

It also includes security features required for file servers and high-end PCs in a corporate environment. NTFS supports data access control and ownership privileges that are important for the integrity of corporate data. While directories shared by a Windows NT server are assigned particular permissions, NTFS files and directories can have assigned permissions whether they are shared or not. NTFS is the only file system on Windows NT that allows you to assign permissions to individual files.

NTFS has a simple, yet very powerful design. From the file system's perspective, everything on the NTFS volume is a file or part of a file. Every sector on an NTFS volume that is allocated belongs to some file. Even the file system metadata (information that describes the file system itself) is part of a file.

This attribute-based file system supports object-oriented applications by treating all files as objects that have user-defined and system-defined attributes.

Master File Table

Each file on an NTFS volume is represented by a record in a special file called the Master File Table (MFT). NTFS reserves the first 16 records of the table for special information. The first record of this table describes the Master File Table itself, followed by a MFT *mirror record*. If the first MFT record is corrupted, NTFS reads the second record to find the MFT mirror file, whose first record is identical to the first record of the MFT. The locations of the data segments for both the MFT and MFT mirror file are recorded in the boot sector. A duplicate of the boot sector is located at the logical center of the disk.

The third record of the MFT is the log file, used for file recovery. The log file is discussed in detail later in this chapter. The seventeenth and following records of the Master File Table are for each file and directory (also viewed as a file by NTFS) on the volume. Figure 5.5 provides a simplified illustration of the MFT structure.

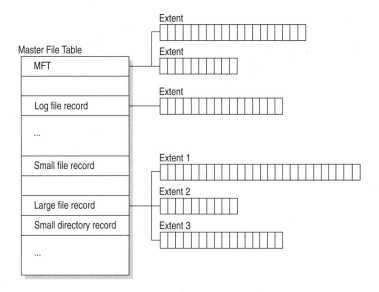

Figure 5.5   Master File Table

The Master File Table allocates a certain amount of space for each file record. The attributes of a file are written to the allocated space in the MFT. Small files and directories (typically 1500 bytes or smaller), such as the file illustrated in Figure 5.6, can be entirely contained within the Master File Table record.

Standard information	File or directory name	Security descriptor	Data or index	

Figure 5.6   MFT Record for a Small File or Directory

This design makes file access very fast. Consider, for example, the FAT file system, which uses a file allocation table to list the names and addresses of each file. FAT directory entries contain an index into the file allocation table. When you want to view a file, FAT first reads the file allocation table and assures that it exists. Then FAT retrieves the file by searching the chain of allocation units assigned to the file. With NTFS, as soon as you look up the file, it's there for you to use.

Directory records are housed within the Master File Table just like file records. Instead of data, directories contain index information. Small directory records reside entirely within the MFT structure. Large directories are organized into B-trees, having records with pointers to external clusters containing directory entries that could not be contained within the MFT structure.

NTFS File Attributes

NTFS views each file (or directory) as a set of file *attributes*. Elements such as the file's name, its security information, and even its data are all file attributes. Each attribute is identified by an attribute type code and, optionally, an attribute name.

When a file's attributes can be written within the MFT file record, they are called *resident* attributes. For example, information such as filename and time stamp are always included in the MFT file record. When a file is too large to fit all of its attributes in the MFT file record, some of its attributes are *nonresident*. The nonresident attributes are allocated one or more runs of disk space elsewhere in the volume. (A *run* of disk space is a contiguous linear area on the disk.)

In general, all attributes can be referenced as a stream of bytes whether they are resident or nonresident.

Table 5.1 lists all of the file attributes currently defined by NTFS. This list is extensible, meaning that other file attributes can be defined in the future.

Table 5.1   NTFS File Attribute Types

Attribute type	Description
Standard Information	Includes time stamps, link count, and so on.
Attribute List	Lists all other attributes in large files only.
Filename	A repeatable attribute for both long and short filenames. The long name of the file can be up to 255 Unicode characters. The short name is the MS-DOS–readable, eight-plus-three, case-insensitive name for this file. Additional names, or *hard links*, required by POSIX may also be included as additional Filename attributes.
Security Descriptor	Shows information about who can access the file, who owns the file, and so on.
Data	Contains file data. NTFS allows for multiple data attributes per file. Each file typically has one unnamed data attribute. In addition, a file can have one or more named data attributes, using a particular syntax.
Index Root	Used to implement directories.
Index Allocation	Used to implement directories.

Table 5.1   NTFS File Attribute Types *(continued)*

Attribute type	Description
Volume Information	Used only in the volume system file and includes, among other things, the version and name of the volume.
Bitmap	Provides a map representing records in use on the MFT or directory.
Extended attribute Information	Used by file servers that are linked with OS/2 systems. This attribute type isn't useful to Windows NT.
Extended attributes	Used by file servers that are linked with OS/2 systems. This attribute type isn't useful to Windows NT.

Long and Short Filenames

One of the improvements HPFS implemented on the MS-DOS design was the ability to use long filenames of up to 255 characters. Unfortunately, files with long names on an HPFS volume couldn't be accessed from an MS-DOS operating system, which has an eight-plus-three filename limitation.

Like HPFS, NTFS allows filenames of up to 255 characters. NTFS filenames use the 16-bit Unicode character set but solve the problem of access from MS-DOS. NTFS automatically generates an MS-DOS–readable (eight-plus-three) name for each file. This way, NTFS files are accessible over a network by MS-DOS and OS/2 operating systems. This is a particularly important feature for file servers, especially in an office using personal computers with two or all three of these operating systems.

By creating eight-plus-three filenames for files, NTFS also allows MS-DOS and Windows 3.*x* applications to recognize and load files that have NTFS long filenames. In addition, when an MS-DOS or Windows 3.*x* application saves a file on an NTFS volume, both the eight-plus-three filename and NTFS long filename are retained.

Note   When saving a file from an MS-DOS or Windows 3.*x* application on an NTFS volume, if that application saves to a temporary file, deletes the original file, and renames the temporary file to the original filename, the long filename is lost. Any unique permissions set on that file are also lost. Permissions are propagated again from the parent directory.

If the long name of a file or directory on an NTFS volume contains spaces, be sure to surround the path name with quotation marks. This is true when specifying a path in Program Manager for the application's icon. For example, suppose Word for Windows is installed in D:\WORD FOR WINDOWS. The Program Item Properties Command Line should be set to D:\WORD FOR WINDOWS\WINWORD.EXE. If the quotation marks were omitted, an error message would display, saying "The path D:\Word is invalid."

This is also true when a path typed at the command line includes spaces, as in the following:

```
move "c:\This month's reports\*.*" "c:\Last month's reports",,
```

Note   Remember to use wildcards such as * and ? carefully in conjunction with **del** and **copy** commands. NTFS searches both long and short filenames for matches to the wildcard combination you specify, which may cause extra files to be deleted or copied.

To copy or move files with case-sensitive long filenames, it is safest to use a mouse in File Manager to identify which files you want to copy or move.

Generating Short Filenames

Because NTFS uses the Unicode character set for its names, there are potentially several "illegal" characters that MS-DOS cannot read in any filename. To generate a short MS-DOS–readable filename for a file, NTFS deletes all of these characters from the long filename and removes any spaces. Then, since an MS-DOS–readable filename can have only one period, NTFS removes all extra periods from the filename. Next, NTFS truncates the filename, if necessary, to six characters and appends a tilde (~) and a number. For example, each nonduplicate filename is appended with **~1**. Duplicate filenames end with **~2**, **~3**, and so on. Filename extensions are truncated to three or fewer characters. Finally, when displaying filenames at the command line, NTFS translates all characters in the filename and extension to uppercase. (File Manager displays these filenames as lowercase.)

Windows NT does not generate short (eight-plus-three) filenames for files created by POSIX applications on an NTFS partition. This means that MS-DOS–based and Windows-based applications cannot view these filenames if they are not valid eight-plus-three filenames. If you want to use files that are created by a POSIX application with MS-DOS–based or Windows-based applications, be sure to use standard MS-DOS eight-plus-three naming conventions.

Viewing Short Filenames

Both File Manager and the **dir** command are able to display either the long NTFS filenames or the short MS-DOS–readable filenames, so you can look up and manipulate files using either long or short filenames.

To see short filenames from File Manager, choose Full File Details.

From the command line, to see both the long and short filenames for each file in the directory, type the following command:

```
dir /x
```

Tip To display both long and short filenames automatically, use the System application in Control Panel to set the **dircmd** variable to the value **/x**.

Multiple Data Streams

NTFS supports multiple data streams. The stream name identifies a new data attribute on the file. Streams have separate opportunistic locks, file locks, allocation sizes, and file sizes, but sharing is per file.

An example of an alternate stream is the following:

```
myfile.dat:stream2
```

This feature permits related data to be managed as a single unit. For example, Macintosh computers use this type of structure to manage resource and data forks. Or, a company might create a program to keep a list of changes to the file in an alternate stream, thus keeping archive information with the current version of the file.

As another example, a library of files might exist where the files are defined as alternate streams, as in the following:

```
library:file1
       :file2
       :file3
```

Suppose a "smart" compiler creates a file structure like the following:

```
program:source_file
       :doc_file
       :object_file
       :executable_file
```

Note Because NTFS is not supported on floppy disks, when you copy an NTFS file to a floppy disk, data streams and other attributes not supported by FAT are lost.

POSIX Compliance

POSIX compliance permits UNIX applications to be ported to Windows NT. Windows NT is fully compliant with the Institute of Electrical and Electronic Engineers (IEEE) standard 1003.1, which is a standard for file naming and identification.

The following POSIX-compliant features are included in NTFS:

- Case-sensitive naming. Under POSIX, README.TXT, Readme.txt, and readme.txt are all different files.
- Hard links. A file can be given more than one name. This allows two different filenames, which can be located in different directories, to point to the same data.
- Additional time stamps. These show when the file was last accessed or modified.

Caution POSIX applications create case-sensitive filenames where two or more filenames can differ only in case, for example, annm.doc and AnnM.Doc.

While NTFS supports both case-preservation and case-sensitivity, you cannot use standard commands with NTFS to manage filenames that differ only in case. (*Standard* commands include those used at the command-line—such as **copy**, **del**, and **move**—and their File Manager equivalents.) For example, both annm.doc and AnnM.Doc are deleted if you type the following at the command prompt:

```
del AnnM.Doc
```

You must use POSIX applications to manage filenames that differ only in case.

For related information, see the section on the POSIX subsystem in Chapter 1, "Windows NT Architecture" and Chapter 25, "POSIX Compatibility."

NTFS Features Used by Macintosh Services Clients

Services for Macintosh is included with Windows NT Advanced Server. These services give Macintosh users access to files residing on a Windows NT Advanced Server, and since these files are available to Windows NT network users, the file server can be easily used for sharing files across platforms.

You must make an NTFS partition available when you enable Services for Macintosh if you want to automatically create the User Authentication Module volumes for Macintosh clients. (The Network Control Panel uses the first NTFS partition to create these default volumes.)

Macintosh clients can use only files on NTFS volumes. Macintosh resource forks and the Finder information for each Macintosh file are stored as NTFS streams. Because NTFS also supports long names, most Macintosh filenames are preserved.

Services for Macintosh stores File Sharing folder privileges as NT permissions, meaning that there is only one set of permissions on a folder or file, which is enforced both for NT users and Macintosh users. However, Macintosh users cannot see file permissions, since AppleShare® supports only folder permissions.

For more information about Services for Macintosh, see the *Windows NT Advanced Server Services for Macintosh Administrator's Guide.*

NTFS System Files

NTFS includes several system files, all of which are hidden from view on the NTFS volume. A *system file* is one used by the file system to store its metadata and to implement the file system. System files are placed on the volume by the Format utility.

The NTFS system files are listed in Table 5.2.

Table 5.2   NTFS System Files

System file	Filename	Description
Master File Table	$Mft	A list of all contents of the NTFS volume.
Master File Table2	$MftMirr	A mirror of the important parts of the MFT, used to guarantee access to the MFT in the case of a single-sector failure.
Log File	$LogFile	A list of transaction steps, used by the Log File System for recoverability.
Volume	$Volume	The name, version, and other information about the volume.
Attribute Definitions	$AttrDef	A table of attribute names, numbers, and descriptions.

Table 5.2   NTFS System Files *(continued)*

System file	Filename	Description
Root Filename Index	$.	Root directory.
Cluster Bitmap	$Bitmap	A representation of the volume showing which allocation units are in use.
Boot File	$Boot	Includes the bootstrap for the volume, if this is a bootable volume.
Bad Cluster File	$BadClus	A location where all the bad clusters in the volume are located.

Comparing NTFS with HPFS and FAT

NTFS takes the best parts of both FAT and HPFS and improves upon those designs. From FAT, NTFS borrowed the "simplicity yields performance" philosophy. Performance increases when the number of disk transfers is minimized for common operations. From HPFS, NTFS borrowed techniques for speed and flexibility. For example, NTFS uses B-trees similar to those used by HPFS to maximize performance.

NTFS supports both long and short (eight-plus-three) filenames for compatibility with MS-DOS, HPFS, and other networked clients including OS/2, UNIX, AppleShare, and NFS. NTFS also provides for multiple extended attributes and allows future applications to define other extended attributes.

NTFS offers data security on fixed and removable hard disks, a feature important to corporate users and other power users.

For example, suppose Joe has a removable hard disk on his computer. That hard disk is formatted as an NTFS volume and has security permissions that allow access only to Joe and to one other coworker in his domain, Ann. Ann works at the company's the branch office. Joe removes the disk from his computer and sends it to Ann, who installs it in her computer. When she accesses the files on the disk, since Ann's computer is in the same domain as Joe's, she sees that the security mechanisms within the domain for the NTFS volume are intact.

Note Be sure to shut down the system before removing a disk containing an NTFS volume.

In addition to these features, NTFS provides a recovery system that is more reliable than either FAT or HPFS, and NTFS meets POSIX requirements.

The following table summarizes key features of FAT, HPFS, and NTFS as implemented on Windows NT:

Table 5.3   Comparison of FAT, HPFS, and NTFS

	FAT file system	HPFS	NTFS
Filename	Eight-plus-three ASCII characters [one period (delimiter) allowed]	254 bytes of double-byte characters [multiple periods (delimiters) allowed]	255 Unicode characters [multiple periods (delimiters) allowed]
File size	2^{32} bytes	2^{32} bytes	2^{64} bytes
Partition	2^{32} bytes	2^{41} bytes	2^{64} bytes
Maximum path length	64	No limit	No limit
Attributes	Only a few bit flags	Bit flags plus up to 64K of extended-attribute information	Everything, including data, is treated as file attributes
Directories	Unsorted	B-tree	B-tree
Philosophy	Simple	Fast	Fast, recoverable, and secure
Built-in security features	No	No	Yes

The next section describes one other difference that distinguishes the FAT, HPFS, and NTFS file systems—that is, the way each file system ensures data integrity on the disk.

Data Integrity and Recoverability with File Systems

Until now, there were two types of file systems—careful-write file systems and lazy-write file systems. NTFS introduces a third type—a recoverable file system.

Careful-Write File Systems

A *careful-write file system* is designed around the idea that it is important to keep the volume structure consistent. Two examples of careful-write file systems are FAT on MS-DOS and Digital ODS 2.

A careful-write file system works this way: When it's modifying the volume structure, it orders the disk writes. Most volume updates are made one at a time. Disk writes for each update are ordered so that if the system failed between two disk writes, the volume would be left in an understandable state with the possibility of an "expected" inconsistency. The disk remains usable. Running utilities such as **chkdsk** is rarely needed for a careful-write file system. (On FAT, for example, **chkdsk** is needed only to recover from system failure and provides a way to restore file system consistency quickly.)

The disadvantage of careful-write file systems is that serialized writes can be slow. This is because the first disk write must be completed and committed before the second disk write can begin, and so on. On a powerful computer, this is not the most efficient use of processing power.

Lazy-Write File Systems

A second kind of file system, such as HPFS and most UNIX file systems, is called a *lazy-write file system*. This type was designed to speed up disk access. Assuming that disk crashes were not a regular occurrence, a lazy-write file system was designed to use an intelligent cache-management strategy and provide a way to recover data (such as the **chkdsk** utility) should something happen to the disk.

All data is accessed via the disk cache. While the user searches directories or reads files, data to be written to disk is allowed to accumulate in the cache. Thus, the user never has to wait while disk-writes are performed. Plus, the user is able to access all the file-system resources that might otherwise be allocated for disk writing. Data gets written to disk when the computer's resources are in low demand, rather than in serial fashion.

If the same data is modified several times, all those modifications are captured in the disk cache. The result is that the file system needs to write to disk only once to update the data. That is, the file system opens the file once and then performs all of the updates together before closing the file.

The disadvantage of a lazy-write file system is that, in the event of a disk crash, recovery could take much longer than with a careful-write file system. This is because a utility such as **chkdsk** must then scan the entire volume to recover, checking what should have been written to disk against what actually was written.

Recoverable File Systems

NTFS is a third kind of file system—a *recoverable file system*. It combines the speed of a lazy-write file system with virtually instant recovery.

NTFS guarantees the consistency of the volume by using standard transaction logging and recovery techniques. It includes a lazy writing technique plus a system of volume recovery that takes typically only a second or two after the computer is rebooted. The transaction logging, which allows NTFS to recover quickly, requires a very small amount of overhead compared with careful-write file systems.

When used on a partition on a single device, NTFS can recover from a system crash, yet it may lose data as the result of an I/O error. In conjunction with the mirroring or parity striping support implemented by the fault tolerance driver (described later in this chapter), NTFS can survive any single point of failure. The NTFS partition still remains accessible, though potentially not bootable. That is, even if the boot sector is lost and the bootstrap cannot transfer control to the NTFS copy of the boot sector, you can still boot the computer from another partition or another physical drive and can still access the NTFS partition.

NTFS also supports hot-fixing, so that if an error occurs because of a bad sector, the file system moves the information to a different sector and marks the original sector as bad. This is transparent to any applications performing disk I/O. Hot-fixing eliminates error messages such as the "Abort, Retry, or Fail?" error message that occurs when a file system such as FAT encounters a bad sector.

However, when NTFS is used on a fault-tolerant device and an error is detected on one copy of a cluster, data can be recovered. The bad cluster is migrated to the Bad Cluster File, and it is replaced by another cluster. Then a copy of the original data is written to the new cluster.

Note   NTFS supports cluster sizes of 512, 1024, 2048, and 4096.

Although the **format** command automatically selects an appropriate cluster size based on its examination of your disk, you can use the **/a** option to specify a particular cluster size. Type **format /?** at the command line for more syntax information.

For more information about using fault tolerance with Windows NT, see "Windows NT Fault Tolerance Mechanisms," later in this chapter.

Data Integrity and Recoverability with NTFS

Each I/O operation that modifies a file on the NTFS volume is viewed by the file system as a transaction and can be managed as an atomic unit.

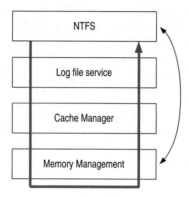

Figure 5.7   Interaction Between NTFS and Other Windows NT Components

When a user updates a file, the Log File Service logs all redo and undo information for the transaction. For recoverability, *redo* is the information that tells NTFS how to repeat the transaction, and *undo* tells how to roll back the transaction that was incomplete or that had an error.

If a transaction completes successfully, the file update is committed. If the transaction is incomplete, NTFS ends or rolls back the transaction by following instructions in the undo information. If NTFS detects an error in the transaction, the transaction is also rolled back.

File system recovery is straightforward with NTFS. If the system crashes, NTFS performs three passes—an analysis pass, a redo pass, and an undo pass. During the analysis pass, NTFS appraises the damage and determines exactly which clusters must now be updated, per the information in the log file. The redo pass performs all transaction steps logged from the last checkpoint. The undo pass backs out any incomplete (uncommitted) transactions.

Lazy Commit

Lazy commit is an important feature of NTFS. It allows NTFS to minimize the cost of logging to maintain high performance.

Lazy commit is similar to lazy write. Instead of using resources to mark a transaction as successfully completed as soon as it is performed, the commitment information is cached and written to the log as a background process. If the power source and/or computer system should fail before the commit is logged, NTFS will recheck the transaction to see whether it was successfully completed. If NTFS cannot guarantee that the transaction was completed successfully, it backs out the transaction. No incomplete modifications to the volume are allowed.

Periodic Log File Checkpoints

Every few seconds, NTFS checks the cache to determine the status of the lazy writer and marks the status as a checkpoint in the log. If the system crashes subsequent to that checkpoint, the system knows to back up to that checkpoint for recovery. This method provides for more expedient recovery times by saving the amount of queries that are required during recovery.

Note   This level of recoverability protects metadata. User data can still be corrupted in the case of power and/or system failure.

Disk Organization and Disk Management

Windows NT offers a number of disk management techniques that you can use to organize and safeguard data on your disks:

- You can choose how many physical disks and logical disk partitions your system will have. You can also choose whether you want to use volume sets or stripe sets to organize data across partitions.

- You can choose from among several fault-tolerance options to ensure data reliability on your system.

- You can employ other data backup and recovery techniques, such as tape backups and use of uninterruptible power supplies, to further safeguard against data loss.

The remainder of this chapter discusses using these techniques to improve disk performance and to ensure data reliability and security.

Logical Organization: Partitions, Volume Sets, and Stripe Sets

A physical disk can be arranged into one or more logical partitions. Each partition or set of partitions is formatted for a particular file system as a volume and assigned a drive letter. The *primary partition* is the portion of a physical disk that can be used by an operating system. Each disk can have as many as four partitions, one of which may be an extended partition.

Extended partitions can be subdivided into logical drives; primary partitions can't be subdivided. The free space in an extended partition can also be used to create volume sets or other kinds of volumes for fault-tolerance purposes. (Fault-tolerance options are described later in this chapter.) So long as the disk does not contain the boot partition, it can be used entirely as an extended partition.

Note On RISC–based computers, the primary partition created by the manufacturer's configuration program must be FAT.

Creating a *volume set* is simply a way of combining multiple areas of free space and formatting it into a single logical disk with a single drive letter. You can use the Disk Administrator utility to create and extend volume sets. Each volume set can include up to 32 areas of free space from one or more physical disks or partitions. Volume sets are organized so that the free space on one disk is filled before free space on the next disk in the set is used. Using volume sets does not increase disk performance. Only volume sets formatted with NTFS can be extended. A volume set cannot contain mirrored or striped components in its composition.

Disk striping (that is, the use of *stripe sets*) is a way to increase disk performance, as shown in Figure 5.8. You can create stripe sets using the Disk Administrator utility. This method increases both read and write performance since multiple I/O commands can be active on the drives at the same time. A striped set can have from 2 to 32 disks. If the disks are different sizes, the smallest is used as the common partition size. The remaining free space may be used individually or in a volume set.

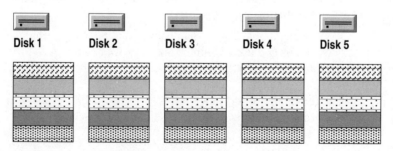

Disk 1   Disk 2   Disk 3   Disk 4   Disk 5

Figure 5.8   Disk Striping Across Physical Disks

Note that disk striping is different from the Windows NT Advanced Server method called *disk striping with parity* (described later in this chapter). Disk striping in Windows NT provides no parity stripe. Because the parity stripe is not present, the set is not fault tolerant. Once a stripe has been lost, there is no way to recover it. Some disk drivers do provide i-drive hot-fix capabilities that can be used to help ensure the safety of the data.

Running chkdsk on an NTFS Volume

Each time you boot Windows NT, it performs an autocheck routine. If this routine detects a dirty volume, it automatically runs the **chkdsk /f** command to fix the inconsistency or error. (Note that it is normal for chkdsk to report consistency errors on an NTFS drive containing the pagefile.) As long as no specific files are listed as being damaged and no other errors are detected, the volume will be marked clean, and there is rarely a need to force a **chkdsk /f**.

If the **chkdsk** command locates files or directories that have lost pointers to their parent directory, they are named FILE###.CHK and DIR###.CHK, respectively, and housed in the FOUND### directory of the NTFS volume.

If you run **chkdsk /f** from the command line and see the message "Cannot lock the current drive," you should simply make another drive current. For example, if you are trying to run **chkdsk /f** for drive D, type **C:** to make drive C the current drive, and then type the following command:

```
chkdsk d: /f
```

Note If Windows NT is unable to run the **chkdsk /f** command (because you want to run it on the boot partition or because someone is accessing the partition from the network, for example), Windows NT asks if you would like the autocheck routine to run with **chkdsk /f** upon reboot.

Changing the File System on a Partition

There are three ways to establish a new file system on a disk partition:

- Specify the file system for the boot partition during the installation process.
- Use the **format** utility and specify the file system for the partition.
- Use the **convert** utility to convert a partition from FAT or HPFS to NTFS. This leaves the existing files intact.

With the **format** utility, you can format a partition as an NTFS volume by specifying the **/fs:ntfs** option. Using the Format utility destroys all existing files on the partition.

With **convert**, you can convert an existing partition from FAT or HPFS to NTFS without losing data. You cannot convert from NTFS to another file system. To convert a volume to the NTFS file system, type the **convert** command using this form, where **E:** is the partition you want to convert:

```
convert e: /fs:ntfs
```

Convert can be used on the boot partition of non-RISC–based computers, as well as on secondary partitions. However, the **convert** utility cannot convert the boot partition while it is in use. Instead, if you specify the active partition, an entry is added to the Registry so that the **convert** utility is run the next time the system is booted.

Caution   You must not convert the boot partition to NTFS on a RISC–based computer. This is because the firmware on RISC-based computers loads the first system files in the Windows NT boot process, and the firmware understands only the FAT file system. Converting the boot partition would therefore make the computer unable to boot. If you want to use NTFS on a RISC-based computer, create a small boot partition (1 MB or larger) to hold HAL.DLL and OSLOADER.EXE. The rest of the disk can be used as an NTFS partition. The installer correctly puts HAL.DLL and OSLOADER on the boot partition.

If someone mistakenly converts the RISC–based boot partition to NTFS, run ARCINST.EXE from the install CD-ROM and reformat the boot partition as FAT.

The **convert** utility works in only one direction, so you cannot use it to change your file system from NTFS back to FAT or HPFS format. Instead, you must reformat the NTFS drive using the **format** command. (Be sure to back up any files you want to preserve before using **format**.)

Remember, though, that you cannot use the Windows NT **format** command on the system partition. If Windows NT is installed on the NTFS partition, you can reformat the drive by following these steps:

1. Start Windows NT Setup.

2. Choose Custom Installation.

3. When Setup prompts you to select the partition where you would like to install Windows NT, highlight the NTFS drive, and type **P** to delete the partition.

4. Continue using the Setup program to recreate and format the partition.

Windows NT Fault-Tolerance Mechanisms

Windows NT Advanced Server offers several fault tolerance mechanisms:

- Tape backup support (available for both Windows NT and Windows NT Advanced Server)
- Uninterruptible Power Supply support
- Disk mirroring
- Disk duplexing
- Disk striping with parity

Some of these can be used within any file system and some with only specific file systems. Restrictions are specified in the following sections, which provide more details about fault tolerance mechanisms offered by Windows NT. (For more information about how to use Windows NT with uninterruptible power supply units and tape backup, see the *Windows NT Advanced Server Concepts and Planning Guide.*

Disk Mirroring

Disk mirroring is a method that protects against hard disk failure. Any file system—including FAT, HPFS, and NTFS—can make use of disk mirroring. Disk mirroring uses two partitions on different drives connected to the same disk controller. All data on the first (primary) partition is mirrored automatically onto the secondary partition. Thus, if the primary disk fails, no data is lost. Instead, the partition on the secondary disk is used.

Mirroring is not restricted to a partition identical to the primary partition in size, number of tracks and cylinders, and so on. This eliminates the problem of acquiring an identical model drive to replace a failed drive when an entire drive is being mirrored. For practical purposes, though, the mirrored partitions will usually be created to be the same size as the primary partition. The mirrored partition cannot be smaller. However, if the mirrored partition is larger than the primary, the extra space will be wasted.

Disk Duplexing

Disk duplexing is simply a mirrored pair with an additional adapter on the secondary drive. This provides fault tolerance for both disk and controller failure. (The use of multiple adapters connecting to one drive is not supported.) In addition to providing fault tolerance, this can also improve performance.

Like mirroring, duplexing is performed at the partition level. To the Windows NT operating system, there is no difference between mirroring and duplexing. It is simply a matter of where the other partition can be found.

Disk Striping with Parity

Disk striping with parity is a method where multiple partitions are combined as a single logical drive (like disk striping, described earlier). As illustrated in Figure 5.9, the partitions are arranged in a way that ensures multiple single points of failure in the array.

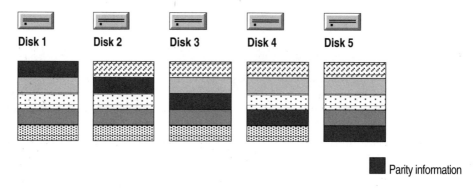

Figure 5.9   Disk Striping with Parity

There must be at least three disks and no more than 32 disks in a striped set with parity. A partition of approximately the same size must be selected from each disk. The disks can be on the same or different controllers. SCSI disks (that is, CD-ROMs) are best since advanced recovery features such as bad block remapping can be used during the recovery process. Data is written in stripes across all partitions in the set. In addition to the data, a parity stripe is written interleaved with the data stripes. The parity stripe is simply a byte parity of the data stripes at a given stripe level or row.

For example, suppose you have five disks in the striped set. At level 0, you have stripe block 0 on disk 0, 1 on 1, 2 on 2, and 3 on 3, and the parity (eXclusive OR, XOR) of the stripe blocks on disk 4. The size of the stripes (also called *striping factor*) is currently 64K. The size of the parity stripe is the size of the data stripes. On the next row the parity stripe is on disk 0. Data is on the rest of the disks. Because the parity stripes are not all on the same disk, there is no single point of failure for the set, and the load is evenly distributed.

When using any of the fault-tolerant disk schemes, Windows NT uses a device driver called FTDISK.SYS to receive commands and respond appropriately based on the type of fault tolerance that is being used. Thus when the file system generates a request to read a section of a file, the normal disk system receives the request from the file system and passes it to the FTDISK.SYS driver. This driver then determines the stripe the data is in. From this and the information on the number of disks in the set, the disk and location on the disk are located. The data is read into memory. Striping can actually increase read performance since each disk in the set can have an outstanding read at the same time.

Writing to a parity striped set is a little more difficult. First the original data from the stripe that is to be written must be read along with the parity information for that stripe level. The differences in the parity information are calculated. The differences are added to the parity stripe. Finally, both the parity and the new information are written to disks. The reads and the writes can be issued concurrently since they must be on different disks, by design.

Fault Tolerance with Parity Striping

There are two general cases of fault tolerance with parity striping.

The first case is when a data stripe is no longer readable. Though the data stripe is not readable, the system may still function. When the bad data stripe is to be read, all of the remaining good data stripes are read along with the parity stripe. Each data stripe is subtracted (with XOR) from the parity stripe; the order isn't important. The result is the missing data stripe. Writing is a little more complicated but works very much the same way. All the data stripes are read and backed out of the parity stripe, leaving the missing data stripe. The modifications needed to the parity stripe can now be calculated and made. Since the system knows the data stripe is bad, it is not written; only the parity stripe is written.

The other general case is when a parity stripe is lost. During data reads this does not present a problem. The parity stripe is not used during normal reads. Writes become much less complicated as well. Since there is no way to maintain the parity stripe, the writes behave as a data stripe write without parity. The parity stripe can be recalculated during regeneration.

Identifying When a Set Is Broken

The process of error detection and recovery is very similar for both mirrored sets and parity striped sets. The exact system response to the problem depends on when the problem occurred.

A *broken set* is defined as any time one or the other partition in a mirrored or duplexed set cannot be written, or any time a stripe can no longer be written.

When an I/O error is first detected, the system performs some routines in an attempt to keep the set from breaking. The system's first priority is to try reassigning the sector that failed. This is done by issuing the a command to remap the sector to the disk.

Windows NT attempts remapping only if the disk is supported by a small computer standard interface (SCSI) controller. SCSI devices are designed to support the concept of remapping. This is why SCSI devices work well as fault-tolerant devices. (Note that some fixed hard disk devices also support the concept of remapping, but there is no standard for this support.)

If the disk does not support sector mapping, or if the other attempts to maintain the set fail, a high severity error is logged to the event log.

The partition that has failed is called an *orphan*. It is important to note that the process of orphaning a partition does not occur during a read, only during writes. This is because the read cannot possibly affect the data on the disks, so performing orphan processing would be superfluous.

During system initialization, if the system cannot locate each partition in a mirrored set, a severe error is recorded in the event log, and the remaining partition of the mirror is used. If the partition is part of a parity striped set, a severe error is recorded in the event log, and the partition is marked as orphan. The system then continues to function using the fault tolerant capabilities inherent in such sets.

If all of the partitions within a set cannot be located, the drive is not activated, but the partitions are not marked orphan. This save the recovery time of simple problems like disconnecting the SCSI chain from the computer.

Recovering Orphans

When a partition is marked as orphan, the system continues processing until a replacement disk or partition is available to recover from the problem and ensure fault tolerance again. A set with an orphan is not fault tolerant. Another failure in the set can, and most likely will, cause the loss of data.

Recovery procedures should be performed as soon as the problem is discovered. To recover, follow these steps:

1. Break the mirror-set relationship using the Break Mirror option in the Disk Administrator utility.

2. This converts the remaining active partition of the set into an "normal" partition. This partition receives the drive letter of the set. The orphan partition receives the next available drive letter.

3. You can then create a new set relationship with existing free space on another disk in the local computer, or replace the orphan drive and reestablish the relationship with space from this disk.

4. Once the relationship is established, restart the computer.

5. During the system initialization, the data from the original good partition is copied over to the new mirrored partition.

When a member of a parity striped set is orphaned, it can be regenerated from the remaining data. This uses the same logic discussed earlier for the dynamic regeneration of data from the parity and remaining stripes. Select a new free space area that is as large as the other members in the set. Then choose the Regenerate command from the Fault Tolerance menu. When the system is restarted, the missing stripes are recalculated and written to the new space provided.

For more information about using Windows NT fault tolerance features, see the *Windows NT Advanced Server Concepts and Planning Guide.*

CHAPTER 6

Printing

For Windows NT users, printer resources seem to be provided automatically from each application. This is because Windows NT is the first operating system that truly supports remote printing. There is no need to install a printer driver on the local workstation before printing with Windows NT. Instead, the Windows NT printing model allows users to simply "point and print."

How Windows NT prints a document is somewhat more complicated than the user's "point and print" perspective. The real power of the Windows NT printing model is in the components that are invisible to the user. This chapter explains how Windows NT prints documents and what each component of the printing model does along the way. The chapter also includes compatibility information about printing from non-Windows NT clients and about printing to non-Windows NT print servers. Finally, the chapter includes information about customizing your printing environment through the use of separator pages, halftoning, and custom forms.

Printing from the User's Perspective

Windows NT maintains for each user a list of favorite printers—those used most regularly—on the network. In addition, users can use Print Manager to browse a list of network printers for a particular printer type and then select a printer to include it in the application's list of available printers. (For example, when you choose Print Setup from Microsoft Word for Windows, the network printer you selected from Print Manager will appear in the Word for Windows Print Setup list.)

When a user selects the destination printer, the application can display a WYSIWYG ("what you see is what you get") rendition of the document, exactly as it will print on the specified printer.

Note Even if the same size paper is used on two different printers, the number of lines on each page may differ because of the printer device's own requirements. Windows NT allows applications to show exactly what will print.

Printing Terms

This section briefly clarifies some terms used throughout the rest of this chapter.

Under Window NT, a *print device* refers to the actual hardware device that produces printed output. A *printer* in Windows NT printing terminology refers to the software interface between the application and print device.

A *queue* is a group of documents waiting to be printed. In the OS/2 environment, queues were the primary software interface between the application and print device, and users submitted print jobs to a queue. With Windows NT the printer is that interface—the job is sent to a printer, not a queue.

Network-interface printers are printers with built-in network cards; they need not be adjacent to a print server since they are directly connected to the network.

Print device resolution is measured in *dots per inch* (DPI). The greater the DPI, the better the resolution.

Computer screen resolution is measured in *pixels*. A pixel is the smallest unit a computer screen can display.

Windows NT Printing Model

The printing model, like other parts of Windows NT, is modular. Figure 6.1 shows the Windows NT printing model and shows how a document sent to the printer is processed through the components of the model.

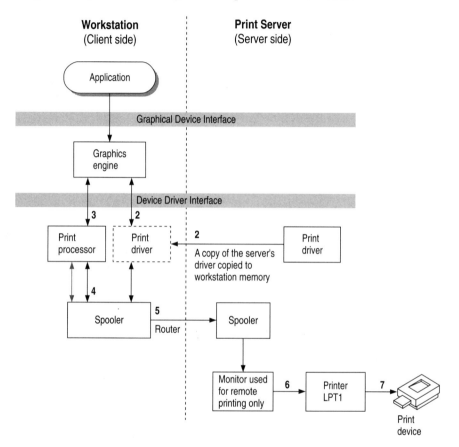

Figure 6.1   Windows NT Printing Model

This figure assumes that the workstation and the server are separate computers and that both are running either Windows NT or Windows NT Advanced Server. (Later in this chapter, how Windows NT works with non-Windows NT clients and print servers is discussed.)

When you instruct a Windows NT-based application to print to a remote printer, you initiate the following sequence of events (the step numbers correspond to those in Figure 6.1):

1. The printer driver for the specified printer is temporarily copied from the print server to the workstation's memory. (If Windows NT finds the driver on the workstation, the local version is used, and the server copy is not downloaded.) This enables the application to query the driver for current printer settings (resolution, color, fonts, and so on) and to produce a WYSIWYG image of the document. The application communicates with the printer driver through the graphics engine.

2. Next, the application generates a description of the requested output using graphical device interface (GDI) commands. These commands specify everything Windows NT needs to know about the content and formatting of the document but do not tell the printer how to print the document.

3. The Windows NT graphics engine translates these GDI calls into Device Driver Interface (DDI) calls. What happens next depends on the command format (*data type*) of the document sent to the print device. If the data type is Journal, the graphics engine writes these calls to a *Journal file* (a collection of DDI calls). The translated calls are passed via the device driver to the spooler.

4. The spooler passes the document to the appropriate print processor. If the data type is Raw, the print processor returns the document to the spooler. If the data type is Journal, the print processor passes the Journal file to the graphics engine, which passes it to the driver for rendering into printer language. The printer driver returns the rendered document to the spooler.

5. The spooler on the client workstation passes the document to the spooler on the print server via the router. (If the client and server are the same computer, this step is skipped.)

6. On the print server, the spooler passes the document to the monitor. The monitor writes the data to the appropriate print destination (such as LPT1, COM1, *server\sharename*, or the address of a network interface printer's network adapter card). Alternately, the spooler can pass the document to a file for printing at a later time.

7. The print device receives the information and produces printed output. Then the monitor displays a message letting the user know the document is printed.

As described in Chapter 1, "Windows NT Architecture," the modular design of Windows NT allows for greater flexibility by allowing components to be added or exchanged. This is true of the printing model, too. Each component provides a certain set of services to the other printing model components, to the applications, and to the print devices. This modular architecture simplifies the design of each individual component. For example, printer drivers are easier to write because many common printing services are already provided by other standard components of the Windows NT printing model.

The next few sections describe how these components work together to process and print a document.

Graphics Engine

The *graphics engine* (GDI32.DLL) is the print component that provides WYSIWYG support across devices. This component sits between two interfaces —the GDI and the DDI. The graphics engine communicates through the GDI to the application and through the DDI to the printer driver.

The first step in the printing process is for the application to pass printing instructions to the graphics engine. These instructions are sent in the form of GDI calls and describe the document. The graphics engine's job is to convert GDI calls into DDI calls, which can be read by other components of the printing model.

As shown by Figure 6.2, the graphics engine provides services to the spooler and the printer driver.

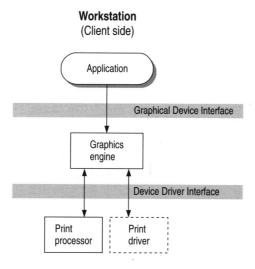

Figure 6.2   Graphics Engine in Relation to Other Printing Components

The graphics engine also communicates with the printer driver to find out what the printer's capabilities are. Then the graphics engine instructs the printer driver about which characters, fonts, locations, and point sizes to print and when.

The graphics engine can also query the printer driver about the fonts supported. Then, using that information, the graphics engine uses other DDI commands to specify the positioning of each character in the document by the print device. The graphics engine also uses DDI commands to define how the printer should draw and fill graphics, and how to manipulate and print bitmaps.

The graphics engine provides services to the printer driver, including compatibility with the environment subsystem (MS-DOS, OS/2, and so on), performance optimization, caching, client-server communications, and ANSI-to-Unicode conversion.

The graphics engine communicates with the spooler to determine which data type the graphics engine should spool. If the specified data type is Raw, the graphics engine calls the printer driver to render the DDI calls. If the data type is Journal, the graphics engine writes a Journal file and does not call the printer driver to render the DDI calls.

When the graphics engine passes the Journal file to the spooler, spooling happens quickly because Journal files are small and there is no wait for printer-specific rendering. (Rendering is done later as a background process.) Although Journal files contain DDI calls rather than printer commands, they are not device-independent.

The graphics engine calls the printer driver and provides information about the type of printer needed and the data type used. In response, the printer driver provides the graphics engine with the printer's fully qualified path name for the printer and printer-setting information. This information is passed to the spooler.

Journal Files

Journal files differ from metafiles. Windows NT does not spool metafiles because they are device-independent and thus do not translate reliably to an individual printer's page layout. Metafiles are pictures, not pages. In addition, metafiles often contain a list of "acceptable" font and color substitutions for a document. For WYSIWYG accuracy, such color and font substitutions are unacceptable.

In contrast, use of Journal files guarantees that Windows NT provides true reproduction of spooled document. Journal files can contain TrueType fonts, so even if the printer server does not have a particular font installed, the actual outlines of the TrueType fonts are already embedded in the Journal file.

Journal files are concise and precise. They only contain calls that make a difference. For example, some applications add hundreds of unnecessary and/or redundant instructions for creating a graphic. The Journal file includes only those necessary to draw that picture.

Journal files are tuned for a particular device; they are not device-independent. For example, a Journal file created for a 150-DPI LaserJet® printer cannot print on a 300-DPI LaserJet printer. A Journal file is created to play back on a specific device and therefore is tuned for the device's specific coordinate space, color space, bits-per-pixel, fonts, and so on.

Halftoning Graphics Support

The Windows NT graphics engine provides *halftoning* support, which is a method of providing higher-quality output and improved color accuracy on a print device or computer screen. The graphics engine provides output devices with the ability to include a rich spectrum of colors, or range of gray tones in the case of monochrome, in printed or displayed graphics.

For more information, see "Using Graphics Halftoning," later in this chapter.

Printer Driver

Printer drivers are stored on a server and are dynamically loaded to the workstation's memory across the network as needed. Printer drivers can also be stored locally on the workstation, which will increase processing speed, but which may cause the printer drivers on the server and workstation to become out of sync if one is updated without the other.

The printer driver retrieves configuration information from the server and provides WYSIWYG support for workstation applications. Some WYSIWYG applications, such as Microsoft Word for Windows, request the printer driver at application startup. Soft fonts can also be loaded from the server to the workstation's memory in the same way.

Note Make sure you have the correct license agreements to use printer drivers and soft fonts across the network.

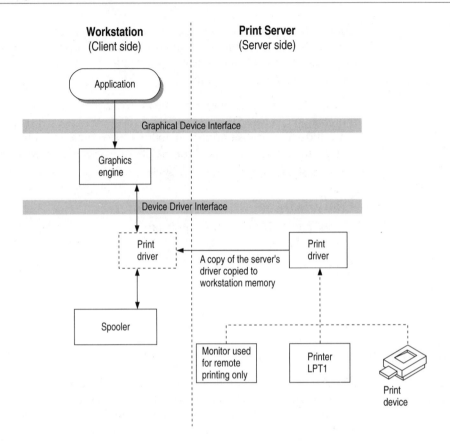

Figure 6.3   Printer Driver in Relation to Other Print Components

Printer drivers are composed of three separate files:

- A printer graphics driver (for example, PSCRIPT.DLL or RASDD.DLL). This dynamic link library (DLL) is responsible for print rendering and management and is called from the GDI server, GDISVR.DLL. It is inaccessible from the application.

- A printer interface driver (for example, PSCRPTUI.DLL or RASDDUI.DLL). This DLL includes the user interface and configuration management. It is called by the client side of the router (WINSPOOL.DRV). The role of the router is described later, in "Router."

- A configuration file (for example, PRINTER.PPD for PostScript) or minidriver (for the Universal printer driver). This component is used by the other two pieces of the print driver as needed. It provides information about the configuration capabilities for the printer. Both .PPD files and minidrivers are source-code compatible across processors and platforms (including R4000, Alpha, x86, Windows version 3.1 and future versions, and Windows NT version 3.1 and future versions).

These three files work together on the client and server side of the printing model. For example, the configuration file might include information about the number of trays the printer has. The user-interface DLL uses this information to specify which form to include in Tray 1. The rendering DLL uses the form information to determine the printable area, the number of lines per page, and the number of characters per line.

Note A Windows NT print server must have the *x*86 and RISC-based printer drivers installed on the print server if client workstations of each platform type will be printing to that print server. This is because a RISC-based computer cannot print using the *x*86 printer driver.

Universal and PostScript Printer Drivers

Windows NT includes two printer drivers—the Universal printer driver and a PostScript® printer driver.

The Universal printer driver is an improved version of the Windows 3.1 driver and supports raster-graphics printing. It includes support for scalable TrueType fonts, device fonts, compression/run length encoding (RLE), and Tag Image File Format (TIFF) version 4.0. It also includes mechanisms that provide for smaller, more efficient bitmaps. These mechanisms include ignoring whitespace and supporting *rules*, which are printable rectangles extracted from the bitmap and sent to the printer as a separate command as supported by Hewlett-Packard LaserJet and compatible printers. The Universal printer driver is also an excellent driver for the LaserJet III printer.

The Windows NT PostScript driver supports Adobe version 4.0-compatible PostScript Printer Description (.PPD) files. (Windows NT does not use the .WPD or .MPD files used by Windows 3.1.) This driver supports key features, including binary transfer compression, from Level II.

Printer Minidrivers

Raster minidrivers are actually DLLs. The Windows NT Raster printer driver can read most Windows 3.1 minidriver DLLs (those created for UNIDRV.DLL) directly with no porting required. Raster minidrivers contain printer-specific information but do not contain executable code, except for a few rare instances (such as Toshiba and C. Itoh drivers).

PostScript minidrivers are actually Adobe PostScript standard .PPD files. These files include printer-specific information for a particular printer model and are available from the printer's manufacturer. Unlike Windows 3.1, the Windows NT PostScript printer driver can directly interpret .PPD files. Because PostScript printers ship with .PPD files, when new PostScript printers become available, they will be ready for use with Windows NT.

Spooler

The *spooler* is a scheduler for the printing process. It coordinates activity among other components of the print model and schedules all print jobs arriving at the print server. An identical spooler runs in background mode on each client Windows NT workstation and coordinates with the spooler on the print server.

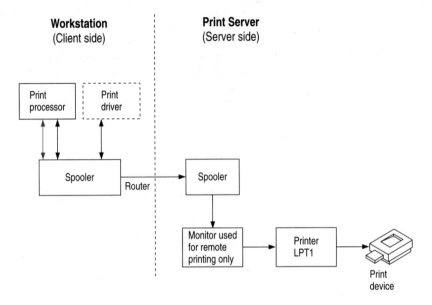

Figure 6.4   Spooler in Relation to Other Print Components

The spooler communicates with the following print components:

- Printer driver. The spooler retrieves data type information for the print processor.

- Print processor. The spooler calls a print processor to interpret a particular data type.

- Print router. This component passes information from the spooler on the client workstation to the server's spooler.

- Print monitor. The spooler queries to see which print monitor manages the appropriate type of printer for the document to be printed and to find out the status of the device.

The spooler fully supports preemptive multitasking. It creates a list of jobs to be printed for a particular printer, using several criteria to determine which is the next job to print, including the status of the device (for example, whether it is busy or paused), the number and priority of other jobs scheduled for that device, and the hours during which the print device may print jobs and during which hours a particular job may be printed.

The spooler also checks whether the printer is physically capable of printing the document. For example, if the print job requires a special form not currently in the paper tray, the spooler will not send the job to print until that form is in the printer.

Spooling Journal Files

When the spooler spools a Journal file, it provides for the following:

- Multiple resources per document (for example, a single document can consist of many very different pages; for example, each with its own color table).

- Multiple forms per document (for example, the first page of a document could be printed on an envelope, the second on letterhead, and the third on plain letter-sized paper).

- Identification of distinct page boundaries, including where a page starts and ends.

- Ability to write to disk as the document is spooled. (That is, the data is not stored in memory as the spooled document is created; rather, it is written out as the size increases, preferably a page at a time.)

- Ability to store Raw data, such as an encapsulated PostScript file.

The spooled data isn't necessarily device-independent. The data spooled is destined and formatted for a particular device and does not need to be printable on a different device.

Forms Database

The spooler maintains a database of forms used by all printers on a particular server. The database includes the name of the form and related information such as form size and printable area.

The spooler checks the printer settings against information maintained in the forms database. A record for each of the printer's default forms is added to the database when the printer driver is installed.

This database is far more flexible than the limited list of forms maintained by Windows 3.1. The Windows NT forms database includes information about several standard forms and is readily expandable so that you can add information about your own custom forms.

For more information about specifying new forms, see "Using Custom Forms," later in this chapter.

Print Processor

A *print processor* is a dynamic link library that interprets data types. It receives information from the spooler and sends the interpreted information to the graphics engine. When a spooled file is sent to print, control is passed from the spooler to the relevant print processor. The spooler only accepts data types that are supported by the print processors installed on the system.

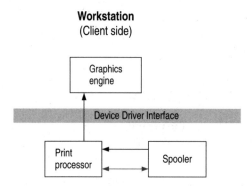

Workstation
(Client side)

Figure 6.5   Print Processor in Relation to Other Print Components

Each print processor can support one or more data types. The Windows NT print processor is called WinPrint (WINPRINT.DLL). This print processor interprets these two default data types:

- Journal files, which are a collection of DDI calls. (The Journal data type is labeled NT JNL 1.000.)

- Raw files, which contain printer-specific commands. (This data type is labeled RAW.)

Another print processor, SFMPSPRT.DLL, is included with Windows NT Advanced Server and provides support for Macintosh clients printing PostScript documents to raster printers. This print processor uses the PSCRIPT1 data type.

Though its main job is to interpret compatible data types, the print processor also provides access to the printing process. You can modify the printing process by substituting a custom program in place of the Windows NT default print processor. A print processor could be used to filter data, to create a special dialog with the printer device, or to interpret a new data type. For example, you might have a print processor that filters ASCII for use on a PostScript printer.

As another example, assume Windows NT has spooled a document to the print server. The print processor sends the Journal file to the graphics engine, which passes it on to the appropriate printer driver for rendering. What happens at this point varies with the print device:

- If the output device is a raster printer, the graphics engine sends the printer driver a series of DDI commands to generate a bitmap. If the computer doesn't have enough memory to accommodate the bitmap, the driver performs *banding,* a process whereby the document is replayed several times to generate the full image.

- If the target device is a PostScript printer, the graphics engine sends DDI commands, which are translated by the PostScript driver into printer commands. All rendering is done by the printer CPU.

After the data type is interpreted, the print processor passes the document back to the spooler. Then the spooler, located on the client workstation, passes the document to the spooler on the print server via the router.

Router

The *router* is the printing model component that locates the requested printer and sends information from the workstation spooler to the print server's spooler.

The server portion of the router comprises three files—SPOOLSS.EXE, SPOOLSS.DLL, and WINSPOOL.DLL. The client side of the router is a DLL called WINSPOOL.DRV. It uses a .DRV extension because when an application tries to print, it sees the client-side router WINSPOOL.DRV and not the printer driver.

When a user selects a network printer through Print Manager, the system tracks its local device name. Then, when a job is sent to that device name, it causes the router to locate the appropriate printer driver on the printer server for the specified device name. Then a copy of the server's printer driver is placed in the workstation's memory, so that the application can display the document as it will be printed.

Print Monitor

The *print monitor* keeps track of printers and print devices. It is the component that receives information from the printer driver via the spooler and sends it on to the printer or destination file. The print monitor tracks physical devices so that the spooler doesn't have to.

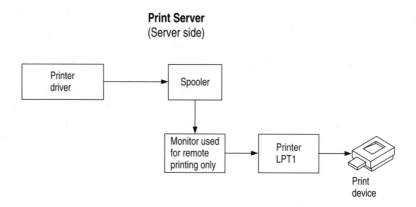

Figure 6.6   Print Monitor in Relation to Other Print Components

Windows NT includes two print monitors:

- LOCALMON.DLL handles output for LPT*x*, COM*x*, FILE:, remote print shares, and named pipes.

- HPMON.DLL provides logical ports for network interface printers, such as HP LaserJet IIIsi and 4si printers. HPMON.DLL may not support other network-interface printers since HPMON.DLL looks for HP-specific strings when the request is broadcast to the network. Most manufacturers of network-interface printers must supply their own print monitor.

Another print monitor, SFMMON.DLL, is included with Windows NT Advanced Server for use with AppleTalk clients. (When you select Network Printers as the port option from the Printer Properties dialog box, this monitor is the one associated with the AppleTalk Printers option that displays in the next Print Destination dialog box.)

If the destination is a port (such as LPT1 or COM1), the monitor opens the port, writes the data, and then closes the port. For serial ports, it also sets the baud rate, parity, and so forth. Because print monitors are integrated with Print Manager, you can use Print Manager to configure or view settings for local and remote printers.

Print monitors receive messages, including unsolicited error messages such as "out of toner," from print devices and pass them directly to be displayed by the application. Print monitors can also provide true end-of-job notification. That is, unlike other printing systems which send end-of-job messages as soon as the job is spooled, Windows NT waits until the last page has actually printed before sending the message, if the print device and monitor both support bidirectional communication.

Print monitors also support printing-error recovery. That is, a print monitor tracks the status of the print device and detects when anything goes wrong. For example, if the printer's cord is unplugged, and then plugged back in, it might cause the print job to terminate midway. When the print monitor detects a problem (even if it can't identify exactly what it is), the print monitor alerts the spooler, causing the print job to reprint from the beginning.

Printers and Print Devices

Remember that under Windows NT, a print device is the hardware device that produces printed output. A printer is the software interface between the application and print device.

Multiple printers can be routed to one print device. For example, you might want to create one printer (using Print Manager) for PostScript jobs and another for HPPCL mode if you have a printer capable of both modes. Each "printer" would use a different printer driver. Certain printers can be given higher priority or even be set up to print during limited hours.

Windows NT allows you to create a printer using either a physical port (such as LPT1 or COM3) or a logical port (such as \\server\printer) as the print destination.

Printer Pools

Windows NT supports printer pooling. This allows you to create a single logical printer for multiple print devices when those devices are identical. The spooler schedules incoming documents to print at the first available print device. Additionally, the spooler can print to all of the print devices within the pool simultaneously.

You can define a printer pool by creating a printer in Print Manager and then associating more than one print device with it. (In the Printer Details dialog box, mark all of the appropriate ports in the Print To Additional Ports list box.)

All printers in the printer pool must be able to use the same printer driver, and because they are identified as a single "printer" to Windows NT, must be able to be defined by a common set of parameters such as memory and separator file.

Some print devices support multiple printer emulation (for example, PostScript and PCL5). Those print devices can participate in multiple printer pools.

When print jobs are sent to the printer for the printer pool, Print Manager routes the job to the first available print device that was designated to receive output, thus using the printers more efficiently. Printer pools have the following characteristics:

- All print devices in the printer pool share the same printer name and act as a single device. Pausing the printer pauses the entire printer pool, and changing any properties affects all print devices in the printer pool.

- The print destinations can all be of the same type or mixed (that is, serial, parallel, and network).

- When a job arrives for the printer pool, the spooler checks to see which print device is available. The spooler checks for available devices based on the order in which they were added to the printer pool in Print Manager. Therefore, if the printer pool consists of mixed print destinations, make sure that the fastest port is selected first when setting up the printer pool, for optimal performance.

Setting Up PostScript Printers

PostScript devices use an ASCII-based print language that offers flexible font capability and high-quality graphics. Documents sent to a PostScript device are rendered in the device CPU rather than by Windows NT. While this means that pages can be sent to the printer very quickly, PostScript devices require a relatively long time to process documents. When setting up a PostScript printer for network use, remember the following:

- Because they are slower than many other printers, PostScript devices usually require longer time-out settings.

- PostScript printers cannot process generic text files. For example, if you try to print a simple ASCII document to a PostScript device from the Windows NT command prompt, you get no output.

- If a separator page is required, make sure you use the special PostScript separator page file, PSCRIPT.SEP.

- Some print devices can switch between PostScript and non-PostScript jobs. If you have such a device, create two printers on your server: one using a PostScript driver and one using the other supported driver. Both printers use the same print destination.

Note If your printer is the HP LaserJet IIIsi, make sure the device's system language switch is set to ON (SYS SWITCH=ON*).

Interacting with Other Providers and Printing Clients

A *print provider* is a software component that allows the client to print to the print server's device. For the spooler to schedule a print job, it calls a print provider (generally the local Windows NT print provider). In the case of printing to a down-level server such as Windows for Workgroups, instead of using the local print provider, the print server's spooler takes care of the print job via a network print provider.

Windows NT includes the following print providers:

- LOCALSPL.DLL provides Windows-style printing, where the data streams are sent to the file system but may be queued for individual ports. This is sometimes referred to as a local spooler.

- WIN32SPL.DLL provides print server services to Windows NT clients (in both directions), including remote administration, browsing, connecting, and so on. This print provider also includes support for OS/2 clients.

- LMSPOOL.DLL provides downlevel clients with access to Windows NT printers. This also provides Windows NT clients access to downlevel servers.

Other print providers can be added to Windows NT, for example, to use with Novell® or Banyan® networks.

Printing to Other Print Servers

Your network may include other types of print servers, such as LAN Manager 2.*x* or Novell NetWare servers. These servers and the printers they control appear when you browse the network using the Connect To Printer dialog box in Print Manager. However, because Windows NT computers cannot use the printer drivers on non-native servers, when you connect to this type of printer, Print Manager prompts you to create a local printer and install a local driver. You can configure the new local printer just as you would any other printer you create.

You must be a member of the Administrators or Power Users group to connect your Windows NT computer to printers managed by other providers. This is because the non-Windows NT server must copy the appropriate printer driver to your disk. Because this is done on your behalf, it means that you must have permission to write to the Windows NT directory tree. If you don't have this permission, when you select Connect To Printer and type the name of a non-Windows NT print server, the following error message displays:

```
You must have Administer privilege on your machine to connect to the
selected printer, since a driver needs to be installed on your local
machine.
```

Notice that this is not an issue when you connect to a Windows NT print server. In this case, the printer driver is copied from the Windows NT server to your computer's memory and not to disk. Because nothing is written to disk, it does not affect anyone else who might log on to the computer later, so there is no security risk.

Printing to Downlevel Print Servers

When you print a document from a Windows NT computer to a non-Windows NT print server, such as a Windows for Workgroups computer, Windows NT creates an alternate spool file. The spool file it creates is kept in the *SystemRoot* \SYSTEM32\SPOOL\PRINTERS directory on the Windows NT computer.

Printing from Windows or MS-DOS Applications on Windows NT

Documents from Windows 3.1-based applications running on a Windows NT computer print in the same way as from Windows NT-based applications. Windows 3.1-based applications use Windows NT printer drivers.

If an MS-DOS application generates graphics, the graphics must be rendered by the application itself, using a local MS-DOS printer driver. (The appropriate MS-DOS printer driver must be located on the workstation.) Once rendered, the document is passed to the Windows NT spooler and processed like other print documents.

Printing from Non-Windows NT Clients

Workstations running MS-DOS or versions of Windows for MS-DOS can access Windows NT printers by redirecting their output ports to the appropriate *\\server\sharename*. However, unlike Windows NT workstations, these types of workstations must have a printer driver installed locally.

Soft fonts and forms available on a Windows NT print server cannot be accessed by non-Windows NT workstations.

Security on Shared Printers

Windows NT security is integrated into Print Manager so that you can specify which printers have which security attributes. For example, you can specify that everyone in your department can print to this printer, and only one or two specified people can administer it.

There are four categories of permissions you can assign to a person or group for a specific Windows NT printer:

- Full control, which allows a user complete access and administrative control
- Manage documents, which allows a person to change the status of anyone's jobs but not of printers
- Print, which enables the user to print on the printer and have control to pause, resume, or delete his or her own jobs
- No access, which denies access to a particular printer

By default, people in the Administrators, Power Users, and Print Operators (on Windows NT Advanced Server) groups are granted Full Control. The Creator Owner is granted Manage Documents, and the Everyone group is granted Print permission by default. To explicitly deny access to a printer, you must specify No Access for a particular group or user.

Print Manager also provides an auditing option for tracking successful or unsuccessful printing and administrative events for particular groups or individuals. To use this option, you must first enable auditing in User Manager. From the Policies menu, select Audit. Next select the Audit These Events option button and choose OK. (You do not need to specify any events in this dialog box to enable print auditing.)

Customizing Printer Output

Windows NT provides dozens of ways for you to customize the way your documents are printed. Most of these are covered in the standard documentation for Windows NT and Windows NT Advanced Server. This section describes how you can use three customizing features—halftoning, forms, and separator pages—for your printed output.

Using Graphics Halftoning

The Windows NT graphics engine provides halftoning support. Halftoning provides the highest quality color and gray-scale reproduction possible on a particular device. It helps to increase visual resolution within a limited set of intensity levels and to improve color correlation among different output devices (including printers, plotters, and screens).

Halftoning is based on optical illusion. For example, the bottom lines of the ophthalmologist's eye chart contains a set of letters, but to many of us, the line looks like a vague gray smudge. Similarly, forested mountains at a certain distance look like large green rocks rather than a collection of individual trees on the rolling landscape.

Halftoning is available for all printer drivers and for your computer screen because it is provided by the Windows NT GDI layer. Windows NT supports a variety of printer resolutions (60 DPI and higher), pixel sizes and shapes, and color resolutions (from monochrome to 24-bit). The graphics engine interprets these adjustments by means of your application and interprets them appropriately for the specific print device.

Print Manager includes two halftone dialog boxes—one to set options for your printer and one to set options for your documents. The first, shown below, sets halftoning options for your printer. (Choose Setup from the Print Properties dialog, and then choose Halftone.)

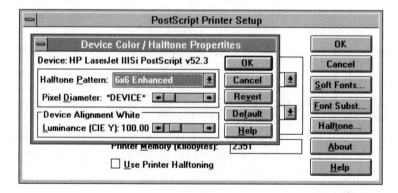

This dialog box lets you choose from among several predefined pattern sizes for print and display output to provide the best possible resolution. The Halftone Pattern field shows options for print output, and the Pixel Diameter field allows you to adjust the pixel size for display output.

Windows NT provides several predefined pattern sizes—from 2x2 to 16x16. It also provides enhanced versions of each of these sizes. Enhanced patterns have different dot-cluster sequences. Using enhanced patterns tends to improve the richness of the color resolution but may cause unwanted *noise* in the image. The halftone pattern size is device-resolution dependent, which means that you should select a resolution that is supported by your print device; otherwise, the image will not be printed at the right size. The following table offers suggestions for halftone patterns that will probably best suit different printers' resolutions.

Print device's DPI	Suggested halftone pattern
Less than 150	4x4
150-400	6x6
400-800	8x8
800-1200	10x10
1200-1800	12x12
1800-2400	14x14
Greater than 2400	16x16

For best results, test the suggested pattern and then test the next smaller pattern. Use the enhanced pattern unless a lot of noise occurs in your image. If it does, use the standard halftone pattern of the same pattern size. If the height and width of the dot pattern for your print device are not equal (for example, a 200x300 dot pattern), you'll need to print a few test images to determine which works best for your print device.

A second dialog box sets halftoning for your document. (Choose Details from the Print Properties dialog box. Then choose Job Defaults to display the Document Properties dialog. From there, choose Halftone.)

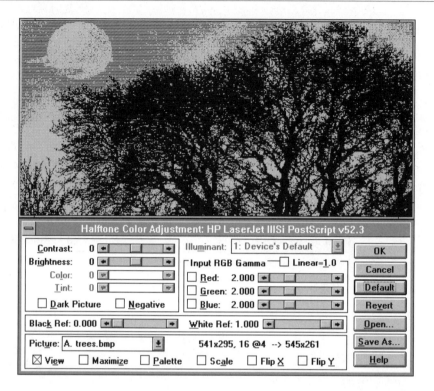

This dialog box lets you adjust color options and other settings for a default to be used with applications that don't have a similar dialog box. You can choose from among several options to provide the best blend of color or gray tones for your graphics.

The color of the output can vary widely depending on the quality of the original bitmap, the scanning method used, the viewing condition (in sunlight, under florescent lighting, as a projected transparency slide), and what kind of ink resolution a particular print device has. In addition, color preference varies from person to person. This dialog box allows for both equipment and personal preference variables.

Windows NT always uses a standard GDI bitmap format. For monochrome devices, it renders 1 bit per pixel. Color devices can be rendered at 4 bits per pixel [for standard red-green-blue (RGB) or cyan-magenta-yellow (CMY)], 8 bits per pixel (such as a display device with special palette management features), or 16 bits per pixel (usually for display devices).

For more information, see online Help for these dialog boxes.

Using Custom Forms

As mentioned earlier, a *form* consists of a physical paper size, margins that define the image area, and a name. Through Print Manager, you can define new forms and add them to the print server's database. For example, you could create a form called Customer Receipt Form that uses letter size paper and nonstandard margins.

To specify a new form, choose Forms from the Printer menu to display the Forms dialog box:

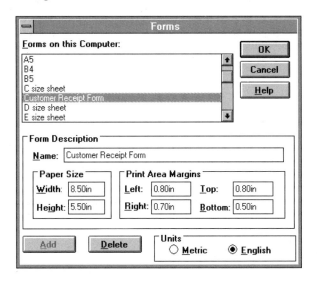

Through this dialog box, anyone with Full Control privilege can add a form and specify the paper size and image area. Forms information is stored per server, not per printer.

On a per-printer basis, you can use the Printer Properties dialog box to specify the paper tray in which your form is located. The Form drop-down list in this dialog box includes only those forms that can be used by your printer; forms of sizes different from what your printer can accommodate aren't listed.

Hint If you want to use an odd-sized form with your printer, specify Manual Feed in the Paper Tray text box.

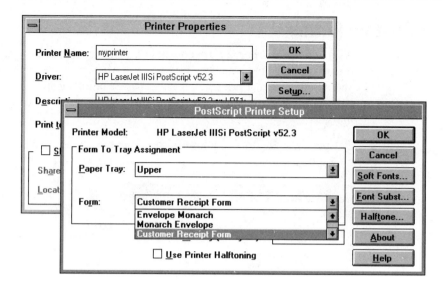

Users who want to print a document can select the new form from the list shown in the application's Print Setup dialog box. The spooler remembers which paper tray contains that form and includes that information in the instructions passed to the print device.

Note With Windows 3.1 and Windows for Workgroups, you set details such as the form name and tray from within an application. For example, in Word for Windows, you would choose Print Setup from the File menu to do this. With Windows NT, these details are set only through Print Manager.

Windows NT applications can use different forms within a document. For example, you might use an envelope for the first page, Letterhead for the second page, and Letter for the third and following pages.

Using Separator Files

You can set up a printer so that one or more separator pages print at the beginning of each job. Separator pages typically show who submitted the job and give the date and time of printing.

By default, separator page files are stored in the *SystemRoot*\SYSTEM32 directory. (DEFAULT.SEP is not a file on disk but rather is built into the program. To use it, type **DEFAULT.SEP** in the Separator File text box of the Printer Details dialog box. To use no separator file, leave this text box blank.) The following separator files are included with Windows NT.

Filename	Purpose	Compatible with	Can be edited?
DEFAULT.SEP	Prints a page before each document	PCL	No
PSLANMAN.SEP	Prints a page before each document	PostScript	Yes
PCL.SEP	Switches printer to PCL printing	PCL	Yes
PSCRIPT.SEP	Switches printer to PostScript printing	PostScript	Yes

The first character of the separator page file must always be the escape character. This character is used throughout the separator page file in escape codes. The program replaces these escape codes with appropriate data, to be sent directly to the printer.

For more information about using and creating separator pages, see Chapter 6 of the *Microsoft Windows NT Advanced Server Concepts and Planning Guide*. This chapter also includes a complete listing of the escape codes that can be used in separator pages.

C H A P T E R   7

Fonts

This chapter examines technical issues related to fonts, focusing on TrueType, the new font technology available in Microsoft Windows NT. This chapter also presents details about using printer fonts with specific types of printers.

About Typography in Windows NT

A *typeface* is a set of characters that share common characteristics such as stroke width and the presence or absence of serifs. For example, Arial and Courier are both typefaces. (Frequently, both the typeface and its name are copyrighted and/or trademarked by the typeface designer or manufacturer.)

In Windows NT, a *font* is the name of a typeface, excluding attributes such as bold or italic (which is a more general definition than in traditional typography). For example, MS Serif is a font in Windows NT.

In Windows NT, a *font family* refers to a group of typefaces with similar characteristics. The families that Windows NT recognizes for font installation and mapping are roman , Swiss, Modern, Script, and Decorative. For example, the sans serif typefaces Arial, Arial Bold, Arial Bold Italic, Arial Italic, Small Fonts, and MS Sans Serif are all part of the Swiss font family.

For printing and display in a computer system, each font has its own character set according to the ASCII, ANSI, or original equipment manufacturer (OEM) standard or other industry standard that defines what character is represented by a specific keystroke. Windows NT uses the ANSI character set. Many non-Windows NT applications use the ASCII character set or the OEM character set.

These basic terms are used in Windows NT to define the appearance of a font in an application:

- *Font style* refers to specific characteristics of the font. The four characteristics you can define for fonts in Windows NT are italic, bold, bold italic, and roman (often called Normal or Regular in Font dialog boxes).

- *Font size* refers to the point size of a font, where a point is about 1/72 of an inch. Typical sizes for text are 10-point and 12-point.

- *Font effects* refers to attributes such as underlining, strikeout, and color that can be applied to text in many applications.

You may also encounter these terms in descriptions of fonts and typefaces:

- *Spacing* can be either fixed or proportional. In a fixed font such as Courier every character occupies the same amount of space. In a proportional font such as Arial or Times New roman ®, character width varies.

- *Pitch* refers to the amount of horizontal space used for each character of fixed-width fonts. This is often specified in characters-per-inch (CPI), typically where 10-pitch = 12-point, 12-pitch = 10-point, and 15-pitch = 8-point type. (Some fonts use other equivalencies.)

- *Serif* and *sans serif* describe specific characteristics of a typeface. Serif fonts such as Times New roman   or Courier have projections that extend from the upper and lower strokes of the letters. Sans serif fonts such as Arial and MS Sans Serif do not have serifs.

- *Slant* refers to the angle of a font's characters, which can be italic or roman (no slant).

- *Weight* refers to the heaviness of the stroke for a specific font, such as Light, Regular, Book, Demi, Heavy, Black, and Extra Bold.

- *Width* refers to whether the standard typeface has been extended or compressed horizontally. The common variations are Condensed, Normal, or Expanded.

- *X-height* refers to the vertical size of lowercase characters.

About Windows NT Fonts

Windows NT provides three basic kinds of fonts, which are categorized according to how the fonts are rendered for screen or print output:

- *Raster fonts* are stored in files as bitmaps and are rendered as an array of dots for displaying on the screen and printing on paper. Raster fonts cannot be cleanly scaled or rotated.

- *Vector fonts* are rendered from a mathematical model, where each character is defined as a set of lines drawn between points. Vector fonts can be scaled to any size or aspect ratio.

- *TrueType fonts* are outline fonts. TrueType fonts can be scaled and rotated.

Besides the font-rendering mechanism, Windows NT fonts are described according to the output device:

- *Screen fonts* are font descriptions that Windows NT uses to represent characters on the display devices. (TrueType fonts, as listed in the following screen display, act as both screen and device fonts.)

- *Printer fonts* are the font descriptions used by the printer to create a font. Windows NT applications can use three kinds of printer fonts—device fonts, downloadable soft fonts, and printable screen fonts, as described in "Printer Fonts and Windows NT," later in this chapter.

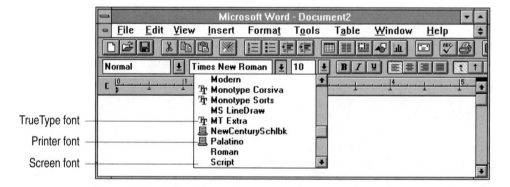

The next sections describe raster, vector, and TrueType fonts. Later sections in this chapter discuss screen fonts and printer fonts used by Windows NT.

Windows NT Raster Fonts

Raster fonts are bitmaps supplied in different sizes for specific video display resolutions. The Windows NT fonts MS Serif, MS Sans Serif, Courier, System, and Terminal are raster fonts.

A raster font file contains data that describes all the characters and style of a typeface for a specific display device. Windows NT provides several raster font sizes for various display devices. For example, MS Serif comes in point sizes 8, 10, 12, and 14 for Video Graphics Array (VGA) and 8514 display devices.

Windows NT can scale raster fonts, but if you try to scale them too far from their original size or style, they become jagged. Bold, italic, underline, and strikeout styles can also be generated from a standard raster font.

The following is a list of the raster fonts installed in Windows NT. Additional raster font sets can be installed by choosing the Fonts icon in Control Panel.

Table 7.1   Windows NT Raster Fonts

Font	Filename	Character set
Courier	COUR*x*.FON	ANSI
MS Sans Serif	SSERIF*x*.FON	ANSI
MS Serif	SERIF*x*.FON	ANSI
Small	SMALL*x*.FON	ANSI
Symbol	SYMBOL*x*.FON	Symbol

The raster font sets for different display resolutions are distinguished by a letter suffix on the font name (represented as *x* in the previous table). Add the letter from the following table that identifies the resolution to the raster font filename to see the files that Windows NT installs for a given display or printer. For example, the resource file for MS Serif fonts for VGA is named SERIFE.FON.

Table 7.2   Raster Font Sizes

Font set and output device	Horizontal resolution	Vertical resolution	Aspect ratio H:V
E = VGA display	96 dpi	96 dpi	1:1
F = 8514 display	120 dpi	120 dpi	1:1

Raster fonts can also be printed if their resolution and aspect ratio are close to what your printer requires. If you do not see raster fonts for your printer in a Fonts dialog box, check your printer's horizontal and vertical resolution, and compare it with the table above. If there is a close match, choose the Fonts icon in Control Panel, and make sure the appropriate font set is installed. If there is no close match, you cannot print the Windows NT raster fonts on your printer.

Note Some applications, such as Microsoft Excel for Windows and Microsoft Paintbrush, work around this problem by sending documents to the printer in the form of bitmaps. This way, the application can ensure that what prints closely matches what you see on the screen.

Other applications, such as desktop publishing packages, allow you to choose only printable fonts.

In general, applications are written so that you can choose either displayable fonts or printable fonts. It is up to the developer of the application to decide which type of font you can choose.

You might be able to print raster fonts in a different resolution, if the other resolution has an aspect ratio that matches your printer. Some printer drivers cannot print raster fonts, regardless of the aspect ratio.

In Windows NT, MS Serif and MS Sans Serif replace the identical raster fonts Tms Rmn and Helv that were installed in Windows 3.0 or earlier versions. Windows NT matches MS Serif to Tms Rmn and MS Sans Serif to Helv using the information stored in the FontSubstitutes key in the Registry:

```
HKEY_LOCAL_MACHINE\SOFTWARE\Microsoft\Windows NT
    \CurrentVersion\FontSubstitutes
```

You will still see the Tms Rmn and Helv typeface names in a Fonts dialog box if, for example, your Hewlett-Packard Printer Control Language (HPPCL) printer uses the Microsoft 1Z font cartridge.

The raster font named Small Font was designed for readable screen display of small fonts. For sizes under 6 points, Small Font is a better choice than any TrueType font for screen display, because it's easier to read.

You can also purchase raster fonts as both screen and printer fonts that work with Windows NT. Font products that work with Windows NT include Bitstream® Fontware®, Hewlett-Packard Type Director™, Adobe Type Library, and SoftCraft WYSIFonts!®. Windows NT raster fonts can also be created using the FontEdit utility from the Windows NT Software Development Kit or the Publisher's Type Foundry™ from ZSoft Corporation.

Windows NT Vector Fonts

Vector fonts are a set of lines drawn between points, like a pen plotter drawing a set of characters. They can be scaled to virtually any size, but generally they do not look as good as raster fonts in the sizes that raster fonts are specifically designed for.

Vector fonts are stored in Windows NT as collections of Graphical Device Interface (GDI) calls and are time-consuming to generate. But these fonts are useful for plotters and other devices where bitmapped characters can't be used. Before TrueType, vector fonts were also used in some applications to create large characters or characters that were rotated or distorted from the baseline.

Some Windows NT applications automatically use vector fonts at larger sizes. Some applications allow you to specify at what point size you want to use vector fonts. For example, the Vector Above setting in Aldus® PageMaker® specifies the point size at which PageMaker will switch to vector fonts.

The Windows NT fonts roman, Modern, and Script are vector fonts. Although the vector fonts use the ANSI character set, they are marked internally as an OEM character set.

Note   Third-party, non-TrueType scalable font products that were supported by Windows 3.1 are not supported by Windows NT. These products include Adobe Type Manager® (ATM®), Bitstream Facelift™, and Atech Publisher's PowerPak.

TrueType and Windows NT

Windows NT includes support for TrueType, an outline font technology. Instead of being composed of bitmaps (as raster fonts are) or lines (as vector fonts are), TrueType fonts are *glyph shapes* that are described by their outlines. A glyph outline consists of a series of contours. A simple glyph may have only one contour. More complex glyphs can have two or more contours. Figure 7.1 shows three glyphs with one, two, and three contours respectively.

Figure 7.1   TrueType Glyphs

Note   Windows NT supports all TrueType fonts that are supported by Windows 3.1.

TrueType has many benefits over other kinds of Windows NT fonts:

- What you see is really what you get, because Windows NT can use the same font for both screen and printer. You don't have to think about whether you have a specific point size for a particular printer or for your display.

- You can scale and rotate TrueType fonts, and they look good in all sizes and on all output devices that Windows NT supports.

- Your document will look the same when printed on different printers. And any printer that uses a Windows NT Universal driver can print TrueType fonts.

- Your document will look the same if you move it across platforms. For example, the text you format in Microsoft Word for Windows will look the same if you open the same document in Word for the Macintosh.

- Each TrueType typeface requires only an .FOT and a .TTF file to create fonts in all point sizes at all resolutions for all output devices. (Many raster font products include one font size per file. The raster fonts that ship with Windows NT are included within a single file.)

- TrueType is integrated with the operating environment, so all Windows NT applications can use TrueType fonts like they do other Windows NT raster fonts.

The TrueType fonts installed with Windows NT are Arial, Courier New, Times New Roman, Symbol, and Wingdings in regular, bold, bold italic, and italic.

How TrueType Works

TrueType fonts are stored as a collection of points and hints that define the character outlines. When a Windows NT application requests a font, TrueType uses the outline and the hints to render a bitmap in the size requested. Hints are algorithms that distort the scaled font outlines to improve how the bitmaps look at specific resolutions and sizes.

For each time you run Windows NT, when you first select a TrueType font size, TrueType renders a bitmap of the selected characters for display or printing. Windows NT stores the rendered bitmaps in a font cache, so each subsequent time the font is used during that Windows NT session, display or printing will be just as fast as for a Windows NT raster font.

The Windows NT Universal printer driver supports TrueType. Any printer that works with the Universal printer driver will support TrueType automatically. (For more information about this printer driver, see Chapter 6, "Printing.")

Using TrueType in Windows NT Applications

TrueType fonts give you a broad range of fonts you can use with your application. In many applications, TrueType fonts appear in the Fonts dialog box with a TT logo beside the typeface name. Typefaces that are device fonts have a printer icon beside their names in the list.

You will also notice that you can specify any size that you want for TrueType fonts, rather than choosing from a limited list of raster or vector font sizes.

Use the TrueType dialog box to specify that you want to use TrueType fonts or restrict all choices to only TrueType. (Choose the Fonts icon in Control Panel, and then choose TrueType.) If you restrict all choices to TrueType, you will ensure that type styles in your documents will print on any dot matrix, HPPCL, or PostScript printer and that your documents can be moved to other platforms easily.

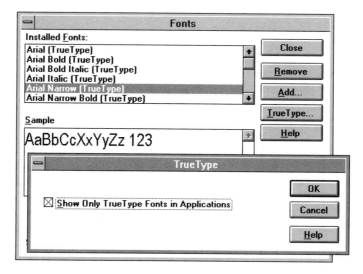

Windows NT does not automatically change fonts in documents that were produced with earlier font technologies. If you want to update old documents to use TrueType fonts, you must update them manually. You might also contact your application vendor to see if there are new utilities available that will assist automatic upgrading of documents to use TrueType.

Note TrueType uses a different character spacing (called ABC widths) than was used for raster fonts. Applications that use this spacing will be able to space characters more accurately, especially for bold and italic text. However, because of this change in spacing, text can sometimes appear inaccurately in applications written for Windows 3.0 or earlier versions. For example, the end of a highlighted text line might look odd on screen.

Disk Space, Memory Use, and Speed

You may notice a performance decrease if your document uses many fonts in many sizes. Rendering many fonts requires a large font cache, which might force more swapping to the hard disk.

Hard disk space can be a problem when using multiple raster fonts, but it is not a problem for TrueType fonts. Any soft fonts you already have on your hard disk will not be affected by the installation of TrueType with Windows NT.

The Windows NT limit on the number of TrueType fonts that can exist simultaneously on your system is limited only by disk space. However, some printers limit the number of fonts you can use on a single page or in a single document.

Installing Fonts

In Windows NT, fonts can be installed in your system in several ways:

- Windows NT installs TrueType and its screen fonts automatically during installation. When you specify a printer and other options in the Printer Properties dialog box, Windows NT includes information about font cartridges and built-in fonts for your printer.

- Install more TrueType fonts from disks by choosing the Add Fonts button in the Font Installer dialog box.

- Install other third-party soft fonts on your hard disk by using the utility supplied by the manufacturer. Then choose the Add Fonts button in the Font Installer dialog box to install the fonts in Windows NT.

- Install a new font cartridge in your printer. In Print Manager, choose Print Properties, then Setup, and choose a new item from the Cartridge list from Print Properties.

- Install PostScript soft fonts by using the Soft Fonts Installer from within the PostScript Printer Setup dialog box.

Adding Fonts

To install additional fonts, choose the Fonts icon in Control Panel. The following dialog box displays:

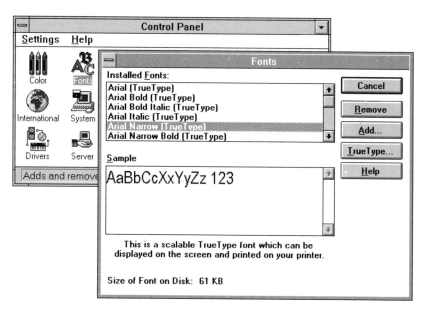

Note The font shown here, Contemporary Brush, is not included with Windows NT but can be purchased separately as part of the Microsoft TrueType Font Pack 2 product.

For more information about using the Font Installer, choose the Help button in the dialog box. Other details about using the Font Installer are discussed in "Printer Fonts and Windows NT," later in this chapter.

Information About Installed Fonts

Information about the fonts installed for your system are kept in the Windows NT Registry. As shown below, most of the information about installed fonts is kept in the HKEY_LOCAL_MACHINE\SOFTWARE key.

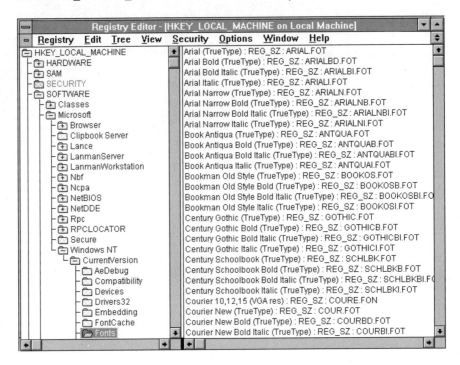

For more information, see "Registry Entries for Fonts" in Chapter 14, "Registry Value Entries."

If you installed Windows NT on a computer that previously had Windows 3.*x* installed, the Registry will include entries showing you where to find that information previously found in the **[Fonts]** and **[FontSubstitutes]** sections of WIN.INI, as shown above. For example, to find information that used to be in the **[Fonts]** section of WIN.INI, look in this location in the Registry:

```
HKEY_LOCAL_MACHINE\SOFTWARE\Microsoft\Windows NT\CurrentVersion\Fonts
```

How Windows NT Matches Fonts

When an application requests characters to print or display, Windows NT must find the appropriate font to use from among the fonts installed on your system. Finding the font can be complex because, for example, your document may contain fonts that aren't available on the current printer, or there may be more than one font with the same name installed on your system.

The basic rules that Windows NT uses for finding a font are these:

- If the font is a TrueType font, TrueType renders the character, and the result is sent to the display or to the printer.
- If the font is not a TrueType font, Windows NT uses the font mapping table to determine the most appropriate device font to use.

When Windows NT uses the font mapping table to match screen fonts to printer fonts, the characteristics used to find the closest match are—in descending order of importance—typeface name, character set, variable versus fixed pitch, family, height, width, weight, slant, underline, and strikeout.

The following table shows which types of Windows NT fonts can be printed on different kinds of printers.

Table 7.3   Windows NT Printable Fonts

Printer type	Device fonts	Raster fonts	Vector fonts	TrueType fonts
Dot Matrix	Yes	Yes	Yes	Yes
HPPCL	Yes	No	Yes	Yes
PostScript	Yes	No	Yes	Yes

The following table lists the character sets installed with Windows NT.

Table 7.4   Windows NT Character Sets

Font	Font type, spacing, and default sizes
Arial Bold Italic	TrueType, proportional, scalable
Arial Bold	TrueType, proportional, scalable
Arial Italic	TrueType, proportional, scalable
Arial	TrueType, proportional, scalable
Courier New Bold Italic	TrueType, fixed, scalable
Courier New Bold	TrueType, fixed, scalable
Courier New Italic	TrueType, fixed, scalable
Courier New	TrueType, fixed, scalable
Courier	Raster, fixed, 10,12,15
Modern	Vector, proportional, scalable
MS Sans Serif	Raster, proportional, 8, 10, 12, 14, 18, 24
MS Serif	Raster, proportional, 6, 7, 8, 10, 12, 14, 18, 24
roman	Vector, proportional, scalable
Script	Vector, proportional, scalable
Small	Raster, proportional, 2, 3, 4,5, 6, 7
Symbol**	Raster, proportional, 8, 10, 12, 14, 18, 24
Symbol**	TrueType, proportional, scalable
System	Raster, proportional, display-dependent size
Terminal*	Raster, fixed, display-dependent size
Times New roman Bold Italic	TrueType, proportional, scalable
Times New roman Bold	TrueType, proportional, scalable
Times New roman Italic	TrueType, proportional, scalable
Times New roman	TrueType, proportional, scalable
Wingdings	TrueType, proportional, scalable

* OEM character set, rather than ANSI character set

** Symbol character set, rather than ANSI character set

Screen Fonts and Windows NT

Windows NT uses special raster fonts as the system screen font for menus, window captions, messages, and other text. A set of system, fixed, and OEM terminal fonts is shipped with Windows NT to match your system's display capabilities (that is, for VGA or 8514 video displays). The default system screen font in Windows NT is System, a proportionally spaced raster font.

The installed system screen fonts are listed in the following Registry keys:

```
HKEY_LOCAL_MACHINE\SOFTWARE\Microsoft\Windows NT
    \CurrentVersion\Fonts
HKEY_LOCAL_MACHINE\SOFTWARE\Microsoft\Windows NT
    \CurrentVersion\GRE_Initialize
```

For information about the display device resolution of specific Windows NT system fonts, see "Font and Printer Files" in Chapter 4, "Windows NT Files."

By default, code page 437 (U.S.) fonts are installed using EGA40WOA.FON, EGA80WOA.FON, and DOSAPP.FON. Other screen font files are included for international language support, identified by the code page number appended to the filename.

Note Windows 3.1 supplied both "small fonts" and "large fonts" variations of each of several display drivers. The major difference between these two variations was the system font set that the Setup program installed: VGAOEM, VGAFIX, and VGASYS are the "small" (VGA-resolution) system fonts, and 8514OEM, 8514FIX, and 8514SYS are the "large" (8514-resolution) system fonts. For display drivers that did not offer this option, some users manually copied another font set and manually altered the SYSTEM.INI file to reference that font set.

With Windows NT, you need a different display driver file as well as a different font set to produce the small fonts/large fonts effect. Simply changing entries in the Registry will not work. Instead, use the Font application from Control Panel to install the appropriate font drivers.

For a list of these files with their associated code page translation tables, see "Font and Printer Files" in Chapter 4, "Windows NT Files."

Printer Fonts and Windows NT

A printer font is any font that can be produced on your printer. There are basically three kinds of printer fonts:

- Device fonts are fonts that actually reside in the hardware of your printer. They can be built into the printer itself or can be provided by a font cartridge or font card.

- Printable screen fonts are Windows NT screen fonts that can be translated for output to the printer (including TrueType).

- Downloadable soft fonts are fonts that reside on your hard disk and are sent to the printer when needed. (Only the characters needed for the particular document are downloaded, not the whole font set.)

Not all printers can use all three types of printer fonts. For example, HPPCL printers cannot print Windows NT screen fonts.

The Windows NT Universal printer driver takes advantage of TrueType and offers other improvements over older dot matrix and HPPCL printer drivers. The Windows NT Universal printer driver is used instead of specific dot matrix or HPPCL printer drivers. Instead of seeing the specific name of your printer in the Printer Properties dialog box in Print Manager, you will see a generic description of your printer.

For more information about setting up printers, see Chapter 6, "Printing."

Mapping Characters

Windows NT uses the Windows ANSI character set. Some printers, such as the IBM Proprinter®, use the IBM (OEM) standard for codes above 128. Other printers might use their own proprietary set of extended character codes.

To be sure you get the characters you want, see your printer documentation for the character set supported by the printer. Then see the online Help for Character Map for instructions on entering codes from the keyboard for special characters.

You can also use the Windows NT Character Map to select and insert special characters in your document.

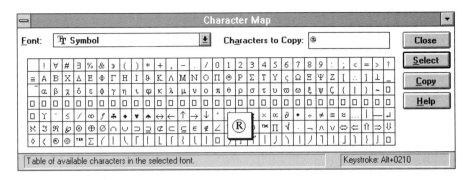

Figure 7.2   Mapping Special Characters

When you insert special characters in a document to print, the character you see on the screen might not be correct, because it is displayed using the Windows ANSI character set and the best matching screen font for the current printer font. However, the printed document will contain the correct character. Conversely, if you type an ANSI character that appears on screen but is not supported in your printer fonts, some other character will be printed, instead.

Dot Matrix Printer Fonts

Dot matrix printers support device fonts and printable screen fonts. Usually, a dot matrix printer includes only a limited range of internal device fonts. Typically fixed-spacing fonts are supplied in a variety of characters-per-inch (CPI) sizes and are conventionally named typeface *xx*CPI, where typeface is the typeface name, and *xx* is the number of characters per inch. Distinguishing a device font on a dot matrix printer is usually as easy as checking for the CPI designation at the end of the font name, such as Courier 10 CPI.

Through the Universal printer driver, dot matrix printers can also support TrueType. When you use TrueType fonts on a dot matrix printer, Windows NT sends a rasterized graphics image to the printer.

Dot matrix printers do not provide any landscape device fonts, but vector and TrueType screen fonts can be printed in any resolution or orientation. Dot matrix device fonts are faster but less flexible than screen fonts.

Dot matrix printers are typically distinguished as either 9-pin or 24-pin printers (but not limited to these):

- 9-pin dot matrix printers such as the Epson 9-pin and IBM Proprinter series usually print in a 1.67:1 aspect ratio. The Windows NT Epson 9-pin driver supports resolutions of 120x72 (1.67:1 aspect ratio), 120x144 (1:1.2), and 240x144 (1.67:1).

- 24-pin dot matrix printers such as the Epson 24-pin and IBM Proprinter 24 series can print in 120x180 resolution (1:1.5 aspect ratio), 180x180 (1:1), and 360x180 (2:1). Some others, such as the NEC 24-pin, provide a 360x360 resolution. The 180x180 resolution is usually best for printing raster screen fonts. In 180x180 resolution, these printers can print 1:1 aspect ratio screen fonts, such as the E set (96x96 dpi) and the F set (120x120 dpi). E set fonts will be available at about 50 percent, and F set fonts at 75 percent of normal point sizes. A true 180x180 dpi screen font set is available by special order from Epson of America.

Some 24-pin dot matrix printers such as the Epson and NEC printers also support font cards or cartridges. You can use these fonts if the Windows NT driver for that printer supports them. Use the printer setup dialog box to specify a font cartridge for your printer. (Choose Printer Properties from Print Manager, and then choose Setup.)

HPPCL Printer Fonts

Printers that use the Hewlett-Packard Printer Control Language (HPPCL) can print several different types of fonts. HPPCL printers can use font cartridges, downloadable soft fonts, vector screen fonts, and TrueType fonts.

HPPCL printers cannot print Windows NT raster screen fonts.

When you use TrueType fonts on an HPPCL printer, TrueType performs all the font rendering in the computer and downloads bitmaps of the fonts to the printer. (Windows NT downloads these bitmaps only if the printer has enough memory.) TrueType downloads only the specific characters needed in a document, not the entire font.

If you use an HP LaserJet-compatible printer, be sure to specify accurately the amount of memory installed in your printer. This is important because the Windows NT HPPCL minidriver tracks the available memory in your printer. You may get an out-of-printer-memory error or other errors if the memory is specified incorrectly.

Font Cartridges

Hewlett-Packard LaserJet-compatible font cartridges are supplied by numerous manufacturers, including Hewlett-Packard, Pacific Data Products, and IQ Engineering. Some cartridge vendors also produce custom font cartridges to your specifications.

Windows NT treats font cartridges as device fonts because they are always with the printer. Font cartridges can be selected in the Printer Properties dialog box. The HPPCL minidriver available with Windows NT can support all HP font cartridges.

If you want to add a font cartridge that came out after the printer driver was written, you may need a printer cartridge metrics (.PCM) file. A .PCM file tells Windows NT the characteristics of the new font and is installed with the Font Installer in the same way as soft fonts. After a .PCM file is installed, a new entry appears in the Cartridges dialog box of the Printer Properties dialog box.

For new HP cartridges, contact Hewlett-Packard or other cartridge vendor for the appropriate .PCM file.

Downloadable Fonts

You can get HP LaserJet-compatible downloadable soft fonts from a number of sources, including Hewlett-Packard, Bitstream, SoftCraft, and CompuGraphics. Some downloadable font utilities also generate raster screen fonts for Windows NT. If an exact screen font match is not available, Windows NT uses one of its own screen fonts.

Hewlett-Packard downloadable fonts are installed with the Font Installer. (To use the Font Installer, choose Fonts from the Printer Properties dialog box.)

Font Limitations for Older HPPCL Printers

Some older model HPPCL printers have a limit of 16 fonts per page. If you send a page that contains more than 16 fonts to an HPPCL printer, a warning message is displayed.

An Error 20 message might appear on the front panel of the HPPCL printer when printing a document that contains soft fonts. This also indicates that you tried to download more fonts than the printer's memory can hold. You can recover from this error by pressing the Continue button on the printer control panel. The soft font that caused the error is not downloaded and will not print.

To avoid this error, reduce the number of fonts that you try to download, or add more memory to your printer. Also make sure you haven't downloaded any permanent soft fonts that are taking up memory in the printer.

The maximum number of soft fonts you can install is limited by the maximum size of WIN.INI, not by the Font Installer itself.

Printer Fonts for HP Printers

Windows NT includes fonts for Hewlett-Packard PCL, DeskJet®, and PaintJet printers.

HP LaserJet Printer Fonts

In Windows NT, all HPPCL (LaserJet) printers are supported by the HPPCL.DLL minidriver. Additional LaserJet III scalable outline fonts are available from Hewlett-Packard as cartridges or downloadable soft fonts. With the HPPCL driver in Windows NT, downloadable outline fonts can be installed with the Font Installer.

HP DeskJet Printer Fonts

The HP DeskJet Printer is an ink-jet printer. The Windows NT driver for the Hewlett-Packard DeskJet printer family supports Windows NT vector screen fonts, DeskJet internal fonts, soft fonts, and TrueType. DeskJet printers can print at resolutions of 75, 150, and 300 dpi. Without font cartridges, the DeskJet includes only the built-in Courier and LinePrinter fonts. Cartridges can be selected in the Printer Properties dialog box. At this time, font cartridges for DeskJet printers are available only from Hewlett-Packard.

DeskJet soft fonts are installed with the Font Installer. To use downloadable fonts on the DeskJet printers, you must install either HP22707A or HP22707B RAM cartridges. When you set printer memory in the Printer Properties dialog box, make sure to specify the total amount of RAM cartridge memory if more than one cartridge is installed.

DeskJet internal, downloadable, and cartridge fonts will not work in landscape orientation. This is a hardware, not a driver, limitation. For landscape mode, print with Windows NT vector screen fonts such as Modern or roman .

HP PaintJet Printer Fonts

The HP PaintJet is a color ink-jet printer. The Hewlett-Packard PaintJet driver in Windows NT composes a full page at a time in 180x180 dpi resolution and outputs the page to the PaintJet as a large bitmap. This produces the highest possible quality of output, but results in very large temporary spool files if you use Print Manager. For improved printing speed, it is recommended that you choose the Fast Printing Direct To Port option in the Connect dialog box in Printer Properties. This option prevents the creation of temporary spool files.

The PaintJet driver supports the printing of PaintJet internal fonts, Windows NT raster and vector screen fonts, PaintJet soft fonts, and TrueType. The same considerations apply for printing raster screen fonts on the PaintJet as for using the 24-pin dot matrix printers in 180x180 dpi resolution (see "Dot Matrix Printer Fonts," earlier in this chapter). PaintJet soft fonts are not downloadable fonts. They are used internally by the driver, which places them as necessary into the full-page bitmap during page composition. The font itself is never sent to the printer, except as part of the full-page bitmap.

PaintJet soft fonts, which have a .PJF filename extension, are installed with the Font Installer. Windows NT supports PaintJet soft fonts for Courier 10-CPI and Letter Gothic 12-CPI and 18-CPI. Additional soft fonts can be obtained from Hewlett-Packard. Scalable PaintJet soft fonts are also available from Hewlett-Packard in the HP Color PrintKit (HP part number 17390A).

PostScript Printer Fonts

All PostScript fonts are scalable outlines that can be printed at any size. PostScript outline fonts can also be rotated to any angle and can be printed in both portrait and landscape modes. However, font size limits are often imposed by applications. A common PostScript font size limit in an application is 127 points.

Most PostScript printers include either the standard Apple LaserWriter Plus set of 35 scalable fonts or the earlier Apple LaserWriter set of 17 fonts.

PostScript soft fonts are installed using the Soft Font Installer dialog box. (For a PostScript printer, choose Properties from the Print Manager Printer menu. Choose Setup; then choose Soft Fonts.) Because the fonts are scalable, if there isn't a comparable screen font, mismatches can occur between screen display and printed output.

PostScript printers can print Windows NT raster screen fonts, vector screen fonts, and TrueType fonts.

LaserWriter Plus Typefaces

The LaserWriter Plus standard font set includes eleven typefaces, including the following eight, which are available in roman, bold, italic, and bold italic:

- AvantGarde Gothic
- Helvetica
- ITC Bookman®
- Palatino®

- Courier
- Helvetica Narrow
- New Century Schoolbook
- Times

The other three typefaces are Symbol, Zapf Chancery, and Zapf Dingbats. The Symbol typeface contains mathematical and scientific symbols; Zapf Chancery is a calligraphic font; and Zapf Dingbats contains decorative bullet characters and embellishments. These typefaces are available only in roman style.

PostScript Printers and TrueType

TrueType fonts are treated as downloaded fonts by the PostScript driver. When you use TrueType fonts on a PostScript printer, scaling and hints are always performed in the computer. Scan conversion can be done in the computer or in the printer, depending on the point size. At smaller point sizes, TrueType performs scan conversion in the computer; at larger point sizes, scan conversion is done in the printer.

You can map a TrueType font to a PostScript font by using the FontSubst option in Print Manager. (Choose Properties from the Printer menu, and then choose Setup to see this option.) This is helpful to view TrueType as a screen font and to get PostScript for the printout font. This will increase printing speed, but the results on the display may not be exactly the same as the printed output.

Alternately, you can choose to download TrueType fonts as soft fonts to the printer, so that the printed output matches the screen display. (In Print Manager, specify your printer and choose Properties from the Printer menu. Then, in order, choose these three command buttons: Details, Job Defaults, Options. Select the Download TrueType Fonts as Softfont option button.)

Substituting PostScript Fonts

You can edit the Substitution Table to specify which PostScript printer fonts you want to print in place of the TrueType fonts in your documents. The changes you make in the Substitution Table only affect the fonts that are printed. The fonts that appear on the screen will not change; the original TrueType fonts are still used to display TrueType text in your document.

To specify which printer fonts to use, choose FontSubst from the Printer Setup dialog box. Then select the TrueType font you want to replace from the For TrueType Font list in the Substitution dialog box. From the Substitute Printer Font list, select the PostScript printer font you want to use instead of the selected TrueType font.

If your printer supports downloaded fonts, you can choose the Download As Soft Font option, as described in the preceding section. In this case, the selected TrueType fonts will be sent to the printer as soft fonts. Repeat these steps until you have selected printer fonts to use in place of all the TrueType fonts in your document.

PostScript Downloadable Outline Fonts

In addition to installed fonts, PostScript printers also accept downloadable outline fonts, which can be scaled to any size and printed in both portrait and landscape orientations. Downloadable PostScript fonts are available from several suppliers, including Adobe and Bitstream.

Although PostScript downloadable outlines can be scaled to any size, Windows NT raster screen fonts cannot. If you specify a PostScript font size that does not have a corresponding screen font, Windows NT substitutes another screen font. This results in a little loss in display quality but no loss in print quality.

Specifying Virtual Printer Memory

You can change the amount of virtual memory that your PostScript printer has available for storing fonts. The PostScript driver uses a default setting recommended by the printer manufacturer for virtual memory.

To adjust the amount of virtual memory for your printer, in the PostScript Printer Setup dialog box, type the amount of virtual memory you want to use in the Printer Memory (kilobytes) box. (Choose the Setup option from the Printer Properties dialog box.)

Questions and Answers About Fonts

This section answers some common questions about using fonts with Windows NT.

I printed the same document with TrueType fonts from two different computers to the same PostScript printer. The two printouts are different. Why?

TrueType font substitution is different on the two computers. Use Print Manager to reconfigure font substitution on one of the computers.

My document looks fine on the screen but prints with a different font. Why?

This may be happening for one of two reasons. Either you specified the wrong printer model during setup, or the downloadable font did not download to the print device. Check the Printer Properties dialog box to see that the printer driver you are using matches the print device. Then choose Setup, and check the amount of memory for your printer. Make sure the amount shown in the Setup dialog box accurately reflects the amount of memory for your print device. If there is too little memory, the print device may not be able to download fonts.

My document prints OK, but it looks funny on the screen. Why?

There is no direct displayable equivalent of a device font that you are using.

I can't select a font that I know is provided by a cartridge installed in the printer. Why?

In Print Manager, make sure that the printer properties lists the correct cartridge.

CHAPTER 8

Microsoft Mail

Windows NT includes an electronic mail application, Microsoft Mail, that can be used to exchange information with other Windows NT computers. Mail also can work interactively with many other Windows-based applications. This chapter describes the components that make up Mail and explains how to use Mail functionality from within other Windows-based applications, such as Microsoft Word for Windows and Microsoft Excel for Windows. This chapter also describes customization features you can use to tailor Mail for your office—custom commands, custom message types, custom menus, and the Messaging Application Program Interface (MAPI).

About Mail

The Mail application provided with Windows NT has a client side, a mail-server side, and an interface between them. The client side includes a visual user interface, made up of viewers for messages, folders, and address lists. The server simply contains a directory structure known as the *postoffice* and has no programmatic components. The interface between client and server manages message storage and retrieval, name validation, and directory access.

A user sends mail to, and receives mail from, a *message store* on his or her own computer. When a user sends a message, it is forwarded from the local computer's message store to the postoffice located on the mail server. The postoffice has a mailbox for each user, giving users access to the messages they've received when they sign in to Mail.

Mail uses a *shared file system*, which means that the postoffice must reside on a share on a computer running Windows NT to which each user in the workgroup has access. The postoffice is a directory structure in which the main directory is called a workgroup postoffice (WGPO). All postoffice file manipulation is handled by the Mail client.

The postoffice is a temporary message store, holding a message until the recipient's workstation retrieves it. Mail is efficient because it stores only one copy of each mail message, even when a message is addressed to multiple recipients. When it is retrieved, the message is removed from the postoffice. A message sent to multiple recipients has a reference count in it. The count is decremented each time a recipient retrieves the message, and the message itself is removed when the reference count drops to 0.

For a description of Mail's features and for information on how to use the application, see the Mail chapter in the *Windows NT System Guide*.

Mail Postoffice

Figure 8.1 shows the postoffice directory structure:

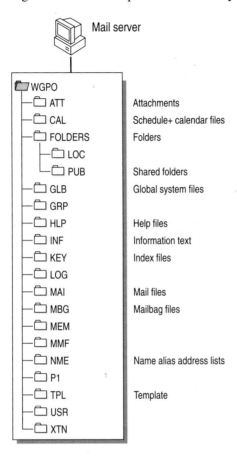

Figure 8.1   Postoffice Directory Structure

All subdirectories must be present for the Mail system to function correctly. The following is a list of what's in each subdirectory of the Mail postoffice:

- The ATT subdirectory contains encrypted file attachments.

- The CAL subdirectory contains Schedule+ calendar files.

- The FOLDERS\PUB subdirectory contains shared folders.

- The GLB subdirectory contains global system files for Mail. These files contain local user logon information and control files to generate mail files.

- The HLP subdirectory contains Mail help files.

- The INF and TPL subdirectories contain information and template files, respectively. ADMIN.INF and ADMIN.TPL contain template information for local postoffice users.

- The KEY subdirectory includes index files that contain pointers to header records in the mailbag (.MBG) files.

- The MAI subdirectory stores Mail messages in encrypted form until the recipients retrieve them.

- The MBG subdirectory contains Mail headers that point to the Mail (.MAI) files. For each file in this directory, there is a matching index (.KEY) file.

- The NME subdirectory contains pointer files for the name alias address lists. ADMIN.NME and ADMINSHD.NME list members of the postoffice address list.

- The FOLDERS\LOC, GRP, LOG, MEM, MMF, P1, USR, and XTN subdirectories are reserved.

Workgroup Postoffice Administration

The workgroup postoffice administrator is responsible for creating and managing the postoffice. The only difference between the administrator and other Mail users is that the administrator can perform the following tasks:

- Back up the postoffice, which should be done on a regular basis
- Add users to the postoffice
- Change user information, including forgotten passwords
- Check the status of shared folders

The workgroup postoffice manager library, WGPOMG32.DLL, is the software component that supports administrative functions such as adding or deleting users and changing passwords.

For more information about performing administrative tasks, see the Mail chapter in the *Windows NT System Guide*.

Interface Between the Mail Client and Postoffice

Mail has a modular architecture. While some of the modules comprise the user interface and postoffice, most make up the interface between the Mail client and the Mail postoffice. Figure 8.2 shows the key components that make up this interface:

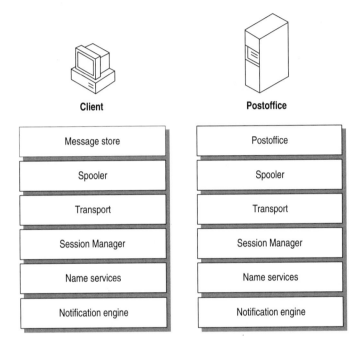

Figure 8.2   Components of the Interface Between Mail Clients and Server

Mail Spooler and Mail Transport

When you have a message to send, the Mail spooler (MAILSP32.EXE) tells the Mail transport (MSSFS32.DLL) to move it from your Outbox to the postoffice. When a message arrives for you at the postoffice, the Mail spooler tells the Mail transport to deliver it to your Inbox .

The Mail spooler's primary job is to parcel out system idle time to the Mail transport. This enables the Mail transport to transfer messages in a timely way but without interfering with the work you really want to do in the foreground. The spooler provides a safety net for the transport by retrying any operations that fail.

The spooler also resolves address book entries, adds message recipients to the personal address book, and generates nondelivery reports. It checks for new mail and deletes mail from the server.

Mail Session Manager

The Mail Session Manager (MAILM32.DLL) validates users' identities and manages connections with the message store, directory, and transport. It is the component that enables you to work even when the Mail server is unavailable (for example, when you work offline). Mail continues to work with the resources that are available at your computer and automatically connects to the server's resources when the server is again available. Maintaining the security of messages across transitions from offline to online and back is another feature of the Mail Session Manager.

The Name Service

The Name service (MAILM32.DLL) manages functions related to browsing and filtering lists of names. At the user interface, the Name service is apparent whenever you browse file folders, specify search criteria, or ask for a recipient's name to be checked.

With the exception of the personal address book, the Name service treats the directories it uses as read-only lists. Addresses as used in Mail consist of three parts:

- Display name, which is usually the full descriptive name of a person, group, or resource. This is the name you most often see in the user interface.

- Mail address type, which helps the transport route mail and provides the syntax of the mail address to the Mail client.

- Mail address, which is the part actually used to identify the routing destination for a message.

Notification Engine

When you receive new mail, the Notification Engine (STORE32.DLL) lets you know that the mail has arrived.

The Notification Engine also works with the Session Manager when you browse or filter messages. Folder management and message searches use the services of the Notification Engine. The message finder detects notification of every change to a message. As the message changes, it is reflected in the appropriate search windows.

For example, you can have multiple windows viewing the same folder. If you delete a message from the folder in one of the windows, it automatically disappears from the others because each window waits for notification of events like messages being deleted.

When a new message arrives and is written to the store by the Mail spooler, the Inbox viewer is updated by the Notification Engine. When you place a message in your Outbox, the Notification Engine alerts the spooler that there is a message to deliver to the postoffice.

Customizing the Mail Client

You can use several Mail features to customize the way Mail works for a user on a Windows NT computer:

- *Custom commands* are commands you add to Mail menus.
- *Custom message types* enable you to define and install mail forms customized for your own requirements.
- *Custom menus* enable you to add a menu name to the Mail menu bar. You may use these menus to group custom commands and/or messages under a single, distinctive menu item.
- The *Messaging Application Program Interface* (MAPI) is a set of calls you can use to easily add Mail-enabled features to other Windows-based applications.

You can install custom commands, message types, and menus for use by a single Mail user on an individual computer or on a network file server to be shared by many Mail users.

Custom Commands

You can add custom functions to your Mail menus with custom commands. A custom command is one that you add to a menu to perform a unique function tailored to your needs.

There is a second type of custom command not associated with any menu, but which can be set to run whenever the user starts Mail, ends Mail, or receives a new message.

A custom command is implemented as a dynamic-link library (DLL). Any executable code—including batch files or applications—can be run from a custom command. Here are some examples of how custom commands can be used to tailor Mail for specific needs:

- Display a window that contains information specific to where the user works, such as a parts list or a list of stock quotes.

- Query a database without leaving Mail.

- Launch another application and open a specific file. For example, users can create a command to open a MEMOS.TXT file in the Windows Notepad application.

Installing Custom Commands

You can install custom commands on the local computer for use by a single user or centrally on the postoffice to be shared by all users. Installing the command on the postoffice eases installation and administrative tasks, and saves space on other users' hard disks.

Once installed, these custom commands can appear to users as built-in features. You can install up to 1000 custom commands in Mail. If you install several custom commands, you can add separator bars between groups of commands to help organize the menu's appearance.

To install custom commands for a user on an individual computer, you need to modify the Registry on that computer for each custom command and supply the appropriate DLLs. To install custom commands for everyone who uses a postoffice, you need to modify the Registry for each user, modify the SHARED32.INI file on the postoffice computer, and add the DLLs to the postoffice computer.

Note Typically, the Setup program that installs the custom commands automatically modifies entries in your computer's Registry and in the postoffice computer's SHARED32.INI file. The information in the following sections is for your reference if you need to make the modifications yourself.

Starting Separate Applications

Mail expects that a custom command will be implemented as a DLL. A custom command can launch an application. The DLL can pass information about the command to the application when it starts.

Although Mail always calls a DLL, the DLL can pass information to an application by using Windows dynamic data exchange (DDE), command line parameters, or a disk file. If the called application is already running, the DLL transfers information most efficiently using DDE. If the DLL uses a disk file, care should be taken so that multiple temporary files are not added to the user's disk. The application that implements the custom command runs independently of Mail.

Installing a Custom Command for a Single User

To install a custom command for a single user on an individual computer, follow these steps:

1. Copy the DLL for the custom command to the *SystemRoot*\SYSTEM32 directory of your hard drive.
2. Add a custom command entry to the Registry on your computer in HKEY_CURRENT_USER\Software\Microsoft\Mail\Custom Commands. For information on how to do this, see "Custom Command Entries for Mail" in Chapter 14, "Registry Value Entries."
3. Quit Mail if it is running, and then restart it. Mail rereads your Registry and adds the custom command.

Installing a Custom Command on the Postoffice

If you have a custom command that you want to make available to multiple users, you can install the command on the postoffice instead of in each user's Registry. When you create a new custom command, you must include a **SharedExtensionsDir** entry in this key in each user's Registry:

```
HKEY_CURRENT_USER\Software\Microsoft\Mail\Microsoft Mail
```

This entry instructs Mail to check the server's SHARED32.INI file for custom command entries.

Mail finds the **SharedExtensionsDir** entry in the user's Registry, then reads entries for custom commands in SHARED32.INI before returning to the user's Registry to read any custom command entries there. For example in Figure 8.3, Mail reads the **SharedExtensionsDir** entry in the user's Registry first. Then it reads the entries in the **[Custom Commands]** section of SHARED32.INI (in this case, the lines labeled **tagA=** and **tagB=**). After reading all of the custom command entries in SHARED32.INI, Mail reads entries in the key of the user's Registry (in this case, the entries labeled **tag1** and **tag2**):

```
HKEY_CURRENT_USER\Software\Microsoft\Mail\Custom Commands
```

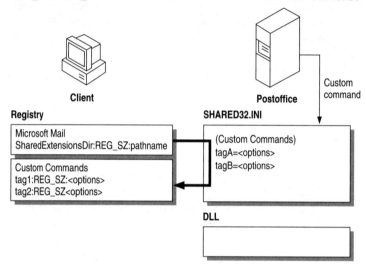

Figure 8.3   File Interaction with Shared Custom Commands

The directory on the postoffice share specified by **SharedExtensionsDir** in the Registry contains the SHARED32.INI file as well as the DLLs that implement shared custom commands.

Mail can check a server for custom commands and custom messages in one of two ways:

- When you use a dynamic connection to the postoffice
- When you manually connect to the postoffice before starting Mail

The syntax you use with the **SharedExtensionsDir** entry in the Registry reflects the way you choose to connect. The **SharedExtensionsDir** entry uses the following syntax:

```
SharedExtensionsDir:REG_SZ:\\server\share\pathname [password]
```

or:

```
SharedExtensionsDir:REG_SZ:pathname
```

When you want to dynamically connect to the server's shared disk, use the
server\share\pathname option with **SharedExtensionsDir**. Use the *pathname*
option with **SharedExtensionsDir** to point to a manual connection to the server's
shared disk.

To install a shared custom command, follow these steps:

1. Create a shared Mail extensions directory on the postoffice.

2. Copy the custom command DLL to the shared extensions directory.

3. A sample SHARED32.INI file is included on the *Windows NT Resource Guide*
   disks. Copy this file to the shared extensions directory.

4. Add custom command entries to the **[Custom Commands]** section of the
   SHARED32.INI file on the postoffice, using this syntax:

   ```
   tag=Mail version; menu; name; position; DLL name; command;
   event map; status text; Help file; Help context
   ```

   (Note that this is a single command line in SHARED32.INI. Don't add any
   carriage returns even if line-wrapping occurs.)

   Values are defined in the following table.

Value	Definition
tag	The descriptive identifier for the command.
version	The version of Mail that the custom command is compatible with.
menu	Names the menu where the custom command is to be added, such as File or Help.
name	The command name that is to appear on the menu. You may include an ampersand just before the letter that is to serve as an ALT+ key accelerator.
position	The zero-relative position within its menu where the command is to appear. A value of **-1** places the command at the end of the menu.
DLL name	Name or path of the DLL where the custom command resides. This entry can optionally be followed by a comma and the ordinal of the entry point to call (default is **,1**).
command	The command string passed as one of the parameters to the DLL entry point for the command.

Value *(continued)*	Definition *(continued)*
event map	A sequence of up to 16 digits identifying the Mail events that the custom command supports. Each can be **0** or **1** to indicate if the DLL is to be called for a specific event. Currently three events are defined; the rest are reserved and must be zero (or this whole section can be empty):
	The first digit means Mail startup. The second digit means Mail exit. The third digit means the arrival of a new message.
status text	Text to be displayed in the Mail status bar when the user moves the cursor to the command in the menu.
Help file	Windows NT Help file to be invoked when the user presses F1 while the command is selected. The specified filename is passed to the Windows NT Help program. (optional)
Help context	Passed to the Windows NT Help program along with the Help file name. Use **-1** (Help file index) if there is no specific entry in the Help file for this command (optional).
	There is one special token that may appear within certain fields:
<ExtsDir>	Expands to the value of **SharedExtensionsDir** in the user's Registry. Used to refer to DLLs that are installed in a shared extensions directory on the network. Valid for the DLL name, command, and Help file subfields.

5. In the Registry on your computer, add a **SharedExtensionsDir** entry to reference the shared extensions directory in the following key:

```
HKEY_CURRENT_USER\Software\Microsoft\Mail\Microsoft Mail
```

   For information about **SharedExtensionsDir**, see "Microsoft Mail Entries" in Chapter 14, "Registry Value Entries."

6. If you have chosen the manual connection method, make the necessary network connection using File Manager.

7. Quit Mail if it is running, and then restart it.

   Mail rereads your Registry and adds the shared custom command to the specified menu.

8. Test the shared custom command.

9. When the custom command works successfully on your computer, modify each user's Registry to have access to the shared extensions directory. (See step 5.)

Custom Message Types

A custom message type is a special type (or class) of message for delivery between two or more Mail recipients or Mail-enabled applications. A custom message type can define a particular way to perform standard Mail operations such as composing, replying to, and forwarding messages. Custom message types can define a message's appearance and content, or the behavior of the forms displayed to the user when sending, reading, and replying to messages of that type.

Most custom message types are received in your Inbox just like standard Mail messages. A second kind of custom message type doesn't appear in the Inbox when it arrives and yet is available to other Mail-enabled applications. This allows Mail-enabled applications to define their own message classes.

Custom message types have many similarities to custom commands. Like custom commands, a command for composing a custom message type can be added to a Mail menu. When the Mail user chooses this command, the custom message type DLL displays a dialog box or form that enables the user to compose a message of the corresponding type. These dialog boxes or forms can include features specific to the message type.

You can install up to 1000 custom message types in Mail.

When a custom-type message arrives in a Mail folder, it can appear in the message list the same as other standard Mail messages. But when read or replied to, the custom dialog boxes or forms associated with the message type can be displayed in place of the standard read or reply form. You can also design a custom message type that doesn't appear in Mail's Inbox when it arrives and yet is available to other Mail-enabled applications.

Note If a custom message type is delivered to a user who does not have that custom message type installed, the message is treated as a standard message type.

Custom message types can provide special messaging functionality such as the following:

- Messages that are composed or read using a special form.
- Messages accessed by the user through an application other than Mail.
- Messages that are preaddressed to a particular recipient.
- Messages that are used to order parts or services or to describe an event. The dialog boxes displayed when the user composes these types of messages can include special structured fields specific to the purpose of the message.
- Messages that help route workflow events.
- Messages that are specific to group scheduling.

- Messages that enable some type of game, such as chess, to be played between two Mail users.

Microsoft Schedule+ is an example of an application that defines its own custom message types. Schedule+ uses the following custom message types:

- IPM.Microsoft Schedule.MtgReq—used to generate the Meeting Request form
- IPM.Microsoft Schedule.MtgRespP—used to generate the Positive Meeting Response form
- IPM.Microsoft Schedule.MtgRespN—used to generate the Negative Meeting Response form
- IPM.Microsoft Schedule.MtgRespA—used to generate the Tentative Meeting Response form
- IPM.Microsoft Schedule.MtgCncl—used to generate a Meeting Cancellation message

For more information about these custom message types, see Chapter 9, "Schedule+."

Installing Custom Message Types

Installing a custom message type is similar to installing a custom command. Just like custom commands, you can install custom message types on an individual computer or on the postoffice as shared custom message types. Typically, though, you'll install them as shared custom message types because you'll want both sending and receiving parties to take advantage of the custom message type.

When you install custom message types on an individual computer, you must modify the Registry on that computer by adding a custom message type entry in this key:

```
HKEY_CURRENT_USER\Software\Microsoft\Mail\Custom Messages
```

For information about how to do this, see "Custom Messages Entries for Mail" in Chapter 14, "Registry Value Entries."

For shared custom message types, you must add a custom message type entry to the postoffice's SHARED32.INI file. Then, on each workstation using the shared custom message type, you must add a **SharedExtensionsDir** entry in the Microsoft Mail subkey Registry. As with custom commands, when Mail sees this entry in the Registry, it reads SHARED32.INI for custom message type entries before reading custom message type entries in the Registry.

Installing Custom Message Types on the Postoffice

To install a shared custom message type on the postoffice, follow these steps:

1. Create a shared Mail extensions directory on the postoffice.
2. Copy the SHARED32.INI file and custom message type DLL (and/or .EXE) to the shared extensions directory.
3. Add custom message type declarations to the **[Custom Messages]** section of the SHARED32.INI file on the postoffice, using this syntax:

```
MessageClassName= Mail version; menu name; command name;
    command position; ExtsDir DLL name; ExtsDir command string;
    operation map; status text; ExtsDir Help file name; Help context;
```

(Note that this is a single command line in SHARED32.INI. Do not add any carriage returns even if line-wrapping occurs.)

Values are defined in the following table.

Value	Definition
class	A string uniquely identifying the message type. Mail places this string in messages and calls custom message DLLs based on its value.
Mail version	Identifies the version of Mail that the custom message is compatible with.
menu name	Names the menu where the custom command for the message type is to be added, such as File or Mail.
command name	The command name that is to appear on the menu. As usual, you may include an ampersand just before the letter that is to serve as an ALT+ key accelerator.
command position	The zero-relative position within its menu at which the command is to appear. A value of **-1** places the command at the end of the menu.
ExtsDir DLL name	The name or path of the DLL in which the custom message resides.
command string	The Command string passed as one of the parameters to the DLL entry point for the command.

Value *(continued)*	Definition *(continued)*
operation map	A sequence of up to 16 digits. Each can be **0**, **1**, or **2**. **0** indicates that Mail is to perform its standard operation on the custom message. **1** indicates that the DLL is to be called to handle the operation. **2** indicates that the operation is to be completely disabled. Currently eight operations are defined; the rest are reserved and must be zero. In the following list, **0** is the leftmost digit:
	0 Compose (menu command defined in this entry)
	1 File.Open
	2 Mail.Reply
	3 Mail.Reply to All
	4 Mail.Forward
	5 File.Print
	6 File.Save as
	7 Arrival of new mail
status text	Text to be displayed in the Mail status bar when the user moves the cursor to the command in the menu.
ExtsDir Help file name	The Windows NT Help file to be invoked when the user presses F1 while the command is selected. The specified filename is passed to the Windows NT help program. (optional)
Help context	Passed to the Windows NT help program along with the Help file name. Use **-1** (Help file index) if there is no specific entry in the Help file for this command. (optional)
	There is one special token that may appear within certain fields:
<ExtsDir>	Expands to the value of **SharedExtensionsDir** in the user's Registry. Used to refer to DLLs that are installed in a shared extensions directory on the network. Valid for the DLL name, command, and Help file subfields.

4. In the Registry on your computer, add a **SharedExtensionsDir** entry to reference the shared extensions directory in the following key:

```
HKEY_CURRENT_USER\Software\Microsoft\Mail\Microsoft Mail
```

   For information about how to do this, see "Microsoft Mail Entries" in Chapter 14, "Registry Value Entries."

5. If you have chosen the manual connection method, make the necessary network connection using File Manager.

6. Quit Mail if it is running, and then restart it.

   Mail rereads your Registry and adds the shared custom message to the specified menu.

7. Restart Mail and test the shared custom message type.

8. When the custom message type works successfully on your computer, modify each user's Registry to have access to the shared extensions directory. (See step 4.)

Custom Menus

You can add menu items to the Mail menu bar by putting custom menu entries in the Custom Menus section of your Registry or in the **[Custom Menus]** section of SHARED32.INI (in the directory specified by the **SharedExtensionsDir** entry in your Registry). SHARED32.INI is examined first.

Each entry specifies a menu name to be added to the Mail menu bar. You may use these menus to group custom commands and/or messages under a single menu item. A description follows of the custom menu entry format for SHARED32.INI. Each entry must occupy a single line. Many subfields are optional. For information on how to add equivalent entries to your Registry, see Chapter 14, "Registry Value Entries."

```
tag=version;name;name to follow;status text
```

For example,

```
tools=3.0;&Tools;Window;Useful development toys
```

Values are defined in the following table.

Value	Definition
tag	Identifies the menu to someone reading the .INI file but serves no other purpose.
version	Identifies the version of Mail with which the command is compatible.
name	The menu name to be added to the menu bar. As usual, you may include an ampersand just before the letter that is to serve as an ALT+ key accelerator.
name to follow	Name of an existing menu. The new menu will be added directly before it.
status text	Text to be displayed in the Mail status bar when the user moves cursor to the menu.

Messaging Application Program Interface (MAPI)

The Messaging Application Program Interface (MAPI) is a set of functions that developers can use to create Mail-enabled applications. Mail includes a subset of 12 functions called *Simple MAPI*. Simple MAPI functions enable developers to send, address, and receive messages from within Windows-based applications.

With Simple MAPI functions, developers can easily add the power of messaging to any Windows-based application. Simple MAPI supports the standard interface for simple integration of a Windows-based application with Mail.

All of the Simple MAPI functions are designed to be called from C or C++ programs, but they can also be called from high-level languages, such as Visual Basic™, Actor®, Smalltalk®, and Object Vision®. Simple MAPI functions can also be called from applications with macro languages that can call a DLL. Two examples of these are Microsoft Excel or Microsoft Word.

Some Simple MAPI functions include a user interface (a dialog box) but can also be called without generating an interface. The seamless integration with Mail is convenient for applications such as word processors and spreadsheets, which manipulate files that users may want to exchange through Mail. The style of the user interface is not defined by Simple MAPI, so you can design your own.

An application developer can incorporate Mail functionality into his or her application by calling the MAPI functions. For example, if an application creates data files that need to be distributed to other users in a workgroup, the application developer can use the **MapiSendDocuments()** function to create a mail message and to send the data files as an attachment to the message. Sending mail messages is fully controlled from the application and the MAPI support library (MAPI32.DLL). The user doesn't need to have the Mail program running to do this.

In this case, one function call is all that is required. The **MapiSendDocuments()** function creates and initializes a message and supplies all the standard Mail dialog boxes for the user to send messages. The function can be compiled into the native code of the application, or if the application includes a macro facility that can link to a DLL, the developer can integrate the DLL as an added macro command.

Simple MAPI consists of the following 12 functions:

Table 8.1 Simple MAPI Functions

Function	Description
MapiAddress()	Addresses a Mail message
MapiDeleteMail()	Deletes a message
MapiDetails()	Displays a recipient details dialog box
MapiFindNext()	Returns the ID of the next (or first) Mail message of a specified type
MapiFreeBuffer()	Frees memory allocated by the messaging system
MapiLogoff()	Ends a session with the messaging system
MapiLogon()	Begins a session with the messaging system
MapiReadMail()	Reads a Mail message
MapiResolveName()	Displays a dialog box to resolve an ambiguous recipient name
MapiSaveMail()	Saves a Mail message
MapiSendDocuments()	Sends a standard Mail message
MapiSendMail()	Sends a Mail message

Integrating Mail and Other Applications

Some applications provide macros and support functions so that users can use the capabilities of Mail directly from within the application. For example, the latest releases of both Microsoft Excel for Windows and Microsoft Word for Windows provide macros to send worksheets and documents, respectively, directly from within these applications.

As an example of how Mail can be integrated with applications, Windows NT provides a File Manager extension to add a Send Mail option to the File Manager menu and toolbar. The Send Mail command displays all the user interface necessary for the user to send the currently selected files or executable files as file attachments to a message. The user can add message text around the file attachment, change the attached files, and address the message as usual.

Tips for Using Mail

This section offers tips for running Mail.

Recreating the Mail Initialization Procedure

When you first run the Mail application, it asks whether you want to use an existing postoffice on the workgroup or to create the postoffice on your computer. If you accidentally select the incorrect option, you can use the following procedure to reinitialize Mail so that these options are available again:

1. Edit your Registry to delete **ServerPath** and **Login** (or edit their values to blank) in the following key:

   ```
   HKEY_CURRENT_USER\Software\Microsoft\Mail\Microsoft Mail
   ```

2. Add or edit the **CustomInitHandler** entry to read as follows:

   ```
   CustomInitHandler:REG_SZ:WGPOM32.DLL, 10
   ```

3. Run Mail. The initialization process will begin and will once again prompt you for the location of the workgroup postoffice.

Changing the Postoffice Administrator

The postoffice administrator is tied to a specific account that is created when the postoffice is created. To change the postoffice administrator, the person who is using that account must abandon it, and the new administrator must take it over. The two persons involved in the exchange must take their Mail folders and Schedule+ data with them. The following procedure describes how to do this.

Future administrator:

1. Sign in to Schedule+, export your appointments, archive your data, and then exit Schedule+.

2. Sign in to Mail, export your folders, and then exit and sign out of Mail.

3. Edit your Registry to include the following entries in HKEY_CURRENT_USER\Software\Microsoft\Mail\Custom Commands.

   ```
   WGPOMgr1:REG_SZ:3.0;Mail;;13
   WGPOMgr2:REG_SZ:3.0;Mail;&Postoffice Manager...;14;WGPOM32.DLL;0;;
       Administer Workgroup
   ```

Current administrator:

4. Sign in to Schedule+, export your appointments, archive your data, and then exit Schedule+.

5. Sign in to Mail and export your folders.

6. Remove the present account of the future administrator.

7. Change the details of the postoffice administrator account (Name, Mailbox, Password, etc.) to those of the future administrator.

8. Create a new account for yourself, using the details from the old administrator account.

9. Exit and sign out of Mail.

10. Edit your Registry to remove the **WGPOMgr1** and **WGPOMgr2** entries from HKEY_CURRENT_USER\Software\Microsoft\Mail\Custom Commands.

11. Sign in to your new Mail account and import the folders that you exported.

12. Sign in to Schedule+ and import your appointments.

New administrator:

13. Sign in to your Mail account, which is now the postoffice administrator account, and import the folders that you exported.

14. Sign in to Schedule+ and import your appointments.

Packaging Objects with UNC Pointers

Windows NT supports the use of the uniform naming convention (UNC) inside packaged objects. This means that you can create an object with the Object Packager utility that includes a pointer to a file located on a network file share.

For example, instead of embedding a 1 MB Word for Windows document into a mail message, you can insert a packaged object that contains a UNC pointer to the document on the network share. When the message is received, the recipient can double-click on the icon created by Object Packager to connect to the share and load the Word for Windows document.

You can create a packaged object containing a UNC pointer to a Word document on a network share by following these steps:

1. In Mail, choose the Insert Object command from the Edit menu.

2. Choose Package from the Insert Object list. This starts Object Packager.

3. In Object Packager, choose the Command Line command from the Edit menu.

4. Type the UNC path and filename of the Word for Windows document file in the command box. For example, you can include something like the following:

   ```
   \\COMPUTER2\WORDDOCS\BUDGET.DOC
   ```

   If the network share requires a password, the recipient will have to know the password to retrieve the package.

5. Select the Insert Icon button, and choose one of the available icons for this object. Choose OK.

6. From the Edit menu, choose Label, and then type a descriptive label for the icon.

7. From the File menu, choose Exit. When asked if you want to update the Mail message, choose Yes.

8. Send the Mail message.

Questions and Answers About Mail

This section answers some common questions about Mail.

How much disk space does Mail's postoffice require?

You should allow approximately 2 MB of storage on the Mail server to start. As the Mail system is used, the amount of space it requires grows based on the number of users and the size of the messages and attachments being stored.

Is there a limit on the size or number of attachments in Mail?

There is a limit to the number of attachments, not the size. The constraint is the size of a single mail message (not including the size of any attachments). The sum (size of the message text in bytes) + (the number of attachments) must always be less than 32K—allowing for many more attachments than most users need to get their message across.

Will the Message Finder search attachments to my mail messages?

Not currently.

Can I retrieve deleted messages?

Mail doesn't actually purge deleted files; it moves them to a Deleted Mail folder. Deleted messages are not deleted until you empty the Deleted Mail folder or quit the program. You can also configure Mail not to delete messages when you quit the program (see the Options selection under the Mail menu).

How do I change my Postoffice location for the Mail client?

In the Registry, edit the **ServerPath** entry in
HKEY_CURRENT_USER\Software\Microsoft\Mail\Microsoft Mail
to redirect where Mail looks for the postoffice.

C H A P T E R   9

Microsoft Schedule+

Microsoft Schedule+ is an application that lets you plan and schedule meetings and appointments with others in your workgroup. It works together with Microsoft Mail to perform key functions, such as sending meeting-request messages to other workgroup members.

This chapter describes the components that make up Schedule+ and shows how the application works with Microsoft Mail. It also describes the custom message types used for Schedule+ and includes a section that answers common questions about Schedule+.

For a description of the features of Schedule+ and information about how to use the application, see the Schedule+ chapter in the *Windows NT System Guide*.

Overview of Schedule+ Architecture

Schedule+ is an example of a Mail-enabled application. It relies on Mail for certain functions, including support for logging on, accessing Mail's address book, and sending and receiving messages.

Because Schedule+ relies on Mail for key functionality, there is no special Schedule+ server. User account information for Mail is automatically translated to Schedule+ accounts.

Figure 9.1 illustrates the key components that make up Schedule+.

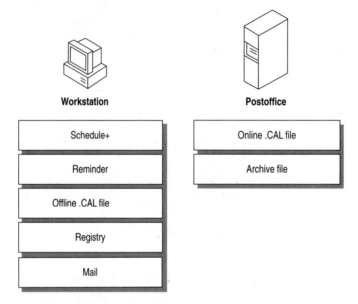

Figure 9.1 Overview of Schedule+

As shown in Figure 9.1, Schedule+ maintains both an online calendar and an offline calendar, so you can use Schedule+ as a stand-alone application or as a networked application. When you start Schedule+ offline, the local calendar file on your hard disk is read by the program. As you make changes to your calendar, those changes are written to disk immediately.

When you use Schedule+ online, it uses the online calendar (.CAL) file in the WGPO\CAL directory of the workgroup postoffice. When run online, Schedule+ uses Mail to send meeting messages and to provide name service and logon support.

A separate program, Reminder (MSRMND32.EXE), is used to notify you of Schedule+ appointments. This application is typically installed in the Windows NT Startup group and runs in the background (it can alternately be launched by Schedule+). When it is included in the Startup group, as soon as you log on to Windows NT you are prompted to supply your Mail logon name and password. The same logon is shared by Reminder, Schedule+, and Mail.

The next few sections discuss the components shown in Figure 9.1 that make up Schedule+.

Registry Entries

The Registry entries for Schedule+ and Mail are found in the following Registry paths:

```
HKEY_CURRENT_USER\Software\Microsoft\Schedule+
```

```
HKEY_CURRENT_USER\Software\Microsoft\Mail
```

In the Schedule+ entries you will find your preferences, such as colors and general options, and the location of your calendar files and archives. When Schedule+ uses Mail functionality, such as for logging on and using custom message types, Mail reads the necessary information from the Registry. SCHMSG32.DLL refers to the Mail entries in the Registry to find out how to launch Schedule+ when you choose the View Schedule button from within the Microsoft Mail client (this button is displayed when you read received meeting requests). For more information, see "Registry Entries for Microsoft Mail" and "Registry Entries for Microsoft Schedule+" in Chapter 14, "Registry Value Entries."

The access privileges you set for Schedule+ are not stored in the Registry. They are stored in your calendar (.CAL) file on the postoffice so that Schedule+ can check for the following types of information:

- When a person wants to look at or modify your calendar—what privileges have you assigned for that person to access your calendar?

- When someone is inviting you to a meeting—do you have an assistant, and what is the assistant's name?

Calendar Files

Schedule+ uses a calendar file, which contains scheduling information. Each user has an offline calendar file (named with the person's logon ID and a .CAL filename extension) and an online calendar file (also having a .CAL filename extension, but with a numeric filename). The offline file resides anywhere you want, by default in your SYSTEM32 directory. The online file location is determined by the Mail transport and resides in the CAL directory on the postoffice.

Whenever you want to access the schedules of another user on the postoffice, Schedule+ reads the data directly from the other user's online .CAL file. (You can prevent others from viewing, reading, or modifying your schedule by setting access privileges for the schedule.) When you schedule a meeting with another user, Schedule+ reads the data in the other user's .CAL file to display his or her busy times.

When you schedule an event with others, Schedule+ automatically creates a Request form that you can send to the others asking them to attend the meeting. For more information about the automatic Request and Response forms, see "Custom Message Types for Schedule+," later in this chapter

Merging Online and Offline Calendars

You can use your online calendar while your computer is connected to the Mail server. If you have an assistant, that person can also make changes to your online calendar. You can also use the offline calendar when the Mail server is unavailable or when you are away from the office.

When you work online, Schedule+ keeps your offline file synchronized with your online file. After you have worked offline and then start up online, Schedule+ merges the calendar files as follows:

- Schedule+ adds all of the appointments that you have added offline to the postoffice file.

- Schedule+ deletes all of the appointments that you have deleted offline from the postoffice file.

- When you change an existing appointment, the changes made to the local file always take precedence over the changes made to the postoffice file. If you change the text of an appointment offline and another person changes the start time, both changes will be applied because these changes are not in conflict. If you change the start time, end time, start date, end date, reminder notification time, or reminder notification date for an appointment, all of these attributes will be set to the values stored in the local file.

- When an overlap occurs as a result of merging the online and offline files, Schedule+ doesn't notify you specifically; instead, both appointments are entered in the calendar. For example, suppose you schedule an appointment on January 1 at noon while working offline and your Schedule+ assistant creates an appointment at the same time on the postoffice file. Because your assistant has authority to add to and modify your scheduled activities, it appears to Schedule+ that you made two changes to the schedule at the same time. Schedule+ enters both appointments in the merged calendar files.

Offsite Calendar Files

As with Microsoft Mail, you can work with Schedule+ offline at home or on a portable computer. You can take a copy of your Schedule+ files from your local computer to work with while you're away from the office.

To take your calendar home or on the road, choose the Move Local File command from the File menu to copy the calendar to a floppy disk. Then load Schedule+ on the destination computer and choose the Move Local File command again. The command moves the calendar file to the location you specify and changes a Registry entry in the Schedule+ key so that it points to your calendar in the new location.

Archiving Old Calendar Information

A calendar file full of scheduling information soon gets cumbersome. Archiving enables you to remove past data from your calendar and store the data for later reference. This minimizes disk space used on the postoffice without having to completely discard past Schedule+ data. You can open and view your archive file as if it were another appointment book.

Custom Message Types for Schedule+

When you invite people to attend a meeting or when you reserve a resource, Schedule+ automatically prepares a Request form. When you respond to someone else's meeting request, Schedule+ generates a Response form. This section describes the forms Schedule+ automatically generates and the custom message types associated with each.

Mail enables you to create and use custom message types to send specific kinds of messages, as described in Chapter 8, "Mail." Schedule+ uses this feature to define meeting requests, meeting responses, and meeting cancellations. In the Registry, Schedule+ defines five message types in the Mail\Custom Messages subkey in the Registry:

- Meeting Request
  (defined as message type IPM.Microsoft Schedule.MtgReq)
- Positive Meeting Response
  (message type IPM.Microsoft Schedule.MtgRespP)
- Negative Meeting Response
  (message type IPM.Microsoft Schedule.MtgRespN)
- Tentative Meeting Response
  (message type IPM.Microsoft Schedule.MtgRespA)
- Meeting Cancellation
  (message type IPM.Microsoft Schedule.MtgCncl)

These message types create special Request and Response forms that you can use to schedule meetings with others in your workgroup. For example, when you add a new appointment, choose a time, and specify attendees, the Send Request form shown in Figure 9.2 is displayed automatically.

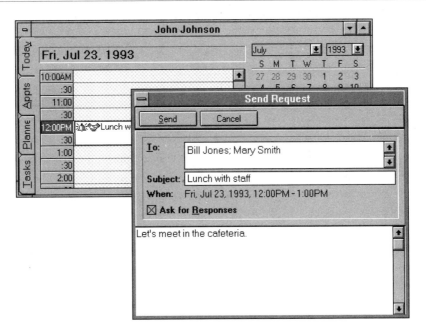

Figure 9.2 Send Request Form for Meeting Request

This message is deposited in the Outbox and sent to users just as any Mail message would be sent.

When a meeting attendee accepts the meeting, another automatic form, called the Response form, is generated and sent as a Mail message. Three variations of the Response form (Positive, Negative, and Tentative) are defined by custom message types defined by Schedule+. These three message types define the Response forms and a portion of the response message (such as "I might attend," shown in the Response form in Figure 9.3). They also add Yes:, No:, or Tentative: to the front of the original request title to create a response-message title. When the messages are displayed in the recipient's Messages window, these custom message types also display symbols (, **X**, or **?**) to the left of each message to make it easy to see responses at a glance.

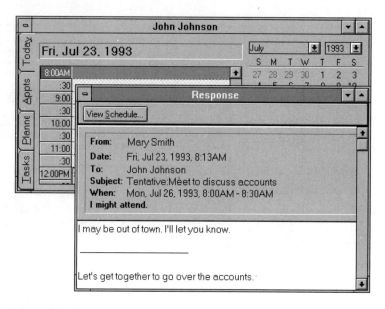

Figure 9.3 Response Forms for Meeting Requests

Because meeting messages are sent using Mail facilities, they can be viewed from within Schedule+ or from within Mail. Only one copy of each message is maintained, however, because what appear to be duplicates are really only pointers to the original. So when you delete the message in one view, it is also deleted in the other.

Schedule+ Interoperability

Schedule+ has a flexible architecture that makes communication with other schedule and calendar systems possible. Developers can modify their schedule and calendar software to share information with Schedule+ by using the Schedule+ Interchange format, described below.

The *Schedule+ Interchange* format is a text file with an .SCH extension. An interchange file can be imported to Schedule+ with the File/Import Appointments command; a Schedule+ calendar can be exported with the File/Export Appointments command. The file format supports importing and exporting projects, tasks, appointments, meetings, and notes.

Interchange Format Syntax

The Interchange format file begins with a header describing the owner of the file (the person to whom the schedule belongs) and when it was exported or created. The header is followed by descriptors for projects, tasks, notes, standard appointments, and recurring appointments. Although meetings are supported in the interchange format, they are not documented here. Meetings can be imported as standard appointments by the scheduling or calendar software that is exchanging data with Schedule+. The order of descriptors is not significant, except that projects must precede tasks.

The following section describes the syntax for individual descriptors.

If you export a Schedule+ calendar to the interchange format, you will find that each descriptor begins with a line defining a field called **aid**. This is an appointment ID defined and maintained by Schedule+; it should not be included in the import file.

Table 9.1   Key to Interchange Format Syntax

⌘ = tab	m = month or minute
italic = required input	d = day
nonitalic = fixed-field definitions	h = hour (24-hour format)
	y = year

Header
SCHEDULE+ EXPORT BY *mailbox name* ON *m/dd/yy* AT *hh:mm AM/PM*

Nonprivate Project
FixedAppt:
⌘ szText
project description
⌘ fTask ⌘ ⌘ ⌘ ⌘ ⌘ T
⌘ aidProject ⌘ ⌘ ⌘ ⌘ ⌘ ⌘ *project id # (integer, number in sequence)*
End

Private Project
FixedAppt:
⌘ szText
project description
⌘ aaplWorld ⌘ ⌘ ⌘ ⌘ ⌘ Read
⌘ fTask ⌘ ⌘ ⌘ ⌘ ⌘ T
⌘ aidProject ⌘ ⌘ ⌘ ⌘ ⌘ ⌘ *project id # (integer, number in sequence)*
End

> **Note** The **fTask** line is present for all projects; other lines, like the **aaplWorld** line above, are present only for private projects.

Standard Task

FixedAppt:
⌘ szText
task description
⌘ fTask ⌘ ⌘ ⌘ ⌘ ⌘ T
⌘ bpri ⌘ ⌘ ⌘ ⌘ ⌘ ⌘ *priority # (1–35, where 1–9 = priority 1–9 and 10–35 = priority A–Z)*
⌘ aidParent ⌘ ⌘ ⌘ ⌘ ⌘ ⌘ *project id # of associated project (integer)*
End

Standard Private Task

FixedAppt:
⌘ szText
task description
⌘ aaplWorld ⌘ ⌘ ⌘ ⌘ ⌘ Read
⌘ fTask ⌘ ⌘ ⌘ ⌘ ⌘ T
⌘ bpri ⌘ ⌘ ⌘ ⌘ ⌘ ⌘ *priority # (1–35, where 1–9 = priority 1–9 and 10–35 = priority A–Z)*
⌘ aidParent ⌘ ⌘ ⌘ ⌘ ⌘ ⌘ *project id # of associated project (integer)*
End

Task with Due Date and Start Work Date

FixedAppt:
⌘ dateStart ⌘ ⌘ ⌘ ⌘ ⌘ ⌘ *due date in format m-d-yyyy hh:mm*
⌘ dateEnd ⌘ ⌘ ⌘ ⌘ ⌘ ⌘ *due date in format m-d-yyyy hh:mm*
⌘ szText
task description
⌘ fTask ⌘ ⌘ ⌘ ⌘ ⌘ T
⌘ nAmtBeforeDeadline ⌘ ⌘ ⌘ ⌘ ⌘ ⌘ *integer # (with unit below, indicates start work before due date)*
⌘ tunitBeforeDeadline ⌘ ⌘ ⌘ ⌘ ⌘ *unit: Day, Week, or Month (indicates start work before due date)*
⌘ bpri ⌘ ⌘ ⌘ ⌘ ⌘ ⌘ *priority # (1–35, where 1–9 = priority 1–9 and 10–35 = priority A–Z)*
⌘ aidParent ⌘ ⌘ ⌘ ⌘ ⌘ ⌘ *project id # of associated project*
End

> **Note** The **dateStart** and **dateEnd** lines ask for *hh:mm*. This must be supplied but won't be used for these date-oriented (rather than time-oriented) tasks. *hh:mm* should be 00:00.

Standard Appointment, Marked Private

FixedAppt:

⌘ dateStart ⌘ ⌘ ⌘ ⌘ ⌘ ⌘ *start date and time in format m-d-yyyy hh:mm (time is 24 hour)*

⌘ dateEnd ⌘ ⌘ ⌘ ⌘ ⌘ ⌘ *end date and time in format m-d-yyyy hh:mm (time is 24 hour)*

⌘ szText

appointment description

⌘ aaplWorld ⌘ ⌘ ⌘ ⌘ ⌘ Read

End

Standard Appointment with Alarm

FixedAppt:

⌘ dateStart ⌘ ⌘ ⌘ ⌘ ⌘ ⌘ *start date and time in format m-d-yyyy hh:mm (time is 24 hour)*

⌘ dateEnd ⌘ ⌘ ⌘ ⌘ ⌘ ⌘ *end date and time in format m-d-yyyy hh:mm (time is 24 hour)*

⌘ szText

appointment description

⌘ dateNotify ⌘ ⌘ ⌘ ⌘ ⌘ ⌘ *specification of alarm in format m-d-yyyy hh:mm (time is 24 hour)*

⌘ nAmt ⌘ ⌘ ⌘ ⌘ ⌘ ⌘ *integer defining how long before an appointment the alarm should go off*

⌘ tunit ⌘ ⌘ ⌘ ⌘ ⌘ *the unit (Minute, Hour, Day, Week, Month) defining the alarm*

End

Note The **dateNotify** line asks for *hh:mm*. Place any time here; a value is required. The actual time used for the alarm is set in the **nAmt** and **tunit** lines. If the alarm is in minutes, the **tunit** line is not required.

Recurring Appointment

RecurAppt:

⌘ ymdStart ⌘ ⌘ ⌘ ⌘ ⌘ *start date of recurrence pattern in format m-d-yyyy*

⌘ ymdEnd ⌘ ⌘ ⌘ ⌘ ⌘ *end date of recurrence pattern in format m-d-yyyy*

⌘ wgrfValidMonths ⌘ ⌘ ⌘ ⌘ ⌘ *used to define recurrence pattern (see next section for detail)*

⌘ bgrfValidDows ⌘ ⌘ ⌘ ⌘ ⌘ ⌘ *used to define recurrence pattern (see next section for detail)*

⌘ trecur ⌘ ⌘ ⌘ ⌘ ⌘ ⌘ *used to define recurrence pattern (see next section for detail)*

⌘ timeStart ⌘ ⌘ ⌘ ⌘ ⌘ *start time in format hh:mm*

⌘ timeEnd ⌘ ⌘ ⌘ ⌘ ⌘ *end time in format hh:mm*

⌘ szText

Recurring appointment description
End

Note The **ymdEnd** line is required only if the recurring appointment has an end date. If it does not, omit the **ymdEnd** line. See the following section for more information about this type of entry.

Notes for One Month

MonthNotes:
⌘ *date of Note in format m-d-yyyy*
note #1 text
⌘ *date of Note in format m-d-yyyy*
note #2 text
End

Note All notes for the month are listed together in sequence.

Recurrence Patterns

The recurrence pattern is defined by three fields that, in combination, define the following recurrence patterns: daily, weekly, biweekly, monthly defined by a pattern, monthly defined by a date, yearly defined by a pattern, and yearly defined by a date.

The three fields used to define the recurrence types and patterns are describe in the following table.

Table 9.2   Recurrence Pattern Fields

Field	Description
wgrfValidMonths *bbbbbbbbbbbb*	Enumerates valid months of the year, where *bbbbbbbbbbbb* is 12 bits, each being either T or F and representing January through December.
	All bits are T in every recurrence type except yearly. In the yearly case, all but one bit will be F. The T bit indicates which month the yearly appointment falls into in either of the yearly recurrence patterns.

Table 9.2 Recurrence Pattern Fields *(continued)*

Field	Description
bgrfValidDows *bbbbbbb*	Enumerates valid days of the week where *bbbbbbb* is 7 bits, T or F, representing Sunday through Saturday. (Note that in this syntax the week always starts on Sunday regardless of the user's start of week designation in Schedule+ Options.) All bits are T in the case of a monthly or yearly recurrence defined by the specific date. In the daily-every weekday recurrence or the monthly or yearly recurrences defined as the *x* weekday, the first and seventh bits are F, and all others are T. In the monthly or yearly recurrence where field 2 is weekend day (see the description of fields below), the first and seventh bits are T and all others are F. In all other recurrence types, one or more bits are T to indicate the days of the week on which the appointment falls.
trecur [**Week** *bb* 0 | **IWeek** *bbbbb* 0 | **Date** *x*]	**trecur** is followed by one of these terms to describe the recurrence type: **Week** *bb* **0**—daily or weekly (*bb* is FF); **trecur** and **bgrfValidDows** are used in conjunction to define the daily or weekly recurrence. The days of the week are indicated as described above. **Week** *bb* **0**—biweekly (if *bb* is TF, this means even weeks; if *bb* is TT, this means odd weeks; based on the start day of the week); **trecur** and **bgrfValidDows** are used in conjunction to define the biweekly recurrence. **IWeek** *bbbbb* **0**—monthly or yearly, defined by a pattern instead of the date. If you look at the choices for the monthly recurrence in Schedule+, you'll see that the pattern is defined by two fields. For example, a monthly appointment can be on the first (field 1) weekday (field 2) of the month. The yearly pattern is defined by three fields. The first two are the same as the monthly fields, and field 3 is the month of the year. **IWeek** is followed by five bits with T or F; only one of these bits can be T. Field 2 of the monthly or yearly recurrence pattern is defined by **bgrfValidDows**. For example, if field 2 is a weekday, **bgrfValidDows** would be FTTTTTF. Field 3 in the yearly pattern is defined by **wgrfValidMonths**. **Date** *x*—monthly or yearly, defined by the date *x* (the day of the month, 1–31). If it is a monthly occurrence, all months are T in **wgrfValidMonths**. If it is a yearly occurrence, one month of the year is indicated by T in **wgrfValidMonths**, and the rest are F.

Sample Schedule+ Interchange Format File

SCHEDULE+ EXPORT BY user1 ON 9/16/1992 AT 10:44 amFixedAppt:
⌘ szText
Personal Projects
⌘ aaplWorld⌘ ⌘ ⌘ ⌘ ⌘ Read
⌘ fTask⌘ ⌘ ⌘ ⌘ ⌘ T
⌘ aidProject⌘ ⌘ ⌘ ⌘ ⌘ ⌘ 1
End
FixedAppt:
⌘ szText
pay bills (belongs to Personal Project)
⌘ aaplWorld⌘ ⌘ ⌘ ⌘ ⌘ Read
⌘ fTask⌘ ⌘ ⌘ ⌘ ⌘ T
⌘ bpri⌘ ⌘ ⌘ ⌘ ⌘ ⌘ 4
⌘ aidParent⌘ ⌘ ⌘ ⌘ ⌘ ⌘ 1
End
FixedAppt:
⌘ dateStart⌘ ⌘ ⌘ ⌘ ⌘ ⌘ 9-27-1992 12:00
⌘ dateEnd⌘ ⌘ ⌘ ⌘ ⌘ ⌘ 9-27-1992 12:00
⌘ szText
confirm presenters
⌘ fTask⌘ ⌘ ⌘ ⌘ ⌘ T
⌘ nAmtBeforeDeadline⌘ ⌘ ⌘ ⌘ ⌘ ⌘ 2
⌘ tunitBeforeDeadline⌘ ⌘ ⌘ ⌘ ⌘ Day
⌘ bpri⌘ ⌘ ⌘ ⌘ ⌘ ⌘ 1
⌘ aidParent⌘ ⌘ ⌘ ⌘ ⌘ ⌘ 2
End
FixedAppt:
⌘ dateStart⌘ ⌘ ⌘ ⌘ ⌘ ⌘ 10-17-1992 08:00
⌘ dateEnd⌘ ⌘ ⌘ ⌘ ⌘ ⌘ 10-17-1992 09:00
szText
meeting with John
⌘ dateNotify⌘ ⌘ ⌘ ⌘ ⌘ ⌘ 10-17-1992 08:00
⌘ nAmt⌘ ⌘ ⌘ ⌘ ⌘ ⌘ 1
⌘ tUnit⌘ ⌘ ⌘ ⌘ ⌘ Month
End

FixedAppt:
⌘ dateStart⌘ ⌘ ⌘ ⌘ ⌘ ⌘ 9-17-1992 14:00
⌘ dateEnd⌘ ⌘ ⌘ ⌘ ⌘ ⌘ 9-17-1992 15:30
⌘ szText
phone call with ABC Corp
⌘ aaplWorld⌘ ⌘ ⌘ ⌘ ⌘ Read
End
RecurAppt:
⌘ ymdStart⌘ ⌘ ⌘ ⌘ ⌘ 9-16-1992
⌘ wgrfValidMonths⌘ ⌘ ⌘ ⌘ ⌘ TTTTTTTTTTTT
⌘ bgrfValidDows⌘ ⌘ ⌘ ⌘ ⌘ ⌘ FFFTFFF
⌘ trecur⌘ ⌘ ⌘ ⌘ ⌘ Week FF 0
⌘ timeStart⌘ ⌘ ⌘ ⌘ ⌘ 16:30
⌘ timeEnd⌘ ⌘ ⌘ ⌘ ⌘ 17:30
szText
Weekly appointment without end date
End
RecurAppt:
⌘ ymdStart⌘ ⌘ ⌘ ⌘ ⌘ 9-01-1992
⌘ ymdEnd⌘ ⌘ ⌘ ⌘ ⌘ 6-01-1993
⌘ wgrfValidMonths⌘ ⌘ ⌘ ⌘ TTTTTTTTTTTT
⌘ bgrfValidDows⌘ ⌘ ⌘ ⌘ ⌘ ⌘ TTTTTTT
⌘ trecur⌘ ⌘ ⌘ ⌘ ⌘ Date 1
⌘ timeStart⌘ ⌘ ⌘ ⌘ ⌘ 16:30
⌘ timeEnd⌘ ⌘ ⌘ ⌘ ⌘ 17:30
szText
Monthly Appointment (the first of each month) with end date
End
MonthNotes:
⌘ 9-17-1992
call dentist
⌘ 10-31-1992
Halloween
End

Questions and Answers About Schedule+

This section answers some common questions about Schedule+:

Does Schedule+ support OLE or attachments (such as a meeting schedule)?

No, but Mail does. You can create a message to invite attendees to a meeting and refer them to a separate Mail message that includes OLE objects and/or attachments.

Does Schedule+ include all hours of each day as valid meeting times when the auto-pick feature is used to search for a meeting time?

To determine a meeting time, auto-pick only looks at weekdays (Monday–Friday) within the time defined by your start-work and end-work settings in the General Options command. Schedule+ looks only at the meeting initiator's settings to determine valid times. Schedule+ doesn't recognize the nonworking hours of other users, and you aren't able to define days other than Saturday or Sunday as nonworking days.

Does Schedule+ support recurring meetings? For example, I'd like to schedule a weekly meeting with my group.

Schedule+ supports recurring *appointments*, but not recurring *meetings*. Schedule+ also doesn't support recurring meeting requests. Instead, you must request the meeting for a single occurrence and then remind the attendees to use the Recurring Appointment command to enter it for each week. Alternately, you can ask everyone attending your weekly meeting to set up their own recurring appointment for that time each week.

Are there options for altering the time and date displays (for example, using a 24-hour clock or a European date format)?

Yes. From the Windows NT Control Panel, select the International icon. In the dialog box, you can specify the format used for the date and the time, which will affect the displays in Schedule+ also.

Does Schedule+ support customized reminder sounds?

Yes. You can modify the sound that is assigned to the Schedule+ Reminders in the Sound option in Control Panel. (You must have a suitable wave output device available.)

Because each resource requires a user account, does this mean that each resource requires a user license?

No. Microsoft's licensing is per computer running the software, not per user account used.

What are the dimensions of the print sizes in Schedule+?

The formats are designed to match the most popular appointment book sizes. They are the following:

- Standard = 8.5 inches by 11.5 inches
- Junior = 5.5 inches by 8.5 inches
- Pocket = 3.75 inches by 6.75 inches

Are meetings scheduled by somebody else distinguished in any way?

Yes. If you double-click an appointment created by someone else, the name of the person who created it will be indicated at the bottom of the appointment details. However, the appointment is not identified differently by an icon or special color in the appointment book.

How can I view or modify someone else's calendar?

Schedule+ enables you to grant access privileges to other users with the Set Access Privileges command from the Options menu. Once you have assigned privileges to another user, that user can view your calendar while signed in under his or her own account by choosing Open Other's Appt. Book from the File menu.

What is the difference between the "Modify" and the "Assistant" privileges?

The modify privilege is part of the set of privileges granted to your assistant. In addition to modifying privileges, the assistant can send meeting messages on your behalf by requesting a meeting while viewing your calendar. The assistant also receives meeting messages designated for you and can respond to them on your behalf.

When I specify someone as my Schedule+ assistant, do we both receive meeting messages for my meetings, or does only my assistant receive them?

You have the ability to specify either of the above. If you choose General Options from the Options menu, you will see a check box that specifies Send Meeting Messages Only To My Assistant.

Because I can view the meeting request messages from Mail or Schedule+, does this mean that there are actually two messages?

No. The Schedule+ Messages box and the Mail Inbox just provide two views of the same message. The message is only stored in one place. When you delete it from one view, it is deleted in the other.

PART IV

Windows NT Registry

Part Four explains the organization of the Windows NT Registry and how to use Registry Editor for configuration management in special cases. Chapter 14 contains an encyclopedia of Registry entry values, with definitions and explanations for setting these values.

C H A P T E R   1 0

Overview of the Windows NT Registry

Every MIS department or local system administrator must meet an enormous challenge in managing hardware, operating systems, and applications on PCs. In Windows NT, the Registry helps simplify the support burden by providing a secure, unified database that stores configuration data in a hierarchical form, so that system administrators can easily provide local or remote support, using the administrative tools in Windows NT.

This part of the *Windows NT Resource Guide* describes the Registry and shows how to use the information in the Registry for troubleshooting and configuration maintenance.

- This chapter presents background information about the structure and contents of the Registry.

- Chapter 11, "The Registry Editor and Registry Administration," provides details about using Registry Editor for viewing and editing Registry entries.

- Chapter 12, "Configuration Management and the Registry," provides specific problem-solving techniques using the Registry.

- Chapter 13, "Initialization Files and the Registry," describes how Windows NT uses files such as WIN.INI and CONFIG.SYS and how this information is mapped to the Registry.

- Chapter 14, "Registry Value Entries," lists the Registry values that can be used for tuning and troubleshooting the network, system components, and the user environment.

Caution Wherever possible, use the administrative tools such as Control Panel and User Manager to make configuration changes, rather than using Registry Editor. Using the administrative tools is safer because these applications know how to properly store values in the Registry. If you make errors while changing values with Registry Editor, you will not be warned, because Registry Editor does not understand or recognize errors in syntax or other semantics.

Getting Started with Registry Editor

To get the most out of the material in this chapter, you will want to run Registry Editor so that you can see the contents of the Registry for your computer. The Registry Editor application, REGEDT32.EXE, does not appear in any default program groups in Program Manager, but it is installed automatically when you install Windows NT or Windows NT Advanced Server on any computer.

▶ **To run Registry Editor**

1. Run REGEDT32.EXE from File Manager or Program Manager.

   Or type **start regedt32** from a command prompt, and press ENTER.

2. From the Options menu, choose the Read Only Mode command.

   This command will protect the Registry contents while you explore its structure and become familiar with the entries.

3. Double-click any folder icon to display the contents of that key.

For details about security and backup measures to take with the Registry and other issues, see Chapter 11, "Registry Editor and Registry Administration."

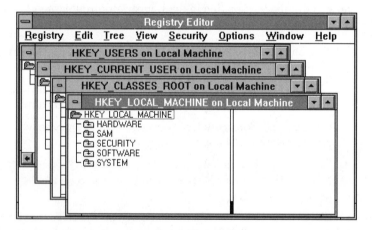

Figure 10 .1   The Registry Editor

Most simply, the Registry is a database, and Registry Editor displays the four subtrees used to access the contents of the database. The hierarchical structure that appears in Registry Editor is similar to how File Manager displays hierarchical directory structures. The information in this chapter will help you understand where specific kinds of information can be found in the Registry (and where you should or should not make changes).

In this chapter, the Registry keys are described in the order they appear in the Registry Editor windows, with a focus on the parts of the Registry where a system administrator might want to view or change entries. Some information is provided merely to explain what is stored in certain keys.

The content or location of a specific Registry key may differ from what is described in this *Resource Guide*, depending on which services and software are installed, whether a computer is running Windows NT or Windows NT Advanced Server, and other factors. However, the general organization described in this chapter will help you understand how to navigate the Registry.

Note Most Registry entries that you might need to examine or edit are found under HKEY_LOCAL_MACHINE\SYSTEM\CurrentControlSet, described later in this chapter. Specific entries are defined in Chapter 15, "Registry Value Entries."

How Windows NT Components Use the Registry

Under versions of Windows for MS-DOS, starting the system, connecting to the network, and running applications involves multiple configuration files with some form of synchronization between them. With Windows NT, the operating system stores and checks the configuration information at only one location—the Registry.

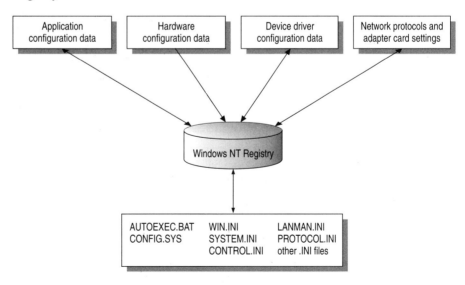

Figure 10.2   Data in the Windows NT Registry

The following figure shows how various Windows NT components and applications use the Registry. The numbered explanations below this illustration provide details.

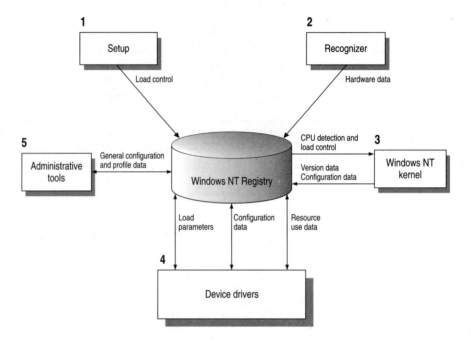

Figure 10.3   How Registry information Is Used by Windows NT

1. Whenever you run the Windows NT Setup program or other setup programs for applications or hardware, the Setup program adds new configuration data to the Registry. For example, new information is added when you install a new SCSI adapter or change the settings for your video display.

2. Each time you start a Windows NT computer, the Hardware Recognizer places hardware configuration data in the Registry. This information includes a list of hardware detected in your system. On *x*86-based computers, this is done by a program called NTDETECT.COM and the Windows NT Kernel (NTOSKRNL.EXE). On RISC-based computers, this information is extracted from the ARC firmware.

3. During system startup, NTOSKRNL extracts information from the Registry, such as the device drivers to load and their load order. NTOSKRNL also passes to the Registry information about the Kernel itself, such as its version number.

4. Device drivers send and receive load parameters and configuration data from the Registry. This data is similar to what you might find on the DEVICE= lines in the CONFIG.SYS file under MS-DOS. A device driver must report system resources that it uses, such as hardware interrupts and DMA channels, so that the system can add this information to the Registry. Applications and device drivers can read this Registry information to provide users with smart installation and configuration programs.

5. The administrative tools in Windows NT, such as those provided in Control Panel and in the Administrative Tools program group, can be used to modify configuration data. The Registry Editor is helpful for viewing and occasionally making detailed changes to the system configuration. You can also use WINMSD.EXE, the diagnostic tool for Windows NT, to view configuration information stored in the Registry. For details, see Chapter 11, "Registry Editor and Registry Administration."

The Registry is analogous to the .INI files used under Windows for MS-DOS, with each key in the Registry similar to a bracketed heading in an .INI file, and entries under the heading similar to values in the Registry. However, Registry keys can contain subkeys, while .INI files do not support nested headings. Registry values can also consist of executable code, rather than the simple strings representing values in .INI files. And individual preferences for multiple users of the same computer can be stored in the Registry, which is not possible with .INI files.

Although Microsoft discourages using .INI files in favor of using Registry entries, some applications (particularly 16-bit Windows-based applications) will continue using .INI files for the time being. Windows NT supports .INI files solely for compatibility with those applications and related tools (such as setup programs). Some form of the files AUTOEXEC.BAT and CONFIG.SYS also still exist to provide compatibility with applications created for MS-DOS and Windows 3.1. For details about how Windows NT uses such files in conjunction with the Registry, see Chapter 14, "Initialization Files and the Registry."

Registry Structure

This section describes the hierarchical organization of the Registry and defines the overall structure of keys, value entries, and hives. Following this section, details are provided about specific Registry keys.

The Registry Hierarchy

The Registry is structured as a set of four subtrees of keys that contain per-computer and per-user databases. The per-computer information includes information about hardware and software installed on the specific computer. The per-user information includes the information in user profiles, such as desktop settings, individual preferences for certain software, and personal printer and network settings. In versions of Windows for MS-DOS, per-computer information was saved in WIN.INI and SYSTEM.INI files, but it was not possible to save separate information for individual users.

In the Windows NT Registry, each individual key can contain data items called *value entries* and can also contain additional *subkeys*. In the Registry structure, keys are analogous to directories, and the value entries are analogous to files.

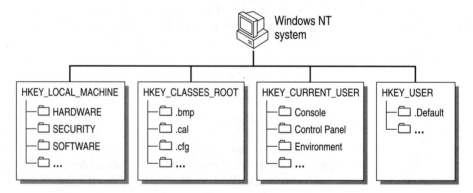

Figure 10.4   The Four Subtrees in the Windows NT Registry

The following table identifies and defines these four subtrees.

Table 10.1   Registry Subtrees

Root key name	Description
HKEY_LOCAL_MACHINE	Contains information about the local computer system, including hardware and operating system data such as bus type, system memory, device drivers, and startup control data.
HKEY_CLASSES_ROOT	Contains object linking and embedding (OLE) and file-class association data (equivalent to the Registry in Windows for MS-DOS).
HKEY_CURRENT_USER	Contains the user profile for the user who is currently logged on, including environment variables, personal program groups, desktop settings, network connections, printers, and application preferences.
HKEY_USERS	Contains all actively loaded user profiles, including HKEY_CURRENT_USER, which always refers to a child of HKEY_USERS, and the default profile. Users who are accessing a server remotely do not have profiles under this key on the server; their profiles are loaded into the Registry on their own computers.

Each of these subtrees is described in detail later in this chapter. Each of the root key names begins with "HKEY_" to indicate to software developers that this is a *handle* that can be used by a program. A handle is a value used to uniquely identify a resource so that a program can access it.

Value Entries in the Registry Keys

Registry data is maintained as value entries under the Registry keys. As shown in the following figure, Registry Editor displays data in two panes. The value entries in the right pane are associated with the selected key in the left pane.

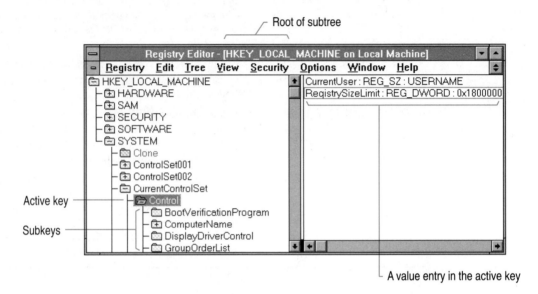

Figure 10.5   Structure of a Key in the Registry

A value entry has three parts: the name of the value, the data type of the value, and the value itself, which can be data of any length. The three parts of value entries always appear in the following order:

DependOnService: REG_MULTI_SZ: Tcpip Nbtsys Streams

A value entry cannot be larger than about 1 MB. Values from 0 to 0x7fffffff are reserved for definition by the system, and applications are encouraged to use these types. Values from 0x80000000 to 0xffffffff are reserved for use by applications.

The table below lists the data types currently defined and used by the system.

Table 10.2   Data Types for Registry Entries

Data type	Description
REG_BINARY	Raw binary data. Most hardware component information is stored as binary data, and can be displayed in Registry Editor in hexadecimal format, or displayed in WinMSD in an easy-to-read format. For example: `Component Information : REG_BINARY : 00 00 00...`
REG_DWORD	Data represented by a number that is 4 bytes long. Many parameters for device driver and services are this type and can be displayed in Registry Editor in binary, hex, or decimal format. For example, entries for service error controls are this type: `ErrorControl : REG_DWORD : 0x1`
REG_EXPAND_SZ	An expandable data string, which is text that contains a variable to be replaced when called by an application. For example, for the following value, the string *%SystemRoot%* will replaced by the actual location of the directory containing the Windows NT system files: `File : REG_EXPAND_SZ : %SystemRoot%\file.exe`
REG_MULTI_SZ	A multiple string. Values that contain lists or multiple values in human readable text are usually this type. Entries are separated by NULL characters. For example, the following value entry specifies the binding rules for a network transport: `bindable : REG_MULTI_SZ : dlcDriver dlcDriver non non 50`
REG_SZ	A sequence of characters representing human readable text. For example, a component's description is usually this type: `DisplayName : REG_SZ : Messenger`

Hives and Files

The Registry is divided into parts called *hives,* named by a Windows NT developer as an analogy for the cellular structure of a beehive. A hive is a discrete body of keys, subkeys, and values that is rooted at the top of the Registry hierarchy. A hive is backed by a single file and a .LOG file.

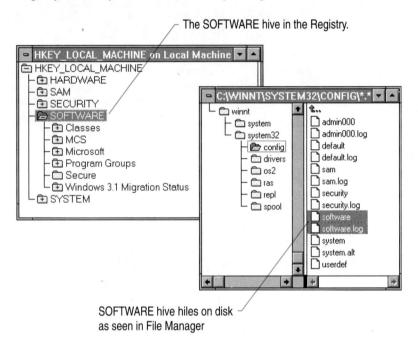

Figure 10.6 SOFTWARE Hive Files

The following table shows the standard hives for a Windows NT computer.

Table 10.3   Standard Hive Files

Registry hive	Filename
HKEY_LOCAL_MACHINE\SAM	SAM and SAM.LOG
HKEY_LOCAL_MACHINE\SECURITY	SECURITY and SECURITY.LOG
HKEY_LOCAL_MACHINE\SOFTWARE	SOFTWARE and SOFTWARE.LOG
HKEY_LOCAL_MACHINE\SYSTEM	SYSTEM and SYSTEM.ALT
HKEY_USERS\.DEFAULT\	DEFAULT and DEFAULT.LOG
HKEY_CURRENT_USER	*USER###* and *USER###.LOG* or ADMIN### and ADMIN###.LOG

By default, all hives are stored in the *SystemRoot*\SYSTEM32\CONFIG subdirectory, which also includes SYSTEM.ALT and the .LOG files that are backup hive files. The hive files for user profiles can be stored in other locations.

Atomicity and Hive Recovery in the Registry

The Registry ensures *atomicity* of individual actions. This means that any single change to a value to set, delete, or save values either works or does not work—even if the system goes down because of power failure, sudden hardware failure, or software problems. However, this applies for single changes. So, for example, if an application sets two value entries, A and B, and the system crashes while this change is being made, you might get new A or new B or both or neither. But you will not get a corrupted mix of old A and new A, or old B and new B. Also, the key containing A and B will have a size, time stamp, and other data that are consistent with what is actually there.

In this version of Windows NT, data is only written to the Registry when a *flush* occurs, which happens after changed data ages past a few seconds, or when an application intentionally flushes the data to the hard disk.

For all hives other than the System hive, this is the flush process:

1. Write all changed data into the hive's .LOG file along with a map of where it is in the hive. Then perform a file system flush on the .LOG file. It is now certain that all changed data is written in the .LOG file.

2. Mark the first sector of the hive file to indicate that the file is in transition.

3. Write the changed data into the hive file.

4. Mark the hive file as done.

If a system crash occurs between steps 2 and 4, when the hive is next loaded at startup (unless it's a profile, which is loaded at logon), the system will see the mark left in step 2, and proceed to recover the hive using the changes in .LOG file. So the .LOG files are not used if the hive is not in transition. If the hive is in transition, it cannot be loaded without the .LOG file.

There is a special case for System hive, because this is so important to starting the system and because it's used too early in startup to be recovered as described above. The SYSTEM and SYSTEM.ALT files are two full copies of the data. At flush time, changes are marked, written, and then marked as done, and then the same process is followed for SYSTEM.ALT. If the system crashes anywhere in this process, one of these files will be good. SYSTEM.ALT isn't that different from a .LOG file, except that at load time, rather than having to reapply the logged changes, the system just switches to SYSTEM.ALT. You don't need SYSTEM.ALT unless the System hive is in transition.

Each time a new user logs onto a computer, a new hive is created for that user. Because each user profile is a separate hive, each profile is also a separate file. User profile hives can be stored in other directories. The system administrator can copy a user profile as a file and view, repair, or copy entries using Registry Editor on another computer. For specific information about how to take advantage of this feature, see "Managing User Profiles Through the Registry" in Chapter 13, "Configuration Management and the Registry." For information about the hive for the default profile, see "HKEY_USERS" later in this chapter.

Registry Size Limits

The total amount of space that can be consumed by Registry data (the hives) is restricted by the Registry size limit, which is a kind of "global quota" for Registry space that prevents an application from filling the paged pool with Registry data. Registry size limits affect both the amount of paged pool the Registry can use and the amount of disk space.

You can view or set the value for **RegistrySizeLimit** under the following key:

```
HKEY_LOCAL_MACHINE\SYSTEM\CurrentControlSet\Control
```

RegistrySizeLimit must have a type of REG_DWORD and a data length of 4 bytes, or it will be ignored. By default, the Registry size limit is 25 percent of the size of the paged pool, which is 32 MB; so the default **RegistrySizeLimit** is 8 MB (which is enough to support about 5000 user accounts). Setting the **PagedPoolSize** value under the CurrentControlSet\Control\Session Manager\Memory Management key also affects the Registry size limit. The system ensures that the value for **RegistrySizeLimit** will be at least 4 MB and no greater than about 80 percent of the size of **PagedPoolSize.**

The **RegistrySizeLimit** limitations are approximate. The **PagedPoolSize** can be set to a maximum of 128 MB, so **RegistrySizeLimit** can be no larger than about 102 MB, supporting about 80,000 users (although other limits prevent a Registry this large from being very useful). Also, **RegistrySizeLimit** sets a maximum, not an allocation (unlike some similar limits in the system). Setting a large value for **RegistrySizeLimit** will not cause the system to use that much space unless it is actually needed by the Registry. A large value also does not guarantee that the maximum space will actually be available for use by the Registry.

The space controlled by **RegistrySizeLimit** includes the hive space, as well as some of the Registry's run-time structures. Other Registry run-time structures are protected by their own size limits or other means.

To ensure that a user can always at least start the system and edit the Registry if the **RegistrySizeLimit** is set wrong, quota checking is not turned on until after the first successful loading of a hive (that is, the loading of a user profile). For more details about **RegistrySizeLimit**, see its entry in Chapter 14, "Registry Value Entries."

HKEY_LOCAL_MACHINE

HKEY_LOCAL_MACHINE contains the configuration data for the local computer. The information in this database is used by applications, device drivers, and the Windows NT system to determine configuration data for the local computer, regardless of which user is logged on and what software is in use.

HKEY_LOCAL_MACHINE contains five subtrees, as listed briefly in the following table. The rest of this section describes these keys.

Table 10.4   Subtrees in HKEY_LOCAL_MACHINE

Subtree key name	Contents
HARDWARE	The database that describes the physical hardware in the computer, the way device drivers use that hardware, and mappings and related data that link kernel-mode drivers with various user-mode code. All data in this subtree is recreated each time the system is started.
	▪ The Description key describes the actual computer hardware.
	▪ The DeviceMap key contains miscellaneous data in formats specific to particular classes of drivers.
	▪ The ResourceMap key describes which device drivers claim which hardware resources. WinMSD can reports on its contents in an easy-to-read form.
SAM	The security information for user and group accounts, and for the domains in Windows NT Advanced Server. (SAM is the Security Account Manager.)
SECURITY	The database that contains the local security policy, such as specific user rights. This key is used only by the Windows NT security subsystem.
SOFTWARE	The per-computer software database. This key contains data about software installed on the local computer, along with various items of miscellaneous configuration data.
SYSTEM	The database that controls system startup, device driver loading, Windows NT services, and operating system behavior.

You can read information in any of these keys, but you can only add or change information in the SOFTWARE and SYSTEM keys.

By convention, if similar data exists under HKEY_CURRENT_USER and under HKEY_LOCAL_MACHINE, the data in HKEY_CURRENT_USER is considered to take precedence. However, values in this key may also extend (rather than replace) data in HKEY_LOCAL_MACHINE. Also, some items (such as device driver loading entries) are meaningless if they occur outside of HKEY_LOCAL_MACHINE.

HKEY_LOCAL_MACHINE\HARDWARE Subtree

The HKEY_LOCAL_MACHINE\HARDWARE subtree contains the hardware data in the Registry that is computed at system startup. This includes information about hardware components on the system board and about the interrupts hooked by specific hardware devices.

The Hardware key contains distinct and important sets of data in three subkeys—Description, DeviceMap, and ResourceMap.

All information in HKEY_LOCAL_MACHINE\HARDWARE is *volatile*, which means that the settings are computed each time the system is started and then discarded when the system is shut down. Applications and device drivers use this key to read information about the system components, store data directly into the DeviceMap section, and store data indirectly into the ResourceMap section.

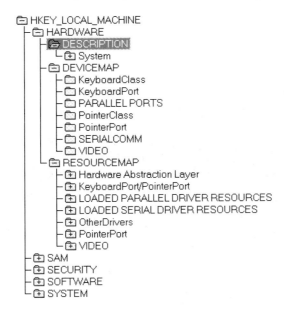

Tip Do not try to edit the data in HKEY_LOCAL_MACHINE\HARDWARE; much of the information appears in binary format, making it difficult to decipher.

To view data about a computer's hardware in an easy-to-read format for troubleshooting, run WinMSD, and choose the Devices button. WinMSD extracts the information from the Registry and renders it in a more readable format.

The Description, DeviceMap, and ResourceMap subkeys are described in the following sections.

Description Subkey

The Description subkey under HKEY_LOCAL_MACHINE\HARDWARE displays information from the hardware database built by the firmware, NTDETECT, and the Executive itself:

- If the computer is a RISC-based computer, this database is a copy of the ARC configuration database taken from the firmware.

- If the computer is an x86-based computer, this database contains the data found by the Hardware Recognizer, which is a program that runs as part of the Windows NT startup sequence. The Hardware Recognizer on x86-based computers is NTDETECT.COM.

- If the target computer is not PC-compatible, the OEM provides its own version of NTDETECT.COM as the Hardware Recognizer.

The Hardware Recognizer for x86-based computers detects the following:

Bus/adapter type	Machine ID	Mouse
Keyboard	Video adapter	Floppy drives
SCSI adapters	Floating point coprocessor	Parallel ports
Communication ports		

Network adapter cards are not detected as part of startup but are instead detected during Windows NT Setup or if you choose the Network icon in Control Panel to install a new network adapter. For details, see "Network Settings in the Registry," later in this chapter.

The *MultifunctionAdapter* subkey under the Description key contains several subkeys, each corresponding to specific bus controllers on the local computer. Each of these subkeys describes a class (or type) of controller, including controllers for disk drives, display, keyboard, parallel ports, pointing devices, serial ports, and SCSI devices. The subkey's path describes the type of component. The numbering for hardware components is 0-based, which means that, for example, the first (or only) disk controller appears under the 0 subkey.

The name of the *MultiFunctionAdapter* key depends on the bus type. For example, the subkey name for ISA and MCA buses appears as MultiFunctionAdapter. For EISA buses, the key name is EisaAdapter, and for TurboChannel buses, the name can be TcAdapter.

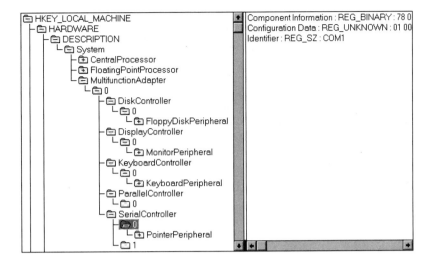

For each detected hardware component, the optional **Component Information** and **Configuration Data** value entries store version and configuration data in binary format. The **Identifier** entry contains the name of a component, if specified. For details about these entries, see "Registry Entries for Device Drivers" in Chapter 14, "Registry Value Entries."

DeviceMap Subkey

Under HKEY_LOCAL_MACHINE\HARDWARE\DeviceMap, each *Device* subkey contains one or more values to specify the location in the Registry for specific driver information for that kind of component.

The following illustration shows an example of the DeviceMap subkey and the value entry for a selected device name.

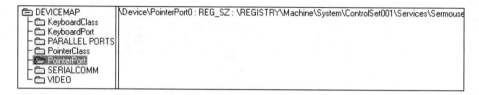

The value for each *Device* subkey describes an actual port name or the path for a *Service* subkey in HKEY_LOCAL_MACHINE\SYSTEM\ControlSet*nnn*\Services, which contains information about a device driver. That *Service* subkey contains the information a system administrator might need for troubleshooting and is also the information presented about the device in WinMSD.

The following shows DeviceMap entries for a computer that has multiple SCSI adapters.

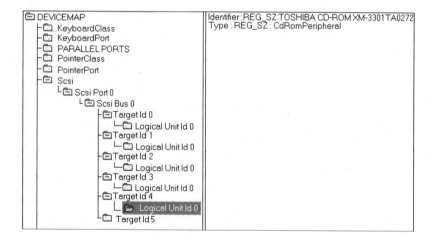

ResourceMap Subkey

The ResourceMap subkey under HKEY_LOCAL_MACHINE\HARDWARE maps device drivers to resources that the drivers use. Each ResourceMap subkey contains data reported by the device driver about its use of I/O ports, I/O memory addresses, interrupts, DMA channels and so on. The data in the ResourceMap subkey is volatile, so this subkey is recreated each time you start Windows NT.

Under the ResourceMap subkey, there are *DeviceClass* subkeys for the general class (or type) of devices. Each of these subkeys contains one or more *DriverName* subkeys with information about a specific driver. For example, in the following illustration, Sermouse is the *DriverName* subkey under the PointerPort *DeviceClass* subkey. (The driver names in these subkeys match the services listed in HKEY_LOCAL_MACHINE\SYSTEM\CurrentControlSet\Services.)

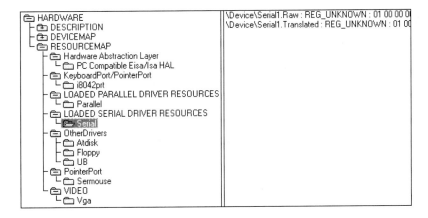

Tip If you need to resolve resource conflicts, use WinMSD to view the data from these subkeys in an easily readable format.

HKEY_LOCAL_MACHINE\SAM Subtree

The HKEY_LOCAL_MACHINE\SAM subtree contains the user and group account information in the Security Account Manager (SAM) database for the local computer. For a computer that is running Windows NT Advanced Server, this key also contains security information for the domain. This information is what you see in User Manager, and it also appears in the lists of users and groups when you use the Security menu commands in File Manager.

This key is mapped to HKEY_LOCAL_MACHINE\SECURITY\SAM, so changes made in one key automatically appear in the other key.

If you want to change user account or global group account information, use User Manager or User Manager For Domains to add or remove users or to change information about any account.

Caution The information in this database is in binary format and should not be changed using Registry Editor. Errors in this database may prevent users from being able to log on to the computer—which is another reason why system administrators should not allow typical users to log on as members of the Administrator group.

System Administrators can use User Manager or User Manager For Domains to change security information for the local computer or for the domain.

HKEY_LOCAL_MACHINE\SECURITY Subtree

The HKEY_LOCAL_MACHINE\SECURITY subtree contains security information for the local computer, including user rights, password policy, and the membership of local groups, as set in User Manager.

The subkey HKEY_LOCAL_MACHINE\SECURITY\SAM is mapped to HKEY_LOCAL_MACHINE\SAM, so changes made in one key automatically appear in the other key.

If you want to change global group membership or other security-related items, use User Manager or User Manager For Domains.

Caution The information in this database is in binary format and should not be changed using Registry Editor. Errors in this database may prevent users from being able to log on to the computer.

HKEY_LOCAL_MACHINE\SOFTWARE Subtree

The HKEY_LOCAL_MACHINE\SOFTWARE subtree contains specific configuration information about software on the local computer. The entries under this handle, which apply for anyone using this particular computer, show what software is installed on the computer and also define file associations and OLE information. The HKEY_CLASSES_ROOT handle is an alias for the subtree rooted at HKEY_LOCAL_MACHINE\SOFTWARE\Classes.

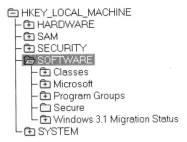

```
HKEY_LOCAL_MACHINE
├─ HARDWARE
├─ SAM
├─ SECURITY
├─ SOFTWARE
│   ├─ Classes
│   ├─ Microsoft
│   ├─ Program Groups
│   ├─ Secure
│   └─ Windows 3.1 Migration Status
└─ SYSTEM
```

This key contains, for example, the information you add by using the Associate command in File Manager, information added during installation for specific Windows-based applications, and information about applications installed with Windows NT.

The HKEY_LOCAL_MACHINE\SOFTWARE subtree contains several subkeys. The Classes, Program Groups, and Secure subkeys are described here, plus general information about the various *Description* subkeys that might appear in a Registry.

The key HKEY_LOCAL_MACHINE\SOFTWARE\Microsoft and its subkey named Windows NT\CurrentVersion are of particular interest. These subkeys contain information about software that supports services built into Windows NT, as well as data about the version and type of the current release (multiprocessor versus uniprocessor). For example, it is possible to run a Windows NT uniprocessor kernel on a multiprocessor computer, but you don't get any multiprocessor benefits by doing so. To quickly check which kernel type is running on a computer, see the data in the Registry under the Windows NT\CurrentVersion subkey.

Classes Subkey

The Classes subkey defines types of documents, providing information on filename-extension associations and OLE information that can be used by Windows shell applications and OLE applications. HKEY_CLASSES_ROOT displays the same information as stored under this subkey.

Important The OLE information must be created by the specific application, so you should not change this information using Registry Editor. If you want to change filename-extension associations, use the Associate command in File Manager.

The Classes subkey contains two kinds of subkeys:

- Filename-extension subkeys, which specify the application associated with files that have the selected extension, as shown in the following illustration.

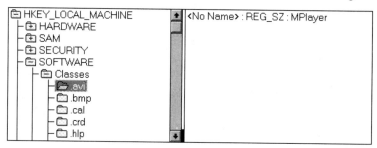

- Class-definition keys, which specify the shell and OLE properties of a class (or type) of document. These subkeys can describe shell and protocol properties for each class of document. If an application supports DDE, the Shell subkey can contain Open and Print subkeys that define DDE commands for opening and printing files, similar to the OLE and DDE information stored in the registry database under versions of Windows for MS-DOS. In the following example, **cardfile.exe /p %1** is the print command, and the **%1** parameter stands for the selected filename in File Manager when the command is carried out.

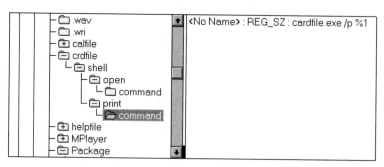

Description Subkeys

The various HKEY_LOCAL_MACHINE\SOFTWARE*Description* subkeys contain the names and version numbers of the software installed on the local computer. (Information about the configuration of these applications is stored on a per-user basis under HKEY_CURRENT_USER.)

During installation, applications record this information in the following form:

```
HKEY_LOCAL_MACHINE\SOFTWARE\<CompanyName>\<ProductName>\<Version>
```

The following example shows some entries under the subkey for Microsoft (a *CompanyName*), which contains entries for the service software installed on the computer:

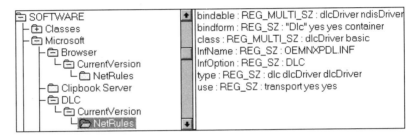

Note   The information in each subkey is added by the related application. Do not edit entries in these subkeys unless directed to do so by your application vendor.

Program Groups Subkey

The Program Groups subkey under HKEY_LOCAL_MACHINE\SOFTWARE contains the common program groups—that is, those used in common by all users of the local computer. (The program groups for an individual user can be viewed under HKEY_CURRENT_USER, and the default personal program groups can be viewed in HKEY_USERS\.DEFAULT.) Each subkey under the Program Groups subkey is the name of a common program group, and its value is binary data describing that program group.

If you want to change the content of common program groups, use the menu commands or mouse techniques provided in Program Manager, or the User Profile Editor in Windows NT Advanced Server.

Secure Subkey

The Secure subkey provides a convenient place for applications to store configuration information that should not be changed by anyone except an administrator.

HKEY_LOCAL_MACHINE\SYSTEM Subtree

All startup-related data that must be stored (rather than computed during startup) is saved in the System hive. A complete copy of the data is also stored in SYSTEM.ALT. The data in HKEY_LOCAL_MACHINE\SYSTEM—which is the System hive—is organized into control sets that contain a complete set of parameters for devices and services as described in this section. You may occasionally need to change entries in the CurrentControlSet subkey, as described in Chapter 12, "Configuration Management and the Registry."

The following example shows the structure of this key:

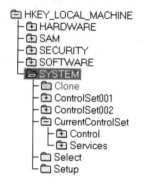

The following sections describe the HKEY_LOCAL_MACHINE\SYSTEM subkeys.

Select, ControlSetnnn, and CurrentControlSet Subkeys

The Registry, particularly data in the System hive, is essential to starting the system. To help ensure that the system can always be started, a kind of backup version is kept, which allows for an Undo of any configuration changes that did not have the intended effect. This section describes how it works.

All of the data required to control startup is gathered into subtrees called control sets in the Registry. Each control set has two parts, a Control key and a Services key. The Control key contains various data items used to control the system, including such things as the computer's network name and the subsystems to start. The Services key contains a list of drivers, file systems, user-mode service programs, and virtual hardware keys. Its data controls the services (drivers, file systems, and so on) to be loaded and their load order. The data in the Services key also controls how the services call each other.

Multiple control sets are saved as subtrees of HKEY_LOCAL_MACHINE
\SYSTEM under names such as ControlSet001 and ControlSet003. Although as
many as four control sets can appear, there are usually two sets. This is similar to
having multiple sets of CONFIG.SYS files under MS-DOS — a current one and a
backup copy known to start the system correctly. However, the work for creating
and maintaining backups is all done automatically by the system.

The Select key describes how the control sets are used in four value entries:

- **Default** specifies the number of the control set (for example, 001 =
  ControlSet001) that the system will use at next startup, barring an error or
  manual invocation by the user of the LastKnownGood control set.

- **Current** specifies the number of the control set actually used to start the
  system this time.

- **LastKnownGood** specifies the number of the control set that is a clean copy
  of the last control set that actually worked.

- **Failed** specifies the control set that was replaced if the LastKnownGood
  control set was used to start the system this time. You can examine this
  control set to learn why the replacement was required.

The CurrentControlSet key is not the root of an actual control set; rather, it is a
symbolic link to the control set indicated by the value of **Current**. It's there so
that constant paths can be used to refer to keys in the currently used control set,
even though the name of that control set may change.

These multiple control sets are used to allow escape from various problems. Each
time the system starts, the control set used to actually start up is saved away
(under Clone). If the startup is declared "good," the old LastKnownGood control
set is discarded, and the Clone subtree is copied to replace it. Administrators can
change how system startup is declared "good," but usually it means no Severe or
Critical errors in starting services and at least one successful logon.

If system startup fails in certain ways or if the user chooses LastKnownGood
from the Configuration Recovery menu, the LastKnownGood control set will be
used to start the system instead of the Default control set. The Default set will
be reserved as Failed, and the LastKnownGood set cloned to make a new
LastKnownGood set. The LastKnownGood set becomes the new Default set. The
effect of all of this is to undo all changes to configuration data stored in a control
set since the last time a startup was declared "good." (User profile data is stored
elsewhere and is therefore unaffected by this.)

> **Tip** You can choose from among control sets on a computer by pressing the
> SPACEBAR immediately after selecting Windows NT at the Boot Loader prompt.
> A message asks if you want to choose to start the system using the current control
> set or the last known good configuration.
>
> To find out whether Default or Last Known Good was used, see the values in the
> Select key.

You can modify the information stored in these subkeys by choosing the Devices,
Network, Server, and Services icons in Control Panel, or by using Server Manager
in Windows NT Advanced Server.

If you need to modify the configuration in Registry Editor, make changes under
the CurrentControlSet subkey.

The Control and Services keys found in each control set are described in the
following sections.

Control Subkey for All Control Sets

The Control subkey contains startup parameters for the system, including
information about the subsystems to load, computer-dependent environment
variables, the size and location of the paging files, and so on. The following
illustration shows the typical Control subkeys, and Table 10.5 describes the
contents of some typical subkeys.

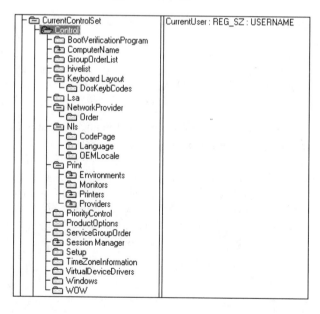

Table 10.5   Typical Subkeys in the Control Key for All Control Sets

Subkey	Contents
BootVerificationProgram	A value that can be set to define a nonstandard mechanism to declare system startup as "good," as described in Chapter 12, "Configuration Management and the Registry."
ComputerName	The names of the default and active computers, stored in two subkeys, ComputerName and ActiveComputerName. The computer name should be set using the Network icon in Control Panel.
GroupOrderList	Specifies the order to load services for all groups that have one, used in combination with Tags. ServiceGroupOrder specifies the order for loading groups.
ServiceGroupOrder	Specifies the order to load various groups of services. Order within groups is specified using Tags and GroupOrderList.
HiveList	The location of the files that contain Registry information. This value should be maintained only by the system.
Keyboard Layout	The DLLs for the keyboard language used as the default layout, plus a subkey named DosKeybCodes that lists the other available keyboard layouts. Settings for keyboard layout should be set by using the International icon in Control Panel.
Lsa	The authentication package for the local security authority. This value should be maintained only by the system—errors may prevent anyone from being able to log on to the computer.
NetworkProvider	Two subkeys, Active and Order, that specify the network provider and the order in which to load providers. Settings for network providers should be set by choosing the Network icon in Control Panel.
Nls	Information on national language support in three subkeys: CodePage, Language, and OEMLocale. Preferences about language and locale in Windows NT should be set using the International icon in Control Panel.

Table 10.5   Typical Subkeys in the Control Key for All Control Sets *(continued)*

Subkey	Contents
Print	Information about the current printers and printing environment, contained in several subkeys:
	▪ Environments, which contains subkeys defining drivers and print processors for system environments such as Windows NT Alpha_AXP, Windows NT R4000, and Windows NT x86.
	▪ Monitors, which can contain subkeys with data for specific network printing monitors.
	▪ Printers, which can contain subkeys describing printer parameters for each installed printer.
	▪ Providers, which can contain subkeys describing DLLs for network print services.
	Printing parameters should be changed by using Print Manager.
PriorityControl	The Win32 priority separation. This value should be set only by using the System icon in Control Panel.
ProductOptions	The product type, such as Winnt. These values should be maintained only by the system.
Session Manager	Global variables used by Session Manager and these keys:
	▪ DOS Devices, which defines the MS-DOS devices AUX, MAILSLOT, NUL, PIPE, PRN, and UNC.
	▪ Environment, which defines the **ComSpec, Path, Os2LibPath,** and **WinDir** variables. User environment variables can be set using the System icon in Control Panel. If you want to change or add to the computer's default path, or add default system environment variables, you must change values in this subkey. For an example, see Chapter 14, "Registry Value Entries."
	▪ FileRenameOperations, which are used during startup to rename certain files so that they can be replaced. These values should be maintained only by the system.
	▪ KnownDLLs, which defines the directories and filenames for the Session Manager DLLs. These values should be maintained only by the system.
	▪ MemoryManagement, which defines paging options. The paging file should be defined by using the System icon in Control Panel.
	▪ SubSystems, which defines information for the Windows NT subsystems. These values should be maintained only by the system.

Table 10.5   Typical Subkeys in the Control Key for All Control Sets *(continued)*

Subkey	Contents
Setup	Hardware setup options. These values should be maintained only by the system. Users can make choices by running Windows NT Setup.
TimeZoneInformation	Values for time zone information. These settings should be set by using the Date/Time icon in Control Panel.
VirtualDeviceDrivers	Virtual device drivers. These values should be maintained only by the system.
Windows	Paths for the Windows NT directory and system directory. These values should be maintained only by the system.
WOW	Options for 16-bit Windows applications running under Windows NT. These settings should be maintained only by the system.

Services Subkey for All Control Sets

The Services subkey in each control set lists all of the Kernel device drivers, file system drivers, and Win32 service drivers that can be loaded by the Boot Loader, the I/O Manager, and the Service Control Manager. The Services subkey also contains subkeys that are static descriptions of hardware to which drivers can be attached. Table 10 .6 describes some typical Services subkeys for a Windows NT computer.

Entries that appear under the DeviceMap subkeys include values that refer to entries in the Services subkey in the control set. For example, for a serial mouse, the following entry might appear under the DeviceMap\PointerPort subkey in HKEY_LOCAL_MACHINE\HARDWARE:

```
\Device\PointerPort0 : \REGISTRY\Machine\System\ControlSet001
    \Services\Sermouse
```

A related Services subkey named Sermouse will define values for the serial mouse driver. For example:

To view this information in an easily readable format, run WinMSD, and then choose the Drivers button and review details about a selected driver. You can choose the Devices icon in Control Panel to change startup and other information for a driver. For suggestions about how a system administrator can use this information for troubleshooting, see Chapter 12, "Configuration Management and the Registry."

Each subkey includes several standard (but optional) entries as shown in the following example, where Alerter is the name of a service that appears in the Services Control database.

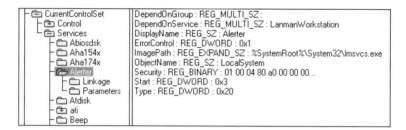

The value entries that govern the behavior of a service include **ErrorControl, Group, DependOnGroup, DependOnService, ImagePath, ObjectName, Start, Tag,** and **Type.** For definitions of these value entries, see "CurrentControlSet \Services Subkeys" in Chapter 14, "Registry Value Entries."

The optional Linkage subkey specifies the binding options for the driver using the **Bind** and **Export** values. The **OtherDependencies** value that appears in the Linkage subkey for some services allows nodes to be loaded in an order related to other specific nodes with which they are closely associated. For example, the NBF transport depends on an NDIS driver. Therefore, to load the NBF protocol stack successfully, an NDIS network card driver must be loaded first. For details about loading order dependencies for network components, see "Dependency Handling for Network Components," later in this chapter.

The Parameters subkey (optional for some Services subkeys such as an adapter entry) contains a set of values to be passed to the driver. These values vary for each device driver. The following shows parameters for the serial mouse driver.

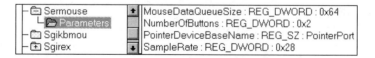

Because the entries in the Services list are Registry keys, no assumptions can be made about their order in an enumeration, so services can explicitly specify load ordering by grouping services and drivers in order by type. For example, the SCSI port driver can be loaded before any of the miniport drivers. The ordering is specified under the \Control\ServiceGroupOrder subkey in a control set.

Settings for the drivers that appear under the Services subkeys can be changed using the Devices, Network, or Services icons in Control Panel or, for network services, User Manager For Domains in Windows NT Advanced Server. Specific parameters for drivers and services are described in Chapter 14, "Registry Values Entries."

Table 10.6 Descriptions of Typical Services Subkeys for a Windows NT Computer

Service name	Description
Abiosdsk	Primary disk[1]
Aha*xxx*	Adaptec SCSI adapters[1]
Alerter	Alerter service for the workstation[3]
AtDisk	Primary disk driver for non-SCSI hard disks[1]
Ati	ATI video display[1]
Beep	Base sound driver[1]
Bowser	Network[1]
Browser	Computer browser used by Workstation and Server services[3]
BusLogic	BusLogic SCSI adapter[1]
Busmouse	Bus mouse pointer[1]
Cdaudio	Filter[1]
Cdfs	SCSI CD-ROM class file system driver[1]
Cdfs_Rec	Recognizer for SCSI CD-ROM class file system[1]
Cirrus	Cirrus Logic video display[1]
ClipSrv	ClipBook (NetDDE service)[3]
Cpqarray	Compaq array driver (no additional Registry values)
Dell_DGX	Dell DGX video display[1]
Diskperf	Filter[1]
DLC	DLC transport[2]
DptScsi	DPT SCSI adapter[1]
Et4000	Tseng ET4000 video display[1]
EventLog	Event log service[3]
Fastfat	FAT boot file system driver[1]
Fat_Rec	Recognizer for FAT boot file system[1]

1 Change settings for this driver using the Devices icon in Control Panel.

2 Change settings for this driver using the Network icon in Control Panel.

3 Change settings for this driver using the Services icon in Control Panel or using Server Manager in Windows NT Advanced Services.

Table 10.6   Descriptions of Typical Services Subkeys. . . *(continued)*

Service name	Description
Fd16_700	Future Domain MCS 600/700, TMC-7000ex, 800-series SCSI adapters[1]
Floppy	Primary disk[1]
Ftdisk	Filter[1]
Hpfs_Rec	Recognizer for HPFS boot file system[1]
i8042pt	Keyboard driver[1]
Inport	Microsoft InPort Mouse pointer[1]
Jazzg*xxx*	Video display[1]
Jzvxl484	Video display[1]
Kbdclss	Keyboard class driver[1]
LanmanServer	Server service[3]
Lanman Workstation	Workstation service[3]
Messenger	Messenger service for workstation[3]
Mouclass	Mouse class driver[1]
Mup	Network[1]
Nbf	NetBEUI transport protocol[1,2]
Ncr*xxx*	NCR SCSI controllers and adapters[1]
NetBIOS	NetBIOS transport interface[1,2]
NetDDE et al.	Network DDE and Network DDE DSDM[3]
NetDetect	Network detection[1]
NetLogon	Network logon for workstation[3]
Ntfs	NTFS file system driver[1]
Nfts_Rec	Recognizer for NTFS file system[1]
Null	Base driver for null port[1]
Oliscsi	Olivetti SCSI adapter[1]
Parallel	Parallel port[1]
Pinball	HPFS file system driver[1]
Qvision	Qvision video display driver[1]
RAS	Remote Access Service[3]
Rdr	Network redirector[1]

[1] Change settings for this driver using the Devices icon in Control Panel.

[2] Change settings for this driver using the Network icon in Control Panel.

[3] Change settings for this driver using the Services icon in Control Panel or using Server Manager in Windows NT Advanced Services.

Table 10.6   Descriptions of Typical Services Subkeys. . . *(continued)*

Service name	Description
Replicator	Directory replicator for workstation and server[3]
RPCLocator	Remote Procedure Call (RPC) locator (name service provider)[3]
RPCSS	Remote Procedure Call (RPC) service[3]
S3	S3 video display[1]
Schedule	Network schedule service[3]
Scsi*xxx*	SCSI class devices, which do not add parameters to the Registry, including Scsicdrm, Scsidisk, Scsiflip, Scsiprnt, and Scsiscan
Serial	Serial port[1]
Sermouse	Serial mouse[1]
Sgikbmou	Silicon Graphics keyboard and mouse driver[1]
Sgirex	Silicon Graphics video display driver[1]
Simbad	Filter[1]
Sparrow	SCSI adapter[1]
Spock	SCSI adapter[1]
Srv	Network server[3]
T128, T13B	Trantor SCSI adapters[1]
Trident	Trident video display[1]
UB*xxx*	Ungermann-Bass NDIS drivers[1,3]
Ultra*xxx*	UltraStore SCSI adapters[1]
UPS	Uninterruptible power supply (UPS)[3,4]
V7vram	Video Seven VRAM video display[1]
Vga	VGA video display[1]
Videoprt	Video display[1]
Wd33c93	Maynard SCSI adapter[1]
Wdvga	Western Digital/Paradise video display[1]
Xga	IBM XGA video display[1]

[1] Change settings for this driver using the Devices icon in Control Panel.

[2] Change settings for this driver using the Network icon in Control Panel.

[3] Change settings for this driver using the Services icon in Control Panel or using Server Manager in Windows NT Advanced Services.

[4] Change settings for this driver using the UPS icon in Control Panel.

Setup Subkey

The Setup subkey under HKEY_LOCAL_MACHINE\SYSTEM is used internally by Windows NT for the setup program. Do not change these value entries. These settings should be maintained only by the system.

HKEY_CLASSES_ROOT

HKEY_CLASSES_ROOT contains information about file associations and OLE. As shown in the following illustration, this is the same data as in the Classes subkey under HKEY_LOCAL_MACHINE\SOFTWARE.

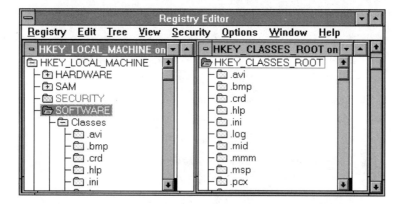

The sole purpose for HKEY_CLASSES_ROOT is to provide compatibility with the Windows 3.1 registration database.

As with Windows for MS-DOS, the Windows NT File Manager includes an Associate dialog box for associating a filename extension with a specific application. Windows NT stores these associations in the Windows NT Registry. The Associate dialog box should be used whenever possible to define filename associations.

HKEY_CURRENT_USER

HKEY_CURRENT_USER contains the database that describes the user profile for the user who is currently logged on the local computer. A user profile contains information that defines the appearance and behavior of the individual user's desktop, network connections, and other environment settings. A user profile ensures that Windows NT will look and act the same at any computer where that user logs on, if that person's profile is available at that computer or on the same domain in Windows NT Advanced Server.

HKEY_CURRENT_USER contains all the information necessary to set up a particular user environment on the computer. Information such as program groups, application preferences, screen colors, and other personal preferences and security rights are included. Many of these settings are the same kind of information that was stored in the WIN.INI file under Windows for MS-DOS.

HKEY_CURRENT_USER includes the default subkeys described in the following table. For details about managing the hives for user profiles, see "Managing User Profiles through the Registry" in Chapter 12, "Configuration Management and the Registry." For details about the contents of subkeys in HKEY_CURRENT_USER, see "Registry Entries for User Preferences" in Chapter 14, "Registry Value Entries."

Table 10.7   Default Subkeys in HKEY_CURRENT_USER

Subkey	Contents
Console	Subkeys that define the options and window size for a console (the interface between the user and character-mode applications). This includes settings for the Windows NT command prompt. These settings should be changed by using the commands in the Control menu for each of the specific non-Windows–based applications. (The subkey for the command prompt does not appear unless the font or screen colors have been changed by the current user.)
Control Panel	Subkeys that have parameters adjusted by applications in Control Panel, for example, the Windows NT Desktop. This includes information that was stored in WIN.INI and CONTROL.INI under Windows for MS-DOS.
Environment	Value entries that correspond to the current user's settings for environment variables. This includes information that was stored in AUTOEXEC.BAT under MS-DOS. Values should be set by using the System icon in Control Panel.
Keyboard Layout	The value entry that gives the current active keyboard layout. This value should be set by using the International icon in Control Panel.

Table 10.7   Default Subkeys in **HKEY_CURRENT_USER** *(continued)*

Subkey	Contents
Printers	Subkeys that describe the printers installed for the current user. These values should be set by using Print Manager.
Program Groups	Subkeys that describe the names and settings for the current user's program groups. Values defining common program groups are stored in HKEY_LOCAL_MACHINE\SOFTWARE\ProgramGroups. Personal program groups should be set by using the menu commands or mouse techniques in Program Manager.
Software	Subkeys that describe the current user's configurable settings for installed software that the user can use. This information has the same structure as HKEY_LOCAL_MACHINE\SOFTWARE. This information contains application-specific information that was stored in WIN.INI or private initialization files under Windows for MS-DOS.

Whenever similar data exists in HKEY_LOCAL_MACHINE and HKEY_CURRENT_USER, the data in HKEY_CURRENT_USER takes precedence, as described earlier, in "HKEY_LOCAL_MACHINE." The most significant example is environment variables, where variables defined for the user who is currently logged on take precedence over system variables, as defined by using the System icon in Control Panel.

HKEY_CURRENT_USER is mapped to HKEY_USER*SID_#*, where *SID_#* is the Security ID string of the current user, as shown in the following example from Registry Editor. The Windows NT logon process builds a user's personal profile environment based upon what it finds in HKEY_USER*SID_#*. If no such data is available, HKEY_CURRENT_USER is built from the data in HKEY_USER\\.DEFAULT.

Note To find the name of the file that goes with a hive, see the HiveList subkey in HKEY_LOCAL_MACHINE\SYSTEM\CurrentControlSet\Control. To find which hive file goes with a user profile (whether or not the user is logged on), see the ProfileList subkey under HKEY_LOCAL_MACHINE\SOFTWARE \Microsoft\Windows NT\CurrentVersion. You can use the Find Key command from the View menu in Registry Editor to locate a specific key quickly.

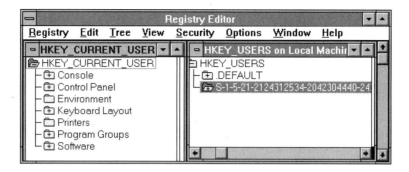

HKEY_USERS

HKEY_USERS contains all actively loaded user profiles. HKEY_USERS has at least two subkeys: .DEFAULT and the Security ID string for the user who is currently logged on. The information in the .DEFAULT subkey is used to create the user profile for a user who logs on without a personal user profile.

The .DEFAULT key contains the Console, Control Panel, Environment, Keyboard Layout, Program Groups, and Software as described in Table 10 .7. For details about the contents of subkeys in HKEY_USERS, see "Registry Entries for User Preferences" in Chapter 14, "Registry Value Entries."

To delete profiles from a computer, choose the Delete User Profiles command from the Options menu in Windows NT Setup.

Network Settings in the Registry

When a network component is installed, various information is added to the Registry. Each network component is represented in two distinct areas of the Registry:

- Software registration keys for the component's driver and adapter card under HKEY_LOCAL_MACHINE\SOFTWARE.

- Service registration keys for the component's driver and adapter under HKEY_LOCAL_MACHINE\SYSTEM.

The following sections describe the general organization and content of the software and service registration information for network components and then conclude with information about bindings for network components and dependency handling.

Note The information in this section is provided for informational purposes, so that you can easily find entries in the Registry. All changes to settings for network adapters and supporting software should be made by choosing the Network icon in Control Panel, not by directly editing values in the Registry.

Network Component Types in the Registry

The following table describes the network component types.

Table 10.8   Network Component Types

Component type	Meaning
Adapter	A piece of hardware
Driver	A software component associated directly with a piece of hardware
Transport	A software component used by services
Service	A software component providing capability directly to user applications
Basic	A token used to represent a fundamental class name (that is, a class with no parent)

Each type of network component requires a subkey for both software and services. Therefore, the installation of a single network card will usually result in the creation of four distinct subkeys in the Registry:

- The software registration key for the driver, found in HKEY_LOCAL_MACHINE\SOFTWARE*Company**ProductName**Version*.

  For example, the path for the driver for an Etherlink adapter will be HKEY_LOCAL_MACHINE\Software\Microsoft\Elinkii\CurrentVersion.

- The software registration key for the network adapter card, found in HKEY_LOCAL_MACHINE\SOFTWARE\Microsoft\Windows NT \CurrentVersion\NetworkCards*netcard#*.

- The service registration key for the driver, found in HKEY_LOCAL_MACHINE\SYSTEM\CurrentControlSet\Services.

- The service registration key for the network adapter card, found in HKEY_LOCAL_MACHINE\SYSTEM\CurrentControlSet\Services.

Software Registration Information for Network Components

Because installation of a network adapter card results in separate Registry entries for the driver and for the adapter, the Software subtree will contain several subkeys to describe the network component. For each network component, a special subkey named NetRules is created in the appropriate driver or adapter registration subkeys. The NetRules subkey identifies the network component as part of the network ensemble.

For example, the standard software registration entry for the Etherlink II driver will appear under this path:

```
HKEY_LOCAL_MACHINE\SOFTWARE\Microsoft   \Elinkii\CurrentVersion
```

The standard entries for the driver might include the following values:

```
Description = 3Com Etherlink II Adapter Driver
InstallDate = 0x2a4e01c5
...
RefCount = 0x1
ServiceName = Elnkii
SoftwareType = driver
Title = 3Com Etherlink II Adapter Driver
```

And under the Etherlink II driver's related NetRules subkey, these value entries might appear:

```
bindable = elnkiiDriver elnkiiAdapter non exclusive
bindform = "ElnkIISys" yes no container
class = REG_MULTI_SZ "elnkiiDriver basic"
Infname = OEMNADE2.INF
InfOption = ELNKII
type = elnkiiSys ndisDriver elnkiiDriver
use = driver
```

The Etherlink adapter is described in a NetworkCards subkey under this path:

```
HKEY_LOCAL_MACHINE\SOFTWARE\Microsoft
    \Windows NT\CurrentVersion\NetworkCards\netcard#
```

The standard entries for the adapter might include these values:

```
Description = 3Com Etherlink II Adapter
InstallDate = 0x2a4e01c5
Manufacturer = Microsoft
ProductName = Elnkii
ServiceName = Elnkii02
Title = [01] 3Com Etherlink II Adapter
```

And these value entries might appear under the adapter's related NetRules subkey:

```
bindform = "Elnkii02" yes yes container
class = "elnkiiAdapter basic"
Infname = OEMNADE2.INF
InfOption = ELNKII
type = elnkii elnkiiAdapter
```

The value entries for the NetRules subkeys are defined in Chapter 14, "Registry Entry Values." The information in the main entries for network adapters and drivers is maintained by the system and should not be changed by users.

Service Registration Information for Network Components

The HKEY_LOCAL_MACHINE\SYSTEM\CurrentControlSet\Services subkey is the service registration area that contains the information used to load a network component into memory. These subkeys contain certain required information, such as the location of the executable file, the service type, and its start criterion.

Each network component's software registration information (as described in the previous section) contains an entry named **ServiceName**, whose value is the name of the service corresponding to the network component. This name acts as a symbolic link to the CurrentControlSet\Services parameters.

Some network components are actually sets of services, each of which has its own subkey in the Services subkey. There is usually a "main" service, with the other services listed as its dependencies.

For example, as shown in the previous section, the Etherlink driver's **ServiceName** is Elnkii, and this name would appear as a Services subkey that defines the location of the driver file, dependencies, and other startup information. The Elnkii key in turn contains subkeys that define the parameters and linkage rules for the driver.

The Etherlink adapter's **ServiceName** is Elnkii02, which also appears as a Services subkey that defines linkage rules for bindings plus physical parameters of the network card, such as its I/O address and interrupt request (IRQ) number, as specified in the Network dialog in Control Panel.

The value entries for the subkeys describing adapters and drivers are defined in "Registry Entries for Network Adapter Cards" in Chapter 14, "Registry Value Entries."

Bindings for Network Components

For the networking software in a computer to operate properly, several different pieces of software must be loaded, and their relationships with other components must be established. These relationships are often called *bindings*. To determine the complete set of optimal bindings among an ensemble of configured network components, the system checks the following information in the Registry:

- The set of network components to be configured
- The types of network components in this set
- The constraining parameters for the network components and their bindings
- The possible bindings that could occur
- The proper way to inform each network component about its bindings

During system startup, the CurrentControlSet\Services subkey is checked for binding information for each service. If any is found, a Linkage subkey is created, and values are stored. For example, these two strings might appear in a value entry under the CurrentControlSet\Services\LanmanWorkstation\Linkage subkey:

```
Bind = \Device\Nbf_Elnkii01  \Device\Nbf_Elnkii02
```

This entry describes the binding information used by the Windows NT Redirector when two separate network cards are present. Each network card's symbolic name is suffixed with a network card index number. This name is joined to the name of the transport through which the network card is accessed. The names are generated by the system according to the constraints defined by the network component's rules.

Bindings have a *usability* requirement that means the binding must terminate at either an adapter (that is, a physical device) or at a *logical end-point*, which is simply a software component that manages all further interconnection information internally. This requirement avoids loading software components that can never be of actual use. For example, a user might have a running network and then choose to remove the adapter card. Without the usability restriction, the bindings would still connect components and prepare them for loading even though the network was entirely unusable.

The following example uses NBF.SYS and SRV.SYS in an ensemble with two Etherlink II network cards and an IBM Token Ring card. First, in the values in the CurrentControlSet\Services\Nbf\Linkage subkey are the following:

```
Bind=    "\Device\ElnkII1"
         "\Device\ElnkII2"
         "\Device\IbmTok1"
Export=  "\Device\Nbf\ElnkII1"
         "\Device\Nbf\ElnkII2"
         "\Device\Nbf\IbmTok1"
Route=   "ElnkIISys ElnkII1"
         "ElnkIISys ElnkII2"
         "IbmtokSys IbmTok1"
```

Under the CurrentControlSet\Services\Srv\Linkage subkey, the following might appear:

```
Bind   = "\Device\Nbf\ElnkII1"
         "\Device\Nbf\ElnkII2"
         "\Device\Nbf\IbmTok1"
Export = "\Device\Srv\Nbf\ElnkII1"
         "\Device\Srv\Nbf\ElnkII2"
         "\Device\Srv\Nbf\IbmTok1"
Route  = "Nbf ElnkIISys ElnkII1"
         "Nbf ElnkIISys ElnkII2"
         "Nbf IbmtokSys IbmTok1"
```

The names in the **Bind** and **Export** entries are based upon the object names defined in the component's NetRules subkey; these entry values can therefore be different from the actual names of the services, although in the previous example, for the sake of clarity, they are not. The names in the **Route** entry are the names of the Services subkeys comprising the full downward route through the bindings protocol.

When the system finishes computing the bindings for network components and the results are stored in the Registry, some network components might need to be informed of changes that occurred. For example, TCP/IP needs to ask the user for an IP address for any network adapter that has been newly configured. If the NetRules subkey for a network component has a value entry named **Review** set to a nonzero value, the .INF file for the network component will be checked every time the bindings are changed.

Dependency Handling for Network Components

Services can be dependent upon other services or drivers, which can be dependent upon others, and so on. The system can establish these types of dependencies:

- Specific dependencies, which are represented by the names of the services upon which a service is dependent
- Group dependencies
- Static dependencies, which are required in all circumstances

Specific Dependencies

A specific dependency is simply the name of a necessary service. By default, the system generates explicit names for all dependent services discovered during bindings generation. Specific dependencies are marked in the Registry as a value of the **Use** entry under the component's NetRules subkey.

For example, assume the Workstation service is dependent upon NBF. NBF is connected to two adapter cards and so is dependent upon their drivers. The system will mark NBF as dependent upon the two network card drivers and will mark the Workstation service as dependent upon the network card drivers and NBF.

Group Dependencies

It often happens that a service should be loaded if any member of a set of dependencies successfully loads. In the previous example, the Workstation service would fail to load if either of the network card drivers failed to initialize.

Groups are used to support this approach. Any service (driver, transport, or whatever) can identify itself as being a member of a service group. All Windows NT network card drivers, for example, are treated as members of the group NDIS.

Group dependencies are marked in the Registry as a value of the **Use** entry under the component's NetRules subkey. Groups are symbolic names listed in the CurrentControlSet\Control\GroupOrderList subkey.

Static Dependencies

A *static dependency* is a required service in all circumstances and is unrelated to how the system otherwise determines bindings.

When the system computes dependencies, it discards any previously listed dependencies. To guarantee that a service is always configured to be dependent upon another service, the value entry **OtherDependencies** can be created under the component's Linkage subkey. **OtherDependencies** is a REG_MULTI_SZ value, so it can contain the names of as many services as needed.

C H A P T E R   1 1

Registry Editor and Registry Administration

You can use the Registry Editor to view Registry entries for the various components in Windows NT. You can also use Registry Editor to modify or add Registry entries. This chapter describes what Registry Editor is and how to use it, with an emphasis on protecting the Registry contents and using Registry Editor to monitor and maintain the system configuration on remote computers. The topics include the following:

- Using Registry Editor and WinMSD, the Windows NT diagnostics tool
- Viewing the Registry for a remote computer
- Editing Registry value entries
- Maintaining the Registry

For more information about the commands and dialog box options that appear in Registry Editor, press F1 to view the online Help.

Microsoft recommends that, wherever possible, you make changes to the system configuration by using Control Panel or the applications in the Administrative Tools group in Program Manager.

Caution You can impair or disable Windows NT with incorrect changes or accidental deletions if you (or other users) use Registry Editor to change the system configuration. Wherever possible, you should use the graphical tools in Windows NT to make changes, and use Registry Editor only as a last resort.

To protect the system configuration, administrators can restrict users' access to the Registry, as described in "Maintaining Registry Security," later in this chapter.

Using Registry Editor and WinMSD

Registry Editor

The Registry Editor application, REGEDT32.EXE, does not appear in any default program groups in Program Manager, although it is installed automatically when you set up Windows NT or Windows NT Advanced Server on any computer.

▶ **To run Registry Editor**

- Run REGEDT32.EXE from File Manager or Program Manager.

  Or type **start regedt32** from a command prompt, and press ENTER.

You can also run Registry Editor from your desktop by placing a program-item icon for REGEDT32.EXE in any program group.

Your ability to make changes to the Registry using Registry Editor depends on your access privileges. In general, you can make the same kinds of changes in Registry Editor as your privileges allow for Control Panel or other administrative tools.

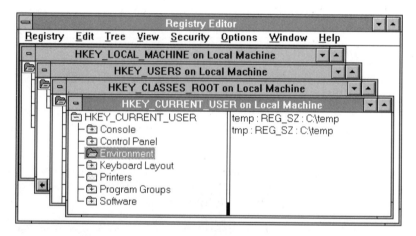

Figure 11.1 Registry Editor

Working in the Registry Editor Windows

You can use the mouse or commands to manipulate the windows and panes in the Registry Editor in the same way as in File Manager. For example:

- Double-click a key name to expand or collapse that entry. Or choose commands from the View and Tree menus to control the display of a selected key and its data.

- Use the mouse or arrow keys to move the vertical split bar in each window to control the size of the left and right panes.

- Choose the Tile or Cascade command from the View menu to arrange the Registry Editor windows. Click the Minimize button, or double-click the particular window icon for the Registry to reduce or restore a window.

- Choose Auto Refresh from the Options menu to update the display continuously. Or choose one of the Refresh commands from the View menu to update the display of Registry information when Auto Refresh is turned off. (Auto Refresh is not available when you are viewing the Registry from a remote computer.)

Tip   Turning off Auto Refresh improves the performance of Registry Editor.

The following table shows some keyboard methods for managing the display of data in each of the Registry Editor windows.

Table 11.1 Keyboard Actions for Viewing Registry Data

Procedure	Keyboard action
Expand one level of a selected Registry key	Press ENTER.
Expand all of the levels of the predefined handle in the active Registry window	Press CTRL + *.
Expand a branch of a selected Registry key	Press the asterisk (*) key on the numeric keypad.
Collapse a branch of a selected Registry key	Press ENTER or the minus (-) sign on the numeric keypad.

Using WinMSD to View System Configuration Data

Windows NT
Diagnostics

You can also use WINMSD.EXE, the diagnostic tool for Windows NT, to view configuration information stored in the Registry. WinMSD is placed in your *SystemRoot*\SYSTEM32 directory when you set up Windows NT. You can run this tool like any executable file in Windows NT. It's a good idea to place a program-item icon for WinMSD in either the Main group or Administrative Tools group in Program Manager.

When you want to browse for system information, WinMSD is the best tool to choose.

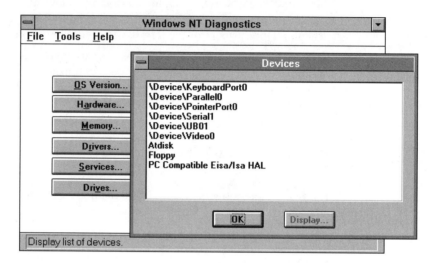

Figure 11.2 WinMSD, the Windows NT Diagnostic Tool

With WinMSD, you choose a button to display specific data from the Registry in an easily readable format.

Tip You cannot edit value entries in WinMSD, so the Registry contents are protected while you browse for information. However, you can select and copy any value if you want to paste information in a Registry Editor edit box or in a text editor.

Viewing the Registry for a Remote Computer

In the same way that you can use Event Viewer or User Manager to view details on another computer, you can use Registry Editor to view and change the contents of another computer's Registry if the Server services on the remote computer are running.

This ability to remotely view a computer's configuration allows you, as a system administrator, to examine a user's startup parameters, desktop configuration, and other parameters. So you can provide troubleshooting or other support assistance over the telephone while you view settings on the other computer from your own workstation.

▶ **To view the Registry for a remote computer**

- From the Registry menu, choose the Select Computer command, and then select or type the name of the computer whose Registry you want to access.

  Or double-click the name of a computer in the Select Computer list. Under Windows NT Advanced Server, the first name in this list represents the name of a domain. If no computer name appears after this domain name, double-click the domain name to view a list of the computers in that domain.

Two Registry windows appear for the remote computer, one for HKEY_USERS and one for HKEY_LOCAL_MACHINE. You can view or modify the information on keys for the remote computer if the access controls defined for the keys allow you to perform such operations. If you are logged on as a member of the Administrators group, you can perform actions on all keys.

Loading Hives from Another Computer

You can use the Load Hive and Unload Hive commands in Registry Editor to display and maintain another computer's Registry without viewing it remotely. You might want to do this to view specific values or to repair certain entries for a computer that is not configured properly or cannot connect to the network.

The hives that make up your computer's Registry are loaded automatically when you start the computer, and you can view the content of these hives in Registry Editor. If you want to view or change the contents of other hive files, you must use the Load Hive command to display its contents in Registry Editor.

The following examples use the Load Hive command:

- Repairing a hive on a computer that temporarily cannot run Windows NT. For details, see "Backing Up and Restoring Registry Hives," later in this chapter.

- Looking at or repairing hives for profiles of people who aren't currently logged on, either on the same computer or a remote PC. For details and examples, see "Managing User Profiles Through the Registry" in Chapter 12, "Configuration Management and the Registry."

- Creating a custom LastKnownGood and other startup controls. For details and examples, see "Making Sure the System Always Starts" in Chapter 12, "Configuration Management and the Registry."

The Load Hive and Unload Hive commands affect only the Registry windows that display HKEY_USERS and HKEY_LOCAL_MACHINE. To use these commands, you must have Restore and Backup privileges, which you have if you are logged on as a member of the Administrators group. The Load Hive command is available only when HKEY_USERS or HKEY_LOCAL_MACHINE is selected. The Unload Hive command is available only when a subkey of one of these handles is selected.

▶ **To load a hive into the Registry Editor**

1. Select the HKEY_LOCAL_MACHINE or HKEY_USERS root.

2. From the Registry menu, choose the Load Hive command.

3. Use the File Name, Drives, and Directories boxes and the Network button of the Load Hive dialog box to select the file that contains the hive you want to load, and then choose the OK button.

   If you are loading a hive on a remote computer, the drive and path in the filename is relative to the remote computer.

Tip You can find the directory location and names of hives on a computer in HKEY_LOCAL_MACHINE\SYSTEM\CurrentControlSet\Control\Hivelist.

This file must have been created with the Save Key command (as described later in this chapter), or it must be one of the default hives. Under the FAT file system, the filename cannot have an extension.

If you are unable to connect to another computer over the network, you can load a hive file that you copied to a floppy disk.

4. In the second Load Hive dialog box, type the name you want to use for the key where the hive will be loaded, and then choose the OK button.

This name creates a new subkey in the Registry. You can specify any name using any characters and including blank spaces. You cannot load to an existing key.

Data from the loaded hive appears as a new subkey under HKEY_USERS or HKEY_LOCAL_MACHINE (whichever handle you selected before loading the hive). A loaded hive remains in the system until it is unloaded.

The Load Hive command creates a new hive in the memory space of the Registry and uses the specified file as the backing hive file for it. The specified file is held open, but nothing is copied to the file unless the information in a key or value entry is changed. Likewise, the Unload Hive command does not copy or create anything; it merely unloads a loaded hive.

▶ **To unload a hive from the Registry Editor**

• Select the key that represents a hive that you previously loaded, and then from the Registry menu, choose the Unload Hive command.

The selected key is removed from the window and is no longer actively available to the system or for editing in Registry Editor.

You cannot unload a hive that was loaded by the system. Also, you won't be able to unload a hive that contains an open key.

Saving and Restoring Keys

The Save Key command lets you save the information in a key and all its subkeys in a hive file. This file can be used by the Restore and Load Key commands.

Changes in the Registry are saved automatically, whether you make changes by using Registry Editor or by changing settings in applications. The Save Key command is used specifically to save portions of the Registry as a file on disk.

To use the Save Key command, you need Backup privileges, which you have if you are logged on as a member of the Administrators group.

You can use the Save Key command on any key. However, this command will not save volatile keys, which are destroyed when you shut down the system. For example, the HKEY_LOCAL_MACHINE\HARDWARE key is volatile, so it is not saved as a hive file. If you want to view the Hardware hive for debugging, you can save it in a text file by choosing the Save Subtree As command from the Registry menu, as described at the end of this chapter.

▶ **To save a Registry key**

1. Select the key that you want to save as a hive file on a disk.

2. From the Registry menu, choose the Save Key command, and then complete the filename information in the Save Key dialog box.

   Under the FAT file system, this filename cannot have an extension.

   If the key that you are saving is in the Registry of a remote computer, the drive and path that you specify for the filename is relative to the remote computer.

The selected key is now saved as a file. When you use the Load Hive command, you can select the filename for any files saved using the Save Key command.

For example, as part of system maintenance, you might use the Save Key command to save a key as a file. When the key that you saved is ready to be returned to the system, you use the Restore command.

You can use the Restore or Restore Volatile command to make a hive file a part of the system configuration. The Restore and Restore Volatile commands let you copy information in a hive file over a specified key. This information copied from the file will overwrite the contents of the specified key, except for the key name.

To use the Restore or Restore Volatile commands, you need Restore privilege—which you have if you are logged on as a member of the Administrators group.

▶ **To restore a key**

1. Select the key where you want to restore the hive.

2. From the Registry menu, choose the Restore command, and then complete the filename information in the Restore Key dialog box to specify the hive you want to restore.

   Under the FAT file system, this filename cannot have an extension.

   If you are restoring a key on a remote computer, the drive and path of the filename is relative to the remote computer.

Note If you want to add a key temporarily to a system, however, you use the Restore Volatile command. If you use this command, the Registry will make a volatile copy, which will disappear when the system is restarted.

You cannot restore to a key that has opened handles or that has subkeys with opened handles. This is why you cannot restore the SAM or SECURITY subtrees, because Windows NT always has handles open in these keys. So the Restore command is used only for special conditions, such as restoration of user profiles on a damaged system. Usually, to switch in a backup version of a hive, you can use the ReplaceKey function in REGREST.EXE (included on the Resource Guide disk).

Editing Registry Value Entries

Within the Registry, you can alter the value entries for a selected key or assign new value entries to keys. This section describes how to find keys and add, edit, or delete keys and value entries.

Finding a Key in the Registry

The location of a Registry key may be different in the tree structure from what is described in this *Resource Guide*, depending on whether a computer is running Windows NT or Windows NT Advanced Server and other factors.

You can search for a specific key name in the Registry tree. Key names appear in the left pane of the Registry Editor windows. The search begins from the currently selected key. Searching from a predefined key will search all its descendant keys.

Each search is local to the tree where the search begins. That is, if you are searching in the windows for HKEY_LOCAL_MACHINE, the search will not include keys found under HKEY_CURRENT_USER.

▶ **To search for a key in Registry Editor**

1. From the View menu, choose the Find Key command, and then in the Find What box of the Find Key dialog box, type the name of the key that you want to find, and choose the Find button.

2. If you want to restrict the scope of the search or define the search direction, select the Match Whole Word Only box, the Match Case option, or select Up or Down in the Direction box.

3. To see the next occurrence of the key name you specified, choose the Find Next button.

   Because key names are not unique, it's a good idea to search for additional occurrences of a specific key name, to be sure you find the key you want.

Tip   Some key names include spaces (such as "Session Manager"), while others use underscores ("Ntfs_rec") or a continuous string ("EventLog"). To ensure that you find the key you want, search for a portion of the name, and make sure that the Match Whole Word Only check box is cleared in the Find dialog box.

You can also use the Registry database provided in the Resource Guide disk to find specific keys or value entries related to specific topics.

▶ **To use the Windows NT Registry Entries database**

• In File Manager, double-click REGENTRY.HLP.

Editing Values in the Registry

Each value entry in Registry Editor appears as a string that consists of three components, as shown in the following figure.

DependOnService: REG_MULTI_SZ: Mup

Figure 11.3 The Three Components of a Value Entry

These rules govern the content of these components:

- The name of the value is a string of up to 16,000 Unicode characters (32K). This name can contain backslash (\) characters. The name itself can be null (that is, "").

- The data type of the value is REG_BINARY, REG_DWORD, REG_EXPAND_SZ, REG_MULTI_SZ, or REG_SZ, as described in Table 10.2 in Chapter 10, "Overview of the Windows NT Registry." Other data types can be defined by programs, but editing of only these five specific data types is supported in Registry Editor.

- The value itself can be data of a size up to 1 MB in any format except DWord, including arbitrary strings and raw binary data. However, values larger than about 2048 bytes should be stored as files with the filenames stored in the Registry, so that the Registry can perform efficiently.

The Registry preserves case as you type it for any entry but ignores case in evaluating the data. The names are case-insensitive. However, the data is defined by specific applications (or users), so it might be case-sensitive, depending on how the program that uses it treats the data.

▶ **To edit any value**

1. In the right pane of the Registry Editor window, double-click the value entry. Or from the Edit menu, choose the String, Binary, DWord, or Multi String command as appropriate for selected value.

2. Edit the value that appears in the related Editor dialog box, and then choose the OK button.

   The Binary and DWord editors give you the flexibility to select the base of a number system in which you want to edit your data. In the Binary editor, you can edit your data as binary (base 2) or hex (base 16). In the DWord editor, you can also edit your data in decimal (base 10). Hex is the default base for both editors. These types of data will always be displayed in hex in the right pane of the Registry Editor.

Tip To view numbers in decimal format, double-click the value entry and select the Decimal format option. Cancel the dialog box when you finish checking the value.

Information stored in a nonvolatile key remains in the Registry until you delete it. Information stored in a volatile key is discarded when you shut down the system. Everything under a volatile key is also volatile. Everything stored under the HKEY_LOCAL_MACHINE\HARDWARE key is volatile.

Note If your Registry becomes quite large, you will want to set a larger value for the value entry named **RegistrySizeLimit,** as described in "The CurrentControlSet\Control Subkeys" in Chapter 14, "Registry Value Entries."

Adding a Key

You can add a key to store data in the Registry. For example, you might add a subkey under CurrentControlSet\Services to start a service process you have written or to install a device driver that doesn't have an installation program.

To do this, you must have Create Subkey access permission for the key under which you are adding a subkey, as described in "Assigning Access Rights to Registry Keys," later in this chapter.

▶ **To add a key to the Registry**

1. Select the key or subkey under which you want the new key to appear, and then choose the Add Key command from the Edit menu, or press the INS key.

2. In the Key Name box of the Add Key dialog box, type the name that you want to assign your key.

   The key name cannot contain a backslash (\), and it must be unique in relation to other subkeys at the same level in the hierarchy. That is, Key1 and Key2 can each have a subkey named Key3, but Key1 cannot have two subkeys named Key3.

3. Leave the Class box blank, as this entry is reserved for future uses.

4. Choose the OK button to display the new key in the Registry Editor window.

Adding a Value Entry to a Registry Key

In Registry Editor, you can assign a new value entry to a key or edit the value entry of an existing key. When you do this, the value that you add appears in the data pane of the selected Registry window.

You may want to add value entries based on tuning or troubleshooting information you find in Chapter 14, "Registry Value Entries," or when advised by technical support personnel for Windows NT or for your application.

▶   **To add a value entry to a Registry key**

1. Select the subkey to which you want to add a value entry.

2. From the Edit menu, choose the Add Value command, or move the focus to the right pane using the TAB key or the mouse, and then press the INS key. In the Value Name box, type the name you want to assign to the new value entry.

3. In the Data Type box, select the type that you want to assign to the value entry, as described in Table 10.2 in Chapter 10, "Overview of the Windows NT Registry."

4. Choose the OK button, and then type the value in the Editor dialog box that appears. Choose the OK button again to display the new entry in the Registry Editor window.

Deleting a Key or a Value Entry

You can use either the Delete command from the Edit menu or press the DELETE key to remove selected keys or value entries from the Registry. However, you cannot delete any of the predefined subtrees or change the name of a key.

Caution   There is no Undo command for deletions. Registry Editor asks you to confirm the deletions if the Confirm On Delete option is checked under the Options menu. However, the message does not include the name of the key you are deleting. Check your selection carefully before proceeding when you delete a key.

The only way to retrieve a key that you mistakenly delete is to restart the computer. Press the spacebar immediately after selecting Windows NT at the Boot Loader prompt, and then choose the Last Known Good option to roll back to an earlier configuration.

You can protect the Registry from accidental deletions in these ways:

- Protect data through read-only mode

  To do this, choose the Read Only command from the Options menu. When this command is checked, Registry Editor will not save any changes made, protecting the data from accidental changes.

- Protect data through confirmation

  To do this, choose the Confirm On Delete command from the Options menu. When this command is checked, the Registry Editor asks you to confirm deletion of any key or value.

Maintaining the Registry

Windows NT enforces access control on Registry files, so it is difficult for users to accidentally or intentionally damage or delete hives on a running system. This is because while the system is running, hive files are kept open by the system for exclusive access on all file systems. If the Windows NT *SystemRoot* is not on an NTFS volume, the Registry files can be tampered with—specifically, users can remove hives for user profiles that aren't currently loaded. With NTFS, such tampering can be prevented.

You should plan how you will protect the Registry for each Windows NT computer at your site. This section describes how to ensure that you will have working Registry files under most conditions.

For more details about how to ensure recoverability under all conditions, see "Making Sure the System Always Starts" in Chapter 12, "Configuration Management and the Registry."

Maintaining Registry Security

Your first line of protection as a system administrator is the simple rule for protection under Windows NT: Don't allow users to log on as members of the Administrators group unless a specific individual has administrative duties.

You might also choose not to put REGEDT32.EXE on workstations, since you can easily administer any workstation from a remote computer. Or place access controls in File Manager on REGEDT32.EXE, limiting the rights of users to start this program.

This section describes additional steps you can take to protect the Registry through the following measures:

- Protecting Registry files
- Assigning access rights to Registry keys
- Auditing Registry activities

Protecting Registry Files for User Profiles

You can protect the Registry hive files for user profiles in the same way that you protect other files in Windows NT—by restricting access through File Manager. If the files are stored on an NTFS volume, you can use the commands on the Security menu in File Manager to assign permissions. For details about using these commands, see the online Help in File Manager.

Caution   You should only change permissions for user profile hives. The permission for other hives are maintained automatically by the system and should not be changed.

For information about safeguarding files with backups, see "Backing Up and Restoring Registry Hives," later in this chapter.

Assigning Access Rights to Registry Keys

To determine who has access to specific Registry data, you can set permissions on the Registry keys to specify the users and groups that can access that key. This is sometimes called *changing ACLs*, in reference to the Access Control Lists that govern who has access to data. You can also add or remove names from the list of users or groups authorized to access the Registry keys.

You can assign access rights to Registry keys regardless of the type of file system on the partition where the Windows NT files are stored.

Caution   Changing the permissions to limit access to a Registry key can have severe consequences. If, for example, you set No Access permissions on a key that the Network Control Panel application needs for configuration, it will cause the application to fail.

At a minimum, ensure that Administrators and the System have full access to the key, to ensure that the system starts and that the Registry key can be repaired by an administrator.

If you change permissions on a Registry key, you should audit the key for failed access attempts. For details, see "Auditing Registry Activities," later in this chapter.

Because assigning permissions on specific keys can have drastic consequences, you should reserve this action for keys that you add to accommodate custom applications or other custom settings. After you change permissions on a Registry key, be sure to turn on auditing in User Manager, and then test the system extensively through a variety of activities while logged on under different user and administrative accounts.

In Registry Editor, the commands on the Security menu for assigning permission and ownership of keys work the same as similar commands in File Manager for assigning access rights for files and directories. For details about these commands, see the online Help in Registry Editor. For a detailed discussion of permissions and ownership, see "Securing Directories and Files" in Chapter 4, "File Manager," in the *Windows NT System Guide.*

▶ **To assign permission on a key**

1. Make a backup copy of the Registry key before making changes.

2. Select the key for which you want to assign access permission, and then from the Security menu, choose the Permissions command.

3. In the Registry Key Permissions dialog box, assign an access level to the selected key by selecting an option in the Type of Access box as described in the following table, and then choose the OK button.

Type of access	Meaning
Read	Allows users on the Permissions list to read the key's contents, but prevents changes from being saved
Full Control	Allows users on the Permissions list to access, edit, or take ownership of the selected key.
Special Access	Allows users on the Permissions list some custom combination of access and edit rights for the selected key. For a description of the Special Access types, see "Auditing Registry Activities," later in this chapter.

4. Turn on auditing in User Manager, and then test the system extensively to ensure that the new access control does not interfere with system or application operations.

As a system administrator, you may need to take ownership of a key to protect access to that key. You take ownership of a Registry key by choosing the Owner command from the Security menu in Registry Editor and then completing the Ownership dialog box. You can also add users or groups to the Permissions list by following the same procedure for managing lists of users and groups as appears throughout Windows NT.

You (or any user) can take ownership of any Registry key if you log onto the computer as a member of the Administrator group. However, if an Administrator takes ownership of a key without being assigned full control by its owner, the key cannot be given back to its original owner, and the event is audited.

Auditing Registry Activities

Auditing Registry activities requires several separate activities:

- Turning on auditing and setting the audit policies in User Manager or User Manager for Domains for the activities you want to audit

- Specifying the groups and users whose activities you want to audit for selected keys, by choosing the Auditing command in Registry Editor

- Viewing the Security log in Event Viewer for a selected computer to see the results of auditing

For each of these activities, you must be logged on as a member of the Administrators group for the specific computer you are auditing. Auditing policies are set on a per-computer basis. Before you can audit activities in Registry keys, you must turn on security auditing for the computer.

▶ **To turn on auditing**

1. In User Manager or User Manager for Domains, choose the Audit command from the Policies menu, and select the Audit These Events option to turn on auditing.

2. Check Success and Failure options for each type of event to be audited, and then choose the OK button.

Note At a minimum, you should check the Failure option for File And Object Access. Choosing the Success option for many items may produce an abundance of meaningless entries in the event log.

You may want to audit actions for a specific Registry key. For example, you might want to audit the following:

- Keys where you want to know about changes being made by users or applications

- Keys you added that you want to test

▶ **To audit user actions for a selected Registry key**

1. From the Security menu in Registry Editor, choose the Auditing command, and then complete the dialog box.

   This command in Registry Editor is similar to the Auditing command in File Manager. For details about the Auditing dialog box, choose online Help in Registry Editor. For a discussion of general issues related to the Auditing command, see "Auditing Files and Directories" in Chapter 4, "File Manager," in the *Windows NT System Guide*.

2. Check the Success or Failure check box for the following activities:

Audit option	Events audited
Create Link	Events that attempt to open a key with Create Link access
Create Subkey	Events that attempt to open a key with Create Value access
Delete	Events that attempt to delete the key
Enumerate Subkeys	Events that attempt to open a key with Enumerate Subkeys access (that is, events that try to find the subkeys of a key)
Notify	Events that attempt to open a key with Notify access
Query Value	Events that attempt to open a key with Query Value access
Read Control	Events that attempt to find the owner of a key
Set Value	Events that attempt to open a key with Set Value access
Write DAC	Events that attempt to determine who has access to the key

▶ **To view the results of auditing**

- Run Event Viewer, select the computer that you are interested in, and then choose the Security command from the Log menu.

Note If you change permission for any Registry key, you should turn on Auditing in User Manager and specify the Failure attempts for File And Object Access to be audited. Then you can check the Security event log for details if any application isn't working because of changes in permissions.

Backing Up and Restoring Registry Hives

You might at some time find it necessary to restore backed up versions of Registry hives. This might occur, for example, when a new computer is to replace an old one, when a disk controller or hard disk has gone bad, or when an electrical failure erased large parts of a disk. This section describes how to back up and restore Registry hives.

How this restoration is done depends on what hardware is available and what file system is in use. You can, of course, only restore what you have backed up.

Important Make frequent and consistent backup sets of all important files, including system files, to tape or to a local or remote hard drive.

Your regular backup routine should include using the Configuration Save command in Disk Administrator to maintain an up-to-date Emergency Repair Disk for restoring the Windows NT system. For details, see the Disk Administrator chapter in the *Windows NT System Guide*.

Backing Up Registry Hives

You might make a Registry hive backup in one of four ways:

- Use a tape drive and the Windows NT Backup program, and select the Backup Local Registry option in the Backup Information dialog box to automatically include a copy of the local Registry files in the backup set. This is the preferred method for creating backups if you have a tape drive. For details, see the Backup chapter in the *Windows NT System Guide.*

- If you don't have a tape drive, run REGBACK.EXE or REPAIR.EXE from the Resource Guide disk, or use another tool that uses the same techniques to back up Registry files.

- Start the computer using a different operating system. Then copy all files in the *SystemRoot*\SYSTEM32\CONFIG directory to a safe backup location. For example, use another instance of Windows NT if the Registry is stored on an NTFS partition, or use MS-DOS if the Registry is stored on a FAT partition.

- Use the Save Key command in Registry Editor (which essentially performs the RegBack procedure manually).

   To do this, for each direct subkey of HKEY_LOCAL_MACHINE and HKEY_USERS, you must choose the Save Key command from the Registry menu, specifying filenames that match the key names. For example, save the SYSTEM key to \BACKDIR\SYSTEM. On the FAT file system, the filename should not have an extension.

   Don't use Save Key with the Hardware hive, which is volatile. You won't get any data, because Save Key cannot save volatile keys to disk.

Restoring Hives from Backup Files

If you have a good set of backup files, which you update regularly, you can restore Registry hives that are damaged or missing.

But you cannot use Registry Editor to fully restore hives, because active parts of the Registry require use of the ReplaceKey operation for restoration, which Registry Editor cannot perform.

To restore a damaged system, you must first restore the basic operating system installation. You might do this by using the Emergency Repair Disk to restore your system to what it looked like just after installation, or simply run Windows NT Setup again. Such a restoration results in a system that starts the computer (which is good) but that lacks changes made since you first set it up (which isn't good). Most of those changes are recovered by copying files from backups by using the Windows NT Backup program for tape backups or by copying from disk backups.

However, you cannot merely copy the backups of Registry hive files, because those files are protected while Windows NT is running. So, after the system and all of the additional files such as device drivers are restored, you must restore the Registry. You might do this in one of the following ways, depending on which backup mechanism you used:

- For tape backups, you can use the Windows NT Restore program to restore the Registry. Then restart the computer. For details, see Chapter 14, "Backup," in the *Windows NT System Guide.*

- Start the computer using an alternate instance of the operating system (or using MS-DOS if the system files are on a FAT partition). Copy back the files to the *SystemRoot*\SYSTEM32\CONFIG directory. Then restart the computer using the regular operating system.

- Use the REPAIR.EXE program from the Resource Guide disk.

- Use the REGREST.EXE program from the Resource Guide disk. The RegRest program performs a ReplaceKey operation, which swaps backup files for the default files that Emergency Repair or Windows NT Setup installed, and saves the default files under other filenames. Restart the computer after running RegRest to see the restored Registry.

Compacting Registry Data

The memory used for the Registry is approximately equal to the size of a hive when it is loaded into memory. Hives vary in size on disk from 20K to over 500K. The amount of space used depends chiefly on how many local user profiles are retained and how much information is stored in each profile.

You should remove unused or out-of-date user profiles from a computer by choosing the Delete User Profiles command in Windows NT Setup. (The Setup program protects you from deleting the profile for the currently logged on user.)

The first release of Windows NT doesn't compact, or shrink, a hive when profiles are deleted or hives are unloaded. But you can use the Save Key command to save a user hive and then use the Restore command so you can use this smaller hive. How much space you gain depends on how much was stored in various user profiles.

This procedure is useful only for user profiles, not for the SAM, Security, Software, or System hives.

Viewing and Printing Registry Data as Text

You might want to examine the contents of a Registry key as text for troubleshooting. You can save a key as a text file, and you can print data from Registry Editor, including a key, its subkeys, and all of the value entries of all of its subkeys.

The Save Subtree As command also works for the HKEY_LOCAL_MACHINE\HARDWARE subtree, which you cannot otherwise save as a hive file.

▶ **To save a Registry key as a text file**

- In a Registry window, select the key you want to save as a text file. Then choose the Save Subtree As command from the Registry menu, and specify a filename.

▶ **To print a Registry key**

- In a Registry window, select the key you want, and then choose the Print Subtree command from the Registry menu.

Summary of Administrative Tools for the Registry

The following table summarizes the tools provided with Windows NT (in addition to Registry Editor and WinMSD) that you can use to administer the Registry.

Table 11.2   Tools in Windows NT for Registry Management

Tool	Description
Backup	Back up Registry hives as part of a tape backup routine
Emergency Repair Disk	Restore default hives to the system
File Manager	Apply access controls to REGEDT32.EXE and hive files

The following table summarizes the tools on the Resource Guide disk that you can use to administer the Registry. For details about these and other utilities provided with the *Windows NT Resource Kit,* see the RKTOOLS.HLP file on your Resource Guide disk.

Table 11.3 Tools on the Resource Guide Disk

Tool	Description
REGBACK.EXE	Creates backups of Registry files
REGENTRY.HLP	Documents Windows NT Registry entries
REGINI.EXE	Makes Registry changes by script
REGREST.EXE	Restores Registry hives using the ReplaceKey function

CHAPTER 12

Configuration Management and the Registry

This chapter provides some examples of problem-solving tasks that involve changes made to the Registry using Registry Editor. The topics here include the following:

- Solving users' environment problems with the Registry
- Making sure the system always starts
- Changing driver and service configuration data
- Managing user profiles through the Registry

Caution Editing entries in the Registry is equivalent to editing raw sectors on a hard disk. This is a dangerous undertaking—you can easily make a computer unbootable.

Wherever possible, you should use Control Panel, the programs in the Administrative Tools group, and Windows NT Setup to change the system configuration.

Use extreme care if you follow any procedures described here for changing the Registry directly using Registry Editor.

Solving Users' Environment Problems with the Registry

Using Registry Editor to view the contents of the Registry for a remote computer makes it easier for Help Desk personnel or a system administrator to solve users' configuration problems. Select the troublesome computer using the Select Computer command in Registry Editor, and then you can browse through Registry entries to find where problems may exist.

You can also load a copy of a hive from another computer to view and change entries, as described in "Loading Hives from Another Computer" in Chapter 11, "Registry Editor and Registry Administration."

This is probably how you will use Registry Editor most often—to find the source of problems, not to edit value entries. After you find the source of a problem, Control Panel or other tools can be used to solve the problem.

For example, you can check the user's desktop settings easily by examining the values under the Console and Control Panel subkeys for the user. The Console subkeys define settings for the command prompt and other character-based applications. The Control Panel subkeys in the Registry define the appearance and behavior of items in the Windows NT desktop.

▶ **To view a user's desktop settings**

1. Focus on the user's computer by choosing the Select Computer command from the Registry menu.

2. Under HKEY_USERS for the selected computer, select the key that represents the profile for the user who is having problems.

   Tip To determine which *SID_#* key represents which user, see the values for **ProfileImagePath** under the ProfileList key in the following Registry path:

   `HKEY_LOCAL_MACHINE\SOFTWARE\MICROSOFT\WINDOWS NT\CurrentVersion`

   The hive file name that is the value for **ProfileImagePath** includes a portion of the username associated with that *SID_#*, so that you can identify the user to which it belongs.

   ---

3. Double-click either the Console or Control Panel subkey, depending on whether the problem is with a character-based screen or a Windows NT window.

4. Check values, as described in the topic "Registry Entries for User Components" in REGENTRY.HLP, which is included on the *Resource Guide* disk.

For example, suppose a user calls for help, complaining that the screen goes black whenever the icon for the command prompt is clicked in Program Manager. You can select this computer in Registry Editor, and then select the following subkey:

```
HKEY_USERS\SID_#\Console\Command Prompt
```

In this example, if the value of **ScreenColors** is 0, both the text and the screen background have been set to black, and this is the source of the user's problem. The user can fix this by running Command Prompt and pressing ALT+SPACEBAR to display the Control menu and choosing the Screen Colors command to select new colors.

Tip To change the colors or the bitmap that appears on the CTRL+ALT+DEL logon screen, change the entries under HKEY_USERS\.DEFAULT\Control Panel\Desktop. For example, if you want a bitmap of your company's logo on the logon screen, change the value of **Wallpaper** to specify the path and filename for that bitmap.

As another example, any user with sufficient access permission can use the System icon in Control Panel to change user environment variables, but the system environment variables can only be set by changing values in the Registry. Such changes to the system environment variables affect all users and can only be made in the Registry if you are logged on as a member of the Administrators group.

▶ **To change system environment variables**

1. In Registry Editor, select the Environment subkey under this Registry path:

   ```
   HKEY_LOCAL_MACHINE\SYSTEM\CurrentControlSet
       \Control\Session Manager\Environment
   ```

2. Double-click an environment variable and change its value, as described in "The CurrentControlSet\Control Subkeys" in REGENTRY.HLP, which is included on the *Resource Guide* disk.

3. Restart the system for these changes to take effect.

For example, if you want to change the path for the Microsoft OS/2 version 1.*x* libraries, change the value of **OS2Lib** under the Environment subkey to specify a new path name, such as D:\OS2\DLL.

Making Sure the System Always Starts

This section discusses three topics:

- Starting a system with configuration problems
- Reconstructing a system with damaged files
- Creating a custom startup verification program

The goal in all of these topics is to make sure a Windows NT system starts correctly each time you turn on the switch. The obvious first steps, of course, involve planning ahead for system safety, with the following activities:

- Protect the Registry hive files on disk and maintain a regular backup program, including backups of Registry hive files, as described in "Maintaining the Registry" in Chapter 11, "Registry Editor and Registry Administration."

- Maintain a handy copy of the Emergency Repair disk created when you installed Windows NT. Each Repair disk works only for the computer where it was made during Setup.

- Install a redundant copy of the operating system to make the system more robust, as described in Chapter 3, "Customizing Windows NT Setup."

You can also rely on Windows NT to automatically recover from damages to startup data. Specifically, to protect from bad sectors occurring in the System hive file, Windows NT automatically creates a backup of the system hive named SYSTEM.ALT, which is stored in the *SystemRoot*\SYSTEM32\CONFIG directory. If any problems are encountered while reading the System hive during startup such as damage to the file, the Boot Loader automatically switches to SYSTEM.ALT to continue starting the system. For more information about SYSTEM.ALT, see "Hives and Files" in Chapter 10, "Overview of the Windows NT Registry."

Starting a System with Configuration Problems

This section describes how to start a computer when hardware or software problems prevent normal system startup.

For a Windows NT computer, the Registry includes several control sets. Each control set is a complete set of system parameters that define startup, system recovery, and driver load controls plus service parameters and other system configuration data. The control set represented as the CurrentControlSet in the Registry is a link to the control set used to start the system for the current session. For details about control sets, see "HKEY_LOCAL_MACHINE\SYSTEM Subtree" in Chapter 10, "Overview of the Windows NT Registry."

Whenever you start Windows NT, the Boot Loader automatically tries to boot using the CurrentControlSet described in the HKEY_LOCAL_MACHINE \SYSTEM\Select subkey. If the system cannot start using this control set (because of erroneous user changes or bad-sector errors on a file), the Boot Loader automatically tries the LastKnownGood control set, as defined in the Select subkey.

You can also switch to a previous system configuration manually, bypassing the automatic process.

▶ **To switch to a previous system configuration manually**

1. Press ENTER to select Windows NT at the startup prompt, and then immediately press the spacebar.

2. From the Configuration Recovery menu, choose the option named Use Last Known Good Configuration, and then press ENTER.

Note   Choosing the Last Known Good option at startup will cause the system to discard all configuration changes made since the computer's last successful startup.

During system startup, you can only choose between the current and the **LastKnownGood** control set. For information about how the **LastKnownGood** control set is selected and stored, see "HKEY_LOCAL_MACHINE\SYSTEM Subtree" in Chapter 10, "Overview of the Windows NT Registry."

Reconstructing a System with Damaged Files

You might need to restore a user's system configuration and working environment, either because of hardware failure or replacement, or because files have been damaged on the hard disk. You can use the Emergency Repair Disk created during Windows NT installation to restore the system files. If you use the Emergency Repair Disk to repair files such as the Registry hives, you will lose any changes that were made to the system after installation (unless you update your Emergency Repair Disk using the REPAIR.EXE program from the *Resource Guide* disk).

You can use one of the following methods to reconstruct the system from backups, as described in "Backing Up and Restoring Registry Hives" in Chapter 11, "Registry Editor and Registry Administration":

- Use the Windows NT Restore program to restore the Registry from tape backups.
- Start the computer using another instance of the operating system (or with MS-DOS for a FAT partition), and then copy the backup files to the *SystemRoot*\SYSTEM32\CONFIG directory.

If you are attempting to restore damaged SAM or Security hives, you must use the method of starting the computer with another operating system and then copying the backup hive files from a disk. You cannot replace these hives while Windows NT is running. This means that if your system files are on an NTFS volume, you must have another instance of Windows NT available on that system to be able to restore the SAM and security hives. Or you can use the Emergency Repair Disk to restore the default SAM and Security hives (and subsequently lose any security changes made since Windows NT was installed).

Creating a Custom Startup Verification Program

System startup is usually declared good if two procedures are complete:

- All startup drivers are loaded.

   When a service fails to load during startup, its **ErrorControl** value is checked, as defined in the CurrentControlSet\Services*serviceName* subkeys. Whether system startup continues depends on this value.

- At least one user successfully logs on the computer by pressing CTRL+ALT+DEL and supplying a valid user name, domain name, and password.

This basic standard for verifying system startup will suit the needs for most situations. But your site might require additional steps before considering a computer to be successfully started and ready to participate in the network.

For example, you might want to redefine startup validation for a server where, normally, no one logs on or where you want system startup to be validated as successful only after a particular process has started.

Or, for a server running Microsoft SQL Server, you might want a system startup to be marked as good only after the SQL server responds to a request. To do this, you might write a program that queries the SQL server and checks the response. If the response is not as expected, the program can call the **NotifyBootConfigStatus()** function with FALSE, causing the system to restart using the **LastKnownGood** control set. Or the program might cause the system to run without saving the current configuration as the **LastKnownGood** control. Conversely, if the SQL server responds as expected, the program can call the **NotifyBootConfigStatus()** function with TRUE, causing the current configuration to be saved as the **LastKnownGood** control.

You can run such a verification program from the command prompt. Or you can have the program run automatically during startup by specifying value entries under **BootVerificationProgram** in the Registry.

▶ **To create a custom startup verification program**

1. Change the value of **ReportBootOK** to 0 under the following Registry path:

   ```
   HKEY_LOCAL_MACHINE\SOFTWARE\Microsoft\Windows NT\CurrentVersion
       \WinLogon
   ```

   The data type for **ReportBootOK** is REG_SZ. When this value is 0, it disables the automatic startup acceptance that happens after the first successful logon.

2. Create the executable program that you want to run as part of startup verification. Then specify its filename as a value for **ImagePath** in the **BootVerificationProgram** subkey under this Registry path:

   ```
   HKEY_LOCAL_MACHINE\SYSTEM\CurrentControlSet
       \Control\BootVerificationProgram
   ```

   The data type for **ImagePath** must be REG_SZ or REG_EXPAND_SZ.

As another example, a computer set up for a turnkey application is a candidate for a custom startup verification routine, where the computer doesn't usually interact directly with users and you therefore don't want a successful user logon to be part of the system startup.

If you want a good system startup to be accepted from a remote computer (either manually or automatically), you can use the service program BOOTVRFY.EXE that is supplied with Windows NT. In this case, the remote computer accepts the system startup by starting the BOOTVRFY.EXE service. You can also write your own verification service that can reject the system startup and revert to the **LastKnownGood** control set to restart the computer.

▶ **To verify system startup from a remote computer**

1. For the local computer, add a **BootVerification** key under this Registry path:

   ```
   HKEY_LOCAL_MACHINE\SYSTEM\CurrentControlSet\Services
   ```

2. Add the following value entries under this new **BootVerification** key:

   ```
   Start : REG_DWORD : 0x00000003
   Type : REG_DWORD : 0x00000020
   ErrorControl : REG_DWORD : 0x00000001
   ImagePath : REG_EXPAND_SZ : bootvrfy.exe
   ObjectName : REG_SZ : LocalSystem
   ```

   For more information about these entries, see "BootVerification Service Entries" in Chapter 14, "Registry Value Entries."

3. Change the value of **ReportBootOK** to 0 under the following Registry path:

   ```
   HKEY_LOCAL_MACHINE\SOFTWARE\Microsoft\Windows NT\CurrentVersion
       \WinLogon
   ```

4. Start the **BootVerification** service from a remote computer.

   This service tells the service controller on the local computer to save the current startup configuration as the **LastKnownGood** configuration, and then it terminates itself.

Important   You cannot use the **BootVerification** service in conjunction with settings in the **BootVerificationProgram** key. These are mutually exclusive methods.

You might also want a good system startup to depend on whether a specific service or driver loads. For example, for a server you might want to cause the Boot Loader to choose the **LastKnownGood** control set if the Server service doesn't start on the computer.

▶ **To change system startup to depend on a service or driver**

1. Select the subkey for the service under this Registry path:

   ```
   HKEY_LOCAL_MACHINE\SYSTEM\CurrentControlSet\Services\ServiceName
   ```

   ServiceName can be any service upon which you want successful system startup to depend.

2. Double-click the service's **ErrorControl** entry, and specify a new value of 2 (to switch to **LastKnownGood** if service doesn't start).

   Rarely, you might want to specify a value of 3 (to fail the attempted startup if the service doesn't start). But this **ErrorControl** value is usually reserved for critical services such as file system drivers.

3. Close Registry Editor, shut down, and restart the computer for these values to take effect.

4. If you do not get the intended effect, restart the computer, and manually choose the **LastKnownGood** control set as described in "Starting a System with Configuration Problems," earlier in this chapter. All changes in the last session will be discarded.

Customizing Windows NT Logon

You can change the Windows NT logon process in two ways:

- Create a custom logon message, especially for secure sites
- Allow automatic logon for a computer

During Windows NT logon, the first message that appears instructs the user to press CTRL+ALT+DEL to log on, and then the Welcome dialog box appears so the user can type a username, domain name, and password.

You can define a custom message to display after the user presses CTRL+ALT+DEL. For example, you might want to warn users that a particular computer is restricted to only certain users. Or, for all computers on the network, you might want to warn against unauthorized attempts to logon.

▶ **To create a custom logon message**

1. In Registry Editor, select this subkey:

   ```
   HKEY_LOCAL_MACHINE\SOFTWARE\Microsoft\Windows NT\CurrentVersion
       \Winlogon
   ```

2. Add a value entry named **LegalNoticeCaption** of type REG_SZ, and type text that will be the caption for the message.

3. Add a value entry named **LegalNoticeText** of type REG_SZ, and type text for the message.

If either **LegalNoticeCaption** or **LegalNoticeText** is defined in the Registry, a user cannot log on to the computer without acknowledging the message by clicking the OK button.

For some computers such as a print server or other special-use systems, you may want to be able to start the system without a user having to supply a username or password. You can define automatic logon for a computer by adding some value entries in the Registry.

▶ **To allow automatic logon for a computer**

1. In Registry Editor, select this subkey:

```
HKEY_LOCAL_MACHINE\SOFTWARE\Microsoft\Windows NT\CurrentVersion
    \Winlogon
```

2. Add a value entry named **AutoAdminLogon** of type REG_SZ, and specify a value of 1.

3. Add a value entry named **DefaultPassword** of type REG_SZ, and enter the password of the user listed under the value **DefaultUserName**.

Changing Driver and Service Configuration Data

The hardware detected on a computer is stored in the volatile HKEY_LOCAL_MACHINE\HARDWARE key. Because this key is destroyed and recreated each time the system starts, you cannot usefully edit hardware settings.

You can use WinMSD to view hardware data in an easy-to-read format, and based on this information you can discover conflicts and their causes or determine how to set up new hardware before installing it. You can also get information about conflicts by looking at the System event log in the Event Viewer.

This section presents some suggestions for solving hardware and related driver problems using Registry Editor.

To carry out some procedures described in this section, you need to follow the instructions for saving keys in "Saving and Restoring Keys" in Chapter 11, "Registry Editor and Registry Administration."

Recovering from an Unsuitable Video Display Choice

You can choose the Windows NT Setup icon in Program Manager to change the type of video driver, the color depth, or the resolution for a display adapter. If you make an unsuitable choice, one of two things happens:

- The driver will not recognize the card and will therefore fail to load at system startup. By default, the system tries to load VGA in base mode as a kind of reserve. So if your video choice fails, the computer will start in VGA. Screen resolution will not be what you'd like, but you can run Windows NT Setup from Program Manager to try another option. (This only happens on an *x*86-based computer.)

- Or the driver will recognize the card and proceed as though the parameters selected are OK. But because they're not (for example, you tried to use 1280x1024 resolution on a monitor that is only capable of 1024x768), you can't see anything on your screen, although the system starts just fine. (This is what always happens on a RISC-based computer when an inappropriate option is chosen but can also occur on an *x*86-based computer.)

If you can't see anything on screen after changing the display settings, do not attempt to log on. Instead, wait for the disk activity to stop, and then use the power switch to restart the computer; then follow the instructions in "Starting a System with Configuration Problems," earlier in this chapter. Then you can run Windows NT Setup from Program Manager to try another choice.

Changing Driver Loading Controls in the Registry

Under most circumstances, you should define the startup behavior of a device or a service by choosing the Devices icon or the Services icon in Control Panel, or by using Server Manager in Windows NT Advanced Server. Use these procedures in specific cases where you cannot define behavior using the other administrative tools.

You can change the basic value entries in the Registry for a specific driver to control driver loading. For example, you can change these things:

- When the driver is loaded or the service is started, including turning off driver loading during startup

- The load order for a driver, a service, or a group during system startup

- Error control for a driver or service, so that startup continues or halts, depending on whether the item is initialized

- Parameters that can be set for a driver or service

▶ **To change the behavior of a driver or service**

1. Select the subkey for the driver or service in the following Registry path:

   ```
   HKEY_LOCAL_MACHINE\SYSTEM\CurrentControlSet
       \Services\DriverName
   ```

2. If you want to change how system startup proceeds if the driver is not loaded or the service is not started, change the value of **ErrorControl** as follows:

Error control	Value	Meaning
Critical	0x3	Fail the attempted system startup
Severe	0x2	Switch to **LastKnownGood** or, if already using **LastKnownGood**, continue on in case of error
Normal	0x1	Continue startup if the driver fails to load, but display a message noting the failure
Ignore	0x0	—

3. If you want to change the dependencies for loading the service, specify new values under **DependOnGroup, DependOnService,** or **Tag.**

4. If you want to change when the service is started or the driver is loaded, change the **Start** value as follows:

Start type	Value	Meaning
Boot	0x0	Loaded by the Boot Loader
System	0x1	Loaded at Kernel initialization
Auto load	0x2	Loaded or started automatically at startup
Load on demand	0x3	Available, but started only by the user
Disabled	0x4	Not to be started under any conditions

5. Close Registry Editor, shut down, and restart the computer for these values to take effect.

For details about **Start** and **ErrorControl** values, see their definitions in "CurrentControlSet\Services Subkeys" in Chapter 14, "Registry Value Entries."

You can also set parameters for many drivers and services, as described in Chapter 14. For example, a modem that includes a National Semiconductor 16550 AUART chip can take advantage of FIFO buffer support. This capability is not turned on by default in Windows NT, however. If you are using such a modem, you can change the value of **ForceFifoEnable** to 1 to turn on FIFO support, under this subkey:

```
HKEY_LOCAL_MACHINE\SYSTEM\CurrentControlSet
   \Services\Serial\Parameters
```

Controlling Multiport Serial I/O Cards

The Microsoft serial driver can be used to control many *dumb* multiport serial cards. *Dumb* indicates that the control includes no onboard processor. Each port of a multiport board has a separate subkey under the CurrentControlSet\Services\Serial subkey in the Registry. In each of these subkeys, you must add values for **DosDevices, Interrupt, InterruptStatus, PortAddress**, and **PortIndex,** because these are not detected by the Hardware Detector. (For descriptions and ranges for these values, see "Disk, Serial, and Parallel Port Entries" in Chapter 14, "Registry Value Entries.")

For example, if you have a four-port COMTROL Hostess 550 board configured to use address 0x500 with an interrupt of 0x2, the values in the Registry would be as follows:

Serial2 subkey:

```
PortAddress = REG_DWORD 0x500
Interrupt = REG_DWORD 2
DosDevices = REG_SZ COM3
InterruptStatus = REG_DWORD 0x507
PortIndex = REG_DWORD 1
```

Serial4 subkey:

```
PortAddress = REG_DWORD 0x510
Interrupt = REG_DWORD 2
DosDevices = REG_SZ COM5
InterruptStatus = REG_DWORD 0x507
PortIndex = REG_DWORD 3
```

Serial3 subkey:

```
PortAddress = REG_DWORD 0x508
Interrupt = REG_DWORD 2
DosDevices = REG_SZ COM4
InterruptStatus = REG_DWORD 0x507
PortIndex = REG_DWORD 2
```

Serial5 subkey:

```
PortAddress = REG_DWORD 0x518
Interrupt = REG_DWORD 2
DosDevices = REG_SZ COM6
InterruptStatus = REG_DWORD 0x507
PortIndex = REG_DWORD 4
```

Certain multiport boards, such as Digiboard non-MCA bus cards, use a different scheme to determine which port is interrupting. These boards should include the **Indexed** value entry in the configuration data for each port under its subkey in CurrentControlSet\Services\Serial. This entry indicates that the board uses an indexed interrupt notification scheme as opposed to a bitmapped method.

For example, if you have an eight-port Digiboard communications board configured to be at address 0x100 with an interrupt of 0x3, the values in the Registry would be as follows:

Serial2 subkey:

```
PortAddress = REG_DWORD 0x100
Interrupt = REG_DWORD 3
DosDevices = REG_SZ COM3
InterruptStatus = REG_DWORD 0x140
Indexed = REG_DWORD 1
PortIndex = REG_DWORD 1
```

Serial3 subkey:

```
PortAddress = REG_DWORD 0x108
Interrupt = REG_DWORD 3
DosDevices = REG_SZ COM4
InterruptStatus = REG_DWORD 0x140
Indexed = REG_DWORD 1
PortIndex = REG_DWORD 2
```

Serial4 subkey:

```
PortAddress = REG_DWORD 0x110
Interrupt = REG_DWORD 3
DosDevices = REG_SZ COM5
InterruptStatus = REG_DWORD 0x140
Indexed = REG_DWORD 1
PortIndex = REG_DWORD 3
```

Serial5 subkey:

```
PortAddress = REG_DWORD 0x118
Interrupt = REG_DWORD 3
DosDevices = REG_SZ COM6
InterruptStatus = REG_DWORD 0x140
Indexed = REG_DWORD 1
PortIndex = REG_DWORD 4
```

Serial6 subkey:

```
PortAddress = REG_DWORD 0x120
Interrupt = REG_DWORD 3
DosDevices = REG_SZ COM7
InterruptStatus = REG_DWORD 0x140
Indexed = REG_DWORD 1
PortIndex = REG_DWORD 5
```

Serial7 subkey:

```
PortAddress = REG_DWORD 0x128
Interrupt = REG_DWORD 3
DosDevices = REG_SZ COM8
InterruptStatus = REG_DWORD 0x140
Indexed = REG_DWORD 1
PortIndex = REG_DWORD 6
```

Serial8 subkey:

```
PortAddress = REG_DWORD 0x130
Interrupt = REG_DWORD 3
DosDevices = REG_SZ COM9
InterruptStatus = REG_DWORD 0x140
Indexed = REG_DWORD 1
PortIndex = REG_DWORD 7
```

Serial9 subkey:

```
PortAddress = REG_DWORD 0x138
Interrupt = REG_DWORD 3
DosDevices = REG_SZ COM10
InterruptStatus = REG_DWORD 0x140
Indexed = REG_DWORD 1
PortIndex = REG_DWORD 8
```

Deleting Serial Ports

You can configure communication ports as described in the previous section or as described in "Serial Subkey Entries in the Services Subkey" in Chapter 14, "Registry Value Entries." You might also need to delete one or more COM ports, which you can only do by deleting the related Registry information in the DeviceMap and Services areas of the Registry. To delete entries in the DeviceMap subkey, you must be logged on as a member of the Administrators group.

▶ **To delete a COM port**

1. In Registry Editor, delete the appropriate value entry for the COM port under the following Registry path:

   ```
   HKEY_LOCAL_MACHINE\Hardware\DeviceMap\SerialComm
   ```

   The value entries in this subkey are used to determine all the communication ports available on the system. The values are of the form **Serial**yyy=COMx, where COMx can be COM1 to COM256, and **Serial**yyy can be from **Serial0** through any large positive number such as Serial15000.

   You can identify the value entry you want to delete based on the list that appears when you choose the Ports icon in Control Panel.

2. Delete the COM port's related **Serial**yyy key in the following Registry path:

   ```
   HKEY_LOCAL_MACHINE\System\CurrentControlSet\Services
       \Serial\Parameters\Serialyyy
   ```

If you do not delete the related Services subkey for **Serial**yyy, the COMx port continues to appear in the Ports list in Control Panel each time the system starts, even though there is no related DeviceMap subkey.

Managing User Profiles Through the Registry

Each user on a Windows NT system is assigned a user profile, which can be set up on a local or remote computer. This user profile contains all the individual preferences and settings for items such as personal program groups, desktop settings, printer connections, user environment variables, and other items.

With Windows NT Advanced Server, you can use the User Profile Editor to move user profiles to other computers, and you can use User Manager for Domains to assign mandatory or individual profiles to users. For information about creating and assigning profiles on local and remote computers, see the *Windows NT Advanced Server System Guide*.

However, you will need to use Registry Editor to edit a profile offline or to manage user profiles when you want to examine a profile on a remote computer (as described earlier in this chapter).

When you edit a profile offline, you need to copy both the related hive and .LOG files, and load them on the computer where you will be working, as described in "Loading Hives from Another Computer" in Chapter 11, "Registry Editor and Registry Administration."

This section describes how hive files are created and how you can move a user profile to another computer when User Profile Editor is not available.

Creating User Profile Hives

With the appropriate access permission, a user can save a locally cached copy of a user profile. The directory and filename of the hive are added as a value under the following Registry key, where *SID_#* represents a key with the same name as the security ID assigned to the user:

```
HKEY_LOCAL_MACHINE\SOFTWARE\Microsoft\Windows NT\CurrentVersion
   \ProfileList\SID_#
```

When the user logs on, the hive defined in the particular **ProfileList*SID_#*** subkey is loaded, with a root key whose name matches the *SID_#* as a child key of HKEY_USERS. HKEY_CURRENT_USER points to this key.

The available user profile hives on a computer will consist of any hives created using User Profile Editor or saved locally by a user who logged on with appropriate permissions, as defined in User Manager for Domains. The **ProfileList** subkeys define all the known user hives on the local computer.

The hive that is loaded when a user logs on depends on whether the user has an assigned profile, as described in the following tables.

Table 12.1   Creating a Hive for a User Without an Assigned Profile

Scenario	How hive is created
If the user has permission to keep a local copy of profile	A copy of the User Default profile (USERDEF) is loaded under the key HKEY_USERS*SID_#*, and a local copy of this profile is saved as the user's profile. This hive is created when you install Windows NT and is saved as *SystemRoot*\SYSTEM32\CONFIG\USERDEF. The user's local copy resides in the same directory. When the user logs off, all changes made to the profile are saved to the local profile just created.
If the user doesn't have permission to keep a local copy of profile (that is, Guest accounts)	USERDEF is copied to a temporary file (*SystemRoot*\SYSTEM32\CONFIG\TMPDEF00) and this copy will be used by the user. When the user logs off, all changes made to the profile are lost.

For a user with an assigned profile, that profile is used whenever possible. Otherwise, the rules in the following tables are used to create a hive.

Table 12.2   Creating a Hive for a User with an Assigned Profile on a Local Computer

Scenario	How hive is created
If the user has a mandatory profile (with a .MAN file-name extension) on a local PC and on a remote PC	The profile is copied to a temporary file in the *SystemRoot*\SYSTEM32\CONFIG directory, and the user will use this temporary profile. All changes made to this profile are lost when the user logs off. If the mandatory profile is not accessible (for example, if the server is down or if there is no access permission for the file), the user is not able to log on.
If the user has a personal profile on a local PC but the profile is not accessible	The user will get a copy of USERDEF.

**Table 12.2   Creating a Hive for a User with an Assigned Profile
on a Local Computer** *(continued)*

Scenario	How hive is created
If the user has a personal profile on a remote PC but doesn't have permission to save a local copy	<ul><li>If the remote profile is accessible, it is saved as a temporary file in *SystemRoot*\SYSTEM32\CONFIG directory. The user's changes are saved back to the remote profile when the user logs off.</li><li>If the remote profile is not accessible (for example, if the server is down or if there is no access permission for the file) and there is no local copy of the user's profile, a copy of USERDEF is saved as a temporary file in the \CONFIG directory. This temporary profile is used for the user's entire logon session. Changes made to the profile are lost when the user logs off.</li></ul>

This last table shows how a hive is created if the user has a personal profile on a remote computer and has permission to save a local copy.

Table 12.3   Creating a Hive for a User with a Profile on a Remote Computer

Scenario	How hive is created
If the remote profile is accessible and there are no local copies of the profile on the local PC	The remote profile is copied as *SystemRoot*\SYSTEM32\CONFIG\USER002. Then this local copy is loaded into the Registry as the user's profile. At logoff, the changes are saved to the local copy, and the local copy is copied back to the remote profile file.
If the remote profile is accessible and a local copy exists	The newest file overwrites the older version, and the file is treated as described above.
If the remote profile is not accessible but a local copy exists	The local copy is loaded into the Registry and used as the user's profile. At logoff, the changes are saved to the local copy, which is copied to the remote profile file at the next log on (if the remote profile is accessible and if the date on the local copy is newer than that for the remote profile).
If the remote profile is not accessible and the local copy does not exist	A copy of USERDEF is saved to the local profile copy path and is loaded in the Registry to be used as the user's profile. At logoff time, the changes made to the profile are saved in the local profile.

Moving User Profile Hives

The hives for user profiles can be located anywhere on a local or remote computer. In some circumstances, you might want to move a user profile hive to another computer when User Profile Editor is not available. You can move a user profile by copying the hive to the new location and then changing the Registry to specify the new location.

▶ **To change a user profile location in the Registry**

1. Log on under a username other than the one for the profile you want to move.

2. Use File Manager to copy the hive and .LOG files for the profile you want to move. This file can be on a floppy disk or on a shared network drive.

3. In Registry Editor, display the Registry for the computer where this hive will be used, and change the value of **ProfileImagePath** under the appropriate **ProfileList***SID*_# subkey to specify the new path and filename for the new hive. The full Registry path for this subkey is the following:

   ```
   HKEY_LOCAL_MACHINE\SOFTWARE\Microsoft\Windows NT\CurrentVersion
       \ProfileList\SID_#
   ```

   The data type for **ProfileImagePath** is REG_EXPAND_SZ, so you can specify a value in the form of %SystemRoot%\system32\config*hiveFilename*. Do not include the double backslash (\\) to specify the UNC path name.

The next time that user logs on, the new user profile will be used.

Important For secure installations, user profile hives should be stored on an NTFS volume where they can be secured by specifying access permission in File Manager.

For more information about the **ProfileList** subkey, see REGENTRY.HLP, which is included on the *Resource Guide* disk.

C H A P T E R   1 3

Initialization Files and the Registry

Although the Registry replaces the initialization (.INI) files used in versions of Microsoft Windows created for MS-DOS, some .INI files still appear in the Windows NT system directory. Also, applications created for 16-bit Microsoft Windows must still be able to read and write .INI values that previously were stored in WIN.INI or SYSTEM.INI.

This chapter describes how .INI files and other configuration files are used under Windows NT and how these values are stored in the Registry. The following are the topics discussed in this chapter:

- How Windows NT uses MS-DOS configuration files
- How .INI files are mapped to the Registry
- Microsoft OS/2 version 1.x entries in the Registry
- POSIX entries in the Registry

Related topics are discussed in the following chapters of the *Windows NT Resource Guide*:

- For details about the SHARED32.INI file, see Chapter 8, "Mail."
- For details about Registry entries for Microsoft Mail and Microsoft Schedule+ initialization values, see Chapter 14, "Registry Value Entries."

How Windows NT Uses MS-DOS Configuration Files

During system startup, Windows NT adds any **Path, Prompt,** and **Set** commands from the C:\AUTOEXEC.BAT file to the Windows NT environment variables and then ignores the rest of the contents of C:\AUTOEXEC.BAT and C:\CONFIG.SYS. If these files are not present when you install Windows NT, the Setup program creates them.

For a RISC-based computer, default AUTOEXEC.NT and CONFIG.NT files are created.

The path and other Windows NT environment information are stored under the following Registry key:

```
HKEY_LOCAL_MACHINE\SYSTEM\CurrentControlSet
   \Control\Session Manager\Environment
```

When an MS-DOS–based application is started, Windows NT executes files specified in the application's PIF or the AUTOEXEC.NT and CONFIG.NT files in the *SystemRoot*\SYSTEM32 directory. Any changes made in one of these files take effect as soon as the file is saved and a new MS-DOS–based application is started that uses that file. You do not need to restart your system after changing the *.NT files.

File	Use in Windows NT
C:\AUTOEXEC.BAT	Path and environment variables are added to the Windows NT environment at system startup.
C:\CONFIG.SYS	Not used by Windows NT.
AUTOEXEC.NT and CONFIG.NT in *SystemRoot*\SYSTEM32	Used every time an MS-DOS–based application is run with the _DEFAULT.PIF. (Custom *.NT files can be created and used when starting an application from another PIF.)

You can use WinMSD to view the contents of AUTOEXEC.NT and CONFIG.NT by choosing commands from the File menu. You can edit the contents of these files using any text editor.

Commands in AUTOEXEC.BAT and CONFIG.SYS for starting applications and initializing drivers are ignored in Windows NT. If you want an application to run automatically when you start Windows NT, place an icon for the application in the Startup group in Program Manager, as described in Chapter 3, "Program Manager," in the *Windows NT System Guide*. For a service or driver, use the Services icon in Control Panel to define the startup type. This setting is saved as the **Start** value in the service's subkey under HKEY_LOCAL_MACHINE \SYSTEM\CurrentControlSet\Services in the Registry.

VDM Sessions

Each MS-DOS and 16-bit Windows application runs in a Windows NT virtual MS-DOS machine (VDM). Windows NT includes the necessary virtual device drivers (VDDs) for the mouse, keyboard, printer, COM ports, and network support. The VDDs are loaded into every VDM based on values stored in the Registry. The Registry path for information about VDDs is the following:

```
HKEY_LOCAL_MACHINE\SYSTEM\CurrentControlSet\Control\VirtualDeviceDrivers
```

Any changes to the VDD entries are managed automatically by the system when you add a device driver using Windows NT Setup.

Windows for MS-DOS on Windows NT

Windows NT is a 32-bit environment, and Windows 3.x for MS-DOS is a 16-bit environment. For a 16-bit Windows-based application, Windows NT runs the application using a VDM and VDDs. This process is called WOW, for *Win16 on Win32*. Using a Win16 VDM, Windows NT translates Windows 3.1 application calls in standard mode for RISC-based computers and in 386 enhanced mode for *x*86 based-computers.

Control parameters for WOW startup and for the WOW application environment are found under the following Registry path:

```
HKEY_LOCAL_MACHINE\SYSTEM\CurrentControlSet\Control\WOW
```

The settings in this key are maintained automatically by the system and should not require manual changes.

The environment settings equivalent to the SYSTEM.INI file for Windows 3.x are found in this Registry path:

```
HKEY_LOCAL_MACHINE\SOFTWARE\Microsoft\Windows NT\CurrentVersion\WOW
```

The WOW subkeys have the same names as headings in the SYSTEM.INI file, and the values are the same items as contained in the old SYSTEM.INI file. For details about these entries, see REGENTRY.HLP on the Resource Guide disk.

How .INI Files Are Mapped to the Registry

If you install Windows NT as an upgrade over Windows 3.1, all the settings from various initialization files are copied into the Registry, including CONTROL.INI, PROGMAN.INI, SYSTEM.INI, WIN.INI, WINFILE.INI, and others. You can see where the Windows initialization files are mapped in the Registry by viewing the subkeys and value entries under this path:

```
HKEY_Local_Machine\SOFTWARE\Microsoft
    \Windows NT\CurrentVersion\IniFileMapping
```

When you install an application created for 16-bit Microsoft Windows, the application's setup program creates its own .INI file or creates entries for the WIN.INI or SYSTEM.INI file in the same way that it does for any versions of Windows for MS-DOS. These entries are not updated in the Registry, because these applications do not know how to access the Windows NT Registry. For this reason, basic SYSTEM.INI, WIN.INI, and WINFILE.INI files appear in the *SystemRoot* directory in Windows NT.

If a Windows-based application tries to write to WIN.INI, SYSTEM.INI, or any other section listed in the **IniFileMapping** key, and if the application uses the Windows NT Registry APIs, the information is stored in the Registry. If the application writes to other sections of the .INI file or tries to open the .INI file directly without using the Windows NT Registry APIs, the information is saved in an .INI file.

To find mapping information in the HKEY_LOCAL_MACHINE\Software key, the system looks up the *filename.ext* of the initialization file. If a match is found, it looks under the mapped key for the specific application name and a variable name, and if necessary it continues to look for keys whose value entries are the variable names. If no mapping for either the application name or filename is found, the system looks for an .INI file to read and write its contents.

Tables 13.1 through 13.3 show where system settings are saved in the Registry in comparison to initialization files used with Windows 3.1 for MS-DOS.

In the entries in the **IniFileMapping** key and in Tables 13.1 through 13.3, the following symbols are used:

Symbol	Meaning
!	Forces all writes to go to both the Registry and to the .INI file on disk.
#	Causes the Registry value to be set to the value in the Windows 3.1 .INI file whenever a new user logs in for the first time after Setup, if Windows NT was installed on a computer that had Windows 3.1 already installed.
@	Prevents any reads from going to the .INI file on disk if the requested data is not found in the Registry.
USR	Stands for HKEY_CURRENT_USER, and the text after the prefix is relative to that key.
SYS	Stands for HKEY_LOCAL_MACHINE\Software, and the text after the prefix is relative to that key.

WIN.INI Settings in the Registry

The information stored in the keys described in Table 13.1 is used by applications that expect to find this information in a WIN.INI file.

Table 13.1   Registry Paths for WIN.INI Sections

WIN.INI section	Registry path	Description
[colors]	#USR\Control Panel\Colors[1]	Defines colors for the Windows display as set using the Colors icon in Control Panel.
[compatibility]	#SYS...\Compatibility[3]	—
[desktop]	#USR\Control Panel\Desktop[1]	Specifies appearance of the desktop as set using the Desktop icon in Control Panel.
[embedding]	#SYS...\Embedding[3]	Lists the server objects used in Object Linking and Embedding (OLE); created during software setup.
[extensions]	#USR...\Extensions[2]	Associates types of files with applications as set by choosing Associate in File Manager.
[fonts] and [fontSubstitutes]	#SYS...\Fonts and \FontSubstitutes[3]	Describes the screen font files loaded by Windows as set using the Fonts icon in Control Panel.
[intl]	#USR\Control Panel\International[1]	Describes items for languages and locales as set using the International icon in Control Panel.
[mci extensions]	SYS...\MCI Extensions[3]	Associates file types with Media Control Interface devices as set using the Control Panel Drivers icon.
[network]	USR...\Network\Persistent Connections[2]; network printers in HKEY_LOCAL_MACHINE \SYSTEM\Control\Print	Describes network printer port settings as set using Print Manager and the persistent network connections as set using File Manager.
[ports]	SYS...\Ports[3]	Lists all available printer and communications ports as set using the Ports icon in Control Panel.
[printerPorts] and [devices]	SYS...\PrinterPorts and \Devices[3]	Lists active and inactive output devices to be accessed by Windows as set using Printer Manager.
[sounds]	#USR \Control Panel\Sounds[1]	Lists the sound files assigned to each system event as set using the Sound icon in Control Panel.
[TrueType]	#USR...\TrueType[2]	Describes options for using TrueType fonts as set using the Fonts icon in Control Panel.
[Windows Help]	USR\Software \Microsoft\Windows Help[1]	Lists settings for the Help window as set using the mouse or menus in any Help window.
[Windows]	#SYS...\Winlogon[3]	Specifies the Windows environment and user startup options as set using the Desktop, Keyboard, and Mouse icons in Control Panel.

[1] Full path = HKEY_CURRENT_USER

[2] Full path = HKEY_CURRENT_USER\SOFTWARE\Microsoft\Windows NT\CurrentVersion

[3] Full path = HKEY_LOCAL_MACHINE\SOFTWARE\Microsoft\Windows NT\CurrentVersion

SYSTEM.INI Settings in the Registry

Entries from a SYSTEM.INI file in Windows for MS-DOS on the computer when you install Windows NT will be preserved as entries under this key:

```
HKEY_LOCAL_MACHINE\Software\Microsoft\Windows NT\CurrentVersion\WOW
```

The following table describes where you can view or edit entries for similar purposes in Windows NT. These entries are used by applications that look for values in the SYSTEM.INI file.

Table 13.2   Registry Paths for SYSTEM.INI Sections

SYSTEM.INI section	Registry path	Description
[boot] and **[boot.description]**	#SYS...\WOW\Boot and \Boot.description[3]; replaced by ...CurrentControlSet\Control	Lists drivers and Windows modules as set using the System icon in Control Panel.
[drivers]	Replaced by #SYS...\Drivers32[3]	Contains a list of aliases (or names) assigned to installable driver files as set using the Drivers and Devices icons in Control Panel.
[keyboard]	#SYS...\WOW\Keyboard[3]; #USR\Keyboard Layout[1]	Contains information about the keyboard as set using the International icon in Control Panel or identified by the Hardware Detector.
[mci] and **[mci32]**	Replaced by #SYS...\MCI and \MCI32[3] and #SYS...\Drivers.desc[3]	Lists Media Control Interface (MCI) drivers as set using the Drivers icon in Control Panel.
[NonWindows App]	#SYS...\WOW\NonWindowsApp[3]	Contains information used by non-Windows–based applications as defined in PIFs for specific applications or in CONFIG.NT.
[standard]	Standard in #SYS...\WOW[3]	Contains information used by Windows for MS-DOS in standard and 386 enhanced mode. All memory management is handled automatically by Windows NT.

[1] Full path = HKEY_CURRENT_USER

[2] Full path = HKEY_CURRENT_USER\SOFTWARE\Microsoft\Windows NT\CurrentVersion

[3] Full path = HKEY_LOCAL_MACHINE\SOFTWARE \Microsoft\Windows NT\CurrentVersion

Other Initialization File Settings in the Registry

The following table describes where you can view or edit Registry entries equivalent to CONTROL.INI, PROGMAN.INI, and WINFILE.INI entries.

Table 13.3   Registry Paths for Other Initialization Files

.INI file section	Registry path	Description
CONTROL.INI **[Current]**, **[Color Schemes]**, **[Custom Colors]**	Color Schemes, Current, and Custom Colors subkeys in #USR \Control Panel[1]	Describes color schemes and custom colors as set using the Colors icon in Control Panel.
CONTROL.INI **[Patterns]** and **[Screen Saver*]**	Patterns and Screen Saver.*x* subkeys in #USR\Control Panel[1]	Describes elements of desktop appearance and behavior as set using the Desktop icon in Control Panel.
CONTROL.INI **[MMCPL]**, **[Drivers.Desc]**, **[Userinstallable.drivers]**	#USR\Control Panel\MMCPL[1]; #SYS...\Drivers.Desc and \Userinstallable.drivers[3]	Contains values for installable drivers and devices used for multimedia as set using the Drivers icon in Control Panel.
PROGMAN.INI **[groups]**, **[restrictions]**, **[settings]**	Groups, Restrictions, and Settings subkeys in #USR...\Program Manager[2]	Describes window appearance, groups and the icons in the groups, and restrictions on Program Manager operations as set using Program Manager; restrictions are set in User Manager for Domains.
MSMAIL32.INI	USR...\Mail[2]	Contains parameters that can be set for Mail.
SCHDPL32.INI	#USR...\Schedule+[2]	Contains parameters that can be set for Schedule+.
WINFILE.INI **[settings]**	#USR...\File Manager[2]	Describes the appearance and behavior of items in File Manager as set using File Manager.

[1] Full path = HKEY_CURRENT_USER

[2] Full path = HKEY_CURRENT_USER\SOFTWARE\Microsoft\Windows NT\CurrentVersion

[3] Full path = HKEY_LOCAL_MACHINE\SOFTWARE \Microsoft\Windows NT\CurrentVersion

Microsoft OS/2 Version 1.*x* Entries in the Registry

The Microsoft OS/2 version 1.*x* subsystem starts whenever a user starts an OS/2 character-based application on an *x*86-based computer. The Registry entries for the OS/2 subsystem are found under this key:

```
HKEY_LOCAL_MACHINE\SYSTEM\CurrentControlSet
    \Control\Session Manager\SubSystems
```

The **Os2** entry in this subkey describes the path to the executable file used to start the OS/2 subsystem. The directory path for the OS/2 library is the **Os2LibPath** value defined under the **Session Manager\Environment** subkey.

When Windows NT is installed on a computer, if Setup finds a copy of CONFIG.SYS for OS/2, a copy is placed in the *SystemRoot*\SYSTEM32 directory. This information is used to configure the OS/2 subsystem whenever an OS/2 application is started. If a CONFIG.SYS file is not found, a substitute is created in the Registry, with the following values:

```
PROTSHELL=C:\os2\pmshell.exe c:\os2\os2.ini c:\os2\os2sys.ini
    %SystemRoot%\system32\cmd.exe
SET COMSPEC=%SystemRoot%\system32\cmd.exe
```

The OS/2 CONFIG.SYS information is stored in the following Registry entry, which appears only after an OS/2 application has been run on the system:

```
HKEY_LOCAL_MACHINE\SOFTWARE\Microsoft\OS/2 Subsystem for NT\config.sys
```

The other subkeys under the OS/2 Subsystem key do not contain entries.

If you subsequently edit the C:\CONFIG.SYS file using a text editor, **LIBPTH=,** **SET PATH=,** and **Set WINDIR=** entries are appended to the end of the file from the Windows NT environment. Any changes made to the path or environment variables take effect after the system is shut down and restarted.

For details about managing this environment under Windows NT, see Chapter 11, "Other Application Environments," in the *Windows NT System Guide*.

You can disable an OS/2 subsystem in Windows NT and still run a bound application under a VDM. Many bound applications run better under a VDM than under the OS/2 subsystem.

▶ **To disable the OS/2 subsystem in Windows NT**

- In Registry Editor, change the value of **GlobalFlag** to 20100000 in the following Registry path:

```
HKEY_LOCAL_MACHINE\SYSTEM\CurrentControlSet\SessionManager
```

You can also use FORCEDOS.EXE, a utility supplied with Windows NT in the *SystemRoot*\SYSTEM32 subdirectory. This allows you to run a bound application under a VDM. To see how to use the ForceDOS utility, type **forcedos /?** at the command prompt.

POSIX Entries in the Registry

The POSIX subsystem starts whenever a user starts a POSIX application. The Registry entries for the POSIX subsystem are found under this key:

```
HKEY_LOCAL_MACHINE\SYSTEM\CurrentControlSet
    \Control\Session Manager\SubSystems
```

The **Posix** entry in this subkey describes the path to the executable file used to start the POSIX subsystem. The POSIX subsystem does not have any parameters or environmental variables that the user can set.

CHAPTER 14

Registry Value Entries

Wherever possible, you should use the Control Panel and the applications in the Administrative Tools program group to make changes to the system configuration. For those occasions when you need to view or adjust a setting, this chapter identifies the Registry entries that you can add or change using the Registry Editor.

In this chapter, entries for Registry values are listed alphabetically within the following groups of topics:

- Summaries of entries in the Select, Control, and Services subkeys in HKEY_LOCAL_MACHINE\SYSTEM\CurrentControlSet
- Network adapter cards, drivers, and bindings
- Device drivers, with entries for disk, serial, and parallel port devices; keyboard and mouse devices; SCSI miniport devices; and video display devices
- Services, with entries for the Alerter, AppleTalk and Macfile, DLC, Eventlog, NetBEUI (NBF) transport, Netlogon, Replicator, Server, NWLink, TCP/IP, UPS, and Workstation services
- Mail and Schedule+
- User preferences
- Fonts and printing
- Windows NT subsystems

Caution Using Registry Editor incorrectly can cause serious problems, including corruptions that may make it necessary to reinstall Windows NT.

Not all entries that appear here may be found in the Registry for a particular computer. For many entries, the system uses the default value unless you add the entry to the Registry and specify another value.

The information in this chapter appears in the following format:

Entry Name   REG_type   Range for value entry
A description of the entry, usually including the conditions under which you might change the value.

Default: *value*
(For value ranges that are Boolean, the value can be **1** for true or "enabled," or **0** for false or "disabled.")

In general, if you change values for any entries in the CurrentControlSet, you must restart the computer for the changes to take effect.

If you change values for entries under HKEY_CURRENT_USER using Registry Editor, you may have to log off and log back on for the changes to take effect.

Note You'll find a navigational hint at the bottom corner of each page, indicating which service or portion of the Registry is described on that page.

CurrentControlSet\Select Subkey

The Select subkey under HKEY_LOCAL_MACHINE\SYSTEM maintains information about the control sets for the currently selected computer. The Select subkey contains the following named values:

Current   REG_DWORD   *0xN, where N identifies a control set*
Identifies the control set from which the CurrentControlSet subkey is derived. If this value is 0x1, for example, the subkey producing the CurrentControlSet is ControlSet001.

Default   REG_DWORD   *0xN, where N identifies a control set*
Identifies the default control set. If this value is 0x1, for example, the default control set is ControlSet001.

Failed   REG_DWORD   *0xN, where N identifies a control set*
Identifies the control set number of the control set that was last rejected and replaced with a LastKnownGood control set.

LastKnownGood   REG_DWORD   *0xN, where N identifies a control set*
Identifies the last control set that successfully started the system. If this value is 0x1, for example, the last control set known to be good is ControlSet001.

CurrentControlSet\Control Subkeys

This key contains parameters that control system startup, such as subsystems to load, the size and location of paging files, and so on.

Note The system must be restarted for any changes in the Control key to take effect.

The Control subkey itself can contain the following value entries:

Current User   REG_SZ   *Username*

Specifies the username for the currently logged-on user.

Default: *Username*

RegistrySizeLimit   REG_DWORD   *Size in bytes*

Specifies the total amount of space that can be consumed by Registry data.

The system ensures that the value for **RegistrySizeLimit** is at least 4 MB and no greater than about 80 percent of the size of **PagedPoolSize.** Setting **RegistrySizeLimit** to 0xffffffff sets the value to be as large as 80 percent of **PagedPoolSize** (under the Control\Session Manager\MemoryManagement key). You can allow for a bigger Registry by setting the initial **PagedPoolSize,** or you can set the value of **RegistrySizeLimit.** If you want a very large Registry, you want to set both. However, for all but a few domain controllers, **RegistrySizeLimit** never needs to be changed.

RegistrySizeLimit must have a type of REG_DWORD and a data length of 4 bytes, or it will be ignored.

Default: 8 MB (That is, 25 percent of the default **PagedPoolSize.**)

SystemStartOptions   REG_SZ   *String*

Contains the text of system arguments passed to the system by the firmware. These values can be used to determine whether the debugger is enabled, the options set for ports and speed, and so on. For example, the following value could be defined for **SystemStartOptions**:

```
c:\winnt="Windows NT" /DebugPort=com1 /DebugBaudRate=56000
```

In this example, "Windows NT" in the first part of the string indicates the *SystemRoot* specified under the Windows NT\CurrentVersion subkey in the Software area of the Registry. The remaining portion of this string is interpreted by the system to define the COM port and baud rate for debugging.

The following standard Control subkeys are found under this Registry path:

`HKEY_LOCAL_MACHINE\SYSTEM\CurrentControlSet\Control`

BootVerificationProgram	Lsa[1]	Session Manager
ComputerName[1]	NetworkProvider	Setup[1]
DisplayDriverControl[1]	Nls	TimeZoneInformation[1]
GroupOrderList	Print[2]	VirtualDeviceDrivers
ServiceGroupO-rder	PriorityControl[1]	Windows
HiveList	ProductOptions[1]	WOW
Keyboard Layout		

[1] These keys contain information used only by the system and should not be edited by users. Because these entries should be maintained only by the system, they are not described here.

[2] See "Registry Entries for Printing," later in this chapter.

BootVerificationProgram Control Entries

The BootVerificationProgram key is used to update the last known good configuration during system startup. This entry describes a program that will be called by the service controller to establish the last known good configuration. Such a program can be written by the system administrator.

The Registry path for this key is the following:

`HKEY_LOCAL_MACHINE\SYSTEM\CurrentControlSet`
`    \Control\BootVerificationProgram`

Any entry added under this subkey must have the following format:

ImagePath   Reg_SZ or REG_EXPAND_SZ   *Filename*
Specifies the filename for a startup verification program.
Default: (no entry)

You must also specify a value of 1 for the **ReportBootOK** entry under the following Registry path:

`HKEY_LOCAL_MACHINE\Software\Windows NT\CurrentVersion\WinLogon`

When the value of **ReportBootOK** is set to 0, it disables the automatic (default) startup acceptance, which happens after the first successful logon.

As an alternative, if you want to verify system startup from a remote location, the BootVerification service supplied with Windows NT can be used instead of the BootVerificationProgram, as described later in this chapter. The BootVerification service cannot be used in conjunction with entries in the BootVerificationProgram subkey.

Note Do not change values in the BootVerificationProgram key unless you need a custom verification program to satisfy specific startup criteria at your site. Otherwise, accept the default procedures for verifying system startup.

GroupOrderList Control Entries

The entries in the GroupOrderList key specify the ordering of services within groups, under the following Registry path:

```
HKEY_LOCAL_MACHINE\SYSTEM\CurrentControlSet\Control\GroupOrderList
```

For a service listed under CurrentControlSet\Services, the value of the **Group** entry plus any **Tag** entry determines the order in which the service is loaded. But not all services have a **Tag** entry, and not all groups have an entry in the GroupOrderList subkey. The ServiceGroupOrder subkey described later in this section specifies the order for loading groups.

The entries in the key are all of type REG_BINARY. These are the default entries that define the order within groups:

Base	Pointer Class	Video
Ndis	SCSI Miniport	Keyboard Port
Primary Disk	Keyboard Class	
Filter	Pointer Port	

HiveList Control Entries

The location of the files that contain Registry information is reported under the following Registry path:

```
HKEY_CURRENT_MACHINE\SYSTEM\CurrentControlSet\Control\hivelist
```

All data types are REG_SZ. The following are the default entries:

\REGISTRY\MACHINE\HARDWARE

\REGISTRY\MACHINE\SAM=
\Device\Harddisk0\Partition1*SystemRoot*\SYSTEM32\CONFIG\SAM

\REGISTRY\MACHINE\SECURITY=
  \Device\Harddisk0\Partition1*SystemRoot*\SYSTEM32\CONFIG\SECURITY

\REGISTRY\MACHINE\SOFTWARE=
  \Device\Harddisk0\Partition1*SystemRoot*\SYSTEM32\CONFIG\SOFTWARE

\REGISTRY\MACHINE\SYSTEM=
  \Device\Harddisk0\Partition1*SystemRoot*\SYSTEM32\CONFIG\SYSTEM

\REGISTRY\USER\.DEFAULT=
  \Device\Harddisk0\Partition1*SystemRoot*\SYSTEM32\CONFIG\DEFAULT

\REGISTRY\USER*SID_#*=
  \Device\Harddisk0\Partition1*SystemRoot*\SYSTEM32\CONFIG\ADMIN000

Keyboard Layout Control Entries

The Keyboard Layout key maintains the mapping of keyboard layout names to keyboard layout DLL names, under the following Registry path:

```
HKEY_LOCAL_MACHINE\SYSTEM\CurrentControlSet\Control\Keyboard Layout
```

The Keyboard Layout key is used by the system to determine which DLL to load. The mapping may contain duplicated keyboard layout DLL names if that DLL implements the layout for more than one language (in other words, a keyboard layout may have more than one name). Individual preferences are stored under HKEY_CURRENT_USER\Keyboard Layout.

The Keyboard Layout key contains an entry in this format:

KeyboardLayout   **REG_SZ**   *DLL filename*
  By convention, a keyboard layout name is a null-terminated string of 8 hexadecimal digits representing a language ID (in the last four digits) and a variation number (in the first four digits).

  For example, the language ID of Swiss German is 0x807, so, by convention, keyboard layout names could be 00000807, 00010807, and so on.

The DosKeybCodes subkey is used by the system to convert Windows NT keyboard layout names into MS-DOS–style two-character keyboard layout names as used by the **kb16** command (equivalent to **keyb** in MS-DOS). The system must automatically switch the VDM keyboard layout whenever the Windows NT keyboard layout is changed. Entries are found under this Registry path:

```
HKEY_LOCAL_MACHINE\SYSTEM\CurrentControlSet\Control
    \Keyboard Layout\DosKeybCodes
```

KeyboardLayout   **REG_SZ**   *Two-character code*

These entries define the two-character equivalent for each keyboard layout. This list summarizes the entries under DosKeybCodes:

00000405=cz	**00000414**=no	**0000080C**=be
00000406=dk	**00000415**=pl	**00000813**=be
00000407=gr	**00000416**=br	**00000816**=po
00000409=us	**00000419**=ru	**00000C0C**=cf
0000040A=sp	**0000041A**=yu	**00001009**=us
0000040B=su	**0000041B**=sl	**0000100C**=sf
0000040C=fr	**0000041D**=sv	**00010409**=dv
0000040E=hu	**00000807**=sg	**0001040A**=sp
0000040F=us	**00000809**=uk	**00010C0C**=cf
00000410=it	**0000080A**=la	**00020409**=us
00000413=nl		

NetworkProvider Control Entries

Windows NT supports a common interface that allows networks from several different vendors (that is, network providers) to operate on a single computer at the same time. The NetworkProvider subkey provides a list of the available network providers that use the Microsoft network-independent APIs. The following value for the Order subkey appears under this Registry path:

```
HKEY_LOCAL_MACHINE\SYSTEM\CurrentControlSet\Control
    \NetworkProvider\Order
```

ProviderOrder   **REG_SZ**   *Comma-separated list of key names*

Specifies the order for accessing available network providers, as defined by choosing the Networks button in the Network dialog box in Control Panel. Each entry in this list is in the form of a Registry Services key name for a service or driver that is associated with a particular network provider. The Services subkey associated with a network provider should contain a **Group** entry with the value of NetworkProvider, and must also contain a NetworkProvider subkey with information for the Multiple Provider Router. For more information, see "NetworkProvider" in the "Registry Entries for Network Services" section later in this chapter.

Default: LanmanWorkstation (when a single network is installed)

Nls Control Entries

This key contains subkeys that define information for languages and code pages.

In the Code Page and Language subkeys, all code pages and languages supported under Windows NT are listed, so applications can check these keys to find all "supported" languages. However, only the entries with filenames in the data fields are actually installed in the system. So applications must check the data fields to find out if a specific code page is actually installed in the system.

CodePage Entries

The entries under the following Registry path identify the files for available code pages. If there is no value following the entry name, that code page is not installed in the system.

```
HKEY_LOCAL_MACHINE\SYSTEM\CurrentControlSet\Control\Nls\CodePage
```

Each entry has the following format:

CodePageID   **REG_SZ**   *Filename*

As shown in the following list, **437**=C_437.NLS indicates the file for code page 437, and **1252**=C_1252.NLS indicates the file for code page 1252, and so on. **ACP** is the default ANSI code page; **OEMCP** is the default OEM code page; and **MACCP** is the default Macintosh code page.

10000=c_10000.nls	**1253**=	**861**=
10006=	**1254**=	**863**=
10007=	**437**=c_437.nls	**865**=
10029=	**500**=	**866**=
1026=	**850**=c_850.nls	**869**=
1250=	**852**=	**875**=
1251=	**855**=	**ACP**=1252
1252=c_1252.nls	**857**=	**MACCP**=10000
	860=	**OEMCP**=437

Language Entries

The entries under the following Registry path identify the files for available languages. If there is no value following the entry name, that language is not installed in the system.

```
HKEY_LOCAL_MACHINE\SYSTEM\CurrentControlSet\Control\Nls\Language
```

Each entry has the following format:

LanguageID   **REG_SZ**   *Filename*

As shown in the following table, l_INTL.NLS is the file for language 0409, l_INTL.NLS is the file for language 0809, and so on.

Default: 0409 (the default language ID)

0405=l_intl.nls	**0414**= l_intl.nls	**0813**=l_intl.nls
0406= l_intl.nls	**0415**=l_intl.nls	**0814**=l_intl.nls
0407=l_intl.nls	**0416**=l_intl.nls	**0816**=l_intl.nls
0408=	**0419**=l_intl.nls	**0c07**= l_intl.nls
0409=l_intl.nls	**041b**=l_intl.nls	**28**=l_intl.nls
040a=l_intl.nls	**041d**=l_intl.nls	**0c0a**=l_intl.nls
040b= l_intl.nls	**041f**=	**0c0c**=l_intl.nls
040c=l_intl.nls	**0807**=l_intl.nls	**1009**=l_intl.nls
040e=l_intl.nls	**0809**=l_intl.nls	**100c**=l_intl.nls
040f=l_intl.nls	**080a**=l_intl.nls	**1409**=l_intl.nls
0410=l_intl.nls	**080c**=l_intl.nls	**1809**=l_intl.nls
0413=l_intl.nls	**0810**=l_intl.nls	

OEMLocale Entries

The following key, if present, can contain entries that an OEM adds to customize its locale:

`HKEY_LOCAL_MACHINE\SYSTEM\CurrentControlSet\Control\Nls\OEMLocale`

This section of the Registry is only checked if a specific locale ID is not found in the default locale file (LOCALE.NLS). If this subkey is present, each entry has the following format:

OEMlocale   **REG_SZ**   *filename*

Specifies the locale ID and a filename for the OEM locale.

Default: This subkey is not present, so there is no default.

ServiceGroupOrder Control Entries

The ServiceGroupOrder key specifies the order to load various groups of services.

Order within groups is specified using the value of **Tag** under the specific Services subkeys and the values in the GroupOrderList subkey. For example, when you start Windows NT, the Boot Loader scans the Registry for drivers with a **Start** value of 0 (which indicates that these drivers should be loaded but not initialized before the Kernel) and a **Type** value of 0x1 (which indicates a Kernel device driver such as a hard disk or other low-level hardware device driver). The drivers are then loaded into memory in the order specified as the **List** value in the ServiceGroupOrder subkey.

```
HKEY_LOCAL_MACHINE\SYSTEM\CurrentControlSet\Control\ServiceGroupOrder
```

List   REG_MULTI_SZ   *Group names*

Specifies the order for loading drivers into memory.

Default:

SCSI miniport
port
Primary disk
SCSI class
SCSI CDROM
class filter
boot file system
Base
Keyboard Port
Pointer Port
Keyboard Class
Pointer Class
Video
file system
Event log
Streams Drivers
NDIS
TDI
NetBIOSGroup
NetDDEGroup
extended base network

Session Manager Control Entries

The Session Manager subkey contains the global variables used by the Session
Manager. These values are stored under the following Registry path:

```
HKEY_LOCAL_MACHINE\SYSTEM\CurrentControlSet\Control\Session Manager
```

BootExecute   REG_MULTI_SZ

Specifies programs to run during startup. For example, if CONVERT.EXE has
been used to convert the file system on a hard disk drive, this value is added to
BootExecute so that conversion occurs when the system is restarted:

```
BootExecute = autocheck autoconv \Dos\Devices\x: /FS:NTFS
```

Default: autocheck autochk *

CriticalSectionTimeout   REG_DWORD

Specifies the deadlock time-out for critical sections. Usually, retail installations of Windows NT will not time-out and detect deadlocks.

Default: 0x278d00

GlobalFlag   REG_DWORD

Controls various Windows NT internal operations. You can change this value to disable the OS/2 subsystem if you want to run bound applications in a VDM, rather than under the OS/2 subsystem. Set this value to 20100000 to disable the OS/2 subsystem.

Default: 0x21100000

ObjectDirectories   REG_MULTI_SZ

Lists the object directories to create during startup. Do not edit these entries.

Default: \DosDevices
\Windows
\RPC Control

DOS Devices Control Entries

The DosDevices subkey lists the built-in symbolic links to create at startup. The values are stored under this subkey:

```
HKEY_LOCAL_MACHINE\SYSTEM\CurrentControlSet
    \Control\Session Manager\DOS Devices
```

Entries in this key have the data type of REG_SZ. The following list shows the default entries under this key.

AUX=\DosDevices\COM1
MAILSLOT=\Device\MailSlot
NUL=\Device\Null
PIPE=\Device\NamedPipe
PRN=\DosDevices\LPT1
TELNET=\Device\Telnet
UNC=\Device\Mup

Environment Control Entries

The Environment subkey defines environment variables that the system creates and that are used by Windows NT Logon and Program Manager.

Caution Use extreme care in changing these entry values. If the operating system cannot find the files specified for a subsystem, you will not be able to run non-Windows NT applications.

The Registry path for these values is the following:

```
HKEY_LOCAL_MACHINE\SYSTEM\CurrentControlSet
    \Control\Session Manager\Environment
```

ComSpec   REG_EXPAND_SZ   *Filename*

Defines the path and filename for the Windows NT command interpreter (the equivalent of MS-DOS COMMAND.COM).

Default: %systemRoot%\SYSTEM32\CMD.EXE

Os2LibPath   REG_EXPAND_SZ   *Filename*

Defines the path for the Microsoft OS/2 version 1.*x* library.

Default: %systemRoot%\SYSTEM32\os2\dll

Path   REG_EXPAND_SZ   *Filename*

Defines the path variable for Windows NT logon and Program Manager.

Default: %systemRoot%\SYSTEM32; %SystemRoot%

Windir   REG_EXPAND_SZ   *Filename*

Defines the path for the executable for WOW, as used by Windows NT logon and Program Manager.

Default: %systemRoot%\SYSTEM32\CMD.EXE

KnownDLLs Control Entries

The KnownDlls key defines the set of DLLs that are first searched during system startup. In general these are system DLLs that are loaded from disk into a section of memory and are checked for integrity. These DLLs consume some resources, even if no application loads them. These appear as separate entries under this Registry path:

```
HKEY_LOCAL_MACHINE\SYSTEM\CurrentControlSet\Control\Session
Manager\KnownDLLs
```

driverName   **REG_SZ**   *DLL Filename*

This series of entries defines a driver name and the corresponding DLL filename. The following shows the default entries:

advapi32=advapi32.dll   **olecli32**=olecli32.dll
comdlg32=comdlg32.dll   **olesvr32**=olesvr32.dll
crtdll=crtdll.dll   **rpcrt4**=rpcrt4.dll
DllDirectory=%SystemRoot%\system32   **shell32**=shell32.dll
gdi32=gdi32.dll   **user32**=user32.dll
kernel32=kernel32.dll   **version**=version.dll
lz32=lz32.dll

Memory Management Control Entries

The Memory Management subkey defines paging options under the following Registry path:

```
HKEY_LOCAL_MACHINE\SYSTEM\CurrentControlSet\Control
    \Session Manager\Memory Management
```

The paging file parameters should be defined by using the System icon in Control Panel and choosing the Virtual Memory button.

Session Manager Control Entries

IoPageLockLimit   REG_DWORD   *Number of bytes*

Specifies the limit of the number of bytes that can be locked for I/O operations. When this value is 0, the system uses the default (512K). The maximum value is about the equivalent of physical memory minus pad, which is 7 MB for a small system and grows as the amount of memory grows. For a 64 MB system, pad is about 16 MB; for a 512 MB system, pad is about 64 MB.

Default: 512K

LargeSystemCache   REG_DWORD   *Number*

Specifies, for a nonzero value, that the system favor the system-cache working set rather than the processes working set. Set this value by choosing the Windows NT Advanced Server installation base.

Default: 0

NonPagedPoolSize   REG_DWORD   *Number of bytes*

Specifies the size of nonpaged pool in bytes. When this value is 0, the system uses the default size (based on physical memory). The maximum amount is about 80 percent of physical memory.

Default: 0

PagedPoolSize   REG_DWORD   *0 to 128 MB*

Specifies the size of paged pool in bytes. When this value is 0, the system uses the default size (32 MB). See also the entry for **RegistrySizeLimit** at the beginning of this section.

Default: 0x3000000 (32 MB)

PagingFiles   REG_MULTI_SZ   *System_Paging_Files*

Specifies page file information set by choosing the System icon in Control Panel.

Default: C:\pagefile.sys 27

Subsystem Startup Control Entries

The following is the Registry path for the subsystem settings established at startup:

```
HKEY_LOCAL_MACHINE\SYSTEM\CurrentControlSet
    \Control\Session Manager\SubSystems
```

These values should only be maintained by the system. You should not need to manually define these settings.

Debug   REG_EXPAND_SZ   *Names*

Default: (no value)

Optional   REG_MULTI_SZ   *Subsystem names*

Defines subsystems that are only loaded when the user starts an application that requires this subsystem.

Default: Os2 Posix

Os2   REG_EXPAND_SZ   *Path and filename*

Defines the path to the executable file used to start the Microsoft OS/2 version 1.*x* subsystem.

Default: %SystemRoot%\system32\os2ss.exe

Posix   REG_EXPAND_SZ   *Path and filename*

Defines the path to the executable file used to start the POSIX subsystem. (There are no additional POSIX entries in the Registry.)

Default: %SystemRoot%\system32\psxss.exe

Required   REG_MULTI_SZ   *Name*

Default: Debug Windows

Windows   REG_EXPAND_SZ   *Path and filename*

Defines the path to the executable file used to start the Win32 subsystem.

Default: %SystemRoot%\system32\csrss.exe ObjectDirectory=\Windows SharedSection=1024,3072 Windows=On SubSystemType=Windows ServerDll=basesrv,1 ServerDll=winsrv:GdiServerDllInitialization,4 ServerDll=winsrv:UserServerDllInitialization,3 ServerDll=winsrv:ConServerDllInitialization,2 ServerDll=mmsndsrv,5 ProfileControl=Off MaxRequestThreads=16

VirtualDeviceDrivers Control Entries

The VirtualDeviceDriver key contains a list of Win32 DLLs that serve as virtual device drivers (VDD). Each **VDD** entry results in loading that VDD when a virtual MS-DOS machine (VDM) is being created for running an application created for MS-DOS or 16-bit versions of Microsoft Windows. This is the Registry path:

```
HKEY_LOCAL_MACHINE\SYSTEM\CurrentControlSet\Control\VirtualDeviceDrivers
```

VDD   REG_MULTI_SZ   *Filenames*

Specifies valid Win32 DLLs that are virtual device drivers.

Default: None—the Windows NT VDDs are built into the system.

Windows Startup Control Entries

This key contains entries that define the system directories for the Win32 subsystem (32-bit Windows) under this path:

```
HKEY_LOCAL_MACHINE\SYSTEM\CurrentControlSet\Control\Windows
```

Directory   REG_EXPAND_SZ   *Directory name*
Defines the directory for Windows NT.

Default: %SystemRoot%

SystemDirectory   REG_EXPAND_SZ   *Directory name*
Defines the directory for the Windows NT system files.

Default: %SystemRoot%\system32

The Registry entries for starting the Win32 subsystem are defined under the **Required** and **Windows** value entries in the Session Manager\Subsystem key, as described earlier in this section.

WOW Startup Control Entries

The following values control startup parameters that affect MS-DOS–based applications and applications created for 16-bit Windows 3.1. The Registry path for these values is the following:

```
HKEY_LOCAL_MACHINE\SYSTEM\CurrentControlSet
    \Control\WOW
```

Cmdline   REG_EXPAND_SZ   *Path and switches*
Defines the command line that runs when an MS-DOS–based application runs under Windows NT. This command line continues to run until the related application is closed. The following switches can be included:

Switch	Meaning
-a	Specifies a command to pass to the VDM
-f	Specifies the directory to find NTVDM.EXE
-m	Hides the VDM console window
-w	Specifies the WOW VDM

Default: %SystemRoot%\system32\ntvdm -f%SystemRoot%\system32 -a

KnownDLLs   REG_SZ   *DLL filenames*

Defines a list of known DLLs for use by the WOW VDM that provide
compatibility for non-Win32 applications. When the system searches for DLLs
to load, it compares the requested DLL with those in the **KnownDLLs** list and
then loads the matching DLL from the *SystemRoot*\SYSTEM32 directory.

If you want to replace a DLL, you must delete the name from this list, so that
the system will search elsewhere for the DLL. The files USER.DLL,
GDI.DLL, and SYSTEM.DRV are not included in this list, because these are
required Windows NT system files and their location cannot be changed.

Default: shell.dll commdlg.dll mmsystem.dll olecli.dll olesvr.dll ddeml.dll
win87em.dll toolhelp.dll lanman.drv netapi.dll pmspl.dll wowdeb.exe

LPT_timeout   REG_SZ   *Number of seconds*

Defines how many seconds after the LPT port has been used that Windows NT
waits before grabbing the port, closing it, and flushing the output. This value
should only be needed for MS-DOS–based applications that use BIOS and do
not close the port.

Default: 15

Size   REG_SZ   *Number in megabytes*

Defines the amount of memory to be given to each individual MS-DOS VDM.
The default of 0 gives the VDM as much memory as Windows NT determines
is necessary, depending upon the memory configuration.

To change this value, change the related value in the PIF file for the
application.

Default: 0

Wowcmdline   REG_EXPAND_SZ   *Path and switches*

Defines the command line that runs when a 16-bit Windows-based application
is started. The switches instruct Windows NT to start either an MS-DOS VDM
or a WOW VDM. See the definitions for allowable switches under **Cmdline**.

Default: %SystemRoot%\system32\ntvdm -m -w -f%SystemRoot%\system32
-a %SystemRoot%\system32\krnl386

Wowsize   REG_SZ   *Up to 16 megabytes*

For RISC-based computers, defines the amount of memory provided in a
VDM when a WOW session is started. This value is not used on *x*86-based
computers, where Windows NT allocates the memory needed when it is
asked for.

WOW Startup Control Entries

The default size chosen for a RISC-based computer depends on the amount of system memory on the computer. For each MB specified, the system uses 1.25 MB, so setting **Wowsize** to 4 MB causes the VDM to allocate 5 MB, although applications can only use 4 MB. You can override the following defaults:

System memory size	Default VDM size
Less than 12 MB (small)	3 MB
12–16 MB (medium)	6 MB
More than 16 MB (large)	8 MB

Caution Setting **Wowsize** to a value lower than 3 MB will cause most applications to fail.

Default: Depends on RISC-based computer's system memory

CurrentControlSet\Services Subkeys

The Services subkeys under the following Registry path contain parameters for the device drivers, file system drivers, and Win32 service drivers:

```
HKEY_LOCAL_MACHINE\SYSTEM\CurrentControlSet\Services
```

The name of each Services subkey is the name of the service, which is also the root of the name of the file from which the service is loaded. For example, for the serial mouse, the service name and Services subkey name is Sermouse. The file from which this is loaded is *SystemRoot*\SYSTEM32\DRIVERS \SERMOUSE.SYS.

All service names are defined under HKEY_LOCAL_MACHINE\SOFTWARE. The names of the Windows NT built-in network services such as the Alerter and Browser services are defined under the Microsoft\Windows NT\CurrentVersion subkey in the Software area of the Registry.

Each Services key can have additional subkeys. Many services have a Linkage subkey, which provides data for binding network components, as described in "Linkage Subkey Entries for Network Components," later in this chapter. Many services also have a Parameters subkey that contains entries defined by the service with values for configuring the specific service.

Values for Parameters subkeys and other service-specific entries are described in these sections in this chapter:

- Registry Entries for Network Adapter Cards
- Registry Entries for Device Drivers
- Registry Entries for Network Services

The following standard value entries appear for each Services subkey:

ErrorControl   REG_DWORD   *Error constant*

Specifies the level of error control for the service as follows:

Error control level	Meaning
0x3 (Critical)	Fail the attempted system startup. If the startup is not using the LastKnownGood control set, switch to LastKnownGood. If the startup attempt is using LastKnownGood, run a bug-check routine.
0x2 (Severe)	If the startup is not using the LastKnownGood control set, switch to LastKnownGood. If the startup attempt is using LastKnownGood, continue on in case of error.
0x1 (Normal)	If the driver fails to load or initialize, startup should proceed, but display a warning.
0x0 (Ignore)	If the driver fails to load or initialize, start up proceeds. No warning is displayed.

Group   REG_DWORD   *Group name*

Specifies the name of the group of which the particular service is a member.

Default: (null)

DependOnGroup   REG_DWORD   *Group name*

Specifies zero or more group names. If one or more groups is listed, at least one service from the named group must be loaded before this service is loaded.

Default: (empty)

DependOnService   REG_DWORD   *Service name*

Specifies zero or more Services subkey names. If a service is listed here, that named service must be loaded before this service is loaded.

Default: (empty)

ImagePath   REG_DWORD   *Path and filename*

Specifies a path name. For adapters, this value is ignored.

Default: For a driver, *systemroot*\SYSTEM32\DRIVERS*driverName*.SYS
For a service, *systemroot*\SYSTEM32*serviceName*.EXE (where *driverName*
or *serviceName* is the same as the related Services subkey name)

ObjectName   REG_DWORD   *Object name*

Specifies an object name. If **Type** specifies a WIN32 Service, this name is the
account name that the service will use to log on when the service runs. If **Type**
specifies a Kernel driver or file system driver, this name is the Windows NT
driver object name that the I/O Manager uses to load the device driver.

Default: *subkeyName*

Start   REG_DWORD   *Start constant*

Specifies the starting values for the service as follows:

Start type	Loader	Meaning
0x0 (Boot)	Kernel	Represents a part of the driver stack for the boot (startup) volume and must therefore be loaded by the Boot Loader.
0x1 (System)	I/O subsystem	Represents a driver to be loaded at Kernel initialization.
0x2 (Auto load)	Service Control Manager	To be loaded or started automatically for all startups, regardless of service type.
0x3 (Load on demand)	Service Control Manager	Available, regardless of type, but will not be started until the user starts it (for example, by using the Devices icon in Control Panel).
0x4 (Disabled)	Service Control Manager	Not to be started under any conditions.

The **Start** value is ignored for adapters. If **Type** is a Win32 Service value (as
described below), the **Start** value must specify an Auto, Demand, or Disabled
value.

Tag   REG_DWORD

Specifies a load order within a given group. The value of **Tag** specifies a number that is unique within the group of which the service is a member. The related *GroupName* entry under the Control\GroupOrderList subkey specifies a list of tags, in load order.

For example, the following services that are members of the Primary Disk group could have these values: **Tag**=4 for the Abiosdsk subkey, **Tag**=2 for Atdisk, **Tag**=1 for Cpqarray, and **Tag**=3 for Floppy. The value for **Primary Disk** under the GroupOrderList subkey will use these **Tag** values to specify the defined order for loading these services. As another example, each SCSI miniport service has a unique **Tag** value that is used as an identifier in the **SCSI miniport** value under the GroupOrderList subkey to define which SCSI adapter to load first.

Type   REG_DWORD   *Type constant*

Specifies the type of service as follows:

Service type	Description
0x1	A Kernel device driver.
0x2	File system driver, which is also a Kernel device driver.
0x4	A set of arguments for an adapter.
0x10	A Win32 program that can be started by the Service Controller and that obeys the service control protocol. This type of Win32 service runs in a process by itself.
0x20	A Win32 service that can share a process with other Win32 services.

For example, when you start Windows NT, the Boot Loader scans the Registry for drivers with a **Start** value of 0 (which indicates that these drivers should be loaded but not initialized before the Kernel) and a **Type** value of 0x1 (which indicates a Kernel device driver such as a hard disk or other low-level hardware device driver). The drivers are then loaded into memory in the order specified as the **List** value in CurrentControlSet\Control\ServiceGroupOrder.

Registry Entries for Network Adapter Cards

This section describes specific Registry entries related to network adapter cards and the drivers for network adapters. Windows NT supports network adapter drivers under the NDIS 3.0 specification (Network Device Interface Specification).

The CurrentControlSet\Services subkey for a network driver or adapter card includes the standard entries found in the Services subkeys, with the following default values:

Value entry	Value
ErrorControl	0x1 (normal)
Start	0x3 (load on demand)
Type	0x1 or 0x4 (driver or adapter)

The following sections describe entries in the other areas of the Registry that contain configuration information for network adapter cards and their drivers, including:

- NetRules subkeys under HKEY_LOCAL_MACHINE\SOFTWARE for drivers and adapters.

- Linkage subkey entries under HKEY_LOCAL_MACHINE\SYSTEM for drivers and adapters, defining information about bindings for the component.

- Parameter subkey entries under HKEY_LOCAL_MACHINE\SYSTEM for network card adapters, defining specific information such as the IRQ number, I/O base address, and other details.

The information provided here is chiefly to be used for informational and troubleshooting purposes. The settings for either the NDIS driver or the network adapter card should be changed using the Network icon in Control Panel.

For information about Registry values other network services, see "Registry Entries for Network Services," later in this chapter. Entries for TCP/IP that are specific to network adapter cards can be found under "TCP/IP Transport Entries," later in this chapter.

NetRules Subkey Entries

During network reconfiguration (that is, when you use the Network icon in Control Panel to make changes), the system reads the values stored in the NetRules subkeys for information used to bind the network components. The Registry path for these value entries is the following:

- For adapter card drivers and network services, where the *driverName* subkey is the name of the network card's driver, as defined by the system:

```
HKEY_LOCAL_MACHINE\SOFTWARE\Microsoft
    \driverName\CurrentVersion\NetRules
```

- For network adapter cards, where the *netcard#* subkey is a number, beginning with 01 for the first network adapter:

```
HKEY_LOCAL_MACHINE\SOFTWARE\Microsoft\Windows NT\CurrentVersion
    \NetworkCards\netcard#\NetRules
```

Bindable   REG_MULTI_SZ   *fromClass toClass Yes|No Yes|No value*

Defines a possible binding and its constraints. For example:

```
bindable = ndisDriver ndisAdapter non exclusive 100
```

This example specifies that components of class "ndisDriver" can be bound to those of class "ndisAdapter." For the other fields in this example:

- Non indicates that the component of class ndisDriver can accept other bindings
- Exclusive indicates that the component of class ndisAdapter cannot accept other bindings
- 100 indicates the relative importance (weight) of this binding; that is, in cases of competition, it will be discarded in favor of other bindings whose weight is greater.

Because this value entry is a REG_MULTI_SZ, as many criteria for binding as necessary can be defined by a single component.

This value entry is optional, because there are a few predefined binding rules, and binding rules defined anywhere in the system apply to all network component classes.

Bindform   REG_SZ   *ObjectName Yes|No Yes|No [container|simple|streams]*

The *ObjectName* field contains the name (or name prefix) by which the component is identified by the system. This value must be the same as the name in the related CurrentControlSet\Services subkey. Names for adapters are created by the system and override the **Bindform** setting.

The first Yes|No pair indicates whether the component is to receive binding information directly in its Linkage subkey. The second Yes|No pair indicates whether the device name is supposed to appear in generated binding strings.

The final optional value in this entry indicates how binding device names are constructed. This value is required for software components.

Class   REG_MULTI_SZ   *NewClassName OldClassName|basic [Yes|No]*

Allows a component to define a new class. As many new classes as necessary can be defined by any component.

Note   These classes are not related to the OLE and DDE classes defined under HKEY_LOCAL_MACHINE\SOFTWARE\Classes.

Class names do not need to be defined within any particular component. The system adds the new definition to its database without regard to origin. The order of **Class** entries is irrelevant. However, results are indeterminate if classes are referred to that are not defined anywhere in the system.

This entry is optional, because there are a few predefined classes, and class definitions made anywhere in the system apply to all network components. Because any network component can define new classes, be careful that the names used are unique within all possible installable network components. The following shows the predefined class names in the first release of Windows NT. This list, of course, cannot be exhaustive.

Predefined class	Adapter card type
ee16Driver; ee16Adapter	Intel EtherExpress™ 16 LAN adapter
elnkiiAdapter; elinkiiDriver	3Com® Etherlink II® adapter
ibmtokDriver; ibmtokAdapter	IBM® Token Ring adapter
lanceDriver; dec101Adapter	DEC® Lance adapter
lt200Driver; lt200Adapter	Daystar Digital LocalTalk adapter
ne2000Driver; ne2000Adapter	Novell® NE2000 adapter
proteonDriver; p1390Adapter	Proteon adapter
ubDriver; ubAdapter	Ungermann-Bass® Ethernet NIUpc adapter
wdlanDriver; smcisaAdapter	SMC® (WD) adapter

The final optional value indicates whether this class is a "logical end-point" for the bindings protocol; the default value is No.

Hidden   REG_DWORD   *0 or 1*

Suppresses the display of the component (adapter or network software) in the Network dialog box in Control Panel.

Usually, all networking components discovered in the Registry are displayed in the two list boxes in the Network dialog box in Control Panel. Setting this value to 1 prevents the item from being displayed, which means it cannot be configured or removed by the user.

Interface   REG_MULTI_SZ

Allows a single component to make available more than one type of capability to other components in the system. The format for this value is:

```
Interface = interfaceName upperClass "objectName" namingMethod
```

Value	Meaning
interfaceName	The tokenized name of the secondary interface.
upperClass	The class to which the interface belongs. (*LowerClass* is the same as the primary interface.)
objectName	The Windows NT device name to be created.
namingMethod	Determines how the bindings appear.

Review   REG_DWORD   *0 or 1*

Indicates whether a component requests bindings review. If set to 1 (or nonzero), the system reinvokes this component's .INF file after bindings have been changed. This allows network components to modify the binding information or request additional information from administrators about the new or altered connections.

Type   REG_SZ   *component className [lowerClass]*

Defines the type of the component in terms of abstract network component classes. If the optional lower class name is absent, the first (or upper level) class type name is used for both its upper and lower classes.

This value is required for network software and network adapter cards.

Component type	Meaning
Adapter	A piece of hardware
Driver	A software component associated directly with a piece of hardware
Transport	A software component used by services
Service	A software component providing capability directly to user applications
Basic	A token used to represent a fundamental class name (that is, a class with no parent)

NetRules Subkey Entries

Use   REG_SZ   *service\driver\transport\adapter [Yes\No] [Yes\No]*

Defines the role played by the component. If this entry is absent, the value of Service is assumed. This value entry only appears for software items.

A hardware device is automatically assumed to be an adapter. Each network component may identify itself as a driver, transport, or service to clarify its role. This distinction is as follows (note the lowercase for the values):

Value	Meaning
driver	Exists only to support one or more adapters. If no bindings are generated (or permitted by the user) that include a particular driver, that driver is not loaded. However, no error is generated, since no "denial of service" has occurred.
service	Provides end-user functionality, and every attempt is made to support its operation. An EventLog entry is generated if a service is present in the system for which there is no available transport (the number of possible bindings is zero).
transport	Exists only to support services. Like a driver, it is not loaded unless necessary.

The final two Yes\No values in this entry are optional; if present, each must be either Yes or No. The first value indicates whether driver group names are used instead of specific driver dependencies. The second value indicates whether transport group names are used instead of specific transport dependencies. These values cause the system to generate references to dependencies based upon their group names, not by their specific service names.

For example, the LanmanServer is marked as Yes Yes; this means that its transport and driver dependencies are at the group level; so LanmanServer will be loaded if any one of its transport dependencies and any one of its driver dependencies successfully load.

Linkage Subkey Entries for Network Components

Each network component that the system determines to be required can be given bindings, which establish the relationships between network software components, as described in "Bindings for Network Components" in Chapter 11, "Overview of the Windows NT Registry." All bindings are created by the system and should not be changed by the user, except by choosing the Bindings button in the Network dialog box in Control Panel.

Whether the bindings actually appear in the Registry depends upon the **Bindform** value for the component in its NetRules subkey.

The binding information is stored in three value entries in the Linkage subkey for a component under the Services subkey. The Registry path for each Linkage subkey is the following:

```
HKEY_LOCAL_MACHINE\SYSTEM\CurrentControlSet\Services
    \ServiceName\Linkage
```

If a binding is disabled, the settings are stored under a Disabled subkey under the Linkage subkey. These values are in exactly the same format as for active bindings.

For a network component, there might be more than one subkey under its Services key: one for the driver and one for the network adapter card, plus additional subkeys for services that might be installed with the network adapter. Also, entries for adapter cards for AppleTalk, DLC (Data Link Control), NWLink, and TCP/IP are described in their respective sections in "Registry Entries for Network Services," later in this chapter.

Bind   REG_MULTI_SZ   *ObjectName ObjectName ...*

Each string in this value entry is the name of a Windows NT object created by the underlying software. The names are based on the object names declared in the **Bindform** entry under the NetRules subkey.

Export   REG_MULTI_SZ   *ObjectName ObjectName ...*

Each string in this value entry indicates the name that should be added in the system to allow access to the corresponding bound object. The names are based on the object names declared in the **Bindform** entry under the NetRules subkey.

Route   REG_MULTI_SZ   *"Name of service" "Name of service"...*

Each string in this value entry indicates the exact path through the binding protocol represented by the binding. The names of services are used, surrounded by quotation marks.

Each element of these multistring values has a one-to-one correspondence with the others; that is, **Bind[1]** is to **Export[1]** and **Route[1]** as **Bind[2]** is to **Export[2]** and **Route[2]**.

In addition to generating binding information, the system determines each network component's complete set of dependencies, and stores them in the related subkey in the CurrentControlSet\Services key. For examples using these value entries, see "Bindings for Network Components" in Chapter 11, "Overview of the Windows NT Registry."

Parameters Subkey Entries for Network Adapter Cards

Each network adapter card has a Parameters subkey with value entries that contain the settings for interrupt number, I/O port, and other parameters. These entries are found under subkeys for specific adapter cards in this Registry path:

```
HKEY_LOCAL_MACHINE\SYSTEM\CurrentControlSet
   \Services\adapter name#\Parameters
```

These values should all be set by choosing the Network icon in Control Panel. These value entries are provided here for informational purposes only. For a list of default values for network adapter card settings, see the table at the end of this section.

BusNumber   REG_DWORD   *Number*

Defines the bus number, beginning with 0 in the common case where the computer has one bus type, whether it is ISA, EISA, MCA, or TurboChannel. For the rare computer that has more than one bus, bus number 2 has the value of 1, and so on.

This value should be maintained by the system. You cannot change it using the Network dialog box in Control Panel.

Default: Usually 0 (depends on the installation)

BusType   REG_DWORD   *Number*

Specifies the bus type for the computer, as in the following list:

Value	Bus type
0	MIPS (Jazz-Internal bus)
1	ISA bus
2	EISA bus
3	MCA bus
4	TcChannel bus

This value should be maintained by the system. You cannot change it using the Network dialog box in Control Panel.

CableType   REG_DWORD   *1 or 2*

Specifies the cable type as unshielded twisted pair (UTP=1) or shielded twisted pair (STP=2), for Proteon 1390 adapter cards.

CardSpeed   REG_DWORD   *4 or 16 megabits per second*

Specifies card speed as 4 or 16 megabits per second in hex (0x4 or 0x10), for Proteon 1390 adapter cards.

CardType   REG_DWORD   *Number*

Specifies the card installed in the system. For some manufacturers, all their network cards use the same driver, which checks the value of **CardType** to determine the network card model number of the installed card. For example:

CardType value	Network card model number
DEC:	
1	DEC100
2	DEC20x
3	DEC PC
4	DEC Station
5	DEC422
7	DEC101
Proteon:	
1	Proteon 1390
2	Proteon 1990
Ungermann-Bass:	
2	UB PC
3	UB EOTP
4	UBPS

This value should be maintained by the system. You cannot change it using the Network dialog box in Control Panel.

DMAChannel   REG_DWORD   *5, 6, or 7*

Specifies the DMA channel used by the adapter card.

InterruptNumber   REG_DWORD   *IRQ number*

Specifies the interrupt level (IRQ) for the adapter card. IRQ5 is a common choice (0x5).

IoBaseAddress   REG_DWORD   *Number in hex*

For some adapters, this entry specifies the I/O port base address as a hexadecimal string. For other adapters, this entry specifies whether this is the primary adapter card (1) or a secondary card (2).

MediaType   REG_DWORD   *Number*

Specifies the network type, as follows:

Value	Network type
1	Ethernet
2	IBM Token Ring
3	ARCnet
4	FDDI network
5	Apple LocalTalk

This value should be maintained by the system. You cannot change it using the Network dialog box in Control Panel.

MaximumPacketSize   REG_DWORD   *Number*

Specifies the maximum packet size that the IBM Token Ring adapter is allowed to transmit. Use this parameter when sending data across bridges that may have smaller packet sizes available on the destination network than on the native network. You cannot change this parameter using the Network dialog box in Control Panel.

MemoryMapped   REG_DWORD   *0 or 1*

Specifies whether the adapter card is memory mapped.

MemoryMappedBaseAddress   REG_DWORD   *Memory address in hex*

Specifies the base memory (I/O) address used by the adapter card. This number must match the card's memory address settings as specified by its manufacturer.

NetworkAddress   REG_SZ   *Number*

Specifies the address the network adapter should use instead of the burned-in address. For example, for the IBM Token Ring card, this value is 40000000203. You can change this value for Token Ring adapters using the Network dialog box in Control Panel, but not for Ethernet adapters.

Transceiver   REG_DWORD   *1 or 2*

Specifies the transceiver as External (1) or OnBoard (2). This value should be 1 for a DEC/Intel/Xerox (DIX) connection.

The following table summarizes default settings for various card types.

Card name	Default setting
3Com [1]:	
EtherLink® II, EtherLink II / TP, EtherLink II/ 16, or EtherLink II/ 16 TP	**InterruptNumber** = 3 **IoBaseAddress** = 0x300 **Transceiver** = Internal **MemoryMapped** = Off
EtherLink 16/16 TP	**InterruptNumber** = 5 **IoBaseAddress** = 0x300 **MemoryMappedAddress** = 0xD0000 **MemorySize** = 16 **Transceiver** = Internal
DEC [1]:	
EtherWORKS Turbo EISA	**SlotNumber** = 1
EtherWORKS LC, EtherWORKS Turbo, or EtherWORKS Turbo / TP	**InterruptNumber** = 5 **MemoryAddress** = 0xD0000 **IoBaseAddress** = Primary
IBM [1]:	
Token Ring 16/4	**IoBaseAddress** = Primary
Novell [1]:	
NE2000	**InterruptNumber** = 3 **IoBaseAddress** = 0x300
Proteon [1]:	
P1390	**InterruptNumber** = 5 **IoBaseAddress** = 0xa20 **DMAChannel** = 5 **CableType** = STP **CardSpeed** = 16
SMC®/Western Digital™:	
8003EP, 8013EWC, or 8013WB	**InterruptNumber** = 3 **MemoryBaseAddress** = 0xD000 **IoBaseAddress** = 0x300
Ungermann-Bass®[1]:	
Ethernet NIUpc (long) or Ethernet NIUpc/EOTP (short)	**InterruptNumber** = 5 **IoBaseAddress** = 0x368 **MemoryMappedAddress** = 0xD8000

[1] Settings are not required for EtherLink / MC, DEC PC, IBM Token Ring 16/4A, Proteon P1990, Novell NE3200, SMC/Western Digital 8013EA, and the Ungermann-Bass Ethernet NIUps (MC) or Ethernet NIUps/EOTP (short MC).

Parameters Subkey Entries for Network Adapter Cards

Registry Entries for Device Drivers

The following device drivers have additional value entries that can be specified in the Registry, in addition to changes that you can make using the Devices or Drivers icon in Control Panel. These types of services and drivers appear in the Registry and are described in this section:

- File system drivers and recognizers
- Disk, serial, and parallel port devices
- Keyboard and mouse devices
- SCSI miniport devices
- Sound cards
- Video display devices

Tip You can view current settings for these device drivers by choosing the Devices button in WinMSD.

File System Drivers and Recognizers

Each file system supported by Windows NT is made up of three components: the file system driver, the file system utility DLL, and the file system recognizer used during startup to determine the file systems present on the system. All necessary elements and settings are recognized automatically by Windows NT. You can configure file system drivers by choosing the Devices icon in Control Panel.

File system driver and recognizer	File System
Cdfs and Cdfs_Rec	Compact disc file system (CDFS)
Fastfat and Fat_Rec	File Allocation Table (FAT)
Ntfs and Ntfs_Rec	Windows NT file system (NTFS)
Pinball and HPFS_Rec	High-performance file system (HPFS)

The Registry path for settings that control file system drivers is the following, where *DriverName* is the file system driver minus the filename extension:

```
HKEY_LOCAL_MACHINE\SYSTEM\CurrentControlSet\Services\DriverName
```

The standard entries for the file system drivers are the following:

Value entry	Default value
ErrorControl	0x1 (Normal)
Group	Boot file system
Start	0x4 (disabled)
Type	0x2 (file system driver)

The file system recognizer determines whether the file system should be loaded. The Registry path for file system recognizers is the following, where *RecognizerName* is the file system driver minus the filename extension:

```
HKEY_LOCAL_MACHINE\SYSTEM\CurrentControlSet\Services\RecognizerName
```

The standard entries for the file system recognizers are the following:

Value entry	Default value
ErrorControl	0 (startup halts)
Group	Boot file system
Start	0x1 (system)
Type	0x8 (file system recognizer)

The file system drivers and recognizers do not add any additional Registry entries besides the standard entries described in "CurrentControlSet\Services Subkeys," earlier in this chapter.

Note If CONVERT.EXE has been used to convert the file system on a hard disk drive, this value is added to CurrentControlSet\Control\SessionManager so that conversion occurs when the system is restarted:

```
BootExecute = autocheck autoconv \Dos\Devices\x: /FS:NTFS
```

Disk, Serial, and Parallel Port Entries

This section provides general information about the Description entries for adapters in the Hardware key. Then specific information is presented about the DeviceMap subkey entries for AtDisk and for serial and parallel ports. Finally, Services subkey entries for parallel and serial ports are described, including specific entries for multiport serial I/O cards.

Description Entries for Adapters

The following shows the path for all *MultifunctionAdapter* entries:

```
HKEY_LOCAL_MACHINE\HARDWARE\Description\System
    \MultifunctionAdapter\0\ControllerName\0.
```

The entries in this portion of the Registry contain data discovered by the Hardware Recognizer or provided from the ARC database that describes controllers for hard disks, display devices, the keyboard, pointing devices, and serial and parallel ports. Administrators cannot usefully modify entries in the Hardware key. This data is volatile (destroyed and recreated each time the system starts) and is useful only for informational purposes. You can use WinMSD to view this information in a more usable format.

Each subkey contains information in the following format:

Component Information   REG_BINARY   *System-defined*
Identifies version information plus other data for the associated subkey entry.

Configuration Data   REG_UNKNOWN   *System-defined*
Contains binary information related to the hardware component, such as I/O port addresses and IRQ number. This entry is not present if no such data is available for a particular subkey.

Identifier   REG_SZ   *Device type name*
Contains the name of a component, if specified.

The following samples from the *MultifunctionAdapter* subkeys describe a system that has a keyboard, a Microsoft InPort® bus mouse or Microsoft Mouse Port mouse, and a Microsoft serial mouse (on COM1), all connected to the ISA bus. This sample is for informational purposes only, since these subkeys are volatile and are therefore recreated each time you start Windows NT.

In the following example, the **Identifier** value specifies the keyboard type name, which is typically PCAT_ENHANCED to indicate a 101/102-key enhanced keyboard. The keyboard type name is mainly informational, since the actual keyboard type and subtype are retrieved from the keyboard-specific data in **Configuration Data.**

```
HKEY_LOCAL_MACHINE\HARDWARE\Description\System\MultifunctionAdapter
    \0\KeyboardController\0\KeyboardPeripheral\0

Configuration Data : REG_UNKNOWN : Device data (keyboard type, subtype)
Identifier : REG_SZ : PCAT_ENHANCED
```

The following two examples show typical **Identifier** values for two basic types of pointer devices. For the first example, the **Identifier** value for the pointer type name can also be MICROSOFT PS2 MOUSE (also known as the Mouse Port mouse) or MICROSOFT BUS MOUSE under this subkey:

```
HKEY_LOCAL_MACHINE\HARDWARE\Description\System\MultifunctionAdapter
    \0\PointerController\0\PointerPeripheral\0

Identifier : REG_SZ : MICROSOFT INPORT MOUSE
```

This example shows a typical entry for a serial mouse, under this subkey:

```
HKEY_LOCAL_MACHINE\HARDWARE\Description\System\MultifunctionAdapter
    \0\SerialController\0\PointerPeripheral\0

Identifier : REG_SZ : MICROSOFT SERIAL MOUSE
```

DeviceMap Subkey Entries for AtDisk

AtDisk is the driver for non-SCSI hard disk controllers on x86-based computers.

Note The Abiosdsk driver has no Hardware key and no parameters that users can set under CurrentControlSet\Services.

The following Registry path can contain subkeys named Controller$x$, where x starts at 0 and increases:

```
HKEY_LOCAL_MACHINE\HARDWARE\DeviceMap\AtDisk
```

These Controller$x$ subkeys are created for each non-SCSI hard disk controller on the system. As with all hardware data, these subkeys are volatile and so are recreated each time you start the system.

Under the Controller*x* subkeys are subkeys named Disk*y*, where *y* starts at 0 (zero) and increases. These subkeys are created for each actual disk controlled by the particular controller.

Under the Disk*y* subkeys are the following value entries, which can be extremely helpful in reporting disk problems:

Firmware revision   REG_SZ   *Free format*
Defined by the disk manufacturer to identify the version of the on-board code used to control the disk.

Identifier   REG_SZ   *Free format*
Defined by the disk manufacturer to identify the make and model of the disk.

Number of cylinders   REG_DWORD   *A hex value*
The number of cylinders on the drive.

Number of heads   REG_DWORD   *A hex value*
The number of heads on the drive.

Sectors per track   REG_DWORD   *A hex value*
The number of sectors that exist on a track. These are typically 512-byte sectors.

The standard entries for AtDisk under the CurrentControlSet\Services subkey are the following:

Value entry	Default value
ErrorControl	0 (startup halts)
Group	Primary disk
Start	0x0 (boot)
Tag	0x2
Type	0x1 (Kernel driver)

DeviceMap Subkey Entries for Serial and Parallel Ports

Remember that the entries in HKEY_LOCAL_MACHINE\HARDWARE are recreated each time the system is started. The entries in these subkeys are described here for informational purposes only.

Parallel*X*   REG_SZ   *A string, typically LPTy*
HKEY_LOCAL_MACHINE\HARDWARE\DEVICEMAP\PARALLEL PORTS

Specifies that the Windows NT Parallel device *X* is the actual device for the MS-DOS name LPT*y*. These value entries are used to determine all the parallel ports available on the system.

Serial*X*   REG_SZ   *A string, typically COMy*
HKEY_LOCAL_MACHINE\HARDWARE\DeviceMap\Serialcomm

Specifies that the Windows NT Serial device *X* is the actual device for the MS-DOS name COM*y*. These value entries are used to determine all the communication ports available on the system.

Parallel Subkey Entries in the Services Subkey

The following subkeys and values can be found under the following key:

HKEY_LOCAL_MACHINE\System\CurrentControlSet\Services\Parallel

Subkeys and values under the Parallel subkey can be used to configure parallel (printer) ports in addition to information that the Hardware Detector finds at system startup.

This can also be used to override values determined by the Hardware Detector. If the **PortAddress** value entry is the same as a system-detected port, this data in the current control set will be used instead of the data found by the system. Entries appear in the System log in Event Viewer if this is occurring.

The Parallel subkey contains a subkey named Parameters, under which is a set of subkeys typically named Parallel*x* where *x* is some whole number. A system administrator must place these subkeys and values into the Registry. There exists no tool other than Registry Editor to define and manipulate these values.

For example, under the Parallel2 subkey, the following value entries can appear.

The first two of these value entries are required. If the section does not include both, the port is not configured and an error appears in the System log in Event Viewer. If an entry is placed into the Registry with just these values, the port will be driven using polling algorithms.

DosDevices   REG_SZ   *Free-form string*
Specifies the name used to access the parallel port from the command prompt or from within an application. A typical value would be LPT3.

PortAddress   REG_DWORD   *A hex value*

Denotes the address of the first register of the parallel port. A typical **PortAddress** in this case would be 0x278.

The following values are optional:

DisablePort   REG_DWORD   *0 or 1*

If the value is a 1, the device will be deleted after the port is reset during initialization. No access to the port will be allowed.

Default: 0

Interrupt   REG_DWORD   *A hex value*

Denotes the IRQ that the particular device would interrupt on. A typical **Interrupt** value in this case would be 0x5.

The standard entries for the Parallel subkey are the following:

Value entry	Default value
ErrorControl	0 (startup halts)
Group	Extended base
Start	0x2 (autoload)
Type	0x1 (Kernel device driver)

Serial Subkey Entries in the Services Subkey

The following subkeys and values can be found under the following key:

```
HKEY_LOCAL_MACHINE\System\CurrentControlSet\Services\Serial
```

Subkeys and values under the CurrentControlSet\Services subkey can be used to configure serial ports in addition to information that the Hardware Detector finds at system startup. This can also be used to override values determined by the Hardware Detector. If the **PortAddress** value entry is the same as a system-detected port, this data in the current control set will be used instead of the data found by the system. Entries appear in the System log in Event Viewer if this is occurring.

The Serial subkey contains a subkey named Parameters, under which is a set of subkeys typically named Serial*X* where *X* is a whole number. A system administrator must place these subkeys and values into the Registry. You can only define and manipulate these values by using Registry Editor.

For example, under the Serial2 subkey, the following value entries can appear.

The first three of these value entries are required. If the subkey does not include all three, the port is not configured, and an error appears in the System log in Event Viewer.

DosDevices **REG_SZ** *Free-form string*

Specifies the name used to access the communication port from the command prompt or from within an application. A typical value would be COM3.

Interrupt **REG_DWORD** *A hex value*

Denotes the IRQ that the particular device would interrupt on. A typical **Interrupt** value in this case would be 0x4.

PortAddress **REG_DWORD** *A hex value*

Denotes the address of the first register of the serial device. A typical **PortAddress** in this case would be 0x3e8.

The following entry values are optional:

DisablePort **REG_DWORD** *0 or 1*

If the value is 1, the device will be deleted after the port is reset during initialization. No access to the port will be allowed.

Default: 0

ForceFifoEnable **REG_DWORD** *0 or 1*

If the value is 1 and the hardware supports a FIFO buffer (for example, the NS 16550AFN), the driver enables the FIFO. Not all FIFOs are reliable. If the application or the user notices lost data or no data transmission, it is recommended that this value be set to 0.

Default: 1

The standard entries for the Serial subkey are the following:

Value entry	Default value
ErrorControl	0 (startup halts)
Group	Extended base
Start	0x2 (autoload)
Type	0x1 (Kernel device driver)

Multiport Serial I/O Card Entries in the Services Subkey

In addition to controlling the standard serial ports included with most PCs, the Microsoft serial driver can be used to control many *dumb* multiport serial cards. Dumb denotes that the control includes no onboard processor.

At least the following two additional value entries are used for each port on the multiport card. Each of these two entries must be included for each port of the multiport board under subkey entries in CurrentControlSet\Services:

InterruptStatus   REG_DWORD   *A hex value*

Denotes the address of the interrupt status register that indicates which port on the multiport card is actually requesting an interrupt. To determine the appropriate value, consult the manufacturer's installation guide.

PortIndex   REG_DWORD   *A hex value*

Denotes which port on the card this information is for. These values start at 1 and increase. Typically these would be the same as the values inscribed on the connector for the multiport.

Certain multiport boards, such as Digiboard non-MCA bus cards, use a different scheme to determine which port is interrupting. These boards should include the following value entry in the configuration data:

Indexed   REG_DWORD   *Should be 1*

Denotes that this board uses an indexed interrupt notification scheme as opposed to a bitmapped method. To determine whether this entry should be included, consult the board's manufacturer.

For detailed examples describing entries for four-port and eight-port communications boards, see "Controlling Multiport Serial I/O Cards" in Chapter 12, "Configuration Management and the Registry."

Mouse and Keyboard Driver Entries

Parameters in this section are for the mouse and keyboard class and port drivers, including these drivers:

Busmouse	Mouclass	Kbdclass
Inport	i8042prt	Sermouse

Microsoft Bus Mouse Port Driver Entries

The following value entries for the Microsoft bus mouse are found in this subkey:

```
HKEY_LOCAL_MACHINE\SYSTEM\CurrentControlSet\Services\Busmouse\Parameters
```

MouseDataQueueSize   **REG_DWORD**   *>= 0x1*

Specifies the number of mouse events to be buffered internally by the driver, in nonpaged pool. The allocated size, in bytes, of the internal buffer is this value times the size of the MOUSE_INPUT_DATA structure (defined in NTDDMOU.H). Consider increasing the size if the System log in Event Viewer frequently contains this message from the Busmouse source: "The ring buffer that stores incoming mouse data has overflowed (buffer size is configurable via the Registry)."

Default: 0x64 (100)

NumberOfButtons   **REG_DWORD**   *>= 0x1*

Specifies the number of buttons on the bus mouse. If the number of buttons detected at startup time and placed in the Registry is incorrect, this value can be used to override it.

Default: 0x2 (two buttons)

PointerDeviceBaseName   **REG_SZ**   *Base port device name*

Specifies the base name for the device object(s) created by the bus mouse port device driver. The device driver also writes information about the device objects into HKEY_LOCAL_MACHINE\HARDWARE\DeviceMap so that the pointer class driver can locate the pointer port device objects.

Default: PointerPort

SampleRate   **REG_DWORD**   *Mouse sample rate in Hz*

Specifies the sample rate for the bus mouse. Intended for future use. This value might have no effect in the first release of Windows NT.

Default: 0x32 (50 Hz)

Intel 8042 Port Driver Entries

The i8042prt driver handles the keyboard and mouse port mouse (also known as a PS/2-compatible mouse) for the Intel 8042 controller. These value entries are found in the following subkey:

```
HKEY_LOCAL_MACHINE\SYSTEM\CurrentControlSet\Services\i8042prt\Parameters
```

KeyboardDataQueueSize   REG_DWORD   >= *0x1*

Specifies the number of keyboard events to be buffered internally by the driver, in nonpaged pool. The allocated size, in bytes, of the internal buffer is this value times the size of the KEYBOARD_INPUT_DATA structure (defined in NTDDKBD.H). Consider increasing the size if the System log in Event Viewer contains the following message from the i8042prt source: "The ring buffer that stores incoming keyboard data has overflowed (buffer size is configurable via the Registry)."

Default: 0x64 (100)

KeyboardDeviceBaseName   REG_SZ   *Base keyboard port device name*

Specifies the base name for the keyboard device object(s) created by the i8042prt device driver. The device driver also writes information about the device objects into HKEY_LOCAL_MACHINE\HARDWARE\DeviceMap so that the keyboard class driver can locate the keyboard port device objects.

Default: KeyboardPort

MouseDataQueueSize   REG_DWORD   >= *0x1*

Specifies the number of mouse events to be buffered internally by the driver, in nonpaged pool. Consider increasing the size if the System log in Event Viewer contains the following message from the i8042prt source: "The ring buffer that stores incoming mouse data has overflowed (buffer size is configurable via the Registry)."

Default: 0x64 (100)

MouseResolution   REG_DWORD   *Mouse resolution specifier*

Used in specifying the mouse port mouse resolution, where 2 to the power of **MouseResolution** specifies counts-per-millimeter.

Default: 0x3

MouseSynchIn100ns   **REG_DWORD**   *Time, in 100 nanosecond units*

Specifies the length of time after which the next mouse interrupt is assumed to indicate the start of a new mouse packet (partial packets are discarded). This allows the driver to synchronize its internal notion of the mouse packet state with the hardware state, in the event that a mouse interrupt has been lost. Consider modifying this value if the system behaves as if there are random mouse events occurring (for example, button clicks when no mouse button has been pressed).

Default: 10000000 (1 second)

NumberOfButtons   **REG_DWORD**   *>= 0x1*

Specifies the number of buttons on the mouse port mouse. If an incorrect number of buttons is detected at startup time and placed in the Registry, this value can be used to override it.

Default: 0x2

PointerDeviceBaseName   **REG_SZ**   *Base mouse port device name*

Specifies the base name for the pointer device object(s) created by the mouse port mouse driver. The device driver also writes information about the device object into HKEY_LOCAL_MACHINE\HARDWARE\DeviceMap so that the pointer class driver can locate the pointer port device objects.

Default: PointerPort

PollStatusIterations   **REG_DWORD**   *Number*

Specifies the maximum number of times to check the i8042 controller status register for interrupt verification before dismissing the interrupt as spurious. This value can be used to work around a problem experienced on some hardware (including the Olivetti MIPS computers) where the keyboard interrupt is raised before the Output Buffer Full bit is set in the i8042 status register.

Increase this value if the system seems to suddenly stop taking keyboard interrupts. This can happen if a keyboard interrupt is mistakenly dismissed as spurious, when instead it just took too long to set Output Buffer Full after raising the interrupt. Increasing the value of **PollStatusIterations** results in a longer execution time for the Interrupt Service Routine if the keyboard interrupt truly is spurious (there is a 1 microsecond delay following each check for Output Buffer Full).

To determine whether the driver is taking keyboard interrupts, press the NUMLOCK key. If the NumLock light on the keyboard turns on or off, this indicates that the i8042prt driver handled the keyboard interrupt correctly.

Default: 1

Mouse and Keyboard Driver Entries

OverrideKeyboardType   REG_DWORD   >= *0x0*

This entry is not usually present. When present, it specifies the keyboard type (overriding the keyboard type detected during system initialization). Add this value entry if the detected keyboard type is incorrect in the Registry. Type values 0x2 and 0x4 indicate an enhanced 101-key or 102-key keyboard, or compatible; other values typically indicate an old-style AT keyboard (83, 84, or 86 keys), or compatible.

Default: 0x4 (Enhanced 101-key or 102-key keyboard)

OverrideKeyboardSubtype   REG_DWORD   >= *0x0*

This entry is not usually present. When present, it specifies the OEM-dependent keyboard subtype (overriding the keyboard subtype detected during system initialization).

Default: 0x0

PollingIterations   REG_DWORD   >= *0x400*

Specifies the standard number of times to poll the hardware (in polling mode) before giving up and timing out the operation. Consider increasing this value if the driver fails to initialize or work correctly and the System log in Event Viewer contains the following message from the i8042prt source: "The operation on ... timed out (time out is configurable via the Registry)."

Default: 0x400

PollingIterationsMaximum   REG_DWORD   >= *0x400*

Specifies the maximum number of times to poll the hardware (in polling mode) before giving up and timing out the operation. This value is used instead of **PollingIterations** when an old-style AT keyboard is detected (see **OverrideKeyboardType**).

Consider increasing this value if the driver fails to initialize or work correctly and the System log in Event Viewer contains the following message from the i8042prt source: "The operation on ... timed out (time out is configurable via the Registry)."

Default: 0x2EE0

ResendIterations   REG_DWORD   >= *0x1*

Specifies the maximum number of times a hardware operation will be retried before timing out. Consider increasing this value if the driver fails to initialize or work correctly and the System log in Event Viewer contains the following message from the i8042prt source: "Exceeded the allowable number of retries (configurable via the Registry) on device ..."

Default: 0x3

Mouse and Keyboard Driver Entries

SampleRate   **REG_DWORD**   *Mouse sample rate in Hz*

Specifies the sample rate for the mouse. Intended for future use. This value might have no effect in the first release of Windows NT.

Default: 0x3C (60 Hz)

Microsoft InPort Bus Mouse Port Driver Entries

The value entries for the Microsoft InPort® bus mouse are found in the following subkey:

```
HKEY_LOCAL_MACHINE\SYSTEM\CurrentControlSet\Services\Inport\Parameters
```

HzMode   **REG_DWORD**   *Mouse sample rate mode specifier*

Specifies the value written to the Microsoft InPort mode register to set the mouse sample rate. Might be used in the first release of Windows NT, but should become obsolete.

Default: 0x2 (selects 50 Hz)

MouseDataQueueSize   **REG_DWORD**   *>= 0x1*

Specifies the number of mouse events to be buffered internally by the driver, in nonpaged pool. The allocated size, in bytes, of the internal buffer is this value times the size of the MOUSE_INPUT_DATA structure (defined in NTDDMOU.H). Consider increasing the size if the System log in Event Viewer contains the following message from the InPort source: "The ring buffer that stores incoming mouse data has overflowed (buffer size is configurable via the Registry)."

Default: 0x64 (100)

NumberOfButtons   **REG_DWORD**   *>= 0x1*

Specifies the number of buttons on the Microsoft InPort bus mouse. If the number of buttons detected at startup time and placed in the Registry is incorrect, this value can be used to override it.

Default: 0x2

PointerDeviceBaseName   **REG_SZ**   *Base port device name*

Specifies the base name for the device object(s) created by the Microsoft InPort bus mouse device driver. The device driver also writes information about the device objects into HKEY_LOCAL_MACHINE\HARDWARE\DeviceMap so that the pointer class driver can locate the pointer port device objects.

Default: PointerPort

SampleRate   REG_DWORD   *Mouse sample rate in Hz*

Specifies the sample rate for the Microsoft InPort bus mouse. Intended for future use. This value might have no effect in the first release of Windows NT.

Default: 0x32 (50 Hz)

Microsoft Serial Mouse Port Driver Entries

The value entries for the Microsoft serial mouse are found in the following subkey:

```
HKEY_LOCAL_MACHINE\SYSTEM\CurrentControlSet\Services\Sermouse\Parameters
```

MouseDataQueueSize   REG_DWORD   *>= 0x1*

Specifies the number of mouse events to be buffered internally by the driver, in nonpaged pool. The allocated size, in bytes, of the internal buffer is this value times the size of the MOUSE_INPUT_DATA structure (defined in NTDDMOU.H). Consider increasing the size if the System log in Event Viewer contains the following message from the Sermouse source: "The ring buffer that stores incoming mouse data has overflowed (buffer size is configurable via the Registry)."

Default: 0x64 (100)

NumberOfButtons   REG_DWORD   *>= 0x1*

Specifies the number of buttons on the serial mouse. If the number of buttons detected at startup time and placed in the Registry is incorrect, this value can be used to override it.

Default: 0x2

OverrideHardwareBitstring   REG_DWORD   *0x1 or 0x2*

This entry is not usually present. When present, it specifies that regardless of whether it was actually detected, a serial mouse is present on the system. Add this value to tell the driver to assume the serial mouse is on COM1 (specified by the value 0x1) or COM2 (specified by the value 0x2). This entry is useful if the serial mouse has not been automatically detected.

PointerDeviceBaseName   REG_SZ   *Base port device name*

Specifies the base name for the device object(s) created by the serial mouse device driver. The device driver also writes information about the device objects into HKEY_LOCAL_MACHINE\HARDWARE\DeviceMap so that the pointer class driver can locate the pointer port device objects.

Default: PointerPort

SampleRate   REG_DWORD   *Mouse sample rate in Hz*

Specifies the sample rate for the serial mouse. Intended for future use. This value might have no effect in the first release of Windows NT.

Default: 0x28 (1200 baud)

Mouse Class Driver Entries

The value entries for the mouse class driver are found in the following subkey:

```
HKEY_LOCAL_MACHINE\SYSTEM\CurrentControlSet\Services\Mouclass\Parameters
```

ConnectMultiplePorts   REG_DWORD   *0x0 or 0x1*

Specifies the type of connection between class and port device objects. This parameter is mainly of interest to device driver writers.

The value 0x0 specifies a 1:1 relationship between class device objects and port device objects. (That is, one class device object is created by the driver and connected to one port device object; the maximum number of objects created and connected to an associated port object is determined by the value of **MaximumPortsServiced.**) The value 0x1 specifies a 1:many relationship between a single class device object and multiple port device objects. (That is, one class device object is created by the driver and then connected to multiple port device objects, up to a maximum specified by **MaximumPortsServiced.**)

Default: 0x1 (The events generated by up to the **MaximumPortsServiced** number of pointing devices on the system will all be fed to the Windows subsystem in a single input stream.)

MaximumPortsServiced   REG_DWORD   *>= 0x1*

Specifies the number of port devices the mouse class device driver will connect to and service. The class device driver handles hardware-independent operations on a specific class of devices (in this case, the mouse and other pointing devices). The port drivers manage the hardware-specific operations.

Default: 0x3 (The class driver will service up to three pointing devices.)

MouseDataQueueSize   REG_DWORD   *>= 0x1*

Specifies the number of mouse events to be buffered internally by the driver, in nonpaged pool. The allocated size, in bytes, of the internal buffer is this value times the size of the MOUSE_INPUT_DATA structure (defined in NTDDMOU.H). Consider increasing the size if the System log in Event Viewer frequently contains the following message from the Mouclass source: "The ring buffer that stores incoming mouse data has overflowed (buffer size is configurable via the Registry)."

Default: 0x64 (100)

PointerDeviceBaseName   REG_SZ   *Base class device name*

Specifies the base name for the device object(s) created by the mouse class device driver. The device driver also writes information about the device object into HKEY_LOCAL_MACHINE\HARDWARE\DeviceMap so that the pointer class device object(s) can be easily located.

Default: PointerClass

Keyboard Class Driver Entries

The value entries for the keyboard class driver are found in the following subkey:

```
HKEY_LOCAL_MACHINE\SYSTEM\CurrentControlSet\Services\Kbdclass\Parameters
```

ConnectMultiplePorts   REG_DWORD   *0x0 or 0x1*

Specifies the type of connection between class and port device objects. This parameter is mainly of interest to device driver writers.

The value 0x0 specifies a 1:1 relationship between class device objects and port device objects. (That is, one class device object is created by the driver and connected to one port device object; the maximum number of objects created and connected to an associated port object is determined by the value of **MaximumPortsServiced.**) The value 0x1 specifies a 1:many relationship between a single class device object and multiple port device objects (That is, one class device object is created by the driver and then connected to multiple port device objects, up to a maximum specified by **MaximumPortsServiced.**)

Default: 0x0 (The events generated by up to the **MaximumPortsServiced** number of keyboard devices on the system will feed separate input streams. In the first release of Windows NT, the Windows subsystem only reads from a single keyboard input stream.)

KeyboardDataQueueSize   REG_DWORD   *>= 0x1*

Specifies the number of keyboard events to be buffered internally by the driver, in nonpaged pool. The allocated size, in bytes, of the internal buffer is this value times the size of the KEYBOARD_INPUT_DATA structure (defined in NTDDKBD.H). Consider increasing the size if the System log in Event Viewer contains the following message from the Kbdclass source: "The ring buffer that stores incoming keyboard data has overflowed (buffer size is configurable via the Registry)."

Default: 0x64 (100)

KeyboardDeviceBaseName   REG_SZ   *Base class device name*

Specifies the base name for the keyboard device object(s) created by the keyboard class device driver. The device driver also writes information about the device objects into HKEY_LOCAL_MACHINE\HARDWARE\DeviceMap so that the keyboard class device objects are easily located.

Default: KeyboardClass

MaximumPortsServiced   REG_DWORD   >= *0x1*

Specifies the number of port devices the keyboard class device driver will connect to and service. The class device driver handles hardware-independent operations on a specific class of devices (in this case, keyboard devices). The port drivers manage the hardware-specific operations.

Default: 0x3 (The class driver will service up to three keyboard devices.)

DeviceMap Entries for the Keyboard and Mouse

The following DeviceMap descriptions are for informational purposes only, since the DeviceMap subkeys are volatile and are recreated each time you start Windows NT. Administrators cannot modify DeviceMap entries.

These DeviceMap entries are used by the Windows subsystem to locate the pointer and keyboard class devices, and by the pointer and keyboard class drivers to locate the associated pointer and keyboard port devices. Information is placed in the DeviceMap subkey by the keyboard and pointer class and port drivers.

The format for each of these entries is the following:

Name of class device object **: REG_SZ :** *Registry path to driver's Services*

The keyboard class information appears in the following Registry path:

```
HKEY_LOCAL_MACHINE\HARDWARE\DeviceMap\KeyboardClass
```

There can be one or more of these entries. Each entry specifies the name of a device object created by the keyboard class driver to represent the class device, followed by the Registry path to the driver's Services subkey.

Default:

```
\Device\KeyboardClass0 : REG_SZ :
\Registry\Machine\System\ControlSet001\Services\Kbdclass
```

The keyboard port information appears in the following Registry path:

```
HKEY_LOCAL_MACHINE\HARDWARE\DeviceMap\KeyboardPort
```

> There can be one or more of these entries. Each entry specifies the name of a device object created by the keyboard port driver(s) to represent the physical keyboard (port) device, followed by the Registry path to the driver's Services subkey.
>
> Default:
>
> ```
> \Device\KeyboardPort0 : REG_SZ :
> \Registry\Machine\System\ControlSet001\Services\i8042prt
> ```

The mouse class information appears in the following Registry path:

```
HKEY_LOCAL_MACHINE\HARDWARE\DeviceMap\PointerClass
```

> There can be one or more of these entries. Each entry specifies the name of a device object created by the pointer (mouse) class driver to represent the class device, followed by the Registry path to the driver's Services subkey.
>
> Default:
>
> ```
> \Device\PointerClass0 : REG_SZ :
> \Registry\Machine\System\ControlSet001\Services\Mouclass
> ```

The mouse port information appears in the following Registry path:

```
HKEY_LOCAL_MACHINE\HARDWARE\DeviceMap\PointerPort
```

> There can be one or more of these entries. Each entry specifies the name of a device object created by the pointer port driver(s) to represent the physical pointing (port) device, followed by the Registry path to the driver's Services subkey.
>
> Default (assumes mouse port, Microsoft InPort, and serial pointing devices are connected):
>
> ```
> \Device\PointerPort0 : REG_SZ :
>     \Registry\Machine\System\ControlSet001\Services\i8042prt
> \Device\PointerPort1 : REG_SZ :
>     \Registry\Machine\System\ControlSet001\Services\Inport
> \Device\PointerPort2 : REG_SZ :
>     \Registry\Machine\System\ControlSet001\Services\Sermouse
> ```

Mouse and Keyboard Driver Entries

SCSI Miniport Driver Entries

The basic SCSI miniport driver entries in the Registry are found under subkeys in the following path:

`HKEY_LOCAL_MACHINE\System\CurrentControlSet\Services`

Each subkey's name is the same as the driver's filename minus the .SYS filename extension; for example, FD8XX, which is the entry for all Future Domain 800-series SCSI adapter. The Registry includes entries for at least the following SCSI miniport device drivers:

Driver name	Description
Aha*xx*	Adaptec 154x and 174x SCSI adapters
DptScsi	DPT SCSI adapter
Fd16_700, Fd7000ex, Fd8xx	Future Domain MCS 600/MCS 700, TMC-7000ex, and 800-series SCSI adapters
Ncr53c9x, Ncrc700, Ncrc710	NCR SCSI controller and adapters
Oliscsi	Olivetti SCSI adapter
Sparrow	SCSI adapter
Spock	SCSI adapter
T128 and T13B	Trantor SCSI adapters
Ultra*xx*	UltraStor 124, 14f, and 24f SCSI adapters
Wd33c93	Maynard SCSI adapter

The contents of a SCSI miniport subkey are standard for all SCSI miniport drivers, with these basic value entries:

Value entry	Value
ErrorControl	0x01—which is the preferred value for **ErrorControl**. With a value of 0x01, the startup process continues if the SCSI miniport driver fails to initialize.
Group	SCSI Miniport.
Start	0x00 (Auto Start).
Tag	Optional (determines the load order of SCSI miniport drivers).
Type	0x01 (device driver).

For each SCSI miniport key, there can be one or more subkeys named Parameters\Device or Parameters\Device*N*, where $N = 0, 1, 2$, and so on. The value of *N* corresponds to the SCSI host adapter number. If the subkey name is Device, the value is globally defined. If the subkey name is Device*N*, the value only pertains to the particular SCSI host adapter.

The SCSI miniport driver recognizes several optional value entries that can be defined under these subkeys, as described in this section.

InitiatorTargetId   REG_DWORD   *Number*

Sets the SCSI bus host adapter ID. It is used by host adapters that can set the initiator ID from software.

Default: Uninitialized

MaximumLogicalUnit   REG_DWORD   *Number*

Controls the number of logical units per target controller that are scanned for by the SCSI miniport driver. Most devices only support one logical unit, and some devices may fail if more than one logical unit is scanned for.

Default: 8

ScsiDebug   REG_DWORD   *Number*

This value is used to set the value of the ScsiDebug variable, which controls the verbosity of DebugPrint, with 0 being the least verbose. This is used for debugging.

Default: 0

The following value entries are used to fix problems such as device time-outs or controller detection errors but will reduce I/O performance. These value entries can be abbreviated. For example, a value entry of **Disable** will cause **DisableSynchronousTransfers, DisableTaggedQueuing, DisableDisconnects,** and **DisableMultipleRequests** to be set.

Note The system must be restarted before these options take effect.

BreakPointOnEntry   REG_DWORD   *0 or 1*

A DbgBreakPoint() call is immediately made inside of SpParseDevice. This is used for debugging.

Default: 0 (disabled)

DisableDisconnects   REG_DWORD   *0 or 1*

Disables disconnects on the SCSI bus. It causes all requests to be executed sequentially.

Default: 1 (enabled)

DisableMultipleRequests   REG_DWORD   *0 or 1*

Prevents the SCSI miniport driver from sending more than one request at a time per SCSI device.

Default: 1 (enabled)

DisableSynchronousTransfers   REG_DWORD   *0 or 1*

Disables synchronous data transfers on the SCSI bus.

Default: 1 (enabled)

DisableTaggedQueuing   REG_DWORD   *0 or 1*

Disables SCSI-II tagged command queuing on the host adapter.

Default: 1 (enabled)

DriverParameter   *Data type is specific to driver   A string*

A pointer to this data is passed to the SCSI miniport driver in a miniportFindAdapter routine. It is the fourth parameter, ArgumentString. A miniport driver uses this data to define the IRQ number for the SCSI host adapter, but other applications for the data are possible.

The data type for this value is defined by the specific SCSI miniport driver developer. If the data type is REG_SZ, the Unicode string is converted to an ANSI string before transferring it to the SCSI miniport driver.

The following drivers currently use the **DriverParameter** value entry:

Driver	Values	Meaning
Wd33c93	**IRQ**=*xx*; **DMA**=*yy*	*xx* is the IRQ the card should use. Valid values are: 3, 4, 5, 10, 11, 12, and 15. The default is 10. *yy* is the DMA channel the card should use. Valid values are: 5, 6, and 7. The default is 6.
Aha154*x*	**BusOnTime**=*xx*	*xx* is the bus on time in microseconds for the card. Valid values are 2–15. The default is 7. The value is usually adjusted downward when DMA transfers from the Adaptec card are interfering with other DMA transfers.
FD8*XX*	**IRQ**=*xx*	*xx* is the IRQ the card should use. Valid values are 0, 3, 4, 5, 10, 11, 12, 14, 15. This value should match the jumper settings on the card. Numbers 0, 3, and 5 are for the short cards (850, 845); the rest are for the 885 card only. A value of 0 indicates the card should not use any interrupts and will poll. The default is 5.

Driver *(continued)*	Values *(continued)*	Meaning *(continued)*
T128	**IRQ=**xx	xx is the IRQ the card should use. Valid values are: 0, 3, 5, 7, 10, 12, 14, and 15. This value should match the jumper settings on the card. Numbers greater than 7 are for the T128F card only. A value of 0 indicates the card should not use any interrupts and will poll. The default is 5.
T13B	**IRQ=**xx	xx is the IRQ the card should use. Valid values are 0, 3, 5, and 7. This value should match the jumper settings on the card. A value of 0 indicates the card should not use any interrupts and will poll. The default is 5.
TMV1	**IRQ=**xx	xx is the IRQ the card should use. Valid values are: 2, 3, 4, 5, 6, 7, 10, 11, 12, and 15. The default is 10.

Sound Card Driver Entries

Usually, sound drivers consist of two parts: a front-end for installation and request processing, consisting of files such as SNDBLST.DLL or SYNTH.DLL; and a kernel driver for communicating with the hardware, consisting of files such as SNDBLST.SYS or SYNTH.SYS.

There is also a helper driver named MMDRV.DLL that transforms most low-level calls to Wave, MIDI, and AUX devices into calls to kernel mode drivers.

These are the installable sound kernel drivers for Windows NT:

Sound driver	Comment
MIPSSND.SYS	MIPS® ARCSystem 100/150 built-in sound
MVAUDIO.SYS	Media Vision Pro Audio Spectrum 16 and Pro Studio 16
MVOPL3.SYS	Synthesizer driver for Media Vision Pro Audio Spectrum 16 and Pro Studio 16
SNDBLST.SYS	SoundBlaster™ 1.5 and compatibles
SNDSYS.SYS	Windows sound system and COMPAQ® Business Audio
SYNTH.SYS	Ad Lib and OPL3 MIDI synthesizer driver

For each installed sound driver, several parameters are stored in the Registry, based on choices made by using the Drivers icon in Control Panel. The following shows the Registry path for sound system driver entries:

```
HKEY_LOCAL_MACHINE\SYSTEM\CurrentControlSet\  Services
    \SoundDriverName\Parameters
```

The actual key name in the Registry is the same as the filename of the related kernel driver. For example, for SNDBLST.SYS, the key name is Sndblst.

Some drivers can write over the values they receive on the basis of information read from the hardware. The following shows some typical values found in the Parameters subkey for sound cards:

Configuration Error   REG_DWORD   *0, 1, 2, 3, or 4*

Specifies an error that occurred during install. This value is only relevant if the driver fails to load. (Not all drivers write this information into the Registry.)

Value	Meaning
0	Nonspecific error
1	Hardware not found (usually the wrong I/O port was assumed)
2	Specified interrupt was incorrect or did not work
3	Specified DMA channel was incorrect or did not work
4	Hardware is present but not working

DmaChannel   REG_DWORD

Defines the DMA channel settings for transferring digitized sound.

Default: Depends on the sound card—not user-configurable.

Interrupt   REG_DWORD   *Interrupt number*

Defines the interrupt number used by the hardware.

Default: 0xa (configured for Interrupt 10)

LeftLineInAtten   REG_DWORD   *Number*

Specifies the current volume level of the left channel of the line-in input.

Port   REG_DWORD   *Address*

Defines the I/O port start address used to communicate with the hardware.

Default: 0x220 for SNDBLST.SYS

RightLineInAtten   REG_DWORD   *Number*

Specifies the current volume level of the right channel of the line-in input.

Video Device Driver Entries

This section describes the entries for video device drivers under the DeviceMap subkey and under the CurrentControlSet\Services subkeys for specific video drivers.

Video Information in the DeviceMap Subkey

The hardware device mapping for video is under the following subkey:

```
HKEY_LOCAL_MACHINE\Hardware\DeviceMap\Video
```

This information is volatile and is reconstructed at startup by the video port driver. It can change from startup to startup based on external factors, such as failure to initialize a video adapter or the addition of other video cards to the system.

This subkey contains the mappings from Windows NT logical video devices to the physical device they represent in the CurrentControlSet\Services subkey. This mapping allows the system to find the right display driver for the currently installed video device.

%device_object_name%   **REG_SZ**   *Registry path for device*

Indicates the first logical video device is the first physical adapter. For example, the following entry indicates that the first logical video device is the second physical XGA adapter:

```
Video\Device0 =
\Registry\Machine\CurrentControlSet\Services\XGA\Device1
```

In this example, the value indicates that the second logical video device is the first physical VGA adapter:

```
Video\Device1 =
\Registry\Machine\CurrentControlSet\Serivces\Vga\Device0
```

These values point to entries in the Services subkey, as described in the next section.

Video Driver Entries in the Services Subkey

The port driver portion of the video driver is hardware-independent and contains operating system-specific code. Therefore, the port driver, VIDEOPRT.SYS, can support one or more video devices. The Services\Videoprt subkey has no added parameters, and its standard entries are the following:

Value entry	Default value
ErrorControl	0x1 (Normal)
Group	Video
Start	0x1 (system)
Type	0x1 (Kernel driver)

The specific subkey for each video driver contains all the information required to initialize and program the device properly. If several adapters can be handled by a single driver, the subkeys Device1, Device2, and so on will contain information for the other devices. The Registry path looks like this, where *VideoDriverName* is the name of a specific video device driver:

```
HKEY_LOCAL_MACHINE\SYSTEM\CurrentControlSet\Services
    \VideoDriverName\Device0
```

The *VideoDriverName* subkeys for drivers in Windows NT include the following. This is not an exhaustive list:

Ati	ET4000	Jazzg*xxx*
S3	Trident	Vga
Wdvga	Xga	

For example, the following subkey contains information for the first logical device of type VGA:

```
HKEY_LOCAL_MACHINE\SYSTEM\CurrentControlSet\Services\Vga\Device0
```

The following values can be set in a video driver subkey.

DefaultSettings.BitsPerPel   **REG_DWORD**   *Number of bits per pixel*
Contains the number of colors for the mode requested by the user. For example, for the v7vram miniport, the following value yields a 256-color mode:

```
DefaultSettings.BitsPerPel = 8
```

DefaultSettings.Interlaced   **REG_DWORD**   *0 or 1*
Determines whether the mode requested by the user is interlaced. For example, for the v7vram miniport:

```
DefaultSettings.Interlaced = 0x0 (FALSE)
```

DefaultSettings.VRefresh   **REG_DWORD**   *Number Hz*
Contains the refresh rate of the mode requested by the user. For example, for the et4000 miniport:

```
DefaultSettings.VRefresh = 72
```

DefaultSettings.XResolution   **REG_DWORD**   *Number of pixels*
Contains the width of the mode requested by the user. For example, for the et4000 miniport:

```
DefaultSettings.Xresolution = 1024
```

DefaultSettings.YResolution   **REG_DWORD**   *Number of pixels*
Contains the height of the mode requested by the user. For example, for the et4000 miniport:

```
DefaultSettings.Yresolution = 768
```

DeviceData   **REG_BINARY**   *Binary code*
Contains binary data specific to the Windows display driver. For example, for the VGA miniport:

```
DeviceData = 05a0 5075 8ef0 8456 c8dd
```

InstalledDisplayDrivers   **REG_MULTI_SZ**   *Driver names*
Contains a list of names of display drivers that can function with this miniport, depending on which mode is selected by the user.

Note Display driver names do not contain the .DLL filename extension.

The system attempts to initialize the adapter by calling each display driver, using the user-selected parameter. If the combination of display driver and monitor do not support the mode requested by the user, the display driver fails to initialize and the system tries the next display driver. If all display drivers fail to initialize, the system calls the first display driver again to set the adapter to any mode it can.

For example, for the et4000 miniport:

```
InstalledDisplayDrivers = "vga" "vga256" "vga64k"
```

For the S3 miniport:

```
InstalledDisplayDrivers = "s3"
```

Monitor   REG_SZ   *Monitor name*

This entry is reserved to contain the name of the VESA VDIF monitor information file for the monitor connected to the adapter. No such files are provided with Windows NT in the current version.

If a file is supplied and a value is added, the miniport can load this file to determine the exact timings of the monitor connected to the physical device.

For example, for the XGA miniport, if a NEC4FS monitor was attached to the XGA card:

```
Monitor = "NEC4fg.vdb"
```

VgaCompatible   REG_DWORD   *0 or 1*

Determines whether the driver supports all of the VGA functionality required to perform full-screen operations.

If this value is 1, the driver supports full-screen applications in x86-based computers. If this value is 0, the VGA miniport (described under the Vga subkey) will also be used to enable and disable full-screen modes for non-Windows applications.

As a general rule, all drivers for SVGA adapters should set this value to 1, because they must implement all the VGA functionality to perform extended save/restore of all registers. A video accelerator designed as an accelerator working independently of the VGA miniport (via pass-through) can set this to 0 and let the VGA miniport do all the full-screen work.

For example, for the et4000 miniport:

```
VgaCompatible = 0x1 (TRUE)
```

Video Device Driver Entries

For the S3 miniport:

```
VgaCompatible = 0x0 (FALSE)
```

This functionality is not required for other computer platforms, such as RISC-based computers, because the VDM sessions are emulated using NTVDM.EXE, and there are no full-screen sessions.

Registry Entries for Network Services

The following services have additional value entries that can be specified in the Registry, in addition to changes that you can make using the Services icon in Control Panel or Server Manager in Windows NT Advanced Server. You can view current settings for these services by choosing the Services button in WinMSD.

Alerter service	NWLink transport
AppleTalk and MacFile services	Redirector (Rdr) service
BootVerification service	Remote Access Service (RAS)
Browser service	Replicator service
DiskPerf service	Schedule service
DLC transport	Server service
EventLog service	TCP/IP (FTP, NBT, Streams, WinSock)
NetBEUI (NBF) transport	UPS service
NetLogon service	Workstation service
NetworkProvider service	

Services that are not included in this section do not have hidden parameters that you can set.

This section describes parameters for these services under the HKEY_LOCAL_MACHINE\SYSTEM\CurrentControlSet\Services subkey.

Some of these services also have configuration information stored under HKEY_LOCAL_MACHINE\SOFTWARE. These values are described in "NetRules Subkey Entries," earlier in this chapter.

Note Wherever possible, choose the Services icon in Control Panel or use Server Manager in Windows NT Advanced Server to change values for these services.

Alerter Service Entries

Entries for this service appear under the following subkey:

`HKEY_LOCAL_MACHINE\SYSTEM\CurrentControlSet\Services\Alerter\Parameters`

AlertNames   REG_MULTI_SZ   *List*

Specifies the list of users to whom administrator alerts are sent. This value can be set using the Server Manager.

Default: NULL

AppleTalk and MacFile Service Entries for SFM

Services For Macintosh (SFM) does not appear in the Registry until you install SFM using the Network icon in Control Panel. After installation, the SFM value entries appear under several Services subkeys: AppleTalk, MacFile, MacPrint, and MacSrv. You should let the system maintain entries in the MacPrint or MacSrv services. However, the AppleTalk and MacFile services contain definable parameters described in this section.

You should use the Network icon in Control Panel to configure SFM, and use File Manager to administer file services, Server Manager to administer server services, and Print Manager to administer print services for SFM.

SFM is included with Windows NT Advanced Server and the AppleTalk transport service is on the Windows NT Resource Guide disk.

AppleTalk Entries for SFM

The values for the AppleTalk service are found in the following Registry path:

`HKEY_LOCAL_MACHINE\SYSTEM\CurrentControlSet\Services\AppleTalk`

For changes to take effect, you must restart the File Server for Macintosh using the Devices icon in Control Panel.

Values for the AppleTalk Parameters and Adapters subkeys are described here. The settings in the Linkage subkey and the TCP/IP settings in the Winsock subkey for AppleTalk are maintained by the system and should not be changed by the user.

AppleTalk Parameter Entries

This is the Registry path for the AppleTalk parameters:

```
HKEY_LOCAL_MACHINE\SYSTEM\CurrentControlSet\Services
    \AppleTalk\Parameters
```

These values set port, zone, and router information.

DefaultPort   EG_SZ   *Adapter name*

Specifies the network on which the SFM service names are registered. If the AppleTalk protocol is not routing, only Macintosh workstations connected to this network can see the file and print services. During initial installation, the default port is set automatically to the first Ethernet adapter found, or to the first Token Ring adapter, or to a LocalTalk adapter (in that order).

Default: the first adapter found.

DesiredZone   REG_SZ   *Zone name*

Specifies the zone in which the SFM service is present. If this value is not set, SFM is present in the default zone for that network.

There is no default.

EnableRouter   REG_DWORD   *0 or 1*

Tells the AppleTalk protocol whether routing needs to be started on this computer. If routing is started, Macintosh workstations connected to any of the networks that this computer is on should be able to use the file and print servers for Macintosh.

Important This value is critical. Unless absolutely essential, do not set this value to 1.

Default: 0

Adapter Card Entries for AppleTalk

The entries for AppleTalk that are specific to network adapter cards are found under the following Registry path:

```
HKEY_LOCAL_MACHINE\SYSTEM\CurrentControlSet\Services
    \AppleTalk\Adapters\adapter_name
```

There is one subkey for each adapter that is AppleTalk-compatible on the computer. These entries are found in each *Adapter_Name* subkey.

AarpRetries   REG_DWORD   *Number*

Specifies the maximum number of AppleTalk address-resolution protocol packets to be sent by the AppleTalk protocol.

Default: 0xa

DdpCheckSums   REG_DWORD   *0 or 1*

Tells the AppleTalk protocol whether to compute checksums in the DDP layer. If this entry is 1, the AppleTalk protocol uses sums in the DDP layer.

Default: 0

DefaultZone   REG_SZ   *Zone name*

Contains the default zone for this network if this adapter is seeding the network. If the adapter is seeding the network, the default zone is chosen when you configure SFM using the Network icon in Control Panel.

There is no default.

NetworkRangeLowerEnd   REG_DWORD   *1 to 65279*

Specifies the lower network number of the network range if this adapter is seeding the network. If the adapter is seeding the network, this number is set by using the Network icon in Control Panel to configure SFM.

There is no default.

NetworkRangeUpperEnd   REG_DWORD   *1 to 65279*

Specifies the upper network number of the network range for this network if this adapter is seeding the network. If the adapter is seeding the network, this number is set by using the Network icon in Control Panel to configure SFM.

There is no default.

PortName   REG_SZ   *AdapterName@ComputerName*

Specifies the name used to identify the AppleTalk protocol running on a particular adapter on a computer.

There is no default.

SeedingNetwork   REG_DWORD   *0 or 1*

Used by the AppleTalk protocol during startup. If this value is 0, this adapter is not seeding the network and the AppleTalk protocol ignores any seeding information for the adapter, if specified. If this value is 1, the AppleTalk protocol reads all seeding information and seeds the network, if valid.

Default: 0.

ZoneList   REG_MULTI_SZ   *List of zones*

This value is relevant only when the adapter is seeding the network. The network is seeded with this list of zones by the AppleTalk protocol. Changes can be made by using the Network icon in Control Panel to configure SFM.

There is no default.

MacFile Entries for SFM

The MacFile subkey contains the main entries for the AppleTalk File Protocol (AFP) server. All configuration information for the file server is in the following subkey:

```
HKEY_LOCAL_MACHINE\SYSTEM\CurrentControlSet\Services\MacFile
```

For changes to take effect, you must restart the computer.

The MacFile\Parameters subkey includes Type_Creators, Icons, and Extensions subkeys. You should let the system maintain entries in the Icons or Extensions subkeys. This section describes value entries for the Parameters and Parameters\Type_Creator subkeys.

MacFile Parameters Entries

The Registry path for MacFile parameters is the following:

```
HKEY_LOCAL_MACHINE\SYSTEM\CurrentControlSet\Services\MacFile\Parameters
```

The following value entries specify server options, which can be set from the Server Manager. All other entries are added to the Registry when changes to the default values occur.

For information about the Macintosh codepage, see the entry for MacCP in the NLS\CodePage subkey.

LoginMsg   REG_SZ   *1–198 characters*

Specifies the message you want Macintosh users to see when they log on to the Windows NT Advanced Server network.

There is no default.

MaxSessions REG_DWORD *1 to unlimited (0xffffffff)*

Specifies the maximum number of user sessions that the file server for Macintosh can accommodate.

Default: 0xff (255in decimal)

PagedMemLimit REG_DWORD *1000K to 256000K*

Specifies the maximum amount of page memory that the file server for Macintosh uses. Performance of the MacFile service increases with an increase in this value. However, the value should not be set lower than 1000 KB. It is especially important that you are well acquainted with memory issues before changing this resource parameter. You cannot change this value from Server Manager.

Default: 0x4e20 (20000 in decimal)

NonPagedMemLimit REG_DWORD *256K to 16000KB*

Specifies the maximum amount of RAM that is available to the file server for Macintosh. Increasing this value helps performance of the file server, but decreases performance of other system resources.

Default: 0xfa0 (4000 in decimal)

ServerName REG_SZ *Server name*

Specifies the name of the server running SFM on a Windows NT Advanced Server network. Use the server's Windows NT Advanced Server name as the default if you need to add this entry.

There is no default.

ServerOptions REG_DWORD

Specifies server options that are set in Server Manager. If needed for repair purposes, change Bits 1 through 3; do not change any of the other bits. When on, Bit 1 allows guest logons, Bit 2 allows cleartext passwords, and Bit 3 allows Macintosh users to save passwords on their workstations.

The defaults are bit 1, 2, and 3 set to on.

***Volume*   REG_MULTI_SZ*   *MaxUses Properties Password Path*

Each entry specifies information about a Macintosh-accessible volume on the server on a Windows NT Advanced Server network. You should add Macintosh-accessible volumes using File Manager.

Value	Meaning
MaxUses	Specifies the maximum number of simultaneous workstations that can be connected to the file server. The upper limit is unlimited. The practical limits are based on the server hardware and network media.
Properties	Specifies security options . When Bit 1 is set to On, the volume is read-only. When Bit 16 is set to On, guests can use this volume. The default is 1000000000000000 (in binary notation) (the volume is read-only; guests can use this volume).
Password	Contains the encrypted password. Do not change this value. If a user forgets a password, you can delete this entry, thus removing a password requirement from the user's account. Then the user can specify a new password at logon.
Path	Specifies the path of the volume's root directory. If a volume has been deleted, the path may still be valid; consequently, you should not delete this value. If volumes are deleted using File Manager, you can delete this value.

Type_Creators Entries for MacFile

The values in the following Registry subkey list all the Macintosh type-creators that are associated with MS-DOS–style filename extensions:

```
HKEY_LOCAL_MACHINE\SYSTEM\CurrentControlSet\Services
    MacFile\Parameters\Type_Creators
```

Change these values from the File Manager by choosing the Associate command from the MacFile menu. The value entries that appear in the Registry for each type of creator have the following format:

REG_MULTI_SZ   **Creator=***Value* **Type=***Value* **Comment=***Value*

The three values appear for each entry. The value for Creator= must have from 1 through 4 characters. The value for Type= must have from 1 through 4 characters. The value for Comment= must have from 0 through 29 characters.

BootVerification Service Entries

The Services subkey for the BootVerification service does not appear by default in the Registry. You can add this key if you want to verify system startup from a remote location using the BOOTVRFY.EXE program provided with Windows NT. This service can be started from a remote computer. The service tells the Windows NT service controller that it should save the current startup system configuration as the LastKnownGood control set, and then the service terminates itself.

When you add the BootVerification key using Registry Editor, add the following value entries:

Value entry	Data type	Value	Comment
ErrorControl	REG_DWORD	0x1	Normal
ImagePath	REG_EXPAND_SZ	bootvrfy.exe	—
ObjectName	REG_SZ	LocalSystem	—
Start	REG_DWORD	0x3	Demand
Type	REG_DWORD	0x2	Win32 shared process

You must also specify a value of 1 for the **ReportBootOK** entry under the following Registry path:

```
HKEY_LOCAL_MACHINE\Software\Windows NT\CurrentVersion\WinLogon
```

When the value of **ReportBootOK** is set to 0, it disables the automatic (default) startup acceptance, which happens after the first successful logon.

This alternative method of verifying system startup cannot be used in conjunction with BootVerificationProgram (as described earlier in this chapter).

Browser Service Entries

The parameters that control network bindings for the Browser service are described in "NetRules Subkey Entries," earlier in this chapter.

Under the following Registry path, two parameters are found:

```
HKEY_LOCAL_MACHINE\SYSTEM\CurrentControlSet\Services\Browser\Parameters
```

CacheHitLimit   **REG_DWORD**   *0 to 256*

Describes the number of NetServerEnum requests required to qualify that the response to a NetServerEnum request be cached. If the browser receives more than **CacheHitLimit** NetServerEnum requests with a particular set of parameters, it caches the response and returns that value to the client.

Default: 1

CacheResponseSize   REG_DWORD   *0 to xfffffff*

Specifies the maximum number of responses kept for each transport. To disable this feature, set this value to 0.

Default: 10

IsDomainMasterBrowser   REG_SZ   *Boolean*

For TCP/IP, specifies a workstation within a workgroup which can be included in global LMHOSTS file. When this parameter is set to Yes, it forces the elevation of a workstation's priority for the browser. This helps with WAN browsing.

This value should be set on a few systems for the workgroup, placing mappings for each in the global LMHOSTS file. For example, in a workgroup with 20 members, set this value on three of the computers to earn a better chance to act as master browsers. This facilitates remote browsing ability for workstations in remote domains whose domain master browser has successful mappings for these special workgroup members.

MaintainServerList   REG_SZ   *Boolean or Auto*

If this value is No, this server is not a browse server. If this value is Yes, this server becomes a browse server. It attempts to contact the Master Browse Server to get a current browse list. If it cannot find the Master Browse Server, it forces an election and is, of course, a candidate to become the master.

If **MaintainServerList** is Auto, this server may or may not become a browse server, depending on the results of the Registry exchange with the Master Browse Server.

If **MaintainServerList** is set to Yes, the computer is configured to always be a backup browser.

Default: Auto, if none is present. (This server contacts the Master Browse Server, and the Master Browse Server tells this server whether it should become a browse server.)

QueryDriverFrequency   REG_DWORD   *0 to 900*

Indicates the time after which a browser maser will invalidate its NetServerEnum response cache and the frequency that a master browser will query the browser driver to retrieve the list of servers. Increasing this time makes browsing somewhat faster, but browse information will not necessarily be 100 percent accurate to the minute. Lowering this time makes browse response more accurate, but will increase the CPU load on the browse master.

Default: 30

The following Browser driver parameters are found under this Registry path for the Datagram Receiver:

```
HKEY_LOCAL_MACHINE\SYSTEM\CurrentControlSet\Services\DGRcvr\Parameters
```

BrowserServerDeletionThreshold   REG_DWORD
BrowserDomainDeletionThreshold   REG_DWORD *0 to 0xffffffff*

If more than **BrowserServerDeletionThreshold** servers (or **BrowserDomainDeletionThreshold**) servers (or domains) are flushed in a 30-second interval, this will cause an event to be generated.

Default: 0xffffffff

FindMasterTimeout   REG_DWORD   *0 to 0xffffff*

Specifies the maximum number of seconds that FindMaster requests should be allowed to take. If you have a slow LAN, you may want to increase this value (but only if directed by Microsoft Product Support services).

Default: 0xffffffff

GetBrowserListThreshold   REG_DWORD   *Number*

Represents the threshold that the Browser uses before logging an error indicating that too many of these requests have been "missed." If more requests than the value of **GetBrowserServerList** are missed in an hour, the Browser logs an event indicating that this has happened.

Default: 0xffffffff (That is, never log events.)

MailslotDatagramThreshold   REG_DWORD   *Number*

Represents the threshold that the Browser uses before logging an error indicating that too many of these requests have been "missed." If more mailslots than the value of **MailslotDatagramThreshold** are missed in an hour, the Browser logs an event indicating that this has happened.

Default: 0xffffffff (That is, never log events.)

DiskPerf Service Entries

The DiskPerf subkey entries determines whether disk performance statistics are maintained by the system. If the **Start** value is 0 (boot), then statistics are counted and are reported by Performance Monitor and similar tools. Collecting disk performance statistics can take up to 1.5 percent of the disk throughput on a system with a slow processor (such as an 20 MHz 80386 computer) but should have negligible impact on a system with a faster processor (such as a 33 MHz i486 and above).

Turn DiskPerf on or off only by using the Diskperf utility; for example, type **diskperf -y** at the command prompt.

The Registry path is the following:

```
HKEY_LOCAL_MACHINE\SYSTEM\CurrentControlSet\Services\DiskPerf
```

There are no parameters that users can set. The following are the default values for the standard entries:

Value entry	Value
ErrorControl	0x1 (Normal)
Group	Filter
Start	0x4 (disabled)
Type	0x1 (Kernel driver)

DLC System Driver Entries

The DLC subkey does not appear unless this service is installed. In Windows NT, the Data Link Control (DLC) protocol only needs to be installed on computers that access IBM mainframes (usually with 3270 applications) or on print servers that print directly to Hewlett-Packard printers. Network printers such as the HP® III si use the DLC protocol, for example, because the frames received are easy to take apart.

The DLC driver depends on an having an NDIS group service available and is bound to the network adapter card through the NDIS device driver. Each adapter that supports the DLC protocol has a subkey under the DLC\Parameters subkey. With Registry Editor, you can modify the following parameters for the DLC system driver. The path for these parameters is the following:

```
HKEY_LOCAL_MACHINE\SYSTEM\CurrentControlSet\Services
    \DLC\Parameters\adapter name
```

The following **TxTick** parameters are multipliers for the T1, T2, and Ti values, which represent time periods in milliseconds that are used when a station or SAP is opened. If the time period value is between 1 and 5, the time delay is computed as follows:

```
(time period) * TxTickOne * 40 milliseconds
```

If the time period value is between 6 and 10, the time delay is computed as follows:

```
(time period - 5) * TxTickTwo * 40 milliseconds
```

When computing the short-tick values (_One) and the long-tick values (_Two), the resulting values for T1, T2, and Ti should generally follow this rule: T2 < T1 < Ti.

T1Tick{One|Two}   REG_DWORD   *1 to 255 milliseconds*

Specifies the delay before retransmitting an I frame if not acknowledged.

Default: **T1TickOne** = 5; **T1TickTwo** = 25

T2Tick{One|Two}   REG_DWORD   *1 to 255 milliseconds*

Specifies the delay before acknowledging frames in the receive window if the receive window has not been filled.

Default: **T2TickOne** = 1; **T2TickTwo** = 10

TiTick{One|Two}   REG_DWORD   *1 to 255 milliseconds*

Specifies the delay before testing an inactive station to determine if it is still active.

Default: **TiTickOne** = 25; **TiTickTwo** = 125

Swap   REG_DWORD   *0 or 1*

Used when talking over Ethernet to support certain Token Ring-to-Ethernet bridges in swapping of the Destination Address when using DLC over a Token Ring network. If this value is 0, the adapter addresses presented at the API interface are not bit-flipped before being put online.

Default: 1

UseDixOverEthernet   REG_DWORD   *0 or 1*

Specifies the default mode for the connection-oriented and connectionless 802.2 LLC (Logical Link Control) frames sent on Ethernet. If this value is 1, the DLC driver users DIX encoding in the frames to be transmitted instead of the 802.3 Ethernet format.

Default: 0

Note Additional parameters that were included in the Microsoft LAN Manager COMTOKR utility are not defined for DLC, because Windows NT does not have the same memory limitations as MS-DOS.

EventLog Service Entries

The Services subkey for EventLog contains at least three subkeys for the three types of logs—Application, Security, and System. These *Logfile* subkeys contain subkeys that define the location of the related event message file and the supported types of events, as follows:

- The Application key contains subkeys for installed applications and services that write to the Application event log.

- The Security key contains subkeys for each of the security subsystem components.

- The System key contains subkeys for device drivers.

Each of the three *Logfile* subkeys for the EventLog service can contain the value entries described in this section. The Registry path for these entries is the following, where *logfile* is System, Application, or Security.

```
HKEY_CURRENT_MACHINE\SYSTEM\CurrentControlSet\Services
    \Eventlog\logfile
```

These entries are described for informational purposes only. This information is usually maintained by Event Viewer. New keys under the Application key can only be added in meaningful ways by using the Win32 Registry APIs.

File   REG_SZ   *Path and filename*

Specifies the fully qualified path name of the file for this log. This value can be set in Event Viewer.

Default: *SystemRoot*\system32\config*filename*

MaxSize   REG_DWORD   *Number in kilobytes*

Specifies the maximum size of the log file. This value can be set using the Event Viewer.

Default: 512

Retention   REG_DWORD   *Number of seconds*

Specifies that records that are newer than this value will not be overwritten. This is what causes a log full event. This value can be set using the Event Viewer.

Default: 604800 (7 days)

Sources   REG_MULTI_SZ   *Names of source applications*

Specifies the applications, services, or groups of applications that write events to this log. Each source is a subkey of the *Logfile* key.

Default: None. This value is dynamically maintained by the EventLog service.

The *Source* subkeys under a *Logfile* key are created by the applications that write events in the related event log. These subkeys contain information specific to the source of the event under the following types of value entries.

EventMessageFile   REG_EXPAND_SZ   *Filename*

Specifies the path and filename for the event identifier message file.

CategoryMessageFile   REG_EXPAND_SZ   *Filename*

Specifies the path and filename for the category message file. The category and event identifier message strings may be in the same file.

CategoryCount   REG_DWORD   *Number*

Specifies the number of categories supported.

TypesSupported   REG_DWORD   *Number*

Specifies a bitmask of supported types.

NBF (NetBEUI) Transport Entries

The startup parameters for the NetBEUI (NBF) transport are found under the following subkey:

```
HKEY_LOCAL_MACHINE\SYSTEM\Services\NBF\Parameters
```

Note The parameters that control network bindings for this service are described in "NetRules Subkey Entries," earlier in this chapter. You should set the Export and Bind parameters by using the Network application in Control Panel.

The **Init***xx* entries for NBF define the initial allocation and the size of free memory for items. The **Max***xxx* entries define the upper limits. Within these ranges, the system autotunes performance. By default, the NBF service uses all the resources necessary to handle client requests, and when it is not actively working, it doesn't use many resources. Set **Init***xx* values to control initial allocation, which can make the system a little faster when you know a server will be busy. Set the **Max***xxx* values to control limits when you don't want the server to be too busy or to use too much memory for networking.

With Registry Editor, you can modify the following startup parameters for the NBF transport:

AddNameQueryRetries   REG_DWORD   *Number*

Specifies the number of times that NBF will retry sending ADD_NAME_QUERY and ADD_GROUP_NAME_QUERY frames. Adjust this parameter only if NBF is registering addresses on a network that drops many packets.

Default: 3

AddNameQueryTimeout   REG_DWORD   *100-nanosecond units*

Specifies the time-out between NBF sending successive ADD_NAME_QUERY and ADD_GROUP_NAME_QUERY frames. Adjust this parameter only if NBF is registering addresses on a network with slow computers or over a slow network.

Default: 5000000

GeneralRetries   REG_DWORD   *Number*

Specifies the number of times that NBF will retry sending STATUS_QUERY and FIND_NAME frames. Adjust this parameter only if NBF is operating on a network that drops many packets.

Default: 3

DefaultT1Timeout   REG_DWORD   *100-nanosecond units*

Specifies the initial value for the T1 timeout. T1 controls the time that NBF waits for a response after sending a logical link control (LLC) poll packet before resending it. Adjust this parameter only if NBF will be connecting over slow networks or to slow remote computers (although NBF does adapt).

Default: 6000000 (600 milliseconds)

DefaultT2Timeout   REG_DWORD   *100-nanosecond units*

Specifies the initial value for the T2 timeout. T2 controls the time that NBF can wait after receiving an LLC poll packet before responding. It must be much less than T1; one-half or less is a good general rule. Adjust this parameter only if NBF will be connecting over slow networks or to slow remote computers.

Default: 1500000 (150 milliseconds)

DefaultTiTimeout   REG_DWORD   *100-nanosecond units*

Specifies the initial value for the Ti timeout. Ti is the inactivity timer. When it expires, NBF sends an LLC poll packet to ensure that the link is still active. Adjust this parameter only if NBF is connecting over networks with unusual reliability characteristics, or over slow networks or to slow computers.

Default: 300000000 (30 seconds)

GeneralTimeout   REG_DWORD   *100-nanosecond units*

Specifies the time-out between NBF sending successive STATUS_QUERY and FIND_NAME requests. Adjust this parameter only if NBF is operating on a network with slow computers or over a slow network.

Default: 5000000

InitAddresses   REG_DWORD   *1 or higher; 0 = no limit*

Specifies the number of initial addresses to allocate within any memory limits that might imposed on NBF. Addresses correspond to NetBIOS names. An address is for the actual name, and an address file is for a TDI (Transport Driver Interface) client using that name; so usually you have the same number, but if two users open the same address, that is two address files but only one address.

Set this parameter if you know that a large number of addresses are needed. Otherwise, the system automatically allocates space for addresses as needed.

Default: 0 (no limit)

InitAddressFiles   REG_DWORD   *1 or higher; 0 = no limit*

Specifies the number of initial address files to allocate within any memory limits that might imposed on NBF. Set this parameter if you know that a large number of address files are needed. Otherwise, the system automatically allocates space for address files as needed.

Default: 0 (no limit)

InitConnections   **REG_DWORD**   *1 or higher; 0 = no limit*

Specifies the number of initial connections (NetBIOS sessions) to allocate within any memory limits that might imposed on NBF. Set this parameter if you know that a large number of connections are needed. Otherwise, the system automatically allocates space for connections as needed.

Default: 1

InitLinks   **REG_DWORD**   *1 or higher; 0 = no limit*

Specifies the number of initial LLC links to allocate within any memory limits that might imposed on NBF. Typically, you have one connection per LLC link to another network adapter card, because the redirector puts all links to a computer into one connection. However, you may have more if two computers are communicating with each other or if a NetBIOS application is running. Set this parameter if you know that a large number of links are needed. Otherwise, the system automatically allocates space for links as needed.

Default: 2

InitReceiveBuffers   **REG_DWORD**   *1 or higher; 0 = no limit*

Specifies the number of initial receive buffers to allocate. Receive buffers are used by NBF when it calls NDIS TransferData for received datagrams. Usually, this value is allocated as needed, but you can use this parameter to preallocate memory if you know a large number of datagram frames will be received.

Default: 5

InitReceivePackets   **REG_DWORD**   *1 or higher; 0 = no limit*

Specifies the number of initial receive packets to allocate. Receive packets are used by NBF when it calls NDIS TransferData for received data. Usually, this value is allocated as needed, but you can use this parameter to preallocate memory if you know a large number of UI frames will be received.

Default: 10

InitRequests   **REG_DWORD**   *1 or higher; 0 = no limit*

Specifies the number of initial requests to allocate within any memory limits that might imposed on NBF. Requests are used for in-progress connect requests, remote adapter status requests, find name requests, and so on. Set this parameter if you know that a large number of requests are needed. Otherwise, the system automatically allocates space for requests as needed.

Default: 5

InitSendPackets   REG_DWORD   *1 or higher; 0 = no limit*

Specifies the number of initial send packets to allocate. Send packets are used by NBF whenever it sends connection-oriented data on behalf of a client. Usually, this value is allocated as needed, but you can use this parameter to preallocate memory if you know a large number of data frames are needed or if you see a lot of "send packets exhausted" messages when using Performance Monitor.

Default: 30

InitUIFrames   REG_DWORD   *1 or higher; 0 = no limit*

Specifies the number of initial UI frames to allocate. UI frames are used by NBF to establish connections and for connectionless services such as datagrams. Usually, this value is allocated as needed, but you can use this parameter to preallocate memory if you know a large number of UI frames are needed.

Default: 5

LLCMaxWindowSize   REG_DWORD   *Number of frames*

Specifies the number of LLC I-frames that NBF can send before polling and waiting for a response from the remote. Adjust this parameter only if NBF is communicating over a network whose reliability often changes suddenly.

Default: 10

LLCRetries   REG_DWORD   *1 or higher; 0 = no limit*

Specifies the number of times that NBF will retry polling a remote workstation after receiving a T1 timeout. After this many retries, NBF closes the link. Adjust this parameter only if NBF is connecting over networks with unusual reliability characteristics.

Default: 8

MaxAddresses   REG_DWORD   *1 or higher; 0 = no limit*

Specifies the maximum number of addresses that NBF allocates within any memory limits that might imposed on NBF. Addresses are NetBIOS names that are registered on the network by NBF. An address is for the actual name, and an address file is for a TDI client using that name.

Use this optional parameter to fine-tune use of NBF memory. Typically this parameter is used to control address resources with an unlimited NBF.

Default: 0 (no limit)

NBF (NetBEUI) Transport Entries

MaxAddressFiles   REG_DWORD   *1 or higher; 0 = no limit*

Specifies maximum number of address files that NBF allocates within any memory limits that might imposed on NBF. Each address file corresponds to a client opening an address.

Use this optional parameter to fine-tune use of NBF memory. Typically this parameter is used to control address files with an unlimited NBF.

Default: 0 (no limit)

MaxConnections   REG_DWORD   *1 or higher; 0 = no limit*

Specifies the maximum number of connections that NBF allocates within any memory limits that might imposed on NBF. Connections are established between NBF clients and similar entities on remote computers.

Use this optional parameter to fine-tune use of NBF memory. Typically this parameter is used to control connection resources with an unlimited NBF.

Default: 0 (no limit)

MaximumIncomingFrames   REG_DWORD   *1 or higher; 0 = off*

Used in some cases to control how many incoming frames NBF will receive before it sends an acknowledgment to a remote machine. In general, NBF automatically senses when to sends acknowledgments, however when communicating with some Microsoft LAN Manager or LAN Server remote computers configured with a very low value for **maxout**, this parameter can be set to an equal or lower value to improve network performance. (This parameter corresponds roughly to the Microsoft LAN Manager **maxin** parameter.) A value of 0 turns off this hint, causing NBF to revert to usual behavior. For communication with most all remotes, this parameter isn't used.

Default: 2

MaxLinks   REG_DWORD   *1 or higher; 0 = no limit*

Specifies the maximum number of links that NBF allocates within any memory limits that might imposed on NBF. Links are established for every remote adapter to which NBF communicates.

Use this optional parameter to fine-tune use of NBF memory. Typically this parameter is used to control link resources with an unlimited NBF.

Default: 0 (no limit)

MaxRequests   REG_DWORD   *1 or higher; 0 = no limit*

Specifies the maximum number of requests that NBF allocates within any memory limits that might imposed on NBF. Requests are used by NBF to control send, receive, connect, and listen operations.

Use this optional parameter to fine-tune use of NBF memory. Typically this parameter is used to control request resources with an unlimited NBF.

Default: 0 (no limit)

NameQueryRetries   REG_DWORD   *Number*

Specifies the number of times that NBF will retry sending NAME_QUERY frames. Adjust this parameter only if NBF is connecting to computers over a network that drops many packets.

Default: 3

NameQueryTimeout   REG_DWORD   *100-nanosecond units*

Specifies the time-out between NBF sending successive NAME_QUERY frames. Adjust this parameter only if NBF is connecting to slow computers or over a slow network.

Default: 5000000

QueryWithoutSourceRouting   REG_DWORD   *0 or 1*

When you are using NBF over a Token Ring driver, this parameter instructs NBF to send half the queries without including source routing information when connecting to a remote computer. This supports bridging hardware that cannot forward frames that contain source routing information.

Default: 0 (false)

UseDixOverEthernet   REG_DWORD   *0 or 1*

Specifies whether NBF should use DIX encoding when bound to an Ethernet MAC. When using DIX encoding is enabled, NBF cannot talk to computers that use the standard IEEE 802.3 encoding.

Default: 0 (false)

WanNameQueryRetries   REG_DWORD   *Number*

Specifies the number of times that NBF will retry sending NAME_QUERY frames when connecting with RAS. Adjust this parameter only if NBF is connecting to computers over a network that drops many packets.

Default: 5

NetLogon Service Entries

The Registry path for the parameters for the NetLogon service is the following:

`HKEY_LOCAL_MACHINE\SYSTEM\CurrentControlSet\Services\Netlogon\Parameters`

Note The NetLogon share name should also be in the path for logon scripts.

PulseInterval   REG_DWORD   *60 to 3600 seconds*

Specifies how long a domain controller waits before sending each update notice to Windows NT Advanced Servers.

When this value is not specified in the Registry, NetLogon determines optimal values depending on the domain controller's load.

Default: 300

Randomize   REG_DWORD   *15 to 120 seconds*

Specifies the amount of time a Windows NT Advanced Server domain controller uses to stagger requests sent to the domain controller. This value is used by every server in the domain. When the domain controller sends update message to the servers, it includes the **Randomize** value in the message. The servers receiving that message will wait a maximum of that many seconds before responding to that message.

When this value is not specified in the Registry, NetLogon determines optimal values depending on the domain controller's load.

Default: 30

Scripts   REG_SZ   *Pathname*

Specifies the fully qualified path name to where logon scripts reside. This value can be set using the Services icon in Control Panel or the Server Manager.

Default: NULL

Update   REG_SZ   *Yes or No*

When this value is set to Yes, NetLogon fully synchronizes the database each time it starts.

Default: No

NetworkProvider Service Entries

If more than one network is present under Windows NT, each network has a Services subkey that include a value for **Group** of NetworkProvider plus its own subkey named NetworkProvider, under the following Registry path:

```
HKEY_LOCAL_MACHINE\SYSTEM\CurrentControlSet
    \Services\Service or Driver Key Name\NetworkProvider
```

The following entry values should appear under the NetworkProvider subkey for each network the computer can use:

ProviderName   **REG_SZ**   *Name*

Specifies the name of the Provider, which is displayed as the network name in Browse dialog boxes. This name is defined by the network vendor, and is usually some variation of the product name.

Default: Defined by network vendor

ProviderPath   **REG_SZ**   *DLL pathname*

Specifies the full path of the DLL that implements the network provider.

Default: Defined by network vendor

The NetworkProvider subkey under CurrentControlSet\Control provides a list of the available network providers.

NWLink Transport Entries (IPX/SPX)

NWLink is an implementation of the IPX/SPX protocols popular in NetWare networks. In addition, the module NWNBLink provides support for the Novell implementation of the NetBIOS protocol. With the Registry Editor, you can modify the following:

- The NetBIOS component of NWNBLink, including modification of parameters supporting the Microsoft extensions to Novell NetBIOS
- The IPX/SPX component of NWLink
- Parameters that affect the use of NWLink in a Token Ring network

Caution All entries have reasonable defaults that usually should not need to be modified. Be careful when modifying an entry, because any change can easily affect the performance of a conversation between the sender and receiver.

The NWLink keys do not appear in the Registry unless this service is installed using the Network icon in Control Panel. After the service is installed, not all entries appear by default in the Registry. If the entry is not there, the default value for that entry is used.

NWNBLink Entries for Microsoft Extensions to Novell NetBIOS

The Microsoft Extensions to Novell NetBIOS are included to enhance the performance of the traditional Novell NetBIOS protocol. NWNBLink can detect automatically whether it is talking to a Novell NetBIOS implementation that does not understand these extensions; in such a case, NWNBLink will fall back to the standard Novell NetBIOS protocol currently used in NetWare networks. However, significant performance gains can be realized if the extensions are used (for example, if the NetBIOS conversation occurs between two Windows NT computers).

The Registry path for these value entries is the following:

```
HKEY_LOCAL_MACHINE\SYSTEM\CurrentControlSet
   \Services\NWNBLink\Parameters
```

AckDelayTime   REG_DWORD   *50 to 65535 milliseconds*
Determines the value of the delayed acknowledgment timer.

Default: 250 (no entry = default)

AckWindow   REG_DWORD   *0 to 65535 frames*
Specifies the number of frames to receive before sending an acknowledgment. The **AckWindow** entry is used as a clocking mechanism on networks in which the sender is networked on a fast LAN, but the receiver is networked on the other side utilizing a slower link. By automatically forcing acknowledgments, the sender can keep sending frames continually. If both the sender and receiver are located on a fast link, you can set **AckWindow** to 0 to turn off sending an acknowledgment to the sender. Alternatively, NWNBLink can be set to dynamically determine whether to use the **AckWindow** parameter based on the setting of **AckWindowThreshold**. Related parameter: **AckWindowThreshold.**

Default: 2 (no entry = default)

AckWindowThreshold   REG_DWORD *0 to 65535 milliseconds*

Specifies the threshold value for the round-trip time that defines when **AckWindow** will be ignored. The round trip time is an estimate of how long it takes for a frame to be sent and received from a workstation. NWNBLink determines this estimate and uses it as a basis for determining whether it is necessary to send automatic acknowledgments. If **AckWindowThreshold** is set to 0, NWNBLink relies on the **AckWindow** entry. Related parameters: **AckWindow.**

Default: 500 (no entry = default)

EnablePiggyBackAck   REG_DWORD *0 or 1*

Allows the receiver to piggyback acknowledgments. Piggybacking acknowledgments can occur when the receiver has detected the end of a NetBIOS message. When the sender and receiver are not participating in two-way NetBIOS traffic, you should set **EnablePiggyBackAck** to 0. An example of one-way traffic is a stock update application, where a server constantly sends NetBIOS messages to clients but the client does not need to respond.

If **EnablePiggyBackAck** is set to 1 but there is no back traffic, NWNBLink waits the number of milliseconds determined by **AckDelayTime** before sending the acknowledgment, and then it turns off support for piggybacking acknowledgments. If the workstation at some point starts sending as well as receiving data, NWNBLink turns support back on for piggybacking acknowledgments. Related parameter: **AckDelayTime.**

Default: 1 (true—enable piggybacking acknowledgments; no entry = default)

Extensions   REG_DWORD *0 or 1*

Specifies whether to use NWNBLink extensions discussed in this section.

Default: 1 (true; no entry = default)

RcvWindowMax   REG_DWORD *1 to 49152 frames*

Specifies the maximum number of frames the receiver can receive at one time. The value specified by **RcvWindowMax** is sent to the sender during session initialization to give the sender an upper bound on the number of frames that can be sent at one time. Related parameters: **AckDelayTime, AckWindow, AckWindowThreshold, EnablePiggyBackAck,** and **RcvWindowMax.**

Default: 4 (no entry = default)

NWNBLink Entries for Novell NetBIOS or Microsoft Extensions

The Registry path for these value entries is the following:

```
HKEY_LOCAL_MACHINE\SYSTEM\CurrentControlSet
    \Services\NWNBLink\Parameters
```

BroadcastCount   **REG_DWORD**   *1 to 65535*

Specifies the number of times to send a broadcast. If **Internet** is set to 1, the **BroadcastCount** is doubled. Related parameter: **BroadcastTimeout.**

Default: 3 (no entry = default)

BroadcastTimeout   **REG_DWORD**   *1 to 65535 half-seconds*

Specifies the time between sending find-name requests. This value is not affected if **Internet** is set to 1. Related parameter: **BroadcastCount.**

Default: 1 (no entry = default)

ConnectionCount   **REG_DWORD**   *1 to 65535*

Specifies the number of times to send a connection probe. A connection probe is sent by the initiator of a session if a connection could not be made to the remote computer. If **Internet** is set to 1, the **ConnectionCount** is doubled. Related parameter: **ConnectionTimeout.**

Default: 5 (no entry = default)

ConnectionTimeout   **REG_DWORD**   *1 to 65535 half-seconds*

Specifies the time between sending connection probes when initiating a session.

Default: 2 (no entry = default)

InitialRetransmissionTime   **REG_DWORD**   *1 to 65535 milliseconds*

Specifies the initial value for the retransmission time. Related parameter: **RetransmitMax.**

Default: 500 (no entry = default)

Internet   **REG_DWORD**   *0 or 1*

Specifies whether to change the packet type from 0x04 to 0x14 (Novell WAN broadcast).

Default: 1 (true; no entry = default)

NWLink Transport Entries (IPX/SPX)

KeepAliveCount   REG_DWORD   *1 to 65535*

Specifies the number of times to send a session-alive frame before timing out if there is no response. Related parameter: **KeepAliveTimeout.**

Default: 8 (no entry = default)

KeepAliveTimeout   REG_DWORD   *1 to 65535 half-seconds*

Specifies the time between sending session-alive frames. Related parameter: **KeepAliveCount.**

Default: 60 (no entry = default)

RetransmitMax   REG_DWORD   *1 to 65535*

Specifies the maximum number of times the sender should retransmit before assuming that something is wrong with the link. Related parameter: **InitialRetransmissionTime.**

Default: 8 (no entry = default)

NWLink Entries for IPX/SPX:
NWLink Parameters for the Network Adapter Card

These parameters are specific for each binding of NWLink to a network adapter card. The Registry path for these value entries is the following:

```
HKEY_LOCAL_MACHINE\SYSTEM\CurrentControlSet\Services
    \NWLinkIPX\NetConfig\Driver01
```

AdapterName   REG_DWORD   *Name*

Specifies the name of the adapter that NWLink will use. This parameter is set when you choose a network adapter card to bind NWLink using the Network icon in Control Panel. In this release, only one card is supported.

BindSap   REG_DWORD   *Type field*

Specifies the Ethertype if the frame format is Ethernet II. The Ethertype field is only relevant if Ethernet II frames are to be sent or received. You can choose the frame type using the Network icon in Control Panel. For more information, see the explanation for the **PktType** entry. Related parameter: **PktType.**

Default: 8137 (in hex)

NWLink Transport Entries (IPX/SPX)

EnableFuncaddr   REG_DWORD   *Boolean*

When set to 1, this parameter specifies that the IPX functional address will be enabled if this card is a Token Ring card. If this value is 0, the IPX functional address will not be added. The IPX functional address is C00000800000 (hex). Novell has been phasing out use of this, but it is still in use in some places. It is up to the application to take advantage of the IPX functional address. In most instances, the broadcast address (FFFFFFFFFFFF hex) is used instead.

Default: 1 (true)

MaxPktSize   REG_DWORD   *0 to 65535*

Specifies the maximum frame size the network adapter card should be allowed to transmit. If this number is 0, NWLink will get this information from the card driver. This parameter allows the administrator to make the maximum transmit size for a card smaller than the card driver allows. A scenario in which you might want to change this entry is in an environment in which the network adapter card on one side of a conversation is on a link that has a larger frame size than the link on the other side of a conversation—for example, if the sending station is linked to a 16 Mbps Token Ring and the receiving station is linked to an Ethernet network.

Default: 0

NetworkNumber   REG_DWORD   *Number*

Specifies the network number (in hex) to be used for this adapter. If this number is 0, the NWLink will get the network number from the network as it is running. This parameter is set using the Network icon in Control Panel. IPX network numbers are 4 bytes (8 hex characters) long. An example of an IPX network number is AABBDDFF. You should not have to enter a specific value because NWLink will determine it for you. Make sure to get the network number for your IPX subnet from the network administrator if you want to enter a specific number.

Default: 0

PktType   REG_DWORD   *0, 1, 2, 3, or 4*

NWLink supports Ethernet, Token Ring, FDDI, and ARCnet topologies. The **PktType** parameter specifies the packet form to use. The valid values are the following:

Value	Packet form
0	Ethernet_II
1	Ethernet_802.3
2	802.2
3	SNAP
4	ARCnet

NWLink Transport Entries (IPX/SPX)

If the adapter is an Ethernet adapter, choose between values 0 through 3. If the adapter is either a Token Ring or FDDI adapter, choose between s 2 and 3. If you are using an ARCnet adapter, choose value 4. If the adapter is a Token Ring or FDDI adapter, values 0 and 1 will work the same as value 2. Related parameter: **BindSap.**

Default: 1 (802.3)

SourceRouteBcast   REG_DWORD   *0 or 1*

Specifies the source route to be used when transmitting a packet to the broadcast MAC (Media Access Control) address (FFFFFFFFFFFF hex). If this value is 0, the packet will be transmitted to the single-route broadcast (0xC2, 0x70). If the value is 1, the packet will be transmitted to the all-routes broadcast (0x82, 0x70). Related parameters: **SourceRouteDef, SourceRouting,** and **SourceRouteMCast**.

Default: 0

SourceRouteDef   REG_DWORD   *0 or 1*

Specifies the source route to be used when transmitting a package to a unique MAC address that is not in the source routing table. If the MAC address is in the source routing table, the route in the table will be used. If this value is 0, the packet will be transmitted to the single-route broadcast (0xC2, 0x70). If the value is not 0, the packet will be transmitted to the all-routes broadcast (0x82, 0x70). Related parameters: **SourceRouteBcast, SourceRouting,** and **SourceRouteMCast**.

Default: 0

SourceRouteMcast   REG_DWORD   *Boolean*

Specifies the source route to be used when transmitting a packet to a multicast MAC address (C000xxxxxxxx). If this value is 0, the packet will be transmitted to the single-route broadcast (0xC2, 0x70). If the value is not 0, the packet will be transmitted to the all-routes broadcast (0x82, 0x70). Related parameters: **SourceRouteBcast, SourceRouteDef,** and **SourceRouting**.

Default: 0

SourceRouting   REG_DWORD   *Boolean*

Specifies whether to use source routing. This parameter is only used if the adapter is a Token Ring adapter. If there are no source routing bridges on the Token Ring, disable this entry to disable all of the source routing logic. Related parameters: **SourceRouteBcast, SourceRouteDef,** and **SourceRouteMCast**.

Default: 0 (false—do not use source routing)

NWLink Entries for IPX/SPX: Global IPX Parameters

The following parameters are global for the entire transport. The Registry path for these value entries is the following:

```
HKEY_LOCAL_MACHINE\SYSTEM\CurrentControlSet
    \Services\NWLinkIPX\Parameters
```

ConnectionCount   REG_DWORD   *1 to 65535*

Specifies the number of times the probe will be sent when SPX is trying to connect to a remote node. If no response is received after the probes are sent, an error will occur. Related parameter: **ConnectionTimeout**.

Default: 10

ConnectionTimeout   REG_DWORD   *1 to 65535 half-seconds*

Specifies the time between connection probes when SPX is trying to connect to a remote node. Related parameter: **ConnectionCount**.

Default: 2 (1 second)

KeepAliveCount   REG_DWORD   *1 to 65535*

Specifies how many times to send a keep-alive probe before timing out if there is no response. Related parameter: **KeepAliveTimeout**.

Default: 8

KeepAliveTimeout   REG_DWORD   *1 to 65535 half-seconds*

Specifies the time that the local side should wait before sending a probe to the remote to verify that the SPX connection is still alive. Related parameter: **KeepAliveCount**.

Default: 12 (6 seconds)

RipAgeTime   REG_DWORD   *1 to 65535 minutes*

IPX maintains an RIP cache in order to locate computers on a remote network. The **RipAgeTime** entry informs IPX how long to wait before requesting an RIP update for an entry. This timer is reset when an RIP announcement is received for an entry in the RIP cache.

Default: 5 minutes

RipCount   REG_DWORD   *1 to 65535*

When the RIP protocol layer is trying to find a route on the network, this parameter specifies how many times to send a request before giving up. Related parameter: **RipTimeout**

Default: 5

RipTimeout   REG_DWORD   *1 to 65535 half-seconds*

Specifies the timeout between RIP request packets being sent out when the RIP protocol layer is trying to find a route on the network. Related parameter: **RipCount**.

Default: 1 (1 half-second)

RipUsageTime   REG_DWORD   *1 to 65535 minutes*

IPX maintains a RIP cache in order to locate computers on a remote network. The **RipUsageTime** entry informs IPX how many minutes to wait before an entry in the RIP cache will be deleted from the cache. This timer is reset when a packet is sent to the remote computer.

Default: 15 minutes

SourceRouteUsageTime   REG_DWORD   *1 to 65535 minutes*

Range: Specifies the number of minutes an unused entry can remain in the Token Ring source routing cache before it is flushed.

Default: 10

WindowSize   REG_DWORD   *1 to 10 SPX packets*

Specifies the window to use in the SPX packets. SPX uses the Allocation field of the SPX packet to tell the remote how many receives are available for receiving data. The **WindowSize** entry specifies what value to put in the SPX Allocation field.

Default: 4

Redirector (Rdr) Service Entries

The subkey for the Rdr (redirector) service has the following Registry path:

```
HKEY_LOCAL_MACHINE\SYSTEM\CurrentControlSet\Services\Rdr\Parameters
```

For the search buffer sizes defined in the following entries: if the buffer passed for the search is less than the **LowerSearchThreshold** value, the system requests **LowerSearchThreshold** bytes of data from the server. If the buffer size is between the value of **LowerSearchThreshold** and **UpperSearchBufferSize,** the system uses the buffer size. On a slow link (such as a RAS link), if it will take more than five seconds to retrieve data, the Redirector service uses the user's requested buffer size.

ConnectTimeout   REG_DWORD   *Number of seconds*

Specifies the maximum amount of time the redirector will wait for a connect or disconnect to complete.

Default: 300 (5 minutes)

LowerSearchBufferSize   REG_DWORD   *Number of kilobytes*

Specifies the number of bytes the redirector will use for small searches.

Default: 16K

LowerSearchThreshold   REG_DWORD   *Number of kilobytes*

Specifies the number of bytes below which the redirector will request a search of **LowerSearchBufferSize.** If the search size is larger than this (but below the **UpperSearchBufferSize**), the redirector will use the **UpperSearchBufferSize.**

Default: 16K

StackSize   REG_DWORD   *Number of kilobytes*

Sets the default IRP stack size for the redirector.

Default: 4

UpperSearchBufferSize   REG_DWORD   *Number of kilobytes*

Specifies the number of bytes the redirector will use for large searches.

Default: 32K

UseAsyncWriteBehind   REG_DWORD   *0 or 1*

Enables the asynchronous-write-behind variation of the write-behind optimization.

Default: 1 (true)

UseWriteBehind   REG_DWORD   *0 or 1*

Enables the write-behind optimization.

Default: 1 (true)

Remote Access Service (RAS) Entries

The RemoteAccess subkey is created in the Registry when you install RAS on a server, using the Network icon in Control Panel. The default values in RemoteAccess and its subkeys work well for all Windows NT operations such as copying files, using network resources, and sending and receiving electronic mail. However, for some systems, you may want to adjust individual parameters to suit your particular performance and security needs.

Initially, there are no value entries in the Registry for the Remote Access key or its subkeys until you add them with new settings. (The only exception is **EnableNetbiosGateway,** the NetBIOS parameter.) Unlisted value entries are set to their default values, as described in this section.

For information on Remote Access configuration files and other parameters, see Appendix B, "Configuration Files," in the *Windows NT Remote Access Service Administrator's Guide.*

The subkeys under the Remote Access key in HKEY_LOCAL_MACHINE \SYSTEM\CurrentControlSet\Services\ include the following:

- RemoteAccess\Parameters
- RemoteAccess\Parameters\NetbiosGateway
- AsyncMac*n*\Parameters
- RasHub\Parameters
- RasMan\Parameters

See also **WanNameQueryRetries** in "NBF (NetBEUI) Transport Entries," earlier in this chapter.

Remote Access Parameters Subkey Entries

The Parameters subkey for Remote Access has the following Registry path:

```
HKEY_LOCAL_MACHINE\SYSTEM\CurrentControlSet\Services
    \RemoteAccess\Parameters
```

For changes to take effect, you must stop and restart the Remote Access service. The functions and settings of these value entries are as follows:

AuthenticateRetries   REG_DWORD   *0 to 10*

Sets the maximum number of unsuccessful retries allowed if the initial attempt at authentication fails.

Default: 2

AuthenticateTime   REG_DWORD   *20 to 600 seconds*

Sets the maximum time limit within which a user must be successfully authenticated. If the client does not initiate the authentication process within this time, the user is disconnected.

Default: 120 seconds

CallbackTime   REG_DWORD   *2 to 12 seconds*

Sets the time interval that the server waits before calling the client back when the Callback feature has been set. Each client communicates the value of its own callback time when connecting to a Remote Access server. If this value is not communicated (that is, if the client does not communicate a value for the callback time, as with Remote Access 1.0 and 1.1 clients), the value of the **CallbackTime** parameter becomes the default.

Default: 2 seconds

EnableAudit   REG_DWORD   *0 or 1*

Determines whether Remote Access auditing is turned on or off. If this feature is enabled, all audits are recorded in the Security event log, which you can view using Event Viewer.

Default: 1 (enabled)

NetbiosGatewayEnabled   REG_DWORD   *0 or 1*

Caution Do not change this value in Registry Editor, because various network bindings must also be changed. This parameter should only be changed by using the RAS Setup program.

Makes the server function like a NetBIOS gateway, allowing clients to access the LAN. If disabled, remote clients can access only the resources on the Remote Access server in a point-to-point connection; dial-in users cannot see the network or access network resources.

Default: 1 (enabled)

RAS NetBIOSGateway Subkey Entries

The Registry path for these entries is the following:

```
HKEY_LOCAL_MACHINE\SYSTEM\CurrentControlSet\Services
    \RemoteAccess\Parameters\NetbiosGateway
```

AutoDisconnect   REG_DWORD   *0 to 60000 seconds (1000 minutes)*

Sets the time interval after which inactive connections are terminated. Inactivity is measured by lack of NetBIOS session data transfer, such as copying files, accessing network resources, and sending and receiving electronic mail. You may want to set this value to 0 seconds if clients are running NetBIOS datagram applications. Setting this value to 0 turns off **AutoDisconnect**.

Default: 1200 seconds (20 minutes)

DisableMcastFwdWhenSessionTraffic   REG_DWORD   *0 or 1*

Allows NetBIOS session traffic (for example, Windows NT applications) to have priority over multicast datagrams (such as server messages). In other words, multicast datagrams are transferred only when there is no session traffic. Unless you're using an application that depends on multicast datagrams, leave this parameter enabled.

Default: 1 (enabled)

EnableBroadcast   REG_DWORD   *0 or 1*

Determines whether broadcast datagrams are forwarded to remote workstations. Broadcast datagrams are not often useful and take up too much bandwidth on a slow link. Unless you're using an application that relies on broadcast datagrams, leave this parameter disabled.

Default: 0 (disabled)

EnableNetbiosSessionsAuditing   REG_DWORD   *0 or 1*

Enable this parameter to record in the event log the establishment of NetBIOS sessions between the remote clients and the LAN servers. Enable this parameter to track the NetBIOS resources accessed on the LAN.

Default: 0 (disabled)

MaxBcastDgBuffered   REG_DWORD   *16 to 255*

Sets the number of broadcast datagrams that the gateway buffers for a client. If you're using an application that communicates extensively through multicast or broadcast datagrams, increase this parameter so that the Remote Access server can deliver all datagrams reliably.

Default: 32

MaxDgBufferedPerGroupName   REG_DWORD   *1 to 255*

Sets the number of datagrams that can be buffered per group name. Increasing this value buffers more datagrams per group name but also takes up more virtual memory.

Default: 10

MaxDynMem   REG_DWORD   *131072 to 4294967295*

Sets the amount of virtual memory used to buffer NetBIOS session data for each remote client.

Because the Remote Access server is a gateway between the slow line and the LAN, data is stored (buffered) in its memory when coming from the fast line (LAN) before it is forwarded to the slow line (asynchronous line).

The Remote Access server minimizes the usage of the system's physical memory by locking only a minimal set of pages (about 64K per client) and making use of virtual memory (up to **MaxDynMem**) to buffer the rest of the data. So, as long as there is enough space on the hard disk to expand PAGEFILE.SYS, you can increase this value if needed.

If you have an application with a LAN (fast) sender and an asynchronous (slow) receiver, and if the sender is sending more data at a time than the Remote Access server can buffer in **MaxDynMem**, the Remote Access server tries to apply a form of NetBIOS level flow control by not submitting NCB.RECEIVE on the session until it has enough buffer space to get incoming data. For this reason, if you have such an application, you should increase your NetBIOS SEND/RECEIVE time-outs so that the fast sender can keep pace with the slow receiver.

Default: 655350

MaxNames   REG_DWORD   *1 to 255*

Sets the number of unique NetBIOS names each client can have, with a limit of 255 names for all clients together.

Remote clients running Windows NT and Windows for Workgroups may need as many as seven or eight names each. To accommodate these workstations, set the **MaxNames** value to 8 and reduce the number of ports on the Remote Access server. If you have Windows NT or Windows for Workgroups clients dialing in to servers running Remote Access version 1.1 or earlier, set this parameter to 8 or greater.

Default: 255

MaxSessions   REG_DWORD   *1 to 255*

Sets the maximum number of simultaneous NetBIOS sessions each client can have, with a limit of 255 sessions for all clients together. If you have multiple clients connecting simultaneously with each running 4 or 5 sessions, decrease the value of this parameter so that the total number of sessions does not exceed 255.

Default: 255

MultiCastForwardRate   REG_DWORD   *−1 (disabled); 0 to 32,676 seconds*

Governs the multicasting of group name datagrams to all remote workstations. This parameter filters datagrams sent on group names by forwarding them at a specified time interval.

The value −1 disables forwarding. The value 0 guarantees delivery of group name datagrams. The value *n* forwards datagrams every *n* seconds, when $1 \leq n \leq 32,676$.

If the **EnableBroadcast** parameter is set to 0, broadcasts are not forwarded even if the **MultiCastForwardRate** parameter is set to a positive number (in this case, only multicast datagrams are forwarded). The line becomes overloaded. If **MultiCastForwardRate** is set to −1, broadcasts are still not forwarded even if **EnableBroadcast** is set to 1. See also **EnableBroadcast**.

To save bandwidth for session traffic, filter the datagrams. However, if you have an application based on multicast datagrams, set this parameter to 0. This value guarantees delivery of all datagrams sent on group names from the LAN to the remote client.

Default: 5

NumRecvQueryIndications   REG_DWORD   *1 to 32*

Allows a Remote Access client to initiate multiple network connections simultaneously. If a remote client is running a NetBIOS application that does multiple NCB.CALL commands simultaneously, increase this parameter to improve performance.

Default: 3

RcvDgSubmittedPerGroupName   REG_DWORD   *1 to 32*

Determines the number of NetBIOS commands of the type Receive Datagram that can be submitted simultaneously per group name on the LAN stack. Keep this setting as small as possible to minimize the amount of memory consumed by system resources. Each datagram command received locks about 1.5K of physical memory in the system.

Default: 3

RemoteListen   REG_DWORD   *0 to 2*

Sets the remote NCB_LISTEN capability.

Value	Meaning
0	Disables a client's ability to post NCB_LISTEN for any NetBIOS name. Because every remote listen posted consumes one session, setting this parameter to 0 saves sessions.
1	Messages. Allows clients to post NCB_LISTEN on Windows NT Advanced Server message aliases only. If a remote client is running the Messenger service, it can then receive messages from LAN users, printers, and the like.
2	All. Enables NCB_LISTEN for all remote client NetBIOS names, allowing clients to run NetBIOS server applications. This setting allows all clients to function as NetBIOS servers on the network.

It is best to leave the **RemoteListen** parameter set to the default, 1 (messages). Allowing NCB_LISTEN capability on remote clients can significantly drain system resources and therefore is not recommended.

If the **RemoteListen** parameter is set to 2, Remote Access posts an NCB_LISTEN on all NetBIOS names of Remote Access clients. Because the average Windows NT Advanced Server workstation has about seven or eight NetBIOS names assigned to it, the total number of NetBIOS names for which an NCB_LISTEN would be posted is 7 or 8 * 64 (the maximum number of clients per Remote Access server), which exceeds the 255 maximum.

Default: 1 (messages)

SizWorkBufs   REG_DWORD   *1024 to 65536*

Sets the size of work buffers. The default setting is optimized for the server message block (SMB) protocol, the protocol between the workstation and the server running on the Windows NT Advanced Server system.

Default: 4500

RAS AsyncMAC Subkey Entries

The Registry path for these entries is the following:

```
HKEY_LOCAL_MACHINE\SYSTEM\CurrentControlSet\Services
    \AsyncMacn\Parameters
```

For changes to take effect, you must restart the computer.

MaxFrameSize   REG_DWORD   *576 to 1514*

Determines the maximum frame size. Use smaller frames for noisy links. A lower setting sends less data per frame, slowing performance. Do not change this parameter for previous versions of the Remote Access service. The value is negotiated between the server and Windows NT clients.

Default: 1514

RAS RasHub Subkey Entries

The Registry path for the RasHub subkey is the following:

```
HKEY_LOCAL_MACHINE\SYSTEM\CurrentControlSet\Services\RasHub\Parameters
```

For changes to take effect, you must restart the computer.

The subkeys RasHub01 and RasHub02 show, for example, that this installation of Remote Access is configured for two COM ports. In configuring ports, you can determine whether clients have access to the Remote Access server only (point-to-point connection) or to the network.

NetworkAddress   **REG_SZ**   *"xxxxxx"*

Reassigns the first four bytes of the 6-byte IEEE address. For example, for the address "03-1F-2C-81-92-34" only the first four bytes are looked at.

Some applications depend on an IEEE adapter address being available. However, because the Remote Access Service uses modems (not real Ethernet adapters), it does not have an IEEE Ethernet address per se. This parameter lets you manually set an IEEE adapter address for Remote Access adapter bindings where applications demand it.

RAS RasMan Subkey Entries

The Registry path for the RasMan key is the following:

```
HKEY_LOCAL_MACHINE\SYSTEM\CurrentControlSet\Services\RasMan\Parameters
```

Logging   **REG_DWORD**   *0 or 1*

Turns on information tracking for the modem using the DEVICE.LOG file. Set this value to 1 if you have modem problems that you cannot solve following documented procedures in the *Microsoft Windows NT Remote Access Administrator's Guide.* Logging begins the next time you dial in to connect through RAS (you do not need to restart your computer for the DEVICE.LOG file to be created).

Replicator Service Entries

The Registry path that contains entries for the Replicator service is the following:

```
HKEY_LOCAL_MACHINE\SYSTEM\CurrentControlSet\Services
    \Replicator\Parameters
```

CrashDir   **REG_SZ**   *First-level directory name*

This item is temporarily recorded in the Registry by the Replicator service. If it remains after a system repair, you can delete this entry using Registry Editor.

ExportList   REG_SZ *List*

Lists an unlimited number of servers or domains that receive notices when the export directory is updated. These servers subsequently replicate from the export server. If no *List* value is specified, the export server sends a notice to its domain. Separate multiple *List* names with a semicolon (;). This value is ignored if the value of **Replicate** is 2 (Import).

Do not use the UNC name when you specify a computername; that is, do not include two backslashes (\\) at the beginning of the name.

Use the Replicator controls in Server Manager or the Server icon in Control Panel to set this value.

Default: (none)

ExportPath   REG_SZ or REG_EXPAND_SZ *Pathname*

Specifies the export path. All files to be replicated must be in a subdirectory of the export directory. This value is ignored if the value of **Replicate** is set to 2 (Import). Use the Replicator controls in Server Manager or the Server icon in Control Panel to set this value, which cannot be a UNC name.

Default: %SystemRoot%\System32\Repl\Export

GuardTime   REG_DWORD *0 to one-half of Interval minutes*

Sets the number of minutes an export directory must be stable (no changes to any files) before import servers can replicate its files.

Default: 2 minutes

ImportList   REG_SZ *List*

Lists an unlimited number of servers or domains that receive notices when the import directory is updated. These servers subsequently replicate from the import server. If no *List* value is specified, updates come from the import server's domain. Separate multiple *List* names with a semicolon (;). This value is ignored if the value of **Replicate** is 1 (Export).

Do not use the UNC name when you specify a computername; that is, do not include two backslashes (\\) at the beginning of the name.

Use the Replicator controls in Server Manager or the Server icon in Control Panel to set this value.

ImportPath   REG_SZ or REG_EXPAND_SZ *Pathname*

Specifies the path on the import server to receive replicas from the export servers. This value is ignored if the value of **Replicate** is 1 (Export). Use the Replicator controls in Server Manager or the Server icon in Control Panel to set this value, which cannot be a UNC name.

Default: %SystemRoot%\System32\Repl\Import

Interval   **REG_DWORD**   *1 to 60 minutes*

Sets how often an export server checks the replicated directories for changes. This option is ignored on import servers.

Default: 5 minutes

Pulse   **REG_DWORD**   *1 to 10 cycles*

Specifies how often the export server repeats sending the last update notice. These repeat notices are sent even when no changes have occurred, so that import servers that missed the original update notice can receive the notice. The server waits the equivalent of (**Pulse * Interval**) minutes before sending each repeat notice.

Default: 3

Random   **REG_DWORD**   *1 to 120 seconds*

Specifies the maximum time that the import servers can wait before requesting an update. An import server uses the export server's value of **Random** to generate a random number of seconds (from 0 to the value of **Random**). The import server waits this long after receiving an update notice before requesting the replica from the export server. This prevents the export server from being overloaded by simultaneous update requests.

Default: 60

Replicate   **REG_DWORD**   *1, 2, or 3*

Specifies the Replicator action, according to the following:

Value	Meaning
1	Export—the server maintains a master tree to be replicated.
2	Import—the server receives update notices from the export server.
3	Both— the server is to export and import directories or files.

Use the Replicator controls in Server Manager or the Server icon in Control Panel to set this value.

Default: 3

Schedule Service Entries

There are no parameters that can be added for the Schedule service in this path:

```
HKEY_LOCAL_MACHINE\SYSTEM\CurrentControlSet\Services
   \Schedule
```

You use the Schedule service to submit a job such as an executable or batch file to run at a later time. You must define access controls on the Schedule key itself if you want to run in an account that is not an Administrator account.

Server Service Entries

With Registry Editor, you can modify the startup parameters for the Server service. Unless otherwise noted, these parameters are found in this path:

```
HKEY_LOCAL_MACHINE\SYSTEM\CurrentControlSet\Services
    \LanmanServer\Parameters
```

The parameters that control network bindings for this service are described in "NetRules Subkey Entries," earlier in this chapter.

AlertSched   REG_DWORD   *1 to 65535 minutes*

Specifies in Microsoft LAN Manager and in Windows NT how often the server checks alert conditions and sends needed alert messages.

Default: 5

Announce   REG_DWORD   *1 to 65535 seconds*

Specifies how often a nonhidden server announces itself to the network. More frequent announcements keep client server tables more up to date, but cost network overhead and processing on client computers, because clients must process every announcement.

Default: 240

AnnDelta   REG_DWORD   *0 to 65535 milliseconds*

Specifies the time by which the announcement period can vary. This helps to prevent several servers from continuously announcing simultaneously, thereby reducing network load peaks.

Default: 3000

Comment   REG_SZ   *Text string*

Provides the server's comment. This is sent in announcements and returned to NetServerGetInfo requests.

Default: NULL

Disc   REG_DWORD   *0 to infinite minutes*

Specifies the amount of idle time that a circuit is allowed before being disconnected. If the virtual circuit has any open files or searches, it is not automatically disconnected. If this parameter is set to a low value, it saves server resources but hinders performance because of clients' overhead in reconnecting. This is equivalent to **autoDisconnect** in Microsoft LAN Manager.

Default: 15 minutes

DiskSpaceThreshold   REG_DWORD   *0 to 99 percent*

Specifies the percentage of free disk space remaining before an alert is sent.

Default: 10 percent

EnableFCBopens   REG_DWORD   *0 or 1*

Specifies whether MS-DOS File Control Blocks (FCBs) are folded together, so multiple remote opens are performed as a single open on the server. This saves resources on the server.

Default: 1 (true)

EnableOplockForceClose   REG_DWORD   *0 or 1*

If a client has an opportunistic lock (oplock) and does not respond to an oplock break, there are two possible behaviors that this parameter selects:

Value	Meaning
0 (false)	Fail the second open, thereby limiting access to the file. (This is typical behavior for a client running LAN Manager version 2.0.)
1 (true)	Force closed the open instance of the client that has the oplock, risking the loss of cached data. (This is typical behavior for a client running LAN Manager version 2.1.)

Default: 0 (false)

EnableOplocks   REG_DWORD   *0 or 1*

Specifies whether the server allows clients to use oplocks on files. Oplocks are a significant performance enhancement, but have the potential to cause lost cached data on some networks, particularly wide-area networks.

Default: 1 (true)

EnableRaw   REG_DWORD   *0 or 1*

Specifies whether the server processes raw Server Message Blocks (SMBs). If enabled, this allows more data to be transferred per transaction and improves performance. However, it is possible that processing raw SMBs can impede performance on certain networks. This parameter is automatically tuned by the server.

Default: 1 (true)

EnableSoftCompat   REG_DWORD   *0 or 1*

Specifies whether the server maps a request to a normal open request with shared-read access when the server receives a compatibility open request with read access. Mapping such requests allows several MS-DOS computers to open a single file for read access. However, this feature can potentially cause functionality problems with some MS-DOS applications.

Default: 1 (true)

ErrorThreshold   REG_DWORD   *1 to 65535*

Sets the number of errors that can occur within an **AlertSched** interval before the server sends an alert message.

Default: 10

Hidden   REG_DWORD   *0 or 1*

If this parameter is disabled, the server's name and comment can be viewed by others on the domain. If enabled, the server's name and comment will not be announced.

Default: 0 (false)

InitConnTable   REG_DWORD   *1 to 128*

Specifies the initial number of tree connections to be allocated in the connection table. The server automatically increases the table as necessary, so setting the parameter to a higher value is an optimization.

Default: 8

InitFileTable   REG_DWORD   *1 to 256*

Specifies the initial number of file entries to be allocated in the file table of each server connection.

Default: 16

InitSearchTable   REG_DWORD   *1 to 2048*

Specifies the initial number of entries in the connection's search table.

Default: 8

InitSessTable   REG_DWORD   *1 to 64*

Specifies the initial number of session entries to be allocated in the session table of each server connection.

Default: 4

InitWorkItems   REG_DWORD   *1 to 512*

Specifies the initial number of receive buffers, or work items, used by the server. Allocating work items costs a certain amount of memory initially, but not as much as having to allocate additional buffers later.

Default: (depends on configuration)

IRPstackSize   REG_DWORD   *1 to 12*

Specifies the number of stack locations in I/O Request Packets (IRPs) used by the server. It may be necessary to increase this number for certain transports, MAC drivers, or local file system drivers. Each increment costs 36 bytes of memory per work item (that is, #work items * 36 bytes = total memory cost).

Default: 4

Server Service Entries

LinkInfoValidTime   REG_DWORD   *0 to 100,000 seconds*

Specifies the amount of time during which the transport link information is still valid. If more than this amount of time has passed since the last query, the server requires transport link information.

Default: 60

MaxFreeConnections   REG_DWORD   *2 to 8 items*

Specifies the maximum number of free connection blocks maintained per endpoint.

Default: Depends upon configuration

MaxLinkDelay   REG_DWORD   *0 to 100,000 seconds*

Specifies the maximum time allowed for a link delay. If delays exceed this number, the server disables raw I/O for this connection.

Default: 60

MaxKeepSearch   REG_DWORD   *10 to 10000 seconds*

Specifies the maximum time during which an incomplete MS-DOS search will be kept by the server. Larger values ensure better interoperability with MS-DOS utilities such as tree-copy and delete-node. However, larger values can cause unusual local behavior (such as a failure of a local directory-delete operation) and higher memory use on the server.

Default: 1800

MaxMpxCt   REG_DWORD   *1 to 100 requests*

Provides a suggested maximum to clients for the number of simultaneous requests outstanding to this server. A higher value can increase server performance but requires higher use of server work items.

Default: 50

MaxNonpagedMemoryUsage   REG_DWORD   *1 MB to infinite bytes*

Specifies the maximum size of nonpaged memory that the server can have allocated at any time. Adjust this parameter if you want to administer memory quota control.

Default: (depends on system and server configuration)

MaxPagedMemoryUsage   REG_DWORD   *1 MB to infinite bytes*

Specifies the maximum size of pageable memory that the server can have allocated at any time. Adjust this parameter if you want to administer memory quota control.

Default: (depends on system and server configuration)

MaxWorkItems   REG_DWORD   *1 to 512 items*

Specifies the maximum number of receive buffers, or work items, the server can allocate. If this limit is reached, the transport must initiate flow control at a significant performance cost.

Default: (depends on configuration)

MaxWorkItemIdleTime   REG_DWORD   *10 to 1800 seconds*

Specifies the amount of time that a work item can stay on the idle queue before it is freed.

Default: 300

MinFreeConnections   REG_DWORD   *2 to 5 items*

Specifies the minimum number of free connection blocks maintained per endpoint.

Default: (depends upon configuration)

MinFreeWorkItems   REG_DWORD   *0 to 10 items*

Specifies the minimum number of available receive work items that are needed for the server to begin processing a potentially blocking SMB. A larger value for this parameter ensures that work items are available more frequently for nonblocking requests, but it also increases the likelihood that blocking requests will be rejected.

Default: 2

MinKeepSearch   REG_DWORD   *5 to 5000 seconds*

Specifies the minimum amount of time that the server will keep incomplete MS-DOS searches, even if more search entries are needed. This parameter only matters when the server is near the maximum number of open searches it is allowed.

Default: 480

MinLinkThroughput   REG_DWORD   *0 to infinite bytes per second*

Specifies the minimum link throughput allowed by the server before it disables raw and opportunistic locks for this connection.

Default: 0

MinRcvQueue   REG_DWORD   *0 to 10 items*

Specifies the minimum number of free receive work items needed by the server before it begins allocating more. A larger value for this parameter helps ensure that there will always be work items available, but a value that is too large is simply inefficient.

Default: 2

NetworkErrorThreshold   REG_DWORD   *1 to 100 percent*

Triggers an alert whenever the percentage of failing network operations relative to total network operations exceeds this value during the **AlertSched** interval.

Default: 5 percent

NumBlockThreads   REG_DWORD   *1 to 10 threads*

Specifies the number of threads set aside by the server to service requests that can block the thread for a significant amount of time. Larger values can increase performance but use more memory. A value that is too large can impede performance by causing excessive task switching.

Default: (depends on configuration)

OpenSearch   REG_DWORD   *1 to 2048 searches*

Specifies the maximum number of outstanding searches on the server, per connection. A single client can have up to the **OpenSearch** number of active searches. This includes all types of searches, including MS-DOS, OS/2, and Windows NT.

Default: 2048

OplockBreakWait   REG_DWORD   *10 to 180 seconds*

Specifies the time that the server waits for a client to respond to an oplock break request. Smaller values can allow detection of crashed clients more quickly but can potentially cause loss of cached data.

Default: 35

RawWorkItems   REG_DWORD   *1 to 512 items*

Specifies the number of special work items for raw I/O that the server uses. A larger value for this parameter can increase performance but costs more memory.

Default: (depends on configuration)

ScavTimeout   REG_DWORD   *1 to 300 seconds*

Specifies the time that the scavenger remains idle before waking up to service requests. A smaller value for this parameter improves the response of the server to various events but costs CPU cycles.

Default: 30

ScavQosInfoUpdateTime   REG_DWORD   *0 to 100,000 seconds*

Specifies the time that can pass before the scavenger goes through the list of active connections to update the link information.

Default: 300

Server Service Entries

SessConns   REG_DWORD   *1 to 2048 connections*

Specifies the maximum number of tree connections that can be made on the server via a single virtual circuit.

Default: 2048

SessOpens   REG_DWORD   *1 to 2048 files*

Specifies the maximum number of files that can be open on a single virtual circuit.

Default: 2048

SessUsers   REG_DWORD   *1 to 64 users*

Specifies the maximum number of users that can be logged on to a server via a single virtual circuit.

Default: 32

SizReqBuf   REG_DWORD   *512 to 65536 bytes*

Specifies the size of request buffers that the server uses. Small buffers use less memory; large buffers may improve performance.

Default: 4356

ThreadCountAdd   REG_DWORD   *0 to 10 threads*

The server uses one worker thread per processor for the computer it is running on. This parameter indicates how many additional threads the server should use. More threads can improve performance but cost memory. Too many threads can hurt performance by causing excessive task switching.

Default: (depends on configuration)

ThreadPriority   REG_DWORD   *0, 1, 2, or 15*

Specifies the priority of all server threads in relation to the base priority of the process. Higher priority can give better server performance at the cost of local responsiveness. Lower priority balances server needs with the needs of other processes on the system. Values 0 to 2 are relative to normal or background processes. The default value of 1 is equivalent to the foreground process. A value of 15 runs the server threads at real-time priority—which is not recommended.

Default: 1

Users   REG_DWORD   *1 to infinite*

Specifies the maximum number of users that can be simultaneously logged on to the server.

Default: 0xFFFFFFFF (infinite)

Server Service Entries

XactMemSize   REG_DWORD   *64 KB to 16 MB0*

Specifies the maximum amount of virtual memory used by the Xactsrv service. A larger value for this parameter helps ensure that memory is available for downlevel clients but costs virtual address space and potentially costs pageable memory.

Default: 1 MB

TCP/IP Transport Entries

The various TCP/IP keys do not appear in the Registry unless TCP/IP is installed using the Network icon in Control Panel.

With Registry Editor, you can modify the following parameters for the TCP/IP transport. This section does not include all the TCP/IP parameters that can be set using the Networks application in Control Panel.

The startup parameters defined in this section are found in these subkeys of HKEY_LOCAL_MACHINE\SYSTEM\System\CurrentControlSet\Services:

- TCPIP\Parameters
- *adapter_name#*\Parameters\TCPIP, where *adapter_name#* indicates a Services subkey for a network adapter card
- Ftpsvc\Parameters
- NBT\Parameters
- Streams\Parameters

Parameters for network bindings for this service are described in "NctRules Subkey Entries," earlier in this chapter. See also **IsDomainMasterBrowser** in "Browser Service Entries," earlier in this chapter.

TCP/IP Parameters Subkey Entries

The entries for TCP/IP parameters appear under the following Registry path:

```
HKEY_LOCAL_MACHINE\SYSTEM\CurrentControlSet\Services\Tcpip\Parameters
```

ArpCacheLife   REG_DWORD   *Number of Seconds*

Determines the default lifetime for entries in the ARP cache table. Once an entry is placed in the ARP cache, it is allowed to remain there until its lifetime expires or until its table entry is reused because it is the oldest entry.

Default: 600 (10 minutes)

ArpCacheSize   REG_DWORD   *Number*

Determines the maximum number of entries that the ARP cache table can hold. The ARP cache is allowed to grow dynamically until this size is reached. After the table reaches this size, new entries can only be added by replacing the oldest entries that exist.

Default: 62

DatabasePath   REG_EXPAND_SZ   *Pathname*

Determines where TCP/IP and NBT look for the hosts, services, networks, protocols, NETRC, and LMHOSTS files.

Default: %SystemRoot%\system32\drivers\etc

IpEnableRouter   REG_DWORD   *0 or 1*

Determines whether IP routing is enabled between local interfaces. IP routing is always enabled for packets generated by the local host. This parameter determines whether, for packets received on an interface and not destined for this host, IP will attempt to actively forward the packets to hosts that can be reached via its other interfaces.

Default: 0 (false)

IpReassemblyTimeout   REG_DWORD   *Number of seconds*

Determines how long IP accepts fragments when attempting to reassemble a previously fragmented packet. That is, if a packet is fragmented, all of the fragments must make it to the destination within this time limit; otherwise, the fragments will be discarded and the packet will be lost.

Default: 60 seconds

TcpDisableReceiveChecksum   REG_DWORD   *0 or 1*

Specifies whether Checksums is disabled on receive.

Default: 0 (false, that is, checksums will be checked on receives)

TcpDisableSendChecksum   REG_DWORD   *0 or 1*

Specifies whether Checksums is disabled on send.

Default: 0 (false, that is, checksums will be generated on sends)

TcpKeepCnt   REG_DWORD   *Number in seconds*

Specifies how often TCP/IP will generate keep-alive traffic. When TCP/IP determines that no activity has occurred on the connection within the specified time, it generates keep-alive traffic to probe the connection. After trying **TcpKeepTries** number of times to deliver the keep-alive traffic without success, it marks the connection as down.

Default: 120

TCP/IP Transport Entries

TcpKeepTries   **REG_DWORD**   *Number*

Specifies the maximum number of times that TCP/IP will attempt to deliver keep-alive traffic before marking a connection as down.

Default: 20

TcpLogLevel   **REG_DWORD**   *Number*

Specifies how verbose TCP/IP should be about logging events in the event log. The highest level of verbosity is 16, and 1 is the lowest level. The following shows general information about these levels.

Level	Events to be included
1	Only the most critical errors
4	Serious protocol violations
8	Nonserious protocol violations
12	Information about unusual events
16	Information about unusual events that some networks normally allow

Default: 16 (log everything)

TcpMaxConnectAttempts   **REG_DWORD**   *Number*

Specifies the maximum number of times TCP/IP attempts to establish a connection before reporting failure. The initial delay between connection attempts is 3 seconds. This delay is doubled after each attempt.

Default: 3

TcpMaxRetransmissionAttempts   **REG_DWORD**   *Number*

Specifies the maximum number of times that TCP/IP attempts to retransmit a piece of data on an established connection before ending the connection. The initial delay before retransmitting is based on the current estimate TCP/IP makes of the round-trip time on the connection. This delay is doubled after each retransmission. Acknowledgment of the data results in a recalculation of the estimate for the round-trip time.

Default: 7

TcpNumConnections   **REG_DWORD**   *Number*

Specifies the maximum number of TCP endpoints.

Default: 64

TcpRecvSegmentSize   **REG_DWORD**   *Bytes*

Specifies the maximum receive segment size.

Default: 1460

TcpSendDownMax   **REG_DWORD**   *Number*

Specifies the maximum number of bytes queued by TCP/IP.

Default: 16384

TcpSendSegmentSize   **REG_DWORD**   *Bytes*

Specifies the maximum send segment size.

Default: 1460

TcpWindowSize   **REG_DWORD**   *Number*

Sets the size of the TCP send and receive windows, which is the amount of
data that can be accepted in a single transaction. This parameter is important in
transferring files between a client and a server and is critical for performance
for one-way traffic, such as for FTP.

Default: 8192

UdpDisableReceiveChecksum **REG_DWORD**   *0 or 1*

Specifies whether Checksums is disabled on receive.

Default: 0 (false, that is, checksums will be checked on receives)

UdpDisableSendChecksum   **REG_DWORD**   *0 or 1*

Specifies whether Checksums is disabled on send.

Default: 0 (false, that is, checksums will be generated on sends)

UdpNumConnections   **REG_DWORD**   *Number*

Specifies the maximum number of UDP endpoints.

Default: 64

Adapter Card Parameters for TCP/IP

These parameters for TCP/IP are specific to individual network adapter cards.
These appear under the following Registry path, where *adapter name#* refers to
the Services subkey for the specific adapter card:

```
HKEY_LOCAL_MACHINE\SYSTEM\CurrentControlSet\Services
   \adapter name#\Parameters\Tcpip
```

BroadcastType   **REG_DWORD**   *0 or 1*

Determines whether broadcast packets contain all 0's or all 1's as the
broadcast address. The most common broadcast type is all 1's. The all-0's
setting is provided for compatibility with BSD 4.2 systems.

Default: 1 (all 1's)

TCP/IP Transport Entries

ForwardBroadcasts   REG_DWORD   *0 or 1*

Specifies whether broadcasts should be forwarded between adapters. If enabled, broadcasts seen by this interface are forwarded to other IP interfaces.

Default: 0 (false)

KeepAlive   REG_DWORD   *0 or 1*

Determines whether TCP connections that request keep-alive packets result in keep-alive packets being sent. This feature is used to determine when inactive connections can be disconnected. When a connection becomes inactive, keep-alive packets are periodically exchanged. When 20 consecutive keep-alive packets go unanswered, the connection is broken. This disconnect is initiated by the endpoint that is sending keep-alive packets.

Default: 1 (true)

MTU   REG_DWORD   *Number in octets*

Specifies the maximum transmission unit size of an interface. Each interface used by TCP/IP may have a different MTU value specified. The MTU is usually determined through negotiation with the lower driver, using that lower driver's value. However, that value may be overridden.

Ideally, the MTU should be large enough to hold any datagram in one frame. The limiting factor is usually the technology making the transfer. Some technologies limit the maximum size to as little as 128; Ethernet limits transfers to 1500; and proNet-10 allows as many as 2044 octets per frame.

Datagrams larger than the MTU value are automatically divided into smaller pieces called fragments; size is a multiple of eight octets. Fragmentation usually occurs somewhere through which the traffic must pass whose MTU is smaller than the encapsulated datagram. If fragmentation occurs, the fragments travel separately to the destination computer, where they are automatically reassembled before the datagram is processed.

Default: 0 (That is, use the value supplied by the adapter.)

RouterMTU   REG_DWORD   *Number in octets*

Specifies the maximum transmission unit size that should be used when the destination IP address is on a different subnet. Each interface used by TCP/IP may have a different **RouterMTU** value specified. In many implementations, the value of **RouterMTU** is set to 576 octets. This is the minimum size that must be supported by any IP node. Because modern routers can usually handle MTUs larger than 576 octets, the default value for this parameter is the same value as that used by **MTU**.

Default: 0 (That is, use the value supplied by the lower interface.)

Trailers   REG_DWORD   *0 or 1*

Specifies whether the trailer format is used. This feature provides compatibility with BSD 4.2 systems. When this feature is enabled, TCP/IP header information follows the data area of IP packets.

Default: 0 (false)

FTP Server Service Entries for TCP/IP

The following Registry path contains parameters that affect the behavior of the FTP server service component:

```
HKEY_LOCAL_MACHINE\SYSTEM\CurrentControlSet\Services\Ftpsvc\Parameters
```

The Ftpsvc subkey does not appear until you install the FTP service using the Network icon in Control Panel. Also, you must restart the FTP server service (Ftpsvc) using the Services icon in Control Panel for any changes to these values to take effect.

There can also be an AccessCheck subkey under Ftpsvc, which allows access to FTP for new users. If the AccessCheck subkey exists, but cannot be opened, the user is refused FTP services. If the subkey exists but can only be opened for read access, the user is granted read-only FTP access. If the subkey does not exist, it is not used to influence FTP access. By default, this subkey does not exist and therefore has no impact on FTP operations. An administrator can create this Registry subkey and attach specific access controls. which will serve to control user access to the FTP service.

AllowAnonymous   REG_DWORD   *0 or 1*

Controls anonymous logons. Anonymous logons are only allowed if this value is nonzero (true).

Default: 1 (true — anonymous logons are allowed)

AnnotateDirectories   REG_DWORD   *0 or 1*

When this value is 1, every time a user changes directories (that is, sends the server a CWD command), an attempt is made to open a file named ~FTPSVC~.CKM in the new directory. If this file is found, its contents are sent to the user as part of the successful reply to the CWD command. This may be used to attach annotations to specific directories.

This value is used as a default for new users. Users can toggle their own personal annotate directories flag with the site-specific CKM command (SITE CKM).

Default: 0 (false —do not send directory annotations)

AnonymousOnly   **REG_DWORD**   *0 or 1*

When this value is 1, only anonymous logons are allowed. Otherwise, nonanonymous logons are allowed as well.

Default: 0 (false —nonanonymous logons are allowed)

AnonymousUserName   **REG_SZ**   *UserName*

Contains the anonymous login alias. When a user attempts an anonymous login, the username specified ("anonymous") is mapped to this Registry value for authentication and impersonation.

Default: "Guest"

ConnectionTimeout   **REG_DWORD**   *Seconds*

Specifies the time to allow clients to remain idle before forcibly disconnecting them. This prevents idle clients from consuming server resources indefinitely.

This value may be set to 0 if time-outs are not to be enforced. If set to 0, idle clients may remain connected indefinitely.

Default: 600 (10 minutes)

ExitMessage   **REG_SZ**   *Message*

Specifies a signoff message sent to an FTP client upon receipt of a QUIT command.

Default: "Goodbye."

GreetingMessage   **REG_MULTI_SZ**   *Strings*

Specifies the message (if this value exists in the Registry) to be sent to new clients after their account has been validated. In accordance with de facto Internet behavior, if a client logs on as anonymous and specifies an identity starting with a "-" (minus), then this greeting message is not sent.

Default: None (no special greeting message)

HomeDirectory   **REG_EXPAND_SZ**   *Path*

Specifies the initial home directory for new clients. After a new client is validated, an attempt is made to change to this directory with the Chdir command. If this directory is inaccessible, the client is refused FTP services. If Chdir is successful, then an attempt is made to change to a directory with the same name as the client's username. If this fails, an attempt is made to change to a directory called DEFAULT. If this fails, the current directory is left at home.

If a new client connects and finds the home directory is inaccessible, an event is written to the event log.

Default: C:\

LogAnonymous   REG_DWORD   *0 or 1*

When this value is 1, all successful anonymous logons are logged to the system event log.

Default: 0 (false —do not log successful anonymous logons)

LogNonAnonymous   REG_DWORD   *0 or 1*

When this value is 1, all successful nonanonymous logons are logged to the system event log.

Default: 0 (false, that is, do not log successful nonanonymous logons)

MaxClientsMessage   REG_SZ   *Message*

Specifies the message (if this value exists in the Registry) to be sent to a client if the maximum number of clients has been reached or exceeded. This indicates that the server is currently servicing the maximum number of simultaneous clients and is refusing additional clients. See **MaxConnections**.

Default: "Maximum clients reached, service unavailable."

MaxConnections   REG_DWORD   *0 or 1*

Specifies the maximum number of simultaneous clients the server will service. This value may be set to 0 if there is to be no limit on simultaneous clients.

Default: 20

MsdosDirOutput   REG_DWORD   *0 or 1*

When this value is 1, the output of the LIST command (usually sent as a result of a DIR command from the client) will look like the output of the MS-DOS **dir** command. If this value is 0, the output of the LIST command looks like the output of the UNIX **ls** command.

This value also controls slash flipping in the path sent by the PWD command. When this value is 1 (true), the path contains backward slashes (\). If this value is 0 (false), the path contains forward slashes (/).

This value is used as a default for new users. Users can toggle their own personal MS-DOS directory output flag with the site-specific DIRSTYLE command (SITE DIRSTYLE).

Default: 1 (true—directory listings will look like MS-DOS)

ReadAccessMask   REG_DWORD   *BitFields*

This value is a bitmask and controls the read ability of the various disk volumes in the system. Drive A corresponds to bit 0, drive B corresponds to bit 1, drive C corresponds to bit 2, and so on. A user may only read from a specific volume if the corresponding bit is set.

Default: 0 (all read access denied)

WriteAccessMask REG_DWORD *BitFields*

This value is a bitmask and controls the write ability of the various disk volumes in the system. Drive A corresponds to bit 0, drive B corresponds to bit 1, drive C corresponds to bit 2, and so on. A user may only write to a specific volume if the corresponding bit is set.

Default: 0 (all write access denied)

NBT Parameters for TCP/IP

NBT is the NetBIOS over TCP/IP service. Parameters for TCP/IP are also configured under NBT in the following Registry path:

`HKEY_LOCAL_MACHINE\SYSTEM\CurrentControlSet\Services\NBT\Parameters`

MaxPreload REG_DWORD *Number*

Specifies the maximum NBT number of entries for LMHOSTS that are preloaded into the NBT NetBIOS name cache. LMHOSTS is a file located in the directory specified by **DatabasePath.**

Default: 100

NbProvider REG_SZ *DLL name*

This value is only present for network services that provide a NetBIOS interface. Its presence causes LanMan information to be maintained for the transport. The value data represents the RPC provider string used to select the proper DLL for interfacing RPC to the transport.

Default: _tcp

NbtKeepAlive REG_DWORD *Number in seconds*

Specifies how often NBT will generate keep-alive traffic. When NBT determines that no activity has occurred on a connection for the specified time interval, it will generate keep-alive traffic to probe the connection. If TCP/IP is unable to deliver this traffic, it marks the connection as down and notifies NBT.

Default: 0 (Do not generate NBT keep-alive traffic.)

PermanentName REG_SZ *Unique name*

Specifies the permanent name of the NetBIOS node for NBT. In many NetBIOS implementations, this is the MAC address. This name must be unique.

Default: The value of *IPAddress* in dotted decimal

Streams Parameters for TCP/IP

The TCP/IP parameter for Streams are found under the following Registry path:

```
HKEY_LOCAL_MACHINE\SYSTEM\CurrentControlSet\Services\Streams\Parameters
```

MaxMemoryUsage   REG_DWORD   *Number of bytes*

Specifies the maximum amount of memory that can be allocated to the Streams environment. Once this limit is reached, Streams will fail allocation requests made by Streams-based drivers.

Default: No limit

Windows Sockets Entries for TCP/IP

All Windows Sockets parameters can be set by choosing the Network icon in Control Panel. These parameters are found in two locations, as shown here.

```
HKEY_LOCAL_MACHINE\SYSTEM\CurrentControlSet \Services
    \Winsock\Parameters
```

Transports   REG_Multi_SZ   *Strings*

Contains the Registry key names of installed transports that support Windows Sockets. If TCP/IP is the only installed transport that supports Windows Sockets, then this value is Tcpip. The Windows Sockets DLL uses the strings in **Transports** to find information about each transport.

Default: Depends on installation

```
HKEY_LOCAL_MACHINE\SYSTEM\CurrentControlSet \Services
    \TCPIP\Parameters\Winsock
```

HelperDllName   REG_EXPAND_SZ   *Path and filename*

Specifies the name of the Windows Sockets helper DLL for the TCP/IP transport. This value is set by the Windows Sockets DLL and is not a user settable parameter.

Default: Depends on the transport; %SystemRoot%\system32\wshtcpip.dll for TCP/IP.

IRPStackSize   REG_DWORD   *Number*

Specifies the number of IRP stack locations needed by AFD, the driver used for Windows Sockets. The default is sufficient for all existing transports, but new transports may be developed that need more IRP stack locations.

Default: 4

Mapping   REG_BINARY

Identifies the address families, socket types, and protocols supported by the transport. This value is set by the Windows Sockets DLL and is not a user settable parameter.

Default: Depends on transport

MaxSockAddrLen   REG_DWORD   *Octets*

Specifies the maximum length of socket addresses for the INET sockets family. This value is set by the Windows Sockets DLL and is not a user settable parameter.

MinSockAddrLen   REG_DWORD   *Octets*

Specifies the minimum length of socket addresses for the INET sockets family. This value is set by the Windows Sockets DLL and is not a user settable parameter.

UPS Service Entries

The Registry does not contain information for the UPS service until the user checks the Uninterruptible Power Supply Is Installed checkbox in the UPS dialog box and then chooses the OK button. Changes to settings should be made by using the UPS icon in Control Panel.

The UPS service will not start unless the UPS subkey is present in the Registry, all parameters are present in the Registry, and all values are within the correct range. If any of these elements are missing or in error, a message announces that the UPS service is not correctly configured. All corrections can be made using the UPS icon in Control Panel.

The UPS parameters remain in the Registry if the user uninstalls UPS.

The path for the UPS subkey is the following:

```
HKEY_LOCAL_MACHINE\SYSTEM\CurrentControlSet\Services\UPS
```

BatteryLife   REG_DWORD   *2 to 720 minutes*

Specifies the life of the UPS backup battery when fully charged.

Default: 2 (minutes)

CommandFile   REG_EXPAND_SZ   *Filename*

Specifies the name of a command file to execute immediately before shutting down.

Default: (empty)

FirstMessageDelay   REG_DWORD   *0 to 120 seconds*

Specifies the number of seconds between initial power failure and the first message sent to the users. If power is restored within the **FirstMessageDelay** time, no message is sent, although the event is logged.

Default: 5 (seconds)

MessageInterval   REG_DWORD   *5 to 300 seconds*

Specifies the number of seconds between messages sent to users to inform them of power failure.

Default: 120 (seconds)

Options   REG_DWORD   *Value*

Defines the bit mask for messages related to options in the UPS dialog box, as the following:

Installed	0x00000001
PowerFailSignal	0x00000002
LowBatterySignal	0x00000004
CanTurnOff	0x00000008
PosSigOnPowerFail	0x00000010
PosSigOnLowBattery	0x00000020
PosSigShutOff	0x00000040
CommandFile	0x00000080

Port   REG_SZ   *Port name*

Specifies the name of the serial port the UPS is connected to.

Default: COM1:

RechargeRate   REG_DWORD   *1 to 250 minutes*

Specifies the recharge rate of the UPS backup battery.

Default: 100 (minutes)

Workstation Service Entries

You can modify the startup parameters for the Workstation service using the Registry Editor. Unless otherwise indicated, these value entries are found in the following Registry path:

```
HKEY_LOCAL_MACHINE\SYSTEM\CurrentControlSet\Services
    \LanmanWorkstation\Parameters
```

The parameters that control network bindings for this service are described in "NetRules Subkey Entries," earlier in this chapter.

BufFilesDenyWrite   REG_DWORD   *0 or 1*

Specifies whether the redirector should cache files that are opened with only FILE_SHARE_READ sharing access. Usually, if a file is opened with FILE_SHARE_READ specified, the file cannot be buffered because other processes may also be reading that file. This optimization allows the redirector to buffer such files. This optimization is safe because no process can write to the file.

Disable this parameter if it is necessary to preserve the strict semantics of the sharing modes specified.

Default: 1 (true)

BufNamedPipes   REG_DWORD   *0 or 1*

Indicates whether the redirector should buffer character-mode named pipes.

Disable this parameter to guarantee that all pipe write operations are flushed to the server immediately and to disable read ahead on character-mode named pipes.

Default: 1 (true)

BufReadOnlyFiles   REG_DWORD   *0 or 1*
`...\CurrentControlSet\Services\LanmanWorkstation`

Specifies whether the redirector should cache files that are read-only. Usually, if a read-only file is opened, the file cannot be buffered because other processes may also be reading that file. This optimization allows the redirector to buffer such files. This optimization is safe because no process can write to the file. However, another user can modify the file to enable writing to the file, causing loss of data.

Disable this parameter if it is necessary to preserve the strict semantics of the sharing modes specified.

Default: 1 (true)

CacheFileTimeout   REG_DWORD   *Number of seconds*

Specifies the maximum time that a file will be left in the cache after the application has closed the file.

Increase the value of this parameter if you are performing operations on the server that could cause files to be reopened more than 10 seconds after the application has closed them. For example, if you are performing a build over the network, you should increase this parameter's value.

Default: 10

CharWait   REG_DWORD   *0 to 65535 milliseconds*

Specifies time to wait for an instance of a named pipe to become available when opening the pipe.

Increase this value if your pipe server application is typically very busy.

Default: 3600

CollectionTime   REG_DWORD   *0 to 65535000 milliseconds*

Specifies the maximum time that write-behind data will remain in a character-mode pipe buffer.

Changing this value may cause a named pipe application's performance to improve (but it does not affect SQL Server applications).

Default: 250

DormantFileLimit   REG_DWORD   *Number of files*

Specifies the maximum number of files that should be left open on a share after the application has closed the file.

This parameter exists because the default configuration of LAN Manager servers only allow a total of 60 open files from remote clients and 50 from each client workstation. Because the Windows NT redirector may keep files open in the cache after an application has closed the file, this means that the redirector may overload a misconfigured LAN Manager server. To correct this problem, either reduce this value, or increase the values for the LAN Manager server's **maxSessopens** and **maxOpens** parameters.

Default: 45

IllegalDatagramResetTime   REG_DWORD   *Number of seconds*

Specifies the span of time during which the number of illegal datagram events is counted. Because Windows NT logs all illegal datagrams, it is possible for the event log to be filled with a proliferation of these in a short amount of time. This entry and the **NumIllegalDatagramEvents** entry work together to limit the number of illegal datagrams that are recorded in the log within a certain span of time.

Default: 60

KeepConn   REG_DWORD   *1 to 65535 seconds*

Specifies the maximum amount of time that a connection can be left dormant. This parameter is the redirector equivalent of the **Disc** parameter in the Services\LanmanServer\Parameters subkey.

As a general rule, try increasing this value if your application closes and opens UNC files to a server less frequently than 10 minutes apart. This decreases the number of reconnections made to a server.

Default: 600

Workstation Service Entries

LockIncrement   REG_DWORD   *Number of milliseconds*

This parameter is not used for Win32 applications. However, if OS/2-based applications request that a lock operation waits forever, and if the lock cannot be immediately granted on a non-LAN Manager version 2.0 server, this parameter controls the rate at which the redirector ramps back the failed lock operations.

This parameter should not be changed unless you are running an OS/2-based application that requests lock operations that might fail.

Default: 10

LockMaximum   REG_DWORD   *Number of milliseconds*

Used to configure the lock backoff package. This parameter exists to prevent an errant application from "swamping" a server with nonblocking requests where there is no data available for the application.

Default: 500

LockQuota   REG_DWORD   *Bytes of data*

Specifies the maximum amount of data that is read for each file using this optimization if the **UseLockReadUnlock** parameter is enabled.

Increase this value if your application performs a significant number of lock-and-read style operations. (This means performing lock operations and immediately reading the contents of the locked data.) It is conceivable that you could cause the system to run out of paged pool, but only by increasing this value to a few megabytes and by using an application that locks millions-of-byte ranges.

Default: 4096 (bytes)

LogElectionPackets   REG_DWORD   *0 or 1*

Specifies whether the Browser should generate events when election packets are received.

Default: 0 (false)

MailslotBuffers   REG_DWORD   *Number of buffers*

Specifies the maximum number of buffers available to process mailslot messages. If your application uses many mailslot operations, set this higher to avoid losing mailslot messages.

Default: 5

MaxCmds   REG_DWORD   *0 to 255*

Specifies the maximum number of work buffers that the redirector reserves for performance reasons.

Increase this value to increase your network throughput. If your application performs more than 15 simultaneous operations, you might want to increase this value. Because this parameter actually controls the number of execution threads that can be simultaneously outstanding at any time, your network performance will not always be improved by increasing this parameter. Each additional execution threads takes about 1K of nonpaged pool if you actually load up the network. Resources will not be consumed, however, unless the user actually makes use of them.

Default: 15

MaxCollectionCount   REG_DWORD   *0 to 65535 bytes*

Specifies the threshold for character-mode named pipes writes. If the write is smaller than this value, the write will be buffered. Adjusting this value may improve performance for a named-pipe application (but it will not affect SQL server applications).

Default: 16

NumIllegalDatagramEvents   REG_DWORD   *Number of events*

Specifies the maximum number of datagram events to be logged within the span of time specified by the **IllegalDatagramResetTime** parameter. Because Windows NT logs all illegal datagrams, the event log can be filled with a proliferation of these in a short time. This entry and the **IllegalDatagramResetTime** entry work together.

Default: 5

OtherDomains   REG_SZ   *DomainNames*

Specifies the Microsoft LAN Manager domains to be listed for browsing.

Default: (none)

PipeIncrement   REG_DWORD   *Number of milliseconds*

Controls the rate at which the redirector "backs off" on failing nonblocking pipe reads.

This parameter is used to prevent an errant application from swamping a server with nonblocking requests where there is no data available for the application. You can use the backoff statistics to tune this parameter to be more efficient for an application that uses nonblocking named pipes (except for SQL Server applications).

Default: 10

PipeMaximum   **REG_DWORD**   *Number of milliseconds*

Controls the maximum time at which the redirector "backs off" on failing nonblocking pipe reads.

This parameter exists to prevent an errant application from swamping a server with nonblocking requests where there is no data available for the application. You can use the backoff statistics to tune this parameter to be more efficient for an application that uses nonblocking named pipes (except for SQL Server applications).

Default: 500

ReadAheadThroughput   **REG_DWORD**   *Kilobytes per second*

Specifies the throughput required on a connection before the cache manager is told to enable read ahead.

Default: 0xffffffff

ServerAnnounceBuffers   **REG_DWORD**   *Number*

Specifies the maximum buffers used to process server announcements. If your network has many servers, you can increase this value to avoid losing server announcements.

This parameter is found under the LanmanWorkstation\Parameters\Static subkey.

Default: 20

SessTimeout   **REG_DWORD**   *10 to 65535 seconds*

Specifies the maximum amount of time that the redirector allows an operation that is not long-term to be outstanding.

Default: 45

SizCharBuf   **REG_DWORD**   *64 to 4096 bytes*

Specifies the maximum number of bytes that will be written into a character-mode pipe buffer. Adjusting this value may improve performance for a named-pipe application (but it will not affect SQL server applications).

Default: 512

Transports   **REG_MULTI_SZ**   *List*

Lists the transports that the redirector services and is found under the LanmanWorkstation\Linkage subkey. You should modify it by choosing the Network icon in Control Panel.

Default: None

Use512ByteMaxTransfer   REG_DWORD   *0 or 1*

Specifies whether the redirector should only send a maximum of 512 bytes in a request to an MS-Net server regardless of the servers-negotiated buffer size. If this parameter is disabled, request transfers from the Windows NT redirector could cause the MS-Net server to crash.

Default: 0 (false)

UseLockReadUnlock   REG_DWORD   *0 or 1*

Indicates whether the redirector uses the lock-and-read and write-and-unlock performance enhancements.

When this value is enabled, it generally provides a significant performance benefit. However, database applications that lock a range and don't allow data within that range to be read will suffer performance degradation unless this parameter is disabled.

Default: 1 (true)

UseOpportunisticLocking   REG_DWORD   *0 or 1*

Indicates whether the redirector should use opportunistic-locking (oplock) performance enhancement. This parameter should be disabled only to isolate problems.

Default: 1 (true)

UseRawRead   REG_DWORD   *0 or 1*

Enables the raw-read optimization. This provides a significant performance enhancement on a local area network

Default: 1 (true)

UseRawWrite   REG_DWORD   *0 or 1*

Enables the raw-write optimization. On a LAN, this provides a significant performance enhancement.

Default: 1 (true)

UseUnlockBehind   REG_DWORD   *0 or 1*

Indicates whether the redirector will complete an unlock operation before it has received confirmation from the server that the unlock operation has completed. Disable this parameter only to isolate problems or to guarantee that all unlock operations complete on the server before completing the application's unlock request.

Default: 1 (true)

UseWriteRawData   **REG_DWORD**   *0 or 1*

Enables the raw-write-with-data optimization. This allows the redirector to send 4 KB of data with each write-raw operation. This provides a significant performance enhancement on a local area network.

Default: 1 (true)

UtilizeNtCaching   **REG_DWORD**   *0 or 1*

Indicates whether the redirector uses the cache manager to cache the contents of files. Disable this parameter only to guarantee that all data is flushed to the server immediately after it is written by the application.

Default: 1 (true)

Registry Entries for Microsoft Mail

The parameters used by the Microsoft Mail application provided with Windows NT appear under this subkey:

```
HKEY_CURRENT_USER\Software\Microsoft\Mail
```

This key includes the following subkeys:

Subkey	Purpose
Address Book	Specifies entries used by the Address Book support functions for the Mail program.
Custom Commands	Specifies a custom command that can be installed into one of the Mail menus at run-time.
Custom Messages	Specifies a custom message type that is installed into a Mail menu at run-time.
Custom Menus	Specifies a custom menu name to be added to the Mail menu bar.
Microsoft Mail	Defines the configuration of the Mail program, and the Microsoft Mail transport and name service.
MMF	Affects the automatic compression of the Mail message file.
Mac File Types	Defines the mapping from Macintosh file type and creator tags to eight-plus-three character filename extensions.
MS Proofing Tools	Defines settings for the speller.
Providers	Defines settings that service providers use with Microsoft Mail front-end programs.

Many of the entries in these subkeys have default values and won't be present in the Mail subkeys. To change the appearance and behavior of the Mail application, use the Mail menu commands instead of editing the Mail entries directly. Some of the options that you specify in the Mail application are stored in your mail message file (.MMF) instead of the Mail Registry entries.

These keys are created in HKEY_CURRENT_USER when you first run Mail. If your system previously contained a Windows for MS-DOS version of MSMAIL.INI, its contents are migrated to the Registry when you first run Mail under Windows NT.

Address Book Entries for Mail

Entries in this subkey are used by the Address Book support functions in the Mail program. Most of the entries for this subkey use default values specified by the Mail program, and the Address Book subkey might not be present under the Mail key. The entries in this subkey control the default address directory displayed in the Address Book. Do not change any of these entries if they appear.

This is the Registry path for this subkey:

```
HKEY_CURRENT_USER\Software\Microsoft\Mail\Address Book
```

Custom Commands Entries for Mail

Each entry under this key specifies a custom command that can be installed into one of the Mail menus at run-time. These entries can appear both in the Microsoft Mail key and in the SHARED32.INI file in the directory defined under the Microsoft Mail subkey as the value of **SharedExtensionsDir**.

This is the Registry path for this subkey:

```
HKEY_CURRENT_USER\Software\Microsoft\Mail\Custom Commands
```

The Custom Commands subkey can contain one or more of the following entries:

tag   REG_SZ

This specifies the descriptive identifier for the command in the following format:

```
tag= version;menu;name;position;DLL name, ordinal;command;
     event map;status text;Help file;help context;
```

For example:

```
IC1= 3.0;help;&Out of Office;10;<ExtsDir>BIN-EXT\OOF32.DLL;3;;
    Out of Office Email Notification
```

Value	Meaning
version	The version of Mail that the custom command is compatible with.
menu	The menu where the custom command is to be added, such as File or Help.
name	The command name to appear on the menu. Include an ampersand just before the letter that is to serve as an ALT+*key* accelerator.
position	The zero-relative position within its menu where the command is to appear. A value of −1 places the command at the end of the menu.
DLL name	Name or path of the DLL where the custom command resides. This entry can optionally be followed by a comma and the ordinal of the entry point to call (default is ,1).
command	The command string passed as one of the parameters to the DLL entry point for the command.
event map	A sequence of up to 16 digits identifying the Mail events that the custom command supports. Each can be 0 or 1 to indicate if the DLL is to be called for a specific event. Currently three events are defined; the rest are reserved and must be zero (or, as in the examples above, this whole section can be empty):
	▪ The first digit means Mail startup.
	▪ The second digit means Mail exit.
	▪ The third digit means the arrival of a new message.
status text	Text to be displayed in the Mail status bar when the user highlights the command in the menu.
Help file	Windows NT Help file to be invoked when the user presses F1 while the command is selected. The specified filename is passed to the Windows NT Help program. (optional)
help context	Passed to the Windows NT help program along with the Help file name. Use −1 (Help file index) if there is no specific entry in the Help file for this command. (optional)
<ExtsDir>	A special token that can appear within certain fields. Expands to the value of **SharedExtensionsDir** in the Microsoft Mail key. Used to refer to DLLs that are installed in a shared extensions directory on the network. Valid for the *DLL name, command,* and *Help file* subfields.

Custom Messages Entries for Mail

This subkey is similar in many ways to the Custom Commands subkey. Each entry specifies a custom message type to be installed into a Mail menu at run-time.

These entries can appear both in the Microsoft Mail key and in the SHARED32.INI file in the directory defined by the **SharedExtensionsDir** entry under the Microsoft Mail key.

This is the Registry path for this subkey:

```
HKEY_CURRENT_USER\Software\Microsoft\Mail\Custom Messages
```

The Custom Messages subkey can contain one or more of the following entries.

class   REG_SZ

Specifies a string uniquely identifying the message type. Mail places this string in messages and calls custom message DLLs based on its value. Each entry is in the following format:

```
class = version;menu;name;position;DLL name;command;operation map;
     status text;Help file;help context;
```

Value	Meaning
version	The version of Mail that the custom message is compatible with.
menu	The menu where the custom command for the message type is to be added, such as File or Mail.
name	The command name to appear on the menu. Include an ampersand just before the letter that is to serve as an ALT+k*ey* accelerator.
position	The zero-relative position within its menu at which the command is to appear. A value of –1 places the command at the end of the menu.
DLL name	Name or path of the DLL in which the custom command resides.
command	Command string passed as one of the parameters to the DLL entry point for the command.

Value *(continued)*	Meaning *(continued)*
operation map	Sequence of up to 16 digits. Each can be 0, 1, or 2, where 0 indicates that Mail is to perform its standard operation on the custom message. 1 indicates that the DLL is to be called to handle the operation. 2 indicates that the operation is to be completely disabled. Currently eight operations are defined; the rest are reserved and must be zero. In the following list, 0 is the leftmost digit:

0   Compose (menu command defined in this entry)
1   File.Open
2   Mail.Reply
3   Mail.Reply to All
4   Mail.Forward
5   File.Print
6   File.Save as
7   Arrival of new mail

Value	Meaning
status text	Text to be displayed in the Mail status bar when the user highlights the command in the menu.
Help file	Windows NT Help file to be invoked when the user presses F1 while the command is selected. The specified filename is passed to the Windows NT Help program. (optional)
help context	Passed to the Windows NT Help program along with the Help filename. Use –1 (Help file index) if there is no specific entry in the Help file for this command. (optional)
<ExtsDir>	A special token that can appear within certain fields. Expands to the value of **SharedExtensionsDir** in the Microsoft Mail key. Used to refer to DLLs that are installed in a shared extensions directory on the network. Valid for the *DLL name, command,* and *Help file* fields.

Custom Menus Entries for Mail

This subkey can contain any number of entries (within reason). You can use these menus to group custom commands and/or messages under a single, distinctive menu item.

This is the Registry path for this subkey:

```
HKEY_CURRENT_USER\Software\Microsoft\Mail\Custom Menus
```

The following information can appear both in the Microsoft Mail key and in SHARED32.INI in the directory defined by **SharedExtensionsDir** under the Microsoft Mail key. The SHARED32.INI file is examined first.

tag   **REG_SZ**

Identifies the menu to someone reading these values but serves no other purpose. Specifies a menu name to be added to the Mail menu bar. This is the format:

```
Tag=version;name;name to follow;status text
```

For example:

```
tools=3.0;&Tools;Window;Useful development toys
```

Value	Meaning
version	The version of Mail with which the menu is compatible; 3.0 is the current version.
name	The menu name to be added to the menu bar. Include an ampersand just before the letter that is to serve as an ALT+*key* accelerator.
name to follow	Name of an existing menu. The new menu is added directly before it.
status text	Text to be displayed in the Mail status bar when the user highlights the menu name.

Microsoft Mail Entries

This subkey is used to define the appearance and behavior of the Mail program. This is the Registry path for this subkey:

```
HKEY_CURRENT_USER\Software\Microsoft\Mail\Microsoft Mail
```

This key also appears under HKEY_USERS\.DEFAULT, but its only contents are **MigrateIni and MigrateIniPrint.**

These are the value entries that can appear in this key:

CheckLatencyInterval   REG_SZ   *seconds*

Affects the mail spooler's latency checking, which is intended to prevent spooler background processing from interfering with foreground work. If the specified length of time passes without the spooler having any work to do, the latency algorithm is reinitialized.

Default: 30 seconds

DemosEnabled   REG_SZ   *0 or 1*

Specifies whether the Demos menu option is to be displayed in the Help menu. If the value of the entry is 1, the Demos menu option is displayed in the Help menu. If this entry is 0, the Demos menu option is not shown.

Default: 0 (The Mail demos are not provided with Windows NT.)

ExportMmfFile   REG_SZ   *filename*

Identifies the path and filename for a .MMF file pointing to the last place a mail folder was exported to. This entry is written by the Mail program and is used as a default value for display in the Export Folder dialog box when you choose Export Folders from the File menu in Mail.

FixedFont   REG_SZ   *facename, size, 0 or 1, 0 or 1*

Identifies the fixed-pitch font used to display the body text of a mail message. This entry has four parts, each separated by a comma: typeface name (not the font file name), point size, flag for bold, and flag for italic. The Change Font command on the View menu toggles between the Normal font and the Fixed font.

Default: Courier New, 9, 0, 0

ForceScanInterval   REG_SZ   *seconds*

Affects the mail spooler's latency checking, which is intended to prevent the spooler background processing from interfering with foreground work. If the designated length of time passes without the spooler getting an opportunity to do outstanding work, idle time is requested more frequently (based on the value of **ScanAgainInterval**), and eventually idle time is used whenever it can.

Default: 300 seconds (5 minutes)

GALOnly   REG_SZ   *0 or 1*

If this entry is set to 1, the Mail address book displays only the Global Address List and the personal address book, thereby providing a flat address list of all the users visible from your postoffice. You must be running against a PC Mail 3.0 or higher postoffice with global address list support for this to work. **GALOnly** is currently supported only by the PC Mail name service provider.

Default: 0

IdleRequiredInterval   REG_SZ   *seconds*

Affects the mail spooler's latency checking, which is intended to prevent the spooler's background processing from interfering with foreground work. The spooler defers its work temporarily if the system has serviced an interactive request such as a keyboard entry or mouse movement within this interval, to avoid starting a transfer when the user is busy.

Default: 2 seconds

Microsoft Mail Entries

LocalMMF   REG_SZ   *0 or 1*

Specifies the location where the user's mail message file (.MMF) is created when the user runs Mail for the first time. If this entry is 0, the user's Mail messages are stored in the postoffice on the server. If this entry is 1, the user's .MMF file is created locally in the *SystemRoot* directory rather than on the postoffice the first time Mail is run. Also, this value set to 1, in conjunction with the **NoServerOptions** entry, prevents .MMF files from being stored in the postoffice.

Default: 1

Login   REG_SZ   *mailbox name*

Identifies the default User Name (up to 10 characters) displayed in the Mail Sign In dialog box used to log into Mail. If you set both the **Login** and **Password** entries, the Login dialog is not displayed when you start Mail, and your mailbox is immediately displayed. If you set just **Login**, Mail prompts for your password only.

Default: (blank)

MailBeep   REG_SZ   *filename*

Specifies the path name of a .WAV file to change the sound that Mail uses to notify the user when new mail arrives. This entry is ignored if the Sound Chime option in the Mail Options dialog box is not checked.

Mail looks at this entry only if it can't find a **MailBeep** entry in the HKEY_CURRENT_USER\Control Panel\Sounds subkey.

Default: (blank)—Mail beeps twice when new mail arrives.

MailTmp   REG_SZ   *Pathname*

Set this entry to a directory where Mail can place temporary copies of attached files. When you launch an application by double-clicking a file attached to a mail message, Mail copies the file to this directory and runs the application.

Default: The value of the TEMP environment variable. If there is no TEMP variable, the default is the *SystemRoot* directory.

MAPIHELP   REG_SZ   *filename*

Specifies the MAPI Help file to be used when the user requests help in any of the dialog boxes displayed by the MAPI support functions. This entry is defined when the Mail program is run for the first time.

Default: The MSMAIL32.HLP file in the user's *SystemRoot*\SYSTEM32 directory (for example, C:\WINNT\SYSTEM32\MSMAIL32.HLP).

Microsoft Mail Entries

MigrateIni   REG_SZ   *0 or 1*

Specifies whether to migrate the Mail .INI files created by a Windows for MS-DOS version of Mail for use under Windows NT. This entry is saved in the HKEY_USERS\.DEFAULT\Software\Microsoft\Mail subkey. In HKEY_CURRENT_USER, this entry is deleted after the user first runs Mail.

Default: 1 (yes)

MigrateIniPrint   REG_SZ   *0 or 1*

Specifies whether to migrate the Mail .INI print information created by a Windows for MS-DOS version of Mail for use under Windows NT. This entry is saved in the HKEY_USERS\.DEFAULT\Software\Microsoft\Mail subkey. In HKEY_CURRENT_USER, this entry is deleted after the user first runs Mail.

Default: 1 (yes)

Multi-Message   REG_SZ   *0 or 1*

Defines the last setting chosen for the Print Multiple Notes On A Page check box in the Print dialog box, which appears when you print messages from Mail. Set this entry to 0 for that option to appear unchecked by default.

Default: 1 (That is, the check box is checked by default.)

NetBios   REG_SZ   *0 or 1*

Enables NetBIOS notification of new mail delivery. When NetBIOS notification is used, the Windows NT computer sending a mail message to another Windows NT computer sends a NetBIOS notification message to the destination computer to tell the Mail program running on that machine that a new mail message was sent to the computer. The Mail program on the destination computer can then check the workgroup postoffice for the new mail message. This entry set to 1 to enable NetBIOS notification also provides quicker response to the arrival of new mail from users on your local postoffice. If this entry is 0 to disable NetBIOS notification, the Mail client needs to regularly check for the arrival of new mail messages on the postoffice.

Default: 1

NewMsgsAtStartup   REG_SZ   *0 or 1*

Specifies whether Mail is to check for new mail messages in the foreground as soon as the user logs in. Set this entry to 1 to have Mail download new messages as quickly as possible when it is started. If this entry is 0, Mail checks for new messages in the background (as is usually the case when the Mail application is being used).

Default: 0

NextOnMoveDelete   REG_SZ   *0 or 1 or –1*

If this entry is 1, Mail automatically opens the next message in a folder after you delete or move an open message. If set to –1, mail automatically opens the previous message. This facilitates quick scanning through the Inbox. If set to 0, Mail closes the Read Note window after you move or delete the message, and you must press ENTER or double-click to open the next message. Use 1 for messages sorted in ascending order (in the order received) and –1 for messages sorted in descending order (most recent message first).

Default: 1

NormalFont   REG_SZ   *facename, size, 0 or 1, 0 or 1*

Identifies the default font (normally proportionally spaced) used to display Mail messages. This entry has four parts, each separated by a comma: typeface name (not the font file name), point size, flag for bold, and flag for italic. The Change Font command in the View menu toggles between the Normal font and the Fixed font. The latter is useful for viewing messages that were created using a fixed-pitch font. Both entries affect only message body text, not the message envelope text or folder lists; Mail uses Helv 8 for that purpose.

Default: Helv, 10, 0, 0 (The FontSubstitutes subkey defines the mapping of the Helv font to a font present on the local computer.)

NoServerOptions   REG_SZ   *0 or 1*

If this entry is 1, the Server button in the Mail Options dialog box is unconditionally disabled. On the Mail server, this button calls up another dialog box that enables the user to relocate the .MMF file. Together with the **LocalMMF** entry, this entry prevents .MMF files from being stored on the postoffice.

Default: 0

OfflineMessages   REG_SZ   *Pathname*

Defines the file location when you choose to store your message file somewhere other than the postoffice. When you start up without connecting to the postoffice, this entry locates the file quickly (without presenting a File Browse dialog box). The entry is removed when you store your message file at the postoffice.

Note If you start online and your .MMF file is not on the postoffice, this entry is not used. Use the Mail Server Options dialog box to move your .MMF file.

Default: The path specified in the Mail Options Server dialog for a local message file.

Microsoft Mail Entries

OldStorePath   REG_SZ   *Pathname*

Contains the original path to a file that was originally stored in a place other than the postoffice. This entry is written temporarily by the Mail transport while you are moving your message file (using the Mail Options Server dialog box). This entry is removed after the move completes successfully and only appears if the system crashes during a move.

Password   REG_SZ   *password*

Use this entry and the **Login** entry to provide Mail with your account information, without being required to type this information into the Mail Sign In dialog box each time. If there is no password, leave the value for this entry blank, but do not omit the entry. Omitting the entry means you want to type your password each time in the Mail Sign In dialog box when you start Mail.

Default: (blank)—you are prompted for a password by the Mail program.

PollingInterval   REG_SZ   *minutes*

Gives the default for the Check for New Mail Every *n* Minutes option in the Mail Options dialog box. The value the user enters in the dialog box is written to the user's mail message file (.MMF)—this value is used to define how often the Mail spooler checks for new mail messages.

Default: 10

Printer   REG_SZ   *printer name, driver name, port*

This is the printer that appears in the Mail Print dialog box and is used by Mail when printing messages.

Default: the default printer specified in Print Manager

PumpCycleInterval   REG_SZ   *seconds*

Permits the spooler to check for new mail more often than once per minute, or to override the polling interval value defined in the user's mail message file.

Default: 60 seconds, or the number of minutes specified in the Mail Options dialog box

ReplyPrefix   REG_SZ   *String*

If this entry is present, Mail distinguishes your comments from the original message when you reply to mail. When you reply, the original message text is copied to the body of the reply message, and each line of the original is prefixed with the string specified by this entry. If the string contains a space, enclose it within double quotation marks (for example, "| "—a vertical bar followed by a space).

Default: (blank)

ScanAgainInterval   REG_SZ   *seconds*

Affects the mail spooler latency checking to prevent spooler background processing from interfering unduly with foreground work. When the spooler defers work because of higher priority, interactive tasks, it rechecks the availability of the system at this interval.

Default: 2

Security   REG_SZ   *0 or 1*

If this entry is 1, Mail prompts for your password whenever its window is restored from its iconic state. That is, if Mail is minimized and you double-click on the icon, you must re-enter your password before you (or anyone else) can see your messages.

Default: 0

ServerPassword   REG_SZ   *password*

Identifies the password used to connect to the server specified by the **ServerPath** entry. This entry should be used to specify the password for the file share if the form of the **ServerPath** entry is specified using the universal naming conventions (UNC) and the server, share, or the path name contains spaces. If this entry is present, the value for the **ServerPath** entry is interpreted literally, and any spaces present in the value for the entry is used when dynamically connecting to the workgroup postoffice.

If the **ServerPassword** entry is used, do not specify a password for the **ServerPath** entry (the password will be misinterpreted, and the resulting path to the workgroup postoffice will be invalid). The **ServerPassword** entry is written by the Mail program when connecting for the first time to the workgroup postoffice and is stored in the Microsoft Mail key file in encrypted format. Do not change this entry.

ServerPath   REG_SZ   *Pathname*
ServerPath   REG_SZ   *\\server\share\path password*
ServerPath   REG_SZ   *server/share:path*

If this entry is present, Mail searches for the postoffice in the specified directory. The first form, with a normal path name, works on all networks—the connection to the file share containing the network postoffice must be made before running the Mail program. The second form (UNC) works only on Windows NT and on Microsoft networks and compatibles. If you use the UNC form, Mail connects dynamically (without using a drive) to the file server where the postoffice resides. (If the specified UNC name contains any spaces, the password for the share needs to be specified for the **ServerPassword** entry.) The third form works only on Novell NetWare networks and uses an unused drive letter to connect dynamically to the NetWare file server where the postoffice resides. If no value is specified for the **ServerPath** entry, Mail asks the user for a path to the workgroup postoffice and writes a new value for this entry.

SharedExtensionsDir   REG_SZ   *Pathname*
SharedExtensionsDir   REG_SZ   *\\server\share\path password*

If this entry is present, Mail searches for shared custom commands and messages in the specified directory. The SHARED32.INI file in that directory identifies the shared extensions to load. Additional extensions can be entered in the Microsoft Mail key. Administrators often provide a common share point for extensions to Mail to simplify updating the extensions, and this entry makes it work. The first form with a normal path name works on all networks. The second form works only on Windows NT and on Microsoft networks and compatibles. If the second form is used, Mail connects dynamically (without using a drive) to the file server where the shared extensions reside.

Default: (blank)

SharedFolders   REG_SZ   *0 or 1*

Enables the use of Mail shared folders. If this entry is 1, the user can access shared folders. If this entry is 0, shared folders are unavailable to the user.

Default: 1

SpoolerBackoffInterval   REG_SZ   *milliseconds*

Specifies the amount of time the mail spooler waits before retrying an operation that has failed because of a transient mail server error condition, such as a locked file.

Default: 2000 (two seconds)

SpoolerReconnectInterval   REG_SZ   *seconds*

Specifies the amount of time the mail spooler waits before retrying an operation that has failed because of a fatal mail server error condition, such as a lost network connection.

Default: 60 (one minute)

StripGatewayHeaders   REG_SZ   *0 or 1*

If this entry is 1, message header text that appears above the dashed line is stripped from PC Mail messages that arrive via a gateway. Set this value to 0 if you want to see the extended information supplied by the gateways, which typically includes items such as message identifiers specific to the foreign mail system.

Message header text supplied by native PC Mail clients is always stripped. Only the PC Mail transport supports this entry.

Default: 1 (That is, you don't see gateway information.)

WG   REG_SZ   *0 or 1*

Specifies whether the version of the Mail program running on the computer is the Mail program provided with Windows NT. This entry is used internally by the Mail application and is written by the Mail program when it is executed.

Default: 1

Window   REG_SZ   *Left Top Right Bottom Zoom Toolbar Statusbar Scrollbars*

Specifies the zero-relative position within its menu where the main Mail window is to appear. This entry consists of eight numbers that govern the display of the main Mail window. This information is written when you exit Mail, and the changes you made while Mail was running are lost.

The format for this entry is as follows:

Value	Definition
Left Top Right Bottom	The first four numbers are pixel coordinates for the four sides of the main window in this order: left, top, right, and bottom.
Zoom	The zoom value is: 1 main window is in a normal (restored) state 2 maximized (zoomed) 3 minimized (by icon)
Toolbar Statusbar Scrollbars	Determines when the toolbar, status bar, and scroll bars are displayed on the main window: 0 corresponding bar is not displayed 1 bar is displayed

Microsoft Mail Entries

Default: window size and location determined by Windows NT, zoom state normal (restored), toolbar on, status bar on, scroll bars on.

MMF Entries for Mail

Most entries under this key affect automatic compression of the Mail message file, which by default has the filename extension of .MMF. When enabled, automatic compression uses idle time on your PC to recover disk space freed by the deleted messages and returns the disk space to the file system. You should not need to change the default values for entries in this subkey.

This is the Registry path for this subkey:

`HKEY_CURRENT_USER\Software\Microsoft\Mail\MMF`

Kb_Free_Start_Compress   REG_SZ   *kilobytes*
Background compression starts when at least this much recoverable space is detected in your message file. Both **Percent_Free_Start_Compress** and this entry are always active. The first entry to trigger starts the compression.
Default: 300

Kb_Free_Stop_Compress   REG_SZ   *kilobytes*
Background compression stops when there is less than the indicated amount of recoverable space in your message file. This avoids the unnecessary difficulty in trying to recover the last little bit of free space. Both this entry and **Percent_Free_Stop_Compress** are always active. The first entry to trigger stops the compression.
Default: 100.

No_Compress   REG_SZ   *0 or 1*
Specifies whether background compression is to be disabled. A value of 1 disables background compression of the .MMF message store.
Default: 0 (That is, background compression is enabled.)

Percent_Free_Start_Compress   REG_SZ   *percent*
Background compression starts when the amount of recoverable space rises above this percentage of the total file size. Both **Kb_Free_Start_Compress** and this entry are always active. The first one to trigger starts the compression.
Default: 10

Percent_Free_Stop_Compress   REG_SZ   *percent*

Background compression stops when the amount of recoverable space falls
below this percentage of the total .MMF file size. Both this entry and
Kb_Free_Stop_Compress are always active. The last one to trigger stops the
compression.

Default: 5

Secs_Till_Fast_Compress   REG_SZ   *seconds*

The background compression algorithm has a fast mode and a slow mode.
Background compression begins in the slow mode to avoid slowing system
response time. After a number of seconds of system inactivity indicated by this
entry, the compression switches to fast mode. Any user activity changes the
setting back to slow mode.

Default: 600 seconds (That is, ten minutes of system inactivity.)

See also the entry for **AppInit_DLLs** in "Windows Software Registration
Entries."

Mac FileTypes Entries for Mail

Entries in this subkey map the Macintosh file type and creator tags to MS-DOS
eight-plus-three filenames. This is the Registry path for this subkey:

```
HKEY_CURRENT_USER\Software\Microsoft\Mail\Mac FileTypes
```

Mail uses these entry values to determine what application to launch on a file
attachment that has been sent from a Macintosh mail client. There are two
alternate forms for the entries:

```
creator:type=extension      or      :type=extension
```

Both the creator and type are sequences of four characters (possibly including
blanks). For example,

```
:TEXT=DOC
```

launches the application associated with the extension .DOC (Word for Windows,
for example) on any Macintosh file of type TEXT.

MS Proofing Tools Entries for Mail

The MS Proofing Tools subkey defines spelling values for Mail. This is the Registry path for this subkey:

```
HKEY_CURRENT_USER\Software\Microsoft\Mail\MS Proofing Tools
```

CustomDict   **REG_SZ**   *entry name*

Specifies the name of an entry in the [MS Proofing Tools] section of the WIN.INI file. That entry in turn gives the fully qualified path to a file containing your custom dictionary. The custom dictionary contains spellings not found in the standard dictionary but that were added using the Add button in the Spelling dialog box. This entry lets Mail take advantage of a custom dictionary you may have already created with another Microsoft application, such as Microsoft Word for Windows.

Default: (no default)

Spelling   **REG_SZ**   *keyname*

Specifies the name of an entry in the MS Proofing Tools subkey that defines filenames for the spelling checker DLL and dictionary. The entries for **Spelling** are in this format:

```
Spelling NNNN,M
```

There is no space after the comma. In this format, *NNNN* is the four-digit language identifier of the current Windows NT version as defined in the Control\NLS\Language subkey, and *M* is the spelling dictionary type.

The Registry path for the key that this entry refers to is the following, by default:

```
HKEY_CURRENT_USER\Software\Microsoft\Mail\MS Proofing Tools
```

This subkey contains an entry in the following form:

Spelling *NNNN*,0   **REG_SZ**   *DLLfilename, Dictionary filename*

Specifies the fully qualified path to the spelling checker DLL and dictionary. This entry lets Mail use the same dictionary you may already be using with another Microsoft application, such as Microsoft Word for Windows. Windows NT does supply a dictionary.

Default: MSPELL32.DLL,MSP32_*XX*.LEX (In these values, *XX* is usually the two letters identifying the language version of Windows NT defined in the DosKeybCodes subkey, as described in "Keyboard Layout Entries," earlier in this chapter.)

Providers Entries for Mail

Entries in the Providers subkey for Mail define settings that service providers use with Microsoft Mail front-end programs. For this release, there are service providers for Microsoft Mail for PC LANs. Service providers for other mail systems may be available later.

This is the Registry path for this subkey:

```
HKEY_CURRENT_USER\Software\Microsoft\Mail\Providers
```

Logon   **REG_SZ**   *DLL name*

Identifies a single DLL that contains the logon and session management code for your mail system. This value is often, but not necessarily, the same as the **Transport** and **Name** entries. This value is the base name of the DLL, without the .DLL filename extension, but include a path if the DLL is not in a directory on the user's path or in the directory containing the Mail executable file.

Default: MSSFS32

Name   **REG_SZ**   *DLL name*

Identifies one or more DLLs that contain functions required to browse system and personal user lists. One of the values is often, but not necessarily, the same as the **Logon** and **Transport** entries. Enter the base name of the DLL, without the .DLL filename extension, but include a path if the DLL is not in a directory on the user's path or in the directory containing the Mail executable file.

The order of providers in this entry is significant. When Mail is attempting to resolve ambiguous names typed in a message and finds an exact match in the first provider in the list, it will not go on to query the rest. Placing the personal address book provider first can save time in that process.

Default: MSSFS32 PABNSP32

SharedFolders   **REG_SZ**   *DLL name*

Identifies a single DLL that contains functions required to read and write messages in Microsoft PC Mail shared folders.

Default: MSSFS32 (It is unlikely that any DLL other than MSSFS will have this functionality.)

Transport   **REG_SZ**   *DLL name*

Identifies a single DLL that contains the functions necessary to send and receive mail on your mail system. It is often, but not necessarily, the same as the **Logon** and **Name** entries. Enter the base name of the DLL, without the .DLL filename extension, but include a path if the DLL is not in a directory on the user's path or in the directory containing the Mail executable file.

Default: MSSFS32

Registry Entries for Microsoft Schedule+

The settings used by Microsoft Schedule+ to track basic information about the user's schedule, such as display and general option settings, current window positions, and printer information are stored under the following key:

HKEY_CURRENT_USER\Software\Microsoft\Schedule+

The Schedule+ key contains the following subkeys:

Subkey	Purpose
Microsoft Schedule	Defines the appearance and behavior of Schedule+.
Microsoft Schedule+ Appt Books	Indicates the number and list of other users' Appointment Books that were open when you exited Schedule+.
Microsoft Schedule+ Archives	Indicates the number and list of Archive files that were open when you exited Schedule+.
Microsoft Schedule+ Exporters	Specifies DLL filenames for exporters.
Microsoft Schedule+ Importers	Specifies DLL filenames for importers.

Most of these entries have built-in defaults. You should not need to change the Schedule+ settings. To change the appearance and behavior of Schedule+, use the appropriate Schedule+ menu commands. Many values are for saving settings between sessions.

These keys are created in HKEY_CURRENT_USER when you first run Schedule+. If your system previously contained a Windows for MS-DOS version of SCHDPLUS.INI, the contents are migrated to the Registry when you first run Schedule+ under Windows NT.

Microsoft Schedule+ Entries

This key defines the appearance and behavior of Microsoft Schedule+. This is the Registry path for this subkey:

```
HKEY_CURRENT_USER\Software\Microsoft\Schedule+\Microsoft Schedule+
```

This key also appears under HKEY_USERS\.DEFAULT, but its only contents are **MigrateIni and MigrateIniPrint.**

These are the value entries that can appear in this key:

AppointmentView   REG_SZ   *state left top right bottom*
Specifies the state (1=normal, 2=maximized, 3=iconic) and the coordinates for the position of the Appointment Book window on the screen. These five numbers are written by the Schedule+ application when you exit and are used to restore the window to the last displayed position. The coordinates are pixel coordinates for the four sides of the Appointment Book window.

AppPath   REG_SZ   *Pathname*
Specifies the location of the Schedule+ program and execution files. Microsoft Mail uses this path to find Schedule+ when you receive a meeting request.
Default: *SystemRoot*\SYSTEM32 directory

ApptBookColor   REG_SZ   *colornumber(1-17)*
Specifies the preference setting for the background color of the Appointment Book. The color number corresponds (in order) to the colors shown in the Display dialog box available from the Options menu, as follows:

1=Black	7=Red	13=Bright green
2=White	8=Violet	14=Bright blue-green
3=Yellow	9=Khaki	15=Bright red
4=Blue	10=Dark gray	16=Bright violet
5=Green	11=Light gray	17= Bright yellow
6=Blue-green	12=Bright blue	

Default: 3 (Yellow)

ApptBookLinesColor   REG_SZ   *colornumber(1-17)*
Specifies the preference setting for the color of the lines in the Appointment Book. The color number corresponds to nondithered colors in the Display dialog box available from the Options menu (as described in the **ApptBookColor** entry).
Default: 1 (Black)

CopyTime   REG_SZ   *minutes*

Specifies the time interval that Schedule+ copies your online .CAL file to your local .CAL file (occurs in idle time).

Default: 15 minutes

CreateFileFirstTime   REG_SZ   *0 or 1*

Specifies whether an online calendar (.CAL) file should be created for a first-time Schedule+ user. If this entry is 1, an online calendar (.CAL) file is created the first time a user signs on to Schedule+. If 0 (as set automatically the first time you run Schedule+), an online calendar file is not created automatically.

Default: 0

DefaultPrinter   REG_SZ   *printer name, driver name, port*

Indicates the current default printer port and its network path as specified in Print Manager. This is the default printer Schedule+ uses for printing schedule information.

DefaultRemindAgain   REG_SZ   *0 or 1*

Defines the default state of the Remind Again check box. If this entry is 1, you are reminded again of your appointments at the requested intervals. If this entry is 0, you are reminded of your appointment only once.

Default: 0

DefaultRemindAgainAmount   REG_SZ   *timeunits*

Specifies the default number of time units to wait (interval) before reminding you of appointments again.

Default: 5

DefaultRemindAgainUnits   REG_SZ   *minutes, hours, days, weeks, or months*

Specifies the type of time units used in the **DefaultRemindAgainAmount** entry.

Default: minutes

DemosEnabled   REG_SZ   *0 or 1*

Specifies whether the Demos menu option is to be displayed in the Help menu. If the entry is 1, the Demos menu option is displayed in Help menu. If this entry is 0, the Demos menu option is not shown.

Default: 0 (The Schedule+ demos are not provided with Windows NT.)

ExportNoNotes   REG_SZ   *0 or 1*

Indicates whether the user chose to export notes. If this entry is 0, notes are exported. If this entry is 1, the notes are not exported.

Default: 0

Microsoft Schedule+ Entries

ExportRange   **REG_SZ**   *0 or 1*

Indicates the range of schedule information to be exported. If this entry is 0, the entire schedule file is exported. If this entry is 1, a particular range is exported.

ExportType   **REG_SZ**   *0 or 1*

Indicates the current default file type for exporting your schedule. If this entry is 0, the default file type for exporting your schedule is the Schedule+ format. If the entry is 1, the file type for export is Text.

Default: 0

ImportDoNotAddDuplicates   **REG_SZ**   *0 or 1*

Indicates whether the user chose to import duplicate appointments. If this entry is 0, duplicate appointments are imported. If this entry is 1, your duplicate appointments are not imported.

Default: 0

ImportDoNotAskAboutConflicts   **REG_SZ**   *0 or 1*

Indicates whether the user chose to be asked about conflicting appointments during the import process. If this entry is 0, you are prompted for each conflicting appointment during the import process—in this case, you are asked whether to add each conflicting appointment. A value of 1 indicates that you are not asked about conflicts; they are added automatically.

Default: 0

ImportType   **REG_SZ**   *0 or 1*

Indicates the current default file type for importing a schedule file. If this entry is 0, the file type for importing your schedule is the Schedule+ format. If the entry is 1, the file type is the Windows NT Calendar format.

Default: 0

LargeFont   **REG_SZ**   *0 or 1*

Specifies the preference setting for the font size of text displayed in the Appointment Book and Planner. If this entry is 1, the font size of text is 10 points. If this entry is 0, the font is 8 points.

Default: 0

LocalPath   **REG_SZ**   *Pathname*

Specifies the location of the last user's local calendar (.CAL) file.

LocalUser   **REG_SZ**   *username*

Specifies the name of the last user to use the Schedule+ software on this computer.

MainWindow   **REG_SZ**   *state left top right bottom*

Specifies the state (1=normal, 2=maximized, 3=iconic) and the coordinates for the position of the Schedule+ application window on the screen. These five numbers are written by the Schedule+ application when you exit, and are used to restore the Schedule+ window to the last displayed position. The coordinates are pixel coordinates for the four sides of the main window.

MigrateIni   **REG_SZ**   *0 or 1*

Specifies whether to migrate the Schedule+ .INI files created by a Windows for MS-DOS version of Schedule+ for use under Windows NT. This entry is saved in the HKEY_USERS\.DEFAULT\Software\Microsoft\Mail subkey. In HKEY_CURRENT_USER, this entry is deleted after the user first runs Mail.

Default: 1 (yes)

MigrateIniPrint   **REG_SZ**   *0 or 1*

Specifies whether to migrate the Schedule+ .INI print information created by a Windows for MS-DOS version of Schedule+ for use under Windows NT. This entry is saved in the HKEY_USERS\.DEFAULT\Software\Microsoft\Mail subkey. In HKEY_CURRENT_USER, this entry is deleted after the user first runs Mail.

Default: 1 (yes)

NoStatusBar   **REG_SZ**   *0 or 1*

Indicates the preference setting for displaying the status bar. If this entry is 1, status bar is not displayed. If set to 0, the status bar is displayed.

Default: 0

OtherColor   **REG_SZ**   *colornumber(1-17)*

Specifies the preference setting for the color of other users' appointments in the Planner. The color number corresponds to nondithered colors in the Display dialog box available from the Options menu (as described in the **ApptBookColor** entry).

Default: 7 (Red)

PageBackgroundColor   **REG_SZ**   *colornumber(1-17)*

Specifies the preference setting for the background color of the Schedule+ window. The color number corresponds to nondithered colors in the Display dialog box available from the Options menu (as described in the **ApptBookColor** entry).

Default: 11 (Gray)

PlannerColor   REG_SZ   *colornumber(1-17)*

Specifies the preference setting for the background color of the Planner window. The color number corresponds to colors in the Display dialog box available from the Options menu (as described in the **ApptBookColor** entry).

Default: 2 (White)

PlannerLinesColor   REG_SZ   *colornumber(1-17)*

Specifies the preference setting for the color of the lines in the Planner. The color number corresponds to nondithered colors in the Display dialog box available from the Options menu (as described in the **ApptBookColor** entry).

Default: 1 (Black)

PollTime   REG_SZ   *centiseconds*

Specifies the frequency for checking the server for schedule file changes.

Default: 6000 centiseconds (one minute)

ReminderPollTime   REG_SZ   *minutes*

Specifies the frequency for polling the server for alarm changes.

Default: 15

RequestSummary   REG_SZ   *state left top right bottom*

Specifies the state (1=normal, 2=maximized, 3=iconic) and the coordinates for the position of the Messages window on the screen. These five numbers are written by the Schedule+ application when you exit and are used to restore the Messages window to the last displayed position. The coordinates are pixel coordinates for the four sides of the Messages window.

ShowActiveTasks   REG_SZ   *0 or 1*

Indicates whether the Task list is showing all tasks or only active tasks, as specified from the Tasks menu. If only active tasks are displayed, this value is 1.

Default: 0 (That is, all tasks are displayed.)

StartupOffline   REG_SZ   *0 or 1*

Specifies whether Schedule+ should start up using the offline scheduling information, or whether the online schedule should be used. If this entry is 1, Schedule+ is started offline.

Default: 0 (That is, Schedule+ is started online.)

TaskSortOrder   REG_SZ   *0, 1, 2, –1, –2, or –3*

Specifies the current sort order for tasks, according to the following:

Value	Meaning
0	Tasks are sorted by priority.
1	Tasks are sorted by due date.
2	Tasks are sorted by description.
–1	Tasks are sorted by reverse description.
–2	Tasks are sorted by reverse due date.
–3	Tasks are sorted by reverse priority.

Default: 0

TaskSortSecond   REG_SZ   *0, 1, 2, –1, –2, or –3*

Specifies the secondary sort order for tasks. If this entry is 0, the second sort order is by priority; if 1 the second sort order, using the same values as specified for **TaskSortOrder**.

Default: 0

UpdatePostOfficeTime   REG_SZ   *centiseconds*

Specifies the frequency for updating the postoffice on the server after a change is made.

Default: 6000 centiseconds (one minute)

UserColor   REG_SZ   *colornumber(1-17)*

Specifies the preference setting for the color of your own appointments in the Planner. The color number corresponds to nondithered colors in the Display dialog box available from the Options menu (as described in the **ApptBookColor** entry).

Default: 4 (Blue)

ViewNotByProject   REG_SZ   *0 or 1*

Indicates whether the tasks in the Task list are currently displayed by project. If this entry is 1, the tasks are not displayed by project.

Default: 0

WindowOrder   REG_SZ   *0 1 or 1 0*

Indicates the current display order of Schedule+ windows. The Schedule+ window is represented by 0, and the Messages window is 1. The first value for the **WindowOrder** entry indicates the window on top, and the second entry identifies the window behind the top window.

Default: 0 1

Microsoft Schedule+ Appt Books Entries

Schedule+ uses this subkey to track the Appointment books of other Schedule+ users that you had open when you exited Schedule+. The following is the Registry path for this subkey:

```
HKEY_CURRENT_USER\Software\Microsoft
    \Schedule+\Microsoft Schedule+ Appt Books
```

Count   REG_SZ   *number*

Indicates the number of other users' Appointment Books you had open when you exited Schedule+. More entries appear in this subkey when the number is nonzero.

Microsoft Schedule+ Archives Entries

Schedule+ uses this subkey to track the Archive files that you had open when you exited Schedule+. This is the Registry path for this subkey:

```
HKEY_CURRENT_USER\Software\Microsoft
    \Schedule+\Microsoft Schedule+ Archives
```

Count   REG_SZ   *number*

Indicates the number of Archive files you had open when you exited Schedule+. More entries appear in this subkey when the number is nonzero.

Microsoft Schedule+ Exporter Entries

Schedule+ uses this subkey to specify settings for exporters. This is the Registry path for this subkey:

```
HKEY_CURRENT_USER\Software\Microsoft
    \Schedule+\Microsoft Schedule+ Exporters
```

Key   REG_SZ   *DLL name*

Identifies a single exporter DLL for Schedule+. The available files can be found on CompuServe. The *Key* name of this entry can be any string.

Microsoft Schedule+ Importer Entries

Schedule+ uses this subkey to specify settings for importers. This is the Registry path for this subkey:

```
HKEY_CURRENT_USER\Software\Microsoft
    \Schedule+\Microsoft Schedule+ Importers
```

Key **REG_SZ**   *DLL name*

Identifies a single importer DLL for Schedule+. The available files can be found on CompuServe. The *Key* name of this entry can be any string.

Registry Entries for User Preferences

Information about Registry entries for user preferences about the following topics can be found in this section:

Hive information for user profiles	International
Console	Keyboard and keyboard layout
Colors, patterns, and screen savers	Mouse
Cursors	Multimedia and sound
Desktop	Network
Environment variables	Program Manager
File Manager	Windows

The information presented here is primarily for troubleshooting, showing the default entry values and explaining the meaning of important entries. There are no hidden values that you can set for user preferences. All of these values can be set using the icons in Control Panel or the tools in the Administrative Tools group, or other programs provided with Windows NT.

All Registry paths shown here are for HKEY_CURRENT_USER, to show how you can view entries for the currently logged on user. However, most of these entries also appear in HKEY_USERS\.DEFAULT, where changing entries will change values for the default user profile.

Hive Information for User Profiles

Information about user profile files appears in the following keys:

- The HiveList subkey lists all hives that are active but not profiles that are not active. (See its entry in "CurrentControlSet\Control Subkeys," earlier in this chapter.)

- The ProfileList subkey lists all the profiles known on the computer, whether or not the profiles are active, under the following Registry path:

```
HKEY_LOCAL_MACHINE\SOFTWARE\Microsoft\Windows NT\CurrentVersion
     \ProfileList\SID_#
```

Each installed user profile has its own subkey under the ProfileList subkey, and that subkey contains the following entry:

ProfileImagePath   REG_EXPAND_SZ   *Profile hive filename*
Specifies the path and filename for the hive for this user. The hive file name that is the value for **ProfileImagePath** includes a portion of the username associated with that *SID_#*, so that you can identify the user to which it belongs.

Default: *%SystemRoot%\system32\config\hiveFilename*

Sid   REG_BINARY   *Number assigned by system*

Console Entries for Users

The Console key contains several subkeys that define screen size and buffer size for character-based screens in Windows NT. These subkeys appear under the following Registry path:

```
HKEY_CURRENT_USER\Console\subkeyNames
```

The Command Prompt subkey does not appear unless the current user has changed the screen colors or font for the command prompt and also checked the Save Configuration options. Use the commands on the Control menu in the command prompt to change these values.

Console subkey	Default value entries
Command Prompt (All data types are REG_DWORD)	**FontFamily**=0x30 **FontSize**=0xc0008 **FullScreen**=0x1 **PopupColors**=0xf5 **QuickEdit**=0 **ScreenBufferSize**=0x190050 **ScreenColors**=0x9f **WindowsPosition**=0x150004 **WindowSize**=0x190050
Configuration (All data types are REG_SZ)	**CommandRecallBufferSize**=50 **FillAttr**=0x07 **ScreenBufferColumns**=80 **ScreenBufferRows**=25 **WindowColumns**=80 **WindowRows**=25
Introducing Windows NT	**FullScreen**=0x1
Microsoft QBASIC	**FullScreen**=0x1

Color, Pattern, and Screen Saver Entries for Users

This section describes the subkeys that contain settings for user preferences related to the desktop.

Colors Entry Values

The Colors subkey specifies the color as a series of three numbers for each area of the Windows screen, in the following Registry path:

```
HKEY_CURRENT_USER\Control Panel\Colors
```

Each entry has a REG_SZ data type. The following lists the defaults for each entry under the Colors subkey:

ActiveBorder=192 192 192
ActiveTitle=0 0 128
AppWorkSpace=255 255 255
Background=255 255 255
ButtonFace=192 192 192
ButtonHilight=255 255 255
ButtonShadow=128 128 128
ButtonText=0 0 0

GrayText=128 128 128
Hilight=0 0 128
HilightText=255 255 255
InactiveBorder=192 192 192
InactiveTitle=192 192 192
InactiveTitleText=0 0 0
Menu=255 255 255
MenuText=0 0 0
Scrollbar=192 192 192
TitleText=255 255 255
Window=255 255 255
WindowFrame=0 0 0
WindowText=0 0 0

Color Schemes Entry Values

The entries in the Color Schemes subkey define the colors for each element of specific color schemes, as set by choosing the Color icon in Control Panel. These entries appear under the following Registry path:

```
HKEY_CURRENT_USER\Control Panel\Color Schemes
```

The Current subkey specifies the current color scheme, based on those listed in the Color Schemes subkey.

The Custom Colors subkey defines the custom colors in the color palette, as set by choosing the Color icon in Control Panel. The entries are designated ColorA through ColorP, and all have the value FFFFFF by default.

Each entry in these subkeys has a REG_SZ data type.

Patterns Entry Values

The Patterns subkey contains entries that define the color values for the bitmap patterns, as set by choosing the Desktop icon. Each value is a set of eight numbers, corresponding to the colors in the eight basic elements of the pattern.

Each entry has a REG_SZ data type.

Screen Saver Subkey Entry Values

The various *Screen Saver* subkeys define user preferences for specific screen savers. All entries have a REG_SZ data type. The following table summarizes the default entries under the *Screen Saver* subkeys.

Screen Save subkey	Default value entries
Screen Saver.Bezier	—
Screen Saver.Marquee	**BackgroundColor**=0 0 128 **CharSet**=0 **Font**=Times New Roman **Mode**=1 **Size**=24 **Speed**=14 **Text**=Your text goes here. **TextColor**=255 0 255
Screen Saver.Mystify	**Active1**=1 **Active2**=1 **Clear Screen**=1 **EndColor1**=255 255 255 **EndColor2**=255 255 255 **Lines1**=7 **Lines2**=12 **StartColor1**=0 0 0 **StartColor2**=0 0 0 **WalkRandom1**=1 **WalkRandom2**=1
Screen Saver.Stars	**Density**=50 **WarpSpeed**=10

Additional screen saver settings are defined in the Desktop subkey, described later in this section.

Cursors Entry Values for Users

The Cursor subkey contains entries that specify the .ANI or .CUR files containing custom cursors defined using the Cursor icon in Control Panel. There are no entries in this key unless the user changes cursor styles in Control Panel. All data types are REG_SZ. The following lists the names for possible default entries:

AppStarting	**No**	**SizeNWSE**
Arrow	**SizeAll**	**SizeWE**
CrossHair	**SizeNESW**	**Wait**
IBeam	**SizeNS**	

Desktop Entry Values for Users

The Desktop key contains entries that control the appearance of the screen background and the position of windows and icons on the screen. The following shows the Registry path:

```
HKEY_CURRENT_USER\Control Panel\Desktop
```

To change most of these entries, use the Desktop icon in Control Panel. The Desktop subkey can contain the following entries:

BorderWidth   REG_SZ   *number*

Sets the width of the borders around all the windows that have sizable borders. The possible range is 1 (narrowest) to 49 (widest).

Default: 3

CoolSwitch   REG_SZ   *Boolean*

Turns fast task switching on or off. To change this entry, choose the Desktop icon from Control Panel, and check or clear the Fast ALT+TAB Switching option in the Task List dialog box.

Default: 1

CursorBlinkRate   REG_SZ   *milliseconds*

Indicates how much time elapses between each blink of the selection cursor.

Default: 530

GridGranularity   REG_SZ   *number*

Specifies the size of the grid used to position windows on the screen. The possible range is 0 through 49, in units of 8 pixels.

Default: 0

IconSpacing   REG_SZ   *pixels*

Specifies the number of pixels that appear horizontally between icons. A larger number increases the space between icons.

Default: 75

IconTitleFaceName   REG_SZ   *fontname*

Specifies the font used to display icon titles. Change this value if the icon title is difficult to read.

Default: Helv

IconTitleSize   REG_SZ   *number*

Specifies the size of the font used to display icon titles. Change this value if the icon title is difficult to read.

Default: 9

IconTitleStyle   REG_SZ   *Boolean*

Default: 0

IconTitleWrap   REG_SZ   *Boolean*

Specifies whether to wrap icon titles. A value of 1 allows icon title wrapping and increases icon vertical spacing by three lines; 0 turns off icon title wrapping.

Default: 1

Pattern   REG_SZ   *b1 b2 b3 b4 b5 b6 b7 b8*

Specifies a pattern for the screen background. The 8 numeric values define a bitmap 8 pixels wide and 8 pixels high. Each decimal value represents a byte, and each byte represents a row of 8 pixels, where 0 sets the corresponding pixel to the background color, and 1 sets the corresponding pixel to the foreground color (specified by the **Background** and **WindowText** values in the Colors subkey, respectively).

For example, if you set the *b1* value to the decimal value 175, the top row of pixels in the bitmap appears as the binary equivalent (10101111).

Default: (None) (This string appears when no pattern is specified.)

ScreenSaveActive   REG_SZ   *Boolean*

Specifies whether a screen saver should be displayed if the system is not actively being used. Set this value to 1 to use a screen saver; 0 turns off the screen saver.

Default: 0

ScreenSaverIsSecure   REG_SZ   *Boolean*

Specifies whether a password is assigned to the screen saver.

Default: 0

ScreenSaveTimeOut   REG_SZ   *seconds*

Specifies the amount of time that the system must be idle before the screen saver appears.

Default: 900

SCRNSAVE.EXE   REG_SZ   *Filename*

Specifies the screen saver executable filename.

Default: (None)

TileWallpaper   REG_SZ   *Boolean*

Specifies that the desktop wallpaper is tiled across the screen if this value is 1, or centered if this value is 0.

Default: 0

Wallpaper   REG_SZ   *bitmap-filename*

Supplies the filename for the bitmap on the screen background. Include the path if the file is not in the *SystemRoot* or *SystemRoot*\SYSTEM32 directory.

Default: "(None)" (This string appears when no pattern is specified.)

Environment Variable Entries for Users

The Environment subkey contains the user environment variables, as defined by choosing the System icon in Control Panel. Changes to these variables take effect the next time a non-Windows NT–based application is run or the command prompt is used. These value entries are found under the following path:

```
HKEY_CURRENT_USER\Environment
```

The default is the environment variables defined in the user's profile at startup.

File Manager Entries for Users

This section describes settings for user preferences in File Manager.

File Manager Software Settings

The File Manager subkey under this Registry path contains the user preferences for the appearance of items in File Manager:

```
HKEY_CURRENT_USER\Software\Microsoft\File Manager\Settings
```

The following entries can appear. Most items have a default setting and do not appear unless the user makes changes in File Manager.

AddOns   REG_SZ   *Boolean*

Default: (none)

ConfirmDelete   REG_SZ   *Boolean*

Specifies whether the user is to be prompted to confirm file deletion requests.

Default: 1 (enabled)

ConfirmFormat   REG_SZ   *Boolean*

Specifies whether the user is to be prompted to confirm formatting requests.

Default: 1 (enabled)

ConfirmMouse   REG_SZ   *Boolean*

Specifies whether the user is to be prompted to confirm mouse drag-and-drop requests.

Default: 1 (enabled)

ConfirmReplace   REG_SZ   *Boolean*

Specifies whether the user is to be prompted to confirm file replacement requests.

Default: 1 (enabled)

ConfirmSubDel   REG_SZ   *Boolean*

Specifies whether the user is to be prompted to confirm subdirectory deletion requests.

Default: 1 (enabled)

ConfirmSystemHiddenReadOnly   REG_SZ   *Boolean*

Specifies whether the user is to be prompted to confirm for system, hidden, or read-only file changes.

Default: 1 (enabled)

dir1   REG_SZ   *Comma-separated list*

The current directory settings.

Default: 0,0,522,249,-1,-1,1,0,202,2033,261,C:\WINNT*.*

Face   REG_SZ   *Typeface*

Specifies the name of the typeface used for desktop items.

Default: MS Sans Serif.

FaceWeight   REG_SZ   *Number*

Specifies 700 for bold or bold italic, 400 for regular or italic.

LowerCase   REG_DWORD   *0, 1, 4, 8*

Specifies values for lowercase variables checked in the Fonts dialog box, as follows:

Value	Meaning
0	No options checked
0x1	Lowercase for FAT drives
0x4	Italic
0x8	Lowercase for all drives

NumButtons   REG_SZ   *Number*

Default: 15000000

File Manager Entries for Users

Size   REG_SZ   *Number*

The point size for the typeface.

Default: 8

ToolbarWindow   REG_SZ

Contains user-defined settings for the toolbar, as defined in the Options menu in File Manager.

Default:
CD000000CE000000FFFFFFFFFE000000FF000000FFFFFFFF91010000920
10000FFFFFFFF940100009501000096010000970100000FFFFFFFF52040000
FFFFFFFF6B0000006A0000006C000000FFFFFFFF5D020000

Window   REG_SZ   *Numbers*

Specifies the size and position of the window and whether it is maximized when opened. Use the mouse to move and size the window.

Default: 0,0,640,480, , ,2

Extensions Entries for Users

The Extensions subkey identifies personal preferences for document files with corresponding command lines, so that opening a document file in File Manager automatically starts the application. The extensions are found in the following Registry path:

```
HKEY_CURRENT_USER\Software\Microsoft\Windows NT\CurrentVersion
      \Extensions
```

The following default entries are defined. All have a REG_SZ data type.

bmp=pbrush.exe ^.bmp
crd=cardfile.exe ^.crd
ini=notepad.exe ^.ini
pcx=pbrush.exe ^.pcx
rec=recorder.exe ^.rec
trm=terminal.exe ^.trm
txt=notepad.exe ^.txt
wri=write.exe ^.wri

Note The extension information for all users can be viewed and modified in HKEY_CLASSES_ROOT. This is where you will find the file types and extension information for File Manager.

International Entry Values for Users

The International subkey describes how to display dates, times, currency, and other items for a specific country, under the following Registry path:

```
HKEY_CURRENT_USER\Control Panel\International
```

The International\Sorting Order key is not used in this version of Windows NT.

The following table summarizes entry values under this subkey. All data types are REG_SZ. To change any of these items, choose the International icon in Control Panel.

iCountry   **REG_SZ**   *country*

Specifies the country code. This number matches the country's international telephone code, except for Canada, which is 2. The U.S. English default is 1.

iCurrDigits   **REG_SZ**   *number*

Specifies the number of digits to put after the decimal separator in currency. The U.S. English default is 2.

iCurrency   **REG_SZ**   *number*

Specifies a positive currency format, where 0 = $2, 1 = 2$, 2 = $ 2, and 3 = 2 $. The U.S. English default is 0. The actual currency symbol is specified by the **sCurrency** value.

iDate   **REG_SZ**   *number*

Specifies a numerical date format for compatibility with Windows 2.x, where 0 = 12/31/90, 1 = 31/12/90, and 2 = 90/12/31. The U.S. English default is 0. The actual date divider is specified by the **sShortDate** value.

iDigits   **REG_SZ**   *number*

Specifies the number of digits to display after the decimal separator in numbers. The U.S. English default is 2.

iLZero   **REG_SZ**   *0 or 1*

Specifies whether to put leading zeros in decimal numbers, where 0 = .7 and 1 = 0.7. The U.S. English default is 1. The actual decimal separator is specified by the **sDecimal** value.

iMeasure   **REG_SZ**   *0 or 1*

Specifies the measurement system as metric or English, where 0 = metric and 1 = English. The U.S. English default is 1.

iNegCurr   REG_SZ   *number*

Specifies a negative number format, where:

0 = ($1)	4 = (1$)	8 = –1 $	12 = $ -1.1
1 = –$1	5 = –1$	9 = –$ 1	13 = 1.1- $
2 = $–1	6 = 1–$	10 = 1 $–	14 ($ 1.1)
3 = $1–	7 = 1$–	11 = $ 1–	15 = (1.1 $)

The U.S. English default is 1. The actual currency symbol is specified by the **sCurrency** value.

iTime   REG_SZ   *number*

Specifies whether to format time using a 12-hour or 24-hour clock, where 0 = 1:00 (12-hour clock) and 1 = 13:00 (24-hour clock). The U.S. English default is 0. The actual time separator is specified by the **sTime** value.

iTLZero   REG_SZ   *number*

Specifies whether to put leading zeros in time, where 0 = 9:15 and 1 = 09:15. The U.S. English default is 0. The actual time separator is specified by the **sTime** value.

Locale   REG_SZ   *number*

Specifies the current user's locale ID for the local language preferences, based on values defined in CurrentControlSet\Control\Nls\Language. The U.S. English default is 00000409.

s1159   REG_SZ   *string*

Specifies the time marker to use in time strings before noon in the 12-hour time format. The U.S. English default is AM.

s2359   REG_SZ   *string*

Specifies the time marker to use in time strings after noon in the 12-hour format or that follows all times in the 24-hour format. The U.S. English default is PM.

sCountry   REG_SZ   *string*

Specifies the name of the country whose standard value you want to use. The U.S. English default is United States.

sCurrency   **REG_SZ**   *string*

Specifies the currency symbol you want to use. The U.S. English default is $.

sDate   **REG_SZ**   *string*

Specifies the symbol separating numbers for the short date. The U.S. English default is /.

sDecimal   **REG_SZ**   *string*

Specifies the punctuation used to separate the fractional part of a decimal number from the whole number part. The U.S. English default is . (a period).

sLanguage   **REG_SZ**   *string*

Specifies the language you want to work in. Windows applications that provide language specific tasks, such as sorting or spell checking, use this entry. The U.S. English default is **enu**. Values for the locales supported for the first version of Windows NT are the following:

csy = Czech	frc = French (Canadian)
dan = Danish	frs = French (Swiss)
deu = German	hun = Hungarian
des = German (Swiss)	isl = Icelandic
dea = German (Austrian)	ita = Italian
ell = Greek	its = Italian (Swiss)
ena = English (Australia)	nlb = Dutch (Belgian)
enc = English (canada)	nld = Dutch
eng = English (U.K.)	non = Norwegian (Nynorsk)
eni = English (Irish)	nor = Norwegian (Bokmal)
enu = English (U.S.)	plk = Polish
enz = English (New Zealand)	ptb = Portuguese (Brazilian)
esm = Spanish (Mexican)	ptg = Portuguese
esn = Modern Spanish	rus = Russian
esp = Castilian Spanish	sky = Slovak
fin = Finnish	svc = Swedish
fra = French	trk = Turkish
frb = French (Belgian)	

sLiisl = Icelandic st   REG_SZ   *string*

ita = ItalianSpecifies the character used to separate items in a list. In U.S. English, the nld = Dutchmost common separator is a comma. The U.S. English default is , (comma).

sLonor = Norwegian ngDate   **REG_SZ**   *format*

ptg = Portuguese   Specifies your choices for the long date formats, including abbreviations for the sve = Swedish words and separators. Control Panel accepts only certain format combinations. Therefore, you should use Control Panel to change these entries. The U.S. English default is dddd, MMMM dd, yyyy (that is, Friday, June 1, 1990). Values are:

d = Day (1–31)
dd = Day (01–31)
ddd = Day (Mon–Sun)
dddd = Day (Monday–Sunday)
M = Month (1–12)
MM = Month (01–12)
MMM = Month (Jan–Dec)
MMMM = Month (January–December)
yy = Year (00–99)
yyyy = Year (1900–2040)

sShortDate   **REG_SZ**   *format*

Specifies a choice for the short date format, including abbreviations for the words and separators, according to the list described for **sLongDate**. Control Panel accepts only certain format combinations. Therefore, you should use Control Panel to change this setting. The U.S. English default is M/d/yy (that is, 6/1/90).

sThousand   **REG_SZ**   *string*

Specifies the symbol used to separate thousands. For example, if the value is a comma, the number appears as 3,000. The U.S. English default is , (comma).

sTime   **REG_SZ**   string

Specifies the character used to separate the hours, minutes, and seconds in time. For example, if the value is a colon, the time appears as 15:29:31. The U.S. English default is : (a colon).

Keyboard and Keyboard Layout Entries for Users

The Keyboard entry contains user preferences as defined by choosing the Keyboard icon in Control Panel. Entries are found under this Registry path:

```
HKEY_CURRENT_USER\Control Panel\Keyboard
```

InitialKeyboardIndicators   REG_SZ   *Number*

Specifies initial values for keys. 0 means that NUMLOCK is turned off after the user logs on; 2 means NUMLOCK is turned on after the user logs on. This value is set during log off or shutdown to preserve the state of the NUMLOCK key at that time.

Default: 0

KeyboardDelay   REG_SZ   *0 to 3*

Establishes how much time elapses after you hold down a key before the key starts to repeat. The values 0 through 3 provide a linear scale from the smallest delay supported by the keyboard driver to the largest delay. Typically, 0 represents 250 milliseconds, and 3 represents 1 second, with a 20 percent accuracy.

Default: 1

KeyboardSpeed   REG_SZ   *0 to 31*

Sets how much time elapses between repetitions of a character on the display when you hold down a keyboard key. The values 0 through 31 provide a linear scale from the slowed repeat rate supported by the keyboard driver to the fastest repeat rate. Typically, 0 represents 2 per second, and 31 represents 30 per second.

Default: 31

The Keyboard Layout key records the user's preferred layout, which is loaded and activated by the system when the user logs on. Entries are found under this Registry path:

```
HKEY_CURRENT_USER\Control Panel\Keyboard Layout
```

When the user logs off, the user's current keyboard layout is stored here. The value for the entry is based on those defined in CurrentControlSet\Control\NLS\KeyboardLayout. To change the keyboard layout, choose the Windows NT Setup icon from the Main program group.

Active   REG_SZ   *KeyboardLayout*
Default: 00000409 (for standard U.S. English)

The Keyboard Layout\Substitutes key is empty by default. This subkey records a mapping between keyboard layout names. The system checks the user's Substitutes subkey when loading the keyboard driver, and if a substitute is specified, the corresponding layout name is substituted. For example, an entry such as the following under the Keyboard Layout\Substitutes subkey indicates that the user prefers the Dvorak U.S. English keyboard layout (00010409) to the standard U.S. English keyboard layout (00000409).

```
00000409 : REG_SZ : 00010409
```

Mouse Entries for Users

To change these entries, choose the Mouse icon from Control Panel.

DoubleClickSpeed   REG_SZ   *milliseconds*
Sets the maximum time between clicks of the mouse button that the system permits for one double-click. The lower the value for this entry, the less time you have to click twice to double-click.

Default: 686

MouseSpeed   REG_SZ   *0 or 1 or 2*
Sets the relationship between mouse and cursor movement when the value of either **MouseThreshold1** or **MouseThreshold2** is exceeded. When this occurs, cursor movement accelerates according to the value of **MouseSpeed**.

Value	Meaning
0	No acceleration.
1	The cursor is moved twice the normal speed when mouse movement exceeds the value of **MouseThreshold1**.
2	The cursor is moved twice the normal speed when the mouse movement exceeds the value of **MouseThreshold1**, or four times the normal speed if mouse movement exceeds **MouseThreshold2**.

Default: 1

MouseThreshold1   REG_SZ   *pixels*
MouseThreshold2   REG_SZ   *pixels*

These entries set the maximum number of pixels that the mouse can move between mouse interrupts before the system alters the relationship between mouse and cursor movement. If the mouse movement exceeds the threshold defined by **MouseThreshold1** and if **MouseSpeed** is greater than 0, the system moves the cursor at twice the normal speed. If the mouse movement exceeds the threshold defined by **MouseThreshold2** and if **MouseSpeed** is 2, the system moves the cursor at four times the normal speed.

Default: **MouseThreshold1**=6
            MouseThreshold2=10

SwapMouseButtons   REG_SZ   *Boolean*

Specifies whether to swap the right and left mouse buttons. If the value is 1, the buttons are swapped.

Default: 0

Multimedia and Sound Entries for Users

Values related to user preferences for multimedia items in Control Panel are found in the following Registry path:

`HKEY_CURRENT_USER\Control Panel`

The information here is for troubleshooting reference. All changes should be made using the Devices, Drivers, MIDI Mapper, and Sound icons in Control Panel. The following lists the default entries. All are REG_SZ data types.

Multimedia subkey	Default value entries
MMCPL	**H**=230 **NumApps**=20 **W**=442 **X**=88 **Y**=84
Sound	**Beep**=yes
Sounds	**Enable**=1 **SystemAsterisk**=chord.wav,Asterisk **SystemDefault**=ding.wav,Default Beep **SystemExclamation**=chord.wav,Exclamation **SystemExit**=chimes.wav,Windows Logoff **SystemHand**=chord.wav,Critical Stop **SystemQuestion**=chord.wav,Question **SystemStart**=tada.wav,Windows Logon

Network Entries for Users

This section describes the user preferences and settings for the network.

Network Connection Entries for Users

The following Registry path contains the list of specific shares to reconnect when the user logs on:

HKEY_CURRENT_USER\Network

The Network subkey does not appear unless you are connected to a shared directory when the Reconnect At Logon option was checked in File Manager. There is a subkey for each shared directory to be reconnected at system startup. The name of the subkey is the drive-letter designated for the connection. Each such subkey can contain the following entries:

ConnectionType   REG_DWORD   *0x1 or 1x2*

Specifies connection types as 0x1 for drive redirection or 0x2 for print redirection.

Default: 0x1

ProviderName   REG_SZ   *Network name*

Specifies the network provider for the path to the shared directory.

Default: Microsoft Windows Network

RemotePath   REG_SZ   *UNC sharename*

Specifies the UNC name for the shared directory.

UserName   REG_SZ   *username*

Specifies the username under whose authority the connection was established. The password is not remembered. This name can appear in the Connect As box in the Connect Network Drive dialog box in File Manager.

Default: (blank) (That is, the name of currently logged on user is assumed.)

Network Software Entries for Users

The following path contains subkeys with settings for user preferences related to Event Viewer, Server Manager, User Manager, and User Manager for Domains:

HKEY_CURRENT_USER\SOFTWARE\Microsoft\Windows NT\CurrentVersion\Network

The following table summarizes default settings in the Network subkeys. All entries have REG_SZ data types.

Network subkey	Default value entries
Event Viewer	**Filter=** (as chosen in the Filter dialog box) **Find=**: (string from Find dialog box) **IfNT=**1 (1=focused on Windows NT server) **LogType=**0 (0=system; 1=security; 2=application; 4=read from a file) **Module=**System (or Security or Application) **SaveSettings=**1 **SortOrder=**0 (0=new events first; 1=old events first) **Window=**132 126 504 282 0 (position and minimize)
Server Manager	**AccountsOnly=**0 **SaveSettings=**1 **View** = 4 (1=view workstations; 2=view servers) **ViewExtension** (file being viewed if **View**=0)
User Manager	**SaveSettings=**1
User Manager for Domains	**Confirmation=**1 **SaveSettings=**1 **SortOrder=**0 (for sort by full name) **Window=**132 90 480 258 0

The following defines most of the common parameters for these applications:

Confirmation   REG_SZ   *Boolean*

Specifies whether the application requests user confirmation for actions such as deletions or other value changes.

SaveSettings   REG_SZ   *Boolean*

Specifies whether options selected in the application are saved when the application is closed.

SortOrder   REG_SZ   *Boolean*

Specifies the sort order followed by the application, where 1 specifies sort by username, and 0 specifies sort by full name.

Window   Reg_SZ   *Pixel location for window*

Specifies window location when application was last closed as four numbers plus 1 or 0 to indicate whether the window was iconized.

The Persistent Connections subkey contains entries that control the restoration of network connections, under this Registry path:

```
HKEY_CURRENT_USER\SOFTWARE\Microsoft\Windows NT\CurrentVersion
    \Network\Persistent Connections
```

DriveMappingLetter   **REG_SZ**   *UNC sharename*

An entry appears for each connection to a shared network directory.

Order   **REG_SZ**   *drive-letter order*

Specifies the order for the shared directory connections.

SaveConnections   **REG_SZ**   *Yes or No*

Contains the value set by the Reconnect At Logon check box in the Connect Network Drive dialog box in File Manager.

Default: Yes

The following Network parameter is found in this Registry path:

```
HKEY_LOCAL_MACHINE\SOFTWARE\Microsoft\Windows NT\CurrentVersion
    \Network\World Full Access Shared Parameters
```

ExpandLogonDomain   **REG_SZ**   *Yes or No*

Specifies whether the Shared Directories list is expanded by default in the Connect Network Drive dialog box. This is the value set in the Connect Network Drive dialog box in File Manager by checking the Expand By Default check box.

Default: Yes

The following parameter is used by the Windows NT administrative applications:

```
HKEY_LOCAL_MACHINE\SOFTWARE\Microsoft\Windows NT\CurrentVersion
    \Network\Shared Parameters
```

Slow Mode   **REG_SZ**   *String*

Stores information about which servers and domains are across a Low Speed Connection. User Manager for Domains, Server Manager, and Event Viewer read this information unless explicitly told whether to start in Low Speed Connection mode. The cache is updated each time one of these applications is started or set to a new, nonlocal focus, or when the user explicitly changes the Low Speed Connection setting. This is an LRU cache of up to 20 focus targets. The first entry is the most recently used.

This is a shared state between users, so if one user changes the cached setting for a target focus, other users get that setting by default. The user must be a member of a group with Power Users or better privileges to have access to this subkey.

Network Entries for Users

Default: "CLOSEDOMAIN;h;FARDOMAIN;l;\\CLOSEMACHINE;h; \\FARMACHINE;1"

Program Manager Entries for Users

Program Groups Entries

The Program Group key contains subkeys that define the contents of all personal program groups in Program Manager, under this Registry path:

`HKEY_CURENT_USER\Program Groups`

Common groups are defined under the following key:

`HKEY_LOCAL_MACHINE\SOFTWARE\Microsoft\Program Groups`

The information stored in these subkeys is in binary format, so you cannot easily edit it from Registry Editor. To change the content of program groups, use the mouse and keyboard techniques in Program Manager.

Program Manager Software Groups Entries

The Groups key specifies group numbers for the defined program groups, under this Registry path:

`Software\Microsoft\Windows NT\CurrentVersion\Program Manager\Groups`

These are the default entries. All data types are REG_SZ.

Group1=Main
Group2=Accessories
Group3=Administrative Tools
Group4=Games
Group5=Startup

Restrictions Entries for Program Manager

The Restrictions subkey defines restrictions for activities in Program Manager, under this Registry path:

`Software\Microsoft\Windows NT\CurrentVersion`
`    \Program Manager\Restrictions`

Restrictions can be defined for users in User Profile Editor.

EditLevel   REG_DWORD   *Number*

Sets restrictions for what users can modify in Program Manager. You can specify one of the following values.

Value	Meaning
0	Allows the user to make any change. (This is the default value.)
1	Prevents the user from creating, deleting, or renaming groups. If you specify this value, the New, Move, Copy, and Delete commands on the File menu are not available when a group is selected.
2	Sets all restrictions in **EditLevel=1** and prevents the user from creating or deleting program items. If you specify this value, the New, Move, Copy, and Delete commands on the File menu are not available at all.
3	Sets all restrictions in **EditLevel=2** and prevents the user from changing command lines for program items. If you specify this value, the text in the Command Line box in the Properties dialog box cannot be changed.
4	Sets all restrictions in **EditLevel=3** and prevents the user from changing any program item information. If you specify this value, none of the areas in the Properties dialog box can be modified. The user can view the dialog box, but all of the areas are dimmed.

Default: 0

NoClose   REG_DWORD   *0 or 1*

Disables the Exit Windows command on the File menu if this value is 1. Users cannot quit Program Manager through the File Menu or the Control menu (the Exit Windows and Close commands will be dimmed), or by using ALT+F4.

Default: 0

NoFileMenu   REG_DWORD   *0 or 1*

Removes the File menu from Program Manager if this value is 1. All of the commands on that menu are unavailable. Users can start the applications in groups by selecting them and pressing ENTER, or by double-clicking the icon. Unless you have also disabled the Exit Windows command, users can still quit Windows by using the Control menu or ALT+F4.

Default: 0

NoRun   REG_DWORD   *0 or 1*

Disables the Run command on the File menu if this value is 1. The Run command is dimmed on the File menu, and the user cannot run applications from Program Manager unless the applications are set up as icons in a group.

Default: 0

NoSaveSettings   REG_DWORD   *0 or 1*

Disables the Save Settings on Exit command on the Options menu if this value is 1. The Save Settings command is dimmed on the Options menu, and any changes that the user makes to the arrangement of windows and icons are not saved when Windows NT is restarted. This setting overrides the **SaveSettings** value in the Program Manager subkey.

Default: 0

Restrictions   REG_DWORD   *0 or 1*

Turns restrictions on or off.

Default: 0

ShowCommonGroups   REG_DWORD   *0 or 1*

Controls whether common program groups are displayed.

Default: 0x1

Program Manager Settings Entries

AutoArrange   REG_DWORD   *0 or 1*

If the AutoArrange command is checked on the Options menu in Program Manager, this value is 1, and the icons in each group are automatically arranged when you run Program Manager.

Default: 0x1

display.drv   REG_SZ   *filename*

Defines the video display driver used.

Default: vga.drv

MinOnRun   REG_DWORD   *0 or 1*

If the Minimize On Use command is checked on the Options menu in Program Manager, this value is 1, and Program Manager is iconized when you run another application.

Default: 0x1

Order   REG_SZ

Default: 5 4 2 1 3

SaveSettings   REG_DWORD   *0 or 1*

If the Save Settings On Exit command on the Options menu is checked in Program Manager, this value is 1, and Program Manager saves the current configuration when you close Windows.

Default: 0x1

Window   REG_SZ

Four numbers that indicate the pixel position of the window when Program Manager is opened, followed by a 1 if the window is maximized.

Default: 68 63 636 421 1

Windows Entries for Users

This section describes values for personal preferences for items that were formerly stored in WIN.INI for versions of Windows for MS-DOS.

```
HKEY_CURRENT_USER\Software\Microsoft\Windows NT\CurrentVersion\Windows
```

device   REG_SZ   *output-device-name, device-driver, port-connection*

Defines the default printer. An explicit port and driver must be assigned to the device. The *device-driver* is the filename (without the extension) of the device driver file. To change this entry, use Print Manager.

Default: *printerName*,winspool,LPT1:

Documents   REG_SZ   *extensions*

Defines files to be considered "documents" by Windows NT. Use this entry to define only document file extensions not listed in the Extensions subkey, because those extensions are automatically considered documents. The extensions listed in this entry are not associated with any application. Separate the filename extensions with a space, and do not include the preceding periods.

Default: (empty)

DosPrint   REG_SZ   *Boolean*

*S*pecifies whether to use MS-DOS interrupts when printing. When this entry is Yes, MS-DOS interrupts are used; if the value is No, printing output is sent directly to the port that the printer is assigned to. The default is No. To change this entry, clear Print Direct To Ports option in the Printer Details dialog box in Print Manager.

Default: No

fPrintFileLine   REG_SZ   *Boolean*

Default: False

fPrintVerbose   REG_SZ   *Boolean*

Default: False

fPromptOnError   REG_SZ   *Boolean*

Default: True

fPromptOnVerbose   **REG_SZ**   *Boolean*
Default: False

fPromptOnWarning   **REG_SZ**   *Boolean*
Default: False

load   **REG_SZ**   *filename(s)*
Specifies the applications to be run as icons when Windows NT is started. This
entry is a list of application filenames, or documents associated with an
application, with each filename separated by a space. Make sure to specify the
path if the file is not located in the *SystemRoot* directory. To change this entry,
add the application to the Startup group in Program Manager, and then check
Minimize On Use in the Properties dialog box.

Default: (empty)

NetMessage   **REG_SZ**   *Boolean*
Specifies whether to display a warning message if the system is configured to
run a network and the network is not running or the wrong network is running.
All Windows network-related options are disabled if the network is disabled or
incorrect. Setting this value to 0 turns off the warning message. The default is
1.

Default: no

NullPort   **REG_SZ**   *string*
Specifies the name used for a null port. This name appears in the Printers
Connect dialog box in Print Manager when a device is installed (that is, the
device driver is present) but is not connected to any port.

Default: None

Programs   **REG_SZ**   *extensions*
Defines which files Windows NT regards as applications. Separate the
filename extensions with a space and do not include the preceding periods.

Default: com exe bat pif cmd

run   **REG_SZ**   *filename(s)*
Tells Windows NT to run the specified applications when Windows NT is
started. The value is a list of application filenames or documents associated
with applications, with each filename separated by a space. Make sure you
specify the complete path if the file is not in the *SystemRoot* directory. To
change this entry, add the application to the Startup group in Program
Manager.

Default: (none)

Registry Entries for Winlogon

The Registry value entries that control the logon sequence for starting Windows NT are found under the following Registry key:

```
HKEY_LOCAL_MACHINE\SOFTWARE\Microsoft\Windows NT\CurrentVersion\Winlogon
```

AutoAdminLogon   **REG_SZ**   *0 or 1*

Specifies automatic logon if this value is 1. You must also add the value entry **DefaultPassword** with a value for the user listed under **DefaultUserName** for automatic logon to work.

When **AutoAdminLogon** is used, Windows NT automatically logs on the specified user when the system is started, bypassing the CTRL+ALT+DEL logon dialog box.

DefaultDomainName   **REG_SZ**   *Domain name*

Specifies the name of the last successfully logged on domain.

Default: NEWDOMAIN

DefaultPassword   **REG_SZ**   *Password*

Specifies the password for the user listed under **DefaultUserName**. Used during automatic logon.

DefaultUserName   **REG_SZ**   *Username*

Specifies the name of the last successfully logged on user. If values are defined for **DefaultPassword** and **AutoAdminLogon**, this is the user who is logged on by default during automatic logon.

LegalNoticeCaption   **REG_SZ**   *String*

Specifies a caption for a message to appear when the user presses CTRL+ALT+DEL during logon. Add this value entry if you want to add a warning to be displayed when a user attempts to log on to a Windows NT system. The user cannot proceed with logging on without acknowledging this message.

To specify text for the message, you must also specify a value for **LegalNoticeText.**

Default: (none)

LegalNoticeText   REG_SZ   *String*

Specifies for a message to appear when the user presses CTRL+ALT+DEL during logon. Add this value entry if you want to add a warning to be displayed when a user attempts to log on to a Windows NT system. The user cannot procede with logging on without acknowledging this message.

To include a caption for the logon notice, you must also specify a value for **LegalNoticeCaption.**

Default: (none)

ReportBootOk   REG_SZ   *0 or 1*

When this value is set to 0, it disables the automatic (default) startup acceptance, which happens after the first successful logon. This value must be 0 if you use alternate settings in the BootVerification or BootVerificationProgram keys.

Default: 1

Shell   REG_SZ   *Executable names*

Specifies executables that are run by USERINIT and that are expected to be in the user's shell program. If for some reason WinLogon cannot start the entries listed in **Userinit**, then WinLogon will execute the entries in **Shell** directly.

Default: taskman,progman,wowexec

System   REG_SZ   *Executable names*

Specifies executables to be run by WinLogon in the system context. These are activated during system initialization.

Default: lsass.exe,spoolss.exe

Userinit   REG_SZ   *Executable names*

Specifies executables to be run by WinLogon when a user logs on. These executables are run in the user context. The first entry (USERINIT) is responsible for executing the shell program. NDDEAGNT.EXE is needed to run NetDDE.

Default: USERINIT,NDDEAGNT.EXE

Registry Entries for Fonts

This section describes entries in subkeys that concern the fonts available to all users on a computer.

Font Drivers Entries

The Font Drivers subkey in the following Registry path can contain references to external font drivers:

```
HKEY_LOCAL_MACHINE\SOFTWARE\Microsoft\Windows NT\CurrentVersion
    \Font Drivers
```

You should not need to modify this entry directly. Your font vendor should supply an installation program for adding and removing drivers.

Driver description   **REG_SZ**   *Driver filename or pathname*
Lists external font drivers installed on the system. Windows NT does not include any external font drivers. The bitmap, vector, and TrueType drivers are built in and do not appear on this list.

FontCache Entries

The FontCache subkey in the following Registry path contains entries that define parameters for font caching:

```
HKEY_LOCAL_MACHINE\SOFTWARE\Microsoft\Windows NT\CurrentVersion
    \FontCache
```

The value entries in the FontCache subkey can greatly influence the amount of memory used by the system. However, these values should not be modified, except in the rare case where you must tune the performance for an international version of Windows NT or for specialized cases such as a print shop, where you may be manipulating large character sets.

MaxSize   REG_DWORD   *Number of kilobytes*
Specifies the maximum amount of address space reserved per font cache.
Default: 0x80

MinIncrSize   REG_DWORD   *Number of kilobytes*
Specifies the minimum amount of memory committed each time a font cache is grown.
Default: 0x4

MinInitSize   **REG_DWORD**   *Number of kilobytes*

Specifies the minimum amount of memory initially committed per font cache at the time of creation.

Default: 0x4

Fonts Entries

The following Registry path is for entries describing the fonts used for displaying information in applications created for Windows NT or versions of Windows for MS-DOS:

HKEY_LOCAL_MACHINE\SOFTWARE\Microsoft\Windows NT\CurrentVersion\Fonts

Entries in the Fonts key have the following format:

Font Name   **REG_SZ**   *font filename*

These value entries define the installed fonts and their related filenames. These are the default value entries:

Arial=ARIAL.FOT
Arial Bold=ARIALBD.FOT
Arial Bold Italic (TrueType)=ARIALBI.FOT
Arial Italic (TrueType)=ARIALI.FOT
Courier 10,12,15 (VGA res)=COURE.FON
Courier New (TrueType)=COUR.FOT
Courier New Bold (TrueType)=COURBD.FOT
Courier New Bold Italic (TrueType)=COURBI.FOT
Courier New Italic (TrueType)=COURI.FOT
Modern (Plotter)=MODERN.FON
MS Sans Serif 8,10,12,14,18,24 (VGA res)=SSERIFE.FON
MS Serif 8,10,12,14,18,24 (VGA res)=SERIFE.FON
Roman (Plotter)=ROMAN.FON
Script (Plotter)=SCRIPT.FON
Small Fonts (VGA res)=SMALLE.FON
Symbol (TrueType)=SYMBOL.FOT
Symbol 8,10,12,14,18,24 (VGA res)=SYMBOLE.FON
Times New Roman (TrueType)=TIMES.FOT
Times New Roman Bold (TrueType)=TIMESBD.FOT
Times New Roman Bold Italic (TrueType)=TIMESBI.FOT
Times New Roman Italic (TrueType)=TIMESI.FOT
WingDings (TrueType)=WINGDING.FOT

GRE_Initialize Entries

The following Registry path is for entries describing the fonts used for character-based programs:

```
HKEY_LOCAL_MACHINE\SOFTWARE\Microsoft\Windows NT\CurrentVersion
    \GRE_Initialize
```

The FONTS.FON and FIXEDFON.FON entries do not affect the console, but they do affect menus and dialog boxes and some applications such as Notepad.

Caution Editing these entries can cause menus and dialog boxes to display improperly.

Unlike versions of Windows from MSD, changing these default fonts will render poor results, because the font set under Windows NT is closely tied to the driver.

FONTS.FON   **REG_SZ**   *Filename*
Specifies the filename of the default system font.

FIXEDFON.FON   **REG_SZ**   *Filename*
Specifies the filename of the default system fixed-width font.

OEMFONT.FON   **REG_SZ**   *Filename*
Specifies the filename of the default OEM (or console) font.

FontSubstitutes Entries

The entries in the FontSubstitutes subkey define substitute typeface names for fonts under the following Registry path:

```
HKEY_LOCAL_MACHINE\SOFTWARE\Microsoft\Windows NT\CurrentVersion
    \FontSubstitutes
```

You should not need to modify these entries. This subkey is usually used by applications with a special need to equate font names.

Alternate name   **REG_SZ**   *Actual name*

Specifies the alternate typeface name. For example, the following entry means that Helv is an alternative typeface name that can be used to refer to the MS Sans Serif font:

```
Helv=MS Sans Serif
```

Default:
Helv=MS Sans Serif
Helvetica=Arial
Times=Times New Roman
Tms Rmn=MS Serif

TrueType Entries for Users

The entries in the TrueType subkey describe options that affect the use and display of TrueType fonts in Windows-based applications. This is the Registry path:

```
HKEY_CURRENT_USER\Software\Microsoft\Windows NT\CurrentVersion\TrueType
```

The TrueType subkey can contain the following entries:

TTEnable   **REG_SZ**   *Boolean*

Controls whether TrueType fonts are available. Setting this value to 1 makes TrueType fonts available in your Windows-based applications. Setting this value to 0 turns off TrueType fonts so they are unavailable in applications.

Default: 1

TTonly   **REG_SZ**   *Boolean*

Specifies whether to make only TrueType fonts available in Windows-based applications. If this value is set to 1, only TrueType fonts are available. If this value is set to 0, all fonts installed on your system are available. To change this entry, choose the Fonts icon from Control Panel.

Default: 0

Registry Entries for Printing

The Registry contains printer information in these locations:

- The per-user settings for the current default printer are stored under this key:

  `HKEY_CURRENT_USER\Printers`

- The hardware-specific information about drivers and print processors is stored under this key, where *Hardware* represents the subkey for a specific Windows NT platform, such as Windows NT x86 or Windows NT R4000:

  `HKEY_LOCAL_MACHINE\SYSTEM\CurrentControlSet`
  `    \Control\Print`

The following illustration indicates what can be found in *Print* subkeys.

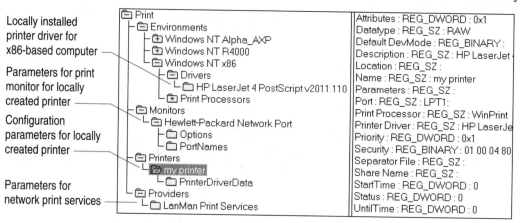

Locally installed printer driver for x86-based computer

Parameters for print monitor for locally created printer

Configuration parameters for locally created printer

Parameters for network print services

Always use Print Manager to change configuration settings for all printers. There are no parameters for printing that can be set only through the Registry.

Registry Entries for Software Classes

Various HKEY_LOCAL_MACHINE\SOFTWARE subkeys contain the names and version numbers of the software installed on the local computer. (Information about the configuration of these applications is stored on a per-user basis under HKEY_CURRENT_USER.)

During installation, applications record this information in the following form:

`HKEY_LOCAL_MACHINE\SOFTWARE\CompanyName\ProductName\Version`

Registry Entries for Subsystems

This section describes software registration entries related to Windows NT subsystems.

Microsoft OS/2 Version 1.x Software Registration Entries

The basic software information for the Microsoft OS/2 version 1.x subsystem is found in the following Registry path:

```
HKEY_LOCAL_MACHINE\SOFTWARE\Microsoft\OS/2 Subsystem for NT
```

The OS/2 Subsystem key contains several subkeys, but initially only the \config.sys subkey contains an entry. This subkey contains the OS/2 CONFIG.SYS information stored after an OS/2 application has been run on the system.

If there is no OS/2 CONFIG.SYS file, this subkey contains the following entry:

```
PROTSHELL=C:\os2\pmshell.exe c:\os2\os2.ini c:\os2\os2sys.ini
    %SystemRoot%\system32\cmd.exe
SET COMSPEC=%SystemRoot%\system32\cmd.exe
```

The Os2 subkey under CurrentControlSet\Control\Session Manager\SubSystems defines the path to the executable file used to start the OS/2 subsystem. The **Os2LibPath** value under the Session Manager\Environment subkey defines the directory path for the OS/2 library. These entries are described in "CurrentControlSet\Control Subkeys," earlier in this chapter.

To disable the OS/2 subsystem, set the value of **GlobalFlag** to 20100000 in the following subkey:

```
HKEY_LOCAL_MACHINE\SYSTEM\CurrentControlSet\Control\Session Manager
```

Windows Software Registration Entries

The Windows subkey under the following path defines some values used by applications created to run under Windows for MS-DOS:

```
HKEY_LOCAL_MACHINE\SOFTWARE\Microsoft\Windows NT\CurrentVersion\Windows
```

AppInit_DLLs   REG_SZ

Causes all the specified DLLs (one or many) to be attached to all Windows-based applications. This means that once this is set for a session, upon restarting the system, all the Windows-based applications that run in that session will load the specified DLLs. For example, an applications developer can use it to attach the Microsoft Call/Attributive Profiler to all Windows-based applications by calling CAPSETUP.EXE, which sets the **AppInit_DLLs** so the user doesn't have to do it through Registry Editor.

Default:

DeviceNotSelectedTimeout   REG_SZ   *Seconds*

Specifies how much time the system waits for a device to be switched on. If the device is not switched on during this time, the system won't print to the device. For some devices, the system immediately posts an error message if the device is not already switched on. This entry only defines the system default value. To change the value for a particular printer, use Print Manager.

Default: 15

Spooler   REG_SZ   *Boolean*

Specifies whether output to the printer is to be sent through Print Manager. Changing this value to No turns off Print Manager.

Default: Yes

swapdisk   REG_SZ   *drive:directory*

Provides the name of the disk drive and directory to which Windows for MS-DOS in standard mode swaps non-Windows–based applications.

Default: The directory pointed to by the TEMP environment variable; if there is no TEMP variable, the default is the boot directory of your first hard disk (usually C:).

TransmissionRetryTimeout REG_SZ *Seconds*

Specifies the default amount of time for attempted transmission retries. If a successful transmission does not occur during this time, Print Manager displays a message stating that the printer is not receiving characters. This setting serves only as the system default value. To change the value for a particular printer, use Print Manager.

Default: 45

WOW Software Registration Entries

Software registration values for the WOW subsystem appear under the following Registry key:

```
HKEY_LOCAL_MACHINE\SOFTWARE\Microsoft\Windows NT\CurrentVersion\WOW
```

The WOW subkeys have the same names as headings in the SYSTEM.INI file, and the values are the same items as were contained in the Windows for MS-DOS SYSTEM.INI file. All are REG_SZ value types.

The information provided here is for troubleshooting only.

WOW subkey	Description and defaults
Boot	Lists drivers and Windows 3.x modules, with these entries and default values to map Windows 3.x drivers to Windows NT.
	Provided for applications that seek this information. Mostly ignored, but drivers are loaded from this source, such as MMSYSTEM.DLL.
	comm.drv = comm.drv **display.drv** = vga.drv **drivers** = mmsystem.dll **fixedfon** = vgafix.fon **keyboard.drv** = keyboard.drv **language.dll** = (empty) **mouse.drv** = mouse.drv **network.drv** = lanman.drv **oemfonts.fon** = vgaoem.fon **shell** = progman.exe **sound.drv** = sound.drv **system.drv** = system.drv

WOW subkey *(continued)*	Description and defaults *(continued)*
boot.description	Provided for applications that seek this information. Not actually used by the WOW subsystem. Lists names of devices that can be changed using Windows 3.*x* Setup, with these kinds of entries and default values: **display.drv** = VGA **keyboard.typ** = Enhanced 101/102 key U.S. and Non U.S. keyboards **language.dll** = English (American) **network.drv** = LAN Support **system.drv** = MS-DOS or PC-DOS System
Compatibility	Used to translate 16-bit Windows APIs and messages to 32-bit equivalents. **MAILSPL** = 0x40000000 (for MS Mail) **SHOPPER** = 0x20000000 (for Clip-Art Windows Shopper) **SHADOW** = 0x10000000 (for BeyondMail installation) **WINPROJ** = 0x80000000 (for Microsoft Project) **ESCAPES** = 0x1000000 (for Micrographix Escapes) **HIRES** = 0x00100000 (for HIRES display cards)
Keyboard	Contains information about the keyboard, provided for applications that seek this information, with these kinds of entries and default values: **keyboard.dll** = (empty) **subtype** = (empty) **type** = 4
NonWindowsApp	Contains information used by non-Windows–based applications. This is handled automatically by Windows NT. Unless you manually added values to SYSTEM.INI in Windows 3.*x*, this subkey is empty.
Standard	Contains entries specific to running Windows 3.*x* in standard mode. Unless you manually added values to SYSTEM.INI in Windows 3.*x*, this subkey is empty.

The [386Enh] section is read from the SYSTEM.INI file for 16-bit Windows-based applications that need it. There is no Registry equivalent, because Windows NT ignores this information.

PART V

Networking

Part Five describes the Windows NT networking architecture and how Windows NT fits into a heterogeneous networking environment. This part describes how the Windows NT security model applies to multidomain networks and suggests ways to prevent problem in resource access and browsing. This part also includes details about the protocols supported by Windows NT. Chapter 22 discusses client-server connectivity under Windows NT, using Microsoft SQL Server and Ingres databases as examples of distributed applications for Windows NT.

CHAPTER 15

Windows NT Networking Architecture

Windows NT is a complete operating system with fully integrated networking capabilities. These capabilities differentiate Windows NT from other operating systems such as MS-DOS, OS/2, and UNIX for which network capabilities are installed separately from the core operating system.

Integrated networking support means that Windows NT offers these features:

- Support for both peer-to-peer and client-server networking. All Windows NT computers can act as both network clients and servers, sharing files and printers with other computers and exchanging messages over the network. Windows NT Advanced Server also includes features needed for full-scale servers, such as domain management tools.

- The ability to easily add networking software and hardware. The networking software integrated into Windows NT lets you easily add protocol drivers, network card drivers, and other network software. Windows NT includes four transport protocols—NBF (Windows NT NetBEUI), DLC, TCP/IP, and NWLink.

- Interoperability with existing networks. Windows NT systems can communicate using a variety of transport protocols and network adapters. It can also communicate over a variety of different vendors' networks.

- Support for distributed applications. Windows NT provides a transparent Remote Procedure Call (RPC) facility. It also supports NetBIOS, Sockets, and the Windows Network (WNet) APIs and named pipes and mailslots, for backward compatibility with LAN Manager installations and applications.

This chapter describes the Windows NT networking architecture and how it achieves each of these goals. For perspective, the next section provides a brief explanation of two industry-standard models for networking—the Open System Interconnection (OSI) reference model and the Institute of Electrical and Electronic Engineers (IEEE) 802 project model. The remainder of the chapter describes the Windows NT networking components as they relate to the OSI and IEEE models and as they relate to the overall Windows NT architecture.

Overview of Networking

In the early years of networking, several large companies, including IBM, Honeywell, and Digital Equipment Corporation (DEC), each had their own standard for how computers could be connected together. These standards described the mechanisms necessary to move data from one computer to another. These early standards, however, were not entirely compatible. Networks adhering to IBM Systems Network Architecture (SNA) could not communicate directly with networks using DEC Digital Network Architecture (DNA), for example.

In later years, standards organizations, including the International Standards Organization (ISO) and the Institute of Electrical and Electronic Engineers (IEEE), developed models that became globally recognized and accepted as the standards for designing any computer network. Both models describe networking in terms of functional layers.

OSI Reference Model

ISO developed a model called the Open Systems Interconnection (OSI) reference model. It is used to describe the flow of data between the physical connection to the network and the end-user application. This model is the best known and most widely used model to describe networking environments.

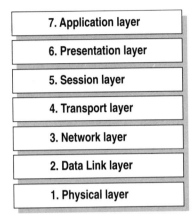

Figure 15.1   OSI Model

As shown in Figure 15.1, the OSI layers are numbered from bottom to top. The most basic functions, such as putting data bits onto the network cable, are on the bottom, while functions attending to the details of applications are at the top.

In the OSI model, the purpose of each layer is to provide services to the next higher layer, shielding the higher layer from the details of how the services are actually implemented. The layers are abstracted in such a way that each layer believes it is communicating with the same layer on the other computer. In reality, each layer communicates only with adjacent layers on one computer. That is, for information to pass from Layer 5 on Computer A to Layer 5 on Computer B, it actually follows the route illustrated by Figure 15.2:

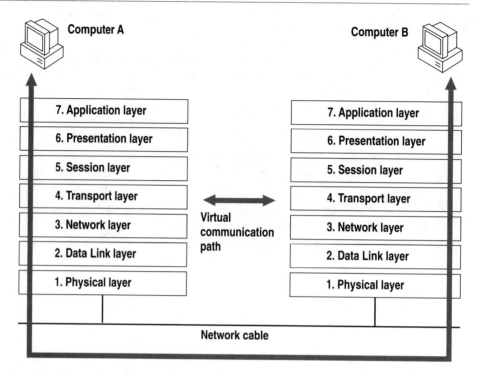

Figure 15.2   Communication Between OSI Layers

The following list describes the purpose of each of the seven layers of the OSI model and identifies services that they provide to adjacent layers.

1. The Physical Layer addresses the transmission of the unstructured raw bit stream over a physical medium (that is, the networking cable). The Physical Layer relates the electrical/optical, mechanical, and functional interfaces to the cable. The Physical Layer also carries the signals that transmit data generated by all the higher layers.

    This layer defines how the cable is attached to the network adapter card. For example, it defines how many pins the connector has and what each pin is used for. It describes the topology used to connect computers together (Token Ring, Ethernet, or some other). It also defines which transmission technique will be used to send data over the network cable.

2. The Data Link Layer packages raw bits from the Physical Layer into *data frames*, which are logical, structured packets in which data can be placed. The exact format of the frame used by the network depends on the topology. That is, a Token Ring network data frame is laid out differently than an Ethernet frame. The Data Link Layer is responsible for providing the error-free transfer of these frames from one computer to another through the Physical Layer. This allows the Network Layer to assume virtually error-free transmission over the network connection. Frames contain source and destination addresses so that the sending and receiving computers can recognize and retrieve their own frames on the network.

3. The Network Layer is responsible for addressing messages and translating logical addresses and names into physical addresses. This layer also determines the route from the source to the destination computer. It determines which path the data should take based on network conditions, priority of service, and other factors. It also manages traffic problems on the network, such as switching, routing, and controlling the congestion of data packets.

   The Network Layer bundles small data frames together for transmission across the network. It also restructures large frames into smaller packets. On the receiving end, the Network Layer reassembles the data packets into their original frame structure.

4. The Transport Layer takes care of error recognition and recovery. It also ensures reliable delivery of host messages originating at the Application Layer. Similar to how the Network Layer handles data frames, this layer repackages messages—dividing long messages into several packets and collecting small messages together in one packet—to provide for their efficient transmission over the network. At the receiving end, the Transport Layer unpacks the messages, reassembles the original messages, and sends an acknowledgment of receipt.

5. The Session Layer allows two applications on different computers to establish, use, and end a connection called a *session*. This layer performs name recognition and the functions needed to allow two applications to communicate over the network, such as security functions.

   The Session Layer provides synchronization between user tasks by placing checkpoints in the data stream. This way, if the network fails, only the data after the last checkpoint has to be retransmitted. This layer also implements dialog control between communicating processes, regulating which side transmits, when, for how long, and so on.

6. The Presentation Layer determines the form used to exchange data between networked computers. It can be called the network's translator. At the sending computer, this layer translates data from a format received from the Application Layer into a commonly recognized, intermediary format. At the receiving end, this layer translates the intermediary format into a format useful to that computer's Application Layer.

The Presentation Layer also manages network security issues by providing services such as data encryption. It also provides rules for data transfer and provides data compression to reduce the number of bits that need to be transmitted.

7. The Application Layer serves as the window for application processes to access network services. This layer represents the services that directly support the user applications such as software for file transfers, database access, and electronic mail.

IEEE 802 Model

Another networking model developed by the IEEE further defines sublayers of the Data Link Layer. The IEEE 802 project (named for the year and month it began— February 1980) defines the *Media Access Control* (MAC) and the *Logical Link Control* (LLC) sublayers.

As Figure 15.3 shows, the Media Access Control sublayer is the lower of the two sublayers, providing shared access for the computers' network adapter cards to the Physical Layer. The MAC Layer communicates directly with the network adapter card and is responsible for delivering error-free data between two computers on the network.

The Logical Link Control sublayer, the upper sublayer, manages data link communication and defines the use of logical interface points [called Service Access Points (SAPs)] that other computers can reference and use to transfer information from the LLC sublayer to the upper OSI layers. Two protocols running on the same computer would use separate SAPs.

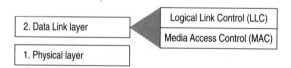

Figure 15.3   Logical Link Control and Media Access Control Sublayers

Project 802 resulted in a number of documents, including three key standards for network topologies:

- 802.3 defines standards for bus networks, such as Ethernet, that use a mechanism called Carrier Sense Multiple Access with Collision Detection (CSMA/CD).

- 802.4 defines standards for token-passing bus networks. (The ArcNet® architecture is similar to this standard in many ways.)

- 802.5 defines standards for Token-Ring networks.

IEEE defined functionality for the LLC Layer in standard 802.2 and defined functionality for the MAC and Physical Layers in standards 802.3, 802.4, and 802.5.

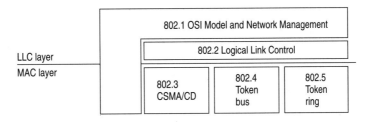

Figure 15.4   Project 802 Standards as Related to LLC and MAC Layers

This chapter describes the layered components of the Windows NT networking architecture, beginning with an overall description of that architecture.

Windows NT Networking Model

As with other architecture components of Windows NT, the networking architecture is built of layers. This helps provide expandability by allowing other functions and services to be added. Figure 15.5 shows all of the components that make up the Windows NT networking model.

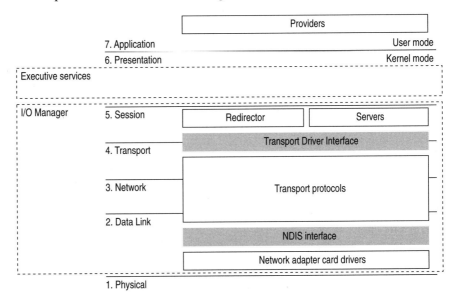

Figure 15.5   Windows NT Networking Model

Each of the Windows NT networking layers performs these functions.

The Windows NT networking model begins at the MAC sublayer where *network adapter card drivers* reside. These link Windows NT to the network via corresponding network adapter cards. Figure 15.5 includes network adapter cards to illustrate that you can use multiple network adapter cards on a computer running Windows NT.

The model also shows a *serial driver* and *serial card*. Windows NT includes RAS to allow network access to computers for people who work at home or on the road. (For more information, see "Remote Access for Windows NT Clients," later in this chapter.)

The network model includes two important interfaces—the *NDIS 3.0 Interface* and the *Transport Driver Interface* (TDI). These interfaces isolate one layer from the next by allowing an adjacent component to be written to a single standard rather than many. For example, a network adapter card driver (below the NDIS interface) does not need to include blocks of code specifically written for each transport protocol it uses. Instead, the driver is written to the NDIS interface, which solicits services from the appropriate NDIS-conformant transport protocol(s). These interfaces are included in the Windows NT networking model to allow for portable, interchangeable modules.

Between the two interfaces are *transport protocols*, which act as data organizers for the network. A transport protocol defines how data should be presented to the next receiving layer and packages the data accordingly. It passes data to the network adapter card driver through the NDIS Interface and to the redirector through the TDI.

Above the TDI are *redirectors,* which "redirect" local requests for network resources to the network.

For interconnectivity with other vendors' networks, Windows NT allows multiple redirectors. For each redirector, the Windows NT computer must also have a corresponding *provider* DLL (supplied by the network vendor). A Multiple Provider Router determines the appropriate provide and then routes the application request via the provider to the corresponding redirector.

The rest of this chapter describes these Windows NT networking components in detail.

NDIS-Compatible Network Adapter Card Drivers

Until the late 1980s, many of the implementations of transport protocols were tied to a proprietary implementation of a MAC-Layer interface defining how the protocol would converse with the network adapter card. This made it difficult for network adapter card vendors to support the different network operating systems available on the market. Each network adapter card vendor had to create proprietary interface drivers to support a variety of protocol implementations for use with several network operating system environments.

In 1989, Microsoft and 3Com jointly developed a standard defining an interface for communication between the MAC Layer and protocol drivers higher in the OSI model. This standard is known as the Network Device Interface Specification (NDIS). NDIS allows for a flexible environment of data exchange. It defines the software interface—called the NDIS interface—used by transport protocols to communicate with the network adapter card driver.

The flexibility of NDIS comes from the standardized implementation used by the network industry. Any NDIS-conformant protocol can pass data to any NDIS-conformant network adapter card driver, and vice versa. A process called *binding* is used to establish the initial communication channel between the protocol driver and the network adapter card driver.

Windows NT currently supports device drivers and transport protocols written to NDIS version 3.0.

NDIS allows multiple network adapter cards on a single computer. Each network adapter card can support multiple transport protocols. The advantage of supporting multiple protocol drivers on a single network card is that Windows NT computers can have simultaneous access to different types of network servers, each using a different transport protocol. For example, a computer can have access to both a Windows NT Advanced Server using NBF (the Windows NT implementation of NetBEUI) and a UNIX server via TCP/IP simultaneously.

Unlike previous NDIS implementations, Windows NT does not need a protocol manager module to link the various components at each layer together. Instead, Windows NT uses the information in the Registry (described in Chapter 10, "Overview of the Windows NT Registry") and a small piece of code called the *NDIS wrapper* that surrounds the network adapter card driver.

Transport Protocols

Sandwiched between the NDIS interface and the TDI are transport protocol
device drivers. These drivers communicate with a network adapter card via
a NDIS-compliant device driver.

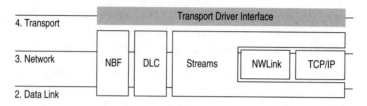

Figure 15.6   Transport Protocols

Windows NT includes these transports:

- NBF is a transport protocol derived from NetBEUI and provides compatibility
  with existing LAN Manager, LAN Server, and MS-Net installations. (For
  more information, see Chapter 18, "Using NBF with Windows NT.")

- TCP/IP is a popular routable protocol for wide-area networks. (For more
  information, see Chapter 19, "Using TCP/IP with Windows NT.")

- NWLink is an NDIS-compliant version of Internetwork Packet Exchange
  (IPX/SPX) compatible protocol. It can be used to establish connections
  between Windows NT computers and either MS-DOS, OS/2, Windows, or
  other Windows NT computers via RPC, Sockets, or Novell NetBIOS. (For
  more information, see Chapter 20, "Using NWLink and NetWare Clients for
  Windows NT.")

- Microsoft Data Link Control (DLC) is provides an interface for access to
  mainframes and network attached printers. (For more information, see Chapter
  21, "Using DLC with Windows NT.")

Note Windows NT Advanced Server also includes the AppleTalk protocol with
its Services for Macintosh.

Transport Protocols and Streams

Windows NT supports Streams-compliant protocols. Two such protocols, TCP/IP and NWLink, are included with Windows NT. These use Streams as an intermediary between the protocol and next interface layer (NDIS on the bottom and TDI on top). Calls to the transport protocol driver must first go through the upper layer of the Streams device driver to the protocol, then back through the lower layer of Streams to the NDIS device driver.

Using Streams makes it easier for developers to port other protocol stacks to Windows NT. It also encourages protocol stacks to be organized in a modular, stackable style, which is in keeping with the original OSI model.

Transport Driver Interface

The Windows NT networking model was designed to provide a platform on which other vendors can develop distributed applications. The NDIS boundary helps to do this by providing a unified interface at a significant break point in the model. At another significant breakpoint, namely the Session Layer of the OSI model, Windows NT includes another boundary layer. The TDI provides a common interface for networking components that communicate at the Session Layer. These boundaries allow software components above and below a level to be mixed and matched without reprogramming.

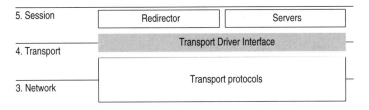

Figure 15.7   The Transport Driver Interface

The TDI is not a single program but a protocol specification to which the upper bounds of transport protocol device drivers are written. (Windows NT also includes a TDI driver that handles IRQ packet traffic from multiple TDI providers.) At this layer, networking software provides a virtual connection between the local redirector and each local or remote destination with which the redirector communicates. Similar connections are made between the server and the sources of the requests it receives.

Windows NT Workstations and Servers

Above all, the goal of a network is to allow users to share resources in one location on the network and to use them from another location on the network. On a network, computers can be organized in one of two ways:

- Networks using a classic *client-server model* have dedicated servers that share resources and workstations that can access those resources.

- The *peer-to-peer networking model* (also called workgroup computing) allows each computer to act as both client workstation and server.

Windows NT allows you to configure your network using either or both of these models.

In the Windows NT architecture, two software components—called the server and the redirector—provide server and workstation functionality. Both of these components reside above the TDI and are implemented as file system drivers.

Being implemented as file system drivers has several benefits. Applications can call a single API (namely, Windows NT I/O functions) to access files on local and remote computers. From the I/O Manager's perspective, there is no difference between accessing files stored on a remote networked computer and accessing those stored locally on a hard disk. The redirector and server can directly call other drivers and other kernel-mode components such as the Cache Manager, thus optimizing performance. Each can be loaded and unloaded dynamically. In addition, the Windows NT redirector can coexist with other redirectors (discussed more fully in the section called "Interoperating with Other Networks," later in this chapter).

Windows NT Redirector

The redirector is the component through which one computer gains access to another computer. The Windows NT redirector allows connection to other Windows NT computers as well as to LAN Manager, LAN Server, and MS-Net servers. This redirector communicates to the protocol stacks to which it is bound via the TDI. Because networking connections are not entirely reliable, it is up to the redirector to reestablish connections when they go down.

As illustrated by Figure 15.8, when a process on a Windows NT workstation tries to open a file on a remote computer, these steps occur:

1. The process calls the I/O Manager, asking for the file to be opened.
2. The I/O Manager recognizes that the request is for a file on a remote computer, so it passes it to the redirector file system driver.
3. The redirector passes the request to lower-level network drivers, which transmit it to the remote server for processing.

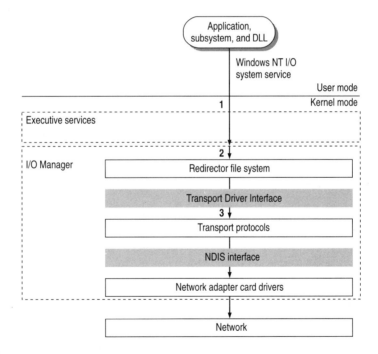

Figure 15.8   Client-Side Processing Using the Redirector

Windows NT Server

The server component entertains the connections requested by client-side redirectors and provides them with access to the resources they request. When a Windows NT server receives a request from a remote workstation to read a file on the server, these steps occur (as shown in Figure 15.9):

1. The low-level network drivers receive the request and pass it to the server driver.
2. The server passes a file-read request to the appropriate local file system driver.
3. The local file system driver calls a lower-level disk driver to access the file.
4. The data is passed back to the local file system driver.
5. The local file system driver passes the data back to the server.
6. The server passes the data to the lower-level network drivers for transmission back to the client computer.

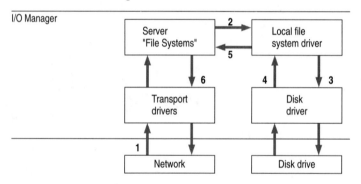

Figure 15.9   Server-Side Processing Using the Server

Interoperating with Other Networks

As mentioned before, the Windows NT redirector allows connections to LAN Manager, LAN Server, and MS-Net servers. It can also coexist with redirectors for other networks, such as Novell NetWare and Banyan VINES®.

While Windows NT includes integrated networking, its open design provides for transparent access to other networks. For example, a Windows NT user can concurrently access files stored on Windows NT and NetWare servers.

For details about interoperating with other networks, see Chapter 16, "Network Interoperability."

Providers and the Provider Interface Layer

For each additional type of network (NetWare, VINES, or some other), you must install a component called a *provider*. The provider is the component that allows a Windows NT computer to communicate with the network. Windows NT includes a provider for the Windows NT network; other provider DLLs are supplied by the alternate networks' vendors.

From the application viewpoint, there are two sets of commands that can cause network traffic—uniform naming convention (UNC) commands and WNet commands.

UNC is a method of identifying a shared resource on a network. UNC names start with two backslashes followed by the server name. All other fields in the name are separated by a single backslash. Although it's enough to simply specify the servername to list a server's shared resources, a full UNC name is in this form:

```
\\server\share\subdirectory\filename
```

WNet is part of the Win32 API and is specifically designed to allow applications on Windows NT workstations to connect to multiple networks, browse the resources of computers on those networks, and transfer data between computers of various networks. File Manager, for example, uses the WNet interface to provide its network browsing and connection facilities.

As shown in Figure 15.10, the provider layer spans the line between kernel and user modes to manage commands that may cause network traffic. The provider layer also includes two components to route UNC and WNet requests to the appropriate provider:

- The Multiple UNC Provider (MUP) receives UNC commands and locates the redirector that can make a connection to the UNC name.
- The Multiple Provider Router (MPR) receives WNet commands and passes the request to each redirector in turn until one is found that can satisfy the request.

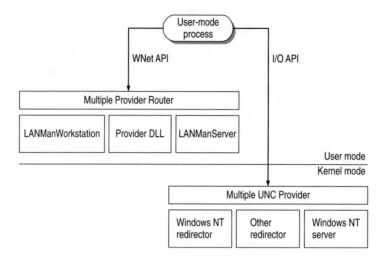

Figure 15.10   Provider Interface Components

Note I/O calls, such as Open, can contain both an UNC name and WNet calls.

Multiple UNC Provider

The MUP is a kernel-mode component whose job is to locate UNC names. When an application sends a command containing UNC names, MUP routes each UNC name to one of the registered UNC providers, including LanmanWorkstation and any others that may be installed. When a provider indicates that it can communicate with the server, MUP sends the remainder of the command to the provider.

When applications make I/O calls that contain UNC names, the MUP directs them to the appropriate redirector file system driver. The call is routed to its redirector based on the handle on the I/O call.

Multiple Provider Router

Through the MPR, Windows NT provides an open interface that enables consistent access to third-party network file systems. The key to the MPR is that all file systems, regardless of type and physical location, are accessible through the same set of file system APIs.

Applications, including File Manager, make file system requests through the Windows NT Win32 API. The MPR ensures that requests are directed to the proper file system. Local file requests are sent to the local disk, remote requests to Windows-based servers are sent to the proper server by the Windows redirector, requests to NetWare-based servers are handled by the NetWare Client for Windows NT and sent to the NetWare server, and so on.

Because applications access all types of files through a single set of APIs, any application can access any kind of server without affecting the user.

Distributed Applications and Windows NT

Any application you run on Windows NT can take advantage of networking resources because networking components are built into Windows NT. In addition, Windows NT includes several mechanisms that support and benefit distributed applications.

A *distributed application* is one that has two parts—a front-end to run on the client computer and a back-end to run on the server. In distributed computing, the goal is to divide the computing task into two sections. The front-end requires minimal resources and runs on the client's workstation. The back-end requires large amounts of data, number crunching, or specialized hardware and runs on the server. A connection between the client and the server at a process-to-process level allows data to flow in both directions between the client and server.

Microsoft Mail, Microsoft Schedule+, SQL Server, and SNA Server are examples of distributed applications.

As described earlier, Windows NT includes NetBIOS and Windows Sockets interfaces for building distributed applications. In addition, Windows NT supports peer-to-peer named pipes, mailslots, and remote procedure calls (RPC). On Windows NT, for example, an electronic mail product could include a messaging service using named pipes and asynchronous communication that runs with any transport protocol or network card.

Of named pipes, mailslots, and RPC, RPC is the most portable mechanism. RPCs use other IPC (interprocess communication) mechanisms—including named pipes and the NetBIOS and Windows Sockets interfaces—to transfer functions and data between client and server computers.

Named pipes and mailslots are implemented to provide backward compatibility with existing LAN Manager installations and applications.

For more information about using distributed applications with Windows NT, see Chapter 22, "Client-Server Connectivity on Windows NT."

NetBIOS and Windows Sockets

Besides redirectors, Windows NT includes two other components that provide links to remote computers—NetBIOS and Windows Sockets. Windows NT includes NetBIOS and Windows Sockets interfaces for building distributed applications. (Windows NT also includes three other interprocess communication mechanisms—Named Pipes, Mailslots, and Remote Procedure Calls—for use by distributed applications. These are described later in this chapter.)

The NetBIOS and Windows Sockets APIs are supplied by separate DLLs. These DLLs communicate with corresponding drivers in the Windows NT Executive. As shown by Figure 15.11, the NetBIOS and Windows Sockets drivers then bypass the Windows NT redirector and communicate with protocol drivers directly using the TDI.

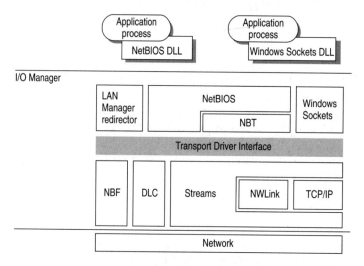

Figure 15.11   NetBIOS and Windows Sockets Support

NetBIOS

NetBIOS is the Network Basic Input/Output System—a high-level interface used by applications to communicate with NetBIOS-compliant transports such as NetBEUI. The network redirector is an example of a NetBIOS application. The NetBIOS interface is responsible for establishing logical names on the network, establishing sessions between two logical names on the network, and supporting reliable data transfer between computers that have established a session.

This Session-Layer interface was originally developed by Sytek, Inc., for IBM's broadband computer network. At that time, NetBIOS was included on a ROM chip on the network adapter card. Sytek also developed a NetBIOS for IBM's Token-Ring network, this time implemented as a device driver. Several other vendors have since produced versions of this interface.

In order to support the emerging network industry standard, Microsoft developed the NetBIOS interface for MS-Net and LAN Manager products, and also included this interface with the Windows for Workgroups product.

NetBIOS uses a unique logical name to identify a workstation for handling communications between nodes. A NetBIOS name is a unique alphanumeric name consisting of one to 15 characters. To carry on two-way communication between computers, NetBIOS establishes a logical connection, or *session*, between them. Once a logical connection is established, computers can then exchange data in the form of NetBIOS requests or in the form of a Server Message Block (SMB).

Server Message Blocks

The SMB protocol (developed jointly by Microsoft, Intel, and IBM) defines a series of commands used to pass information between networked computers and can be broken into four message types—session control, file, printer, and message. Session control consists of commands that start and end a redirector connection to a shared resource at the server. The file SMB messages are used by the redirector to gain access to files at the server. The printer SMB messages are used by the redirector to send data to a print queue at a server and to get status information about the print queue. The message SMB type allows an application to send messages to or receive messages from another workstation.

The redirector packages SMB requests meant for remote computers in a structure known as a Network Control Block (NCB). NCBs can be sent over the network to a remote device. The redirector also uses NCBs to make requests to the protocol stack of the local computer, such as "Create a session with the file server."

The provider DLL listens for SMB messages destined for it and removes the data portion of the SMB request so that it can be processed by a local device.

SMBs provide interoperability between different versions of the Microsoft family of networking products and other networks that use SMBs, including these:

MS OS/2 LAN Manager	DEC Pathworks
Microsoft Windows for Workgroups	Microsoft LAN Manager for UNIX
IBM LAN Server	3Com 3+Open
MS-DOS LAN Manager	MS-Net

Windows Sockets

Windows Sockets is a Windows implementation of the widely used UC Berkeley
Sockets API. Microsoft TCP/IP, NWLink, and AppleTalk protocols use this
interface.

A *socket* provides an endpoint to a connection; two sockets form a complete path.
A socket works as a bidirectional pipe for incoming and outgoing data between
networked computers. The Windows Sockets API is a networking API tailored for
use by programmers using the Microsoft Windows family of products. Windows
Sockets is a public specification based on Berkeley UNIX Sockets and aims to do
the following:

- Provide a familiar networking API to programmers using Windows or UNIX
- Offer binary compatibility between heterogeneous Windows-based TCP/IP
  stack and utilities vendors
- Support both connection-oriented and connectionless protocols

Most users will use programs that comply with Windows Sockets, such as FTP
or Telnet. (However, developers who are interested in developing a Windows
Sockets application can find specifications for Windows Sockets on the Internet.)

Named Pipes and Mailslots

Named pipes and mailslots are actually written as file systems, unlike other IPC
mechanisms. Thus, the Registry lists entries for the Named Pipes File System
(NPFS) and the Mailslot File System (MSFS). As file systems they share common
functionality, such as caching, with the other file systems. Additionally, processes
on the local computer can use named pipes and mailslots to communicate with
one another without going through networking components. Remote access to
named pipes and mailslots, as with all of the file systems, is provided through
the redirector.

Named pipes are based on OS/2 API calls, but in Windows NT they include
additional asynchronous support and increased security.

Another new feature added to named pipes is impersonation, which allows a
server to change its security identifier so that it matches the client's. For example,
suppose a database server system uses named pipes to receive read and write
requests from clients. When a request comes in, the database server program can
impersonate the client before attempting to perform the request. So even if the
server program does have authority to perform the function, the client may not,
and the request would be denied. (For more information on impersonation, see
Chapter 2, "Windows NT Security Model.")

Mailslot APIs in Windows NT are a subset of those in Microsoft OS/2 LAN Manager. Windows NT implements only second-class mailslots, not first-class mailslots. Second-class mailslots provide *connectionless* messaging for broadcast messages and so on. Delivery of the message is not guaranteed, although the delivery rate on most networks is very high. Second-class mailslots are most useful for identifying other computers or services on a network and for wide-scale notification of a service.

Remote Procedure Calls

Much of the original design work for an RPC facility was started by Sun Microsystems®. This work was continued by the Open Software Foundation (OSF) as part of their overall Data Communications Exchange (DCE) standard. The Microsoft RPC facility is compatible with the OSF/DCE-standard RPC. It is important to note that it is compatible and not compliant. Compliance in this case means starting with the OSF source code and building on it. The Microsoft RPC facility is completely interoperable with other DCE-based RPC systems such as the ones for HP and IBM AIX® systems.

The RPC mechanism is unique because it uses the other IPC mechanisms to establish communications between the client and the server. RPC can use named pipes, NetBIOS, or Windows Sockets to communicate with remote systems. If the client and server are on the same computer, it can use the Local Procedure Call (LPC) facility to transfer information between processes and subsystems. This makes RPC the most flexible and portable of the Windows NT IPC mechanisms.

RPC is based on the concepts used for creating structured programs, which can be viewed as having a "backbone" to which a series of "ribs" can be attached. The backbone is the mainstream logic of the program, which should rarely change. The ribs are the procedures the backbone calls on to do work or perform functions.

In traditional programs, these ribs are statically linked. By using DLLs, structured programs can dynamically link the ribs. With DLLs, the procedure code and the backbone code are in different modules. The DLL can thus be modified or updated without changes to the backbone. RPC means that the backbone and the ribs can exist on different computers, as shown in Figure 15.12.

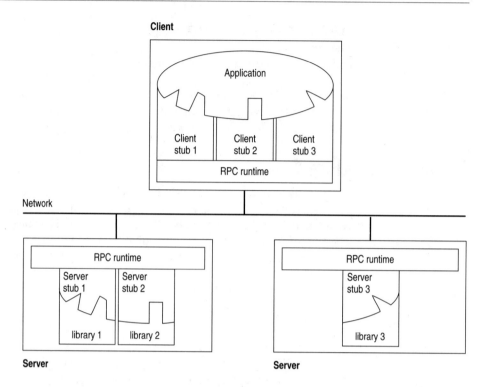

Figure 15.12   Remote Procedure Call Facility

In this figure, the client application was developed with a specially compiled *stub* library. The client application thinks it is calling its own subroutines. In reality, these stubs transfer the data and the function down to a module called the RPC Runtime. This module is responsible for finding the server that can satisfy the RPC command. Once found, the function and data are sent to the server, where it is picked up by the RPC Runtime module on the server. The server piece then loads the needed library for the function, builds the appropriate data structure, and calls the function. The function thinks it is being called by the client application. When the function is completed, any return values are collected, formatted, and sent back to the client via the RPC Runtime modules. When the function returns to the client application it has the appropriate returned data, or it has an indication that the function failed in stream.

Other Client Services for Windows NT

Windows NT Advanced Server includes two additional client services:

- Services for Macintosh, a connectivity service for Macintosh users
- RAS, a dial-up service for remote users

Note The Windows NT base product also offers limited RAS functionality. These limitations are identified in "Remote Access for Windows NT Clients," later in this chapter.

Services for Macintosh

Through Windows NT Services for Macintosh, Macintosh users can connect to a Windows NT server the same way they would connect to an AppleShare server. Windows NT Services for Macintosh will support up to 255 simultaneous AFP™ connections to a Windows NT server, and Macintosh sessions will be integrated with Windows NT sessions. The per-session memory overhead is approximately 15K.

Existing versions of LAN Manager Services for the Macintosh can be easily upgraded to Windows NT Services for Macintosh. OS/2-based volumes that already exist are converted with permissions intact. In addition, graphical installation, administration, and configuration utilities are integrated with existing Windows NT administration tools. Windows NT Services for Macintosh requires System 6.0.7 or higher and is AFP 2.1-compliant; however, AFP 2.0 clients are supported. AFP 2.1 compliance provides support for logon messages and server messages.

Support for Macintosh networking is built into the core operating system for Windows NT Advanced Server. Windows NT Services for Macintosh includes a full AFP 2.0 file server. All Macintosh file system attributes, such as resource data forks, 32-bit directory IDs, and so on, are supported. As a file server, all filenames, icons, and access permissions are intelligently managed for different networks. For example, a Word for Windows file will appear on the Macintosh with the correct Word for Macintosh icons. These applications can also be launched from the File Server as Macintosh applications. When files are deleted, there will be no orphaned resource forks left to be cleaned up.

Windows NT Services for Macintosh fully supports and complies with Windows NT security. It presents the AFP security model to Macintosh users and allows them to access files on volumes that reside on CD-ROM or other read-only media. The AFP server also supports both cleartext and encrypted passwords at logon time. The administrator has the option to configure the server not to accept cleartext passwords.

Services for Macintosh can be administered from Control Panel and can be started transparently if the administrator has configured the server to use this facility.

Macintosh-accessible volumes can be created from File Manager. Services for Macintosh automatically creates a Public Files volume at installation time. Windows NT file and directory permissions are automatically translated into corresponding Macintosh permissions.

Windows NT Services for Macintosh has the same functionality as the LAN Manager Services for Macintosh 1.0 MacPrint. In addition, administration and configuration are easier. There is a user interface for publishing a print queue on AppleTalk and a user interface for choosing an AppleTalk printer as a destination device. The Windows NT print subsystem handles AppleTalk despooling errors gracefully, and uses the built-in printer support in Windows NT. (The PPD file scheme of Macintosh Services 1.0 is not used.) Services for Macintosh also has a PostScript-compatible engine that allows Macintoshes to print to any Windows NT printer as if they were printing to a LaserWriter.

Remote Access for Windows NT Clients

Windows NT Remote Access Service (RAS) extends your local-area network to remote workstations. Business travelers and people working from home can access Windows NT servers through the RAS. In a sense, the RAS turns your modem into a network adapter card.

Windows NT RAS offers these features:

- Full network access for remote PCs. Remote users can access resources on all Windows NT-based, LAN Manager (OS/2, UNIX, and VMS), and Windows for Workgroups computers on the network, including files and print resources and client-server applications.

- Access client-server applications. RAS is optimized for client-server applications, providing an excellent foundation for solutions that span several sites.

- Integrated administration. There is no administrative difference between remote users and on-site users. Remote access is a permission in the user accounts database. In addition, you can perform all administrative tasks such as monitoring server performance, managing user accounts, and starting and stopping services, from a remote computers.

- Advanced security. RAS implements full Windows NT security authentication before allowing remote users access to the network. Network administrators can select the level of call-back on an account-by-account basis. For additional security, Windows NT Remote Access supports dial-up security hosts.

RAS Clients and Servers

A remote access scenario includes three key computers:

- The Remote Access client workstation. This workstation uses one of a number of means (including various asynchronous modems, a null modem cable, X.25, or ISDN) and the RAS software to dial in to a RAS server. The remote workstation can be running MS-DOS LAN Manager, Windows 3.1 running LAN Manager, Windows for Workgroups, OS/1 LAN Manager 1.3, Windows NT, or Windows NT Advanced Server.

- The Remote Access server. A Remote Access server running Windows NT Advanced Server has as many as 64 ports for connecting to remote workstations (compared to Remote Access with LAN Manager, which supported 16 ports). A RAS server running Windows NT can have one port. Any server on the network can be used as a RAS server, it does not need to be dedicated to RAS. The RAS server can have multiple network protocol stacks to allow the workstation to connect to the target server.

- The target server, which can be the same computer as the Remote Access server or any other server on the network. This server does not need to know that the workstation is communicating via the Remote Access server.

The Windows NT platform contains both client and server software. The difference between Windows NT and Windows NT Advanced Server is the number of ports supported (1 for Windows NT and 64 for Windows NT Advanced Server). Figure 15.13 gives a detailed view of the components used by the Remote Access client and server.

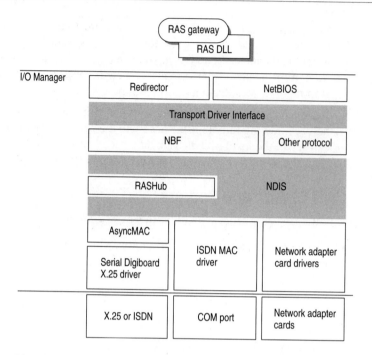

Figure 15.13   Remote Access Client and Server Computers

Briefly, here's how information flows between the remote client and the Remote Access server (see Figure 15.13):

The person at the client computer uses the RAS Phone application to dial the Remote Access server. RAS Phone communicates with the client's modem through a MAC-Layer serial driver called AsyncMAC. (Alternately, instead of using modems, the client and server can communicate through X.25 or ISDN.)

Windows NT includes a standard Serial Interface, similar to NDIS, to which serial drivers are written.

On the server side, the serial driver, through the serial interface, communicates with AsyncMAC. Alternately, if the communication is via ISDN, it is received directly by the ISDN MAC driver. In either case, the communication from the client is passed next to a component called RAS Hub.

RAS Hub routes frames from various RAS endpoints to various transport protocols. This component is implemented as a device driver that is surrounded by an NDIS wrapper. To protocols, RAS Hub behaves like a MAC-Layer driver. (Remote clients enter the network through these MAC-Layer drivers.) To MAC-Layer drivers, RAS Hub behaves like a protocol.

RAS Hub passes the information to the redirector. If the client's request is to use a resource on the local server, the redirector passes the request to the appropriate local component. If the request is for a resource elsewhere on the network, the redirector passes the request to the RAS Gateway, which routes it to the appropriate network destination.

Remote Access Server as a Gateway to Other Networks

The Remote Access server component acts as a gateway. Different from routers, b-routers, and bridges, a gateway performs the transfer function at the application Layer. This allows the Physical, Data Link, Network, Transport, and Session Layers between the two transferring protocol stacks to be different. Because the RAS server was designed as an accessory for LAN Manager, which is based on NetBIOS at the Session Layer, the RAS server requires the Session Layers to be NetBIOS. Other Transport and Network Layer components (such as TCP/IP and XNS®) can be used between the RAS server and the target server.

Once a session is established with a target server, frames from the remote workstation are received at the COM port and work their way up the protocol stack until the frames are received by the RAS server component in the form of a NetBIOS control block (NCB). The Remote Access server then determines which LAN stack is to be retransmitted upon and sends the data. Traffic from the target server to the remote workstation follows a similar path, but in reverse.

Remote Access Authentication

It is important to note that RAS includes security safeguards that assure proper authorization before access is granted to any remote user.

As described in Chapter 2, "Windows NT Security Model," Windows NT performs a standard logon validation process for each user logging on to a Windows NT computer. This process requires a user to provide a recognized username and password combination before being allowed to use the computer. In addition, Windows NT performs authentication-checking (called discretionary access control) whenever the user attempts to access a resource on the computer or on the network. If the user is not granted the appropriate permissions, Windows NT will not allow the user to access the resource.

As illustrated by Figure 15.13, Windows NT RAS adds another layer of security to the model described in Chapter 2. Before the user even logs on, RAS checks to see whether the user has permission to access the server via a dial-in RAS account. The password for remote access is different from the user's logon password and is encrypted.

Windows NT RAS also supports third-party security hosts. For more information, see the *Windows NT Advanced Server RAS Administrator's Guide*.

Note If you do not have this manual, see the *Windows NT System Guide*. Then see Appendix B, "Remote Access Server Administration." This appendix includes all of the information found in the Windows NT Advanced Server documentation but not in the Windows NT-based documentation set.

Callback Options

As part of the RAS authentication process, network administrators can choose from two call-back options:

- The dial-in server can be instructed to hang up and call back to a phone number designated by the administrator for tighter security. This option is ideal for people who travel and dial in from client offices or hotels.

- The server can be set to call a number supplied by the user after validation. This option helps to efficiently manage telephone costs and works well for people who work from home or from a satellite office.

The administrator can set up the RAS server so that users who are permitted access can use only those resources on the server. Or, the administrator can set up the RAS server as a gateway to the network. (Note that this option is set at server level, not account by account for individual users.)

Tip By changing the binding of RAS, you can restrict dial-in users from accessing certain portions of the network. For example, you could unbind the Remote Access server from TCP/IP to disallow access from Remote Access clients to remote UNIX mainframe computers.

Additional Reading

For additional information on topics related to networking and the Windows NT networking model, see the following resources:

ANSI/IEEE standard 802.2 - 1985 (ISO/DIS 8802/2): *IEEE Standards for Local Area Networks—Logical Link Control Standard.*

ANSI/IEEE standard 802.3 - 1985 (ISO/DIS 8802/3): *IEEE Standards for Local Area Networks—Carrier Sense Multiple Access with Collision Detection (CSMA/CD) Access Method and Physical Layer Specifications*; American National Standards Institute; January 12, 1989.

ANSI/IEEE standard 802.4 - 1985 (ISO/DIS 8802/4): *IEEE Standards for Local Area Networks—Token-Passing Bus Access Method and Physical Layer Specifications*; American National Standards Institute; December 17, 1984.

ANSI/IEEE standard 802.5 - 1985 (ISO/DIS 8802/5): *IEEE Standards for Local Area Networks—Token-Ring Access Method and Physical Layer Specifications*; American National Standards Institute; June 2, 1989.

Beatty, Dana. "Programming to the OS/2 IEEE 802.2 API." *OS/2 Notebook.* Ed. Dick Conklin. Redmond, WA: Microsoft Press, 1990.

Haugdahl, J. Scott. *Inside NetBIOS.* Minneapolis: Architecture Technology Corporation, 1990.

Haugdahl, J. Scott. *Inside NetBIOS (2nd Edition).* Minneapolis, Minn: Architecture Technology Corporation, 1988.

Haugdahl, J. Scott. *Inside Token-Ring (3rd Edition).* Minneapolis, Minn: Architecture Technology Corporation, 1990.

IBM Token-Ring Network Architecture Reference (6165877), November 1985.

IBM Token-Ring Network PC Adapter Technical Reference (69X7830).

International Business Machines. *Local Area Network: Technical Reference (SC30-3383-2).* New York: 1988.

International Standard 7498: *Information processing systems—Open Systems Interconnection—Basic Reference Model (First edition)*; American National Standards Institute, November 15, 1984. The OSI model.

Martin, James. *Local Areas Networks: Architecture and Implementations.* Englewood Cliffs, NJ: Prentice Hall: 1989.

Microsoft Corporation, 3Com Corporation. *SMB Specification.* This may be obtained from the files library in the Microsoft Client Server Computing forum on CompuServe (GO MSNETWORK).

Microsoft Corporation. *Microsoft LAN Manager Resource Kit.* Microsoft Corporation, 1992.

Microsoft. *Computer Dictionary.* Redmond, WA: Microsoft Press, 1991.

Microsoft. *Microsoft LAN Manager MS-DLC Protocol Driver.* Redmond, WA: Microsoft Press, 1991.

Microsoft. *Microsoft/3Com LAN Manager Network Driver Interface Specification.* Redmond, WA: Microsoft Press, 1990.

Miller, Mark. *LAN Protocol Handbook.* Redwood City, CA: M & T Books, 1990.

Miller, Mark. *LAN Troubleshooting Handbook.* Redwood City, CA: M & T Books, 1990.

Tanenbaum, Andrew. *Computer Networks (2nd Edition).* Englewood Cliffs, NJ: Prentice Hall, 1988

The Ethernet. A Local Area Network. (Data Link Layer and Physical Layer Specifications); version 2.0, November 1982. Also known as the "Ethernet Blue Book."

C H A P T E R   1 6

Network Interoperability

In addition to Windows networking, Windows NT supports network interoperability with computers running a wide range of operating systems and network protocols. This makes it easy to incorporate computers running Windows NT into existing networks so you can take advantage of the advanced features of Windows NT without disrupting your enterprise.

The networking architecture of Windows NT plays an important role in making Windows NT a powerful member of many different types of networks. The architecture itself is protocol-independent, providing standard interfaces for applications (such as Windows Sockets, RPC, and NetBIOS) and device drivers. Besides making it easier to implement a particular protocol stack for Windows NT, this architecture also allows a Windows NT computer to run multiple protocols on a single network adapter card. As a result, a Windows NT computer can simultaneously communicate with a number of different network systems.

Of particular interest to most network administrators is how to provide access by and to computers running Windows NT and Windows NT Advanced Server in the following environments:

- Novell NetWare networks
- UNIX networks
- IBM mainframes and minicomputers

This chapter provides an overview of some of the issues and benefits involved in using Windows NT computers in these environments.

Using Windows NT with NetWare

Windows NT computers can easily be integrated into a predominantly NetWare environment, making the benefits of an advanced operating system available to an existing network.

A network administrator contemplating a mixed network environment is naturally concerned about how the various components will be able to communicate with each other. In the case of a mixed Windows networking and NetWare environment, the network administrator wants to ensure that Windows NT workstations added to the network are able to use file and print resources on existing NetWare servers, and that existing NetWare clients can access client-server applications running on Windows NT Advanced Servers. The following figure shows how the various components of the network relate to each other.

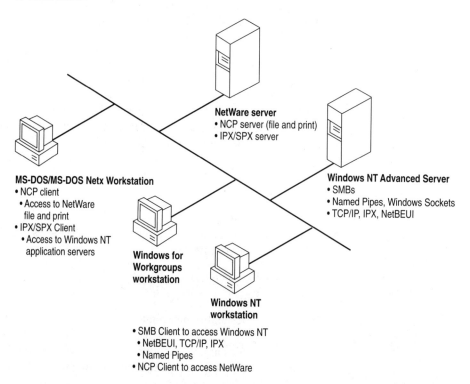

NetWare server
- NCP server (file and print)
- IPX/SPX server

MS-DOS/MS-DOS Netx Workstation
- NCP client
  - Access to NetWare file and print
- IPX/SPX Client
  - Access to Windows NT application servers

Windows NT Advanced Server
- SMBs
- Named Pipes, Windows Sockets
- TCP/IP, IPX, NetBEUI

Windows for Workgroups workstation

Windows NT workstation
- SMB Client to access Windows NT
- NetBEUI, TCP/IP, IPX
- Named Pipes
- NCP Client to access NetWare

The following sections discuss how Windows NT computers can effectively function either as a client of NetWare servers or as an application server for NetWare clients.

Windows NT Advanced Servers on a NetWare Network

Many organizations that use NetWare are seeking solutions for downsizing or reengineering existing applications that run on minicomputers or mainframes. NetWare servers are designed to function primarily as file and print servers, and so they do not support such business-critical applications well. NetWare servers do not feature preemptive multitasking or protected virtual memory, essential features for client-server applications. On the other hand, Windows NT Advanced Server makes an ideal platform for such demanding applications because of its scalability, fault tolerance, 32-bit architecture, and threaded, preemptive multitasking with full memory protection.

NetWare administrators can take advantage of the advanced features of Windows NT Advanced Servers on an existing NetWare network without interfering with client systems' access to file and printer resources on NetWare servers. For example, a NetWare administrator can add Windows NT Advanced Server computers running SQL Server to the network so client workstations can take advantage of a distributed high-performance relational database system while still being able to use files and printers shared by their usual NetWare servers. Such a solution requires no additional hardware or software to provide the necessary connectivity.

To function as an application server for NetWare clients, a computer running Windows NT Advanced Server must be running the built-in NWLink protocol stack. NWLink is an IPX/SPX-compatible transport protocol through which Windows NT computers can be connected to computers running MS-DOS, Windows, OS/2, or Windows NT. The connection can be made via Remote Procedure Calls (RPC), Sockets, or Novell NetBIOS. Because NWLink is NDIS-compliant, the Windows NT computer can simultaneously run other protocol stacks (such as NBF or TCP/IP) through which it can communicate with non-NetWare computers.

Windows NT Clients on a NetWare Network

Because it was designed from the start to be on a network, Windows NT makes an excellent network client. Its open design enables third-party network redirectors to integrate seamlessly with the operating system. An example of one such third-party redirector is NetWare Client for Windows NT developed by Novell. NetWare Client allows a Windows NT computer to access file and print resources on NetWare servers as easily as it accesses resources on Windows-networking servers.

For example, File Manager allows the user to browse and connect to any NetWare or Windows-networking server on the network. Because the network support built into Windows NT is independent of the underlying network system, the same user interface and tools work with all networks that run on Windows NT.

The Windows NT architecture includes an open interface called the multiple provider router (MPR) that enables consistent access to third-party network file systems. The MPR makes all file systems, regardless of type and physical location, accessible through the same set of file-system APIs. Applications (and components of the Windows NT shell) make file-system requests through the Windows NT Win32 API. The MPR ensures that requests are directed to the proper file system: local file requests are sent to the local disk, remote requests to Windows-based servers are sent to the proper server by the Windows redirector, and requests to NetWare servers are sent to the appropriate server by the NetWare Client for Windows NT.

NetWare Client for Windows NT is based on the ODI device-driver standard rather than the NDIS standard used by most Windows NT network software. Even though only one device driver can be bound to a particular network adapter card, both NetWare Client for Windows NT and NDIS-based transports (such as NBF and TCP/IP) can access the network on a single network adapter card. This is possible because NetWare Client for Windows NT includes ODINSUP, a device driver that converts requests from NDIS-based software into ODI requests (and back).

For more information about NWLink and NetWare Client for Windows, see Chapter 20, "Using NWLink and NetWare Client for Windows NT."

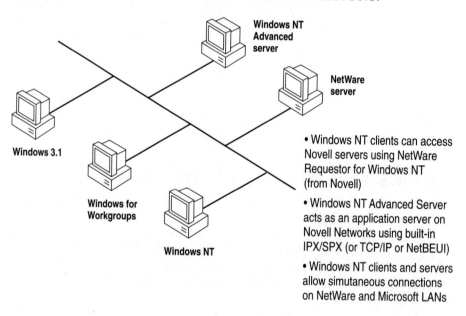

Figure 16.1   Windows NT Computers as NetWare Clients or Application Servers

Additional Considerations

Before adding computers running Windows NT (or other non-NetWare operating systems) to a NetWare network, a NetWare administrator should anticipate some of the potential problems that might arise.

One source of possible difficulty for NetWare administrators is the fact that Windows NT NetWare clients do not run NetWare logon scripts. However, Windows NT is able to run its own logon scripts, and the ability of Windows NT to maintain persistent connections provides much the same functionality as NetWare logon scripts in many instances.

Another area of difficulty is backing up Windows NT NetWare clients. Novell servers cannot provide tape backup services for Windows NT computers. However, a Windows NT computer equipped with a supported tape drive can back up other Windows NT computers, as well as NetWare servers and computers running Windows networking software.

Finally, Windows NT can act as a client only for a NetWare server running NetWare version 3.*x* and earlier. Windows NT can access servers running Netware 4.*x* through the server's Bindery Emulation Mode that emulates version 3.*x*.

Integrating Windows NT and UNIX Systems

As an advanced operating system, Windows NT is especially suited for integrating with most of the UNIX variants that are likely to be found on many networks. Among the Windows NT features that make it easy to interoperate with UNIX systems are:

- Built-in TCP/IP protocol and utilities.
- Support for character and graphics terminal emulation.
- Advanced file transfer and data sharing capabilities.
- Distributed processing support.
- Application portability.

The following sections provide further information about these features.

TCP/IP Protocol

At the protocol level, Windows NT includes the Transport Control Protocol/Internet Protocol (TCP/IP) protocol stack, the most commonly used protocol among UNIX systems. This allows Windows NT computers to communicate with UNIX systems without requiring additional networking software. (TCP/IP also provides efficient communication on wide-area networks even when no UNIX systems are involved.) The TCP/IP protocol stack for Windows NT is NDIS-compliant and so can be used in conjunction with NBF and other NDIS-compliant protocols.

In addition to the TCP/IP protocol itself, Windows NT also includes more than a dozen TCP/IP utilities that make it easier for experienced UNIX users to access UNIX systems from Windows NT and to administer the TCP/IP networking on their own computer.

Windows NT also provides facilities for integrating computers running Windows NT into networks managed through Simple Network Management Protocol (SNMP), which is commonly used to manage TCP/IP networks. Through its SNMP service, a Windows NT computer can report its current status to an SNMP management system on a TCP/IP network, either in response to a request from a management system or automatically when a significant event occurs on the Windows NT computer.

For more information, see Chapter 19, "TCP/IP on Windows NT."

Character and Graphics Terminal Support

The TCP/IP Telnet utility is built into the Windows Terminal accessory to make it easy for a Windows NT computer to have character-oriented terminal access to UNIX systems via TCP/IP. Telnet provides basic terminal emulation of TTY (scrolling), as well as emulation of DEC VT-100 (ANSI) and VT-52 terminals. Because Telnet is implemented as a service, it can be used by third-party terminal emulation programs.

Even in the traditionally character-oriented UNIX environment, many applications are moving to graphical user interfaces. X Windows is a commonly used standard for graphical interfaces in networked UNIX environments. A number of third-party companies are also developing X Servers to allow Windows NT users to access and run X-based applications on UNIX systems. (In X Windows terminology, an X Server runs on a client workstation to provide graphics output on behalf of an X Client program running on an applications server.) Several third parties are also developing X Client libraries for Windows NT as well; this will eventually allow UNIX (or other systems with X Server capabilities) to access client-server applications running on a Windows NT computer.

File Transfer and Data Sharing

One of the fundamental reasons for connecting computers on a network is to allow them to exchange files and data. Windows NT supports standard facilities for transferring files and sharing data between Windows NT and UNIX systems.

Included with Windows NT itself are both client and server versions of File Transfer Protocol (FTP). FTP makes it possible for Windows NT computers to exchange files with diverse systems, particularly UNIX systems.

Where more advanced data sharing capabilities are required, computers running Windows NT can access data on UNIX systems (including data on remotely mountable file systems, such as NFS, RFS, and AFS) through Microsoft LAN Manager for UNIX (LMU), an implementation of Microsoft Windows networking for servers running UNIX variants. LMU is based on SMBs, a set of protocols developed by Microsoft that are now part of the X/Open standard.

Finally, a number of third-party companies (including SunSelect) are developing versions of Sun's Network File System (NFS) for Windows NT. NFS is a widely used tool for sharing files among various UNIX systems.

Distributed Processing Support

As more and more enterprises adopt the client-server paradigm for their networks, standards-based distributed processing becomes a key factor in the success of that effort. Windows NT provides direct support for several types of industry-standard distributed processing.

The Remote Procedure Call (RPC) facility of Windows NT is wire-compatible with the Open Software Foundation's Distributed Computing Environment (DCE) RPC. Using this RPC, developers can create applications that include not only Windows NT computers, but all systems that support DCE-compatible RPCs, such as systems from Hewlett Packard and Digital Equipment Corporation.

In addition to RPCs, Windows NT supports Windows Sockets. Windows Sockets provides an API that is compatible with Berkeley-style sockets, a mechanism that is widely used by different UNIX versions for distributed computing.

For more information about RPC and Windows Sockets, see Chapter 15, "Windows NT Networking Architecture."

Perhaps most importantly, Windows Open Services Architecture (WOSA), whose development is being led by Microsoft, specifies an open set of APIs for integrating Windows computers with back-end services on a broad range of vendors' systems. WOSA consists of an extensible set of APIs that allow Windows-based desktop applications to access available information without having to know anything about the type of network in use, the types of computers in the enterprise, or the types of back-end services available. As a result, should the network, computers, or services change, desktop applications built using WOSA won't require rewriting. The first two WOSA components address database and electronic messaging: Open Database Connectivity (ODBC) and Messaging API (MAPI). Work is underway for additional standards, including directory, security, and software licensing services.

Common Application Support

For most users, the key measure of interoperability is the ability to run the same applications on multiple platforms. Three key factors are furthering this type of interoperability between UNIX systems and Windows NT.

The first factor is the relative ease with which many UNIX ISVs are able to port their high-end business and technical applications to the Win32 API of Windows NT. Aiding this process is the fact that most UNIX applications are written in standard C and so are readily adapted to other operating systems (such as Windows NT) for which standard C libraries have been developed. A wide variety of third-party porting aids (including items as diverse asXlibs, GNU tools, and X Client libraries) are available through commercial sources and from Internet. Because application developers are finding it so easy to port their traditionally UNIX-based applications to Windows NT, increasing numbers of such applications will be available for both UNIX platforms and for computers running Windows NT.

Secondly, Windows NT fully supports programs that conform to the IEEE 1003.1-1990 standard commonly known as POSIX.1 (derived from Portable Operating System Interface). This standard defines a basic set of operating-system services available to character-based applications. Programs that adhere to the POSIX standard can be easily ported from one operating system to another. See Chapter 24, "POSIX Compatibility," for more information.

Thirdly, Microsoft has recently announced that it will license Windows source and test code to third parties to allow them to develop products (called Windows Libraries for UNIX) that will allow UNIX to run Windows applications.

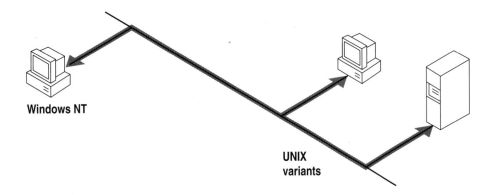

Figure 16.2   Integration of Windows NT and UNIX Systems

Connecting Windows NT and IBM Mainframes

A growing trend in many types of enterprises is downsizing mainframe-based applications to run on PC client-server networks. Many of these downsized applications will still require access to data and applications residing on mainframes and minicomputers. Companies have invested large amounts of money, time, and effort in their mainframe systems and so want to be able to make the best use of that investment even as they move toward distributed client-server computing. This section discusses how Windows NT can be integrated with IBM mainframe and minicomputers to leverage the high capacity of mainframes in a distributed environment.

Basic Connectivity Using the Built-In DLC Protocol

A computer running Windows NT can communicate with IBM mainframe computers (as well as other network devices) across an Ethernet or Token Ring LAN through the Data Link Control (DLC) protocol that is built into Windows NT. The DLC protocol device driver allows a basic level of connectivity with other computers running the DLC protocol stack. For example, a Windows NT computer can connect to and communicate with an IBM mainframe through its 37x5 Front-end processor (FEP) using a 3270 terminal emulator and the DLC protocol. See Chapter 21, "Using DLC with Windows NT," for more information.

SNA Server for Windows NT

Although such simple one-to-one connections may suffice for many basic operations, most enterprises require more flexible connectivity between IBM host computers and their local-area networks (LANs). To meet this need, SNA Server for Windows NT exploits client-server architecture to link desktop PCs to IBM mainframe computers that are accessible using the Systems Network Architecture (SNA) protocols. The PCs can be running Windows NT, Windows, MS-DOS, OS/2, or the Macintosh operating system and can use standard LAN protocols to connect to the server; only the computer running SNA Server must run the SNA protocol. Each PC user can have multiple 3270 and 5250 sessions for concurrent terminal and printer emulation, including file-transfer and Emulator High-Level Language API (EHLLAPI) applications. SNA Server for Windows NT also provides support on the PC for the following APIs for distributed SNA applications:

- Advanced Program-to-Program Communications (APPC) for applications that communicate peer-to-peer with other APPC applications using the LU 6.2 protocol

- Common Programming Interface for Communications (CPI-C) for applications that communicate peer-to-peer with IBM SAA applications using the LU 6.2 protocol

- Common Service Verbs (CSV) for applications that communicate with NetView and enable tracing of API calls

- Logical Unit APIs (LUA) for applications (using LUA/Request Unit Interface or LUA/Session Level Interface APIs) that need direct access to LU 0, 1, 2, and 3 data streams

The client-server architecture of SNA Server for Windows NT makes it possible to off-load communications processing from client systems, permitting them to use their system resources more efficiently. Client PCs do not have to run multiple protocols to access their LAN and IBM hosts. Instead, they can run any combination of NBF, TCP/IP, or IPX/SPX to access the SNA Server, which routes the connection to the appropriate host computer via the SNA protocol. The SNA Server automatically balances the user load across multiple host connections and servers to provide optimal throughput.

The client-server architecture also provides Windows NT-based applications with the ability to access information on IBM mainframes and minicomputers. For example, using SNA Server, mail servers can access PROFS and Microsoft SQL Server can access DB2 information.

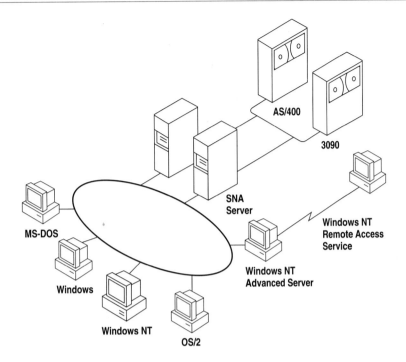

Figure 16.3   SNA Server Connecting LANs to IBM Host Computers

DSPU Support

In addition to standard PC connections, SNA Server for Windows NT supports Downstream Physical Units (DSPUs), devices or PCs running a full PU2 (SNA cluster controller) protocol stack. These systems use the SNA Server as a concentrator gateway for connecting to IBM hosts. The DSPU support provided by SNA Server includes third-party support for full PU2 stack clients connecting to the Windows NT server. Examples of some of the clients that SNA Server for Windows NT supports are IBM OS/2 Extended Services and DCA IRMA Workstation for the Macintosh. The DSPU protocols that SNA Server for Windows NT supports are DLC over Token Ring or Ethernet, Synchronous Data Link Control (SDLC), and OSI-standard X.25/QLLC (Qualified Logical Link Control).

NetView Support

SNA Server for Windows NT provides API support for bidirectional communications with NetView, IBM's mainframe-centered network management system. NetView can be notified of any significant events that occur on Windows NT via NetView alerts. For example, if an SNA Server database is stopped on the LAN, an alert can be sent to the NetView console. A data center operator can then send a command from the NetView console to the Windows NT computer to restart the server.

SNA Server also supports Response-Time Monitor (RTM) and user-defined alerts for third-party 3270 emulators. SNA Server sends application- or system-defined Windows NT event-log messages to NetView and allows Windows NT commands to be executed from the NetView console.

Centralized Management

Network administrators can administer all SNA servers from a centralized location, such as from a LAN workstation or a NetView console. For example, a company with offices in several cities could have one or more SNA Servers at each site. The MIS department at corporate headquarters can manage all of these SNA Servers, performing all administrative functions remotely.

Integration with Windows NT

SNA Server relies on the built-in security of Windows NT, allowing users to log on both the Windows NT network and SNA Server using a single username and password, and administrators need to manage a single set of user accounts.

SNA Server for Windows NT is completely 32 bit and multithreaded for maximum performance, scalability, and reliability. SNA Server also is fully integrated with Windows NT system monitoring and management services, and provides automatic server and connection fault tolerance.

SNA Server is fully compliant with Microsoft's Windows Open Services Architecture (WOSA), providing a consistent interface to enterprise computing environments and hiding the complexities of connectivity from applications.

Server Capabilities

SNA Server provides for as many as 50 simultaneous host connections by each server and up to 250 users and 500 sessions per server.

CHAPTER 17

Network Security and Administration

Each domain and each computer in a workgroup maintains its own user accounts information. Even on a multidomain network, by coordinating account information for an individual user across all parts of the network that he or she must use, the user can access those servers and domains with a single logon. If the user's accounts are allowed to become unsynchronized, problems can occur in which the user:

- Can't browse a domain or server for which he or she has permissions.
- Can't access a shared resource.
- Must type a password each time he or she browses or tries to access a resource.

For the most part, these problems can be avoided by good planning and good network maintenance. Before reading this chapter, be sure to read the *Windows NT Advanced Server Concepts and Planning Guide* for a thorough discussion of domain organization strategies and user environment management techniques.

This chapter provides you with information that can help you avoid problems related to network logon. It also describes how user accounts and other security information are maintained within workgroups and domains. It describes how security information can be shared by trusted domains. Finally, it discusses how the Windows NT Computer Browser service allows network browsing by domain and by server.

Windows NT User Accounts

Windows NT needs only a single logon, even for a heterogeneous networking environment, in part because security in Windows NT is assigned per user rather than per resource. (Per-resource security models require a separate password for each resource a user wants to access.)

In Windows NT, the network administrator creates a user account for each user wanting to use network resources. As described in Chapter 2, "Windows NT Security Model," Windows NT maintains a user account containing a unique security ID within the user accounts database. Windows NT also keeps track of permissions and user rights for the user. When a person logs on, the Security Accounts Manager (SAM) checks the user's logon information against data in its user accounts database to validate the logon. Then, when access is granted, the Local Security Authority (LSA) creates a security access token for that user.

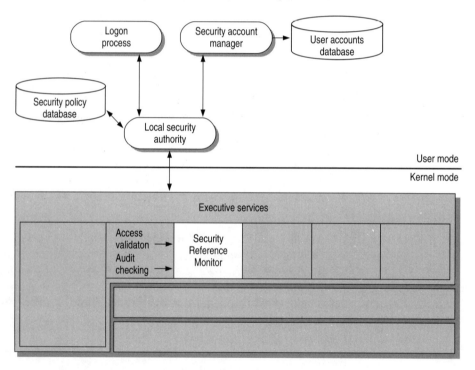

Figure 17.1   Windows NT Security Model

Note A user who forgets his or her password might assume that he or she can gain access to a resource via the Guest account; this is not the case. Because Windows NT recognizes the username, it compares the user's logon information only with the account information for that username. If the password does not match, no access is granted.

As described in the *Windows NT Advanced Server Concepts and Planning Guide*, Windows NT uses the Guest account for people with an unrecognized user account (including users logging on from untrusted domains). By default, the Guest account is disabled so that only those users with recognized accounts can access the system.

Depending on the way your corporation's network is organized, you might in fact have more than one account, granting access to workstation computers and domains on the network. The user account database used to validate a logon doesn't necessarily reside on the user's local computer. Its location depends on whether the computer is part of a workgroup or a domain and whether the user is logging on to the local computer, to the home domain, or to another (trusted) domain.

Workgroups and Domains

Windows NT Advanced Servers are always part of a domain, while Windows NT workstations can join a domain or a workgroup.

A *workgroup* is simply an organizational unit, a way to group workstations that don't belong to a domain. In a workgroup, each computer keeps track of its own user and group account information. For Windows NT computers, each one that participates in a workgroup maintain its own security policy and security account databases.

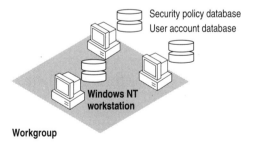

Figure 17.2   Computers Participating in a Workgroup

A *domain* is a group of servers that share common security policy and user accounts databases. One server, running Windows NT Advanced Server, acts as the domain controller and maintains the centralized security databases for the domain. Other servers in the domain function as backup domain controllers and can validate logon requests. Domains can also contain Windows NT computers, LAN Manager 2.*x* servers, and other workstations such as those running Windows for Workgroups and MS-DOS.

With Windows NT, administrators have full centralized control over security, and on a Windows NT domain, the user account database is automatically replicated among servers to eliminate any single point of failure.

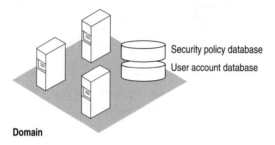

Security policy database
User account database

Domain

Figure 17.3   Computers Participating in a Domain

Domains and workgroups can interoperate and are identical in terms of browsing. If a Windows NT workstation is not participating in a domain, it is by default part of a workgroup (even if the workgroup is only one computer) and can be browsed as part of that workgroup. For more information, see "Network Browsing," later in this chapter.

LAN Manager 2.*x* Domains

A Windows NT computer can connect to standalone LAN Manager 2.*x* servers and LAN Manager 2.*x* servers participating in a LAN Manager 2.*x* domain. LAN Manager 2.*x* and Windows NT computers interoperate because they both use Server Message Blocks (SMBs) to communicate between the redirector and server software. Also the NBF (NetBEUI) and TCP/IP protocols used by Windows NT are interoperable with NetBEUI and TCP/IP protocols written for LAN Manager 2.*x*.

Note LAN Manager 2.*x* servers can act as backup domain controllers in a Windows NT domain.

Trusted Domains

Windows NT Advanced Server allows the user accounts from one domain to be used in another domain. When a domain is configured to allow accounts from another domain to have access to its resources, it effectively *trusts* the other domain. The *trusted* domain has made its accounts available to be used in the first domain. (Trust relationship information is maintained in the domain's security policy database.) These trusted accounts are available on Windows NT Advanced Servers and Windows NT computers participating in the domain.

Hint By using trust relationships in your multidomain network, you reduce the need for duplicate user account information and reduce the risk of problems caused by unsynchronized account information.

The *trust relationship* is the link between two domains allowing them to effectively share account information. The following figure illustrates a trust relationship between two domains, where the London domain trusts the Topeka domain.

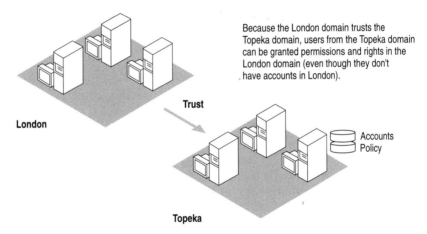

Because the London domain trusts the Topeka domain, users from the Topeka domain can be granted permissions and rights in the London domain (even though they don't have accounts in London).

Trust

London

Accounts Policy

Topeka

Figure 17.4   Trusted Domain

In this example, because London trusts Topeka, the following two statements are true:

- Users defined in the Topeka domain can access resources in the London domain without creating an account within that domain.
- London appears in the From box at the initial logon screen of Windows NT computers in the Topeka domain. Thus a user from the Topeka domain can log on at a computer in the London domain.

Trust relationships allow user accounts and global groups to be given rights and permissions in domains other than the domain where these accounts are located. This makes administration much easier, because you need to create each user account only once on your entire network, and it can be given access to any computer on your network (provided you set up domains and trust relationships correctly).

Note Trust relationships can only be configured between two Windows NT Advanced Server domains. Workgroups and LAN Manager 2.*x* domains cannot be configured to use trust relationships.

For more information about setting up trust relationships and managing user accounts and groups used by trusted domains, see the *Windows NT Advanced Server Concepts and Planning Guide*.

Logons and Validation

When you log on to a workgroup computer, your logon information is compared with the local user accounts database. When you log on to a computer that participates in a domain, you choose whether to log on locally, or to the domain. (If your domain trusts another domain, you can alternately choose to log on there.)

Note Windows NT Advanced Servers do not maintain local stored accounts and require you to log on using a domain account.

For example, suppose AnnM has an account on a domain (MyDomain), as well as an account on a Windows NT workstation (MyWksta) belonging to that domain. When AnnM logs onto her workstation account, the local validation software uses the information stored in the workstation user accounts database to validate the logon. If AnnM logs onto the domain from that workstation, the local validation software sends the logon request to the domain for validation. Although they share the same username, each account has a unique security ID.

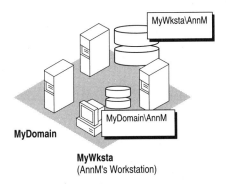

Figure 17.5   Logging On Locally Versus Logging On to the Domain

As described in Chapter 2, "Windows NT Security Model," the Local Security Authority (LSA) creates a security access token for each user accessing the system. This happens when the user logs on and is validated (that is, during interactive logon). The LSA also creates a security access token, if none currently exists for the user, when a user establishes a connection from a remote computer. This is called *remote logon*.

For example, suppose AnnM logs on and is validated by her local computer and then wants to access a printer controlled by a Windows NT Advanced Server in MyDomain. When she tries to connect to the printer (assuming she hasn't already connected to some other resource in the domain), she is actually performing a remote logon. One of the servers in MyDomain checks the domain's central user accounts database for information to validate her account for the domain and then creates a security access token for AnnM, and allows AnnM access.

Note This type of scenario becomes complex when AnnM uses different passwords for different accounts. For example, if her local password doesn't match the password for her domain account, when she tries to browse the domain or connect to a resource in the domain, a message like the following will display:

```
Incorrect password or unknown username
```

(While tools such as File Manager will prompt for a valid password, the command-line interface and some applications will simply deny access.)

From an administrative viewpoint, it is important to understand where the user account information is stored. A user's account will either be in a private local user accounts database or in a domain user accounts database shared by all the Windows NT Advanced Servers in the domain.

Common Problems Associated with Logon

There are two categories of typical problems users may face that relate to logons:

- Problems when trying to view a server's shared resources
- Problems when trying to access one of those resources

Viewing a Server's Shared Resources

Suppose AnnM logged on to a Windows NT domain with the password Yippee. She wants to view the shared resources on a server named \\PRODUCTS, but her password there is Yahoo. Because of this, Ann sees this message:

```
Error 5: Access has been denied.
```

AnnM asks the administrator of \\PRODUCTS to change her password, but the administrator leaves the User Must Change Password At Next Logon checkbox checked. When AnnM tries to view the server's shared resources this time, she sees this message:

```
Error 2242: The password of this user has expired.
```

When the administrator of \\PRODUCTS clears the User Must Change Password At Next Logon checkbox, AnnM is finally able to see the server's shared resources.

Accessing a Server's Shared Resources

Suppose AnnM is logged on to a Windows NT domain with the password Yippee but wants to connect to a shared directory on \\PRODUCTS, where her password is Yahoo. Even though \\PRODUCTS has a Guest account, because there is an account for AnnM, she is not allowed to gain access via the Guest account. Instead, Windows NT prompts AnnM for the valid password on \\PRODUCTS.

On the other hand, JeffH wants to access the same shared directory and has no account on \\PRODUCTS. He is allowed access to this resource via the Guest account for \\PRODUCTS and is assigned the permissions associated with that account.

The next few sections describe different interactive logon and remote logon scenarios and where the user account information is located for each scenario. By understanding where logon information is processed in each case, you will have a better understanding of how to resolve logon problems that users might experience.

Interactive Logon

The interactive logon can occur in any user accounts database where a user has an account. Depending on the type of Windows NT computer and how it has been configured, the From box (in the Logon dialog box) lists the local computer and/or domains where user accounts can be validated.

The following examples describe various interactive logon scenarios in a Windows NT environment.

Example 1: Logging On at a Local Computer

For a computer running Windows NT and participating in a workgroup, the logon information is compared with the local user accounts database. So when a user logs on, the From box lists only the name of the local computer. The user cannot specify another workgroup or domain for logon.

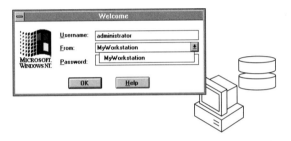

Figure 17.6   Initial Logon and Local Databases for a Windows NT Workstation

After successful validation, the username and password are cached by the computer's redirector for use when connecting to remote resources.

Example 2: Logging On to the Home Domain

From a Windows NT computer participating in a domain, a user can choose to have his or her logon information validated by the local computer or by a Windows NT Advanced Server in its domain. If the user account is a domain account, a Windows NT Advanced Server SAM for the home domain or a trusted domain validates the initial logon.

The From box lists the name of the local computer, the name of the home domain in which the computer participates, and the names of any trusted domains.

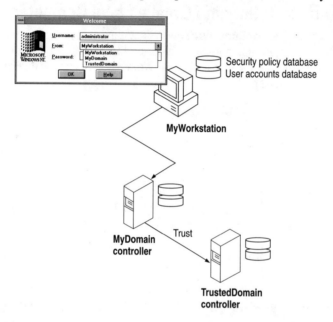

Figure 17.7   Logging On from a Domain Workstation

The security access token generated in an interactive logon is maintained on the computer where the user is logging on.

Example 3: Logging On to a Trusted Domain

If the user logging on is participating in another domain, a Windows NT Advanced Server in the trusted domain can validate the initial logon.

The From box lists the domain and trusted domains for this computer.

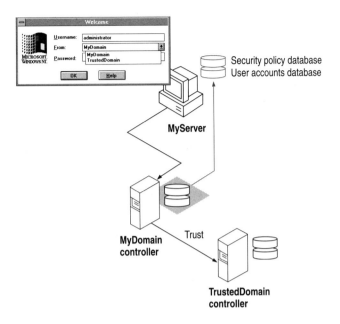

Figure 17.8   Validation by a Trusted Domain Controller

Summary of Interactive Logon Validation

The following table shows the logon options for someone using a Windows NT computer in a workgroup, a domain, and a domain with a trust relationship. The unique identifier used by Windows NT after logon depends on the location of the database used to log on the user. The third column in this table describes the unique identifier used in each case. Any network connection requests sent elsewhere on the network include this unique identifier.

Computer is in	User can logon at	Unique identifier
Workgroup	Local database	Computername and username
Domain	Local database	Computername and username
	Domain database	Domain name and username
Domain with a trust relationship	Local database	Computername and username
	Home domain database	Domain name and username
	Trusted domain database	Trusted domain name and username

Remote Logon

When a user tries to access a resource, the server checks to see if the user is already logged on. Windows NT does this by checking to see if a security access token already exists for that user. (If the server is part of a workgroup, it checks on the local computer. For a domain, it checks the domain's centralized user accounts information.) If no security access token exists, it means that the user's interactive logon was validated by some other domain or workgroup computer. In this case, the server's SAM compares the username and password from the user's process (the one establishing the connection) with the user accounts database. If these match, the server's LSA creates a security access token for the user, which the server and/or domain can use to later validate access request to resources from that user.

A security access token created at interactive logon is assigned to the initial process created for the user. A security access token created at remote logon is placed in a table in the remote server process. The server process creates a security ID for the user and maps it to the user's security access token. This security ID is sent back to the client redirector and is used in all further SMB communication between the server and client. Whenever a resource request comes in from the client, the security ID identifies the user to the server process. The security access token that maps to the user ID identifies the user to the remote security subsystem.

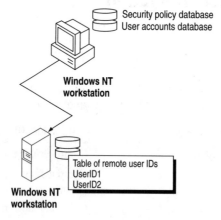

Figure 17.9   Remote Logon

The following list shows the steps in a successful remote logon at a Windows NT computer or Windows NT Advanced Server.

1. The username, password, and computername of the logged on user are sent from the user's computer to the remote Windows NT server.

   If the logon computer is in a domain, its domain name is also passed to the validating server. If it is in a workgroup, there is no domain name, so the validating server uses its computername instead.

   If the validating Windows NT computer is part of a workgroup, only the username and password are used for validation.

2. The validating computer's SAM compares the logon username and password with information in the user accounts database.

3. If the access is authorized, the validating computer's LSA constructs a security access token and passes it to the server process, which creates a user ID referencing the security access token.

4. The user ID is then returned to the client computer for use in all subsequent requests to the server.

   After the session has been created, the client computer will send requests marked with the user ID it received during session setup. The server will match the user ID with the proper access token kept in an internal table. This security access token at the remote computer is used for access validation at the remote computer by that user.

Pass-Through Validation

Pass-through validation occurs when a user account must be validated, but the local computer can't validate the account itself. In this case, the username and password are forwarded to a Windows NT Advanced Server that can validate the user, and the user's information is returned to the requesting computer.

Pass-through validation occurs in these cases:

- At interactive logon when a user is logging into a domain or trusted domain of the Windows NT domain workstation.
- At remote logon when the user account does not exist in the remote computers accounts database.

Figure 17.10 illustrates pass-through validation. Here, AnnM wants to access a computer in the London domain. Because London trusts AnnM's home domain (Topeka), London asks Topeka to validate AnnM's account information.

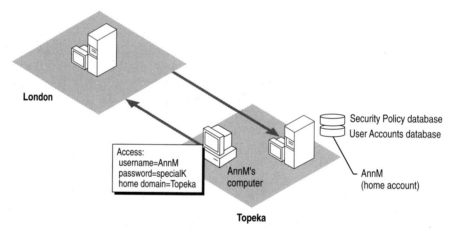

London

Access:
username=AnnM
password=specialK
home domain=Topeka

AnnM's
computer

Security Policy database
User Accounts database

AnnM
(home account)

Topeka

Figure 17.10   Pass-Through Validation

Notes Trust relationships are one-way. If A trusts B, it does not imply that B trusts A. Another trust relationship must be constructed to allow B to trust A.

Trust relationships are direct, not implied. That is, if A trusts B and B trusts C, A does not automatically trust C.

The Netlogon service provides this pass-through validation. Each Windows NT computer participating in the domain must be running the Netlogon and Workstation services. (Netlogon is dependent on the Workstation service.) The Netlogon service communicates with the Netlogon service on the remote computer, as illustrated in Figure 17.11.

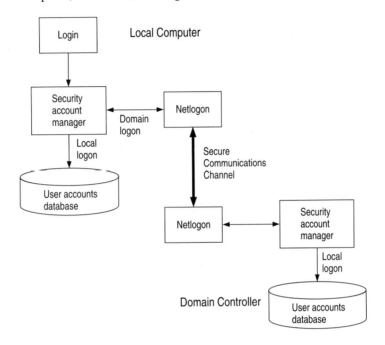

Figure 17.11   Netlogon Requirements for Domain Logons

If the user account is in a trusted domain, the request must first be passed from the Windows NT domain workstation to a Windows NT Advanced Server in the domain. The Windows NT Advanced Server then passes the request to a Windows NT Advanced Server in the trusted domain, which validates the user account information and then returns the user information by the reverse route.

Using a Secure Communication Channel

To communicate with the Netlogon service on the remote computer, the Netlogon service sets up a *secure communication channel*. This communication channel is used to pass the username and encrypted password during pass-through validation to a Windows NT Advanced Server.

Windows NT computers maintain security on these communication channels by using user-level security to create the channel. Special internal user accounts are created for the following:

- Workstation trust accounts, allowing a domain workstation to perform pass-through validation to a Windows NT Advanced Server in the domain
- Server trust accounts, allowing Windows NT Advanced Servers to get copies of the master domain database from the domain controller
- Inter-domain trust accounts, allowing a Windows NT Advanced Server to perform pass-through validation to another domain

The Netlogon service attempts to set up a secure channel when it is started. Failing that, Netlogon will retry every 15 minutes or whenever an action requiring pass-through validation occurs.

Note If the secure channel cannot be created at logon (for example, because the domain controllers are offline), the Netlogon service will start anyway. If the user's interactive logon used the same domain name and username, the user's remote logon will be successfully completed using cached credentials.

Remote Logon at a LAN Manager 2.x Server

Remote logon at a LAN Manager 2.x server is basically the same as remote logon to a Windows NT computer. However, instead of comparing the user's logon information against a centralized user accounts database, the LAN Manager 2.x server compares the information with its local user accounts database. This database may be the server's own standalone database or a domain database shared by a group of servers. LAN Manager 2.x servers cannot use pass-through validation.

Accessing resources on a LAN Manager 2.x server is similar to accessing resources on a Windows NT computer,, except that the LAN Manager 2.x server does not use a security access token to identify resource requests. Instead, the security ID maps to the username, which is used when granting resource requests.

If the LAN Manager 2.x server is in the same domain as the Windows NT Advanced Server, the server logon is identical to accessing another Windows NT Advanced Server (except that the LAN Manager 2.x server does not generate or use security access tokens).

If the LAN Manager 2.x server is in another domain, the server logon is identical to logon for a Windows NT workgroup computer. This is true even for a trusted domain, since LAN Manager 2.x servers don't understand trust relationships. An account must exist either in the LAN Manager 2.x server's domain or at the stand-alone server itself.

Summary of Remote Logon Authentication

The following summarizes remote logon scenarios:

▶ **Workgroup computer connecting to a Windows NT computer in a domain**

Interactive logon for the user at the workgroup computer (the client) was performed by the local user accounts database.

In the domain, a Windows NT Advanced Server checks the client's computername and username. It rejects the remote logon request because the client's computername doesn't match home domain name.

Next, the client's username and password are passed to the specific server in the domain to which the client is trying to connect. This server checks the username and password with information in its local user accounts database. If there is a match, access to this server is allowed.

▶ **Domain computer connecting to a Windows NT computer in the same domain**

Interactive logon for the user at the client computer was performed by the domain's user accounts database.

The client's domain name, username, and password are passed to the computer being accessed, which passes them to a Windows NT Advanced Server in the domain.

The Windows NT Advanced Server verifies that the domain name for the client matches this domain.

Next the Windows NT Advanced Server check the username and password against the domain's user accounts database. If there is a match, access is allowed.

▶ **Domain client in a trusted domain connecting to a Windows NT computer**

Interactive logon for the user at the client computer was performed by the domain's user accounts database.

The client's domain name, username, and password are passed to the computer being accessed. That computer passes the logon information to a Windows NT Advanced Serve in the domain.

The Windows NT Advanced Server verifies that the client's domain is a trusted domain and then passes the client's identification information to a Windows NT Advanced Server in that trusted domain.

A Windows NT Advanced Server in the trusted domain (that is, the same domain as the client computer) checks the username and password against the domain's user accounts database. If there is a match, access is allowed.

Network Browsing

Per-user security is also used to determine which parts of the network the user can and can't browse. If the user has a validated account in a particular domain, he or she can browse servers and resources there.

In Windows NT, the Computer Browser service maintains an up-to-date list of domains, workgroups, and computers and provides the list to applications when requested. It provides the lists that are displayed in the Select Computer and Select Domain dialog boxes; anywhere Windows NT presents lists of domains, workgroups, or computers (for example, in the main Server Manager window); and of course, by the **net view** command.

The list can contain the names of domains, workgroups, and computers that are running the server service, including the following:

- Windows NT Advanced Server controllers and servers
- Windows NT workstations
- Windows for Workgroups computers
- Windows NT workgroups
- Windows for Workgroups workgroups
- LAN Manager 2x domains and servers

For each domain or workgroup, the master copy of this list is maintained by a computer that is designated the master browser, and a copy of that list is maintained by one or more computers designated to be backup browsers. If there is only one designated browser, Windows NT also identifies one backup browser for every 32 computers running the server service in the domain or workgroup. (If more that one server is identified as a designated browser, Windows NT does not assign extra backup browsers.) The master browser and the backup browsers are elected automatically, by the system. Backup browsers, and to a limited extent master browsers, can be designated by adding the **IsDomainMasterBrowser** and **MaintainServerList** entries in the Browser key. For more information, see "Browser Service Entries" in Chapter 14, "Registry Value Entries."

In a Windows NT Advanced Server domain, the master browser will usually be the domain controller, and the backup browsers will usually be Windows NT Advanced Servers, but Windows NT workstations and Windows for Workgroups computers can also act as backup browsers.

In a workgroup, the master browser and backup browsers will be Windows NT workstations or Windows for Workgroups computers.

In the event that a domain spans multiple broadcast regions, multiple master browsers are elected for the domain, one per broadcast region. This may be the case, for example, if you use the TCP/IP protocol to participate on an internet. In this case, the master browsers will compare browsing information periodically to keep their lists synchronized. The master browser for the domain also acts as a well-known master browser for inter-domain browsing (that is, the ability to list the servers within another domain or workgroup).

A LAN Manager 2.x domain is known to the browser only if at least one Windows for Workgroups computer, or at least one Windows NT workstation, is a member of that LAN Manager 2.x domain.

Or, for the browser to know about the LAN Manager 2.x domain, you can use the Control Panel of the Windows NT Advanced Server domain controller. In the Network option in Control Panel, enter the LAN Manager 2.x domain name in the Browser Configuration dialog box. The browser then knows that LAN Manager 2.x domain.

For a Windows NT Advanced Server domain to be browsable by LAN Manager 2.x clients, you can use the Network option in Control Panel to configure the Server service and mark the box labeled Make Browser Broadcasts To LAN Manager 2.x Clients.

C H A P T E R   1 8

Using NBF with Windows NT

NBF is the NetBIOS Extended User Interface (NetBEUI) protocol driver used in Windows NT. This protocol provides compatibility with existing LANs that use the NetBEUI protocol.

This chapter describes how NBF handles connection-oriented and connectionless network traffic, and it also describes NBF's unique method for handling resources to create a virtually infinite number of connections. The topics include the following:

- Overview of NetBEUI and NBF
- NBF and network traffic
- NBF and sessions
- Session limits

Overview of NetBEUI and NBF

The NetBEUI protocol, first introduced by IBM in 1985, was written to the NetBIOS interface and designed as a small, efficient protocol for use on department-sized LANs of 20 to 200 workstations. This original design assumed that broader connectivity services could be added by including gateways as the network grew. (As described later in this chapter, NBF breaks the session limit that restricted NetBEUI's reach.)

The NetBEUI protocol provides powerful flow control and tuning parameters plus robust error detection. Microsoft has supported the NetBEUI protocol in all of its networking products since Microsoft's first networking product, MS-Net, was introduced in the mid-1980s.

NetBEUI is the precursor to the NBF protocol included with Windows NT. NBF provides compatibility with existing LAN Manager and MS-Net installations, and with IBM LAN Server installations. On Windows NT, the NetBIOS interface is supported under MS-DOS, 16-bit Windows, and Win32 subsystem environments.

NBF and Network Traffic

NBF, like NetBEUI, provides for both connectionless or connection-oriented traffic. Connectionless communications can be either unreliable or reliable. NBF and NetBEUI only provide *unreliable connectionless*, not reliable connectionless communications.

Unreliable communication is similar to sending a letter in the mail. No response is generated by the receiver of the letter to ensure the sender that the letter made it to its destination. In comparison, reliable connectionless communications is like a registered letter whose sender is notified that the letter arrived.

Connection-oriented communications provide reliable communications between two computers in a way that is analogous to a phone call, where two callers connect, a conversation occurs, and the connection is dropped when the conversation ends. Providing a reliable connection requires more overhead than for connectionless communications.

NBF communicates via the NDIS interface at the LLC layer. A connection at the LLC layer is called a *link*, which is uniquely defined by the adapter's address and the destination service access point (DSAP). A service access point (SAP) can be thought of as the address of a port to a layer as defined by the OSI model. Because NBF is a NetBIOS implementation, it uses the NetBIOS SAP (0xF0). While the 802.2 protocol governs the overall flow of data, the primitives are responsible for passing the data from one layer to the next. The primitives are passed through the SAPs between layers.

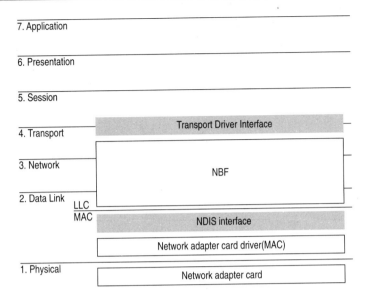

Figure 18.1   NBF Protocol

Connectionless Traffic

For connectionless traffic that requires a response from a remote computer, NBF sends out a certain number of frames, depending on the command. The total number is based on *retry* Registry value entries, such as **NameQueryRetries**. The time between sending each frame is determined by *timeout* Registry entries, such as **NameQueryTimeout**.

Three types of NetBIOS commands generate connectionless traffic: name claim and resolution, datagrams, and miscellaneous commands. These are sent as UI (Unnumbered Information) frames at the LLC sublayer.

To see how Windows NT uses retry and timeout values from the Registry, consider what happens when Windows NT registers computernames via NBF using the NetBIOS Add.Name command. When NBF receives the Add.Name command, it broadcasts ADD_NAME_QUERY frames a total of **AddNameQueryRetries** times and sends these broadcasts at a time interval of **AddNameQueryTimeout**. This allows computers on the network enough time to inform the sending computer whether the name is already registered as a unique name on another computer or a group name on the network.

Note All Registry values discussed in this chapter are found under the following Registry path:

```
HKEY_LOCAL_MACHINE\SYSTEM\CurrentControlSet\Services\Nbf
```

Connection-Oriented Traffic

The **net use** command is an example of a connection oriented communication, as illustrated in Figure 18.2.

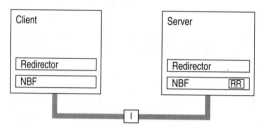

Figure 18.2   Connection-Oriented Network Traffic

When a user types **net use** at the command line to connect to a shared resource, NBF must first locate the server by sending UI-frames and then initialize the link. This is handled by the redirector when it makes a connection to the NBF drivers via the Transport Driver Interface (TDI) boundary. NBF begins the sequence by generating a NetBIOS Find Name frame. Once the server is found, a session is set up with UC Class-II frames following the standard 802.2 protocol (802.2 governs the overall flow of data).

The client computer sends an SABME (Set Asynchronous Balance Mode Extended) frame, and the server returns a UA (Unnumbered Acknowledgment) frame. Then the client sends an RR (Receive Ready) frame, notifying the server that it is ready to receive I-frames whose sequence number is currently 0. The server acknowledges this frame.

Once the LLC-level session is established, additional NetBEUI-level information is exchanged. The client sends a Session Initialize frame, and the server responds with a Session Confirm frame. At this point, the NetBEUI-level session is ready to handle application-level frames (SMBs).

Reliable transfer is achieved with link-oriented frames by numbering the I-frames. This allows the receiving computer to determine whether the frames were lost and in what order they were received.

NBF uses two techniques to improve performance for connection-oriented traffic: use of adaptive sliding windows and use of link timers. These are described in the next two sections.

Adaptive Sliding Window Protocol

NBF uses an adaptive sliding window algorithm to improve performance while reducing network congestion and providing flow control. A sliding window algorithm allows a sender to dynamically tune the number of LLC frames sent before an acknowledgment is requested. Figure 18.3 shows frames traveling through a two-way pipe.

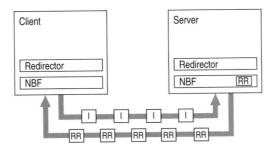

Figure 18.3   Adaptive Sliding Window

If the sender could only feed one frame into the pipe and would then have to wait for an acknowledgment (ACK), the sender's pipe would be underused. If the sender can send multiple frames before an ACK is returned, the sender can keep the pipe full, thereby using the full bandwidth of the pipe. The frames would travel forward, and ACKs for the received frames would travel back. The number of frames that the sender is allowed to send before it must wait for an ACK is referred to as the *send window*. In general, NBF has no receive window, unless it detects that the remote is a version of IBM Lan Server, which never polls; in this case, NBF uses a receive window based on the value of **MaximumIncomingFrames** in the Registry.

The adaptive sliding window protocol tries to determine the best sizes for the send window for the current network conditions. Ideally, the windows should be big enough so that maximum throughput can be realized. However, if the window gets too big, the receiver could get overloaded and drop frames. For big windows, dropped frames cause significant network traffic because more frames have to be retransmitted. Lost frames might be a problem on slow links or when frames have to pass over multiple hops to find the receiving station. Lost frames coupled with large send windows generate multiple retransmissions. This traffic overhead may make an already congested network worse. By limiting the send window size, traffic is throttled, and congestion control is exercised.

Link Timers

NBF uses the three timers: the response timer (T1), the acknowledgment timer (T2), and the inactivity timer (Ti). These timers help regulate network traffic and are controlled by the values of the **DefaultT1Timeout, DefaultT2Timeout,** and **DefaultTiTimeout** Registry entries, respectively.

The response timer is used to determine how long the sender should wait before it assumes the I-frame is lost. After T1 milliseconds, NBF sends an RR frame that has not been ACKed and doubles the value for T1. If the RR frame is not ACKed after the number of retries defined by the value of **LLCRetries**, the link is dropped.

Where the return traffic does not allow the receiver to send an I-frame within a legitimate time period, the acknowledgment timer begins, and the ACK is sent. The value for this timer is set by the T2 variable, with a default value of 150 milliseconds. If the sender has to wait until the T2 timer starts in order to receive a response, the link will be underused while the sender waits for the ACK. This rare situation can occur over slow links. On the other hand, if the timer value is too low, the timer starts and sends unnecessary ACKs, generating excess traffic. NBF is optimized so that the last frame the sender wants to send is sent with the POLL bit turned on. This forces the receiver to send an ACK immediately.

The inactivity timer, Ti, is used to detect whether the link has gone down. The default value for Ti is 30 seconds. If Ti milliseconds pass without activity on the link, NBF sends an I-frame for polling. This is then ACKed, and the link is maintained.

Note   Remember that T2 <= T1 <= Ti.

NBF and Sessions

Each process within Windows NT can communicate with up to 254 different computers. The implementation of NetBIOS under Windows NT requires the application to do a few more things than have traditionally been done on other platforms, but the capacity for doing up to 254 sessions from within each process is well worth the price. Prior implementations of NetBIOS had the 254-session limit for the entire computer, including the workstation and server components.

Note that the 254-session limit does not apply to the default workstation or server components. The workstation and server services avoid the problem by writing directly to the TDI rather than calling NetBIOS directly. This is a handle-based (32-bit) interface.

NBF also has a unique method of handling resources to create a virtually infinite (memory permitting) number of connections, as described in the next section.

Session Limits

The 254-session limit is based on a key variable in the NetBIOS architecture called the Local Session Number (LSN). This is a one-byte number (0 to 255) with several numbers reserved for system use. When two computers establish a session via NBF, there is an exchange of Least Significant Numbers (LSN).

The LSN numbers on the two computers may be different. They do not have to match, but a computer always uses the same LSN for a given session. This number is assigned when a program issues a CALL NCB (Network Control Block). The number is actually shared between the two computers in the initial frame sent from the calling computer to the listening computer. Figure 18.4 shows this session creation frame exchange.

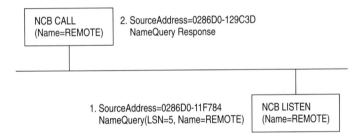

Figure 18.4   Broadcast of NameQuery

The initial frame is a NameQuery frame. In previous implementations of NBF, this frame was broadcast onto the network. All computers read the frame and check to see if they have the name in their name space and if there is a LISTEN NCB pending on the name. If there is a LISTEN NCB, the computer assigns a new LSN for itself, and then adds it to the response frame and satisfies the LISTEN NCB, which now contains just the LSN used on that computer. Even though both computers know the LSN of the other, the information is not used. The more important information for the two communicating partners is the network addresses that are part of the frames. As the frames are exchanged, each partner picks up the address of the other in the source address component of the frame received. The NBF protocol keeps the network address of the remote partner so that subsequent frames can be addressed directly.

Note This process applies for NBF connections. NetBIOS connections established via TCP/IP and RFC1001/1002 or NBP are handled differently.

Windows NT has to use the same NameQuery frame to establish connections with remote computers via NBF; otherwise, it would not be able to talk to existing workstations and servers. The NameQuery frame transmitted must contain the 1-byte-wide LSN to be used.

Breaking the 254-Session Limit

NBF breaks the 254-session barrier by using a combination of two matrices, one maintained by NBF, and one maintained by NetBIOS.

The NBF system maintains a two-dimensional matrix, as shown in Figure 18.2. Along the side of this matrix are the LSN numbers 1 to 254. Across the top are the network addresses for the different computers that it has sessions with. In the cell defined by the LSN and network address is the TDI handle, which relates back to the process that established the connection (either the CALL or LISTEN).

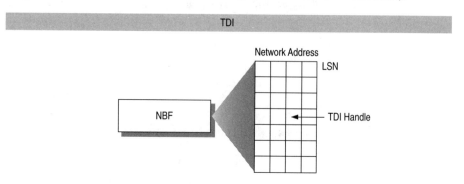

Figure 18.5   NBF and Its LSN Matrix

Note   The matrix concept and its contents are for illustration only. The physical storage algorithm and exact contents are beyond the scope of this document.

The NAME_QUERY frame from Windows NT contains the LSN number associated with the TDI handle that satisfies either the NCB CALL or the LISTEN. In the case of a CALL, it is not broadcast but is addressed directly to the recipient.

The remaining mystery is how NBF gets the network address of the recipient to add to its matrix when doing the CALL. (It's easy on the LISTEN side because the address is in the NameQuery frame received.)

As shown in Figure 18.6, NBF uses two NAME_QUERY frames.

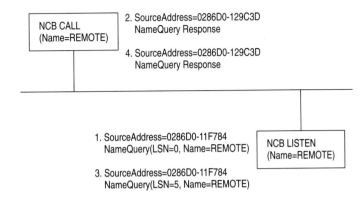

Figure 18.6   Two NameQueries in Windows NT NBF

For the numbered items in Figure 18.6:

1. The first frame is the FindName format of the NAME_QUERY.
    However, an LSN of 0 is special; it indicates that it is a FindName. The
    FindName is broadcast, and, when the remote computer responds to the
    frame, NBF has the network address it needs to add an entry to the table.

2. The second NAME_QUERY is then sent directly to the remote station, with
    the LSN filled in as a CALL command. The FindName will be successfully
    returned by the remote computer, even if no LISTEN NCB is posted against
    the name.

3. If no LISTEN NCB is posted against the name, frame (3) is sent.

4. The same frame is responded to by frame (4).

NBF must also address another problem—the LSN from the NBF table cannot be
the one returned to the process issuing the CALL or LISTEN commands. NBF
may have established connections with multiple remote computers with LSN=5,
for example. Windows NT must return each process an LSN number that uniquely
defines its session.

As stated earlier, NBF uses the TDI handle to know which LSN and network
address to send frames to, and each process has its own set of LSNs available to
it. Therefore, there must be a component between the originating process and the
TDI interface of NBF that translates a process ID and an LSN into a TDI handle.
The component in the middle is called NETBIOS.SYS

This concept is illustrated in Figure 18.7, although the table maintained by
NETBIOS.SYS is actually 254 LSNs per LANA number per process. (In
Windows NT, each binding path is represented by a LANA number). In reality,
each process can have up to 254 sessions per LANA number, not just a total of
254 sessions.

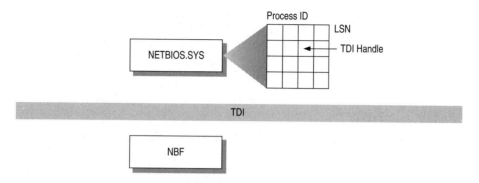

Figure 18.7   NETBIOS.SYS Matrix

NETBIOS.SYS builds a second matrix that has LSNs down the side, process IDs along the top, and TDI handles in the cells. It is the LSN from this table that is passed back to the originating process.

Figure 18.8 presents a top-down view of the architecture.

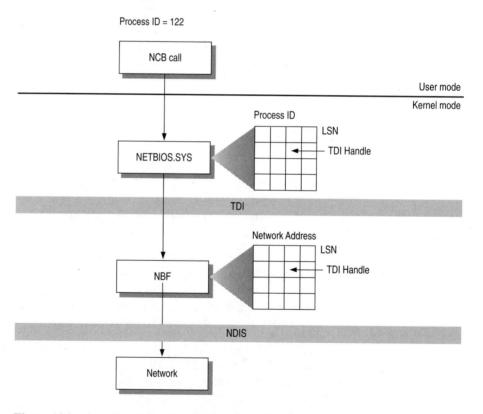

Figure 18.8   Another View of the NetBIOS Architecture

For example, suppose a process needs to establish a session with a remote computer. Before the process can issue the CALL NCB, it must issue a RESET NCB. This command signals NETBIOS.SYS to allocate space in its TDI handle table, among other things. Once the RESET is satisfied, the process issues a CALL NCB to make a connection with a specific remote computer. This NCB is directed down to the NETBIOS.SYS device driver. The driver opens a new TDI handle to NBF and sends the command to NBF.

NBF issues the first NAME_QUERY with LSN=0 to find the remote computer. When the remote computer responds, the network address is extracted from the frame, and a column in the NBF table is created. The second NAME_QUERY with an LSN is sent directly to the remote computer. When that frame is returned successfully, NBF returns from the TDI call to the NETBIOS.SYS driver with a successful status code.

NETBIOS.SYS then fills in the LSN from its table into the NCB and satisfies it back to the calling process.

C H A P T E R   1 9

TCP/IP on Windows NT

Microsoft TCP/IP on Windows NT offers several benefits to Windows NT systems in enterprise networks, providing a standard, routable networking transport for Windows NT networking.

This chapter describes the functionality of the TCP/IP services offered as part of Windows NT networking. It also describes how you can best take advantage of Microsoft TCP/IP in an enterprise network and explains how TCP/IP interacts with the advanced networking components of Windows NT. Topics include the following:

- Components of TCP/IP on Windows NT
- Windows NT TCP/IP architecture
- Using and administering TCP/IP with Windows NT
- Using IP routing under Windows NT
- Using Windows NT TCP/IP as a connectivity protocol
- Tips for Using TCP/IP
- Using SNMP

For details about using TCP/IP, see the *Windows NT Advanced Server TCP/IP Guide*. Online Help is available for all the TCP/IP connectivity utilities through the Windows NT Command Reference Help.

Components of TCP/IP on Windows NT

All the networking features of Windows NT—including file sharing, print sharing, remote administration, domain management, RPC applications, and so on—are offered over native TCP/IP protocols. Microsoft TCP/IP also provides connectivity to foreign hosts running the TCP/IP protocol suite and provides common application-level protocols such as FTP and Telnet. Connectivity utilities included with Windows NT provide terminal emulation, file transfer, network diagnostics, and so on. These applications allow Windows NT users to share information with users of other operating systems such as UNIX®, SunOS™, and VMS®.

Microsoft TCP/IP provides cross-platform connectivity and a client-server development framework that many software vendors and corporate developers are using to develop distributed and client-server applications in heterogeneous enterprise networks over TCP/IP.

This section describes the various components of the Internet protocol suite, IP addressing, subnet masks, routing, and NetBIOS over TCP/IP. For additional information about any of the topics discussed here, see *Internetworking with TCP/IP, Volume I,* by Douglas E. Comer (Prentice Hall, 1991).

Internet Protocol Suite

TCP/IP refers to the Internet suite of protocols. It includes a set of standards that specify how computers communicate and gives conventions for connecting networks and routing traffic through the connections. It is used to connect the Internet—a worldwide internetwork connecting universities, research labs, Department of Defense installations, and corporations. (According to convention, Internet begins with a capital I when referring to the worldwide, connected internet.)

The Internet protocols are a result of a Defense Advanced Research Projects Agency (DARPA) research project on network interconnection in the late 1970s. It was mandated on all United States defense long-haul networks in 1983 but was not widely accepted until the integration with 4.2 BSD (Berkeley Software Distribution) UNIX. The popularity of TCP/IP is based on:

- Robust client-server framework. TCP/IP is an excellent client-server application platform, especially in wide-area network (WAN) environments.

- Information sharing. Thousands of academic, defense, scientific, and commercial organizations share data, electronic mail, and services on the connected Internet using TCP/IP.

- General availability. Implementations of TCP/IP are available on nearly every popular computer operating system. Source code is widely available for many implementations. Additionally, bridge, router, and network analyzer vendors all offer support for the TCP/IP protocol family within their products.

The following discussion introduces the components of the IP protocol suite. Although many of the details discussed are transparent to users, knowledge of the architecture and interaction between the components is useful.

Transmission Control Protocol and Internet Protocol

Transmission Control Protocol (TCP) and Internet Protocol (IP) are only two members of the IP protocol suite. IP is a protocol that provides packet delivery for all of the other protocols within the TCP/IP family. It provides a best-effort, connectionless delivery system for computer data. That is, IP packets are not guaranteed to arrive at their destination, nor are they guaranteed to be received in the sequence in which they were sent. The protocol's checksum feature confirms only the IP header's integrity. Thus, responsibility for the data contained within the IP packet (and the sequencing) is assured only by using higher-level protocols.

The most common higher-level IP protocol is TCP. TCP supplies a reliable, connection-based protocol over (or encapsulated within) IP. TCP guarantees the delivery of packets, ensures proper sequencing of the data, and provides a checksum feature that validates both the packet header and its data for accuracy. In the event that IP corrupts or loses a TCP/IP packet, TCP is responsible for retransmitting the faulty packets. This reliability defines TCP/IP as the protocol of choice for session-based data transmission, client-server applications, and critical services such as electronic mail.

This reliability does not come without a price. TCP headers require the use of additional bits to provide proper sequencing information, as well as a mandatory checksum to ensure reliability of both the TCP header and the packet data. To guarantee successful data delivery, the protocol also requires the recipient to acknowledge successful receipt of data. Such acknowledgments (or ACKs) generate additional network traffic, diminishing the level of data throughput in favor of reliability. To reduce the impact on performance, TCP implements a throttle mechanism that allows the required frequency of ACKs to vary with the reliability of the data link. This permits highly reliable connections to use fewer ACKs and less computing power.

User Datagram Protocol

If reliability is not essential, the TCP complement, *user datagram protocol* (UDP), offers a connectionless datagram service that guarantees neither delivery nor correct sequencing of delivered packets (much like IP). Higher-level protocols or applications provide many reliability mechanisms in addition to UDP/IP. UDP data checksums are optional, providing a manner in which to exchange data over highly reliable networks without unnecessarily consuming processing time or network resources. When UDP checksums are used, they validate both header and data. ACKs are also not enforced by the UDP protocol; this is left to higher-level protocols.

Address Resolution Protocol and Internet Control Message Protocol

Although not directly related to the transport of user or application data, two other protocols in the IP suite perform important functions: *address resolution protocol* (ARP) and *internet control message protocol* (ICMP). These two protocols are maintenance protocols that support the IP framework and are generally invisible to users and to applications.

Although IP packets contain both source and destination IP addresses, the hardware address of the destination node must also be known. (This section assumes that the transmission type is Ethernet. Ethernet adapters contain a 48-bit, globally unique address in permanent memory.) IP can acquire a node's hardware address by broadcasting a special inquiry packet (an ARP *request packet*) containing the IP address of the node with which it is attempting to communicate.

All of the ARP-enabled nodes on the IP network detect these broadcasts, and the node that owns the IP address in question replies by sending its hardware address to the requesting node in an ARP reply packet. The hardware/IP address mapping is then stored in the requesting node's ARP cache for subsequent use. Because the ARP reply can also be broadcast to the network, it is likely that other nodes on the network can use this information to update their own ARP caches.

ICMP allows two nodes on an IP network to share IP status and error information. This information can be used by higher-level protocols to recover from transmission problems or by network administrators to detect network trouble. Although ICMP packets are encapsulated within IP packets, they are not considered to be a higher-level protocol (ICMP is required in every TCP/IP implementation). The **ping** utility makes use of the ICMP *echo request* and *echo reply* packets to determine whether a particular IP node on a network is functional. This is useful for diagnosing IP network or gateway failures.

IP Addressing

Every host system on a TCP/IP network is identified by a unique IP address. This address is used to identify a node on a network; it also specifies routing information in an internetwork. IP addresses are 32-bit values typically represented in dotted decimal notation. Dotted decimal notation depicts each octet (or byte) of an IP address by its decimal value, separating each by a period, as in 102.54.94.97. IP addresses are used to provide nodes on a network with a unique address without relying on the underlying hardware to ensure unique addressing.

Because IP addresses identify nodes on an interconnected network, each node on the internet must be assigned a unique IP address.

Although represented as a single value, IP addresses provide two pieces of information: the network ID and the host ID for a node. The *network ID* (which must be unique among all networks within a connected internet) specifies the network to which a node is attached. The *host ID* (which is unique among nodes within a network) identifies the node within its network. Networks that connect to the public Internet must obtain an official network ID from Defense Data Network-Network Information Center (DDN-NIC) to protect IP network ID uniqueness. Once assigned a network ID, the local network administrator must assign unique host IDs for computers within the network. Although private networks that are not connected to the Internet can choose to use their own network identifier, obtaining a valid network ID from DDN-NIC allows a private network to connect to the Internet in the future without reassigning addresses.

The Internet community has defined address *classes* to accommodate networks of varying sizes. Each network class is easily derived by the first octet (byte) of its IP address. The following table summarizes the relationship between the first octet of a given address and its host and network ID fields. It also identifies the total number of network and host IDs for each address class that participates in the Internet addressing scheme.

Table 19.1   IP Address Classes[1]

Class	w values[1] (inclusive)	Net ID	Host ID	Available nets	Available Hosts per net
A	1-126	w	x.y.z	126	16,777,214
B	128-191	w.x	y.z	16,384	65,534
C	192-223	w.x.y	z	2,097,151	254

[1] This sample uses IP address w.x.y.z.

[2] The network address 127 is reserved for loopback testing and interprocess communication on the local computer; it is not a network address.

A node uses the network and host IDs to determine which packets it should receive or ignore and to determine the scope of the transmissions it produces (only nodes with the same network ID accept one another's IP-level broadcasts). Because the sender's IP address is included in every outgoing IP packet, it is useful for the receiving node to derive the originating network and host ID from the IP address field. This is accomplished using *subnet masks*.

Subnet Masks

Subnet masks are 32-bit values that allow the recipient of IP packets to distinguish the network ID portion of the IP address from the host ID. Like an IP address, the value of a subnet mask is frequently represented in dotted decimal notation. Subnet masks are determined by assigning 1's to bits that belong to the network ID and 0's to the bits that belong to the host ID. Once the bits are in place, the 32-bit value is converted to dotted decimal notation (as shown earlier, in Table 19.1).

Table 19.2   Examples of Subnet Masks for Standard IP Address Classes

Class	Default subnet mask
A	255.0.0.0
B	255.255.0.0
C	255.255.255.0

Although configuring a host with a subnet mask might seem redundant after examining this table, subnet masks are also used to further segment an assigned network ID among several local networks. For example, suppose a network is assigned the Class-B network address 144.100. Table 19.1 shows that this is one of over 16,000 Class-B addresses capable of serving more than 65,000 nodes. However, the worldwide corporate network to which this ID is assigned is composed of 12 international LANs with 75 to 100 nodes each.

Instead of applying for 11 more network IDs, it is better to use subnetting to make more effective use of the assigned ID 144.100. The third octet of the IP address can be used as a *subnet ID*, to define the subnet mask 255.255.255.0. This splits the Class-B address into 256 subnets: 144.100.0, 144.100.1, . . ., 144.100.255, each of which can have 254 nodes. (Host IDs 0 and 255 should not be assigned to a workstation; they are used as broadcast addresses, which are typically recognized by all workstations.) Any 12 of these network addresses could be assigned to the international LANs in this example. Within each LAN, each computer is assigned a unique host ID, and they all have the subnet mask 255.255.255.0.

The preceding example demonstrates a simple (and common) subnet scheme for Class-B addresses. Sometimes it is necessary to segment only portions of an octet, using only a few bits to specify subnet IDs (such as when subnets exceed 256 nodes). Be sure to check with your local network administrator to determine your network's subnet policy and your correct subnet mask.

Important   All computers on a physical network should use the same subnet mask and network ID; otherwise, addressing and routing problems can occur.

Routing

When individual IP subnets are connected to an internet, IP gateways or IP routers are used to provide *routing* (packet delivery) between the networks. When a TCP/IP node attempts to communicate with a different network (when source and destination network IDs differ), a gateway (or a series of gateways) must forward the packet to the appropriate destination network. A gateway maintains routing tables that specify the *direction* (address of the next gateway) a packet should take to reach its destination, as well as a table of local hosts on the networks it interconnects.

Typically, gateways are IP *routers*, or computers with two or more network adapters that are running some type of IP routing software; each adapter is connected to a different physical network. On networks that are not part of an internet, IP gateways are not required. If a network is part of an internet and a node does not specify a default gateway (or the gateway computer is not operating properly), only communication beyond the local subnet is impaired.

Microsoft TCP/IP recognizes only a single default gateway per node. That is, each TCP/IP node must rely on a single gateway to deliver packets to other networks. The network administrator provides users with the address of the local gateway. The Microsoft TCP/IP installation software checks to ensure that the network ID for the default gateway matches the network ID of the local IP address. For more information, see "Using IP Routing under Windows NT," later in this chapter.

Windows NT TCP/IP Architecture

When TCP/IP is installed on a Windows NT computer, several drivers and services provide a rich set of capabilities for end users and network applications. This section describes the various components that make up Windows NT TCP/IP:

- Streams environment and the Registry
- User-mode interfaces to TCP/IP (Windows Sockets, named pipes, and NetBIOS)
- Windows NT TCP/IP drivers and services

The following figure shows TCP/IP architecture within the Windows NT networking model.

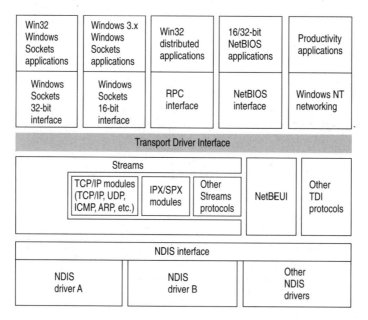

Figure 19.1   TCP/IP and Windows NT Network Architecture

Streams Environment and the Registry

Windows NT TCP/IP takes advantage of NDIS and TDI by means of the Streams environment, which is based on the Streams architecture used in many UNIX implementations.

When TCP/IP is installed and configured, many entries are added to the Windows NT Registry, especially for Streams. The following key in the Registry contains several basic parameters that affect TCP/IP on Windows NT:

```
HKEY_LOCAL_MACHINE\SYSTEM\CurrentControlSet\Services\Tcpip
```

Under the TCP/IP key, the AdapterTypes subkey contains several subkeys for the different media that TCP/IP on Windows NT supports. The NetConfig subkey contains information specific to the TCP/IP building blocks for Streams. Together, the parameters in these keys ensure that the TCP/IP modules connect correctly in the Streams environment.

Other Registry keys created during TCP/IP installation can be used to modify the behavior of Windows NT TCP/IP. For a description of the Registry value entries for Windows NT TCP/IP, see "TCP/IP Transport Entries" in Chapter 14, "Registry Value Entries."

User-Mode Interfaces to TCP/IP

Windows NT TCP/IP supports three user-mode interfaces to TCP/IP: Windows Sockets, named pipes, and NetBIOS. Although RPC and Network DDE can also be used to develop network-aware applications that run over TCP/IP, these interfaces do not offer the same level of network control as the Windows Sockets, named pipes, or NetBIOS.

For details about these protocols, see Chapter 15, "Windows NT Networking Architecture."

NetBIOS over TCP/IP (NBT) is a protocol module that provides NetBIOS naming services over TCP/IP. This layer allows NetBIOS applications (which rely on names to establish connections and deliver data) to function over TCP/IP (which relies on IP addresses). Using NBT, NetBIOS applications can locate other NetBIOS computers by name and simultaneously acquire the computers' IP addresses. For details, see "Name Resolution and NetBIOS over TCP/IP," later in this chapter.

Windows NT TCP/IP Drivers and Services

This section lists the files installed on your system when Windows NT TCP/IP is installed. Details about these files can be found in Chapter 4, "Windows NT Files."

Several driver files included with Windows NT are loaded by the system at initialization time or as needed by other modules. These drivers are copied to the *SystemRoot*\SYSTEM32\DRIVERS directory during installation:

AFD.SYS	TELNET.SYS	TCPIP.SYS
STREAMS.SYS	NBT.SYS	

Several helper dynamic-link libraries (DLLs) handle service controller requests (for example, **net start** and Services in the Control Panel) and provide event logging and support functions for drivers. Other DLLs (such as WINSOCK.DLL) provide an interface or additional functionality. These DLLs are copied to the *SystemRoot*\SYSTEM32 directory during installation:

FTPSMX.DLL[1]	NBTSVC.DLL	WINSOCK.DLL
FTPSVC.DLL[1]	SOCKUTIL.DLL	WINSTRM.DLL
ICMP.DLL	TCPIPSVC.DLL	WSHTCPIP.DLL
LMHSVC.DLL	TELNET.DLL	WSOCK32.DLL

[1] Conditionally installed with the FTP Server service

These executable files are copied to the *SystemRoot*\SYSTEM32 directory during installation to support the TCP/IP utilities:

ARP.EXE	HOSTNAME.EXE	REXEC.EXE
FINGER.EXE	NBTSTAT.EXE	ROUTE.EXE
FTPMGR.CPL[1]	NETSTAT.EXE	RSH.EXE
FTPSVC.EXE[1]	PING.EXE	TELNET.EXE
FTP.EXE	RCP.EXE	TFTP.EXE

[1] Conditionally installed with the FTP Server service

Several UNIX-style database files support TCP/IP-based network applications. These files, modeled after their UNIX counterparts, allow configuration files maintained on UNIX systems to be copied and used on a Windows NT system without modification. These files are copied during installation to the *SystemRoot*\SYSTEM32\DRIVERS\ETC directory:

HOSTS	SERVICES	PROTOCOLS
NETWORKS	LMHOSTS	TELNET.TRM

Using and Administering TCP/IP with Windows NT

Before using Microsoft TCP/IP on Windows NT networking, you should know certain configuration information such as the IP address, subnet mask, and default gateway. If you have a *multihomed* workstation (that is, your system has multiple network adapters), you need valid IP addresses and subnet masks for each network the computer is connected to, and you need to determine which networks you want to use NBT. Windows networking (that is, the Windows NT redirector and server) can only be bound to a single network adapter and NBT binding.

These configuration parameters are all set using the Network icon in Control Panel. For more information on these parameters, installation, and configuration of TCP/IP, see the *Windows NT Advanced Server TCP/IP Guide*.

The Domain Name Service (DNS) provides a way to look up name mappings when connecting a workstation to foreign hosts by way of applications such as FTP. To use the DNS, you must enable the domain name resolver module in the TCP/IP Connectivity Configuration dialog box. For details, see the *Windows NT System Guide* or *Windows NT Advanced Server System Guide*.

NBT provides a dynamic way for locating Windows NT and LAN Manager computers on the local network. For Windows NT-based systems located on remote subnets, the LMHOSTS file is needed to provide computer name-to-IP address mappings.

Topics in this section include the following:

- Name resolution and NBT
- The LMHOSTS file
- Network browsing with Windows NT TCP/IP

Name Resolution and NetBIOS over TCP/IP (NBT)

TCP/IP communication relies on IP addresses as endpoint identifiers; however, users like to refer to networked systems by simple names. TCP/IP workstations running Windows NT use NetBIOS over TCP/IP, an open standard, for name resolution.

Requests for comments (RFCs), which are official documents that detail the IP protocol suite, provide a specification for dynamic NetBIOS name resolution over the TCP/IP protocol suite in RFC 1001 and 1002. Microsoft TCP/IP complies with RFC 1001/1002. These RFCs describe three specific protocols:

- b-node (broadcast)
- p-node (point-to-point)
- m-node (mixed b-node and p-node)

The Windows NT implementation of NetBIOS over TCP/IP uses a modified b-node protocol.

NetBIOS network naming involves three parts: registration, resolution, and release, as described in this section.

Name Registration

NetBIOS over TCP/IP relies on IP-level broadcasts to register a name by announcing its existence to the network. If another node in the IP-broadcast area has already registered the same name, it contests (or challenges) the name, causing the duplicate name registration to fail. If no workstation in the broadcast area has contested the name after a specified timeout, the workstation is said to have *claimed* the name.

Name Resolution

Once a workstation has claimed a name, it is responsible for contesting duplicate name-registration attempts and for responding to name queries on its registered names. Name queries are generated when a user (or process) requests a connection with a remote Windows NT computer on a network. For example, typing **net use x: \\rhino\sources** causes a *name query request* for the computername rhino. The name query request is broadcast on the network over UDP/IP to locate the specified system (in this example, querying the name rhino).

All workstations running NBT in the broadcast area are responsible for examining the contents of the *name query* packet. If the name in the name query packet matches the workstation's computername, it responds with a *positive name query response*. This response contains the IP address of the remote workstation, and the two systems are able to establish a TCP session.

Name Release

In the b-node protocol, when a name is released, a broadcast is made to allow any systems on the network that might have cached the name to remove it. Upon receiving name query packets specifying the deleted name, the workstation ignores the requests, allowing other workstations on the network to acquire the name that it has released.

The b-node protocol provides a simple, dynamic mechanism for locating resources on a TCP/IP network by name. However, because the b-node protocol relies on IP-level broadcasts to locate resources, unwanted effects can result in routed IP topologies. In particular, resources located on remote subnets (that is, outside of the local IP-broadcast area) are effectively unresponsive to name query requests, because routers do not pass IP-level broadcasts.

For this reason, Windows NT uses an enhanced b-node protocol, allowing users to manually provide computername and IP address mappings for remote resources by using an LMHOSTS file, as described in the following section.

The LMHOSTS File

The HOSTS and LMHOSTS files contain lists of known IP addresses. Each of these files is also known as a *host table*. The LMHOSTS and HOSTS files are located in the *SystemRoot*\SYSTEM32\DRIVERS\ETC directory and can be edited using any ASCII editor (such as Notepad or Edit, which are part of Windows NT).

- The Hosts file is the local host table, which maps remote host names to IP addresses. The HOSTS file format is the same as the format for host tables in the 4.3 BSD (Berkeley Software Distribution) UNIX */etc/hosts* file. For example, the entry for a node with an address of 192.102.73.6 and a host name of trey-research.com looks like this:

```
192.102.73.6        trey-research.com
```

  A sample HOSTS file is created when you install Microsoft TCP/IP for Windows NT. Edit this file to include remote host names and their IP addresses for each computer with which you will communicate. This sample file also explains the syntax of the HOSTS file.

- The LMHOSTS file is a local text file that maps IP addresses to NetBIOS names of Windows NT computers outside the local subnet. LMHOSTS is read when the workstation is started, and specified entries are stored in a system cache. When a name must be resolved, NBT checks this cache before doing a b-node name discovery. For example, the LMHOSTS table file entry for a node with an address of 192.45.36.5 and a host name of CPQ386 looks like this:

```
192.45.36.5     CPQ386
```

  For LMHOSTS file syntax, see the comments at the beginning of the sample LMHOSTS file in the *SystemRoot*\SYSTEM32\DRIVERS\ETC directory.

When you are using the replication service, LMHOSTS entries are required on import and export servers for any computers on different subnets participating in the replication.

When you use a host table file, be sure to keep it up-to-date and organized. Follow these guidelines:

- Update the host table file whenever a workstation is changed, added to, or removed from the network.

- Because host table files are searched one line at a time from the beginning, list remote workstations in priority order, with the ones used most often at the top of the file. This arrangement increases the speed of searches for the most often used entries.

The following sections describe how the LMHOSTS file can be used to enhance Windows NT in routed environments.

Specifying Remote Servers with LMHOSTS

With LMHOSTS, users resolve the names of systems outside their local broadcast area with computername and IP address mappings in the LMHOSTS file. For example, computer ClientA wants to connect to computer ServerB, which is outside its IP broadcast area. Both systems are configured with Windows NT TCP/IP.

Under a strict b-node implementation, ClientA's name query request for ServerB would ultimately time out, because ServerB is located on a remote subnet and does not respond to ClientA's broadcast requests. So an alternate method is provided to resolve the name into an IP address.

In LAN Manager 2.x, all the mappings in the LMHOSTS file are preloaded into a cache at initialization time. Before a name query request is generated for a given name (in this case, ServerB), the cache is examined, and if the name is present, it is resolved without querying the network. Besides initializing the cache, LAN Manager also provides the **addname** utility, allowing users to manipulate the cache post-initialization. The name cache can contain only 64 entries.

In Windows NT, a limited cache of computername and IP address mappings is initialized at system startup time and, as with LAN Manager, the cache is examined first during name resolution. If there is no match in the cache, Windows NT uses the b-node protocol. If the b-node protocol fails because the target computer is outside of the broadcast area or does not exist, TCP/IP searches for the name in the LMHOSTS file. If this last method fails, the name goes unresolved, and an error message is displayed.

This allows the LMHOSTS file to contain a large number of mappings without requiring a large chunk of static memory for an infrequently used cache. Entries in the LMHOSTS file can represent Windows NT workstations, LAN Manager servers, or Windows for Workgroups servers running Microsoft TCP/IP. There is no need to distinguish between these different platforms in LMHOSTS. At initialization time, the cache is preloaded only with entries from the LMHOSTS file that are tagged with the #PRE keyword. The #PRE tag ensures backward compatibility with LAN Manager 2.x LMHOSTS files, where the # character identifies a comment so that all trailing characters are ignored under LAN Manager.

For example, the LMHOSTS file could contain the following:

```
102.54.94.91    Accounting    #accounting server
102.54.94.94    Payroll       #payroll server
102.54.94.97    Thezoo        #PRE    #stock quote server
102.54.94.102   Printqueue    #print server in 1/1088
```

In this example, the server named Thezoo would be preloaded into the name cache because it is tagged with the #PRE keyword. The servers Accounting, Payroll, and Printqueue are resolved only after the cache entries fails to match and after b-node protocol fails to locate them. Once non-#PRE entries are resolved (either by b-node or by parsing), their mappings are cached for a period of time for reuse.

By default, Windows NT imposes a limit of 100 entries in its preload name cache, which only affects entries marked with the #PRE tag that cannot fit in the cache. If you specify more than 100 preload entries, there are two alternatives:

- Accept that only the first 100 #PRE entries will be preloaded. Any entries beyond 100 tagged with #PRE will be ignored at initialization, but will be resolved after the b-node protocol fails and after NBT parses the LMHOSTS file.

- Increase the size of the preload cache by adding the Registry value entry **MaxPreload** as type REG_DWORD under the HKEY_LOCAL_MACHINE \ SYSTEM\CurrentControlSet\Services\Nbt\Parameters key. Then specify the number of entries that you want to allocate at initialization time. This allows the preloaded cache to exceed 100 entries.

Finally, the **nbtstat** command can be used to reprime the name cache. The **nbtstat -R** command flushes the name cache, rereads the LMHOSTS file, and inserts name mappings tagged with the #PRE tag. Use the **nbtstat** command to remove or correct a preload entry that may have been mistyped, and to clear any names cached due to b-node resolution.

Although NBT parses arbitrarily large LMHOSTS files successfully, TDI imposes a timeout of 15 seconds in redirector connection requests. The connection request results in failure if NBT is unable to resolve a name in the 15-second period (either because of length or #INCLUDE problems, as described in "Using Centralized LMHOSTS Files," later in this chapter). This imposes a limit on the number of names or #INCLUDEs that you can use in LMHOSTS. The number of entries that can be processed is limited to the speed of your system and any remote systems that you rely on. In any event, NBT should be able to process about 1,000 entries without difficulty.

Designating Domain Controllers using #DOM

The most common use of the LMHOSTS file is for locating remote servers for file, print, and RPC services. However, under Windows NT, LMHOSTS can be used to distinguish domain controllers running TCP/IP in routed environments. Domain controllers maintain the user account security database, authenticate users, manage password changes, and manage other network-related services. As large domains can span multiple IP-layer subnets, situations arise where routers separate the domain controllers from one another or separate workstations from domain controllers.

The #DOM keyword can be used in LMHOSTS files to distinguish a Windows NT domain controller from a Windows NT workstation, a LAN Manager server, or a Windows for Workgroups computer. To use the #DOM tag, follow the name and IP address mapping in LMHOSTS with the #DOM keyword, followed by a colon and the domain in which the domain controller participates, for example:

```
102.54.94.97    rhinodc #DOM:rhino  #The rhino domain controller
```

> **Note** The #DOM tag does not imply preloading of the computername and IP address mapping. For domain controller entries that you expect to access frequently (such as servers in your local domain that are the home of useful files), use the #PRE, followed by #DOM (order is unimportant).

Specifying a domain controller using the #DOM tag builds entries into a special name cache known as the *internet group name cache*. To limit wide scale distribution of domain controller-centered requests in internets, domain controllers register a special internet group name. This special internet group name consists of the domain name padded to byte 15 with space characters (hex 20), with a 16th byte 1c hex. Only the domain controllers for the domain register this special name; servers and workstations do not.

Domain controller-centered activities include domain controller pulses (used for account database synchronization), logon authentication, password changes, master browser list synchronization, and other domain management activities.

When domain controller-centered activity takes place, the request is sent on the special internet group name. In the local IP-broadcast area, the request is sent only once (as a group multicast to the special name) and picked up by any local domain controllers. However, when domain controllers are specified in the LMHOSTS file using the #DOM tag, Windows NT TCP/IP also forwards the requests (using directed datagrams, not using broadcasts) to domain controllers located on remote subnets.

For domains that span subnets, the LMHOSTS file must be used in mapping the important members of the domain (domain controllers). The following presents some guidelines for doing this:

- Windows NT workstations that are members of a domain should have #DOM entries for all the computers that can be domain controllers in their domain and that are located on remote subnets. This ensures that logon authentication, password changes, browsing, and so on all function properly for the local domain. Any alternate domains that the workstation can log onto (including trusted domains) should contain entries for its remote domain controllers. These requirements represent the minimum set of entries necessary to allow an Windows NT system to participate in a Windows networking internet.

- For LMHOSTS files on servers that can be domain controllers, all servers should have at least the primary domain controller's name and IP address mapping in their LMHOSTS file. The mappings for other domain controller names and IP addresses should also be stored in the local file so that promotion of a server to domain controller does not affect the ability to offer domain controller services to members of the domain.

- If trust relationships exist between domains, all domain controllers for all trusted domains should also be provided in the local LMHOSTS file.

- For domains that you want to browse from your local domain, you need at least the name and IP address mapping for the domain controller in the remote domain. Again, Windows NT servers should also be included so that promotion of such a server to a domain controller does not impair the ability to browse remote domains. For more details, see "Network Browsing with Windows NT TCP/IP," later in this chapter.

For small-sized to medium-sized networks with less than 20 domains, a single common LMHOSTS file usually satisfies all workstations and servers on the internet. To achieve this, use the built-in replicator service to maintain synchronized local copies of the global LMHOSTS, or use the centralized LMHOSTS support described in the following section.

Using Centralized LMHOSTS Files

Windows NT provides the ability to include other LMHOSTS files from local and remote systems. The primary LMHOSTS file is always located in the *SystemRoot*\SYSTEM32\DRIVERS\ETC directory on the local system. As most networks will have an LMHOSTS file maintained by the network administrator, the administrator should maintain one or more global LMHOSTS files that users can rely on. To do this, use the #INCLUDE keyword to include other LMHOSTS files.

Usually a global LMHOSTS file is stored on a server (or set of servers) for global access. Rather than copying the global file locally, use the #INCLUDE keyword to define a pointer to the global LMHOSTS file, and use the replicator service to distribute multiple copies of the global files to multiple servers for reliable access.

To provide a redundant list of alternative LMHOSTS pointers (that is, multiple servers maintaining copies of the same LMHOSTS file), use the #BEGIN_ALTERATE and #END_ALTERNATE keywords. This is known as a *block inclusion*, which allows multiple servers to be searched for a valid copy of a specific file. The following example shows the use of these keywords:

```
102.54.94.97    rhinodc #DOM:rhino  #domain controller in rhino domain
102.54.94.99    zoobdc  #DOM:rhino  #server in the rhino domain

#INCLUDE    c:\private\lmhosts      #include a local lmhosts

#BEGIN_ALTERNATE
#INCLUDE    \\rhinodc\public\lmhosts    #source for global file
#INCLUDE    \\zoobdc\public\lmhosts     #backup source
#INCLUDE    \\local\public\lmhosts      #backup source
#END_ALTERNATE
```

This example shows how a local LMHOSTS file in the C:\PRIVATE directory is included by the local LMHOSTS file. Although specifying local files is allowed, this feature should never be used to #INCLUDE a remote file from a redirected drive. This is dangerous for two reasons:

- The LMHOSTS file is shared between local users who have different profiles and different logon scripts.
- Even on single-user systems, redirected drive mappings can change between logon sessions.

Instead, use the UNC name for a fully qualified path.

In the above example, rhinodc and zoobdc are located on remote subnets from the workstation that owns the file. The local user has decided to include a list of preferred domain controllers in a local LMHOSTS file located in the C:\PRIVATE directory. During name resolution, TCP/IP first includes this private file, then fetches the global LMHOSTS file from one of three locations: rhinodc, zoobdc, or local. This example assumes that rhinodc and zoobdc are both remote systems, so it was therefore necessary to provide their mappings before using them as the source for an #INCLUDE statement.

Assuming that the server named local is either defined in the user's private LMHOSTS file or is located in the IP-broadcast area, and assuming the name can be resolved by using the b-node protocol, then if one of the three sources for the global LMHOSTS is available, the block inclusion is satisfied and no other server is used. If no server is available, or for some reason the LMHOSTS file or path is incorrect, an event is logged in the System event log stating that the block inclusion failed.

Tip Because both the LMHOSTS file and cache are searched sequentially, it is best to locate frequently used servers near the top of the file, then less frequently used servers, followed by remote #INCLUDEs. Finally, the #PRE entries should be left for the end of the file, because these are preloaded into the cache at initialization time and are not accessed later.

Embedding Nonprintable Characters in LMHOSTS Computernames

Under Windows NT, the LMHOSTS service offers the ability to specify names containing nonprintable characters. This allows some custom applications that make use of special names to function properly in routed topologies. To use this feature, enclose the name in quotation marks, and specify nonprintable characters using either the \nn or \0xnn hex notation, for example:

```
102.54.94.97    rhinodc #DOM:rhino  #domain controller in rhino domain
11.14.21.96     "appl\0x1f"         #internal db application gateway
```

Note By using the special naming extension for the Windows NT LMHOSTS, you surrender backward compatibility with LAN Manager, because the LAN Manager TCP/IP implementation does not recognize the hex format.

Using LMHOSTS to Join a Domain over a Router

Because the process of joining a domain requires that the workstation contact a domain controller, it is sometimes necessary to provide an LMHOSTS file to a new system installing Windows NT. Two situations require this:

- Adding a server to a domain on an IP subnet other than the domain controller's IP subnet
- Adding a workstation to a domain on an IP subnet that contains no domain controllers for the domain

▶ **To join a domain with no local domain controllers**

1. In the Network dialog box under Control Panel, select TCP/IP Protocol in the Installed Network Software list, and then choose the Configure button.
2. Choose the Import LMHOSTS button in the TCP/IP Configuration dialog box.
3. Specify the filename of the LMHOSTS file that contains at least one domain controller for the domain to be joined (specified by the #DOM keyword), and then choose the Import button.

This copies the specified LMHOSTS file to the local system and allows the Windows NT networking software to connect to a domain controller so that the workstation can be added to the domain.

Note On workstations, you can install Windows NT without joining a domain and then join the domain later. However, when installing Windows NT on a server, the server must be able to establish communication with its domain controller. If the domain controller is not on the local IP subnet, you must import an LMHOSTS file during installation in order to join the domain.

Network Browsing with Windows NT TCP/IP

The Computer Browser service supports applications that present lists of servers available in domains and workgroups. The Computer Browser service is provided by a collection of dynamically elected systems that maintain a list of servers for their domain or workgroup and periodically exchange these lists with each another.

The Windows NT browser architecture is straightforward in a single domain. Elections are held on a per-broadcast-area basis to elect a master browser and possible backup browsers for the domain. These elections take place in the background, without any user intervention. If a domain spans multiple broadcast regions, multiple master browsers are elected for the domain, one per broadcast region. Because there can be multiple master browsers within an internet, the information that they maintain must be kept synchronized. To do this, the domain controller always acts as a *domain master browser*, responsible for keeping in sync all the master browsers for its domain in the internet.

Every 15 minutes, the master browsers contact the domain master browser and feed it a list of changes on their local subnets. The master browsers then download a list of changes from the domain master browser, which has built a master list for the entire domain. This allows all the browsers to remain in sync and accurate within approximately a 45-minute window.

Besides keeping the server list for a domain in sync, the domain master also acts as a master browser for interdomain browsing, which allows users to find the servers within another domain or workgroup. Domain and workgroup server lists are generated when master browsers periodically announce their domain's existence to all local browsers in a broadcast area. During synchronization with their domain masters, master browsers replicate the existence of the domains and master browsers for the new domains. So, when a workstation gets a list of domains and workgroups in the network, it usually represents domains and workgroups with members located on both local and remote subnets.

When a workstation attempts to browse a domain or subnet in which it doesn't belong, it first attempts to contact the master browser for the specified domain or workgroup on the local subnet. If this fails, it contacts its local master browser (in its own domain or workgroup), asking for a list of servers for the remote workgroup or domain. The local master browser then attempts to contact a master browser on the remote workgroup or domain to get the list of servers. This mechanism is referred to as a *double hop*.

If the workstation fails to locate a master browser for the remote domain, why would contacting its own master browser help the situation? The domain master for a given domain is always the domain controller. Provided that the local master browser can resolve a mapping for the remote domain master in the other domain (or any of the master browsers), it can make the double hop. For this reason, on systems that you know will be browsers (that is, domain controllers), keep a list in the LMHOSTS file of servers tagged with #DOM. Again, Windows NT is using the special internet group name that the domain controllers register.

Double hops are more difficult in situations where all members of a workgroup are located on an isolated subnet (that is, one with no members in any domain). This is because all members of a workgroup are considered equal during browser elections, and any workgroup workstation can act as the workstation browser. In the domain model, servers always act as browsers—always winning local elections over workstations in the domain.

In workgroups, all Windows NT systems participate and are equal in an election (although they win over Windows for Workgroups systems), and thus have equal opportunity to serve as master browsers for their workgroup. To do a double hop from a domain to a workgroup, the browser attempting the double hop must have a mapping for all the workstations in the workgroup (because any may be acting as the master browser for the workgroup).

Because no particular Windows NT system is guaranteed to win in this situation, do one of the following:

- Include all the workgroup members' mappings in the LMHOSTS files of any workstation that might want to do a double hop.

- Give priority to some workstations within the workgroup that can be included in global LMHOSTS files.

Because this restriction might not be ideal, a Registry parameter was added to elevate the chances of a workgroup member to win the browser election.

▶ **To elevate a workgroup member in the browser election**

1. For a selected computer, use Registry Editor to add a value entry named **IsDomainMasterBrowser** as type REG_SZ under this key:

   ```
   HKEY_LOCAL_MACHINE\SYSTEM\CurrentControlSet\Services
       \Browser\Parameters
   ```

2. Enter Yes as the value of the string.

3. Restart the computer for the change to take effect.

A computer with this parameter set will force an election to take place and will win over computers without this parameter set.

This value entry should be added on a few systems for the workgroup and mappings for each should be placed in the global LMHOSTS file. For example, in a workgroup with 20 members, you can add the **IsDomainMasterBrowser** value entry on three of the systems and include these three mappings in the LMHOSTS files maintained by remote domains. By doing this, you gain the functionality of remote workgroup browsing over internets.

Using IP Routing Under Windows NT

Windows NT offers basic IP routing and the ability to configure systems for multiple default gateways, so Windows NT can be used as a low-volume router in larger networks and can take advantage of network infrastructures that maintain many routers to provide redundant routes in cases of failure. The IP routing functionality support under Windows NT supports only local and nonsubnetted routing.

This section describes when IP routing might be used and how to configure it to take advantage of multiple default gateways.

Using a Multihomed Windows NT Workstation as an IP Router

Windows NT TCP/IP supports IP routing, but it is disabled by default. You can enable routing on a multihomed host. A properly configured multihomed Windows NT system automatically routes IP packets between all subnets to which it has interfaces with valid IP addresses and subnet masks.

▶ **To enable IP routing on a multihomed host**

1. Use Registry Editor to add a value entry called **IpEnableRouter** as a REG_DWORD under this Registry key:

   `HKEY_LOCAL_MACHINE\SYSTEM\CurrentControlSet\Services\Tcpip\Parameters`

2. Enter a value of 1 to enable this parameter. A value of 0 disables IP routing.

3. Restart the computer for the change to take effect.

There is no support for interrouting protocols such as RIP or OSPF on Windows NT. However, the **route** utility can be used to build static routes into your system's routing table. ROUTE.EXE is installed in the *SystemRoot*\SYSTEM32 directory when you install TCP/IP under Windows NT. The following figure shows how Windows NT can route IP packets between subnets.

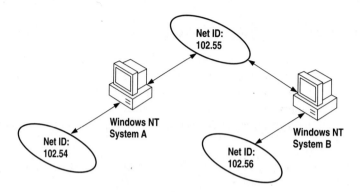

Figure 19.2   Using Windows NT to Route IP Packets Between Subnets

First, for System A, if the system is properly connected and configured on both subnets 102.54 and 102.55 and the **IpEnableRouter** value is 1, the system successfully routes packets between the two subnets to which it is connected. Connecting and configuring System B on both 102.55 and 102.56 and setting **IsRouterEnabled** to 1 will allow System B to route packets between these two nets. However, these steps alone do not allow packets to be routed between 102.54 and 102.56. To do this, entries must be added to each system's routing tables.

When the multihomed systems were configured as routers, the IP software learned of the networks the systems were connected to. Specifically, System A learned of two networks: 102.54 and 102.55. Similarly, System B learned of 102.55 and 102.56. To allow System A to know about 102.56 and System B to know about 102.54, you must use the **route** utility.

If the IP address of System B's interface to the 102.55 network is 102.55.0.2, the following command line adds a routing table entry for System A to allow it to route packets from the 102.54 net to the 102.56 net through System B:

route add 102.56   102.55.0.2

Next, add a routing table entry on System B to allow it to route packets to net 102.54 through System A. If System A's interface on the 102.55 network is 102.55.0.1, the following command allows System B to route IP packets from the 102.56 net to the 102.54 net through System A:

route add 102.54   102.55.0.1

By taking these steps, the three subnet internetworks in Figure 19.2 are now connected. That is, systems on network 102.54 can communicate with systems on network 102.56, and vice versa. The **route** utility can also be used to check the routing table entries on System B. For the command **route print,** the following values would appear:

```
Network Address  Gateway Address       Redirect    Life
102.54           102.55.0.1
```

This example shows how Windows NT systems can be used in place of dedicated IP router hardware systems. This situation might be useful in relatively small TCP/IP networks; however, a more common situation is to use Windows NT to connect a small network to a larger, established TCP/IP internet. The following example shows a topology where this might be effective:

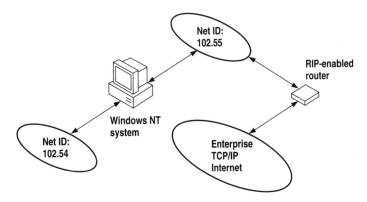

Figure 19.3   Connecting a Remote Subnet to an Established TCP/IP Internet with Windows NT

In this example, the network represented by the enterprise TCP/IP internet, the RIP-enabled router, and the 102.55 network have been established and maintained for some time. The enterprise internet consists of several IP routers using the RIP protocol to maintain their routing tables, and network 102.54 comprises twelve Windows NT workstations used by a few engineers for CAD applications. To enhance productivity, the engineers connected to the enterprise internet, allowing them to access e-mail, remote printers, and so on from their Windows NT workstations.

Instead of using a costly IP router to connect this small group, a Windows NT workstation could be configured to be attached to both the 102.54 and 102.55 networks. Once attached and configured for routing as described earlier in this section, the Windows NT system can successfully route IP packets between the 102.54 and 102.55 networks. However, because Windows NT does not provide native support for RIP, it is necessary to inform it of networks in the enterprise internet, and vice versa.

In this example, because all traffic from the engineers' network needs to pass through the RIP-enabled router, routing table entries could be added for all the remote networks in the enterprise internet. Depending on the number of networks, this could be extremely time-consuming. Also, the routers in the enterprise internet must be configured to recognize the Windows NT system as the gateway to 102.54.

The simpler approach is to configure the Windows NT system to use the local IP router as the default gateway to other networks. In this example, the network administrator configures the 102.55.0.2 interface of the RIP-enabled router to act as the default gateway for all the networks in the enterprise internet. This allows all packets originating from 102.54 and destined for the enterprise internet to be routed properly, because the default gateway knows all the networks in the enterprise internet. However, to allow systems in the enterprise internet to reach systems on the 102.54 network, the RIP-enabled router must be statically configured with the 102.55.0.1 address of the Windows NT system to act as the gateway for packets destined for 102.54. The means for adding this static route vary among routers.

Note Because the RIP-enabled routers periodically exchange lists of known networks (and routes to those networks), RIP usually propagates this information to the other routers in the enterprise internet. However, some RIP implementations do not propagate static routes to other routers through RIP. If this is the case, it may be necessary to statically configure the remote routers in the enterprise internet to know about Windows NT system gateways.

Taking Advantage of Multiple Default Gateways

In more complex network topologies, internetworks are frequently configured to offer alternate routes between some systems in the internet. The following figure shows a simple internetwork that offers exactly two routes from any source to any given remote (off-subnet) destination:

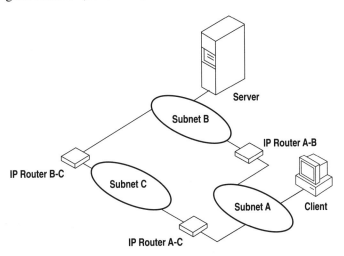

Figure 19.4   Internetwork with Redundant Routes

In this example, the client located on Subnet A can follow two different routes to the server located on Subnet B:

- Client ➔ Router A–B ➔ Server
- Client ➔ Router A–C ➔ Router B–C ➔ Server

It is better to follow the first single-hop route, rather than the second double-hop route. In a situation where a system on Subnet A does most of the internet communication with systems on Subnet B, the system's default gateway should be configured to use Router A-B to deliver all traffic. If such a system wants to deliver traffic to Subnet B, it will be routed by Router A-B. When this same system wants to send packets to Subnet C, it will send the initial packet to Router A-B, which will generally respond with an ICMP Redirect message, telling the system to use Router A-C (a better route). The system will then direct all traffic destined for Subnet C through Router A-C.

Because the routers all periodically exchange routing information, configuring a system with a single default gateway generally allows a system to communicate with all systems reachable on its internet. Either its default gateway can deliver the data directly or it redirects the system to use another, better router to deliver the data. This configuration is fine as long as all the routers remain available.

If a system's default gateway becomes unavailable, it cannot communicate with systems outside its own subnet (aside from those it has established connections with on remote subnets prior to failure). For example, if Router A-B is out of commission when Client1 starts and if Client1 wants to connect to Server2, its default gateway is unavailable, and so it cannot be redirected to Router A-C to connect to Server2. Multiple default gateways can help in situations like this.

▶ **To configure a Windows NT system to use multiple default gateways**

1. Use Registry Editor to add a new REG_MULTI_SZ value entry called **AdditionalGateways** under this Registry key:

    `HKEY_LOCAL_MACHINE\System\CurrentControlSet\Services\Tcpip\Parameters`

2. For this value entry, enter a list of strings representing additional default gateways to use if the default gateway becomes unavailable. (The default gateway is configured using the Network icon in Control Panel.)

    These entries should be added in order of preference. In the above example, only Router A-C would be added to this list.

The list under **AdditionalGateways** can be in dotted decimal format (for example, 102.54.94.97), or it can be a fully qualified domain name (FQDN) that can be resolved by either the HOSTS file or by DNS (for example, rhino.microsoft.com).

When a Windows NT system is configured in this way, retransmission problems at the TCP layer cause the IP routing software to try the routers in the **AdditionalGateways** list. In this example, if Client1 and Server2 had a session established and Router A-B went down, TCP would send a message to IP telling it to try one of the additional routers. IP would then try Router A-C and use the double-hop route to continue exchanging data between Client1 and Server2. When Router A-B becomes available, the interrouting protocol forces Router A-C (the current first hop router in the path from Client1 to Server2) to redirect Client1 to use Router A-B for traffic destined for Server2.

The **route** utility can be used to display the currently active default (or smart) gateway; the **route -s print** command prints the currently active default gateway, and the **route print** command prints all current routes in the routing tables, identifying all default gateways in the table in order of preference.

Use the **route -s add** command to add default gateways after the system has initialized. Any gateways added in this way are appended to the existing list. The **route** command does not provide a way to order the gateways, so you must use **route -f** to flush all the routing table entries and then add entries in the order of preference. However, remember that any changes made to the routing tables using the **route** utility are not added to the Registry. To permanently affect the default gateway routing tables, you must add **AdditionalGateways** values to the Registry.

Using Windows NT TCP/IP as a Connectivity Protocol

Because many users want to use TCP/IP to connect Windows NT systems to heterogeneous systems on networks, some client-side connectivity utilities are provided for file transfer, terminal emulation, and network diagnostics. The following table summarizes the utilities included with Windows NT. For more information, see *Windows NT Advanced Server TCP/IP Guide* and the Windows NT Command Reference Help.

Table 19.3   Windows NT Connectivity Utilities

Utility	Description
arp	Allows a user to view and modify the address resolution protocol (ARP) table entries on the local system.
finger	Allows a user to retrieve system information on remote systems supporting TCP/IP and a finger service.
ftp	Offers file transfer services to remote systems supporting File Transfer Protocol (FTP). **ftp** supports a host of commands allowing bidirectional transfer of binary and ASCII files between systems. The **ftp** commands are explained in online Help.
ftpsvc	The FTP Server service provides an FTP server for Windows NT. The FTP Server is not installed by default when installing Windows NT TCP/IP, because of security considerations described after this table. The FTP Server service is installed by using the Network icon in Control Panel.
hostname	Returns the local workstation's hostname used for authentication by the **rcp**, **rexec**, and **rsh** TCP/IP utilities. This value defaults to the workstation's computername, but can be changed using the Network icon in Control Panel.
nbtstat	Provides network statistics for NBT active and pending connections.
netstat	Provides network statistics for all TCP/IP active and pending connections.

Table 19.3   Windows NT Connectivity Utilities *(continued)*

Utility	Description
ping	Provides a mechanism for determining whether a remote TCP/IP system is reachable. **Ping** is generally used to determine whether a particular system is functioning properly in the TCP/IP network, for example, to determine whether it can see systems located on remote subnets.
rcp	Provides a mechanism for unidirectionally copying files between two systems. One or both systems can be remote. Rcp provides rudimentary security in that the protocol passes both the username (on Windows NT, the locally logged on user) and the hostname of the system for authentication. The remote systems generally must be configured to trust the **rcp** requests by configuring a file (in many cases, the .RHOSTS file in the user's local directory).
rexec	Provides a mechanism for running a process on a remote system that supports remote process execution over TCP/IP. **rexec** is identical to the functionality provided by **rsh**, with the addition of cleartext password authentication.
rsh	Provides a mechanism for executing a process on a remote system that supports running remote processes over TCP/IP. **rsh** provides the same level of security as **rcp**, but it does not support redirection of **stdin** (that is, only output from the remotely run command is displayed; local keystrokes are not passed to the remote system).
telnet	Offers basic terminal emulation to remote systems that support the Telnet protocol over TCP/IP. **telnet** is implemented as a Windows NT service, which allows **telnet** to be used by terminal emulation programs such as the Windows Terminal accessory. **telnet** can be invoked from the command line by typing **telnet** (which starts the service) or **net start telnet** or by using the Services tool in Control Panel, followed by starting Windows Terminal and choosing the TELNET connector. (Other terminal emulation products can also support the TELNET port connector).
tftp	Provides a subset of **ftp** that uses the UDP protocol rather than TCP. **tftp** allows the unidirectional transfer of files between local and remote systems with no security provisions, relying on the world readability or writability of the files on the remote system for access.

> **Important** **ftp**, **ftpsvc**, **rexec**, and **telnet** all rely on password authentication by
> the remote system, passing in cleartext the network authentication passwords
> specified for the user. Microsoft Windows, Windows NT, and LAN Manager
> networking never permit this policy with Microsoft logon credentials. This
> allows a malicious user equipped with a network analyzer on the same network
> to steal a user's remote account password. For this reason, it is strongly
> recommended that users of these utilities choose different passwords for their
> Windows NT workgroup, workstation, or domain than on systems they are
> connecting to that are not Microsoft systems.

Tips for Using TCP/IP

This section covers some details of the Windows NT TCP/IP software not covered
in the *Windows NT Advanced Server TCP/IP Guide.* Topics include the following:

- Using IPINFO.INF to prevent configuration errors
- Using additional features of the FTP Server service
- Using TCP/IP utilities to diagnose network problems

Using IPINFO.INF to Prevent Configuration Errors

The IPINFO.INF file provides "smart" defaults for TCP/IP parameters under
Windows NT. If you provide users with a way to install Windows NT over the
network or create custom installation floppies, you can set smart defaults for
the subnet mask and the default gateway by using the IPINFO.INF file and IP
addresses.

Under Windows NT, .INF files are used during installation to specify how files
should be copied and to provide configuration data for software components.
These files are plain ASCII files that can be edited using Edit or Notepad. For
descriptions of these files, see Chapter 3, "Customizing Windows NT Setup."

▶ **To alter IPINFO.INF to provide smart defaults for parameters**

- Change the **[DefaultIPInfo]** section of IPINFO.INF to specify the settings
  you want.

By default, the TCP/IP installation program bases the default subnet mask on the address class of the workstation's IP address. For example, a network administrator who has subnetted a class B address on the third octet and defined a global default gateway might modify the **[DefaultIPInfo]** section in IPINFO.INF in the following way:

```
[DefaultIPInfo]
    DefaultGateway="102.54.94.97"
    NumberOfIPAddresses=1
    IPAddress1=""
    SubnetMask="255.255.255.0"
```

The IPINFO.INF file can be used to provide custom Windows NT TCP/IP installation floppies with specific IP addresses for users. The complete syntax for IPINFO.INF can be found in the default file in the *SystemRoot*\SYSTEM32 directory.

Using Additional Features of the FTP Server Service

This section describes additional FTP Server features beyond what is available when you choose the FTP Server icon or the Network icon in Control Panel. The Registry value entries described in this section are found under the following Registry key:

```
HKEY_LOCAL_MACHINE\SYSTEM\CurrentControlSet\Services\Ftpsvc\Parameters
```

Controlling the FTP Server and User Access

The FTP Server configuration variable, Maximum Connections, can be set to a value between 0 and 50 by using the Network icon in Control Panel. Any value from 1 to 50 restricts concurrent FTP sessions to the value specified. A value of 0 allows unlimited connections to be established to the FTP Server until the system exhausts the available memory.

If the maximum number of concurrent connections is reached, new connection attempts receive the message, "Maximum clients reached, service unavailable." This message can be customized.

▶ **To customize the "Maximum clients reached" message for the FTP Server**

1. Use Registry Editor to add a REG_SZ value entry named **MaxClientsMessage** under ..\FtpSvc\Parameters

2. Enter a replacement message.

When making any configuration changes to the FTP Server (with the exception of security configuration), you must restart the FTP Server by either restarting the computer or manually stopping and restarting the server.

► **To restart the FTP Server service**

- Use the Services icon in Control Panel. Or type **net stop ftpsvc** followed by **net start ftpsvc** at the command line.

Restarting the service in this way disconnects any users presently connected to the FTP Server without warning—so first use the FTP Server icon in Control Panel to determine if any users are connected.

Pausing the FTP Server (using the **net pause ftpsvr** command or the Services icon in Control Panel) prevents any more users from connecting to the FTP Server but does not disconnect the currently logged in users. This feature is useful when you want to restart the server without disconnecting current users. After the users disconnect on their own, you can safely shut down the server without worrying that users will lose work. When attempting to connect to a Windows NT FTP Server that has been paused, clients receive the message, "421- Service not available, closing control connection."

Annotating Directories for FTP Users

You can add directory descriptions to inform FTP users of the contents of a particular directory on the server.

► **To annotate director for FTP users**

- Create a file called **~ftpsvc~.ckm** in the directory where you want to annotate with the information to be displayed to the user.

  You can make this file hidden so that directory listings do not display this file. To do this, enter the command **attrib +h ~ftpsvc~.ckm** from the command line.

Directory annotation can be toggled by FTP users on a user-by-user basis with a built-in, site-specific command called **ckm**. On most FTP client implementations (including the Windows NT FTP client), users enter a command similar to **quote site ckm** to get this effect. The administrator can control the default behavior of this feature for newly connected users by setting a value for **AnnotateDirectories** under ..\FtpSvc\Parameters in the Registry. A value of 0 indicates that directory annotation is off by default; a value of 1 indicates that it is on.

Formatting Directory Listings with FTP

Some FTP client software makes assumptions based on the format of directory listing information. The Windows NT FTP Server provides some flexibility for client software that requires directory formatting similar to UNIX systems.

▶ **To change the directory listing format**

- Use Registry Editor to change the Registry value entry **MsDosDirOutput** in the ..\FtpSvc\Parameters key.

  A value of 0 defines a UNIX-style listing. The default value of 1 formats a directory listing in MS-DOS–style.

This value entry identifies the default listing type for new users. Users can toggle this setting with the site-specific command **dirstyle**. On most FTP client implementations (including the Windows NT FTP client), users enter a command similar to **quote site dirstyle** to get this effect.

Customizing FTP Greeting and Exit Messages

You can define custom greeting and exit messages for when users connect or disconnect from the FTP Server.

▶ **To add a custom greeting message**

1. Use Registry Editor to add a value entry named **GreetingMessage** of type REG_MULTI_SZ under the ..\FtpSvc\Parameters key.

2. Edit the multiline string to display a welcome message of your choice.

Similarly, you can create an exit message by adding a value entry called **ExitMessage** in the ..\FtpSvc\Parameters key and specifying a string to display to users when they exit. By default, these value entries are not in the Registry, so you must add and modify them.

Logging Incoming Connections with FTP

You can optionally log oncoming connections, both from anonymous and nonanonymous users, by creating REG_DWORD value entries called **LogAnonymous** and **LogNonAnonymous** under the ..\FtpSvc\Parameters key in the Registry. Set these values to 1 to turn on logging. Connections are then logged to the System event log and can be viewed using Event Viewer.

Monitoring FTP Server Traffic with Performance Monitor

The *Resource Guide* disks include the necessary DLL and installation software to monitor and graph various FTP Server statistics using Performance Monitor. Among the statistics that can be graphed are bytes transferred per second, connected users, maximum concurrent users, and files transferred. Because Performance Monitor can be used to view the activity on remote Windows NT systems, this can make FTP Server administration more convenient if you are administering multiple Windows NT FTP Servers.

Using SNMP

This section explains the Microsoft Simple Network Management Protocol (SNMP) service for Windows NT and lists the LAN Manager MIB II objects designed to support computers running Windows NT. For information about installing and configuring the SNMP service, see Chapter 2, "Installing and Configuring Microsoft TCP/IP and SNMP," in *Windows NT Advanced Server TCP/IP Guide.*

This section assumes that you are familiar with network management, TCP/IP, and SNMP. It also assumes that you are familiar with the concept of a *management information base* (MIB). If you are not familiar with TCP/IP or the Internet MIB 2, see *Internetworking with TCP/IP* by Douglas E. Comer (Prentice Hall, 1991) and *The Simple Book* by Marshall T. Rose (Prentice Hall, 1991).

SNMP is a network management protocol heavily used in TCP/IP networks. Network management protocols are used to communicate between a management program run by an administrator and the network management program running on a host or gateway. These protocols define the form and meaning of the messages exchanged, the representation of names and values in the messages, and administrative relationships among the gateways being managed.

SNMP is a standard protocol used to monitor IP gateways and the networks to which they attach. SNMP defines a set of variables that the gateway must keep and specifies that all operations on the gateway are side-effects of fetching or storing the data variables.

How Does the SNMP Service Work?

With the Microsoft SNMP service, a Windows NT computer can report its current status to an SNMP management system on a TCP/IP network. The service sends status information to a host in two instances:

- When a management system requests such information
- When a significant event occurs on the Windows NT computer

The SNMP service can handle requests from one or more hosts. The SNMP service can also report network-management information to one or more hosts in discrete blocks of data called *traps*.

On TCP/IP networks, each device has a unique name and IP address. The SNMP service uses host names and IP addresses to recognize the host or hosts to which it reports information and from which it receives requests.

When a network manager requests information about a device on the network, SNMP management software can be used to determine object values that represent network status. MIB objects represent various types of information about the device. For example, the management station might request an object called **SvStatOpen**, which would be the total number of files open on the Windows NT computer.

Because different network-management services are used for different types of devices or for different network-management protocols, each service has its own set of objects. The entire set of objects that any service or protocol uses is referred to as its *management information base* (MIB). The SNMP service for Windows NT supports multiple MIBs through an extension agent API interface. At SNMP service startup time, the SNMP service loads all of the extension-agent DLLs defined in the Windows NT Registry.

There are two extension-agent DLLs that come with Windows NT; others may be developed and added separately. The SNMP service supports the Internet MIB II and a subset of the LAN Manager MIB II objects.

LAN Manager MIB II for Windows NT Objects

The LAN Manager MIB II for Windows NT contains a set of objects specifically designed to support computers running Windows NT. This section lists the objects in the MIB and provides a brief description of each. Note there are fewer objects in the LAN Manager MIB II for Windows NT than the LAN Manager MIB II for OS/2 because of differences in the operating system.

All objects apply to Windows NT and Windows NT Advanced Server computers.

Common Group

comVersionMaj {common 1}
The major release version number of the Windows NT software.

comVersionMin {common 2}
The minor release version number of the Windows NT software.

comType {common 3}
The type of Windows NT software this system is running.

comStatStart {common 4}

The time, in seconds, since January 1, 1970, at which time the Windows NT statistics on this node were last cleared. The **comStatStart** object applies to the following statistical objects:

comStatNumNetIOs	**svStatErrorOuts**	**wkstaStatSessStarts**
comStatFiNetIOs	**svStatPwErrors**	**wkstaStatSessFails**
comStatFcNetIOs	**svStatPermErrors**	**wkstaStatUses**
svStatOpens	**svStatSysErrors**	**wkstaStatUseFails**
svStatDevOpens	**svStatSentBytes**	**wkstaStatAutoRecs**
svStatJobsQueued	**svStatRcvdBytes**	
svStatSOpens	**svStatAvResponse**	

comStatNumNetIOs {common 5}

The number of network I/O operations submitted on this node.

comStatFiNetIOs {common 6}

The number of network I/O operations on this node that failed issue.

comStatFcNetIOs {common 7}

The number of network I/O operations on this node that failed completion.

Server Group

svDescription {server 1}

A comment describing the server.

svSvcNumber {server 2}

The number of network services installed on the server.

svSvcTable {server 3}

A list of service entries describing the network service installed on the server.

svSvcEntry {svSvcTable 1}

The names of the network services installed on the server.

svSvcName {svSvcEntry 1}

The name of a Windows NT network service.

svSvcInstalledState {svSvcEntry 2}

The installation status of a network.

svSvcOperatingState {svSvcEntry 3}

The operating status of a network service.

svSvcCanBeUninstalled {svSvcEntry 4}

Indicates whether the network service specified by this entry can be removed.

svSvcCanBePaused {svSvcEntry 5}

Indicates whether the network service specified by this entry can be paused.

svStatsOpen {server 4}

The total number of files that were opened on the server.

svStatDevOpens {server 5}

The total number of communication devices that were opened on the server.

svStatQueuedJobs {server 6}

The total number of print jobs that were spooled on the server.

svStatSOpens {server 7}

The number of sessions that were started on the server.

svStatErrorOuts {server 8}

The number of sessions disconnected because of an error on the server.

svStatPwErrors {server 9}

The number of password violations encountered on the server.

svStatPermErrors {server 10}

The number of access-permission violations encountered on the server.

svStatSysErrors {server 11}

The number of system errors encountered on the server.

svStatSentBytes {server 12}

The number of bytes sent by the server.

svStatRcvdBytes {server 13}

The number of bytes received by the server.

svStatAvResponse {server 14}

The mean number of milliseconds it took the server to process a workstation I/O request (for example, the average time an NCB sat at the server).

svSecurityMode {server 15}

The type of security running on the server.

svUsers {server 16}

The number of concurrent users the server can support.

svStatReqBufsNeeded {server 17}

The number of concurrent users the server can support.

svStatBigBufsNeeded {server 18}

The number of times the server needed but could not allocate a big buffer while processing a client request.

svSessionNumber {server 19}

The number of sessions on the server.

svSessionTable {server 20}

A list of session entries corresponding to the current sessions that clients have with the server.

svSessionEntry {svSessionTable 1}

A session that is currently established on the server.

svSesClientName {svSessionEntry 1}
The name of the remote computer that established the session.

svSesUserName {svSessionEntry 2}
The number of connections to server resources that are active in the current session.

svSesNumConns {svSessionEntry 3}
The number of connections to server resources that are active in the current session.

svSesNumOpens {svSessionEntry 4}
The number of files, devices, and pipes that are open in the current session.

svSesTime {svSessionEntry 5}
The length of time, in seconds, since the current session began.

svSesIdleTime {svSessionEntry 6}
The length of time, in seconds, that the session has been idle.

svClientType {svSessionEntry 7}
The type of client that established the session.

svSesState {svSessionEntry 8}
The state of the current session. (Setting the state of an active session to **deleted** by using **netSessionDel** deletes the client session. The session state cannot be set to **active**.)

svAutoDisconnects {server 21}
The number of sessions that the server automatically disconnected because of inactivity.

svDisConTime {server 22}
The number of seconds the server waits before disconnecting an idle session.

svAuditLogSize {server 23}
The maximum size, in kilobytes, of the server's audit log.

svUserNumber {server 24}
The number of users who have accounts on the server.

svUserTable {server 25}
A table of active user accounts on the server.

svUserEntry {svUserTable 1}
A user account on the server.

svUserName {svUserEntry 1}
The name of a user account.

svShareNumber {server 26}
The number of shared resources on the server.

svShareTable {server 27}
A table of the shared resources on the server.

svShareEntry {svShareTable 1}
A table corresponding to a single shared resource on the server.

svShareName {svShareEntry 1}
The name of a shared resource.

svSharePath {svShareEntry 2}
The local name of a shared resource.

svShareComment {svShareEntry 3}
A comment associated with a shared resource.

svPrintQNumber {server 28}
The number of printer queues on the server.

svPrintQTable {server 29}
A table of the printer queues on the server.

svPrintQEntry {svPrintQTable 1}
A table entry corresponding to a single printer queue on the server.

svPrintQName {svPrintQEntry 1}
The name of a printer queue.

svPrintQNumJobs {svPrintQEntry 2}
The number of jobs currently in a printer.

Workstation Group

wkstaStatSessStarts {workstation 1}
The number of sessions the workstation initiated.

wkstaStatSessFails {workstation 2}
The number of failed sessions the workstation had.

wkstaStatUses {workstation 3}
The number of connections the workstation initiated.

wkstaStatUseFails {workstation 4}
The number of failed connections the workstation had.

wkstaStatAutoRecs {workstation 5}
The number of sessions that were broken and then automatically reestablished.

wkstaErrorLogSize {workstation 6}
The maximum size, in kilobytes, of the workstation error log.

wkstaUseNumber {workstation 7}
This object will always return the value 0.

Domain Group

domPrimaryDomain {domain 1}
The name of the primary domain to which the computer belongs.

C H A P T E R   2 0

Using NWLink and NetWare Client for Windows NT

This chapter discusses the two major software components for integrating Windows NT into Novell NetWare environments—NWLink protocol and NetWare Client for Windows NT.

Both NetWare Client for Windows NT and NWLink work seamlessly with Windows NT. With NWLink, Windows NT servers can be accessed by NetWare client computers. With Novell NetWare Client for Windows NT, Windows NT computers can access NetWare servers.

NWLink Protocol

NWLink is an IPX/SPX-compatible transport protocol for Windows NT. It can be used to establish connections between Windows NT computers and either MS-DOS, OS/2, Windows, or other Windows NT computers via RPC, Sockets (either Windows Sockets or NetWare sockets), or Novell NetBIOS. It does not, however, allow a Windows NT computer to connect to a Novell NetWare server or to act as a server to a Novell NetWare client. To connect to a Novell NetWare server, you need to purchase Novell's NetWare Client for Windows NT (described later in this chapter).

NWLink is useful if you have NetWare client applications that use the IPX/SPX API or if you have applications which use NetBIOS or Novell NetBIOS. NWLink can also serve as the protocol used by the default redirector and server for Windows NT and Windows NT Advanced Server.

NWLink and Streams

NWLink protocol drivers are Streams-based and rely on Streams to provide many of the basic services to the protocol device drivers. This is similar to the TCP/IP implementation for Windows NT. The Streams wrapper controls the interface to the higher-level file system and device drivers. It also controls the interface to the NDIS device driver at the lower end.

Because NWLink uses Streams, which in turn uses NDIS 3.0, the NWLink protocol can be run on any network adapter card that uses an NDIS-compatible driver.

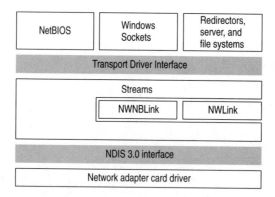

Figure 20.1   NWLink, NWNBLink, and Streams

There are two software components which reside within the Streams wrapper.

- NWLink is responsible for the IPX and SPX protocols.
- NWNBLink is responsible for formatting NetBIOS-level requests and passing them to the NWLink component for transmission on the network.

File system modules reside above the TDI layer and use this common interface to communicate with NWLink.

The default Windows NT server and redirector components use Server Message Blocks (SMB) to perform file and print services. These components can use NWLink to communicate to other Windows NT and Windows for Workgroups computers that use the Novell NetBIOS and IPX protocol.

NetBIOS and Windows Sockets

User-mode applications can use RPC, NetBIOS APIs, or Windows Sockets APIs to access the network via NWLink or other IPX/SPX protocol drivers. Both NetBIOS and Windows Sockets are supported in the Windows 32-bit, Windows 16-bit, and MS-DOS environments. Programs that run in the OS/2 environment can use NetBIOS but not Windows Sockets APIs. All subsystems and VDMs can use logical drives that are established by the redirector via NWLink.

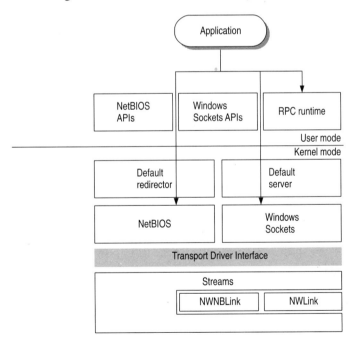

Figure 20.2   Communication via NetBIOS, Sockets, and RPC

NetBIOS Over IPX

The NetBIOS over IPX is compatible with the NetBIOS support provided by Novell. In addition, NWNBLink includes certain enhancements to improve performance when using NetBIOS.

These performance enhancements include acknowledgment of previous frames included in response frames (called PiggyBackAck). They also include use of a "sliding window" acknowledgment mechanism (described in Chapter 18, "Using NBF with Windows NT"). These performance enhancements are used only when communicating with NWNBLink computers.

When a Windows NT computer communicates with a computer using NetWare NetBIOS, the Windows NT computer must also use Novell NetBIOS. The NetBIOS provided by Novell acknowledges each frame received. Over highly reliable media such as a local-area network, this extra amount of precaution is unnecessary.

NWLink and Network Topologies

NWLink can be run on Ethernet, Token Ring, FDDI, and ArcNet topologies.

Each topology requires a different frame formats. Ethernet supports Ethernet_II, raw 802.3, 802.2, or SNAP frame formats. Token Ring and FDDI supports 802.2 and SNAP. ArcNet supports raw ArcNet framing only.

It is important to make sure that the NWLink on the Windows NT computers is using the same framing used by the client computer. On Ethernet networks, the standard frame format for NetWare 2.2 and NetWare 3.1 is 802.3. Starting with NetWare 4.0, the default frame format is 802.2.

Note The most likely problem on a Windows NT computer running with NWLink is caused by mismatched frame protocols. If two computers are not communicating, make sure that both are using the same frame protocol. You can determine the frame protocol on your Windows NT computer by viewing the configuration settings for NWLink through Network Control Panel.

For information about adjusting Registry entries used by NWLink and NWNBLink, see "NWLink Transport Registry Entries" Chapter 14, "Registry Value Entries."

NetWare Client for Windows NT

By installing Novell NetWare Client for Windows NT on your Windows NT computer, you can access NetWare servers. (Novell NetWare Client for Windows NT is available from Novell.) As shown by Figure 20.3, the architecture of NetWare Client for Windows NT is well integrated into the Windows NT networking architecture.

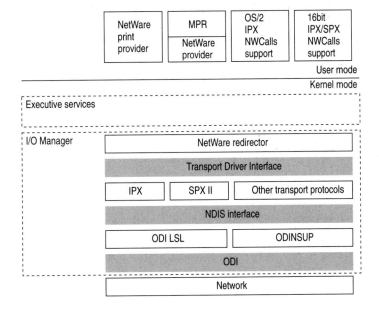

Figure 20.3   NetWare Client for Windows NT Architecture

NetWare Client for Windows NT includes a printer provider in user-mode memory. This component allows the Windows NT printer system to use a NetWare server's printers.

NetWare Client for Windows NT also includes the NetWare Redirector, the NetWare Provider, and the ODINSUP converter device driver. These components are described in the following sections.

NetWare Redirector

The NetWare Redirector, with the NetWare Provider, supports file and print services from NetWare Client for Windows NT, NetWare 2.*x*, 3.*x*, and 4.*x* servers.

The Redirector can support unlimited number of connections. The auto-reconnect feature is also supported so that users don't need to remember previously established connections.

Like the default Windows NT Redirector, the NetWare Redirector is implemented as a file system driver. This allows the NetWare Redirector to have efficient access to the other file system drivers such as FAT and NTFS.

The NetWare Redirector takes advantage of several file-system services, including cache management, offered by Windows NT. Cache management helps increase the performance of the system by reading ahead during sequential file access and buffering multiple operations to reduce the amount of network traffic.

The Redirector communicates with transport protocols through the Transport Device Interface (TDI). NetWare Client for Windows NT support both IPX and SPX II protocols. Unlike the default protocols provided with Windows NT (including TCP/IP, NBF, and DLC), the IPX and SPX protocols use the Open Device Interface (ODI) in place of NDIS.

NetWare Provider

NetWare Provider resides in user mode and provides an interface for user interaction with the network. This component creates extensions in File Manager, allowing users to manage connections and mappings made with NetWare server. NetWare Provider also allows users to browse NetWare resources on the network.

NetWare Provider creates extensions in Control Panel, allowing users to collect information about connections and to manage NetWare Client for Windows NT servers. NetWare Provider works with the MPR to accept and run WNet API calls from Win32 and Windows 16-bit applications.

NetWare Provider communicates with the Win32 subsystem via the Multiple Provider Router (MPR). Programmatic interfaces for the MS-DOS, Windows 16-bit, and OS/2 environments are also provided.

ODINSUP Converter

To allow NDIS-based protocol stacks access to the network adapter card via the ODI MAC-level driver, the NetWare Client for Windows NT system provides a converter driver called ODINSUP. With this device driver, users can simultaneously run the NetWare Client for Windows NT system and TCP/IP, NBF, or DLC on the same network adapter card.

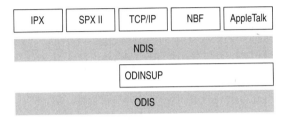

Figure 20.4   ODI and ODINSUP Converter

As mentioned earlier, the IPX and SPX protocols provided with the NetWare Redirector use ODI to communicate to the network adapter card. Since only one device driver can be bound to a network adapter card at a time, this presents a problem for users who want to use both the NetWare Redirector with IPX/SPX to communicate with NetWare servers and the default TCP/IP protocol stack to communicate with UNIX hosts. To allow this type of configuration, the converter driver, ODINSUP, is provided with the NetWare Redirector. This driver translates from NDIS to ODI and vice versa. This allows NDIS protocol drivers to be bound to network adapter cards via ODI-compliant MAC-level device drivers.

C H A P T E R   2 1

Using DLC with Windows NT

A Data Link Control (DLC) protocol interface device driver is provided in each Windows NT and Windows NT Advanced Server computer. The DLC protocol is traditionally used to provide connectivity to IBM mainframes. It is also used to provide connectivity to local-area network printers that are directly attached to the network, instead of to a specific computer.

This chapter provides details about the DLC protocol device driver for Windows NT.

Overview

The Data Link Control (DLC) protocol driver provided with Windows NT and Windows NT Advanced Server allows the computer to communicate with other computers running the DLC protocol stack (for example, an IBM mainframe) and other network peripherals (for example, printers such as a Hewlett-Packard HP 4Si that use a network adapter card to connect directly to the network).

Windows NT DLC contains an 802.2 Logical Link Control (LLC) Finite State Machine, which is used when transmitting and receiving type 2 connection-oriented frames. DLC can also transmit and receive type 1 connectionless frames, such as Unnumbered Information (UI) frames. Type 1 and 2 frames can be transmitted and received simultaneously.

Windows NT DLC works with either Token Ring or Ethernet MAC drivers and can transmit and receive DIX format frames when bound to an Ethernet MAC.

The DLC interface can be accessed from 32-bit Windows NT programs and from 16-bit MS-DOS and 16-bit Windows programs. The 32-bit interface conforms largely to the CCB2 interface, the segmented 16-bit pointers being replaced with flat 32-bit pointers. The 16-bit interface conforms to the CCB1 interface.

Note For definitions of the CCB interfaces, see the *IBM Local Area Network Technical Reference*.

Loading the DLC Driver on Windows NT

The DLC driver can be loaded when the system is first installed, or any time thereafter, using the Network Control Panel.

The order of the bindings section is significant to DLC because an adapter is specified at the DLC interface as a number—typically 0 or 1 (although Windows NT DLC can support up to 16 physical adapters). The number corresponds to the index of the adapter in the DLC bindings section. If you only have one network adapter card installed, DLC applications use a value of 0 to refer to this adapter, and you need not make any changes to the bindings.

If you have more than one adapter card, you may want to modify the bindings. To change the order of the bindings, follow these steps

1. From the Network Control Panel, choose Bindings.

2. From the Show Bindings For box, choose DLC Protocol.

3. You will see a list of bindings, such as the following.

```
DLC Protocol -> ARC Built-in Ethernet Adapter Driver ->
   [01] ARC Built-in Ethernet Adapter
DLC Protocol -> IBM Token Ring Adapter Driver ->
   [02] IBM Token Ring Adapter
```

The numbers in brackets refer to the order in which the adapters were installed. In this example, currently DLC refers to the Ethernet adapter as adapter #0 and the Token Ring adapter as adapter #1.

If you have software (such as a 3270 emulator program) that allows you to specify an adapter number at run time, you may decide to keep the current setup and change the adapter number when you run the software. Typically, however, the software uses adapter #0, expecting an IBM Token Ring card to be the primary adapter. In this case, you will need to change the order of the bindings list.

4. To change the order of an item in the list, highlight the item, and then use the up- and down-arrow buttons to reposition it in the list.

   For example, suppose you wanted to change the above bindings so that the IBM Token Ring adapter corresponds to adapter #0 and the ARC Ethernet adapter corresponds to adapter #1. Highlight the line containing IBM Token Ring Adapter Driver, and click once on the up-arrow button. The bindings are now correctly ordered for your application software, and you do not need to modify the program configuration.

5. Choose OK to keep the modified bindings list.

DLC Driver Parameters in the Registry

Unlike other Windows NT protocol drivers, DLC does not bind to a MAC driver until an adapter open command is issued. When an adapter is opened for the first time, the DLC protocol driver writes some default values into the Registry for that adapter. These values control the various timers that DLC uses, whether DIX (Digital.Intel.Xerox) frames should be used over an Ethernet link and whether bits in a destination address should be swapped (used when going over a bridge that swaps destination addresses).

The timer entries in the Registry are supplied because program-supplied timer values may not be sufficient. There are three timers used by DLC link communication:

- T1 is the response timer
- T2 is the acknowledgment delay timer
- Ti is the inactivity timer

Each timer is split into two groups—**TxTickOne** and **TxTickTwo**, where x is 1, 2, or i.

Typically, these timer values are set when a program opens an adapter and/or creates a Service Access Point (SAP).

The Registry contains entries used to modify timer values. Registry entries for DLC are found in the following location:

```
HKEY_LOCAL_MACHINE\SYSTEM\CurrentControlSet\Services\DLC\Parameters
    \<Adapter Name>
```

When you edit a timer entry value, the change takes effect the next time the adapter is opened (for example, by rerunning the application). For more information, including the ranges and default values for the timers, see "DLC System Driver Entries" in Chapter 14, "Registry Value Entries."

Communicating with Mainframes Using DLC and SNA

One of the major uses of the DLC protocol today is connecting computers to large mainframe computers. With the increased popularity of local area networks in the mid-1980s, IBM introduced a new connectivity option for its 37x5 Front-end processors (FEP). The Token Ring Interface Connection (TIC) allows IBM mainframes to participate as a node on a local-area Token Ring network.

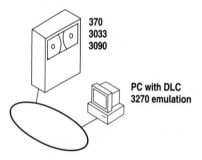

Figure 21.1   Mainframe Connectivity Path Using Token Ring

The mainframes already possessed a rich protocol stack in Systems Network Architecture (SNA). SNA provides equivalent functionality to the Network, Transport, Session, and Presentation services in the mainframe (though functionality may differ at each level). The DLC layer and the OSI Data Link layer are almost identical in functionality. Because of this, a programming interface was developed for the DLC layer and exposed to programmers wanting to use this level of interface.

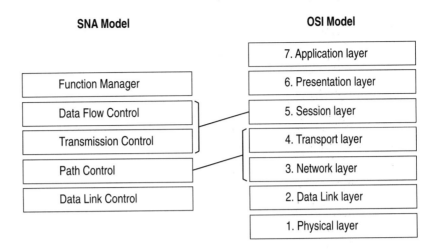

Figure 21.2   Comparison of SNA and OSI Models

SNA Server for Windows NT uses the DLC protocol device driver when communicating to mainframes via the Token Ring interface. Detailed configuration and installation information is provided in the *SNA Server for Windows NT Administrator Guide.*

Using DLC to Connect to HP Printers

DLC is used to provide connectivity to local-area network printers that are directly attached to the network, not to a specific computer.

Printing via the DLC protocol device driver starts by creating a printer that uses the HPMON.DLL printer driver. All commands are performed in the Print Manager utility.

First create a printer from within Print Manager by choosing Create Printer from the Printer menu. From the Print To list box, select the Network Printer. From the Print Destination panel, select the Hewlett-Packard Network Port. The Add Hewlett-Packard Network Peripheral Port dialog box causes Windows NT to automatically search for printers connected to your network. The dialog box also allows you to select the network adapter to be used to used to connect to the server and adjust the DLC Timers for this application. (DLC timers are described earlier, in "DLC Driver Parameters in the Registry.")

For more specific information, see the online Help associated with the Add Hewlett-Packard Network Peripheral Port dialog box.

Changing the Locally Administered Address

There may be times when you want to change or override the network address of the network adapter card when running the DLC protocol. You may want to do this, for example, when communicating directly to a mainframe. Certain configurations of mainframe software require the network address of the devices connecting to it to follow a set format, so it may be necessary to change the card's network address. You can do this through the Registry Editor.

Note   This example is for an IBM Token Ring adapter. This parameter is supported on other network adapters as well, but not necessarily all.

The following instructions do not apply when connecting to a mainframe via SNA Server for Windows NT. The modifications needed to the network address are handled during the installation process.

---

1. Run REGEDT32.EXE.

2. Select the following key:

   `HKEY_LOCAL_MACHINE\SYSTEM\CurrentControlSet\Services\ibmTOKMC01`

3. From the Edit menu, choose Add Value. For Value, type **NetworkAddress,** and select REG_SZ for data. Choose OK.

4. Type the string. This should be the 12-digit Locally Administered Address (LAA) that you need to communicate to the mainframe. If you don't know this address, see your network administrator or operations group.

5. Exit Registry Editor and reboot your computer. (You must reboot for the modification to take effect.)

6. Once rebooted, from the command prompt run the following command:

   `net config rdr`

   This will report the active MAC address so you can confirm that the LAA has taken effect.

For more information about using Registry Editor, see Chapter 11, "Registry Editor and Registry Administration." For information about specific DLC-related Registry Entries, see Chapter 14, "Registry Value Entries."

CHAPTER 22

Client-Server Connectivity on Windows NT

The ability to access data that resides on different hardware platforms, different operating systems, different network operating systems, and different database management systems (DBMSs) is a fundamental need for client-server computing. The purpose of this chapter is to discuss specifically how client workstations communicate with Windows NT databases. Primarily, this chapter covers details about MS-DOS, Windows, Windows NT, and OS/2 client workstations.

Note As of this writing, the client-server databases in the process of being released on the Windows NT platform include Microsoft SQL Server, Ingres Server, Oracle Server, Informix Server, SQLBase, and Versant. A general invitation was sent from Microsoft to all of the Windows NT database vendors to gather information about how their database engines work with Windows NT. Ingres and Microsoft SQL Server agreed to participate. The other database companies were unable to provide details for this chapter before our press date.

This chapter provides details about Microsoft SQL Server and Ingres database products running on Windows NT.

Overview

Microsoft Windows NT is an ideal platform for DBMSs. This platform provides a high level of performance, scalable hardware, and a secure foundation for distributed computing. Features such as preemptive multitasking, multithreading, fault tolerance, and security help meet the growing demands of client-server computing.

Windows NT provides a full 32-bit architecture with a flat memory model, which does away with managing memory in segments, for increased performance. Windows NT and the Win32 API allow for programs, such as DBMSs, that deal with large amounts of data by providing access to 2 GB of address space. The operating system and other processes have their own protected memory spaces so that one process cannot bring another process down.

With preemptive scheduling and an asynchronous input/output model, the operating system, rather than the application, is in control. Windows NT automatically gives high priority to applications running in the foreground and to processes receiving input or completing input/output operations. Multiple threads of execution allow applications to be more powerful and responsive. An application does not have the ability to tie up the system, even when the application is loading, processing data, printing, and so on. The system is always available to the user.

Windows NT was designed from the ground up to support symmetric multiprocessing. The operating system can allocate application and system threads within the same process to different processors. The net benefit to you is improved performance and transparent scalability of your corporate DBMS.

These features within Windows NT provide a powerful platform for mission-critical database applications. Each DBMS for Windows NT implements this architecture differently and may or may not use all of the features available within Windows NT.

SQL Server for Windows NT

Microsoft SQL Server version 4.2 for Windows NT extends intelligent client-server database management to your corporate network, offering an industrial strength platform for the delivery of critical business applications. Microsoft SQL Server has been completely reengineered for Windows NT.

SQL Server for Windows NT includes the following enhancements and performance improvements that were not part of the previous versions of SQL Server:

- A new Symmetric Server architecture allows SQL Server to scale from notebook computers to symmetric multiprocessor servers, with support for *x*86 and RISC processors. This architecture dynamically balances the processor load across multiple CPUs and provides a preemptive multithreaded design for improved performance and reliability.

- Preemptive scheduling, virtual paged memory management, symmetric multiprocessing, and asynchronous I/O are the foundations needed for a mission-critical database server platform. Windows NT provides these services, and SQL Server uses them fully. Integration with the Windows NT operating system improves operational control and ease of use. Administrators have the ability to manage multiple SQL Servers across distributed networks using graphical tools for configuration, security, database administration, performance monitoring, event notification, and unattended backup.

- Unified logon security with Windows NT security means that authorized users do not have to maintain separate SQL Server logon passwords and can bypass a separate logon process for SQL Server. Additionally, SQL Server applications can take advantage of Windows NT security features, which include encrypted passwords, password aging, domain-wide user accounts, and Windows-based user administration.

- Windows NT provides an ideal platform for building powerful 32-bit client-server applications for Microsoft SQL Server. The *SQL Server Programmer's Toolkit for Windows NT* contains a 32-bit Win32-based version of DB-Library™.

- SQL Server for Windows NT is fully interoperable with Microsoft SQL Server for OS/2 as well as SYBASE SQL Server for the UNIX and VMS operating systems. Existing applications will work unchanged. SQL Server on OS/2 database file formats are identical, allowing easy migration of corporate data to the Windows NT platform. SQL Server for Windows NT operates across all corporate network environments, including Novell NetWare and TCP/IP-based LANs.

The key to enterprise interoperability is network independence. SQL Server for Windows NT can support clients communicating over multiple heterogeneous networks simultaneously, with no need for additional integration products. SQL Server communicates on named pipes (over either NetBEUI or TCP/IP network protocols) with Windows, Windows NT, MS-DOS, and OS/2 clients.
In addition, SQL Server for NT can simultaneously support TCP/IP Sockets for communication with Macintosh, UNIX, or VMS clients and SPX Sockets for communications in a Novell NetWare environment. SQL Server for Windows NT will support Banyan VINES as soon as the networking components become available for Windows NT. Microsoft SQL Server for Windows NT leverages the power, ease of use, and scalability offered by the Windows NT operating system to manage large databases for mission-critical applications.

Data Access Mechanisms

Figure 22.1 illustrates the key interfaces used to access data in a Microsoft SQL Server client-server environment. These include application programming interfaces (APIs), data stream protocols, interprocess communication (IPC) mechanisms, and network protocols.

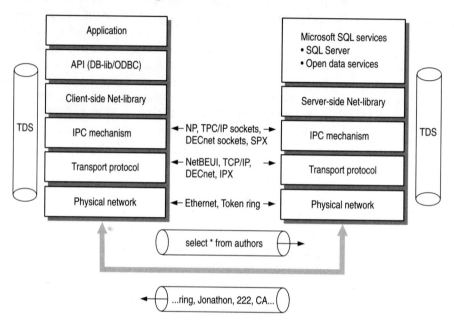

Figure 22.1   Levels and Interfaces Within the SQL Server for Windows NT Architecture

The following sections describe each of these interfaces to SQL Server.

Application Programming Interfaces

Each back-end database typically has its own API through which it communicates with clients. A client application needing to access multiple back-end databases must be able to transform requests and data transfers into each of the corresponding API interfaces. Client-server applications communicate with SQL Server for Windows NT through two APIs—Open Database Connectivity (ODBC) and DB-Library.

ODBC is an API for generic database connectivity for Windows, Windows NT, and, in the future, Macintosh platforms. It is designed to be a general-purpose Call-Level Interface (CLI) for any database back-end, including nonrelational DBMSs. The ODBC interface provides the needed functionality for applications that must access multiple DBMSs from different vendors. Application developers can develop, compile, and ship an application without targeting a specific DBMS, provided that DBMS-specific features are not used. ODBC ensures interoperability by forcing all clients to adhere to a standard interface. The ODBC driver automatically interprets a command for a specific data source.

DB-Library is a set of API calls designed specifically for SQL Server and allows applications to interact with SQL Server. DB-Library provides connectivity between multiplatform clients and SQL Server. DB-Library provides the needed functionality for applications requiring client support for MS-DOS and/or OS/2. DB-Library is also equivalent to the SYBASE Open Client interface on UNIX, VMS, and Macintosh systems.

Data Stream Protocols

Every DBMS uses a data stream protocol that enables the transfer of requests, data, status, error messages, and so on, between the DBMS and its clients: This can be thought of as a "logical" protocol. The API uses interprocess communication (IPC) mechanisms supported by the operating system and network to package and transport this logical protocol.

The Microsoft SQL Server data stream protocol is called Tabular Data Stream (TDS). TDS is also used by Open Data Services and SYBASE software to transfer requests and responses between the client and the server. TDS is a logical data stream protocol and must be supported by physical network IPC mechanisms. The Net-Library architecture (described later in this chapter) provides a method of sending TDS across a physical network connection.

Each database's data stream protocol is typically a proprietary one that is developed and optimized to work exclusively with that DBMS. This means that an application accessing multiple databases must be able to use multiple data stream protocols. Using ODBC helps resolve this problem for application developers.

With ODBC implementations, the data stream protocol differences are resolved at the driver level. That is, each driver emits the data stream using the protocol established by the server. The SQL Server ODBC driver emits TDS directly—it does not translate or otherwise encapsulate DB-Library function calls.

Efforts are underway to establish common data stream protocols. IBM's DRDA architecture has defined a data stream protocol known as FD:OCA. The International Standard Organization (ISO) has proposed another data stream standard, RDA (ISO RDA).

Interprocess Communication Mechanisms

The choice of IPC mechanism is constrained by the operating system and network being used. For example, Microsoft SQL Server on OS/2 uses named pipes as its IPC mechanism, SYBASE SQL Server on UNIX uses TCP/IP sockets, and SYBASE on VMS uses DECnet™ Sockets. In a heterogeneous environment, multiple IPC mechanisms may be used on a single computer.

SQL Server for Windows NT has the ability to communicate over multiple IPC mechanisms. SQL Server communicates on named pipes (over either NetBEUI or TCP/IP network protocols) with Windows, Windows NT, MS-DOS, and OS/2 clients. It can also simultaneously support TCP/IP Sockets for communication with Macintosh, UNIX, or VMS clients and SPX sockets for communications in a Novell NetWare environment. As the networking components for Banyan VINES become available for Windows NT, SQL Server for Windows NT will support it as well.

Network Protocols

A network protocol is used to transport the data stream protocol over a network. It can be considered as the "plumbing" that supports the IPC mechanisms used to implement the data stream protocol, as well as supporting basic network operations such as file transfers and print sharing.

Back-end databases can reside on a local-area network (LAN) that connects it with the client application, or it can reside at a remote site, connected via a wide-area network (WAN) and/or gateway. In both cases, it is possible that the network protocol(s) and/or physical network supported by the various back-end databases are different from that supported by the client or each other. In these cases, a client application must use different network protocols to communicate with various back-end databases.

The network transport protocols supported within SQL Server for Windows NT include NetBEUI, TCP/IP, SPX/IPX using NWLink, and VINES IP.

Net-Library Architecture

Microsoft SQL Server Net-Library architecture for client-server applications is based on the Net-Library concept that abstracts the client and server applications from the underlying network protocols being used. Figure 22.2 shows how SQL Server and related products can be accessed from practically any network environment.

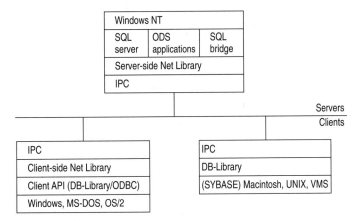

Figure 22.2   Net-Library Architecture

The Net-Library architecture provides a method of sending TDS (used by Microsoft SQL Server, Open Data Services, and SYBASE) across a physical network connection. The Net-Library architecture also provides a transparent interface to the DB-Library APIs and the SQL Server driver for ODBC.

Net-Libraries are linked dynamically at run-time. With the Microsoft Windows NT, Windows, and OS/2 operating systems, Net-Libraries are implemented as DLLs, and multiple Net-Libraries can be loaded simultaneously. With MS-DOS, Net-Libraries are implemented as terminate-and-stay-resident (TSR) programs, and only one can be loaded at a time.

The Net-Library architecture can be divided into two components—server-side Net-Libraries and client-side Net-Libraries.

Server-Side Net-Library Architecture

Server-side Net-Libraries were first introduced with Microsoft SQL Bridge. They are also used by Network Manager in the *Microsoft SQL Server Network Integration Kit for Novell NetWare Networks* and in the *Microsoft SQL Server Network Integration Kit for Banyan VINES Networks*. SQL Server on the Windows NT platform uses this same architecture and has the ability to accept client requests across multiple network protocols at the same time.

Figure 22.3 illustrates the integration of server-side Net-Libraries with the various SQL Server–based products on the Windows NT platform.

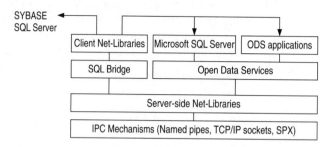

Figure 22.3   Server-Side Net-Library Architecture on the Windows NT Platform

The default Net-Library is named pipes.

When a server-side Net-Library is loaded by an application such as SQL Server for Windows NT, Net-Library implements a network-specific way of establishing communication with clients and, in some cases, registers its presence on the network. SQL Server looks at the Windows NT Registry to determine which Net-Library to load on startup and which parameters to pass them. The SQL Server Monitor process also uses server-side Net-Library to communicate with clients and to search the following Registry key for network-specific parameters:

`HKEY_LOCAL_MACHINE\SOFTWARE\Microsoft\SQL Server`

At startup, SQL Server specifies a value for the *server_name* parameter in the SRV_CONFIG structure of Open Data Services. This value identifies which Registry key SQL Server will search for values of the **ListenOn** and *connection_string* Registry entries. (By default, SQL Server looks in HKEY_LOCAL_MACHINE\SOFTWARE\Microsoft\SQLServer\Server.)

Each *connection_string* Registry value is read and passed on to the associated Net-Library (for example, named pipes) that is listed in the **ListenOn** field in the Server subkey. Each Net-Library acts upon the *connection_string* differently.

If there is no *connection_string* associated with the Net-Library, SQL Server does one of the following:

- If the Registry entry is under the SQL#Server\Server subkey, no connection string is passed as the default.

- If the Registry entry is not under SQL#Server\Server, *server_name* is passed as the default.

If the *server_name* subkey and the SQL#Server\Server subtree do not exist, or the Registry cannot be accessed, SQL Server assumes that the named pipes DLL (for the default Net-Library) is loaded, and no parameter is passed. (Named pipes access can be turned off by using the Registry Editor to explicitly delete the named pipes entry from the SQL#Server\Server subkey.)

Net-Libraries uses the GetComputerName() API to determine the computername of the Windows NT server.

Remote stored procedure calls and the Microsoft SQL Administrator tool (which use named pipes under OS/2) also use the DB-Library/Net-Library architecture under Windows NT.

Client-Side Net-Library Architecture

When a call is made to open a connection to SQL Server, the API involved (DB-Library or the SQL Server driver for ODBC) determines which client-side Net-Library should be loaded to communicate with SQL Server or Open Data Services. (This process is described in more detail later in this chapter.)

Figure 22.4 shows client-side Net-Libraries used to communicate with SQL Server for Windows NT on the server side.

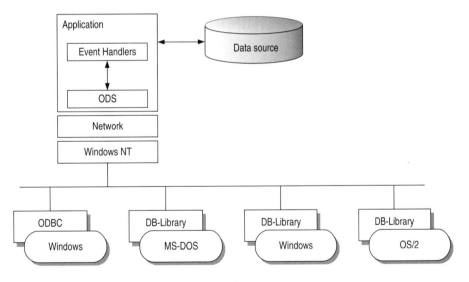

Figure 22.4   Client-Side Net-Library Architecture

Win32 DB-Library Architecture

Internally, the Win32 version of the DB-Library DLL is implemented similarly to the version for OS/2. In Win32, as in OS/2, a separate operating system thread is spawned for each connection that DB-Library makes with SQL Server. Each instance of the DB-Library DLL that is loaded by a calling process gets a private data area, while sharing code.

The Win32 DB-Library architecture differs from the implementation with Windows 3.*x*. In Windows 3.*x*, the DB-Library DLL has a single data segment that is shared among all calling processes. W3DBLIB.DLL maintains DB-Library connections as a linked list of connections in a single data segment. This architecture is required, because in Windows 3.*x* DLLs have a single data segment that is shared among all calling processes. This necessitates the initialization and clean up of the DB-Library DLL data structures through calls to the **dbinit** and **dbwinexit** functions.

The DB-Library functions for Win32 are located in NTWDBLIB.DLL, and the named pipe driver is located in DBNMPNTW.DLL. (Be sure to set the PATH environment variable to include the directory where the DLLs reside.)

Another file, NTWDBLIB.LIB, contains import definitions that your applications for the Win32 API use. Set the LIB environment variable to include the directory where NTWDBLIB.LIB resides.

DB-Library resolves server names differently depending on the client platform.

Resolving Server Names for Clients Based on Windows, Windows NT, and OS/2

When **dbopen** (the DB-Library function that initiates a client conversation with SQL Server) is called with the name of a SQL Server to connect to, DB-Library uses configuration information to determine which client-side Net-Library to load.

The client-side Net-Library configuration is stored in the following locations:

Client	Net-Library configuration is stored in
Windows 3.*x*	WIN.INI
OS/2	OS2.INI
Windows NT	Windows NT Registry

DB-Library scans the **[SQLSERVER]** section of WIN.INI, OS2.INI, or the \SQLServer\Client\ConnectTo subtree of the Windows NT Registry looking for a logical name that matches the *servername* parameter specified in the call to **dbopen**. All items in the **[SQLSERVER]** section of the .INI file or in the Registry subtree have this format:

```
<logical-name> = <Net-Lib-DLL-name> [, <network-specific-parameters>]
```

Note Although some Net-Libraries need values for <*network-specific-parameters*>, this is optional for others that instead use defaults or determine the network-specific information required themselves.

DB-Library uses the following logic to determine which Net-Library to load:

- If a matching logical name is found in the .INI file or in the Windows NT Registry, DB-Library loads the specified Net-Library DLL. If network-specific parameters are present in the .INI entry or the Windows NT Registry, these are passed unmodified by DB-Library to the Net-Library DLL.

- If no matching logical name is found in the .INI file or in the Windows NT Registry, the DLL name (and optionally, the network-specific parameters) of the entry named DSQUERY will be used to load the required Net-Library. So, if you don't have a specific servername but do have a DSQUERY entry, that entry will be used as the default.

- If there is neither a specific logical name nor a DSQUERY entry in the .INI file or in the Windows NT Registry, DB-Library loads the named pipes Net-Library (for example, DBNMPP3.DLL for the Windows operating system) and passes it the *servername* parameter from **dbopen**. With Microsoft SQL Server using named pipes, you typically never need to make a .INI entry. If you use any other Net-Library, you must make at least one entry.

The following examples illustrate this logic:

- **forecast=dbnmp3**

  The Windows named pipe Net-Library is used, and it connects to SQL Server \\Forecast using the standard named pipe, \pipe\sql\query.

- **sales=dbnmp3,\\server1\pipe\sql2\query**

  The Windows named pipe Net-Library is used, and it connects to \\server1, where SQL Server has been started using an alternate named pipe, \pipe\sql2\query.

Note SQL Server can be directed to use an alternate pipe by adding an entry to the ListenOn field in the Registry under the following tree:

`HKEY_LOCAL_MACHINE\SOFTWARE\Microsoft\SQL Server\Server`

- **dsquery=dbmsspx3**

  The SPX Net-Library is used, and the *servername* parameter from **dbopen** is used. This Net-Library requires no specific network connection information because it queries the NetWare Bindery to determine the location of the server running the Network Manager service specified in the *servername* parameter.

- **unixsrv=sybtcpw,131,107.005.21,3180**

  The SYBASE TCP/IP Net-Library is used, and DB-Library passes the IP address and port number contained in the initialization string to the Net-Library.

Note The SQL Server ODBC driver uses the same Net-Libraries as DB-Library to communicate with SQL Server, Open Data Services, and SQL Bridge.

Resolving Server Names for MS-DOS–Based Clients

With MS-DOS, only one Net-Library TSR can be loaded, so there is no .INI configuration. Instead, MS-DOS environment variables are used to specify any network-specific connection information. Environment variables have the following format:

`<logical-name> = <network-specific-parameters>`

The Net-Library used is the currently loaded TSR. If the *servername* parameter passed to **dbopen** corresponds to a currently set environment variable, DB-Library passes the information contained in the environment string to the currently loaded Net-Library. In turn, Net-Library uses this information to determine server location and network-specific information parameters, if present. If no environment variable matches the *servername* passed to **dbopen**, DB-Library passes the *servername* parameter from **dbopen** to the currently loaded Net-Library.

New DB-Library Function Identifies SQL Servers

DB-Library version 4.20.20 and above includes a new function (**dbenumserver**) that enables applications to identify SQL Servers available on the network, regardless of which network operating system is being used.

```
dbenumserver(   ushort        SearchMode,
                char    *     ServNameBuf,
                ushort        SizeServNameBuf
                ushort  *     NumEntries);
```

The following table defines the variables used here:

Variable	Meaning
SearchMode	Specifies the type of search (local and/or remote). Defines whether server names should be checked for locally (using name entries in WIN.INI, OS2.INI, or in the Windows NT Registry) and/or by interrogating the specific Net-Library. Both options can be chosen by using a logical OR with both options.
ServNameBuf	Identifies the buffer in which to store returned names.
SizeServNameBuf	Specifies the size of the buffer.
NumEntries	Holds the count of entries.

Configuration of the Net-Library Architecture

The Net-Library DLLs and IPCs for each network protocol supported by SQL Server for Windows NT are listed in the following table. These files are installed automatically using the SQL Server Setup utility on the server side and the SQL Client Configuration Utility on the Windows, Windows NT, and OS/2 client side. The AUTOEXEC.BAT file is used to load the MS-DOS client Net-Library.

The server-side Net-Library is used by SQL Server and ODS applications. If SQL Server and ODS are on the same computer, ODS uses an alternate pipe.

Table 22.1 shows which files you need when installing SQL Server on various network operating systems with various network protocols. Use the following table to determine exactly which files need to be in place for servers and clients.

You can also use this table for troubleshooting, should there be difficulty in connecting a client workstation to SQL Server for Windows NT.

Table 22.1   Server-Side and Client-Side Net-Library Files

Network interface	Network protocol	Network clients supported	Client-side Net-Library	Server-side Net-Library	Comments
Named Pipes	NetBEUI or TCP/IP	LAN Manager, Windows for Workgroups, and Windows NT clients	DBNMPIPE.EXE (MS-DOS), DBNMP3.DLL (Windows), DBNMPP.DLL (OS/2), DBNMPNTW.DLL (Windows NT)	SSNMPNTW.DLL	This network setup will provide SQL Server Integrated Security with the Windows NT User Account Database.
	NWLink	Windows NT clients	DBNMPNTW.DLL (Windows NT)	SSNMPNTW.DLL	
Windows Sockets	TCP/IP	UNIX and MAC clients	Part of SYBASE Open Client	SSMSSOCN.DLL	This configuration provides multiple vendor integration.
		PC clients: FTP PC/TCP, HP ARPA Services, Wollongong PathWay, Novell LAN WorkPlace, AT&T StarGroup, Sun PC-NFS, DEC Pathworks (DECnet), Microsoft TCP/IP for LAN Manager, and so on	SYBASE Net-Libraries	SSMSSOCN.DLL	with SYBASE. The corresponding Net-Libraries are available from SYBASE.
Windows Sockets	NWLink (IPX/SPX)	Novell NetWare 3.10+ (MS-DOS and Windows) and OS/2 Requestor, NSD004 (OS/2) clients	DBMSSPX.EXE (DOS), DBMSSPX3.DLL (Windows), DBMSSPXP.DLL (OS/2)	Novell: SSMSSPXN.DLL	The servername is registered with the Novell bindery service.

Table 22.1   Server-Side and Client-Side Net-Library Files *(continued)*

Network interface	Network protocol	Network clients supported	Client-side Net-Library	Server-side Net-Library	Comments
		NWLink	DBMSSPXN.DLL (Windows NT)		
Vines Sockets	Vines IP	Banyan Vines, 4.11 (rev.5)+ and Windows NT clients	DBMSVINE.EXE (DOS), DBMSVIN3.DLL (Windows), DBMSVINP.DLL (OS/2), DBMSVINN.DLL (Windows NT)	Banyan VINES: SSMSVINN.DLL	Registers to Street talk as the given service. Banyan VINES will automatically handle look ups of partial names or nicknames.

Notes NWLink is a Microsoft implementation of the IPX/SPX protocol. Alternative software available through Novell is fully expected sometime in the near future.

The Banyan Vines Net-Libraries listed in the table above may not be available in the first release of SQL Server for Windows NT.

Using NetBEUI as the network protocol, the client workstation always uses a broadcast to locate the SQL Server(s) on the network. Also, with TCP/IP the client workstation always uses a broadcast to locate the SQL Server(s), provided that the servername and IP address are not located in the LMHOST file on the workstations.

Novell Connectivity

As shown by Table 22.1, in a Novell NetWare environment, the Windows NT SQL Server requires NWLink (installed through Network Control Panel) and the SSMSSPXN.DLL. This DLL is automatically installed on the server side, with the appropriate Registry entries, when you use SQL Server Setup and choose Change Network Support, then NWLink IPX/SPX.

(For more information about NWLink, see Chapter 19, "Using NWLink and the NetWare Redirector with Windows NT.")

The following is a sample of what is added to the Registry for SQL Server for Windows NT on a Novell Network:

```
HKEY_LOCAL_MACHINE\SOFTWARE\Microsoft\SQLServer\Server
ListenOn: REG_MULTI_SZ: SSNMPNTW, \\.\pipe\sql\query
     SSMSSPXN, CORAL (computername)
```

Windows and OS/2 client workstations require the Novell NetWare 3.10 or higher level of IPX. The SQL Client Configuration Utility that ships with SQL Server for Windows NT is used to specify the default network that the Windows and OS/2 clients will use. By choosing Novell IPX/SPX, the required DBMSSPX3.DLL is automatically installed on the Windows client side, and DBMSSPXP.DLL is installed on the OS/2 client side. This will add the appropriate entries in the WIN.INI file or the OS/2.INI file, respectively.

The following is a sample of what is added to the WIN.INI for Windows clients communicating with SQL Server for Windows NT on a Novell Network:

```
[SQLSERVER]
DSQUERY=DBMSSPX3
```

MS-DOS clients require the same level of IPX that the Windows workstations do. DBMSSPX.EXE must be installed on the MS-DOS computer. This TSR can be loaded either manually or from AUOTEXEC.BAT.

Windows NT client workstations use NWLink, which is installed through Network Control Panel. After installation, use the Client Configuration Utility to specify that the default network is Novell IPX/SPX. This, in turn, installs the required DBMSSPXN.DLL on the Windows NT client side.

The following is a sample Registry entry for Windows NT clients communicating with SQL Server for Windows NT on a Novell Network:

```
HKEY_LOCAL_MACHINE\SOFTWARE\Microsoft\SQLServer\Client\ConnectTo
DSQUERY: REG_SZ: DBMSSPXN
```

Ingres for Windows NT Client-Server Architecture

The heart of Ingres architecture is the General Communication Architecture (GCA). This architecture enables the Ingres Intelligent Database and related products to operate as efficiently in a stand-alone environment as in networking environments.

Figure 22.5 illustrates the Ingres client-server architecture.

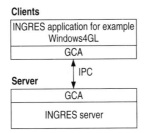

Figure 22.5   Ingres Client-Server Architecture

The basis of the Ingres client-server architecture is the solid separation of the client and server applications. In Windows 3.*x*, a client or a server is implemented as a Windows application. In Windows NT, a client or a server is implemented in an independent process, exploiting Windows NT support of multiple processes. All Ingres server products are multithreaded by design. This allows a single server to simultaneously service multiple clients. Conversely, a client application may request service from multiple servers at the same time. Ingres server threads are built on Windows NT lightweight thread supports. The separation of the clients and servers makes the installation, administration, and maintenance of the software completely independent from each other. For developers, it promotes the modular design of applications. For users, it makes incremental upgrades convenient.

Ingres General Communication Architecture

GCA specifies a set of services and protocols transparently used by all components of INGRES client-server products to communicate with each other, regardless of the interconnection mechanism and circumstances. GCA provides all communication services for a single computer and for networking computers, with homogeneous and heterogeneous architectures.

In a stand-alone (non-networking) environments, GCA is implemented as a run-time library that is part of all Ingres products. GCA provides IPC between client and server. For Windows NT, this is done through the named pipe support. Since Windows NT named pipes span across the network, the implementation of stand-alone GCA on Windows NT can, in fact, be extended over the network of homogeneous computers.

In all other networking environments, GCA uses the Ingres connectivity product, Ingres/Net, to communicate over the network. Ingres/Net handles all network navigation, data conversion, network protocol selection, and other communication details. Figure 22.6 shows Ingres GCA in a networking environment.

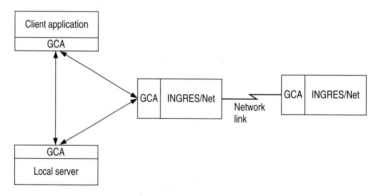

Figure 22.6   Ingres General Communication Architecture

With this architecture, the Ingres applications are shielded from the servers, data locations, and networking intricacies. GCA ensures client-server and server-server interoperability, whatever the underlying hardware and operating system software. By using GCA, any Ingres client can easily connect to any Ingres server (whether it is a Windows NT, or other Ingres servers), without any code changes.

Ingres Open Connectivity Products

Ingres connectivity is built upon the GCA described earlier. Connectivity is made up of three separate pieces—Ingres/Net, Ingres/Star, and Ingres/Gateways.

Ingres/Gateways provide users with the capability of accessing and manipulating data in both Ingres and non-Ingres databases. This section focuses on distributed database connectivity using Ingres/Net and Ingres/Star.

Ingres/Net

Ingres/Net allows applications on one computer to transparently access data on a remote computer. Ingres/Net handles all network navigation, data conversion, network protocol selection, and other communication details. Ingres/Net makes remote data appear as if it resides on the local computer. Ingres/Net has two parts—the server side and the client side.

Because Ingres/Net provides multiple access to one or more servers, a client application on one computer can simultaneously access database servers on multiple computers. Conversely, a server database process on one computer can service multiple client applications from many remote computers. Distributed access is provided while maintaining full concurrency and security controls of the database on the server computers.

The same Ingres/Net communication server handles requests for many servers on the local node, whether they are Ingres Intelligent Database servers, Ingres/Star distributed database servers, or Ingres/Gateway servers. In addition to client-server access (where the application communicates with a database server), Ingres/Net also supports server-server access, which permits the Ingres/Star distributed database server to access other Ingres servers on remote nodes.

To avoid the overhead of loading new copy of the networking code for each client-server connection, Ingres/Net has been designed with reentrant code. A single copy of Ingres/Net simultaneously services multiple clients. Each client can also have multiple connections to remote computers. Furthermore, the same copy of Ingres/Net can simultaneously service client-type and server-type requests.

The reentrant nature of Ingres/Net allows it to exploit the native Windows NT thread support to manage each client-server connection. Each connection is implemented as a lightweight Windows NT thread. Ingres/Net benefits from concurrently running Windows NT threads while leaving to Windows NT the overhead of thread management such as task switching, synchronization of access to shared resources, and management of private resources.

As shown in Figure 22.7, Ingres/Net is an implementation of the upper four layers of the OSI model. (For more information about the OSI model, see Chapter 15, "Network Architecture.") Ingres/Net routes messages through the Network-layer components provided by independent vendors. The Ingres/Net OSI-based design allows it also to work efficiently over the many OSI and non-OSI networks available today, including TCP/IP, IBM LU0 and LU6.2, Digital DECnet, NetBIOS, Novell SPX/IPX, and asynchronous (dial-up) networks.

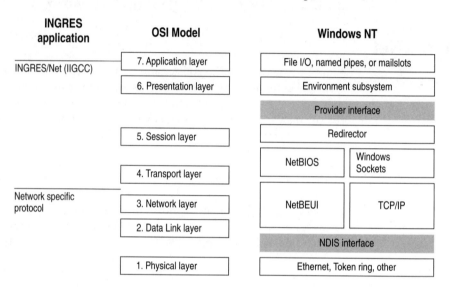

Figure 22.7   OSI, Ingres/Net, and Windows NT Networking

With respect to the networking services provided in Windows NT, Ingres/Net communicates through the Windows Sockets or LAN Manager (NetBIOS) interfaces provided by Microsoft. By using these standard Windows NT interfaces, Ingres applications can access the network using TCP/IP or NetBEUI over many industry-standard NDIS compatible network adapter cards. For other environments, Ingres/Net writes to the available protocols and interfaces, thereby shielding the application developer from the underlying networking.

Ingres/Net modules are developed to support multiple PC networking protocols. This underlying network interface software must be purchased from the third-party networking vendor. Users select the protocol they want when installing the software. This provides the developer with a more simplified development environment, because Ingres client applications are built to a standard set of GCA calls that communicate with the Ingres/Net server, and do not have to be modified to support each network protocol used. The applications built to the Ingres/Net interface also provide the highest level of portability since the standard set of networking calls is found on each platform supported by Ingres. By using the GCA architecture, an Ingres user could move a database and applications from a UNIX server to a Windows NT server without changing one line of application code. Other products, such as Microsoft Excel, can also have the same flexibility when using the Ingres ODBC driver (provided in Ingres/Net for Windows).

MS-DOS-Based Networking Applications

Ingres supports a wide range of Ingres/Net modules for use with its current MS-DOS–based tools. Current Ingres/Net modules support the protocols shown in Table 22.2.

Table 22.2   Protocols Supported by Current Ingres/Net Modules

Company	Product	Protocol	Version
Microsoft	LAN Manager	NetBIOS	2.x
Novell	NetWare	SPX/IPX	2.1x, 3.x
FTP	PC/TCP	TCP/IP	2.04
Sun	PC-NFS	TCP/IP	3.x, 4.x
Wollongong	Pathway Access	TCP/IP	1.x, 2.x
HP/Microsoft	LM/X	TCP/IP	2.1
Ungermann-Bass	UB TCP	TCP/IP	16.4
DEC	Pathworks	DECnet	4.x
Novell	LAN Workplace	TCP/IP	4.x

Networking Windows-based Applications

Ingres/Net protocols includes a suite of protocols (shown in Table 22.3) for the Windows 3.1 environment.

These protocols are available with Windows 3.1 clients. With Windows NT, The ASK Group supports Microsoft TCP/IP and NetBIOS using 32-bit APIs. Other protocols will be supported as they are provided by their manufacturers.

Table 22.3   Protocols Supported in a Windows 3.1 Environment

Company	Product	Protocol	Version
Microsoft	LAN Manager	NetBIOS	2.x
Wollongong	Pathway Access	TCP/IP	1.x, 2.x
HP/Microsoft	LM/X	TCP/IP	2.1
DEC	Pathworks	DECnet	4.x
Novell	NetWare	SPX/IPX	2.1x, 3.x
Novell	LAN Workplace	TCP/IP	4.x
FTP	PC/TCP	TCP/IP	2.04, 3.0
Sun	PC-NFS	TCP/IP	3.x, 4.x

Ingres/Star

Ingres/Star is the distributed portion of the Ingres DBMS. Ingres/Star provides the ability to distribute a database across several geographically dispersed locations and allows user applications to access those locations as though they were a single local database. Ingres/Star provides transparent access across heterogeneous operating system environments with full local security and concurrency controls. The basic Ingres database server includes two-phase commit and multiple connection capabilities. Ingres/Star transparently manages these capabilities for its clients—the application code is written as if all tables were in one local database.

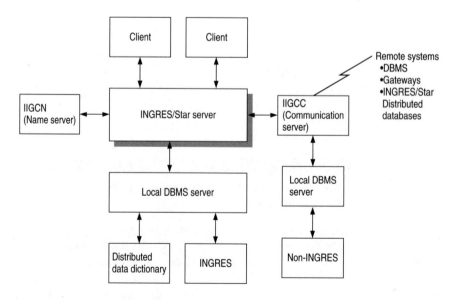

Figure 22.8   Ingres/Star Architecture

Ingres applications on Windows NT act as client to an Ingres/Star server. Since GCA makes communication between clients and servers transparent, the Ingres Windows NT application will never know if it is communicating with a local server or with an Ingres/Star server. Ingres applications are indifferent and can be run concurrently to local or Ingres/Star servers. When an Ingres Intelligent Database server runs on Windows NT, it does not differentiate between a local client and an Ingres/Star client. In addition, the Ingres Intelligent Database server has the only histogram-based query optimizer to automatically determine the most efficient way to satisfy a database request. This is crucial in a distributed environment where network traffic is a consideration.

The Ingres/Star distributed data manager provides all the features needed for effective distributed data management. Ingres/Star is the nerve-center of a distributed database system. It receives a SQL query from an application, breaks it into subqueries, and routes the subqueries to the appropriate local data managers and gateways. Then each local data manager runs the subquery it receives and returns the selected data to the application.

With Ingres/Star, data stored in different computers can be transparently joined and combined using any of the Ingres SQL user interfaces or application development tools, such as Ingres/Windows4GL.

The Ingres/Star server facilities, which are illustrated in Figure 22.9, include the following:

- Transaction Processing Facility, which monitors the state of a distributed transaction and tracks participating servers (Gateways, DBMSs, and other Ingres/Star servers). It also maintains Ingres/Star transaction recovery log.

- Remote Query Facility, which receives locally sufficient subqueries from QEF or TPF, sends queries off through GCF, and returns results to the requestor.

- Relational Description Facility, which performs remote catalog access and caches information in the Star coordinator database.

- Query Execution Facility, which runs Ingres/Star query plans, and coordinates other Ingres/Star components. It also manages direct connections to an underlying DBMS server.

- Optimizer Facility, which adjusts for the amount of data to be moved, network speed, storage structures, keys, indexes, database statistics, query strategies, CPU, and disk I/O.

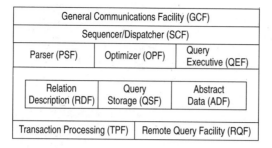

Figure 22.9   Ingres/Star Server Facilities

Client-Server Applications Using GCA Architecture

With the Microsoft Windows family, many client-server applications exist that can utilize the Ingres GCA architecture, from Ingres front-end products to other vendor's products, such as Microsoft Excel and Microsoft Visual Basic.

Ingres/Windows4GL is a native Ingres applications that uses the GCA architecture. It draws from several technologies in order to address the challenges faced by developers of graphical applications. These technologies are fourth-generation languages (4GLs), object-oriented programming, SQL databases, and graphical user interfaces.

Ingres/Windows4GL combines Portable Graphical User Interface, Object-Oriented 4GL, and Application Manager to provide the following:

- Full control over graphical user interface features including mouse, menus, buttons, images, multiple windows, and other windows system features.

- Complete portability for applications between different graphical user interfaces on different systems. A single application can run across GUIs without recoding.

- Reduced work by developers to build graphical applications. It can do to one tenth of what it would take using a third-generation language (3GL) with windowing toolkit.

- Controlled access to application elements for multiple developers working on the same application.

To be able to run a single copy of an Ingres/Windows4GL application on different windowing system, Ingres/Windows4GL provides an abstraction of the native windowing system objects and events. Ingres/Windows4GL visual objects are dynamically mapped at run-time to the native objects of the windowing system. The object-manipulation functions are mapped into the corresponding API functions. The abstraction also enhances the programmability of the user interface by transforming the low-level objects and events into higher-level events that are more convenient to handle. Some of the abstracted objects are mapped one-to-one to native objects. For example, an Ingres/Windows4GL entry field is mapped to a Windows NT edit control. On the other hand, more complex objects, such as table fields, are mapped into an aggregate of different kinds of native objects.

Handling of user interactions consists basically of mapping the native events into Ingres/Windows4GL abstracted events. For this purpose, Windows NT messages of interest are translated into Ingres/Windows4GL events, which are passed to the application. The Ingres/Windows4GL developer uses 4GL code in the application to specify the events to which the program will respond.

Ingres/Windows4GL provides complete facilities for application flow control, data manipulation, and database access. For developers who want to incorporate 3GL routines into their applications, Ingres/Windows4GL provides interfaces to all major 3GLs, including C, COBOL, Pascal, FORTRAN, and C++.

In addition, applications developed in a 3GL can integrate with Ingres databases through Ingres/ESQL. Ingres provides complete access to all databases and forms run-time commands from 3GLs on Windows NT.

Embedded SQL (ESQL) preprocessors translate the ESQL calls contained in the programs into GCA function calls, which can then be compiled and linked into an executable image.

ODBC-Compliant Third Party Front-Ends

ODCB (described earlier in the SQL Server section called "Application Programming Interfaces") allows applications running under Microsoft Windows or Windows NT to communicate easily with both relational and nonrelational database management systems. ODBC provides a set of standard calls that allows an application to establish a connection with a database environment, execute SQL statements, and retrieve results. There are additional standard calls for accessing data, formatting SQL data, and error codes.

Ingres has released an ODBC driver that enables third-party, Microsoft Windows 3.1-based client tools to connect to Ingres/Net on desktop computers. This will allow third-party client applications to connect to all Ingres servers including the Ingres Intelligent Database, Ingres/Star, and Ingres/Gateways. This support was delivered in April 1993 and represents another technological first for The ASK Group. The ASK Group was able to easily deliver the ODBC driver because of the Ingres GCA architecture.

The GCA architecture is also the enabling technology behind ODBC-enabled applications accessing distributed data through Ingres/Star and non-Ingres data through Ingres/Gateways.

Ingres Data Management

The Ingres Intelligent Database lets organizations model their business by managing data, knowledge, and objects.

- Data Management provides the ability to establish multiple, multithreaded servers to access and update the same shared database, reducing the per-user DBMS overhead and using multiprocessor computers.

- Knowledge Management centrally enforces business policies and referential integrity constraints so that database integrity remains intact.

- Object Management allows users to define complex or user-defined objects specific to their business and manipulate them using standard SQL commands.

The Ingres client-multiple server architecture provides the ability to establish multiple, multithreaded DBMS servers to access the same shared databases. The benefits of the client-multiple server architecture include the following:

- Reduced per-user overhead. Multithreading reduces per-user DBMS overhead to 30 to 50K on basic transaction processing applications. Single-threaded DBMSs typically require more than 200 to 400K in these same environments. On Windows NT, multithreading is implemented using Windows NT threads.

- Maximum configurability. Multiple DBMS servers can be established on single or multiprocessor computers to provide maximum configurability of the environment. For example, critical online transaction processing servers can be established at higher priorities than concurrent decision support and reporting servers.

When considering file systems in Windows NT, Ingres can take advantage of the functionality in all three (FAT, HPFS, and NTFS). NTFS supports asynchronous I/O, which multiple threads in the Ingres server take advantage of. However, because FAT is a synchronous read-write facility, the Ingres/Intelligent Database server cannot use its multithreaded capabilities. For this performance reason, Ingres recommends that all Ingres Windows NT database servers use NTFS.

P A R T V I

Migration and Compatibility

Part Six discusses migration and compatibility issues for Windows 3.*x*
for MS-DOS, Microsoft OS/2 version 1.*x*, and POSIX applications.
These chapters describe details about running applications and how
the subsystems are implemented.

CHAPTER 23

Windows 3.*x* Compatibility

This chapter discusses the compatibility of the 16-bit Windows subsystem with the actual Windows 3.1 product. It explains how the subsystem is implemented and describes the restrictions on applications run under it.

Running Applications

The 16-bit Windows subsystem runs 16-bit Windows applications, which you can launch from Program Manager, File Manager, or the command prompt. There are no user-visible distinctions between 16-bit and 32-bit Windows applications.

Restrictions

This section describes the few restrictions that apply to running applications under the 16-bit Windows subsystem.

Direct access to floppy disk drives is supported. Direct access to a hard disk is supported, if the user is an administrator and no one else is using the disk at that time.

All MS-DOS functions except task-switching APIs (Application Programming Interface functions) are supported.

Block mode device drivers are not supported (block devices are not supported, so MS-DOS IOCTL APIs that deal with block devices and SETDPB functions are not supported).

Interrupt 10 function 1A returns 0; all other functions are passed to the ROM.

Interrupt 13 calls that deal with prohibited disk access are not supported.

Interrupt 18 (ROM Basic) generates a message that says ROM Basic is not supported.

Interrupt 19 will not reboot the computer, but will cleanly terminate the current VDM.

Interrupt 2F dealing with DOSKEY call outs (AX = 4800) is not supported.

Microsoft CD-ROM Extensions (MSCDEX) functions 2, 3, 4, 5, 8, E, and F are not supported.

The 16-bit Windows subsystem on an X86 computer supports Enhanced mode applications; it does not, however, support 16-bit VXDs (virtual device drivers). The subsystem on a non-X86 computer supports only Standard mode 16-bit applications.

Terminating the Subsystem

If an ill-behaved application locks up the 16-bit Windows subsystem, bring up the Task List, select the application, and press End Task. If problems persist, logoff from Windows NT and then log back in to cleanly restart the system.

Interoperating Windows NT with a Previous Version of Windows

If you have a previous version of Windows (Windows 3.*x*, Windows for Workgroups) installed on your computer, and you want to run your installed applications from both the previous version of Windows and from Windows NT, then install Windows NT in the same directory as the previous version of Windows. This allows Windows NT to configure the Windows environment based on the existing environment and allows Windows NT to support the features of currently installed applications.

When the first logon occurs on the newly-installed Windows NT computer, the system migrates REG.DAT and portions of WIN.INI from the previous version of Windows to the Registry in Windows NT. The status of each step in the migration is logged in the Application Log, which can be viewed with Event Viewer.

The first time each new user logs in, Windows NT presents a dialog box that lets him or her select the parts of the previous version of Windows to migrate into the Windows NT environment. The user can select whether to migrate the .INI files and/or the Program Manager .GRP files to the Registry. If the user cancels the dialog box and later would like to migrate the files, he or she must delete the following key from the Registry and then log off and log back into Windows NT:

```
HKEY_CURRENT_USER\Windows 3.1 Migration Status
```

Refer to Chapters 11 through 14 for information on the Registry and its entries.

The per-user dialog box and migration do not happen for the usernames Administrator, Guest, and System.

If a user migrated the .INI files, then each time he or she logs into Windows NT, the system reads WIN.INI and SYSTEM.INI and stores the information in the Registry. When the user logs off from Windows NT, the system updates WIN.INI and SYSTEM.INI with any changes made to the environment. This keeps the configuration of Windows NT and the previous version of Windows synchronized with each other.

If Windows NT is not installed in the same directory as the previous version of Windows, then configuration changes made under one version of Windows are not available to the other version. The same is true if the previous version of Windows is installed after Windows NT. In these situations, a user in Windows NT may not be able to run some applications installed under the previous version of Windows. The applications will have to be reinstalled under Windows NT (into the same directories into which they are installed under the previous version of Windows).

Regardless of where Windows NT is installed, changes made to the Desktop or to the arrangement of the Program Groups are not synchronized with the previous version of Windows.

Caution   Setup installs TrueType font and font header files in *SystemRoot*\SYSTEM. Be careful not to delete the TrueType files from this directory. These files are used by Windows NT 32-bit applications as well as 16-bit applications. For more information on the TrueType font and font header files included with Windows NT, refer to Chapter 4, "Windows NT Files."

What Is Migrated at the First Logon

The following items are migrated to the Registry when the first logon occurs on the newly-installed Windows NT computer.

1. All of the OLE (Object Linking and Embedding) information kept in the Windows 3.*x* registry (REG.DAT).

2. The following sections and variables from WIN.INI:

   [Compatibility]

   [Embedding] (except SoundRec, Package, and PBrush)

   [Fonts]

   [FontSubstitutes]

   [Windows]
   DeviceNotSelectedTimeout
   Spooler
   TransmissionRetryTimeout

When Each User First Logs On

What Is Migrated

The following items are migrated the first time each new user logs in, if he or she selects to migrate the .INI files and the .GRP files. This per-user migration does not happen for the usernames Administrator, Guest, and System.

1. The following sections and variables from WIN.INI:

   [Clock]

   [Colors]

   [Cursors]

   [DeskTop]

   [Extensions]

   [Intl]

   [Sounds]

   [Terminal]

   [TrueType]

   [Windows]
   - Beep
   - BorderWidth
   - CursorBlinkRate
   - DoubleClickSpeed
   - KeyboardDelay
   - KeyboardSpeed
   - MouseSpeed
   - MouseThreshold1
   - MouseThreshold2
   - ScreenSaveActive
   - ScreenSaveTimeOut
   - SwapMouseButtons

2. The following sections and variables from CONTROL.INI:

   [Color Schemes]

   [Current]

   [Custom Colors]

   [Patterns]

   [Screen Saver.Marquee]

   [Screen Saver.Mystify]

   [Screen Saver.Stars]

3. The following section from WINFILE.INI:

   [Settings]

4. All 16-bit Windows 3.*x* Program Manager group files listed in PROGMAN.INI. If a group name (contained in the group file, not the actual .GRP filename) matches the name of a 32-bit Windows NT Personal or Common group, then that 16-bit group will not be migrated (for example, Accessories, Games, Main, and Startup). Each group is migrated as is, and the show state is set to Minimized.

5. The Country setting in the International applications.

What Is Not Migrated

The following items are not migrated:

1. Persistent shares and users from Windows for Workgroups.

2. Default domain and user ID from Windows for Workgroups or LANMAN.INI.

3. Per-user profiles maintained by the WINLOGIN addon product for Windows for Workgroups.

4. Any changes that the user has made to his or her Accessories, Games, Main, and Startup groups in Windows 3.*x*. These groups are not migrated because their names match the names of 32-bit Windows NT groups.

5. MS-DOS drive letters. If you have FAT partitions and HPFS or NTFS partitions on a computer that dual-boots MS-DOS and Windows NT, use Disk Administrator to assign drive letters to your non-FAT partitions. Begin with the first drive letter after the one that MS-DOS assigns to your last FAT partition. This ensures that the FAT partition drive letters are the same for both systems and that any migrated path names are valid.

6. The options Auto Arrange, Minimize on Run, and Save Settings on Exit from PROGMAN.INI.

7. Font information for character-mode command windows.

8. The Language and Keyboard settings in the International applications.

9. The default screen saver in **[BOOT]**SCRNSAVE.EXE of SYSTEM.INI. 16-bit screen savers are ill-behaved under Windows NT.

Implementation of the Subsystem

VDM Structure

The 16-bit Windows subsystem is implemented as a Virtual DOS Machine (VDM) with a layer that emulates Windows 3.1 functionality. All 16-bit Windows applications run in the same VDM, which is a multithreaded Win32 process in which each application runs in its own thread. Below is a diagram of the 16-bit Windows subsystem VDM. A description of each layer follows.

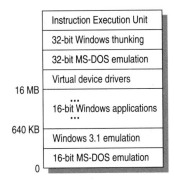

16-bit Windows Subsystem VDM

The 16-bit MS-DOS emulation layer contains all the information to emulate BIOS calls and tables. Some 16-bit Windows applications depend upon BIOS calls, since 16-bit Windows is built on top of MS-DOS.

The Windows 3.1 emulation layer provides the functionality of the Windows 3.1 kernel and 16-bit API stubs. A 16-bit application cannot call a 32-bit API routine. When an application calls a 16-bit API routine, that call is made to a stub routine, which in turn calls a 32-bit API routine. The 32-bit API routine performs the required action, and the result is transformed back into the format expected by the 16-bit API stub, which returns the result to the application. The transformation between 16-bit and 32-bit formats is known as *thunking*, and is carried out by a separate layer in the VDM.

16-bit Windows applications use the memory from 640 KB to 16 MB for their own purposes.

Windows NT does not support 16-bit device drivers that have unrestricted access to hardware (character-mode device drivers that do not depend on special hardware are supported). A secure and robust multitasking operating system cannot let user-level applications talk directly with the hardware because they could completely bypass security and crash the system (there are exceptions to this, however; refer to *Restrictions*, at the beginning of this chapter). The VDM contains a layer of Virtual Device Drivers (VDDs) that allow the sharing of hardware and provide the necessary functionality in a way that is consistent with the design of Windows NT.

The 32-bit MS-DOS emulation layer is for the DOS Protect Mode Interface (DPMI) and 32-bit memory access. This layer replaces calls made to the MS-DOS-level functions for extended and expanded memory with Windows NT memory calls. Windows NT then makes the appropriate conversions so that the 16-bit application sees segmented memory as it normally would.

The purpose of the 32-bit Windows thunking layer was described above.

For Windows NT running on a non-X86 computer, the Instruction Execution Unit emulates the Intel 80286 instruction set, which lets the computer run the binary application. The 16-bit Windows subsystem (or any other VDM) on a non-X86 computer supports only Standard mode 16-bit applications.

On an X86 computer the Instruction Execution Unit acts as a trap handler, capturing instructions that cause hardware traps and transferring control to the code that handles them. A VDM (such as the 16-bit Windows subsystem) on an X86 computer supports Enhanced mode applications; it does not, however, support 16-bit VXDs (virtual device drivers).

Input Queue

Under Windows NT, each application has its own input queue. This eliminates lockups due to programs freezing up the queue. Under Windows 3.*x*, all applications receive input from the same queue. As in Windows 3.*x*, the 16-bit Windows subsystem provides just one input queue. A 16-bit Windows application can lock up the subsystem by freezing up the queue. This does not affect any 32-bit applications running under Windows NT, as they each have their own input queue.

Scheduling

Within the 16-bit Windows subsystem, the applications (threads) are scheduled non-preemptively. Because the applications share memory, a single input queue, and are scheduled non-preemptively, an ill-behaved application can cause the subsystem to lock up. This will not affect the rest of Windows NT, since Windows NT treats the 16-bit Windows subsystem as a whole just like any other 32-bit Windows NT application. The subsystem is scheduled preemptively along with all of the other 32-bit applications.

Files Used

The following are the principal files used by the 16-bit Windows subsystem.

File	Purpose
NTVDM.EXE	The main loader for a VDM.
WOWEXEC.EXE	Provides the Windows 3.1 emulation for the VDM. When you log onto Windows NT, WOWEXEC is loaded by the running NTVDM, which makes that VDM the 16-bit Windows subsystem.
WOW32.DLL	Provides the DLL portion of the Windows 3.1 emulation layer. When you use PViewer to look at running NTVDM processes, you can identify the one that is the 16-bit Windows subsystem by WOW32.DLL being listed in its memory detail.
AUTOEXEC.NT CONFIG.NT	Used to boot the files necessary for running 16-bit Windows applications. AUTOEXEC.NT and CONFIG.NT are usually in \SYSTEM32, but you can change this location with _DEFAULT.PIF. Windows NT creates AUTOEXEC.NT from AUTOEXEC.BAT and creates CONFIG.NT from scratch. It writes comments into AUTOEXEC.BAT and CONFIG.SYS that describe the .NT versions. Refer to the *System Guide* for more information.

Communication with Other Subsystems

An application running under the 16-bit Windows subsystem can communicate with applications in other subsystems (as well as 32-bit applications running under Windows NT) through the usual mechanisms of Object Linking and Embedding (OLE), Dynamic Data Exchange (DDE), and named pipes.

CHAPTER 2 4

OS/2 Compatibility

This chapter describes the OS/2 subsystem in the first release of Windows NT. It describes the kind of applications that the subsystem supports, as well as those that it does not currently support. It describes the supported, unsupported, and partially supported OS/2 APIs (Application Programming Interface functions). The chapter also describes how the OS/2 subsystem is implemented.

Running Applications

The OS/2 subsystem allows OS/2 16-bit character-based applications to run directly under Windows NT with essentially no modification. You can launch a character-based or VIO (Video I/O) application from the Windows NT command prompt, File Manager, Program Manager, or from invocation within a Win32 or OS/2 application. You can create a single batch file that can launch any combination of MS-DOS, Windows, or OS/2 programs. Windows NT recognizes an OS/2 application from information stored in the header of the executable file; it then calls the OS/2 subsystem to load the application.

If you never run an OS/2 application, the subsystem does not use any Windows NT resources. When you run an application, the process OS2SRV is loaded and continues to exist even after the application is finished. To free the minimal resources that OS2SRV uses, run PViewer (provided on the utilities disk for this book) and kill the OS2SRV process. If you later run another OS/2 application, OS2SRV will be reloaded.

Supported Applications

You can run following types of applications under the OS/2 subsystem.

- OS/2 1.*x* 16-bit applications on X86 computers only
- Character-based applications

Unsupported Applications

You cannot run following types of applications under the OS/2 subsystem.

- OS/2 2.*x* applications
- Presentation Manager applications
- AVIO (Advanced VIO) applications.
- OS/2 applications on RISC computers
- Applications that directly access hardware memory or I/O ports at Ring 2 or below. For example, applications that directly access video memory to manipulate text or graphics are not supported. Applications that rely on the statement IOPL=YES in CONFIG.SYS to gain access to Ring 2 I/O privileges are not supported.
- Custom device drivers (those not included with OS/2 itself). These must be rewritten to the Windows NT device driver interface.

If you want to run an OS/2 application that is not supported, you have the following choices:

- If this is a bound application (one that can run under both OS/2 and MS-DOS), you can try to run it under the MS-DOS subsystem. To do so, run FORCEDOS from the command line:

```
FORCEDOS [/D directory] filename [parameters]
```

where:

Variable	Description
/D directory	the current directory for the application to use
filename	the application to start
parameters	the parameters to pass to the application

- If this is not a bound application and you have the source code, you can recompile the source without the unsupported APIs (which are specified in the error message that displays when you try to run the application). If you don't have the source, contact the application's developer.

Partially Supported Applications

VIO (Video Input/Output) applications are partially supported. Some will work and some will not, depending upon the API functions that the applications use. The robustness and security of Windows NT restrict access to physical hardware, which restricts the use of VIO physical buffer APIs, certain DosDevIOCtl functions, and I/O Privilege Level (IOPL). See the description of APIs, below, for more detail.

APIs

A complete list of the APIs that are supported, unsupported, and partially supported is provided in the file OS2API.TXT on the utilities disk for this book.

Supported APIs

APIs with the following prefixes are supported:

- Dos (except DosDevIOCtl and DosDevIOCtl2, which are partially supported)
- Kbd (except those that conflict with the security and robustness of Windows NT)
- Mou (except those that require PM or AVIO)
- Vio (except those that conflict with the security of Windows NT by accessing the physical video hardware and those that require PM or AVIO)
- WinQueryProfile and WinWriteProfile
- Net (selected APIs based on their commercial use)

Unsupported APIs

APIs with the following prefixes are not supported:

- Dev
- Gpi
- Kbd (those that conflict with the security and robustness of Windows NT)
- Mou (those that require PM or AVIO)
- Vio (those that conflict with the security of Windows NT by accessing the physical video hardware and those that require PM or AVIO)
- Win (except WinQueryProfile and WinWriteProfile APIs)

Partially Supported APIs

The following APIs are partially supported:

- DosDevIOCtl, DosDevIOCtl2
- VioGetConfig
- VioGetMode, VioSetMode
- VioGetState, VioSetState

Implementation of Subsystem

This section describes how the OS/2 subsystem is implemented.

Memory Map of an OS/2 Application

The following is a map of memory usage while the OS/2 subsystem is running an application.

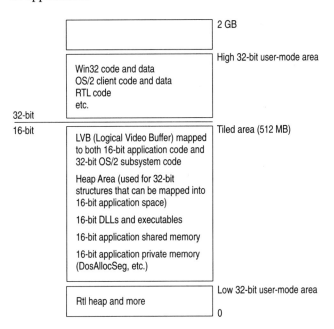

OS/2 Subsystem Memory Map

The Tiled Area is 512 MB of virtual address space that is reserved up front and then committed or decommitted when 16-bit applications need segments. The OS/2 subsystem maintains an LDT (local descriptor table) for each process, with shared memory segments at the same LDT slot for all OS/2 processes.

Architecture Diagram

The OS/2 subsystem is implemented as a protected server; OS/2 applications communicate with the subsystem by using the local procedure call (LPC) message-passing facility. The subsystem and each application run in their own protected address space, which protects them from other processes running on Windows NT.

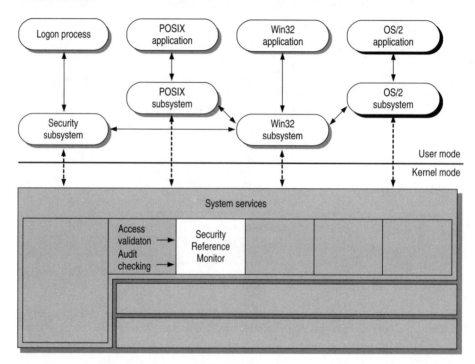

OS/2 Subsystem in Windows NT

In native OS/2, applications run in user mode (Ring 3) and communicate with the OS/2 kernel by using calls to the DLLs. Some application programs and DLLs contain I/O privilege segments and are allowed to perform I/O operations in Ring 2. Programs that use the I/O privilege mechanism violate the robustness features of Windows NT and do not run under the OS/2 subsystem.

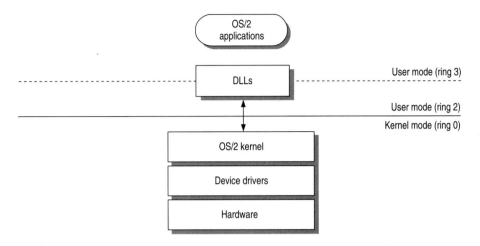

Native OS/2

Multitasking

Process

The OS/2 subsystem uses OS/2 semantics to maintain the various OS/2 objects. Examples include process IDs, the process tree, handles, local and global infosegs, thread-1 semantics, exitlist processing, signals, and semaphores. Windows NT objects are used only when they are relevant; they are then embedded inside OS/2 objects (file handles, for example).

The process tree records the descendant processes of a given process. The subsystem uses the process tree in all related operations, such as ending a program with CTRL+C.

Thread

Every thread created by an OS/2 application is implemented with a Windows NT thread in the same process. The thread gets the priority and ID relevant under OS/2. The exact OS/2 semantics (such as contents of the register and the stack) are held when the thread function starts.

Scheduler

The Windows NT scheduler handles the scheduling of OS/2 threads, with the OS/2 priorities 0-63 mapping to Windows NT variable priorities 0-15 (OS/2 priorities are changed only by the application; they are not changed by the scheduler). OS/2 threads never receive Windows NT real-time priorities 16-31.

User Interface

VIO

The VIO interface is partially supported. Applications can not get direct control of the video hardware. The use of a logical video buffer, as opposed to a physical video buffer, is allowed. See the lists of APIs for specific information.

AVIO

Not currently supported.

Presentation Manager

Not currently supported.

Dynamic Linking

The OS/2 subsystem implements a full OS/2 loader, which loads DLLs, executables, and resources in exactly the same way as under OS/2. Static linking, load-time dynamic linking, and runtime dynamic linking all function as they do under OS/2.

Memory Management

Protection Model

The OS/2 subsystem implements the protection between OS/2 applications. It constructs their address spaces (both the flat address space and LDTs) and implements the same protection as exists under OS/2.

Some of the memory management limitations of OS/2 1.x are removed. The most important of these is the limit of 16 MB of physical RAM; the OS/2 subsystem uses the large memory capability of Windows NT. This translates into increased performance for applications that can use the additional memory, such as Microsoft's SQL Server. SQL Server asks for the physical memory available in the system at setup time. It then uses this number to determine the level of caching it will use. Under OS/2 you can't use more than 16 MB; under the OS/2 subsystem in Windows NT, you can use, for example, 32 MB and double your caching capability.

Segment Swapping

The OS/2 subsystem uses the Windows NT paging mechanism; no segment swapping is performed. Segment swapping is inferior to paging and exists in OS/2 only to support the 80286 processor, which is not supported for Windows NT.

Interprocess Communication

The OS/2 subsystem implements all OS/2 IPC mechanisms (semaphores, pipes, shared memory, queues, and signals).

Named Pipes

The OS/2 subsystem implements named pipes on top of the Windows NT named pipe file system. They are supported transparently between Win32, MS-DOS, Win16, and OS/2 applications, both locally and remotely. All of LM 2.x named pipe functionality is supported.

Anonymous Pipes

Anonymous pipes are fully supported, including inheritance. They are integrated into the OS/2 file handle space.

Shared Memory

The full functionality of OS/2 1.x shared memory, including Get and Give semantics, is implemented using Windows NT shared memory features. The discardable segments property is ignored, invisible to the OS/2 application.

Semaphores

The OS/2 subsystem supports the full range of OS/2 1.x semaphore APIs, including RAM semaphores in private and shared memory, system semaphores, and fast-safe RAM semaphores. Association of semaphores with timers and named pipes is fully supported. The OS/2 subsystem uses a combination of the Windows NT semaphore object and the Windows NT event object to implement and OS/2 semaphore.

Queues

OS/2 1.x queues are fully supported, using shared memory between OS/2 processes and OS/2 semaphores as required.

Signals

OS/2 signals are fully supported, using Windows NT APIs to manipulate thread context. The OS/2 subsystem controls the address space of OS/2 processes and uses it to manipulate the register content and the stack of thread 1 of the process to be signaled.

I/O Architecture

Device Drivers

Existing private OS/2 device drivers will not be supported in the OS/2 subsystem directly, but must be rewritten for the Windows NT device driver model. In this context, private device driver means a driver that a particular application requires but is not included in the OS/2 operating system itself. Examples of such drivers include those that provide custom support for security, FAX, MIDI, or 3270 communication cards. Once the OS/2 device driver has been rewritten for the Windows NT model, however, an OS/2 application can communicate with that device driver using the same OS/2 API, DosDevIoctl. Therefore, no changes will be required within the application itself. Additionally, support exists for the native device drivers that Windows NT includes, such as the display, printer, disk, communications, keyboard, and mouse devices.

As an example, suppose a corporation has written a custom device driver to control a security card. The OS/2 device driver for this card uses an internal name, SECDEV, and an entry for this device driver appears in the CONFIG.SYS file. Under OS/2, the operating system reads the CONFIG.SYS file and adds SECDEV to the device driver list. When an application calls the OS/2 API, DosOpen, this list is searched first. The OS/2 subsystem will read this file during initialization and add symbolic links that will allow the OS/2 application to call the Windows NT device driver from the subsystem. See "OS/2 Configuration," later in this chapter, for details on how to set CONFIG.SYS for the OS/2 subsystem to load a Windows NT device driver.

The OS/2 application code, as opposed to the device driver code, can still load and run binary compatible because the device-specific parameters passed by DosDevIoctl(2) APIs are just PVOID buffers. Of course, the new Windows NT version of the ported device driver would have to be compatible with the original by accepting the same set of parameters within the buffers. Other related OS/2 APIs, such as DosOpen, are supported compatibly, just as they are for supporting the native Windows NT system device drivers like the communications device, keyboard, and screen.

File System Name Space

OS/2 HPFS supports long names. The OS/2 subsystem supports long names and extended attributes. The subsystem treats an NTFS volume as an HPFS volume (it does not utilize or expose recoverability and C2 security functions).

Network Connectivity

The OS/2 subsystem implements some LAN Manager APIs. It also implements NetBIOS (both version 2.x and version 3.0 functionality), named pipes, and mailslots.

The OS/2 subsystem maintains remote drives compatible with OS/2. With these, any OS/2 application can use redirected drives transparently with the file I/O APIs. UNC naming is supported as well. Redirected drives of various network operating systems can be used, provided that the related Win32 Windows NT device drivers (redirectors) are installed.

I/O Privilege Mechanism

The OS/2 IOPL=YES mechanism lets an application have direct control over the CPU, interrupt activity, and so on. This violates the robustness features of Windows NT. Therefore, IOPL is not granted to OS/2 applications, and all of the code runs in Ring 3. An application that tries to use one of the privileged mechanisms will fault and be ended.

Filters

Filters are supported and are integrated with Win32 and MS-DOS; that is, you can redirect output and input between OS/2, MS-DOS, and Win32 applications transparently.

Device Monitors

Device monitors are a feature that OS/2 provides in the device driver level, which violates Windows NT security if given across the system. Therefore, the OS/2 subsystem implements device monitors within an OS/2 session (an OS/2 application and all of its descendants). Within the session the implementation of device monitors is complete and compatible with OS/2. The vast majority of OS/2 applications use monitors within a session already.

Printing

Printing from the OS/2 subsystem is identical to base level printing on OS/2. For example, you can connect to a remote printer using

```
NET USE LPT1: \\myprinter\pscript
```

You can then use the dialogs from within an application to set up a printer and print.

Security

The OS/2 subsystem is subject to the security measures imposed by Windows NT. OS/2 processes, among themselves, have only the security restrictions of OS/2 (no ACLs attached, and so on). OS/2 processes run under the logged-on user token, just as with Win32.

Communication with Other Subsystems

Subsystems communicate by passing messages to one another. When an OS/2 application calls an API routine, for example, the OS/2 subsystem receives a message and implements it by calling Windows NT system services or by passing messages to other subsystems. When finished, the OS/2 subsystem sends a message containing the return values back to the application. The message passing and other activities of the subsystem are invisible to the user.

Communication between OS/2 and Windows NT processes can be accomplished through named pipes, mailslots, NetBIOS, files, and COM devices. The Win32 subsystem directs user input to an OS/2 application; it handles all screen I/O for OS/2 applications.

OS/2 Configuration

The OS/2 subsystem handles OS2.INI compatibly with OS/2. The WIN*xxx* APIs supported in this release of Windows NT are provided for this purpose. STARTUP.CMD is just a batch file; if you want it to be run, add it to the Startup group in the Windows NT Program Manager.

When the OS/2 subsystem starts for the first time, it checks the registry for OS/2 subsystem configuration information. If it doesn't find any, it looks for information in the original CONFIG.SYS file and adds the information to the registry. If the original CONFIG.SYS file does not exist or is not an OS/2 configuration file, the subsystem adds the following default information to the Registry in the key shown in the following figure:

```
PROTSHELL=c:\os2\pmshell.exe c:\os2\os2.ini c:\os2\os2sys.ini
    %SystemRoot%\system32\cmd.exe
SET COMSPEC=%SystemRoot%\system32\cmd.exe
```

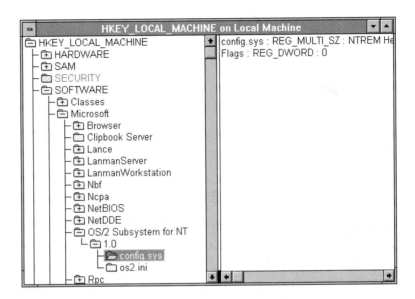

Registry Information for OS/2 Subsystem

The subsystem updates the environment variable **Os2LibPath** with LIBPATH information found in the original CONFIG.SYS file. The updated value for **Os2LibPath** is *<SystemRoot>*\SYSTEM32\OS2\DLL concatenated with the list of directories specified in the LIBPATH line of the original CONFIG.SYS file.

The PATH information found in the original CONFIG.SYS is not entered automatically into the default Windows NT path. To add the location of OS/2 applications, use the System application in Control Panel to add a PATH variable to the User Environment Variables. This information is appended automatically by Windows NT each time a user logs on to the system.

Windows NT supports the OS/2 configuration commands shown in the table below. If you use commands that are not supported, Windows NT ignores them.

Command	Function
protshell	Specifies the command interpreter. Only the Windows NT command interpreter is supported.
devicename	Specifies a user-defined Windows NT device driver used by OS/2 applications.
libpath	Specifies the location of OS/2 16-bit dynamic link libraries.
set	Sets environment variables.
country	Sets a country code that defines country-dependent information such as time, date, and currency conventions.
codepage	Specifies which code pages your system is prepared to use.
devinfo=KBD	Specifies the information the keyboard needs in order to use a particular code page.

The **libpath**, **set**, and **devicename** commands are processed as follows:

- **libpath** appends path information to the OS/2 library path in the Windows NT environment. At the command prompt, you can change the library path for OS/2 applications by using the **os2libpath** command.

- The following **set** commands are ignored:

set path	**set comspec**	**set video_devices**
set vio_ibmvga	**set vio_vga**	**set prompt**

- **devicename** specifies a device driver compatible with Windows NT for use with an OS/2 application. The syntax of the command is:

```
DEVICENAME=OS/2devicename [[path][NTdevicename]]
```

Devicename is the logical name OS/2 applications use to address the device. *Path* and *NTdevicename* specify the Windows NT device driver to which the OS/2 device name is mapped. If these are not specified, the device is mapped to \DEVICE*os/2devicename*.

Changing OS/2 Configuration Information

Although the OS/2 configuration information is stored in the registry, you can edit that information just as you would edit an OS/2 CONFIG.SYS file. To edit the information, you must use an OS/2 text editor.

To change configuration information, you must be logged on as a member of the Administrators group.

▶ **To change configuration information**

1. While running Windows NT, start an OS/2 text editor in a window.

2. Open a file called C:\CONFIG.SYS.

   Windows NT retrieves the configuration information from the Registry and stores it in a temporary file that you can edit.

3. Edit the configuration information.

4. Save and close the file.

5. Exit the editor.

   Windows NT stores the new information in the registry.

6. Log off from Windows NT and restart your computer.

File List

The main files that make up the OS/2 subsystem are:

File	Purpose
OS2SRV.EXE	This file is the subsystem server. It is invoked when you run the first OS/2 application and stays to serve new applications as they are run.
OS2.EXE	This file is the client side of every OS/2 application. There is an instance of OS2.EXE for each OS/2 application running.
DOSCALLS.DLL	This file (in SYSTEM32\OS2\DLL) contains the DOS*xxx* APIs. The other DLLs that are used in OS/2 (such as KBDCALLS and VIOCALLS) are provided in memory by the OS/2 subsystem.

CHAPTER 25

POSIX Compatibility

This chapter discusses the POSIX subsystem in the first release of Windows NT. It includes information about the following:

- Definition of POSIX
- Conformance and compliance to POSIX.1
- Running applications
- Implementation of subsystem
- Windows NT POSIX files

This chapter is not intended to be a POSIX tutorial.

Definition of POSIX

POSIX stands for *Portable Operating System Interface* for computing environments. POSIX began as an effort by the IEEE community to promote the portability of applications across UNIX environments by developing a clear, consistent and unambiguous set of standards. POSIX is not limited to the UNIX environment, however. It can be implemented on non-UNIX operating systems, as was done with the IEEE Std. 1003.1-1990 (POSIX.1) implementation on VMS, MPE, and CTOS operating systems. POSIX actually consists of a set of standards that range from POSIX.1 to POSIX.12.

As the following table shows, most of these standards are still in the proposed state. This section deals with the Windows NT implementation of a POSIX subsystem to support the international ISO/IEC IS 9945-1:1990 standard (also called POSIX.1). POSIX.1 defines a C-language source-code-level application programming interface (API) to an operating system environment.

Family of POSIX Standards

Standard	ISO Standard	Description
POSIX.0	No	A guide to POSIX Open Systems Environment. This is not a standard in the same sense as POSIX.1 or POSIX.2. It is more of an introduction and overview of the other standards.
POSIX.1	Yes	Systems application programming interface (API) [C language]
POSIX.2	No	Shell and tools (IEEE approved standard)
POSIX.3	No	Testing and verification
POSIX.4	No	Real-time and threads
POSIX.5	Yes	ADA language bindings to POSIX.1
POSIX.6	No	System security
POSIX.7	No	System administration
POSIX.8	No	Networking A. Transparent file access B. Protocol-independent network interface C. Remote Procedure Calls (RPC) D. Open system interconnect protocol-dependent application interfaces
POSIX.9	Yes	FORTRAN language bindings to POSIX.1
POSIX.10	No	Super-computing Application Environment Profile (AEP)
POSIX.11	No	Transaction Processing AEP
POSIX.12	No	Graphical user interface

POSIX Conformance

For a system to be given a certificate of POSIX.1 conformance it must meet the following requirements:

- The system must support all of the interfaces as defined in the ISO/IEC 9945-1.
- The vendor must supply a POSIX.1 Conformance Document (PCD) with the vendor's implementation as specified in ISP/IEC 9945-1.
- The implementation must pass the appropriate National Institute of Standards and Technology (NIST) test suite.

Windows NT is in the process of being verified for POSIX.1 conformance, and will be submitted to NIST for the Federal Information Processing Standards (FIPS) Publication 151-2 certification. FIPS 151-2 incorporates POSIX.1 as a reference standard and also requires a number of the optional features defined in POSIX.1 to promote application portability among conforming implementations. An implementation that conforms to FIPS 151-2 also conforms to POSIX.1. Note that conformance is specific to the manufacturer, hardware platform, and model number on which the implementation is tested.

POSIX.1 is a source-level standard; it does not provide any binary compatibility.

Application Compliance to POSIX.1

For POSIX.1, there are four categories of compliance, ranging from a very strict compliance to a very loose compliance. The various categories are outlined below.

Strictly Conforming POSIX.1 Applications

A *strictly conforming POSIX.1 application* requires only the facilities described in the POSIX.1 standard and applicable language standards. This type of application accepts the following:

- Any behavior described in ISO/IEC 9945-1 as unspecified or implementation-defined
- Symbolic constants
- Any value in the range permitted in ISO/IEC 9945-1

This is the strictest level of application conformance, and applications at this level should be able to move across implementations with just a recompilation. At this time, the only language interface that has been standardized for POSIX.1 is the C-language interface. (As shown in the figure below, a strictly conforming POSIX application can use 110 calls from the standard C libraries.)

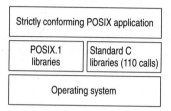

Applications Conforming to ISO/IEC and POSIX.1

An *ISO/IEC-conforming POSIX.1 application* is one that uses only the facilities described ISO/IEC 9945-1 and approved conforming language bindings for ISO or IEC standard. This type of application must include a statement of conformance that documents all options and limit dependencies, and all other ISO or IEC standards used.

```
┌─────────────────────────────────────────────────┐
│      ISO/IEC conforming POSIX application         │
├───────────┬────────────────────┬──────────────────┤
│ POSIX.1   │ Standard C         │ Other ISO/EC     │
│ libraries │ libraries (110 calls)│ standard libraries│
├───────────┴────────────────────┴──────────────────┤
│              Operating system                     │
└─────────────────────────────────────────────────┘
```

This level of conformance is not as strict as the previous one for two reasons. First, it allows a POSIX.1 application to make use of other ISO or IEC standards, such as GKS. Second, it allows POSIX.1 applications within this level to require options or limit values beyond the minimum. For example, such an application could require that the implementation support filenames of at least 16 characters. The POSIX.1 minimum is 14 characters.

Applications Conforming to POSIX.1 and <National Body>

A *<National Body> conforming POSIX.1 application* differs from an ISO/IEC-conforming POSIX.1 application in that this type of application may also use specific standards of a single ISO/IEC organization, such as ANSI or BSI (British Standards Institute). This type of application must include a statement of conformance that documents all options and limit dependencies, and all other *<National Body>* standards used.

For example, you could have a *<National Body>* Conforming POSIX Application that used calls from a BSI-standard set of calls.

```
+------------------------------------------------------------+
|        <National Body> conforming POSIX application        |
+------------------------------------------------------------+
+-------------+-------------------+----------------------------+
|  POSIX.1    |  Standard C       | Standard libraries adopted |
|  libraries  |  libraries (110 calls) | by a single member body |
+-------------+-------------------+----------------------------+
|                   Operating system                          |
+------------------------------------------------------------+
```

POSIX.1-Conformant Applications That Use Extensions

A *conforming POSIX.1 application using extensions* is an application that differs from a conforming POSIX.1 application only because it uses nonstandard facilities that are consistent with ISO/IEC 9945-1. Such an application must fully document its requirements for these extended facilities.

```
+------------------------------------------------------------+
|        Conforming POSIX application with extensions        |
+------------------------------------------------------------+
+-------------+-------------------+----------------------+
|  POSIX.1    |  Standard C       |     Arbitrary        |
|  libraries  |  libraries (110 calls) |  C libraries     |
+-------------+-------------------+----------------------+
|                   Operating system                   |
+------------------------------------------------------+
```

This is the lowest level of conformance; almost any C program could satisfy this with the appropriate documentation. The current release of Windows NT supports Strictly Conforming POSIX.1 applications and ISO/IEC Conforming POSIX.1 applications. Windows NT supports the latter by virtue of the fact that only 110 of the 149 functions of standard C are part of POSIX.1, and standard C is itself an ISO standard (ISO/IEC 9899).

Running Applications

POSIX applications can be started from a Windows NT console window (command prompt), the File Manager, Program Manager, or by invocation from within another POSIX application.

File Systems

POSIX requires a certain amount of functionality from the file system, such as the ability for a file to have more than one name (or *hard links*) and case-sensitive file naming. Neither FAT nor HPFS supports these features, which is another reason why a new file system was required for Windows NT. NTFS supports both hard links and case-sensitive naming. If you want to run in a POSIX-conforming environment, you need at least one NTFS disk partition on your computer.

You can run POSIX applications from any Windows NT file system. If the application does not need to access the file system, the application will run with no problems. However, if the application does require access to the file system, it may not behave correctly on a non-NTFS disk partition.

Bypass Traverse Checking

By default, when you install Windows NT for the first time, the user right Bypass Traverse Checking is granted to everyone. This right allows a user to change directories through a directory tree even if the user has no permission for those directories.

If you want to run in a POSIX-conforming environment, you must disable this privilege for your account by using either the User Manager or User Manager for Domains tool as follows (you must be an administrator to do this):

Select the account, and then choose User Rights from the Policies menu to display the following dialog box. (Be sure the Show Advanced User Rights check box is marked.) Specify the Bypass traverse checking right and choose Remove.

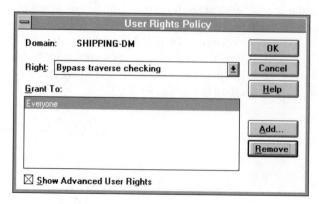

Printing

The POSIX subsystem itself does not directly support printing, but Windows NT supports redirection and piping between subsystems. If your POSIX application writes to **stdout**, and you have connected or redirected either your serial or parallel ports to a printer, you can redirect the output of a POSIX application to that printer. For example, the following sequence of commands will send to a network printer the output of a POSIX application that writes to **stdout**.

```
NET USE LPT1: \\MYSERVER\PRINTER
POSIXAPP.EXE > LPT1:
```

Network Access

The POSIX.1 specification does not have a requirement for access to remote file systems, but as with any of the other subsystems, the POSIX subsystem and POSIX applications have transparent access to any Win32 remotely connected file system.

Restrictions on POSIX Applications

With this release of Windows NT, POSIX applications have no direct access to any of the facilities and features of the Win32 subsystem, such as memory mapped files, networking, graphics, or dynamic data exchange.

Implementation of Subsystem

The POSIX subsystem is implemented in Windows NT as a protected server. POSIX applications communicate with the POSIX subsystem through a message-passing facility in the Executive known as a Local Procedure Call (LPC).

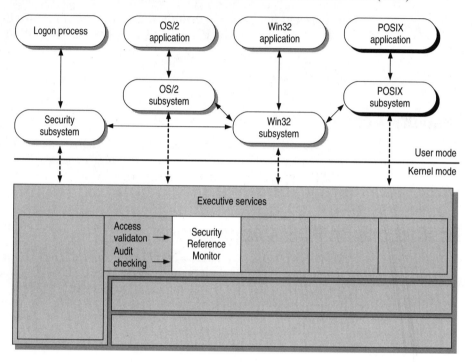

POSIX Subsystem in Windows NT

The POSIX subsystem and each POSIX application run in their own protected address space, which protects them from any other application that might be running on Windows NT. POSIX application are preemptively multitasked with respect to each other, and with respect to other applications running in the system.

Files Used

The following table lists the principal files used by the POSIX subsystem, and the figure shows how they interact.

File	Purpose
PSXSS.EXE	The POSIX subsystem server
POSIX.EXE	The POSIX console session manager
PSXDLL.DLL	The POSIX dynamic link library

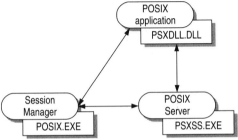

Communicating with Other Subsystems

Windows NT supports a common command processor that can run commands from any of the subsystems. In addition, Windows NT supports piped input and output between commands of different subsystems. For example, you could run the **ls** utility and pipe the results through the **more** command to the console:

```
ls -l | more
```

The following figure illustrates how a POSIX application interacts with other components of the Windows NT operating system.

Further Information

For further information on the POSIX standards, contact either or both of the following resources.

- For information on POSIX.1 (ANSI/IEEE 1003.1-1990, ISO/IEC 9945-1:1990):

  Publication Sales
  IEEE Service Center
  P.O. Box 1331
  445 Hoes Lane
  Piscataway, NJ 08855-1331

- For information on other POSIX standards:

  IEEE Computer Society
  Attention Assistant Director/Standards
  1730 Massachusetts Avenue Northwest
  Washington, DC 20036

P A R T V I I

Troubleshooting

Part Seven provides specific information for troubleshooting problems with Windows NT, showing the key steps for isolating and solving common problems. At the end of Chapter 26, a series of flowcharts lead you step-by-step to solutions for problems that you might encounter.

C H A P T E R   2 6

Troubleshooting

This chapter discusses how to troubleshoot problems that might arise while installing, booting, logging onto, and running Windows NT. At the end of the chapter is a set of flowcharts that you can step through while trying to solve various problems.

Before you use this chapter, you should try to resolve your problem by reading the information files that ship with Windows NT (README.WRI, NETWORK.WRI, and PRINTER.WRI. These files contain material not available in this book, in the *Windows NT System Guide*, or in online Help. They contain important information for troubleshooting problems relating to specific hardware, software, and system configurations.

Very often you can solve a problem by referring to online Help. You can access Help by selecting the Help button, pressing F1, or through the Windows NT Help utility in the Main program group.

You can look up explanations for error and informational messages in the book *Windows NT Messages*, which comes with the Resource Kit. The Windows NT Messages database is the online version of the book. The online Messages database also provides some additional messages that are not in the printed version and includes a run-time version of Microsoft Access with a customized graphical user interface. The file README.WRI contains a section that explains how to set up and use the online Messages database.

Windows NT and the Windows NT Resource Kit provide utilities that can help you diagnose problems with your computer. The Introduction to this book contains a description of the utilities shipped with the Resource Kit, and the documentation that comes with Windows NT describes the utilities that ship with the operating system.

Performance

If your computer is working correctly, but you believe it is not performing as well as it should, you may need to optimize its performance. The Performance Monitor in Administrative Tools lets you track key system metrics while your computer is running so you can find out where bottlenecks occur.

The book *Optimizing Windows NT* takes you step by step through all the basic performance management techniques. It includes chapters with tips for writing and tuning high-performance Windows NT applications, adding extra performance counters to the system, and writing your own customized performance monitoring application. It covers all facets of system performance, including processors, memory, disks, video, and networking. *Optimizing Windows NT* is an indispensable tool that helps all levels of users understand and manage Windows NT system performance; refer to it for any performance tuning on your computer.

Hardware Configuration

The following sections discuss common hardware problems that can prevent Windows NT from installing, starting, or operating properly. See also "Network Problems," later in this chapter, the flowchart "General Hardware Conflicts," and the information file README.WRI.

SCSI

Make sure the SCSI bus is set up properly (refer to your hardware documentation for specific details):

- The ends of the SCSI bus must have terminating resistor packs (also called *terminators*) installed. If you have only internal or only external SCSI devices, the ends of the bus are probably the SCSI adapter and the last device on the cable. If you have both internal and external SCSI devices, the adapter probably is in the middle of the bus and should not have terminators installed.

- If you disconnect a device that has terminators installed (such as an external CD-ROM drive), be sure to install terminators on whatever device then becomes the last one on the bus.

- One of the devices on the SCSI bus, usually the adapter, should be configured to provide termination power to the bus.

Make sure the SCSI ID of the CD-ROM drive is not 0 or 1. Some SCSI adapters reserve IDs 0 and 1 for hard drives. If your CD-ROM drive has an ID of 0 or 1, you may see an extra partition that does not exist. The SCSI ID is usually set by jumpers on the device.

Adapters

Devices cannot share interrupt request (IRQ) numbers, memory buffer addresses, or ROM addresses. Make sure there are no conflicts among adapters or between the system board and adapters. Sometimes the settings are specified with jumpers or switches on the hardware (refer to your hardware documentation for specific details); sometimes they are specified with software. If the network card can be configured through software, you can do so with Windows NT Setup. For more information on network adapter card settings, see "Network Adapter Card Settings," later in this chapter.

If the video controller is not one currently supported, have the manufacturer's disk ready for selection of resolution parameters, if different from standard VGA (640x480x16).

See also the flowchart "General Hardware Conflicts."

Network Cabling

Make sure your network adapter is configured for the network cable you are using.

Installing Windows NT

If you are installing Windows NT onto an MS-DOS–based system, make sure you have a bootable MS-DOS diskette for your drive A that contains copies of your current CONFIG.SYS and AUTOEXEC.BAT files. If major errors occur during installation, you may not be able to boot from the hard drive and will need the diskette to recover your system.

See also the flowchart "Windows NT Setup."

Booting Windows NT

Windows NT boots in the following sequence:

1. When Windows NT is installed, it alters the boot disk's boot record to run a program called NTLDR.
2. NTLDR reads BOOT.INI and builds a menu of the operating systems that you can boot.

BOOT.INI is a text file that has two sections; the first specifies the default operating system that will boot after a timeout value has expired, and the second specifies the operating systems that you can boot. The directory specifications for Windows NT are in the ARC syntax for addressing drives (see "Understanding ARC Names," later in this chapter). The contents of a typical BOOT.INI looks like the following:

```
[boot loader]
timeout=30
default=multi(0)disk(0)rdisk(0)partition(1)\WINDOWS

[operating systems]
multi(0)disk(0)rdisk(0)partition(1)\WINDOWS="Windows NT"
c:\="MS-DOS"
```

The choices that NTLDR displays in the menu consist of the text that appears between quotes in the operating systems section. You can edit this to customize the menu.

3. Either highlight and select an operating system to boot; otherwise, the time counts down to 0, and NTLDR boots the default operating system.

   If you don't see the menu and the default operating system automatically boots, the timeout value has been set to 0. If the default operating system is not Windows NT, to be able to boot Windows NT, you will have to edit BOOT.INI and set the timeout value to something other than 0.

4. Windows NT loads and displays the Welcome screen.

As you change your configuration and accounts, maintain current backups. If you have to use the Emergency Repair Disk that you made when you installed Windows NT to restore the system, the configuration may revert to what it was when the system was first installed. Rather than having to reconfigure the system and recreate all the accounts, you can just restore the configuration from your backup.

If Windows NT does not boot, make sure that the statements in BOOT.INI (found in the root directory of your system partition) correctly specify the path where Windows NT is installed (usually either \WINDOWS or \WINNT).

For x86-based systems, do not delete BOOT.INI, NTLDR, BOOTSECT.DOS, NTDETECT.COM, or NTBOOTDD.SYS (if Windows NT is installed on a SCSI disk) in the root directory of the system partition. For RISC systems, do not delete HAL.DLL or OSLOADER.EXE in \OS\NT. If these files are deleted, the system will not boot. Use the repair disk to recover these files.

If you made changes to a system that used to boot Windows NT successfully, and now it doesn't boot, you can return to your previous configuration (undo the changes you made) and boot Windows NT by doing the following:

1. If your system boots both Windows NT and another operating system, press the SPACE BAR immediately after selecting Windows NT from the Boot Loader menu. If your system boots directly into Windows NT, press the SPACE BAR when the words OS Loader appear.

   A menu appears that lets you select one of the following choices:

   - Use Current Startup Configuration
   - Use Last Known Good Configuration
   - Restart computer

2. The Last Known Good Configuration is the configuration that last successfully booted Windows NT. Select it to boot Windows NT as it was configured before you made the changes that prevented it from booting.

If Windows NT still won't boot, use the Emergency Repair Disk to recover the system. To use the Emergency Repair Disk, run Setup as you did when you installed Windows NT. At the Welcome screen, press R to attempt repairs on a damaged Windows NT system. Setup will ask you to insert the Emergency Repair Disk. Follow the instructions on the screen. If the Emergency Repair Disk doesn't recover the system, reinstall Windows NT. See Chapter 12, "System Maintenance with Windows NT Setup," of the *Windows NT System Guide* for more information.

Note   You must use the Emergency Repair Disk that was created for your specific computer.

If a device driver fails to properly initialize, Windows NT may attempt to automatically boot the LastKnownGood configuration. This depends upon the Error Control value that is recorded in the Registry for that device driver.

For more information on boot configurations and Last Known Good, see Chapter 12, "Configuration Management and the Registry."

See also the flowchart "Boot Sequence."

Understanding ARC Names

ARC names are a generic method of identifying devices within the ARC environment. For disk devices, ARC names are constructed as follows:

<component>(*x*)**disk**(*y*)**rdisk**(*z*)**partition**(*a*)

where

<component> identifies the hardware adapter for the device. The two valid values for this field are **scsi** and **multi**, where **scsi** indicates a SCSI disk and **multi** indicates a disk interface other than SCSI. For Windows NT, this could be a disk supported by the AtDisk driver or one supported by AbiosDsk or CpqArray.

x is the ordinal number of the adapter. For example, if there are two SCSI adapters in the system, the first to load and initialize is assigned the ordinal **0** and the next number assigned is **1**. This continues for all adapter drivers that initialize.

y is, for **scsi**, the SCSI bus number for multiple-bus SCSI adapters times 32 plus the SCSI ID of the disk. For **multi**, this is always **0**.

z is, for **scsi**, the device's logical unit number. For **multi**, this is the ordinal for the disk on the adapter.

a is the partition ordinal for the partition used on the disk. All partitions receive a number, except type 5 (MS-DOS Extended) and type 0 (unused) partitions.

For example, if the Windows NT tree is located on the fourth partition on a SCSI disk with the SCSI ID of 3 on the second SCSI controller in the system, the ARC name is:

scsi(1)disk(3)rdisk(0)partition(4)

Booting an Alternate Operating System

UNIX cannot be an alternate operating system; only MS-DOS and OS/2 can be used as alternates.

For an MS-DOS system, you must have an AUTOEXEC.BAT and CONFIG.SYS file in the root directory of your system partition. If these files did not exist before you ran Windows NT Setup, you can create them in Windows NT using a nonformatting text editor such as Notepad. Save the files in the root directory of drive C; then reboot your computer.

If the alternate operating system does not boot, make sure that the statements in BOOT.INI (which must be in the root directory of your boot partition) specify the correct path for that operating system. You cannot boot an alternate operating system if the boot partition is NTFS; it should be FAT for MS-DOS or OS/2, or HPFS for OS/2.

The file BOOTSECT.DOS contains the boot record for the alternate operating system (even if the alternate is not MS-DOS). The boot fails if the system cannot find BOOTSECT.DOS in the root directory of the system partition. Use the Repair Disk to recover BOOTSECT.DOS.

Logging On

There are a variety of reasons why you may not be able to log on to Windows NT. An administrator can use Event Viewer in Administrative Tools to look at the audit trail of security events to determine why you were not able to log on, and can use User Manager to resolve problems with your account or password. The Audit policies for your account must include Failure For Logon and Logoff events in order for such problems to be displayed in the security log. When viewing the security log, the administrator should filter out all events except Failure Audit.

Some of the possible problems with logging on include the following:

- Passwords are case-sensitive and you used the wrong case. For example, if your password is Test, you cannot use a password of test to log on.

- You forgot your password. There is no way to determine your old password. An administrator can give you a new password.

- Your account or your password may be expired.

- You were required to enter a new password, and you may have entered one that is less than the minimum length set for the account. Also, there may be a restriction on your account concerning the reuse of an old password.

- Your account may be disabled.

- The workstation may be locked by a previous user. Only that person can unlock the workstation.

- You may be trying to log on at a time during which you are not allowed.

- If you are logging on remotely from a workstation:
    - You may be allowed to log on only at certain computers.
    - You may be trying to log onto the wrong domain for your account.
    - The network may be down.

See also the flowchart "Local Logon to Windows NT Workstation."

Network Problems

Common network problems include hardware problems with the network itself, incompatible protocols running on different devices in the network, duplicate computernames, and IRQ number conflicts.

If network problems persist, use Event Viewer from the Administrative Tools group to review the error log information generated during startup. Details in the system error log will reveal possible interrupt conflicts or other driver problems.

See also the flowcharts "Network Connection or Net View Errors" and "Network Configuration" and the information file NETWORK.WRI.

There are a number of books that can help in troubleshooting LANs, including

- *LAN Protocol Handbook* by Mark Miller, ISBN 1-55851-099-0.
- *LAN Troubleshooting* by Mark Miller, ISBN 1-55851-054-0.

A LAN analyzer, such as a Data General Sniffer or a Novell Lanalyzer, can tell you a great deal of information about the actual activity on the network.

Network Hardware Problems

There may be physical problems with the cabling and other hardware that prevents the network from operating properly. Standard tools are available for troubleshooting such problems, for example **ping**, **nbping**, and **wnbstat**. The **ping** utility determines if a network path can be made between two computers (TCP/IP only); **nbping** does the same for NetBEUI; **wnbstat** is the Win32 version of **nbping**. Refer to the documentation provided with these tools for information on how to use them.

Network Adapter Card Settings

If your network adapter card can accept more than one type of cable, make sure that the card is configured for the cable that you are plugging into it. Refer to the documentation that came with the card for details.

When you configure the network adapter card, you must select the correct IRQ number, I/O port base address, and memory buffer address. On older network cards, you set jumpers or switches for each of these items; with newer cards, you can program them with the driver software using only the I/O port address. For information about the settings on specific network cards, see the file NETWORK.WRI or the Help file NTCARD.HLP, which is included on a diskette that ships with this book (in File Manager, double-click on NTCARD.HLP).

If you are not sure about which network card is installed in your computer or what its settings are, accept the defaults proposed by Windows NT Setup. After Setup is complete, you can use the Networks applet in Control Panel to install and configure network settings. For information about completing any options in the dialog boxes that appear during the network portion of Setup or when you run the Networks tool, use the Help button.

For the correct settings for your particular hardware, see the documentation for your network card and other devices such as SCSI adapters, or contact your hardware manufacturer.

You do not have to specify settings for built-in Ethernet capabilities on RISC-based computers from Acer, MIPS, and Olivetti.

Network Adapter Card Interrupts

The IRQ that you assign to a network adapter card should be unique; that is, it should not be used by any other device in the system. The standard assignments for IRQs in x86-based computers include the following:

IRQ	Used for	IRQ	Used for
0	Timer	8	Clock
1	Keyboard	9	—
2	(cascade)	10	—
3	COM2	11	—
4	COM1	12	—
5	LPT2	13	Math coprocessor
6	Floppy controller	14	Hard drive
7	LPT1	15	—

A network card should not be assigned an IRQ that is used by an active serial or parallel port, even if no device is currently attached to the port. Most newer x86-based computers let you disable the built-in serial or parallel ports. After you disable a port, you can assign its associated IRQ to another device, such as a network card.

For example, if you use only a network printer, you can usually disable the built-in parallel printer ports for both LPT1 and LPT2. Network software does not use these interfaces when the underlying devices are redirected.

For information on disabling serial or parallel ports, see the documentation for your computer.

If you do not disable the serial ports, COM1 (IRQ 4) and COM2 (IRQ 3) are usually poor choices because most *x86*-based computers come with two active serial ports. For example, a typical computer with a mouse on COM1 and a modem on COM2 cannot use IRQ 3 or 4 for a network adapter card. IRQ 5 is often a safe choice, because *x86*-based computers usually do not have two parallel printer ports.

If you have two or more COM ports on your computer, you might find that a network adapter card (especially an EtherLink II card) will conflict with one port. Two common symptoms are that the workstation fails to start and that an error attributed to the network adapter card is logged in Event Viewer.

▶ **To change the interrupt of a network adapter card**

1. Run the Networks tool in Control Panel.
2. Double-click the correct entry in the list of Adapter Cards.
3. In the Configuration dialog box, change the interrupt number from its current value to an available interrupt, such as 5 or 10.

   Make sure that the interrupt you choose is not being used by another device.

Assigning I/O Port Base Addresses

Most devices have unique default I/O port base addresses. In the rare case that an I/O port appears to be in conflict, it can usually be moved to another setting without harm. The following table shows some common I/O port addresses:

I/O address	Used for	I/O address	Used for
3F8	COM1	300	—
3BC	—	2F8	COM2
378	LPT1	278	LPT2

Refer to the documentation for your network adapter card and other hardware devices to find what I/O addresses are required or settable for your system.

Assigning Memory Buffer Addresses

No two devices can share memory buffers. Make sure that the network adapter card buffer address is not already used by another device, such as a SCSI adapter card or hard disk controller. Check the installation guide for your computer or peripherals to verify the setting of the memory buffer address.

Some SCSI and network adapters use conflicting memory addresses, such as an Adaptec or Future Domain SCSI adapter and a DEC EtherWORKS Turbo TP network adapter. This requires reconfiguring the hardware by changing jumpers.

You can use the **WinMSD** utility to check how memory buffers are being used.

Duplicate Computernames

Each computer on a network must have a unique name. If you specify a computername that is the same as another computer on the network or the same as a workgroup or a domain, the network will not start when you run Windows NT.

Shared Resources

If you can see the name of a shared resource, but cannot see or use its contents, you probably do not have sufficient permissions to access the resource. The owner of the resource can resolve this for you. It is also possible that the target server has just gone down or is having network problems.

If you cannot connect to a resource that you think you have permission to use, there are two likely possibilities:

- Your computer is not running a protocol that is running on the target computer.
- You logged on with a username that the target computer recognizes and a password that it doesn't recognize. A common example is to log on to your computer as Administrator and then try to connect to a server that has its own Administrator account established.

If you try to view the shared resource for a server that you know exists but receive a message that says it doesn't exist, there are several possibilities:

- The server is not running.
- The server is configured to be hidden from computer browsers.
- Your Browser service may not be started.
- The server is in a domain that is not in the list of domains to be browsed. Use the Network tool in Control Panel to reconfigure the Browser service.

Using TCP/IP Utilities to Diagnose Network Problems

The **arp, ping, netstat,** and **nbtstat** utilities can provide useful information when you are trying to determine the cause of TCP/IP networking problems. Below is a list of some possible TCP/IP symptoms with recommendations for using these utilities to diagnose the problems. Although this is not a complete list, these examples show how you might use these utilities to track down problems on the network.

Determining if TCP/IP Is Installed Correctly

Try using **ping** on the local system by typing the IP loopback address of 127.0.0.1 from the command line: **ping 127.0.0.1**. The system should respond immediately. If **ping** is not found or the command fails, check the System event log with Event Viewer, and look for problems reported by Setup or the TCP/IP service. You should also attempt to **ping** the IP addresses of your local interfaces to determine whether you configured IP properly. Successful use of **ping** indicates that the IP layer on the target system is probably functional.

Determining if the FTP Server Service Is Installed Correctly

Try using **ftp** on the local system by typing the IP loopback address from the command line, for example, **ftp 127.0.0.1**. The interaction with the server locally is identical to the interaction expected for other Windows NT (and most UNIX) clients. This can also be used to determine whether the FTP Server service directories, permissions, and so on are configured properly.

Error 53

Error 53 is returned when the computername specified cannot be resolved. If the computer is on the local subnet, confirm that the name is spelled correctly and that the target system (Windows NT, Windows for Workgroups, or LAN Manager server) is running TCP/IP as well. If the computer is not on the local subnet, be sure that the mapping for its name and IP address is available in the LMHOSTS file. If everything appears to be installed properly, try using **ping** with the remote system to be sure that its TCP/IP software is functional.

Adding a New Mapping to the LMHOSTS File

A large LMHOSTS file with an entry at the end of the file, possibly following some #INCLUDEs, could cause an unusually long time to elapse when connecting to the server. Two things can be done to reduce the connection time:

- Mark the entry as a preload entry by following the mapping with the #PRE tag, and use the **nbtstat -R** command to update the local name cache immediately.

- Place the mapping higher in the LMHOSTS file. As discussed in "LMHOSTS File" in Chapter 19, "TCP/IP on Windows NT," the LMHOSTS file is parsed sequentially to locate entries without the #PRE keyword. Therefore, it is best to place frequently used entries near the top of the file and the #PRE entries near the bottom.

Difficulty Connecting to a Particular Server

Use the **nbtstat -N** command to determine authoritatively) what name the server registered on the network. The output of this command lists several names that the system has registered using NBT. One resembling the system's computername should be present. If not, try one of the other unique names displayed. The **nbtstat** command can also display the cached entries for remote systems, either preloaded from LMHOSTS or recently resolved names from current network activity. If the name the remote users are using is the same and the other systems are on a remote subnet, be sure that they have the system's mapping in their LMHOSTS file.

Can Connect to Foreign Systems with Hostnames Using IP Addresses Only

Check the hostname resolution configuration to be sure that the appropriate hosts and DNS setup has been configured for the system. To do this, choose the Network icon in Control Panel, select TCP/IP Protocol in the Installed Network Software list, choose the Configure button, and then choose the TCP/IP Connectivity button. If you are using the HOSTS file, be sure that the remote system is spelled the same way in the file as it is being used by the application. If you are using DNS, be sure that the IP addresses of the DNS servers are correct and in the proper order. Try using **ping** with the remote system by typing both the hostname and IP address to determine whether the hostname is being resolved properly.

Banner Displayed When Using Telnet Is Wrong

This usually occurs when two systems on the same network are mistakenly configured with the same IP address. The Ethernet and IP address mapping is done by the ARP (address resolution protocol) module, which believes the first response it receives. So the impostor computer's reply sometimes comes back before the intended computer's reply. These problems are difficult to isolate and track down. The command **arp -g** displays the mappings in the ARP cache. If you know the Ethernet address for the intended remote system, you can easily determine if the two match. If not, try using **arp -d** to delete the entry; then **ping** the same address (forcing an ARP), and check the Ethernet address in the cache again using **arp -g.** Chances are that if both systems are on the same network, you will eventually get a different response. If not, it may be necessary to filter the traffic from the impostor host to determine the owner or location of the system.

TCP/IP Connection Appears to Be Frozen

The **netstat -a** command shows the status of all activity on TCP and UDP ports on the local system. The state of a good TCP connection is usually established with 0 bytes in the send and receive queues. If data is blocked in either queue or if the state is irregular, there is probably a problem with the connection. If not, you are probably experiencing network or application delay.

Default Gateway Does Not Belong to One of the Configured Interfaces

If the TCP/IP configuration dialog reports that "Your default gateway does not belong to one of the configured interfaces" and prompts if you want to change it, the default gateway is not located on the same logical network as any of the installed interfaces on the system. This is determined by comparing the net ID portion of the default gateway (by computing a bitwise AND operation between the subnet mask and the default gateway) and the net IDs of any of the installed interfaces. For example, a system with a single interface configured with an IP address of 102.54.0.1 and a subnet mask of 255.255.0.0 requires that the default gateway be of the form 102.54.a.b because the net ID portion of the IP interface is 102.54.

Services or Subsystems Not Starting

If services or subsystems do not start properly, use the Services and Devices tools in Control Panel to check their status. You can try to start them with those tools. Check the system log in Event Viewer for entries relating to the problem.

Mail

Several different Microsoft Mail-related errors may be reported if you run out of disk space on the drive that contains your .MMF file or on the drive where Windows NT is loaded. If Mail stops working properly, check to see if your disk is full.

For other problems with Mail, see the flowcharts "Mail Connections" and "Mail Usage."

ANSI Escape Sequences

Windows NT supports the use of ANSI.SYS for backward compatibility with MS-DOS–based applications that require it. However, when you start a Command Prompt, you are not running ANSI.SYS, so escape sequences do not function. To use escape sequences, do the following:

1. Add a line to CONFIG.NT in *SystemRoot*\SYSTEM32:

```
device=%systemroot%\system32\ansi.sys
```

2. Start a command prompt.
3. Run COMMAND.COM from MS-DOS 5.0. Note: This must be the version that comes with MS-DOS 5.0. If you just type **command**, the system starts another CMD.EXE from Windows NT. Check the version with the VER command. It should be MS-DOS 5.00, not Windows NT Version 3.10. Remember to include extra environment space if you are going to use the PROMPT variable.

You should now be able to send ANSI escape sequences. To test this, try the following example, which should clear the screen:

```
prompt $e[J
```

When you type EXIT at the command prompt, only COMMAND.COM is exited; type EXIT a second time to close the Windows NT command prompt.

Booting MS-DOS

If MS-DOS is an alternate operating system on your computer, you can boot directly into MS-DOS by using the System applet in Control Panel to change BOOT.INI. Change the timeout parameter to 0 and the default operating system to C:\. After you are done, the contents of BOOT.INI should be similar to the following:

```
[boot loader]
timeout=0
default=c:\

[operating systems]
multi(0)disk(0)rdisk(0)partition(1)\WINDOWS="Windows NT"
c:\="MS-DOS"
```

To remove Windows NT from your computer that boots from a FAT partition, do the following.

1. Boot MS-DOS from a diskette and run

   ```
   sys c:
   ```

   This will replace the Windows NT boot sector (which starts up NTLDR) with the MS-DOS boot sector (which boots your computer straight into MS-DOS).

2. Delete the following files, which are left in the root directory:
   - BOOT.INI
   - NTBOOTDD.SYS (if this is a SCSI disk)
   - NTDETECT.COM
   - NTLDR
   - PAGEFILE.SYS (may not be in the root directory)

See also the flowchart "Remove Windows NT and Replace MS-DOS."

Removing an NTFS Partition

If Windows NT is not installed on the NTFS partition, you can use the FORMAT command from a Windows NT command prompt.

Windows NT will not let you format the drive that it is installed on. If Windows NT is installed on an NTFS partition and you want to reformat the drive, do the following:

1. If you can boot MS-DOS, do it and run the DELPART utility (included in the Resource Kit) to remove the partition. Use FORMAT to reformat the drive.

2. If you cannot boot MS-DOS, run the Windows NT Setup program as you did when you installed Windows NT.

3. When the screen appears that asks whether you want to install Windows NT on a particular partition, or want to create or delete a partition, highlight the NTFS partition and type "P" to delete it.

4. Either continue installing Windows NT or press F3 to exit the setup program.

General Hardware Conflicts (Part 1)

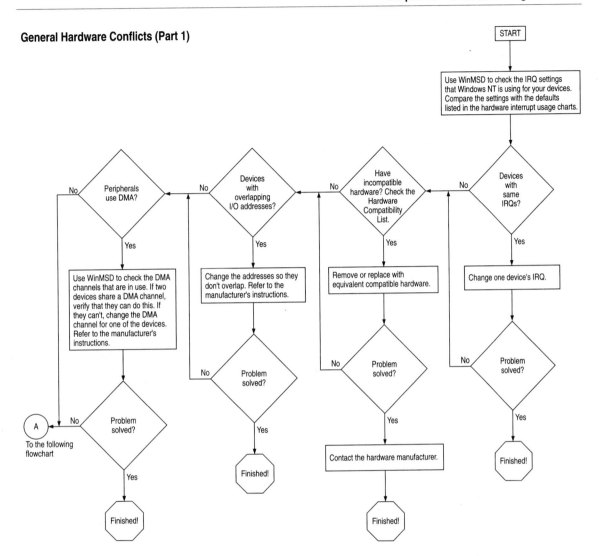

START

Use WinMSD to check the IRQ settings that Windows NT is using for your devices. Compare the settings with the defaults listed in the hardware interrupt usage charts.

Devices with same IRQs?

No → Have incompatible hardware? Check the Hardware Compatibility List.

No → Devices with overlapping I/O addresses?

No → Peripherals use DMA?

No → A To the following flowchart

Devices with same IRQs? Yes → Change one device's IRQ.

Have incompatible hardware? Yes → Remove or replace with equivalent compatible hardware.

Devices with overlapping I/O addresses? Yes → Change the addresses so they don't overlap. Refer to the manufacturer's instructions.

Peripherals use DMA? Yes → Use WinMSD to check the DMA channels that are in use. If two devices share a DMA channel, verify that they can do this. If they can't, change the DMA channel for one of the devices. Refer to the manufacturer's instructions.

Change one device's IRQ. → Problem solved? No → (back to Have incompatible hardware)
Problem solved? Yes → Finished!

Remove or replace with equivalent compatible hardware. → Problem solved? No → (back to Devices with overlapping I/O addresses)
Problem solved? Yes → Contact the hardware manufacturer. → Finished!

Change the addresses so they don't overlap. → Problem solved? No → (back to Peripherals use DMA)
Problem solved? Yes → Finished!

Use WinMSD to check the DMA channels... → Problem solved? No → A
Problem solved? Yes → Finished!

General Hardware Conflicts (Part 2)

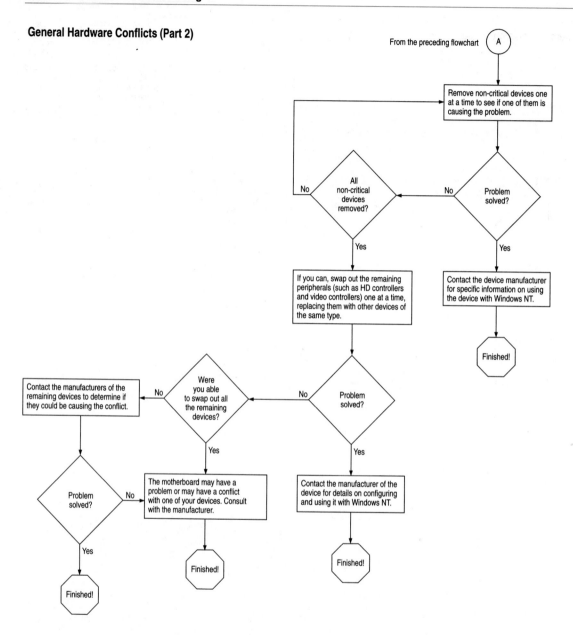

Windows NT Setup

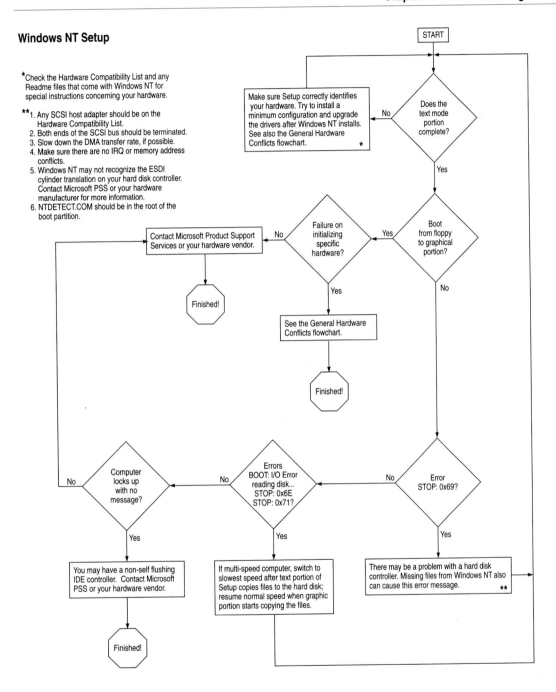

*Check the Hardware Compatibility List and any Readme files that come with Windows NT for special instructions concerning your hardware.

**1. Any SCSI host adapter should be on the Hardware Compatibility List.
2. Both ends of the SCSI bus should be terminated.
3. Slow down the DMA transfer rate, if possible.
4. Make sure there are no IRQ or memory address conflicts.
5. Windows NT may not recognize the ESDI cylinder translation on your hard disk controller. Contact Microsoft PSS or your hardware manufacturer for more information.
6. NTDETECT.COM should be in the root of the boot partition.

START

Does the text mode portion complete?

No → Make sure Setup correctly identifies your hardware. Try to install a minimum configuration and upgrade the drivers after Windows NT installs. See also the General Hardware Conflicts flowchart. *

Yes

Boot from floppy to graphical portion?

Yes → Failure on initializing specific hardware?

No → Contact Microsoft Product Support Services or your hardware vendor.

Finished!

Yes → See the General Hardware Conflicts flowchart.

Finished!

No

Error STOP: 0x69?

No → Errors BOOT: I/O Error reading disk... STOP: 0x6E STOP: 0x71?

No → Computer locks up with no message?

Yes → You may have a non-self flushing IDE controller. Contact Microsoft PSS or your hardware vendor.

Finished!

Yes → If multi-speed computer, switch to slowest speed after text portion of Setup copies files to the hard disk; resume normal speed when graphic portion starts copying the files.

Yes → There may be a problem with a hard disk controller. Missing files from Windows NT also can cause this error message. **

Local Logon to Windows NT Workstation

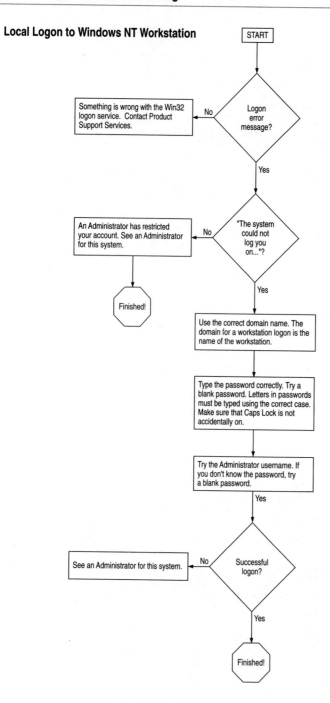

Loggin on to a Windows NT Domain from a Windows NT Workstation (Part 1)

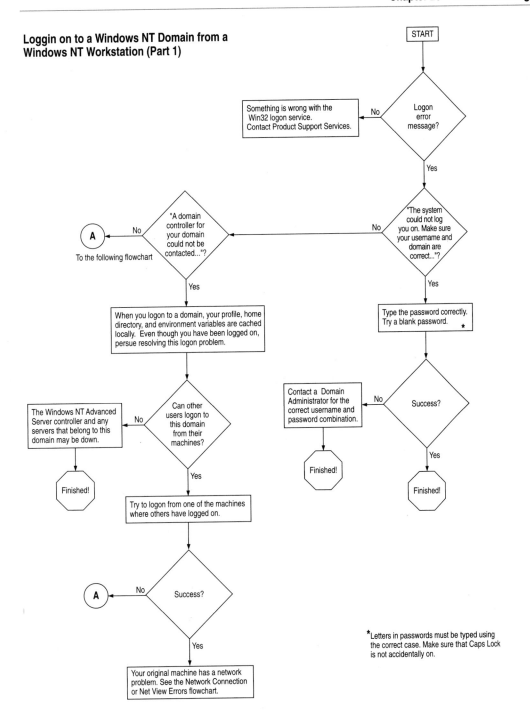

START

Logon error message?

No → Something is wrong with the Win32 logon service. Contact Product Support Services.

Yes

"The system could not log you on. Make sure your username and domain are correct..."?

No → "A domain controller for your domain could not be contacted..."?

No → **A** To the following flowchart

Yes ↓

When you logon to a domain, your profile, home directory, and environment variables are cached locally. Even though you have been logged on, persue resolving this logon problem.

Can other users logon to this domain from their machines?

No → The Windows NT Advanced Server controller and any servers that belong to this domain may be down.

Finished!

Yes ↓

Try to logon from one of the machines where others have logged on.

Success?

No → **A**

Yes ↓

Your original machine has a network problem. See the Network Connection or Net View Errors flowchart.

Yes ↓ (from "The system could not log you on...")

Type the password correctly. Try a blank password.   *

Success?

No → Contact a Domain Administrator for the correct username and password combination.

Finished!

Yes ↓

Finished!

*Letters in passwords must be typed using the correct case. Make sure that Caps Lock is not accidentally on.

Logging on to a Windows NT Domain from a Windows NT Workstation (Part 2)

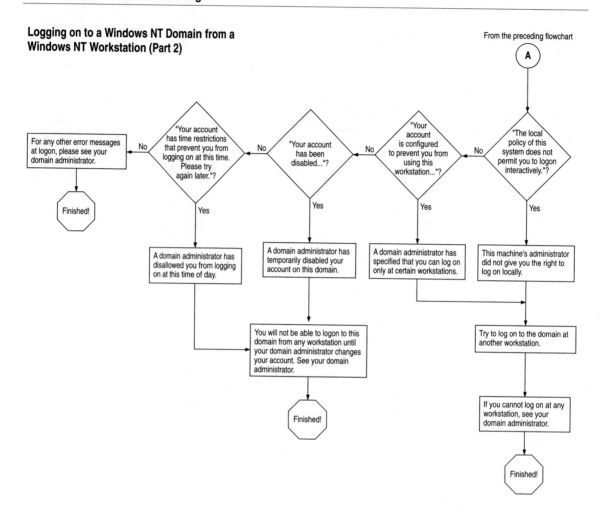

From the preceding flowchart

A

"The local policy of this system does not permit you to logon interactively."?

No → "Your account is configured to prevent you from using this workstation..."?

No → "Your account has been disabled..."?

No → "Your account has time restrictions that prevent you from logging on at this time. Please try again later."?

No → For any other error messages at logon, please see your domain administrator.

Finished!

Yes (time restrictions) → A domain administrator has disallowed you from logging on at this time of day.

Yes (disabled) → A domain administrator has temporarily disabled your account on this domain.

Yes (workstation) → A domain administrator has specified that you can log on only at certain workstations.

Yes (local policy) → This machine's administrator did not give you the right to log on locally.

You will not be able to logon to this domain from any workstation until your domain administrator changes your account. See your domain administrator.

Finished!

Try to log on to the domain at another workstation.

If you cannot log on at any workstation, see your domain administrator.

Finished!

Mice and Other Pointing Devices

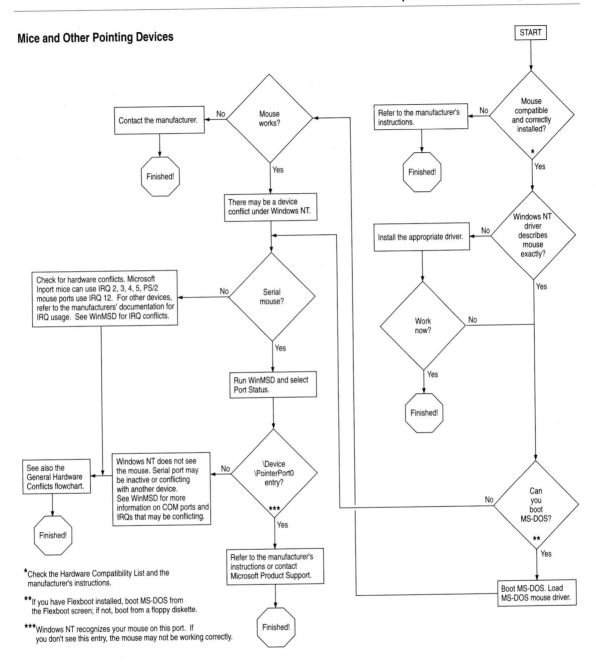

START

Mouse compatible and correctly installed?
*

No → Refer to the manufacturer's instructions. → Finished!

Yes ↓

Windows NT driver describes mouse exactly?

No → Install the appropriate driver. → Work now?

No →

Yes → Finished!

Yes ↓

Mouse works?

No → Contact the manufacturer. → Finished!

Yes ↓

There may be a device conflict under Windows NT.

Serial mouse?

No → Check for hardware conflicts. Microsoft Inport mice can use IRQ 2, 3, 4, 5, PS/2 mouse ports use IRQ 12. For other devices, refer to the manufacturers' documentation for IRQ usage. See WinMSD for IRQ conflicts.

Yes ↓

Run WinMSD and select Port Status.

\Device \PointerPort0 entry?
***

No → Windows NT does not see the mouse. Serial port may be inactive or conflicting with another device. See WinMSD for more information on COM ports and IRQs that may be conflicting.

→ See also the General Hardware Conflicts flowchart. → Finished!

Yes ↓

Refer to the manufacturer's instructions or contact Microsoft Product Support. → Finished!

Can you boot MS-DOS?
**

No →

Yes → Boot MS-DOS. Load MS-DOS mouse driver.

*Check the Hardware Compatibility List and the manufacturer's instructions.

**If you have Flexboot installed, boot MS-DOS from the Flexboot screen; if not, boot from a floppy diskette.

***Windows NT recognizes your mouse on this port. If you don't see this entry, the mouse may not be working correctly.

Serial Port Complications (Part 1)

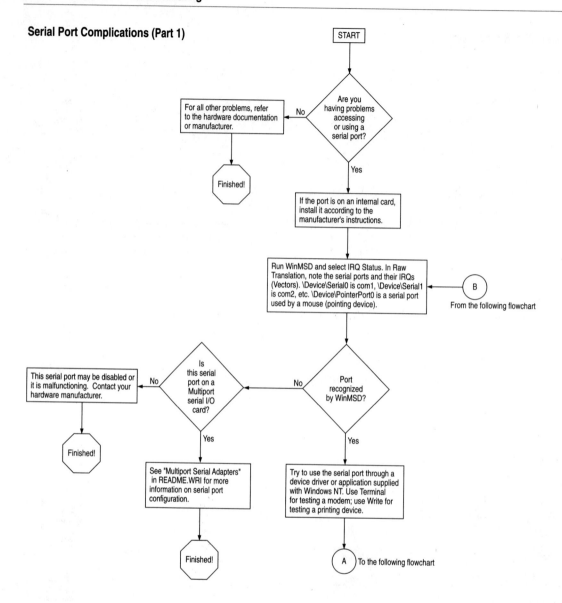

Serial Port Complications (Part 2)

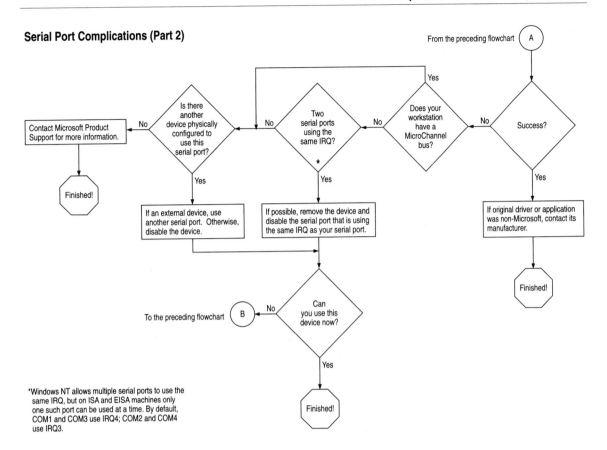

From the preceding flowchart (A)

Does your workstation have a MicroChannel bus?

Success?

— No →

— Yes →

Two serial ports using the same IRQ?

*

Is there another device physically configured to use this serial port?

Contact Microsoft Product Support for more information.

Finished!

If an external device, use another serial port. Otherwise, disable the device.

If possible, remove the device and disable the serial port that is using the same IRQ as your serial port.

If original driver or application was non-Microsoft, contact its manufacturer.

Finished!

To the preceding flowchart (B) ← No —

Can you use this device now?

Yes

Finished!

*Windows NT allows multiple serial ports to use the same IRQ, but on ISA and EISA machines only one such port can be used at a time. By default, COM1 and COM3 use IRQ4; COM2 and COM4 use IRQ3.

Converting File Systems

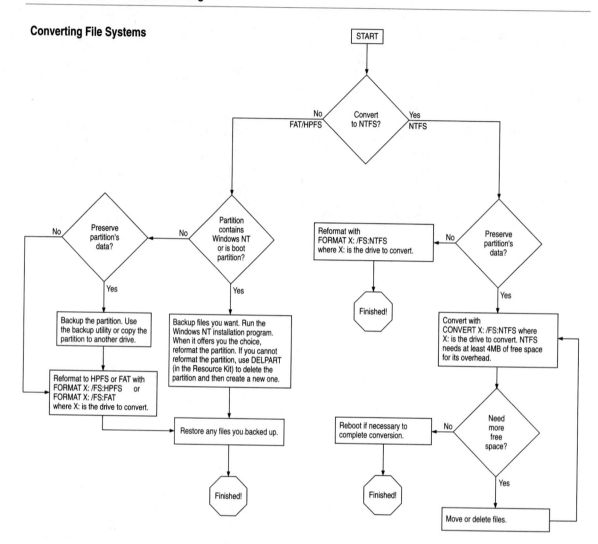

Corruption on an NTFS, HPFS, or FAT Volume

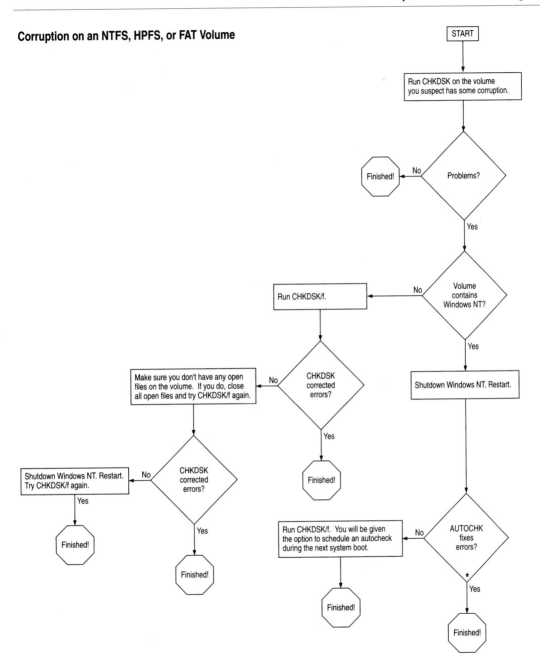

*AUTOCHK runs when Windows NT boots.

Remove Windows NT and Replace MS-DOS

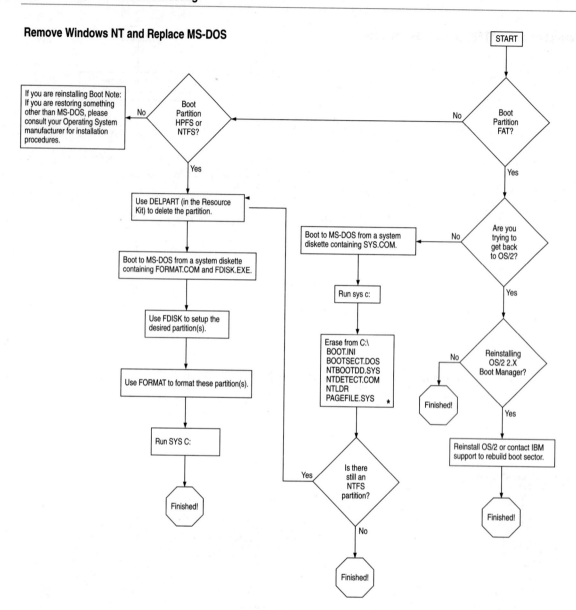

If you are reinstalling Boot Note: If you are restoring something other than MS-DOS, please consult your Operating System manufacturer for installation procedures.

START

Boot Partition FAT?

No → Boot Partition HPFS or NTFS?

No → If you are reinstalling Boot Note...

Yes → Use DELPART (in the Resource Kit) to delete the partition.

→ Boot to MS-DOS from a system diskette containing FORMAT.COM and FDISK.EXE.

→ Use FDISK to setup the desired partition(s).

→ Use FORMAT to format these partition(s).

→ Run SYS C:

→ Finished!

Yes → Are you trying to get back to OS/2?

No → Boot to MS-DOS from a system diskette containing SYS.COM.

→ Run sys c:

→ Erase from C:\
BOOT.INI
BOOTSECT.DOS
NTBOOTDD.SYS
NTDETECT.COM
NTLDR
PAGEFILE.SYS   *

→ Is there still an NTFS partition?

Yes → (back to Use DELPART)

No → Finished!

Yes → Reinstalling OS/2 2.X Boot Manager?

No → Finished!

Yes → Reinstall OS/2 or contact IBM support to rebuild boot sector.

→ Finished!

*Some of the files may not exist. You may have to reset Hidden, Read-only, or System attributes before deleting. PAGEFILE.SYS may not be in C:\.

Local Data Transmission

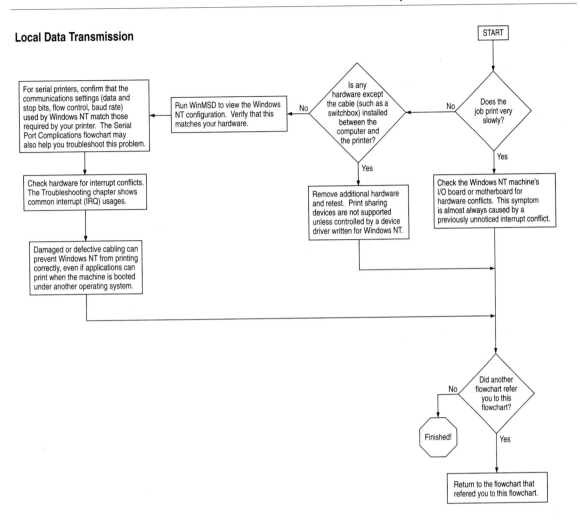

START

Does the job print very slowly?

No →

Is any hardware except the cable (such as a switchbox) installed between the computer and the printer?

No →

Run WinMSD to view the Windows NT configuration. Verify that this matches your hardware.

←

For serial printers, confirm that the communications settings (data and stop bits, flow control, baud rate) used by Windows NT match those required by your printer. The Serial Port Complications flowchart may also help you troubleshoot this problem.

Check hardware for interrupt conflicts. The Troubleshooting chapter shows common interrupt (IRQ) usages.

Damaged or defective cabling can prevent Windows NT from printing correctly, even if applications can print when the machine is booted under another operating system.

Yes (from "Is any hardware...")

Remove additional hardware and retest. Print sharing devices are not supported unless controlled by a device driver written for Windows NT.

Yes (from "Does the job print very slowly?")

Check the Windows NT machine's I/O board or motherboard for hardware conflicts. This symptom is almost always caused by a previously unnoticed interrupt conflict.

Did another flowchart refer you to this flowchart?

No → Finished!

Yes → Return to the flowchart that refered you to this flowchart.

Printer Driver (Part 1)

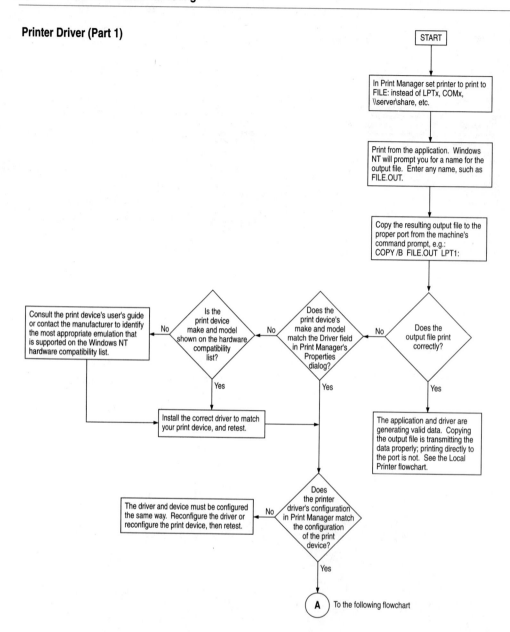

START

In Print Manager set printer to print to FILE: instead of LPTx, COMx, \\server\share, etc.

Print from the application. Windows NT will prompt you for a name for the output file. Enter any name, such as FILE.OUT.

Copy the resulting output file to the proper port from the machine's command prompt, e.g.: COPY /B FILE.OUT LPT1:

Does the output file print correctly?

Does the print device's make and model match the Driver field in Print Manager's Properties dialog?

Is the print device make and model shown on the hardware compatibility list?

Consult the print device's user's guide or contact the manufacturer to identify the most appropriate emulation that is supported on the Windows NT hardware compatibility list.

Install the correct driver to match your print device, and retest.

The application and driver are generating valid data. Copying the output file is transmitting the data properly; printing directly to the port is not. See the Local Printer flowchart.

Does the printer driver's configuration in Print Manager match the configuration of the print device?

The driver and device must be configured the same way. Reconfigure the driver or reconfigure the print device, then retest.

A   To the following flowchart

Printer Driver (Part 2)

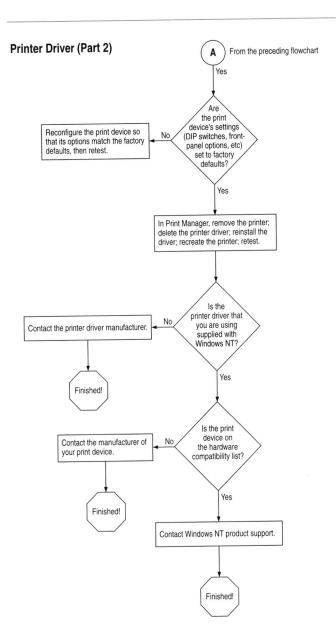

General Printer Troubleshooting

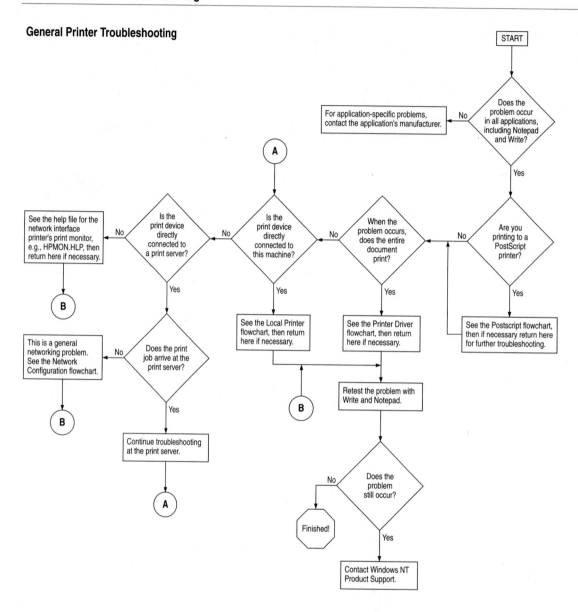

Cannot Select Font in Application (Part 1)

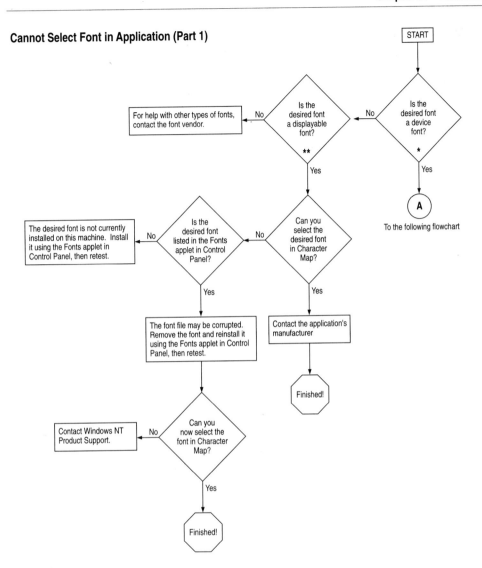

*Device fonts include those built into the print device, those supplied by a font cartridge, and soft fonts downloaded to the print device by the computer.

**Displayable fonts include TrueType fonts, raster fonts, and vector fonts. Other font vendors may create other types of displayable fonts.
Some applications (such as Character Map and Paintbrush) let you select only displayable fonts. Other applications (such as Write) let you select only printable fonts. Some applications let you select both types of fonts.

Cannot Select Font in Application (Part 2)

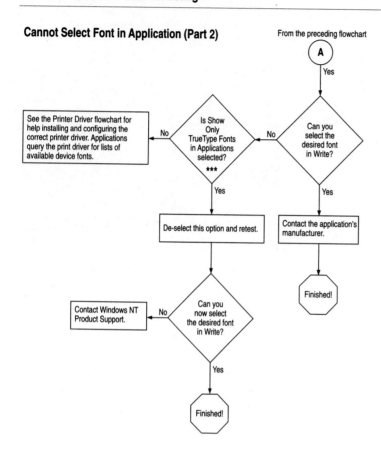

From the preceding flowchart

A

Yes

Can you select the desired font in Write?

No → Is Show Only TrueType Fonts in Applications selected?
***

No → See the Printer Driver flowchart for help installing and configuring the correct printer driver. Applications query the print driver for lists of available device fonts.

Yes ↓

De-select this option and retest.

Yes ↓

Contact the application's manufacturer.

Finished!

Can you now select the desired font in Write?

No → Contact Windows NT Product Support.

Yes ↓

Finished!

***In the Fonts applet in Control Panel.

Network Connection or Net View Errors

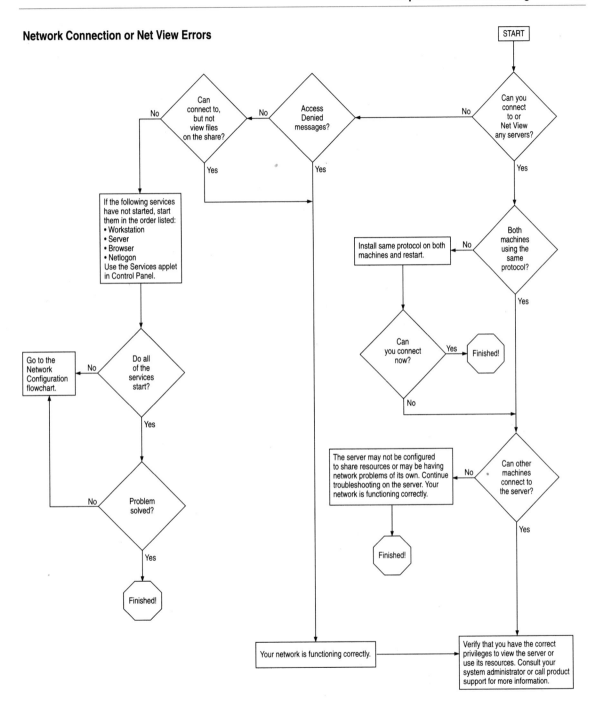

Network Configuration (Part 1)

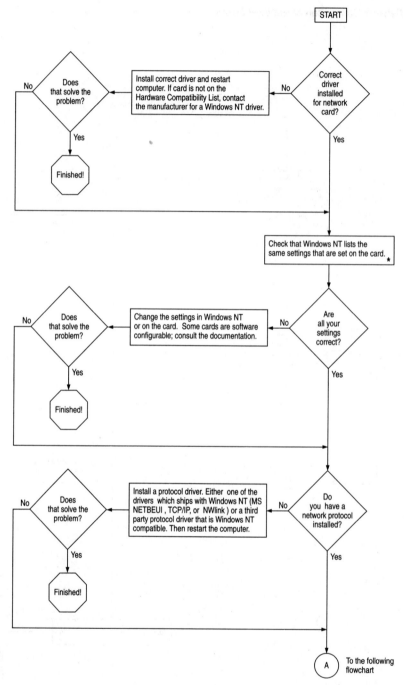

*Use the Network applet in Control Panel. Check the IRQ, I/O base address, memory base address, whether the card has an internal or external transceiver, etc.

Network Configuration (Part 2)

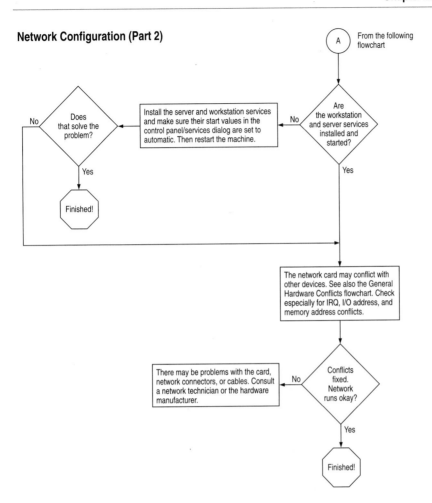

TCP/IP Host Access 1

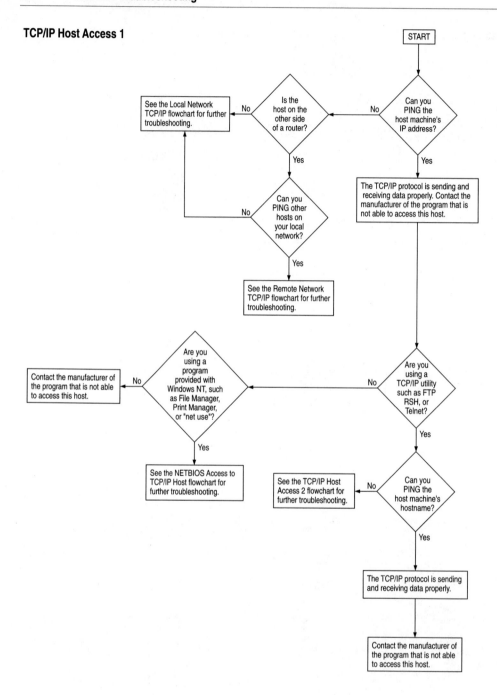

TCP/IP Host Access using Hostname

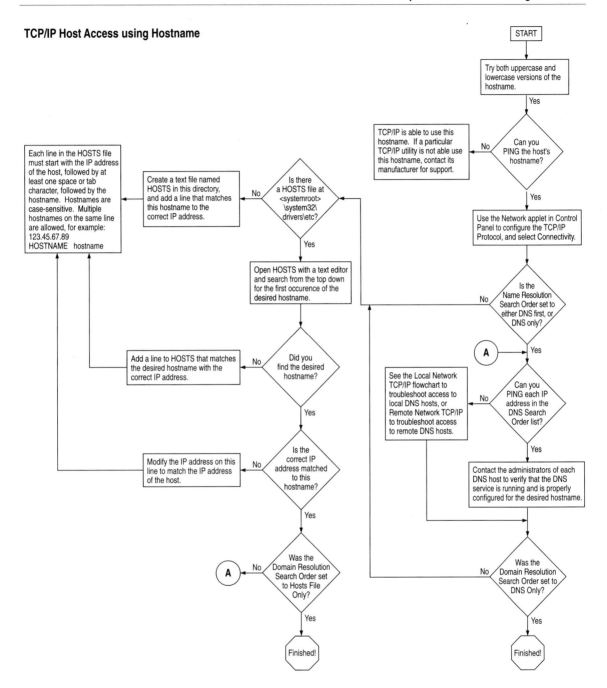

NetBIOSAccess to TCP/IP Host

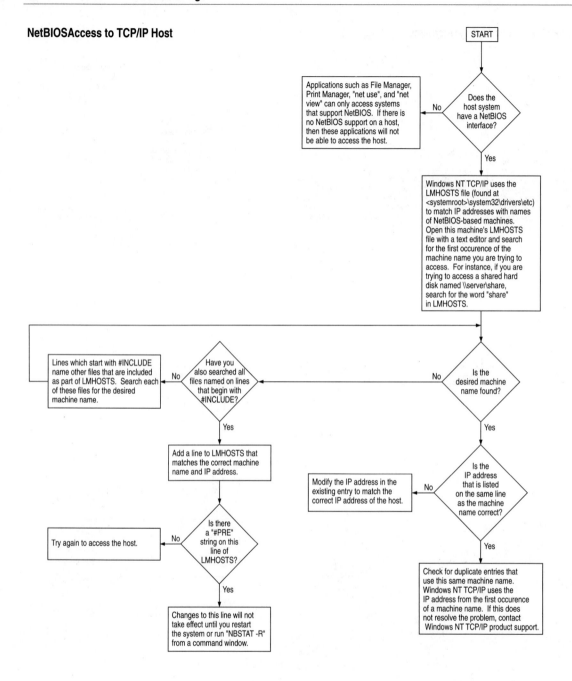

Local Network TCP/IP Problems

START

Make sure you have restarted this machine since installing TCP/IP. Look for binding errors in the Event Viewer, and use the Network applet in Control Panel to verify TCP/IP is currently bound to the correct network adapter. Look for service startup errors in the Event Viewer.

No ← Can you PING the address 127.0.0.1?

No ← Can you PING IP addresses of other hosts on your local network?

Yes

Run the Network applet in Control Panel, and configure the TCP/IP Protocol. Verify that this machine's IP address and subnet mask are correct.

Yes

The target host may be powered off, or may be unable to connect to the network because of a hardware or software problem. The TCP/IP protocol may not be installed on the host, or it may be misconfigured or disabled, or it may not be running, or the host may not have been restarted after the TCP/IP installation. If the host is running Windows NT, check its Event Viewer for error messages.

Remote Network TCP/IP Problems

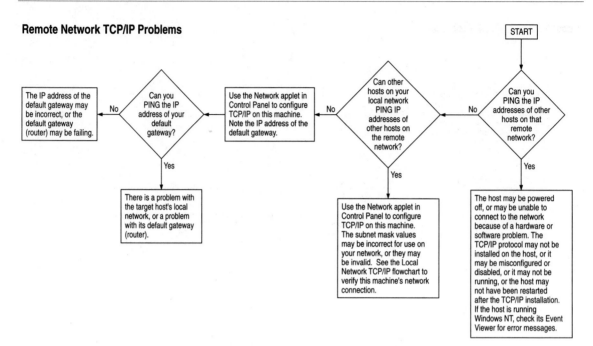

The IP address of the default gateway may be incorrect, or the default gateway (router) may be failing.

No — Can you PING the IP address of your default gateway?

Use the Network applet in Control Panel to configure TCP/IP on this machine. Note the IP address of the default gateway.

No — Can other hosts on your local network PING IP addresses of other hosts on the remote network?

No — Can you PING the IP addresses of other hosts on that remote network?

START

Yes — There is a problem with the target host's local network, or a problem with its default gateway (router).

Yes — Use the Network applet in Control Panel to configure TCP/IP on this machine. The subnet mask values may be incorrect for use on your network, or they may be invalid. See the Local Network TCP/IP flowchart to verify this machine's network connection.

Yes — The host may be powered off, or may be unable to connect to the network because of a hardware or software problem. The TCP/IP protocol may not be installed on the host, or it may be misconfigured or disabled, or it may not be running, or the host may not have been restarted after the TCP/IP installation. If the host is running Windows NT, check its Event Viewer for error messages.

NTDLC (Part 1)

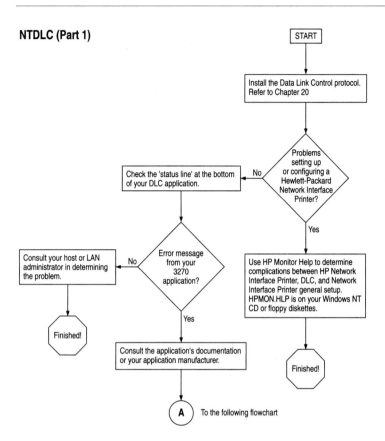

START

Install the Data Link Control protocol. Refer to Chapter 20

Problems setting up or configuring a Hewlett-Packard Network Interface Printer?

No → Check the 'status line' at the bottom of your DLC application.

Yes ↓

Use HP Monitor Help to determine complications between HP Network Interface Printer, DLC, and Network Interface Printer general setup. HPMON.HLP is on your Windows NT CD or floppy diskettes.

Finished!

Error message from your 3270 application?

No → Consult your host or LAN administrator in determining the problem.

Finished!

Yes ↓

Consult the application's documentation or your application manufacturer.

A   To the following flowchart

NTDLC (Part 2)

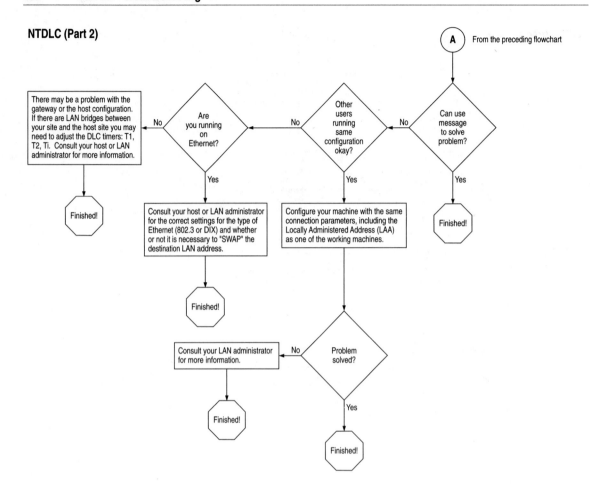

NetDDE Errors

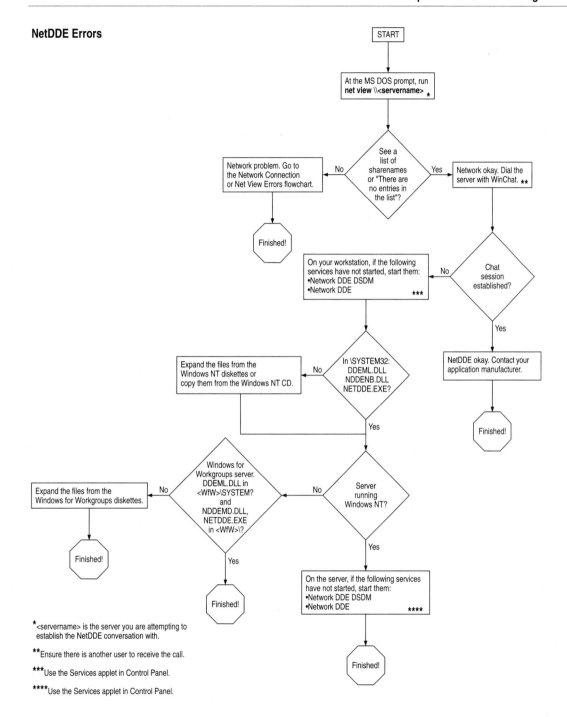

START

At the MS DOS prompt, run
net view \\\\<servername> *

See a list of sharenames or "There are no entries in the list"?

Network problem. Go to the Network Connection or Net View Errors flowchart. — No

Finished!

Yes — Network okay. Dial the server with WinChat. **

Chat session established?

No — On your workstation, if the following services have not started, start them:
•Network DDE DSDM
•Network DDE   ***

Yes — NetDDE okay. Contact your application manufacturer.

Finished!

In \SYSTEM32: DDEML.DLL NDDENB.DLL NETDDE.EXE?

No — Expand the files from the Windows NT diskettes or copy them from the Windows NT CD.

Yes

Server running Windows NT?

No — Windows for Workgroups server. DDEML.DLL in <WfW>\SYSTEM? and NDDEMD.DLL, NETDDE.EXE in <WfW>\?

No — Expand the files from the Windows for Workgroups diskettes.

Finished!

Yes — Finished!

Yes — On the server, if the following services have not started, start them:
•Network DDE DSDM
•Network DDE   ****

Finished!

*<servername> is the server you are attempting to establish the NetDDE conversation with.

**Ensure there is another user to receive the call.

***Use the Services applet in Control Panel.

****Use the Services applet in Control Panel.

Object Linking and Embedding

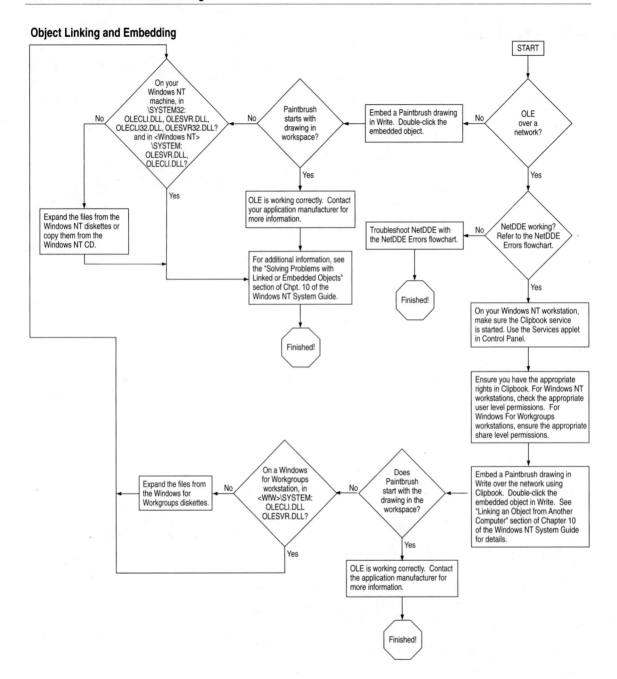

.WAV File Playback

*Check the Hardware Compatibility List and the manufacturer's instructions.

**Look in the Event Viewer logs.

***Check the hardware settings. Make sure that DMA, IRQ, and I/O port addresses are configured properly and do not conflict with other hardware. See also the General Hardware Conflicts flowchart.

****Use the Drivers applet in Control Panel. You may have to contact the hardware manufacturer for updated drivers for Windows NT.

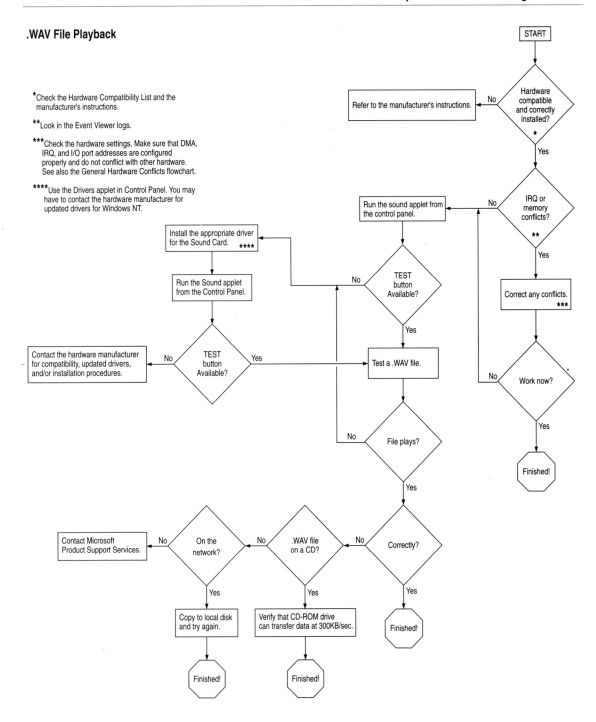

Sound Recorder

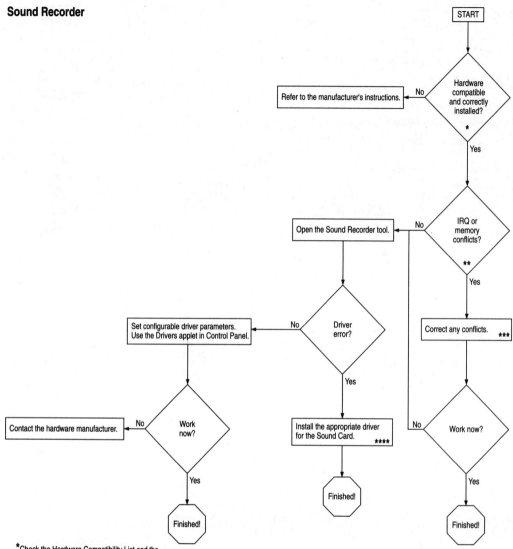

START

Hardware compatible and correctly installed? *

No → Refer to the manufacturer's instructions.

Yes ↓

IRQ or memory conflicts? **

No → Open the Sound Recorder tool.

Yes ↓

Correct any conflicts. ***

Open the Sound Recorder tool. ↓

Driver error?

No → Set configurable driver parameters. Use the Drivers applet in Control Panel.

Yes ↓

Install the appropriate driver for the Sound Card. ****

Finished!

Set configurable driver parameters. Use the Drivers applet in Control Panel. ↓

Work now?

No → Contact the hardware manufacturer.

Yes ↓

Finished!

Correct any conflicts. ↓

Work now?

No

Yes ↓

Finished!

*Check the Hardware Compatibility List and the manufacturer's instructions.

**Look in the Event Viewer logs.

***Check the hardware settings. Make sure that DMA, IRQ, and I/O port addresses are configured properly and do not conflict with other hardware.

****Use the Drivers applet in Control Panel. You may have to contact the hardware manufacturer for updated drivers for Windows NT. See also the General Hardware Conflicts flowchart.

Deleting a File from a local NTFS Partition (Part 1)

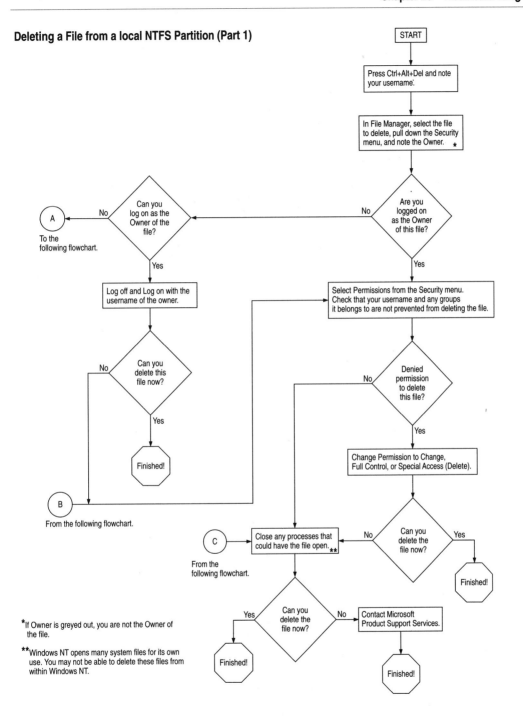

*If Owner is greyed out, you are not the Owner of the file.

**Windows NT opens many system files for its own use. You may not be able to delete these files from within Windows NT.

Deleting a File from a local NTFS Partition (Part 2)

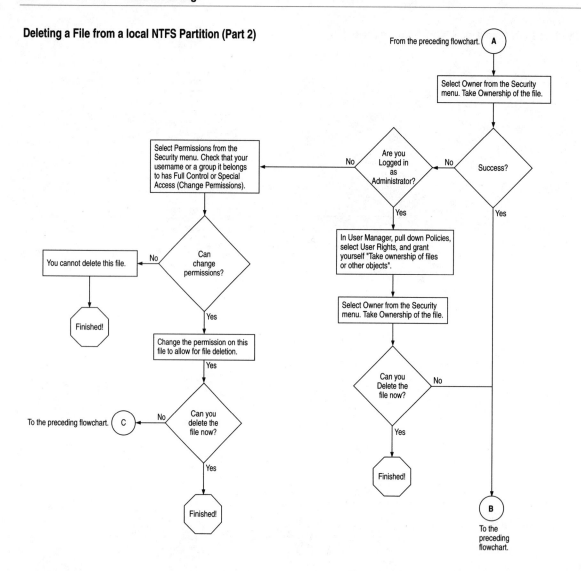

MS-DOS Applications

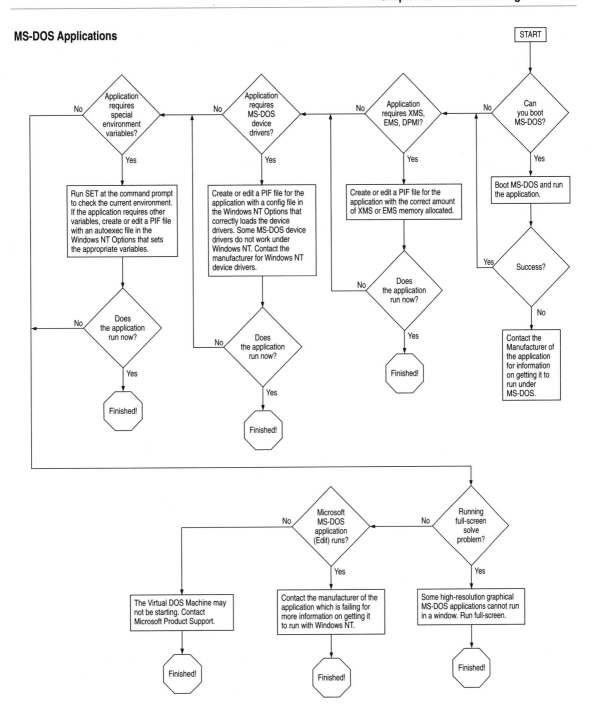

16-Bit Windows Applications

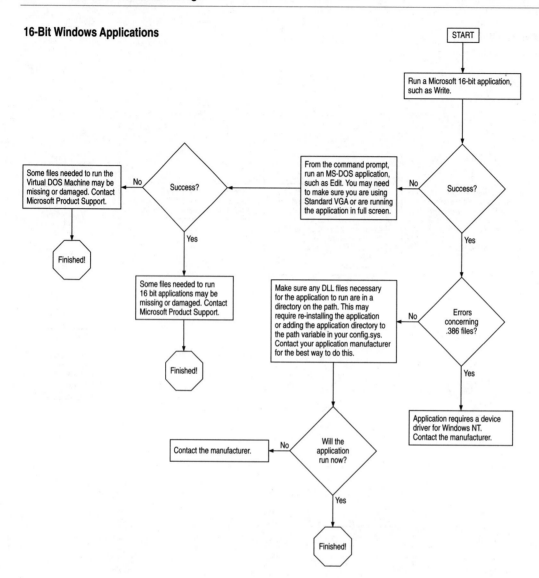

Mail Connections
(Cannot Connect to the Workgroup Postoffice)

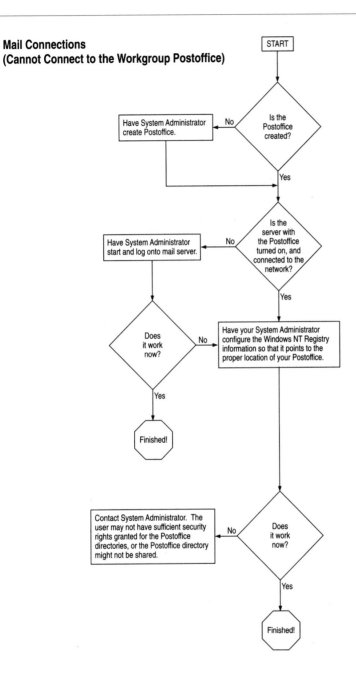

Mail Connections
(Cannot Create a Workgroup Postoffice)

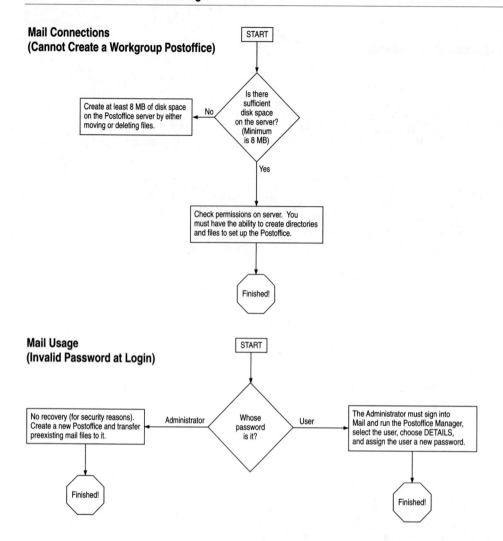

START

Is there sufficient disk space on the server? (Minimum is 8 MB)

No → Create at least 8 MB of disk space on the Postoffice server by either moving or deleting files.

Yes ↓

Check permissions on server. You must have the ability to create directories and files to set up the Postoffice.

Finished!

Mail Usage
(Invalid Password at Login)

START

Whose password is it?

Administrator → No recovery (for security reasons). Create a new Postoffice and transfer preexisting mail files to it.

Finished!

User → The Administrator must sign into Mail and run the Postoffice Manager, select the user, choose DETAILS, and assign the user a new password.

Finished!

**Mail Usage
(Cannot Move or Delete Messages)**

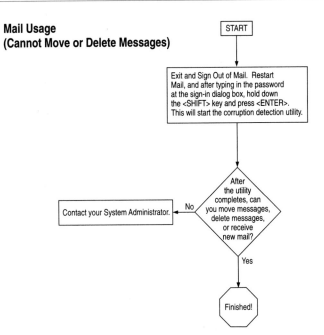

START

Exit and Sign Out of Mail. Restart
Mail, and after typing in the password
at the sign-in dialog box, hold down
the <SHIFT> key and press <ENTER>.
This will start the corruption detection utility.

After
the utility
completes, can
you move messages,
delete messages,
or receive
new mail?

No → Contact your System Administrator.

Yes

Finished!

Media Player Application

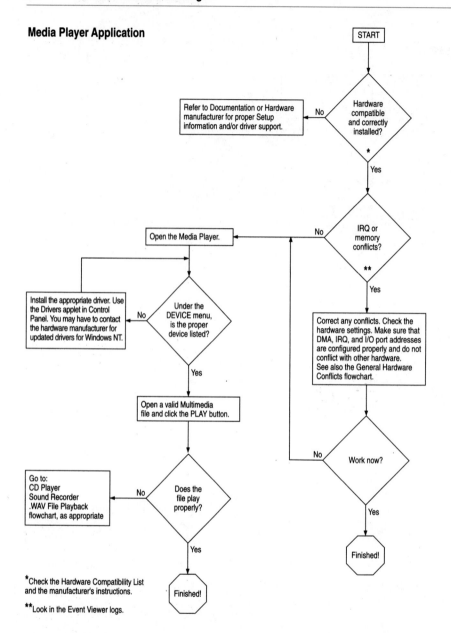

START

Hardware compatible and correctly installed?
*

No → Refer to Documentation or Hardware manufacturer for proper Setup information and/or driver support.

Yes

IRQ or memory conflicts?
**

No → Open the Media Player.

Yes

Correct any conflicts. Check the hardware settings. Make sure that DMA, IRQ, and I/O port addresses are configured properly and do not conflict with other hardware. See also the General Hardware Conflicts flowchart.

Open the Media Player.

Under the DEVICE menu, is the proper device listed?

No → Install the appropriate driver. Use the Drivers applet in Control Panel. You may have to contact the hardware manufacturer for updated drivers for Windows NT.

Yes

Open a valid Multimedia file and click the PLAY button.

Does the file play properly?

No → Go to:
CD Player
Sound Recorder
.WAV File Playback
flowchart, as appropriate

Yes

Finished!

Work now?

No

Yes

Finished!

*Check the Hardware Compatibility List and the manufacturer's instructions.

**Look in the Event Viewer logs.

CD Player (Part 1)

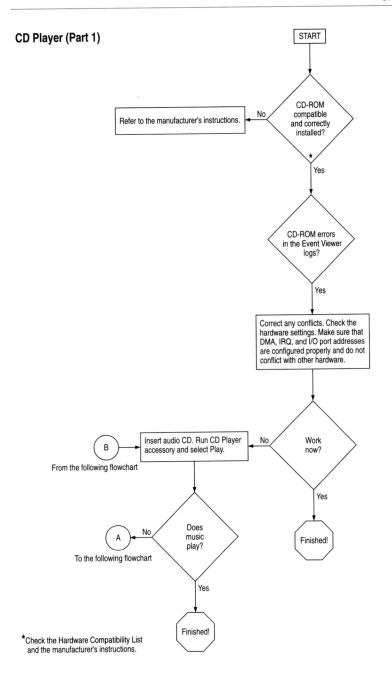

START

CD-ROM compatible and correctly installed?

No → Refer to the manufacturer's instructions.

*

Yes

CD-ROM errors in the Event Viewer logs?

Yes

Correct any conflicts. Check the hardware settings. Make sure that DMA, IRQ, and I/O port addresses are configured properly and do not conflict with other hardware.

Work now?

No → Insert audio CD. Run CD Player accessory and select Play.

B — From the following flowchart

Yes → Finished!

Does music play?

No → A — To the following flowchart

Yes → Finished!

*Check the Hardware Compatibility List and the manufacturer's instructions.

CD Player (Part 2)

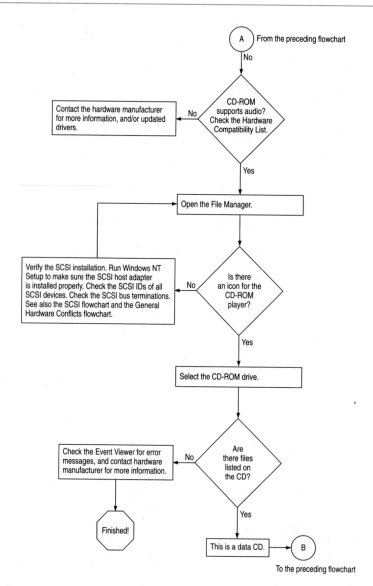

PostScript

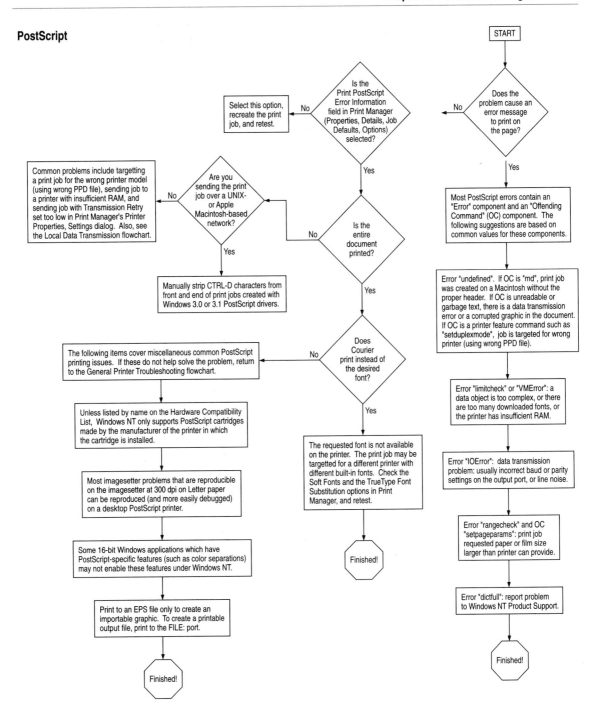

START

Does the problem cause an error message to print on the page? → **No** →

↓ **Yes**

Most PostScript errors contain an "Error" component and an "Offending Command" (OC) component. The following suggestions are based on common values for these components.

Error "undefined". If OC is "md", print job was created on a Macintosh without the proper header. If OC is unreadable or garbage text, there is a data transmission error or a corrupted graphic in the document. If OC is a printer feature command such as "setduplexmode", job is targeted for wrong printer (using wrong PPD file).

Error "limitcheck" or "VMError": a data object is too complex, or there are too many downloaded fonts, or the printer has insufficient RAM.

Error "IOError": data transmission problem: usually incorrect baud or parity settings on the output port, or line noise.

Error "rangecheck" and OC "setpageparams": print job requested paper or film size larger than printer can provide.

Error "dictfull": report problem to Windows NT Product Support.

Finished!

Is the Print PostScript Error Information field in Print Manager (Properties, Details, Job Defaults, Options) selected? → **No** → Select this option, recreate the print job, and retest.

↓ **Yes**

Is the entire document printed? → **No** → Are you sending the print job over a UNIX- or Apple Macintosh-based network?

No → Common problems include targetting a print job for the wrong printer model (using wrong PPD file), sending job to a printer with insufficient RAM, and sending job with Transmission Retry set too low in Print Manager's Printer Properties, Settings dialog. Also, see the Local Data Transmission flowchart.

Yes → Manually strip CTRL-D characters from front and end of print jobs created with Windows 3.0 or 3.1 PostScript drivers.

↓ **Yes**

Does Courier print instead of the desired font? → **No** → The following items cover miscellaneous common PostScript printing issues. If these do not help solve the problem, return to the General Printer Troubleshooting flowchart.

↓ **Yes**

The requested font is not available on the printer. The print job may be targetted for a different printer with different built-in fonts. Check the Soft Fonts and the TrueType Font Substitution options in Print Manager, and retest.

Finished!

Unless listed by name on the Hardware Compatibility List, Windows NT only supports PostScript cartridges made by the manufacturer of the printer in which the cartridge is installed.

Most imagesetter problems that are reproducible on the imagesetter at 300 dpi on Letter paper can be reproduced (and more easily debugged) on a desktop PostScript printer.

Some 16-bit Windows applications which have PostScript-specific features (such as color separations) may not enable these features under Windows NT.

Print to an EPS file only to create an importable graphic. To create a printable output file, print to the FILE: port.

Finished!

Boot Sequence (Part 1)

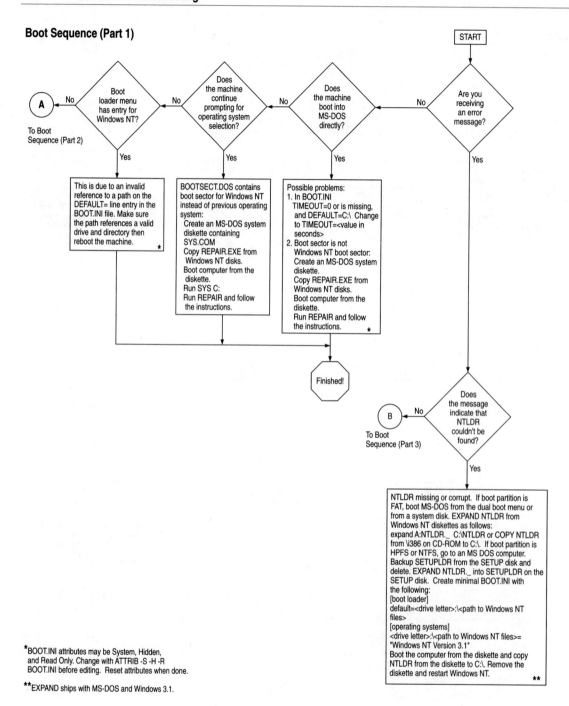

This is due to an invalid reference to a path on the DEFAULT= line entry in the BOOT.INI file. Make sure the path references a valid drive and directory then reboot the machine. *

BOOTSECT.DOS contains boot sector for Windows NT instead of previous operating system:
  Create an MS-DOS system diskette containing SYS.COM
  Copy REPAIR.EXE from Windows NT disks.
  Boot computer from the diskette.
  Run SYS C:
  Run REPAIR and follow the instructions.

Possible problems:
1. In BOOT.INI TIMEOUT=0 or is missing, and DEFAULT=C:\ Change to TIMEOUT=<value in seconds>
2. Boot sector is not Windows NT boot sector: Create an MS-DOS system diskette. Copy REPAIR.EXE from Windows NT disks. Boot computer from the diskette. Run REPAIR and follow the instructions. *

NTLDR missing or corrupt. If boot partition is FAT, boot MS-DOS from the dual boot menu or from a system disk. EXPAND NTLDR from Windows NT diskettes as follows:
expand A:NTLDR._ C:\NTLDR or COPY NTLDR from \i386 on CD-ROM to C:\. If boot partition is HPFS or NTFS, go to an MS DOS computer. Backup SETUPLDR from the SETUP disk and delete. EXPAND NTLDR._ into SETUPLDR on the SETUP disk. Create minimal BOOT.INI with the following:
[boot loader]
default=<drive letter>:\<path to Windows NT files>
[operating systems]
<drive letter>:\<path to Windows NT files>= "Windows NT Version 3.1"
Boot the computer from the diskette and copy NTLDR from the diskette to C:\. Remove the diskette and restart Windows NT. **

*BOOT.INI attributes may be System, Hidden, and Read Only. Change with ATTRIB -S -H -R BOOT.INI before editing. Reset attributes when done.

**EXPAND ships with MS-DOS and Windows 3.1.

Boot Sequence (Part 2)

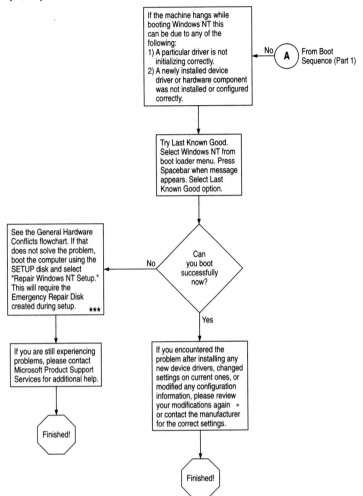

If the machine hangs while booting Windows NT this can be due to any of the following:
1) A particular driver is not initializing correctly.
2) A newly installed device driver or hardware component was not installed or configured correctly.

No ← **A** ← From Boot Sequence (Part 1)

Try Last Known Good. Select Windows NT from boot loader menu. Press Spacebar when message appears. Select Last Known Good option.

Can you boot successfully now?

No →

See the General Hardware Conflicts flowchart. If that does not solve the problem, boot the computer using the SETUP disk and select "Repair Windows NT Setup." This will require the Emergency Repair Disk created during setup.   ***

Yes

If you are still experiencing problems, please contact Microsoft Product Support Services for additional help.

If you encountered the problem after installing any new device drivers, changed settings on current ones, or modified any configuration information, please review your modifications again   ● or contact the manufacturer for the correct settings.

Finished!

Finished!

***You cannot use the Emergency Repair Disk if you installed Windows NT using a non-supported SCSI controller, or if you used the WINNT method.

Boot Sequence (Part 3)

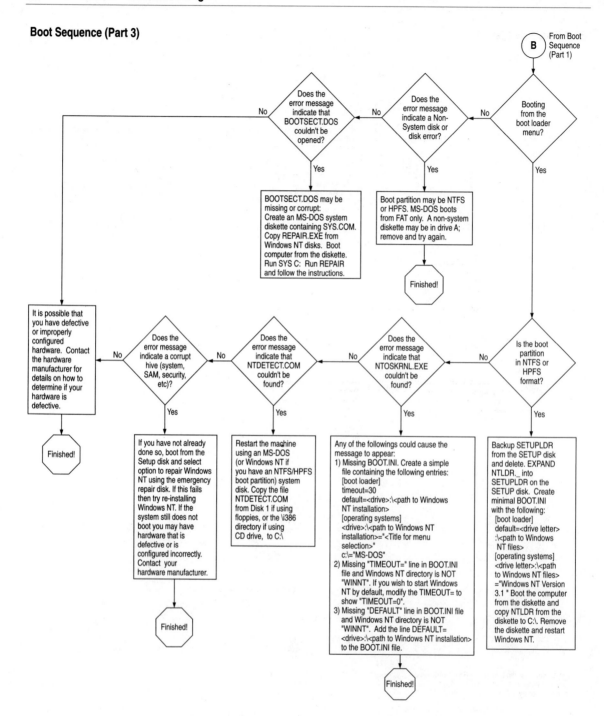

It is possible that you have defective or improperly configured hardware. Contact the hardware manufacturer for details on how to determine if your hardware is defective.

From Boot Sequence (Part 1) — **B**

Booting from the boot loader menu? — No — Does the error message indicate a Non-System disk or disk error? — No — Does the error message indicate that BOOTSECT.DOS couldn't be opened? — No →

Does the error message indicate that BOOTSECT.DOS couldn't be opened? Yes:

BOOTSECT.DOS may be missing or corrupt: Create an MS-DOS system diskette containing SYS.COM. Copy REPAIR.EXE from Windows NT disks. Boot computer from the diskette. Run SYS C: Run REPAIR and follow the instructions.

Does the error message indicate a Non-System disk or disk error? Yes:

Boot partition may be NTFS or HPFS. MS-DOS boots from FAT only. A non-system diskette may be in drive A; remove and try again.

Finished!

Booting from the boot loader menu? Yes — Is the boot partition in NTFS or HPFS format? — No — Does the error message indicate that NTOSKRNL.EXE couldn't be found? — No — Does the error message indicate that NTDETECT.COM couldn't be found? — No — Does the error message indicate a corrupt hive (system, SAM, security, etc)? — No →

Does the error message indicate a corrupt hive (system, SAM, security, etc)? Yes:

If you have not already done so, boot from the Setup disk and select option to repair Windows NT using the emergency repair disk. If this fails then try re-installing Windows NT. If the system still does not boot you may have hardware that is defective or is configured incorrectly. Contact your hardware manufacturer.

Finished!

Does the error message indicate that NTDETECT.COM couldn't be found? Yes:

Restart the machine using an MS-DOS (or Windows NT if you have an NTFS/HPFS boot partition) system disk. Copy the file NTDETECT.COM from Disk 1 if using floppies, or the \i386 directory if using CD drive, to C:\

Does the error message indicate that NTOSKRNL.EXE couldn't be found? Yes:

Any of the followings could cause the message to appear:
1) Missing BOOT.INI. Create a simple file containing the following entries:
[boot loader]
timeout=30
default=<drive>:\<path to Windows NT installation>
[operating systems]
<drive>:\<path to Windows NT installation>="<Title for menu selection>"
c:\="MS-DOS"
2) Missing "TIMEOUT=" line in BOOT.INI file and Windows NT directory is NOT "WINNT". If you wish to start Windows NT by default, modify the TIMEOUT= to show "TIMEOUT=0".
3) Missing "DEFAULT" line in BOOT.INI file and Windows NT directory is NOT "WINNT". Add the line DEFAULT= <drive>:\<path to Windows NT installation> to the BOOT.INI file.

Finished!

Is the boot partition in NTFS or HPFS format? Yes:

Backup SETUPLDR from the SETUP disk and delete. EXPAND NTLDR._ into SETUPLDR on the SETUP disk. Create minimal BOOT.INI with the following:
[boot loader]
default=<drive letter>:\<path to Windows NT files>
[operating systems]
<drive letter>:\<path to Windows NT files> ="Windows NT Version 3.1 " Boot the computer from the diskette and copy NTLDR from the diskette to C:\. Remove the diskette and restart Windows NT.

Finished!

PART VIII

Appendixes

Part Eight includes appendixes with information on additional resources, RAS administration, accessibility for users with disabilities, international issues, and a hardware compatibility list. A glossary of terms used in the *Resource Guide* follows.

APPENDIX A

Windows NT Resource Directory

This appendix describes how to get answers to your technical questions. It also contains a list of resources to support learning and using Windows NT.

With Windows accepted as a standard for PC computing, many companies are making products and services available to enhance the Windows and Windows for Workgroups environment. Microsoft also offers a wide array of support services.

Getting Answers to Your Technical Questions

For answers to your questions and help with technical problems regarding Windows NT:

- First, check online Help (press the F1 key), the printed documentation set, and the information in the README.TXT files.

- Check the Messages database, available on the floppy disks that accompany *Microsoft Windows NT Resource Kit Volume 2: Windows NT Messages.*

- For fast answers to common questions and a library of technical notes delivered by recording or fax, call Microsoft FastTips for Windows NT at (206) 635-7245, available seven days a week, 24 hours a day, including holidays. Microsoft FastTips is an automated system, accessible by touch-tone phone.

- Use CompuServe to interact with other users and Microsoft Product Support Services engineers, or access the Microsoft Knowledge Base of product information. For CompuServe members, type **GO WINNT** to access the forum for Windows NT; or type **GO MSKB** to access the Microsoft Knowledge Base at any ! prompt. For an introductory CompuServe membership kit, call (800) 848-8199 and ask for operator 463.

- Use the Microsoft Download Service (MSDL) to access the latest technical notes on common support issues for Windows NT and to access the Windows NT Driver Library via modem. The MSDL is at (206) 936-6735, available seven days a week, 24 hours a day, including holidays (1200, 2400, or 9600 baud; no parity, 8 data bits, 1 stop bit).

- Use the Internet to access the Windows NT Driver Library and the Microsoft Knowledge Base for information on Windows NT. The Internet FTP archive host for Windows NT, gowinnt.microsoft.com, supports anonymous login. When logging in as anonymous, use your complete e-mail name as your password.

- Contact a Microsoft Solution Provider for installation services and follow-up product support. These companies have individuals who have been certified as Microsoft Certified Professionals on Windows NT. To be referred to a Microsoft Solution Provider in your area, please call Microsoft at (800) 227-4679.

- Get technical support from a Microsoft engineer. Microsoft offers pay-as-you-go telephone support for Windows NT from a Microsoft engineer, available seven days a week, 24 hours a day, except holidays. Please have the serial number from this support card ready when you call. Choose from these options:
  - Dial (900) 555-2100. Service charge of $150.00 per call. Charges appear on your telephone bill.

- Dial (206) 635-7022. Service charge of $150.00 per call. Charges billed to your Visa, MasterCard, or American Express.

- Special Introductory Offer for No-Charge Support! Microsoft will provide you telephone support for installation and setup issues for Windows NT at no charge, via a toll line, for 30 days. The 30-day period begins the day of your first call. Call (206) 635-7018 between 6:00 a.m. and 6:00 p.m. Pacific time, Monday through Friday, except holidays. This offer is not available for Windows NT Advanced Server, and is applicable in the United States only. Offer expires December 31, 1993.

- Annual plans: Contact Microsoft Product Support Services Sales group at (800) 227-4679 for more information on Microsoft support options for Windows NT.

- Microsoft Text Telephone (TT/TDD) services are available for people who are deaf or hard of hearing. Using a special TT/TDD modem, dial (206) 635-4948, between 6:00 a.m. and 6:00 p.m. Pacific time, Monday through Friday.

The following sections provide more information about support and services provided by Microsoft and Microsoft partners for Windows NT.

Microsoft Technical Training

Supporting Microsoft Windows NT is a comprehensive five-day course for systems support professionals. Students gain the knowledge and skills needed to install, configure, and implement Windows NT on a workstation or in a workgroup. Topics covered through instructor-led modules include security, performance tuning, and troubleshooting for Windows NT, along with configuring Windows NT–based network components. Hands-on lab work and product demonstrations help to reinforce concepts. This course and courses on the Win32 application programming interface and Windows NT Advanced Server are available at Microsoft Training Partner locations throughout the United States. For more detailed information about Windows NT–related courses and pricing, please call Microsoft at (800) 227-4679.

The following two tables list the Microsoft Training Partners in the United States and Canada. For more information about classes related to Windows NT, contact the Microsoft Training Partner near you.

U.S. Training Partners

Training Partner name	City, state	Phone
Bull HN	Phoenix, AZ	602-862-5777
MIDAK International	Phoenix, AZ	602-577-2661
Micro Professional Training	Scottsdale, AZ	602-945-0992
Training Solutions, Inc.	Tempe, AZ	602-431-1100
MIDAK International	Tucson, AZ	602-577-2661
Infotec Development	Camarillo, CA	800-282-7990
American Digital	Costa Mesa, CA	714-433-1300
General Technology	Costa Mesa, CA	714-646-5519
Data Wiz International	Foster City, CA	415-571-1300
Quickstart Technologies, Inc.	Huntington Beach, CA	714-894-1448
California Community Colleges	Irvine, CA	714-559-9300
Digital Equipment Corporation	Los Angeles, CA	800-332-5656
Hi-Tech Resources, Inc.	Los Angeles, CA	800-882-6420
Quickstart Technologies, Inc.	Los Angeles, CA	714-894-1448
TechData Corp	Los Angeles, CA	800-553-7951
Vortex	Los Angeles, CA	310-826-5055
ContractEd Computer Training	Los Angeles, CA	310-827-0303
Accelerated Computer Training	Los Angeles , CA	213-388-2942
Innovative Solutions, Inc.	Sacramento, CA	916-928-1700
Netbase Computing, Inc.	San Francisco, CA	310-214-8181
Kennedy and Associates	San Diego, CA	619-483-1692
Clarity Technologies	San Francisco, CA	415-394-7373
Dublin Group, Inc.	San Francisco, CA	415-227-4777
PC Etcetera, Inc.	San Francisco, CA	415-291-0325
Wordlink, Inc.	San Francisco, CA	415-392-5465
Clarity Technologies	San Jose, CA	408-453-6300
TechData Corp	San Mateo, CA	800-553-7951
Infotec Development	Santa Ana, CA	800-282-7990
New Horizons Computer Learning Center, Inc.	Santa Ana, CA	714-556-1220
Digital Equipment Corporation	Santa Clara, CA	800-332-5656
Infotec Development	Santa Clara, CA	800-282-7990
Technology Transfer Institute	Santa Monica, CA	310-394-8305
Netbase Computing, Inc.	Torrance, CA	310-214-8181

Training Partner name (continued)	City, state (continued)	Phone (continued)
The Tompkins Group	Vista, CA	619-941-7294
Semiotix, Inc.	Aurora, CO	303-743-1400
Digital Equipment Corporation	Colorado Springs, CO	800-332-5656
Digital Equipment Corporation	Denver, CO	800-332-5656
SofTeach	Denver, CO	303-759-1127
Linc Systems	Bloomfield, CT	203-286-9060
Aetna	Hartford, CT	MSU CAP
Yale University	New Haven, CT	203-432-6600
Desai Consulting	West Hartford, CT	203-233-8050
CGI Systems, Inc.	Washington, DC	800-969-1980
Digital Equipment Corporation	Washington, DC	800-332-5656
JWP Information Services	Washington, DC	202-429-1922
TechData Corp	Clearwater, FL	800-553-7951
Computer Savvy	Ft. Lauderdale, FL	305-486-0644
Network Education Centers, Inc.	Miami, FL	800-745-4380
TechData Corp	Miami, FL	800-553-7951
Network Education Centers, Inc.	Tampa, FL	800-745-4380
Technology Advantage	Alpharetta, GA	404-751-0978
Network Education Center	Atlanta, GA	813-2820380
Digital Equipment Corporation	Atlanta, GA	800-332-5656
Hi-Tech Resources, Inc.	Atlanta, GA	800-882-6420
Omni Training Centers	Atlanta, GA	404-395-0055
The Computer Group	Augusta, GA	803-798-3424
TechData Corp	Norcross, GA	800-553-7951
Century Systems	Des Moines, IA	515-223-3160
Valcom/Silver Creek Computers	Boise, ID	208-322-5770
Wordlink, Inc.	Champaign, IL	217-359-9378
Check POINT, Inc.	Chicago, IL	312-441-1220
LANmind	Chicago, IL	312-935-9900
PPI/Professional Training Center	Chicago, IL	312-332-3865
Wordlink, Inc.	Chicago, IL	708-397-4000
PPI/Professional Training Centers	Deerfield, IL	312-332-3865
DC Systems	Elmhurst, IL	708-834-2095
PPI/Professional Training Center	Hinsdale, IL	312-332-3865

Training Partner name *(continued)*	City, state *(continued)*	Phone *(continued)*
Productivity Point International	Hinsdale, IL	708-920-0980
Timothy McBreen	Naperville, IL	619-941-7294
Applied Computer Services, Inc.	Orlando Park, IL	708-614-4900
PPI/Professional Training Centers	Rolling Meadows, IL	312-332-3865
Greenbriar & Russel	Schaumburg, IL	708-706-4000
Wordlink, Inc.	Schaumburg, IL	708-397-4000
SEA Group	Springfield, IL	217-523-1717
TechData Corp	Woodale, IL	800-553-7951
Lead Associates	Carmel, IN	317-848-6370
The Future Now	Indianapolis, IN	800-842-3693
PPI/ Micro Advantage	Indianapolis, IN	317-573-2320
PPI/ByteWrite	Olathe, KS	913-829-7300
Digital Equipment Corporation	Boston, MA	800-332-5656
Hi-Tech Resources, Inc.	Boston, MA	800-882-6420
JWP Information Services	Boston, MA	202-429-1922
PPI/Computer Tutor	Boston, MA	617-964-5858
Digital Equipment Corporation	Stow, MA	800-332-5656
Boston University	Tyngsboro, MA	508-649-9731
Valinor	Westford, MA	603-430-9541
MWI Training Services	Hunt Valley, MD	410-185-6300
Hi-Tech Resources, Inc.	Rockville, MD	800-882-6420
PPI/Englehart Training Centers	Grand Rapids, MI	616-285-6898
Stratagem, Inc.	Southfield, MI	313-353-5671
Fourth Wave Technologies, Inc.	Troy, MI	313-362-2288
PPI/Professional Training Centers	Bloomington, MN	312-332-3865
Benchmark Network Systems	Minneapolis, MN	612-830-9920
PPI/Professional Training Center	Minneapolis, MN	612-341-0750
Connect Computer	Minneapolis, MN	612-944-0181
Bridge Data	Minnetonka, MN	612-933-3336
JWP Information Services	Plymouth, MN	612-557-7544
Danka	Kansas City, MO	816-221-2900
Empower Trainers and Consultants	Kansas City, MO	816-753-8885
Solutech	St. Charles, MO	314-947-9393
Wordlink, Inc.	St. Louis, MO	314-878-1422

Training Partner name *(continued)*	City, state *(continued)*	Phone *(continued)*
Cedalion Systems, Inc.	Charlotte, NC	800-277-4526
The Computer Group	Charlotte, NC	803-798-3424
The Computer Group	Greensboro, NC	803-798-3424
The Computer Group	Morrisville, NC	803-798-3424
Cedalion Systems, Inc.	Research Triangle Park, NC	800-277-4526
Valinor	Manchester, NH	603-668-1776
UCI Corporation	Port Smith, NH	603-430-9541
Landau and Associates	Baskin Ridge, NJ	908-766-5717
PPI/Micro Trek	Iselin, NJ	908-603-6278
CHUBB Advanced Training	Parsippany, NJ	201-682-4904
TechData Corp	Paulsboro, NJ	800-553-7951
Alpha Technologies	Piscataway, NJ	908-819-8811
Quickstart Technologies, Inc.	Albuquerque, NM	714-894-1448
CGI Systems, Inc.	New York, NY	800-969-1980
Digital Equipment Corporation	New York, NY	800-332-5656
Network Management, Inc.	New York, NY	212-797-3800
PPI/Micro Trek	New York, NY	212-398-6410
Buller, Owens & Associates	New York, NY	212-921-0774
Computer Applications Learning Center	New York, NY	212-765-8062
PC Etcetera, Inc.	New York, NY	212-736-9046
Logical Operations	Rochester, NY	716-482-7700
PPI/Micro Trek	Uniondale, NY	516-229-2725
Network Compatibility Group	Columbus, OH	614-436-2962
Blue Chip Computers	Dayton, OH	513-299-4594
Babbage-Simmel & Associates	Dublin (Columbus), OH	614-764-8777
TechData Corp	Twinsburg, OH	800-553-7951
Sequent Computer Systems	Beaverton, OR	503-578-4165
Pacific Dataware	Lake Oswego, OR	503-620-9858
CTR Business Systems, Inc.	Portland, OR	503-248-9918
TriLogic Corporation	Canonsburg, PA	412-745-0200
Information Technologists	Conshohocken, PA	215-832-1000
MicroAge of Exton	Exton, PA	215-524-6665
Professional Training Services, Inc.	King of Prussian, PA	215-337-8878
Computer Resources & Training	Philadelphia, PA	215-569-9100

Training Partner name *(continued)*	City, state *(continued)*	Phone *(continued)*
Micro Endeavors	Philadelphia, PA	215-524-6665
MicroAge of Exton	Philadelphia, PA	215-524-6665
Ziff Technologies	Wayne, PA	215-293-4630
PPI/Computer Consulting Group	Columbia, SC	803-782-2825
The Computer Group	Columbia, SC	803-798-3424
PPI/Computer Consulting Group	Greenville, SC	803-277-0123
The Computer Group	Greenville, SC	803-798-3424
The Computer Group	North Charleston, SC	803-798-3424
Computer Learning Center	Knoxville, TN	615-691-1515
The Future Now	Memphis, TN	317-846-5996
TechData Corp	Carillon, TX	800-553-7951
CompuCom Education Center	Dallas, TX	800-783-7894
Edutech	Dallas, TX	214-392-7733
AMRIS	Ft. Worth, TX	800-842-3693
Bridgeworks Integration, Inc.	Houston, TX	713-956-7200
BSG	Houston, TX	713-965-9000
Edutech	Houston, TX	713-827-1314
Netbase Computing	Houston, TX	310-214-8181
Electronic Data Systems	Plano, TX	214-503-5574
Spectrum Integrated Services	Richardson, TX	214-231-6173
Intelogic Trace	San Antonio, TX	210-593-2603
PPI/Squier Computer Services, Inc.	San Antonio, TX	210-342-6500
Erudite Software and Consulting	Orem, UT	801-224-5400
Gestalt Systems	Herndon, VA	703-471-6842
Network Management, Inc.	Rosslyn, VA	703-385-4774
Clarity, Inc	Bellevue, WA	206-828-7498
Synerlogic, Inc.	Bellevue, WA	206-641-4029
SQLSoft	Kirkland, WA	206-822-1287
Synaptix	Seattle, WA	206-527-2468
Fox Valley Technical College	Appleton, WI	414-735-2485
Allied Computer Group	Milwaukee, WI	414-223-1607

Canadian Training Partners

Training Partner name	City, province	Phone
Learning Technologies of Canada	Burlington, ON	(800) 668-0316
Crowntek Learning Centre	Calgary, AB	(416) 507-5313
Digital Equipment Corporation	Calgary, AB	(800) 465-2226
Northwest Digital	Calgary, AB	(204) 957-7795
Informatique Mulihexa	Chicoutimi, PC	(418) 690-0270
PBSC Computer Training	Edmonton, AB	(403) 423-3710
Object Art	London, ON	(519) 663-9697
EDS Canada	Ottawa, ON	(613) 786-7059
Learnserve	Ottawa, ON	(613) 825-1875
Netvision	Ottawa, ON	(613) 739-8030
Remuera Corporation	Ottawa, ON	(613) 235-2321
Institute of Computer Studies	Toronto, ON	(416) 499-9022
Learnix Limited	Toronto, ON	(613) 828-8649
Santronic Sales	Vancouver, BC	(604) 294-9877

TechNet

Microsoft TechNet is the single comprehensive source of technical information for implementing and supporting Microsoft-based solutions. This worldwide information service is available to individuals on an annual subscription basis ($295 per user, $40 for each additional licensee) and is delivered through several advanced delivery mechanisms, including CD-ROM technology and a dedicated CompuServe forum.

Microsoft TechNet is designed for those who support or educate end-users, administer networks or databases, create automated solutions, and recommend or evaluate information technology solutions. Microsoft TechNet makes a wealth of in-depth technical information easily accessible so that subscribers can get fast, accurate answers directly and immediately from a single source. It's a great tool for in-house use by MIS and HELP Desks supporting multiple products in today's complex, integrated software environments as well as for companies providing support and integration services to their customers.

Details on each of the membership benefits are as follows:

The Microsoft TechNet CD-ROM (Monthly)

The Microsoft TechNet CD is packed with valuable and accessible technical information, and monthly editions are cumulative, adding fresh information. This worldwide CD includes:

- The Microsoft KnowledgeBase, which gives you answers to support questions by providing you easy access to the same extensive library of technical support information used by Microsoft Product Support Specialists every day. No need to call, no need to wait, which saves you time and money. There are country-specific KnowledgeBases with the July CD, including the US and French versions, with many more to come in future months.

- Resource Kits packed with technical references, troubleshooting information, utilities, and accessories to aid in installing and supporting Microsoft products. Would you like to know the optimal configuration for your network? The Resource Kits provide you with the answer.

- Technical information that tells you how you to get the most use out of products. Microsoft products are designed to be easy to use and very powerful; however, sometimes this "how to" information is hard to find. The TechNet CD gives you the "tips and tricks" you need to increase your productivity.

- Migration information that helps you move people in an organization from one product to another or from one environment to another. What are the issues involved in migrating from a mainframe based e-mail system to one that is LAN based? TechNet helps you.

- Product facts and features to assist you in evaluating Microsoft products. You can compare versions of products to better understand the advantages of upgrading.

- Educational materials such as tutorials, training guides and training session slides with notes. Windows NT training materials are included.

- Customer solution profiles that detail how your colleagues solve real information technology problems. See how the Orlando Health Care Group developed a central database repository for access by 1800 PCs using a client-server architecture. Or, read how the insurance and legal industries are creating state-of-the-art solutions.

- Strategic information to keep you up to date on the direction Microsoft and its products are taking now and in the future. If you wonder about the overall direction that Microsoft is taking, or need more information on such topics as multimedia, ODBC, MAPI, or WOSA, TechNet brings you the information. Press releases are included.

- Conference session notes from key Microsoft conferences. As part of our effort to provide timely up-to-date information, the TechNet CD delivers technical information not found in a book or a magazine, but rather, straight from the technical professionals themselves. This allows you to stay one step ahead.

- The Software Library, which gives you drivers, utilities, macros and patches.

- The Microsoft Services Directory, a "one stop shop" technical services directory for those who develop, implement and support Microsoft-based solutions in the United States. This directory provides you with information on exactly where you need to go (or what you need to do) to get the following:

  - Training and certification on Microsoft products

  - Product support

  - Ongoing technical information

  - Third-party programs

  - Consulting services

  - Microsoft Press books

Other technical information on the CD includes:

- Using OLE and Word

- Ultimate Printer Manual

- Windows 3.1 and Networks

- Microsoft Excel Functions

- Word Setup and Troubleshooting Guide

- Works Troubleshooting Guide

- Windows Hyper Guide

The simple and easy-to-use interface for the Microsoft TechNet CD-ROM allows you to gain access to relevant information quickly:

- Instant look-up. A powerful, full-text Boolean search engine developed by Microsoft lets you look up the technical information that you need quickly and effortlessly. Simply type in a word or phrase on the information you want. You decide how specific or general you want the information to be, and the search engine will do the rest.

- Intuitive interface. The wealth of information contained on your Microsoft TechNet CD is easy to read, annotate, search, and browse because it's based on the Microsoft Multimedia Viewer. The intuitive Microsoft Windows-based interface allows you to view formatted text and graphics and print topics. A source index lists the CD contents hierarchically by information type, making it easy for you to browse documents on the CD.

- One source of information. No longer will you need to read through piles of papers, search through endless help files, and then cross-reference those same topics. Instead, the Microsoft TechNet CD gathers all the information in one place.

Dedicated Microsoft TechNet CompuServe Forum

The Microsoft TechNet forum on CompuServe (**go technet**) gives you up-to-the-minute news flashes, online connections to the Microsoft TechNet community, and the ability to download the latest technical information from Microsoft. You can also exchange information with other experts and peers across the country and around the world.

Membership in Microsoft

TechNet includes WinCIM, an easy-to-use Microsoft Windows-based front-end application to access CompuServe forums. This greatly simplifies the logon, viewing, and download process.

CD-ROM Disc Drive Offer

A CD-ROM disc drive offer is included in the Welcome Kit of every TechNet membership. The offer is sponsored by CD Technology, and includes the CD Porta-Drive, Model T3401 series.

Specifications

Drive mechanism:	Toshiba XM-3401
System interface:	SCSIe-2/SCSI
Capacity:	683MB
Average access time:	200 milliseconds
Memory buffer:	256K Cache
Reliability:	50,000 hours MTBF
Compatibility:	IBM PC/XT/AT/386/486, PS/2
Transfer rate:	330 K

How to Order TechNet

Microsoft TechNet is priced at cost-of-goods and is an exceptional value, especially when compared to competing products. The fee for annual membership in Microsoft TechNet is $295 (US), plus tax. We're so sure this is a support professional's panacea, that we're offering a 90-day, money-back guarantee. To enroll, using your credit card, call 1-800-344-2121 seven days a week, 24 hours a day.

For international orders, call (206)936-8661 for local contact information.

Microsoft Developer Network

The Microsoft Developer Network is a club for all developers who write applications for the Microsoft Windows operating system or who use Microsoft tools for development purposes. The Microsoft Developer Network has two main goals: to write and publish information on programming for Windows, and to establish two-way communication with the development community. By joining the Microsoft Developer Network, you will become a registered developer with Microsoft and receive technical and strategic information through three channels: the Microsoft Developer Network CD, the Microsoft Developer Network News, and the Microsoft Developer Network Forum on CompuServe.

The Developer Network CD

The Microsoft Developer Network CD is a comprehensive source of information for developers of Windows-based applications. The CD provides new, in-depth articles on programming created in response to developers' inquiries.

To create the content for the Developer Network CD, we assembled a team of programmers, each experienced in specific areas of Windows (GDI, User, Kernel, Win32, multimedia, and so on), and asked them to document the architecture of Windows, addressing known areas of complexity.

The Developer Network CD uses a powerful, Windows-based search engine that lets you search the contents of the entire CD by source, by subject, or by keyword. You can create precise queries, print topics, and import source code into your application.

The Newspaper

The Microsoft Developer Network News is a quarterly newspaper with helpful, timely information for all programmers. The newspaper provides the latest news on Microsoft development tools, operating systems, and Windows functions, as well as programming tips, strategic information, and key Microsoft phone numbers.

The Forum

The Microsoft Developer Network posts all new technical articles and sample code on CompuServe, in the Microsoft Developer Network Forum. You can access this area by typing GO MSDNLIB at the CompuServe ! prompt. You can communicate with the Microsoft Developer Network through forum messages and electronic mail.

Enrollment Information

For more information, call the Microsoft Developer Services Team at
(800) 227-4679, extension 11771, between 6:30 a.m. and 5:30 p.m. Pacific time.
Outside the U.S., contact your Microsoft subsidiary or call (206) 936-8661 for
local contact information.

Mail: Microsoft Developer Network
        One Microsoft Way
        Redmond, WA 98052-6399

Fax: (206) 936-7329, Attn: Developer Network

Internet: devnetwk@Microsoft.com

Microsoft Solution Providers

A key group of independent vendors have a business relationship with Microsoft
to provide technical services centered around Microsoft products. Known as
Microsoft Solution Providers, these companies collectively offer a wide variety
of technical skills and products and services, such as product support and
installation services, application development, vertical industry applications,
integration services, project management, and consulting and training. To locate a
Microsoft Solution Provider with the expertise to meet your needs, call Microsoft
at (800) 227-4679.

Microsoft Certified Professional Program

This program is designed for support coordinators, system engineers, consultants,
trainers, network administrators, or anyone who needs to demonstrate technical
expertise and support Microsoft products. Upon successful completion of a
series of standardized tests, you'll be recognized as a product expert and receive
a Product Certification certificate, a camera-ready logo for your business, a
membership card, and more. To get information about the program and how to
prepare and sign up for exams, call Microsoft at (800) 227-4679. Or see MCP.ZIP
from Section 1 of the "MS Windows Advanced Users" forum on CompuServe (**go
winadv**).

Obtain recognition for your expertise on the Microsoft Windows NT operating
system by becoming a Microsoft Certified Professional (MCP). The MCP
Program supplies you with the guidelines to efficiently support your customers
or your company's personnel on Microsoft products.

The Microsoft Certified Professional (MCP) Program certifies your ability to implement and support Microsoft products by passing a series of standardized exams. If you are a support coordinator, systems engineer, consultant, trainer, network administrator, or anyone else who must gain and display technical expertise concerning Microsoft Windows NT, you owe it to yourself and your company to become Microsoft Windows NT Support Certified. As an MCP, you will be recognized as a **product expert** and as a source for the latest information about Microsoft Windows NT.

To become Microsoft Windows NT version 3.1 Support Certified, you must register for and pass a closed-book exam that tests expertise and experience on Microsoft Windows NT.

- Review the back of this page, which contains information on how to prepare for the exam and includes detailed exam topics.
- Prepare for and pass the Microsoft Windows NT version 3.1 Installation and Support exam.

You can register for the exam by calling Drake Training and Technologies at (800) 755-EXAM (3926). Each exam costs $100 U.S. You may take the exam at a Drake Training and Technologies site near you. When you call Drake to register, be sure to ask about test sites in your area.

Upon successful completion of the exam(s), you will receive an MCP Program certificate, membership card, camera-ready logo for advertising purposes, access to up-to-date information from Microsoft and industry experts, a CompuServe® Intro Kit, an invitation to be listed in the MCP Directory, discounts for the Technical Information Network, and invitations to technical conferences and forums.

Additional Benefits

Solutions Channels participants with Microsoft Certified Professionals on staff receive credits toward purchasing products and training videos, and listing in the Solutions Channels Directory. Consulting Channels participants receive referrals, Microsoft Developer Network discounts, plus more. VAR/Systems Integrator Channels participants may be authorized to resell Microsoft LAN Manager, SQL Server, and Microsoft Mail with the appropriate MCPs on staff. Training Channels participants may qualify their company to offer Microsoft University courses.

Call Microsoft at (800) 227-4679 for a complete copy of the Microsoft Certified Professional Program brochure or the Microsoft Certified Professional Corporate Backgrounder. The brochure contains detailed information on the current certifications, including Microsoft Windows NT Support, Microsoft Windows, Microsoft Windows for Workgroups, Microsoft LAN Manager, SQL Server, Microsoft Mail, Microsoft Excel for Windows and Macintosh, Microsoft Project for Windows and Macintosh, and Microsoft Word for Windows and Macintosh. The Microsoft Certified Professional Corporate Backgrounder explains how certification and periodic assessment of an individual's technical knowledge is essential to ensuring quality service and effective career development. You can obtain the latest copy of the Microsoft Certified Professional brochure electronically as MCP.ZIP from Section 1 of the "MS Windows Advanced Users" Forum on CompuServe (**go winadv**).

How to Prepare for the Installation and Support Exam

This exam is designed to test your expertise on Microsoft Windows NT version 3.1. Results have shown that people who prepare for the exams typically attain higher scores. To prepare for the Microsoft Windows NT version 3.1 Installation and Support exam, we recommend that you do the following:

- Take the five-day Microsoft University course, Supporting Microsoft Windows NT, or equivalent course offered by Training Partners. (Mention code MCP93 when you call to a Microsoft University Training Partner in your area register.)

- Use Microsoft Windows NT version 3.1. Be sure to read the following documentation contained in the Microsoft Windows NT beta product:

  Microsoft Windows NT System Guide

  Microsoft Windows NT Release Notes

- Read about Microsoft Windows NT. Resources include *Inside Windows NT* by Helen Custer (Microsoft Press) ISBN 1-55615-481-X.

Exam Topics

Architecture

- Flat mode memory
- Asymmetric and symmetric multiprocessing

The Role of the Subsystems

- Subsystems available in Windows NT
- Use of threads in the different subsystems

Installation

- Minimum hardware configuration for installation of Windows NT in an Intel platform
- Disk partitioning and formatting for dual booting of MS-DOS and/or OS/2
- Workgroup and Domain during installation
- Emergency disk

Configuration

- CONFIGNT and AUTOEXECNT
- Changing the system display driver
- Changing the system mouse device
- Installing and removing Windows NT components
- Deleting user profiles

Boot Sequence

- Components of the multiple-boot system
- Power on and the multiple-boot menu
- Boot files on an Intel computer and a MIPS computer

Configuration of Networking

- Installing and configuring a network card and network software component using the Control Panel

Security

- Trusted domains
- Access Control Entry (ACE) purpose and functionality
- Access mask
- Security context

Use of the User Admin tool

- Default groups
- Main properties of a user
- Modifying more than one user at a time
- Major account policies
- Changing the account policies and user rights policies

NTFS

- NTFS, HPFS, and FAT in relationship to file security
- Limitations of long names
- Volume striping

Fault Tolerance

- Value of UPS on a system
- Disk duplexing

Use of the Program Manager

- Logging on to Windows NT
- Active components after the user logs off
- Individual and common program groups
- Startup group properties
- Starting a program using the Program Manager

Registry

- Location of boot sequence information and security database
- Automatically loading the MS-DOS Subsystem at bootup
- Saving a copy of the registry tree to disk
- Changing permissions on registry objects
- Hive
- Definition of registry and viewing from a remote computer

Use of the File Manager

- Shared directory properties
- Closing shared files
- Sharing security available on NTFS volumes
- Setting the file and directory permissions
- Establishing file and directory auditing

Backup

- Setting tape options
- Establishing full log options
- Restoring a file from a tape
- Definition of tape catalog and tape sets
- Partial and rotating tape backup schemes

Microsoft Consulting Services

Microsoft Consulting Services (MCS) consultants are system architects with experience and expertise in Microsoft technology, methodologies, and tools, chartered to help organizations capitalize on the benefits of the most powerful platform for client-server computing—the Microsoft Windows NT operating system. MCS consultants focus on transferring knowledge and skills to corporations, government organizations, and third-party Microsoft Solution Providers worldwide. MCS, in conjunction with third-party solution providers, offer organizations a number of services customized to their unique information technology environment including planning, design, development, integration, and implementation. For more information about Microsoft Consulting Services, please call (800) 922-9446.

For more information about Microsoft Consulting Services, please contact an MCS office near you.

In the United States:		Canada (416) 568-0434
Central Region	(708) 495-5550	Australia(61) (2) 870-2200
Northeast Region	(617) 487-6500	France (33) (1) 6986-4480
South Region	(214) 458-1739	Germany(49) (89) 3176-0
West Region	(206) 635-1980	Italy (39) (2) 210-7361
		United Kingdom (44) (734) 270-001

Free Focus on Microsoft Windows Newsletter

This newsletter offers the latest information about Microsoft Windows NT, Windows NT Advanced Server, other members of the Windows family of operating systems, and applications for Windows. Included are tips and tricks, answers to common questions, information on new products and services, and strategies for optimizing Windows NT and making the most of Windows-based applications. For your free subscription, please complete and return the enclosed registration card.

Other Microsoft Press Books

Choose from a diverse range of timely books on both technical and nontechnical topics for users of Microsoft Windows NT at every level. Titles include *Inside Windows NT*, *Windows NT Answer Book*, *Running Windows NT*, and the *Microsoft Win32 Programmer's Guide and Reference*. Microsoft Press books are available wherever computer books are sold or direct from Microsoft Press at (800) MSPRESS, between 8:00 a.m. and 5:00 p.m. Central time. In Alaska and Hawaii, call (615) 793-5090.

Windows NT Driver Library

This service is updated regularly to provide the most current Windows NT–compatible device drivers for printers, displays, networks, and other devices not included in the retail package for Windows NT. All drivers are tested by Microsoft for compatibility with the Windows NT operating system. The Windows NT Driver Library is distributed through the Microsoft Download Service (MSDL) at (206) 936-MSDL, available seven days a week, 24 hours a day, including holidays; the library is also available via anonymous login over the Internet file transfer protocol (FTP) archive host, **gowinnt.microsoft.com** (please use your full email name as the password) and through CompuServe and GEnie.

A P P E N D I X B

Remote Access Server Administration

This appendix includes portions from the *Microsoft Windows NT Advanced Server Remote Access Server Administrator's Guide.* Additional information from the *Administrator's Guide* is available in Appendix B of the *Windows NT System Guide.*

Features

Microsoft Windows NT Advanced Server Remote Access Service offers the following features:

- Transparent access to the network for telecommuters, mobile workers, and remote system administrators, including:
    - Support for named pipes, Remote Procedure Call (RPC), and the LAN Manager application programming interface (API).
    - Client access to resources on application servers such as SQL Server, SNA Server for Windows NT, and Lotus Notes®.
- Compatibility with workstations and servers running previous versions of the Remote Access Service.
- Support for public telephone, X.25, and Integrated Services Digital Network (ISDN) wide-area networks.
- Support for data compression and error control on modems.
- Software compression.
- Security:
    - Integration with Windows NT Advanced Server security
    - Domain-based and trusted domain-based security
    - Encrypted authentication at connect time
    - Support for third-party security hosts that authenticate users
    - Callback for either added security or user convenience
    - Central administration of servers and users
- Up to 64 simultaneous connections per Windows NT Advanced Server (or one connection for Windows NT).
- Support for over 100 modems. (See Appendix E, "Hardware Compatibility List.")
- Local network protocol independence, allowing a Remote Access client to log on to any server on any network to which the Remote Access server is connected, regardless of the target server's network protocol, as long as the Remote Access server has the same NetBIOS protocol as the target server.

Choosing and Configuring Modems

To make sure that your modems work with the Remote Access Service, select them from the list of supported modems in the Microsoft Windows NT Advanced Server Hardware Compatibility List. Microsoft has tested and verified these modems with the Remote Access Service.

Supported Modems

Modems that Remote Access supports do not necessarily work in all modes with other modems in the list. For example, the Hayes® V-Series 9600 modem connects at 9600 bits per second (bps) only with another Hayes V-Series 9600 modem. So if you install this modem on a Remote Access server, make sure that Remote Access clients also have Hayes V-Series 9600 modems. Otherwise, connections will probably be made at 2400 bps.

Note To ensure compatibility, have clients get the same kind of modems as the server's modem. Getting the same kind is less critical if you choose modems that conform to industry standards. But still it is safer to choose the same model for both clients and server.

▶ **To troubleshoot a supported modem**

If you are using one of the modems listed when you set up Remote Access and cannot connect, follow these steps:

1. Make sure your cabling is correct (see "Cabling," later in this appendix).

2. If you still cannot connect, check the modem's documentation to verify that the modem has been correctly installed.

3. If it has, then use a terminal emulator program, such as Windows NT Terminal, to see if you can issue commands to the modem.

4. If the modem still does not work with the Remote Access Service, call Microsoft Product Support Services (PSS) for assistance.

Unsupported Modems

Modems other than those supported by Microsoft may also work with the Remote Access Service, even though they have not yet been tested with the software. If you choose unsupported modems, for best results, make sure they conform to the following industry standards established by the International Consultative Committee for Telephone and Telegraph (CCITT).

Table B.1   Industry Standards for Modems

Speed in bps	CCITT standard
1200	V.22 or Bell 212A
2400	V.22bis
9600	V.32
14,400	V.32bis

For details about industry standard protocols, see the glossary in online Help.

When configuring an unsupported modem for the Remote Access Service, you will have to select from the list of supported modems a modem that matches yours as closely as possible. For best results, make your choice by first comparing entries in the MODEM.INF file with commands for your modem. You can find these commands in your modem's documentation.

▶ **To configure an unsupported modem**

1. In the Windows NT Advanced Server Control Panel, double-click the Network icon.

2. In the Installed Network Software box on the Network Settings screen, select Remote Access Service.

3. Click Configure.

4. On the Remote Access Setup screen select the port you want to configure for the unsupported modem, and click Configure.

5. From the list of modems, select the modem that is as similar to your modem as possible.

6. Click OK, and then click Continue.

7. On the Network Settings screen, click OK.

8. If you configure a new port for the unsupported modem, restart your computer.

   If you reconfigure a port already in use, you don't need to restart your computer, but you do need to restart the Remote Access Service.

If you have trouble connecting through an unsupported modem, test the modem's compatibility.

▶ **To test a modem's compatibility**

1. Check the modem's documentation to make sure you have installed and configured the modem correctly.

2. Make sure that your modem is connected to a serial communication (COM) port on your computer and that your software is set for the same port.

3. Turn on your modem.

4. Check to see if the modem works properly with Windows NT Terminal. For instructions, see the following procedure.

   If the test works, you can assume the modem is not malfunctioning.

5. If the modem still does not work after you have verified that it works with Windows NT Terminal, contact your modem's manufacturer and request a modem command file compatible with the Remote Access Service MODEM.INF file.

   For information about creating a correct modem command file, see "Adding a New Modem to MODEM.INF," later in this appendix.

▶ **To test a modem with Windows NT Terminal**

1. From the Accessories group, double-click the Terminal icon.

2. From the Terminal screen, select Settings.

3. From the Settings menu, choose Communications.

4. In the Communications dialog box, select the bps at which your modem sends and receives data, and select the COM port your modem is connected to. Click OK.

5. On the Terminal screen, type **at** and press ENTER.

   Your modem should return OK, which is echoed on the screen. Some modems return 0, depending on their result code settings.

6. If your modem won't work through Terminal, call the modem's manufacturer.

Compatibility and Speed

Modems from different manufacturers, and even different models from the same manufacturer, may not be completely compatible in all settings and circumstances. Even modems that claim to follow the Hayes AT command set may not be able to communicate with other Hayes-compatible modems under every circumstance.

High-speed modems may perform their own error-correction and data compression, which you can take advantage of by setting modem features during setup on a server or through the Phone Book on a client.

Compatibility problems increase when you begin to consider high-speed modems of 9600 bps or above because some modems achieve high speeds in different ways. Even modems that follow the same standards for compression and error correction may be unable to communicate with each other at 9600 bps and therefore may fall back to 2400 bps. So, if you buy 9600-bps modems from different manufacturers to benefit from high data-exchange rates, you may be disappointed.

If you plan to connect more than one type of modem to a server, you can assign a different telephone number to each modem. That way, users can choose exactly which modem to connect to. The disadvantage is that users may have to dial several different modems before finding one that is not in use.

Note For rates of 12,000 bps and higher, modem manufacturers often require that computer-to-modem communication occur at 19,200 bps. For this reason, the Remote Access software assumes that modems able to connect at 12,000 or 14,400 bps can function at the computer-to-modem speeds of 19,200 bps or faster. Virtually all high-speed modems can do so.

Direct Serial Connections

You can select a NULL modem to establish a direct serial connection between two computers. Although a direct serial connection eliminates the need for a network adapter card, it is a slow link, and password authentication is still required. A NULL modem configuration works best only for computers physically near each other.

▶ **To configure your system for a direct serial connection**

- Select a NULL modem from the list of modems during setup when configuring the COM ports for a serial connection. A null modem must be configured on both the client and the server.

Important For information about cabling required for NULL modems, see "Cabling," later in this appendix.

Modem-Pooling Equipment

▶ **To configure a server to work with modem-pooling equipment**

1. Configure the equipment to behave like one of the modem types listed in the Setup program.

   In other words, the modem-pooling equipment must generate and accept command strings as if it were a modem of the chosen type. The switching equipment must also have the same RS-232 signal behavior as the specified modem.

2. Connect COM ports to this equipment, and specify the modem type in the Remote Access Setup program.

   Microsoft suggests that the equipment be configured as a Hayes-compatible modem, a widely known standard.

Remote Access Security Features

Domain-based security
> Remote Access servers participating in the same domain have identical copies of the user account database, ensuring easy administration and identical security restrictions for all access points to the network.

Remote Access permission
> To connect to the network through Remote Access, a user must have a valid Windows NT Advanced Server user account that has been given Remote Access permission. You can grant or revoke Remote Access permissions as needed from the Remote Access Administrator's utility.

Remote Access authentication
> Remote users must be authenticated by a Remote Access server before they can access or generate traffic on the network. This authentication is a separate step from logging on to Windows NT Advanced Server. User passwords and the authentication procedure are encrypted when transmitted over the phone lines.

Callback security
> You can configure individual user accounts so that the Remote Access server calls the user back at a preset number before allowing access to the network.

Support for security hosts
> You can add another level of security to your Remote Access configuration by connecting an intermediary security host between remote clients and the server. For details, see "Support for Security Hosts and Switches" in Appendix B of the *Windows NT System Guide*.

Auditing
> The Remote Access Service generates audit trails of remote connections. With this feature, you can audit all Remote Access activity. For more information about audits, see "Maintenance" and "Troubleshooting," later in this appendix.

Disconnecting users
> Through the Administrator's utility, you can disconnect users without shutting down the Remote Access Service or interrupting authorized users.

Restricted network access
> To restrict access to specific network resources, you can make all or specified networks unavailable to remote clients.

Security for Windows NT Advanced Server and Remote Access

This section describes restricting remote users' access to the network and to the Remote Access server.

Restricting Access to the Network

Using the Remote Access Setup program, you can restrict remote users to resources on the Remote Access server and allow remote users to see and access the network.

Using the Windows NT Advanced Server Network Control Panel, you can restrict remote users to specific parts of the network.

Restricting Users to the Dial-in Server

Although the Remote Access server may be connected to a network, you can restrict remote users to the server they dial in to, making the network unavailable to them (see Figure B.1).

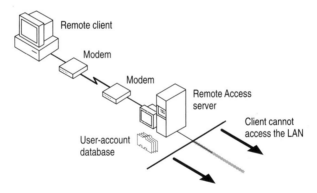

Figure B.1   Remote Users Restricted to the Dial-in Server

Allowing Users to Access the Network

You can let remote users see and access all or part of the network by enabling or disabling sets of protocols and adapters called *bindings*. Figure B.2 shows a configuration with two bindings that allow remote users to see and access all connections in the Remote Access gateway:

- TCP/IP and Adapter 1
- NetBEUI and Adapter 2

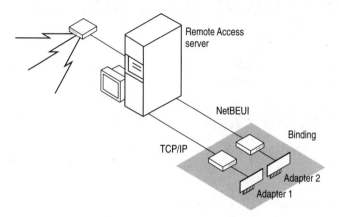

Figure B.2   Remote Users Allowed Access to the Network

Restricting Users to a Part of the Network

Through the Windows NT Advanced Server's Network Control Panel, you can disable some of the bindings, making specific paths unavailable to remote users. This feature lets you limit remote users' access to only the server(s) they need.

For information about disabling bindings, see the *Microsoft Windows NT Advanced Server System Guide*.

How Security Works at Connection Time

The following list shows how a remote user accesses resources on the network:

1. Through the Remote Access Phone Book, a client dials a Remote Access server.
2. The server sends a challenge to the client.
3. The client sends an encrypted response to the server.
4. The server checks the response against the user database.
5. If the account is valid, the server checks for Remote Access permission.
6. If Remote Access permission has been granted, the server connects the client.

   If callback is enabled, the server calls the client back and repeats steps 2–5.

Configuring Callback

When a user connects to a server from a client configured for callback, the server calls the user either at a preset number or at a number supplied by the user at connection time. You can configure each user's callback privilege when you grant them Remote Access permission. (For information about granting permission, see "Setting Up the Remote Access Service" in Appendix B of the *Windows NT System Guide* and online Help for the Administrator's utility.)

In the Administrator's utility, the Remote Access Permissions dialog box contains three callback options:

- Preset To
- Set by Caller
- No Callback (the default)

Choose one of these options to set up a user's callback privilege. The default is No Callback.

Note   Until the user has been authenticated and called back (if Callback is set), no data from the remote client or the Remote Access server is transferred.

▶ **To change a user's callback option**

1. Start the Remote Access Administrator's utility.
2. From the Users menu, choose Permissions.
3. Select a user.
4. Assign a different callback option.

Preset To

Select Preset To for maximum security, and type the number of the phone to which the user's modem is connected. When the user's call reaches the Remote Access server, the server takes the following steps:

1. It determines whether the user name and password are correct.
2. If they are, the server responds with a message announcing that the user will be called back.
3. It disconnects and calls the user back at the preset number.

Set this option for stationary remote computers, such as those in home offices.

Set By Caller

This option is for the convenience of a remote user who calls from various places. It is not a security feature. Select Set By Caller for clients that call from various locations and different phone numbers. When the user's call reaches the Remote Access server, the following steps occur:

1. The server first determines if the user name and password are correct.
2. If they are, the Callback dialog box appears on the user's computer.
3. The user types the current callback number in the dialog box and waits for the server to return the call.

Set this option to minimize telephone charges for anyone calling in from various locations, such as field representatives.

No Callback

If the user account has not been configured for callback, the Remote Access Service establishes a connection as soon as the user's name and password is authenticated.

Network Access Permission

After passing Remote Access authentication and connecting to the LAN, users can access resources on the application server for which they have permission. For example, they can:

- Do anything on the network for which they have sufficient privilege.
- Use any network resource for which they have permission such as:
  - Use the File Manager to access files on the LAN server.
  - Access client-server applications such as electronic mail, SQL Server, and so on.

Remote users are also subject to the Windows NT Advanced Server security, just as they are at the office. In other words, they cannot do anything for which they lack sufficient privilege, nor can they access resources for which they do not have permission.

Note Remote Access authentication does not negate security restrictions on the file or application server.

Maintenance

Once you have installed the Remote Access Service, routine maintenance consists of the following tasks:

- Monitoring servers and users systematically.
- Reviewing the Windows NT Advanced Server event viewer regularly to see whether network security is intact. (See "Troubleshooting" and "Audits" later in this chapter. For complete information about using the Event Viewer, see the *Microsoft Windows NT Advanced Server System Guide*.)

By conveying real-time information about users, ports, modems, and data transmissions, the Remote Access Administrator's utility simplifies monitoring servers and users and gives valuable clues to assist in troubleshooting. By having the utility running continuously, you can track activity on your Remote Access servers and respond promptly to problems with user accounts and hardware.

With the Remote Access Administrator's utility, you can look at a Remote Access Service domain in two ways:

- The Remote Access servers in a domain: This view of the domain lets you manage multiple Remote Access servers from a central location.
- All the users who are connected to those servers: This view lets you monitor user activity on all Remote Access servers in the domain.

Each time you start the utility, the default view is servers, and the Remote Access server(s) screen lists all the servers in the logon domain. You can set focus on a different domain, or you can focus on a single server in the current domain.

Troubleshooting

The Administrator's utility provides real-time information about active users and current connections and is therefore often the place to begin troubleshooting problems.

For example:

- You may notice on the Remote Access server(s) screen that fewer than the expected number of ports are consistently in use on a server, suggesting that one or more of them may not be operating properly.
- If users cannot make a connection, you can ask them to attempt to reconnect while you monitor their efforts in the Port Status dialog box.

When real-time data is insufficient to solve a problem, you can refer to the audit and error messages generated by Remote Access. The Windows NT Advanced Server Event Viewer records all the audits and error messages for Remote Access.

Events are classified into three main categories:

Event	Description
Audit	Normal behavior recorded for administration, for example, information about a connected client — user name, connection time, and current status.
Warning	An irregular or unexpected condition that doesn't affect the system's functionality.
Error	Something wrong that happens; for example, a major function fails or a network error occurs.

Audits are further divided into two categories:

Category of Audit	Example
Success audit	Client connects and disconnects normally.
Failure audit	Server disconnects a client that's been inactive too long, or a client tries to connect with the wrong password.

Audits

The Windows NT Advanced Server Event Viewer records activity on each Remote Access server. Because the audits recorded in the log are the best evidence of possible attempts to violate network security, be sure to review them regularly. For information about using the Event Viewer and the Event Viewer, see the *Microsoft Windows NT Advanced Server System Guide*.

To enable audits, make sure the **EnableAudits** parameter is set to the default value 1. The Remote Access Service generates the following audit records.

Success Audits

Message	Explanation
The user *username* has connected and has been successfully authenticated on port *portname*.	This message signifies a normal connection by a certain user on a given port.
User *username* has disconnected from port *portname*.	This message records a successful disconnection initiated by the user.

Failure Audits

Message	Explanation
The user connected to port *portname* has been disconnected because of inactivity.	The line was idle for a period longer than configured using the **AutoDisconnect** parameter in the Registry.
The user has connected and failed to authenticate on port *portname*. The line has been disconnected.	The user supplied an incorrect username, password, or both. The number of failed authentications before access is denied and the line is dropped depends on the value of the **AuthenticateRetries** parameter in the Registry.
The user connected to port *portname* has been disconnected because of authentication timeout.	Authentication took longer than the value set for timing out. You may need to increase the value of the **AuthenticateTime** parameter.
The user connected to port *portname* has been disconnected because there was a transport-level error during the authentication conversation.	Too many errors occurred during the authentication conversation, possibly because of noisy lines or incompatible modems. Ask the user to try connecting with a lower initial speed.
The user connected to port *portname* has been disconnected because it could not be projected onto the network.	Most likely the user's workstation name already exists on the network. Ask the user to configure the remote workstation with a different computer name, or to make sure the workstation isn't already connected to the network through another means, such as the Ethernet or token ring.

Note If the Remote Access Service fails to start, check the Event Viewer for a description of the error that occurred at the time you tried to start Remote Access. For information about using the Event Viewer, see the *Microsoft Windows NT Advanced Server System Guide*. Once you have found the error, look it up in the error messages in Microsoft Windows NT Advanced Server Messages, and take the recommended corrective action.

Client Problems

Because client problems usually stem from improper hardware or software configuration on the workstation, first check the error message and audit logs for clues. If this doesn't help, see "Answers to Common Questions" in the Remote Access online help.

Security Hosts

A security host is a third-party authentication device that verifies whether a caller from a remote client is authorized to connect to the Remote Access server. This verification supplements security already supplied by the Remote Access Service and Windows NT Advanced Server.

For example, one kind of security system consists of two hardware devices, the security host and security card. The security host is installed between the Remote Access server and its modem. The security card is a small unit the size of a credit-card, resembling a pocket calculator without keys. The security card displays in its window a different access number every minute. This number is synchronized with the same number calculated in the security host every minute. When connecting, the remote user sends the number on the security card to the host. If the number is correct, the security host connects the remote user with the Remote Access server.

Another kind prompts the remote user to type in a username (which may or may not be the same as the Remote Access username) and a password (which differs from the Remote Access password).

Note As of this printing, only the Security Dynamics ACM/400 had been tested with the Windows NT Advanced Server Remote Access Service. Please consult the Microsoft Windows NT Advanced Server Hardware Compatibility List for other supported security hosts.

▶ **To make third-party security devices work with the Remote Access Service**

1. If the Remote Access server's modem is different from the modem in the security host's section in MODEM.INF, the MODEM.INF file on the Remote Access server needs to be customized to link the security host to the server's modem.

2. The remote user needs to activate Terminal mode to interact with the security host.

Customizing the Remote Access Server's MODEM.INF

When you install a security host between the Remote Access server and its modem(s), the server's modem and the security host act together as a new type of modem. The MODEM.INF file is shipped with a template for each supported security host paired with a particular modem. For example, the ACM/400 is paired with an AT&T Comsphere 3820 modem.

To use the security host with a different modem, you will have to modify the MODEM.INF file. For further details, see "Understanding MODEM.INF," later in this appendix.

▶ **To customize MODEM.INF**

1. Make a backup copy of the MODEM.INF file.

2. In the security host's section, replace all of the values for the **_on** and **_off** macros (such as **speaker_on=M1**) with the values from the section for the modem you'll be using.

3. In the security host's section, replace all COMMAND_INIT= lines with the COMMAND_INIT= lines from the section for the modem you'll be using.

The security host section must have the same number of COMMAND_INIT lines as the section for the modem you want to use. Do not change any other line in the security host section.

Note LOOP= lines are not needed for all modems. However, if you are in doubt, leave them in.

After customizing the security host section in MODEM.INF, install the security host and modem on the Remote Access server through the Windows NT Advanced Server Network Control Panel.

▶ **To install a security device**

1. In the Windows NT Advanced Server Control Panel, click the Network icon.

2. In the Installed Network Software window, select Remote Access Service.

3. Click Configure.

4. On the Remote Access Setup screen, select the security device connected between the Remote Access server and its modem, and click Continue.

5. On the Network Setting screen, click OK.

6. Click Yes.

Activating Terminal Mode on the Client

Remote Access Terminal lets the remote user send the correct access number to the security device. If the number is correct, the user is connected to the Remote Access server.

▶ **To prepare the client for Terminal mode**

1. In the Remote Access Phone Book, select the entry you want to connect to.
2. Click Edit.
3. Click Advanced.
4. Click Switch.
5. In the Post-connect Script field, select Terminal.
6. Click OK.

▶ **To connect to the Remote Access server**

1. Select the entry you have just prepared for Terminal mode.
2. Click Dial.

   When prompted, type your username and password, and click OK.
3. When the Terminal screen appears, type the access information required by your security host, for example, your personal identification number, followed by the number on the screen of the security card, or a username and password.
4. As soon as the security host indicates that you have been authenticated, click Done. The indication varies from one security host to another. For example, you may get an OK, or the cursor may just drop to the next line.

Authentication on the Remote Access server begins.

Backward Compatibility

For backward compatibility, the Remote Access servers, version 1.1 or earlier, should contain the following minimal configuration.

LANMAN.INI File

```
[remoteaccess]
MaxNames=8  ;For extra NetBIOS names on Windows NT workstations.
remotelisten=all ;Enables the peer capabilities of Windows NT
                 ;workstations through the Remote Access server.
```

PROTOCOL.INI File

```
[netbeui_xif]
sessions=160
ncbs=180
names=160
[tcpip_xif]
nbsessions=100
numnames=127          ;This is the maximum for the TCP/IP stack.
;numncbs=85           ;Commenting out the numncbs line lets the TCP/IP
                      ;stack assume the highest value possible.
```

If servers with earlier versions of the Remote Access Server do not have this minimal configuration, Windows NT–based workstations will get the following error message when dialing in:

```
The server cannot allocate NetBIOS resources needed to support the
client.
```

Cabling

Most ISA and EISA computers have one of the following serial port connectors:

- 25-pin male D-shell connectors
- 9-pin male connectors

Most off-the-shelf cables will work with your modems, but not all. Some cables do not have all the pins connected as shown in the following tables. When purchasing cables, tell your dealer exactly what you need, and provide the information in these tables to be sure you have the correct match.

Note Do not use the 9-to-25-pin converters that come with most mouse hardware, because some of them do not carry modem signals.

25-Pin Cabling

As Table B.2 shows, pins 1 through 8 on the serial port connector are wired to their counterparts on the modem connector. Ribbon cables usually have all 25 pins wired straight across, but they can cause interference to TVs, radios, and VCRs. Shielded RS-232 cable normally corrects this problem.

Table B.2   25-Pin Cable Wiring

25-pin serial port connector	25-pin modem connector	Signal
1	1	Chassis Ground
2	2	Transmit Data
3	3	Receive Data
4	4	Request To Send
5	5	Clear To Send
6	6	Data Set Ready
7	7	Signal Ground
8	8	Carrier Detect
20	20	Data Terminal Ready

9-Pin Cabling

The following table shows how to connect a 9-pin serial port connector on a computer to a 25-pin connector on a modem. Again, if you buy an off-the-shelf cable, be sure all pins are connected, as shown Table B.3.

Table B.3 9-Pin Cable Wiring

9-pin serial port connector	25-pin modem connector	Signal
1	8	Carrier Detect
2	3	Receive Data
3	2	Transmit Data
4	20	Data Terminal Ready
5	7	Signal Ground
6	6	Data Set Ready
7	4	Request To Send
8	5	Clear To Send
9	22	Ring Indicator (optional)

Note Some modems have the Data Set Ready (DSR) signal physically tied to the Data Carrier Detect (DCD) signal. Some 1200-bps modems and other 2400-bps modems have DIP switches default to this setting as well. As a result, if such a modem loses power while listening for a call, the Remote Access server cannot detect the condition because the DSR will not change, as it does with other modems.

Serial Cabling Requirements

The Remote Access Service requires the following pins on the RS-232 cable:

RX	Receive
TX	Transmit
CTS	Clear To Send
RTS	Ready To Send
DTR	Data Terminal Ready
DSR	Data Set Ready
DCD	Data Carrier Detected

Note All the pins listed above must be present. The Remote Access Service does not work if any of the seven pins is missing. If any pins are not present and working, the Remote Access Service reports a hardware error.

NULL Modem Cabling

If you are using a NULL modem to make a direct serial connection between two computers, your cable must be wired as shown in tables B.4 and B.5.

Table B.4   9-Pin NULL Modem Cabling

Remote host serial port connector	Calling system serial port connector	Signal
3	2	Transmit Data
2	3	Receive Data
7	8	Request To Send
8	7	Clear To Send
6, 1	4	Data Set Ready and Carrier Detect
5	5	Signal Ground
4	6, 1	Data Terminal Ready

Table B.5   25-Pin NULL Modem Cabling

Remote host serial port connector	Calling system serial port connector	Signal
2	3	Transmit Data
3	2	Receive Data
4	5	Request To Send
5	4	Clear To Send
6, 8	20	Data Set Ready and Carrier Detect
7	7	Signal Ground
20	6, 8	Data Terminal Ready

Off-the-shelf NULL modem cables may not be wired properly. Be sure to tell your dealer that your NULL modem cables must be wired as shown in Table B.5.

Understanding MODEM.INF

If you want to configure an unsupported modem to work with the Remote Access Service, you must add an entry for that modem in the MODEM.INF file.

Adding a New Modem to MODEM.INF

If you are using a modem that is not explicitly supported in MODEM.INF, you can append a new section containing the command strings required by your modem. The name of the section should be the name of your modem and should be enclosed in brackets. For information about macros used in building a new section, see "Substitution Macros," later in this appendix.

Note To minimize the risk of corrupting existing modem sections, add any new sections to the end of the MODEM.INF file.

▶ **To edit MODEM.INF for a new modem**

1. Back up your existing MODEM.INF file.
2. Copy an existing section to the end of MODEM.INF, and rename the section header of the copy to the name of your modem. For information about section headers, see "Section Headers" in "Syntax," later in this appendix.

3. Change **MAXCONNECTBPS** and **MAXCARRIERBPS** to the values of the new modem, and set values for **CALLBACKTIME** and **DEFAULTOFF**. For example:

```
MAXCARRIERBPS=9600
MAXCONNECTBPS=19200
CALLBACKTIME=10
DEFAULTOFF=speaker compression
```

Configuration parameter	Description
MAXCARRIERBPS	The maximum speed at which the client's modem and the Remote Access server's modem exchange data (bps rate on the telephone line). This speed is always equal to or less than **MAXCONNECTBPS**.
MAXCONNECTBPS	The maximum speed at which a modem talks to the computer (DTE to DCE bps transfer rate). Set this value to the maximum serial port bps that the modem can support.
CALLBACKTIME	The time in seconds that the server waits before calling the client back. This delay allows the client's modem to reset itself. Start with 10 seconds, and increase this number if there are problems.
DEFAULTOFF	A list of all the on/off macros that you want set to off by default, until turned on by RASPHONE.EXE.

4. Change the command strings for **hwflowcontrol**, **protocol** (error control), **compression**, and **speaker**. Check your modem's documentation for the correct values.

For example:

```
<hwflowcontrol_off>=&K0
<hwflowcontrol_on>=&K3
<protocol_off>=&Q0 S36=1
<protocol_on>=&Q5 S36=5 S46=138
<compression_off>=*DC0
<compression_on>=*DC1
<speaker_on>=M1
<speaker_off>=M0
```

Note If you don't find values for these commands in your modem's documentation, contact the modem's manufacturer. If a modem does not support these features, these macros may be omitted from MODEM.INF. (If you omit a macro definition in step 4, be sure to also omit the same macro in the COMMAND_INIT string in step 5.) Also, **protocol** means error control.

5. And finally, change the commands in the following example. Again, check your modem's documentation for the correct values.

```
COMMAND_INIT=AT&F&C1&D2 v1 s0=0 s2=128 s7=55 w1<cr>
COMMAND_INIT=AT<hwflowcontrol><protocol><compression><speaker><cr>
COMMAND_LISTEN=ATS0=1<cr>
COMMAND_DIAL=ATDT<phonenumber><cr>
```

Command	Description
COMMAND_INIT	Initializes the modem.
COMMAND_LISTEN	Sets the modem to autoanswer mode. Check your modem's documentation for the value that makes the modem answer after the first ring. Insert this value for Remote Access servers and clients configured for callback.
COMMAND_DIAL	Dials the phone number and connects. Do not enter an actual phone number here. Enter **<phonenumber>**, as shown in the example.

The following table lists the modes to which you should initialize your modem. The codes in the left column show examples of each mode. Codes like these form the **COMMAND_INIT** string. For the codes used by your modem, consult the modem's documentation.

Table B.6   Sample COMMAND_INIT Codes

Code	Meaning
&F	Restores factory settings.
&C1	Causes DCD to track the presence of a data carrier.
&D2	Hangs up and disables autoanswer when the DTR signal goes from on to off (high to low).
V1	Allows verbose (English words) return codes.
L1	Lowers the speaker volume.
Q0	Lets the modem return result codes.
E1	Enables character echo in the command state.
S0	Answers on a certain ring number: S0=0 for **COMMAND_INIT**, S0=1 for **COMMAND_LISTEN**.
S2=128	Disables the escape character.
S7=55	Sets the carrier waiting time (to about 55 seconds).
W1	Enables negotiation progress messages.
S95=44	Allows carrier, protocol, and compression messages.

Being meticulous when you create a new modem section can save a lot of debugging time later. Microsoft also recommends that you document your work so that others can quickly understand the entries in case you are not available, or so you can remember later what you did and why you did it. Be sure to type a semicolon (;) at the beginning of each comment line.

Important Microsoft PSS supports only the version of MODEM.INF that ships with the Microsoft Windows NT Advanced Server Remote Access Service. If you edit the file and your new modem does not work, restore the original version of the file, and use one of the modems listed in the Remote Access Setup program.

MODEM.INF

The MODEM.INF file lists all the modems supported by Remote Access, along with the command and response strings each modem needs for correct operation. When you select a modem during Remote Access installation, the Setup program associates the selected modem with the specified communication port. Remote Access connection utilities read MODEM.INF to obtain the command strings for the modem associated with each communication port. You can find MODEM.INF in the \WINNT\SYSTEM32\RAS directory.

The MODEM.INF file consists of two main parts:

- A global **[Responses]** section
- Individual sections for each supported modem, such as **[Hayes V 9600]**

Each section contains the following four components. The first three must appear in the order given. Comment lines can appear anywhere.

Component	Quantity
Section header	Only one
Configuration parameters and substitution macros	Zero or more
Commands	One or more
Comment lines	Zero or more

Responses

A *command-response set* consists of one command followed by zero or more responses. Responses are strings that are expected to be received from the device and can contain macros. Responses take the form:

keyword=value_string

The MODEM.INF file contains two types of responses:

Type of response	Location
Global	In the **[Responses]** section.
Private	Immediately following the command line that is expected to produce the response, and before the next command line.

A modem can match any response. Normally, if the modem returns only carrier bps, put the expected responses in the private modem section. If the modem returns connect bps or both carrier bps and connect bps, put the expected responses in the global section. To find out which bps string(s) your modem returns, see your modem's documentation.

Global Responses

Responses used by most modems are in the global **[Responses]** section of MODEM.INF. For example:

```
[Responses]
    LOOP=<cr><lf>RING<cr><lf>
    CONNECT_V42=<cr><lf>CONNECT <connectbps> RELIABLE  EC=(LAPM) \
        DC=(None)<cr><lf>
    ERROR=<cr><lf>ERROR<cr><lf>
```

The only information contained by LOOP is that another response is coming. Remote Access then waits for that response before moving on. Any response keyword beginning with LOOP or LOOP_ acts this way.

Private Responses

Specific MODEM.INF sections can contain private response strings. Remote Access checks for private responses first. If it doesn't find a response string to match the actual string returned by the modem, it continues checking in the global response section. There is one exception, however. If the first part of a string containing an **<append>** macro is matched in the private section, the global section will not be searched. Instead, Remote Access waits a few seconds for the rest of the string to arrive from the modem.

For information about adding an entry to MODEM.INF, see "Adding a New Modem to MODEM.INF" earlier in this appendix.

The following example shows a section with private responses. Microsoft encourages you to use this method of inserting responses for any section you add.

```
COMMAND_LISTEN=ATS0=1<cr>
CONNECT=<cr><lf>CONNECT <carrierbps><cr><lf>
CONNECT_EC=<cr><lf>CONNECT <carrierbps>/MNP<cr><lf>
CONNECT_EC=<cr><lf>CONNECT <carrierbps>/MNP/COMPRESSED<cr><lf>
CONNECT_EC=<cr><lf>CONNECT <carrierbps>/MNP COMPRESSED<cr><lf>
CONNECT_EC=<cr><lf>CONNECT <carrierbps>/V42<cr><lf>
CONNECT_EC=<cr><lf>CONNECT <carrierbps>/V42BIS<cr><lf>
```

Syntax

This section explains the components that make up the syntax of the MODEM.INF file.

Section Headers

Section headers identify the specific device to which the section applies. In MODEM.INF it is normally a name that identifies the modem make and model. A section header is a string of up to 32 characters between square brackets, and it occupies the first line in each section, for example, **[Hayes V 9600]**.

Configuration Parameters

Remote Access works with the modem through these parameters. They take the following form:

parameter_name=value_string

For example:

```
MAXCARRIERBPS=9600
CALLBACKTIME=8
```

Substitution Macros

Substitution macros are placeholders that are replaced by their values in command strings. Macros follow these rules:

- In the MODEM.INF file, macros must come before the first command, and by convention, after the configuration parameters.
- Macro names must be enclosed in angle brackets (< >).

For example:

```
<reset>=&F
<speaker_on>=M1
<speaker_off>=M0
```

There are two types of macros:

Macro type	Form
Unary	*<macro_name>=value_string*
Binary	*<macro_name_ON>=value_string*
	<macro_name_OFF>=value_string

The command AT<reset><cr> would be sent as AT&F<cr>. Binary macro placeholders are replaced according to instructions from the user. For example, if the user disables the speaker, the command AT<speaker><cr> is sent as ATM0<cr>. If the user enables the speaker, it is sent as ATM1<cr>.

Some responses can also use macros. Most macros in response strings behave the same way as in commands. However, certain macros, such as <carrierbps> and <diagnostics>, capture information such as baud rate from the device response string.

Nested macros are not allowed. Two adjacent left angle brackets are always interpreted as a less-than sign, and two adjacent right angle brackets are always interpreted as a greater-than sign. Interpreting angle brackets this way allows greater-than and less-than symbols in a command string, when required.

The macros in the following list are *reserved words*, which means you cannot define them in MODEM.INF when creating a new macro. Reserved words are case-insensitive.

- **carrierbps**
- **message**
- **cr**
- **match**
- **append**
- **ignore**

- **connectbps**
- **phonenumber**
- **lf**
- **?**
- **h***xx*

Note These macros are defined internally, so they do not need to be defined in MODEM.INF. However, they can be used in MODEM.INF, as **phonenumber** is used in the COMMAND_DIAL= string.

For additional reserved words, see "PAD.INF Format" in Appendix B of the *Windows NT System Guide*.

Table B.7 lists macros defined in the files MODEM.INF. Always enclose these macros in angle brackets (< >).

Table B.7   Macros Defined in MODEM.INF

Macro	Function
speaker	Turns the modem speaker on or off.
protocol	Turns the error correction protocol on or off.
compression	Turns modem compression on or off.
hwflowcontrol	Tells the modem whether to use hardware flow control between the COM port and modem.
cr	Inserts a carriage return.
lf	Inserts a linefeed.
match	Reports a match if the string enclosed in quotation marks is found in the device response. For example, <match>"Smith" matches Jane Smith and John Smith III.
?	Inserts a wildcard character, for example, CO<?><?>2 matches COOL2 or COAT2, but not COOL3.
append	Causes information to be broken into two segments and received from the modem one segment at a time. The client expects delays between the segments and waits until all the information has arrived. See the sample MODEM.INF file for an example.
hxx (*xx* are hexadecimal digits.)	Allows any hexadecimal character to appear in a string including the zero byte, <h00>.
ignore	Ignores the rest of a response from the macro on. For example, <cr><lf>CONNECTV-<ignore> reads the following responses as the same: "crlfCONNECTV-1.1" and "crlfCONNECTV-2.3".

In Table B.7, the first four macros (**speaker**, **protocol**, **compression**, and **hwflowcontrol**) are binary macros. Define them as shown with **speaker** in the first example in this section.

As values, use them as shown in the following example:

```
COMMAND_INIT=AT<speaker><cr>
```

This command sends ATM1<cr> to the modem if the speaker is to be turned on and ATM0<cr> if the speaker is to be turned off. Through the Remote Access Phone Book, the user determines which macros are to be on or off. The Phone Book then reads the MODEM.INF file to find out which value string to send to the modem. Note that value strings sometimes differ among modems.

The Remote Access Service uses the last five macros in the Table B.7 (**match**, **?**, **append**, **h**xx, and **ignore**) in response strings to recognize responses from a modem or another device.

Commands

Commands are strings of characters sent to the modem. These strings can contain macros and take the following form:

command_keyword=value_string

The set of command keywords (or *types*) is:

- **COMMAND_INIT**
- **COMMAND_DIAL**
- **COMMAND_LISTEN**

The MODEM.INF file initializes the modem, dials a phone number, and puts the modem into answer mode with the command types **COMMAND_INIT**, **COMMAND_DIAL**, and **COMMAND_LISTEN**. Commands of a specific type are executed in the order found in the MODEM.INF file. By convention commands of the same type are grouped together, as shown in the following example from MODEM.INF:

```
COMMAND_INIT=AT&F&C1&D2 V1 S0=0 S2=128 S7=55 W0 S95=44<cr>
COMMAND_INIT=AT<speaker><protocol><compression><hwflowcontrol><cr>
COMMAND_LISTEN=ATS0=1<cr>
COMMAND_DIAL=ATDT<phonenumber><cr>
```

Multiple Command Strings

Because most modems accept strings of about 50 characters, the Remote Access Service supports multiple command strings. That way you can break up long commands into strings the modem can accept.

For example, the first line could be rewritten as a multiple command string:

```
COMMAND_INIT=AT&F&C1&D2 V1 S0=0 S2=128 S7=55 W0 \
    S95=44<speaker><protocol><compression><hwflowcontrol><cr>

COMMAND_INIT=AT&F&C1&D2 V1 S0=0 S2=128 S7=55 W0 S95=44<cr>
COMMAND_INIT=AT<speaker><protocol><compression><hwflowcontrol><cr>
```

Notice that each string:

- Is a command in its own right.
- Begins with AT and ends with a carriage return (<cr>).
- Gets a response before going to the next string.

Comment Lines

Comment lines begin with a semicolon (;), and they can appear anywhere in the file. Comment lines convey important information to those who maintain the .INF files. For example:

```
; Explanation of modem commands
; &F  Reset modem to factory default settings
; &C1 DCD tracks presence of modem carrier
; &D2 Hangup & disable autoanswer when DTR goes from ON TO OFF
```

Line Continuation

A backslash (\) signals a line continuation. This mark indicates commands or responses are continued on the next line, making files more legible. A double backslash (\\) denotes a backslash.

For example:

```
CONNECT_EC=\
<cr><lf>CARRIER <carrierbps><cr><lf><append>\
<cr><lf>PROTOCOL: V.42/LAPM<cr><lf>\
<cr><lf>COMPRESSION: NONE<cr><lf>\
<cr><lf>CONNECT <connectbps><cr><lf>

<protocol_on>=K0
<protocol_off>=K1
```

Assigning an Alias

If a modem's command strings are identical to those already listed for another modem, the name of the latter modem can be used as an alias for the former.

For example:

```
[QT Modem]
ALIAS=Codex 326X Fast
```

In this example, the QT modem uses command strings of a Codex 326X Fast modem.

An alias to an alias is not allowed. In other words, you cannot nest aliases. For example, if you want to alias two modems to another modem, you must alias them directly:

```
[Modem 1]
;Modem 1's normal entries go here
[Modem 2]
ALIAS=Modem 1
[Modem 3]
ALIAS=Modem 1
;You cannot say ALIAS=Modem 2
```

Wide-Area Network Adapters

For a list of specific products supported by the Remote Access Service, see Appendix E, "Hardware Compatibility List."

For Digiboard serial and ISDN cards, contact Digiboard at the following address:

Digiboard
6400 Flying Cloud Drive
Eden Prairie, MN 55344
USA

Telephone: (612) 943-9020

For Eicon X.25 smart cards, contact Eicon at the following address:

Eicon Technology Corporation
14755 Preston Road, Suite 620
Dallas, TX 75240
USA

Telephone: (214) 239-3270
Fax: (214) 239-3304

Eicon Technical Corporation
Kingsway Business Park
Oldfield Road
Hampton, Middlesex TW12 2HD
United Kingdom

Telephone: 44 (81) 941-7122
Fax: 44 (81) 941-0548

Eicon Technical Corporation
2196 32nd Avenue
Montreal, Quebec
Canada H8T 3H7

Telephone: (514) 631-2592
Fax: (514) 631-3092

A P P E N D I X   C

Windows NT User Rights

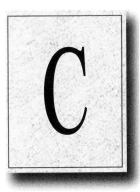

This appendix describes the advanced user rights defined by Windows NT. The descriptions shown in the Policy column appear in the User Rights Policy dialog box of User Manager. The description column also identifies which users are granted this user right by default.

User Right	Policy	Description
SeTcbPrivilege	Act as part of the operating system	The user can use to perform as a secure, trusted part of the operating system. Some subsystems are granted this privilege. Granted by default: None
SeChangeNotifyPrivilege	Bypass traverse checking	The user can traverse directory trees. Deny access to users using POSIX applications. Granted by default: Everyone
SeCreatePagefilePrivilege	Create a pagefile	The user can create a page file (not available in this version of Windows NT). Security is determined by a users access to the **..\CurrentControlSet\ Control\Session Management** key. Granted by default: None
SeCreateTokenPrivilege	Create a token object	Required to create access tokens. Only the Local Security Authority can do this. Granted by default: None
SeCreatePermanentPrivilege	Create permanent shared objects	Required to create special permanent objects, such as \\Device, which are used within Windows NT. Granted by default: None
SeDebugPrivilege	Debug programs	The user can debug various low-level objects such as threads. Granted by default: Administrators

User Right (*continued*)	**Policy** (*continued*)	**Description** (*continued*)
SeAuditPrivilege	Generate security audits	Required to generate security audit log entries. Granted by default: None
SeIncreaseQuotaPrivilege	Increase quotas	Required to increase object quotas (not available in this version of Windows NT). Granted by default: None
SeIncreaseBasePriorityPrivilege	Increase scheduling priority	The user can boost the priority of a process. Granted by default: Administrators and Power Users
SeLoadDriverPrivilege	Load and unload device drivers	The user can load an unload device drivers. Granted by default: None
SeLockMemoryPrivilege	Lock pages in memory	The user can lock pages in memory so they cannot be paged out to a backing store such as PAGEFILE.SYS. As physical memory is a limited resource, locking pages can lead to greater disk thrashing as essentially the amount of physical pages available to other applications is reduced. Granted by default: None
No Name	Log on as a batch job	The user can log on using a batch queue facility (not available in this version of Windows NT). Granted by default: None
No Name	Log on as a service	The user can perform security services. Granted by default: None
SeSystemEnvironmentPrivilege	Modify Firmware environment variables	The user can modify system environment variables (not user environment variables). Granted by default: Administrators
SeProfileSingleProcessPrivilege	Profile single process	The user can use the profiling (performance sampling) capabilities of Windows NT on a process. Granted by default: Administrators and Power Users
SeSystemProfilePrivilege	Profile system performance	The user can use the profiling capabilities of Windows NT on the system. (This can slow the system down.) Granted by default: Administrators
SeUnsolicitedInputPrivilege	Receive unsolicited device input	Required to read unsolicited data from a terminal device. Granted by default: None
SeAssignPrimaryTokenPrivilege	Replace a process level token	Required to modify a process's security access token. This is a powerful privilege used only by the system. Granted by default: None

APPENDIX   D

International Considerations

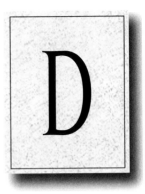

This appendix includes information about using Windows NT international features, including code pages and local keyboards.

Specifying International Preferences

Users can specify preferences related to the user's country and language. This list of preferences is known as the *locale* for that user.

You can specify these preferences by choosing the International icon from Control Panel. There you can specify your preference for the following:

Country	List Separator
Language	Date and time formats
Keyboard Layout	Number and currency formats
Measurement	

Note The Country and Language settings determine how alphabetical lists will be sorted. For example, in English D is followed by E. In Icelandic, an eth (ð) comes between D and E. Spanish CH sorts as a unique character between C and D; Danish AE is a unique letter after Z and before Ø. Swedish Å looks like A, but it is a unique letter that sorts after Z and before Ä (another unique letter in Swedish). In French, the ordering of basic diacritics is:

```
acute < grave < circumflex < diaeresis
```

For more information about specific fields in the International dialog box, see the online Help.

Windows NT supports the following locales:

Language	Code page	Language	Code page
Czech	852	German (Swiss)	850, 437
Danish	850, 865	Hungarian	852
Dutch (Belgian)	850, 437	Icelandic	850, 861
Dutch (Standard)	850, 437	Italian (Standard)	850, 437
English (American)	437, 850	Italian (Swiss)	850, 437
English (Australian)	850, 437	Norwegian (Bokmal)	850, 865
English (British)	850, 437	Norwegian (Nynorsk)	850, 865
English (Canadian)	863, 850	Polish	852
English (Irish)	850, 437	Portuguese (Brazilian)	850, 860
English (New Zealand)	850, 437	Portuguese (Standard)	850, 860
Finnish	850, 437	Russian	866, 855

Language	Code page	Language	Code page
French (Belgian)	850, 437	Slovak	852
French (Canadian)	850, 863	Spanish (Mexican)	850, 437
French (Standard)	850, 437	Spanish (modern sort)	850, 437
French (Swiss)	850, 437	Spanish (traditional sort)	850, 437
German (Austrian)	850, 437	Swedish	850, 865
German (Standard)	850, 437	Turkish	857, 852
Greek	869		

Code Pages and Unicode

A *code page* is an ordering or encoding of a standard set of characters within a specific locale. This encoding provides a consistent way for computer devices to exchange and process data. Each code page includes a common set of core characters (the first 128 characters of the code page). Windows NT supports several code pages, including ANSI and OEM code pages. ANSI code pages are supported for Windows 3.1 compatibility; OEM code pages are supported for MS-DOS and OS/2 compatibility. Other code pages are available, based on the installed locale, for use in data translation. These include secondary OEM code pages, MAC code pages, and EBCDIC code pages.

The following table shows the various code pages supported in Windows NT.

Code page name	Number	Type
Windows 3.1 Eastern European	1250	ANSI
Windows 3.1 Cyrillic	1251	ANSI
Windows 3.1 US (ANSI)	1252	ANSI
Windows 3.1 Greek	1253	ANSI
Windows 3.1 Turkish	1254	ANSI
MS-DOS United States	437	OEM
MS-DOS Multilingual (Latin I)	850	OEM
MS-DOS Slavic (Latin II)	852	OEM
IBM Cyrillic (primarily Russian)	855	OEM
IBM Turkish	857	OEM
MS-DOS Portuguese	860	OEM
MS-DOS Icelandic	861	OEM
MS-DOS Canadian-French	863	OEM
MS-DOS Nordic	865	OEM
MS-DOS Russian (former USSR)	866	OEM

Code page name (continued)	Number (continued)	Type (continued)
IBM Modern Greek	869	OEM
Macintosh Roman	10000	
Macintosh Greek I	10006	
Macintosh Cyrillic	10007	
Macintosh Latin 2	10029	
EBCDIC	037	
EBCDIC "500V1"	500	
EBCDIC	1026	
EBCDIC	875	

Windows NT uses Unicode (BMP of ISO 10646) for all internal text processing. *Unicode* is a 16-bit, fixed-width character encoding standard, with sufficient encoding space to accommodate most of the world's modern characters. All character sets and code pages supported by Windows NT can be mapped to Unicode.

By using Unicode-enabled applications, users can benefit from multilingual processing and a rich selection of characters.

For more information, see *The Unicode Standard* (version 1.0); The Unicode Consortium, Addison-Wesley Publishing Company, Inc.; 1991

Note Most code pages have a core set of characters in common (ASCII characters–the first 128 characters in the code page). In addition, each code page includes some unique "extended" characters not available on other code pages. Be sure not to use these extended characters in server names, computer names, and share names. Also, don't use these extended characters with applications used across the network. The FAT and HPFS file systems, which use the OEM code page, must translate the characters they don't recognize in the filename to a best-fit character, no character, or some non-recognized character.

Common Code Pages

The following show the character sets of two of the most commonly-used code pages 437 and 850.

0	32	64 @	96 `	128 Ç	160 á	192 L	224 α
1 ☺	33 !	65 A	97 a	129 ü	161 í	193 ⊥	225 ß
2 ☻	34 "	66 B	98 b	130 é	162 ó	194 T	226 Γ
3 ♥	35 #	67 C	99 c	131 â	163 ú	195 ├	227 π
4 ♦	36 $	68 D	100 d	132 ä	164 ñ	196 —	228 Σ
5 ♣	37 %	69 E	101 e	133 à	165 Ñ	197 ┼	229 σ
6 ♠	38 &	70 F	102 f	134 å	166 ª	198 ╞	230 μ
7 •	39 '	71 G	103 g	135 ç	167 º	199 ╟	231 τ
8 ◘	40 (	72 H	104 h	136 ê	168 ¿	200 ╚	232 Φ
9 ○	41)	73 I	105 i	137 ë	169 ⌐	201 ╔	233 Θ
10 ◙	42 *	74 J	106 j	138 è	170 ¬	202 ╩	234 Ω
11 ♂	43 +	75 K	107 k	139 ï	171 ½	203 ╦	235 δ
12 ♀	44 ,	76 L	108 l	140 î	172 ¼	204 ╠	236 ∞
13 ♪	45 -	77 M	109 m	141 ì	173 ¡	205 =	237 φ
14 ♫	46 .	78 N	110 n	142 Ä	174 «	206 ╬	238 ε
15 ☀	47 /	79 O	111 o	143 Å	175 »	207 ⊥	239 ∩
16 ▶	48 0	80 P	112 p	144 É	176 ░	208 ╨	240 ≡
17 ◀	49 1	81 Q	113 q	145 æ	177 ▒	209 T	241 ±
18 ↕	50 2	82 R	114 r	146 Æ	178 ▓	210 π	242 ≥
19 ‼	51 3	83 S	115 s	147 ô	179 │	211 ╙	243 ≤
20 ¶	52 4	84 T	116 t	148 ö	180 ┤	212 L	244 ⌠
21 §	53 5	85 U	117 u	149 ò	181 ╡	213 Γ	245 ⌡
22 ▬	54 6	86 V	118 v	150 û	182 ╢	214 ╓	246 ÷
23 ↨	55 7	87 W	119 w	151 ù	183 ╖	215 ╫	247 ≈
24 ↑	56 8	88 X	120 x	152 ÿ	184 ╕	216 ╪	248 °
25 ↓	57 9	89 Y	121 y	153 Ö	185 ╣	217 ┘	249 ·
26 →	58 :	90 Z	122 z	154 Ü	186 ║	218 Γ	250 ·
27 ←	59 ;	91 [	123 {	155 ¢	187 ╗	219 █	251 √
28 ∟	60 <	92 \	124 ¦	156 £	188 ╝	220 ▄	252 ⁿ
29 ↔	61 =	93]	125 }	157 ¥	189 ╜	221 ▌	253 ²
30 ▲	62 >	94 ^	126 ~	158 ₧	190 ╛	222 ▐	254 ■
31 ▼	63 ?	95 _	127 ⌂	159 ƒ	191 ┐	223 ▀	255

437   United States

0		32		64	@	96	`	128	Ç	160	á	192	└	224	Ó
1	☺	33	!	65	A	97	a	129	ü	161	í	193	┴	225	ß
2	☻	34	"	66	B	98	b	130	é	162	ó	194	┬	226	Ô
3	♥	35	#	67	C	99	c	131	â	163	ú	195	├	227	Ò
4	♦	36	$	68	D	100	d	132	ä	164	ñ	196	─	228	õ
5	♣	37	%	69	E	101	e	133	à	165	Ñ	197	┼	229	Õ
6	♠	38	&	70	F	102	f	134	å	166	ª	198	ã	230	µ
7	•	39	'	71	G	103	g	135	ç	167	º	199	Ã	231	þ
8	◘	40	(	72	H	104	h	136	ê	168	¿	200	╚	232	Þ
9	○	41	)	73	I	105	i	137	ë	169	®	201	╔	233	Ú
10	◙	42	*	74	J	106	j	138	è	170	¬	202	╩	234	Û
11	♂	43	+	75	K	107	k	139	ï	171	½	203	╦	235	Ù
12	♀	44	,	76	L	108	l	140	î	172	¼	204	╠	236	ý
13	♪	45	-	77	M	109	m	141	ì	173	¡	205	═	237	Ý
14	♫	46	.	78	N	110	n	142	Ä	174	«	206	╬	238	¯
15	☼	47	/	79	O	111	o	143	Å	175	»	207	¤	239	´
16	►	48	0	80	P	112	p	144	É	176	░	208	ð	240	
17	◄	49	1	81	Q	113	q	145	æ	177	▒	209	Ð	241	±
18	↕	50	2	82	R	114	r	146	Æ	178	▓	210	Ê	242	‗
19	‼	51	3	83	S	115	s	147	ô	179	│	211	Ë	243	¾
20	¶	52	4	84	T	116	t	148	ö	180	┤	212	È	244	¶
21	§	53	5	85	U	117	u	149	ò	181	Á	213	ı	245	§
22	▬	54	6	86	V	118	v	150	û	182	Â	214	Í	246	÷
23	↨	55	7	87	W	119	w	151	ù	183	À	215	Î	247	¸
24	↑	56	8	88	X	120	x	152	ÿ	184	©	216	Ï	248	°
25	↓	57	9	89	Y	121	y	153	Ö	185	╣	217	┘	249	¨
26	→	58	:	90	Z	122	z	154	Ü	186	║	218	┌	250	·
27	←	59	;	91	[	123	{	155	ø	187	╗	219	█	251	¹
28	∟	60	<	92	\	124	|	156	£	188	╝	220	▄	252	³
29	↔	61	=	93	]	125	}	157	Ø	189	¢	221	¦	253	²
30	▲	62	>	94	^	126	~	158	×	190	¥	222	Ì	254	■
31	▼	63	?	95	_	127	⌂	159	ƒ	191	┐	223	▀	255	

850 Multilingual (Latin I)

MS-DOS National Language Support Information

Windows NT supports the following MS-DOS 5.0 National Language Support (NLS) commands. (Note that printer device code page commands are not supported.)

- **chcp**. This command lists the code page used by the system. (Using this command to change code pages is not supported in this release of Windows NT.)
- **mode**. This command displays standard information about the active code pages in the system.
- **keyb**. This command specifies the keyboard layout used.

Windows NT maintains its configuration information in the Registry. However, when CONFIG.SYS changes, the system automatically changes entries in the Registry, which take effect when the system is restarted. These CONFIG.SYS commands are related to NLS. Changes to them will cause changes in the Windows NT Registry:

- **install=c:\dos\keyb.com** *xx,nnn,***filename**
- **device=c:\dos\display.sys**...
- **device=c:\dos\printer.sys**...
- **country=***xxx,***nnn,filename**
- **install=c:\dos\nlsfunc.exe**

NLS Information in the OS/2 Subsystem

The OS/2 subsystem typically inherits the NLS parameters (such as language, country code, and code page) from the parent process. If any of the NLS commands from OS/2 CONFIG.SYS exist, these values will supersede the Windows NT values. To create or edit an OS/2 version 1.0 CONFIG.SYS file, use an OS/2 editor to make any changes to the file; then save the file and exit the editor program. The edits you make will automatically cause the Registry to be updated.

The following OS/2 NLS commands are supported by Windows NT:

- **codepage**. This command specifies one or two code pages that the OS2SS has set up for use as its primary and secondary code pages.
- **country**. This command specifies the country code.
- **devinfo**. This command identifies the keyboard layout selection. This defines the keyboard layout table for translating keystrokes into characters encoded according to a code page based on ASCII.

If no COUNTRY entry is found in the Registry, the OS/2 subsystem takes the current locale country code for each OS/2 application, inherited from the application's parent process.

If the Registry includes a COUNTRY entry but no CODEPAGE entry, the subsystem uses the default code page for the current country. If neither line is present, the subsystem uses the Windows NT primary OEM code page.

If no DEVINFO entry is found, the subsystem uses the default keyboard layout for the country.

APPENDIX E

Hardware Compatibility List

The following computers and peripherals have passed Windows NT 3.1 compatibility testing as of July 1993. Some computers may be sold with additional peripherals that are not yet supported by Windows NT. If your computer or device is not listed below, contact the manufacturer for more information. We have not tested every computer and/or device in all possible configurations. Please refer to the file SETUP.TXT on the install media for additional compatibility information when installing Windows NT.

Items listed with ++ are supported with device drivers available in the Windows NT Driver Library.

Updates to this list will appear in November, 1993, and February, 1994, in Library 1 of the WINNT forum (GO WINNT) or Library 17 of the MSWin32 forum (GO MSWIN32) on Compuserve Information Services.

x86 Architecture Uniprocessor Computers

The following systems have been tested.

Absolute Computer 486/66 VL/EISA
ACD OPTIMA 486 DX 33 VL
ACD OPTIMA 486 DX 50 VL
ACD OPTIMA 486 DX2 66 VL
ACER 1100-33
ACER 1120sx
ACER 1170
ACER AcerFrame 1000 (Model 1733)
ACER AcerFrame 1000 (Model 1766)
ACER AcerFrame 300
ACER AcerFrame 500 (Model F433TE)
ACER AcerFrame 500 (Model FT50TE)
ACER AcerFrame 500 (Model FT66TE)
ACER AcerPower 425s
ACER AcerPower 486/33

ACMA 486/33 TI-VLB
ACMA 486/50 TS-E
ACMA 486/50-2 TI-VLB
ACMA 486/66-2 TI-VLB
ACMA 486/66-2 TS-E
ACMA 486/66-2 TS-VLB
ACS Meritel 486-50SF
ACS Meritel 486-66SF
Actech ACTion EISA 486DX-50
Actech ACTion EISA 486DX/2-66
Actech ACTion ISA 486DX-33
Actech ACTion ISA 486DX/2-50
Actech ACTion ISA 486DX/2-66
Actech ACTion ISA 486SX-25
Actech ACTion ISA 486DX-50

Actech ACTion VLB 486DX-33
Actech ACTion VLB 486DX-50
Actech ACTion VLB 486DX/2-50
Actech ACTion VLB 486DX/2-66
Actech ACTion VLB 486SX-25
Adaptive Data System Pro 3/486-40
Adaptive Data System Pro 486/33 VESA
Adaptive Data System Pro 486/33DX
Adaptive Data System Pro series 486/50
Adaptive Data System TAI 386DX/40CF
    System
Adaptive Data System TAI 486DX/50CS
    System
ADD-X 486 All In One 33 MHz
ADD-X Systemes 486/33MHz ISA bus
ADPS 486 Power Notebook 486DX2-50MHz
ADPS 486 Power Notebook Color 486-33MHz
ADPS Ambassador
ADPS Bat Computer-33MHz
ADPS Bat Computer-50MHz
ADPS Local Bus 33
ADPS Medallion
ADPS Multimedia Power House
ADPS Power Notebook 486-33MHz
ADPS System 3000
ADPS System 4000
ADPS System 5000
ADPS System 6000 EISA
ADPS System 6000 Plus
ADPS System 6000 Plus EISA
ADS Upgradeable 3/486
AIC STM 386DX-33MHz
AIC STM 486DX-33MHz
AIC STM 486DX2-66MHz
AIC STM 486DX2-66MHz Local Bus
Alfa Deltacom 486-33
Alfa Deltacom 486-50
Alfa Deltacom 486SX-25
Alfa Deltacom EISA 486-50
Alfa VESA 486DX2-66
ALR® BusinessVEISA 3/33
ALR BusinessVEISA 4/33D
ALR BusinessVEISA 4/66D

ALR Evolution IV 4/25s
ALR Evolution IV 4/33
ALR Evolution IV 4/33s
ALR Evolution IV 4/66d
ALR Evolution IV 4E/25s
ALR Evolution IV 4E/33
ALR Evolution IV 4E/33s
ALR Evolution IV 4E/66d
ALR Evolution V-Q/60
ALR Evolution V-Q/66
ALR Evolution V/60
ALR Evolution V/66
ALR Flyer 32LCT 4/50D
ALR Flyer 32LCT 4/66D
ALR Flyer 32LCT 4DX/33
ALR Flyer SD32 4/33
ALR Flyer SD32 4/66d
ALR Flyer VL 4/33d
ALR Flyer VL 4/66d
ALR Modular Processor System 486DX2/66
ALR PowerCache 4 33e
ALR POWERPRO VM/64
ALR POWERPRO/MC SMP 4/50D
ALR PROVEISA V/66
ALR RANGER M4/25
ALR RANGER MC4/25S
ALR RANGER MC4DX/25
ALR RANGER MCT4/25
AMAX 486/2-50 VESAmax Power Station
AMAX 486/33 VESAmax Power Station
AMAX 486/50 EISAmax Power Station
AMAX 486/66 EISAmax Power Station
AMAX 486/66 VESAmax Power Station
Ambra 486DX/50
AMI Enterprise III
AMI Enterprise IV
AMI Omni Business Partner
AMI Super Voyager LC
AMI Super Voyager VLB
AMI Super Voyager VLB II
AMSYS UPG VLbus DX2-50 DT
Apricot® FTe 486DX2/66
Apricot FTs 486DX2/66

Apricot XEN-LS II

Ares 486-33 VLB

Ariel 486DX2-66EVS

Ariel 486DX2-66VLS

Asem DP 486/66 II

Asem DS 486/33 II

ASL 433

Aspect 3/486 386DX-40 ISA

Aspect 3/486DX-33 ISA

Aspect 3/486DX-50 ISA

Aspect 3/486DX2-66 ISA

Aspect EISA 486DX-33

Aspect EISA 486DX-50

Aspect EISA 486DX2-66

Aspect ISA 486DX-33

Aspect ISA 486DX-50

Aspect ISA 486DX2-66

Aspect ISA 486SX-33

Aspect VESA 486DX-33

Aspect VESA 486DX-33F

Aspect VESA 486DX-50

Aspect VESA 486DX-50F

Aspect VESA 486DX2-66

Aspect VESA 486DX2-66F

Aspect VESA 486SX-33

Aspect VESA 486SX-33F

AST® Advantage! Plus 486DX/33

AST Advantage! Pro 486SX/25 Model 173

AST Bravo 3/25s Model 3V

AST Bravo LC 4/33

AST Bravo LC 4/50d

AST Bravo LC 4/66d

AST Bravo LP 4/33

AST PowerExec 4/25SL

AST Power Premium 4/50d

AST Power Premium 486/33 EISA

AST Premium 386/33T

AST Premium II 386/33 Model 213V

AST Premium II 486/33

AST Premium SE 4/33 Model 333

AST Premium SE 4/50

AST Premium SE 4/50d

AST Premium SE 4/66d

AST Premium SE 486/33

AST Premmia 4/33

AST Premmia 4/33SX

AST Premmia 4/66d

Athena ALM 486 DX 33

Athena ALM 486 DX 50

Athena ALM 486 DX 66

Athena HQ / ISA 486DLC 40

Athena HQ / ISA 486DX2/66

Athena HQ / ISA 486DX33

Athena HQ / ISA 486DX50

Athena HQ / VESA 486DX 33

Athena HQ / VESA 486DX2 50

Athena HQ / VESA 486DX2 66

Austin 486/50 EISA Tower PATRIOT

Austin 486/50 VESA-LB PATRIOT

Austin 486/50 VESA-LB PATRIOT PLUS

Austin 486DLC

Austin 486DX/33 VESA-LB PATRIOT

Austin 486DX/33 VESA-LB PATRIOT PLUS

Austin 486DX2/66 VESA-LB PATRIOT PLUS

Austin Winstation 486DX2 66

Brett ExecEISA

Brett Executive

Brett Pro VLB

CAF CT-02 L737/486DX-33

Caliber 3/486 386DX-40 ISA

Caliber 3/486DX-33 ISA

Caliber 3/486DX-50 ISA

Caliber 3/486DX2-66 ISA

Caliber EISA 486DX-33

Caliber EISA 486DX-50

Caliber EISA 486DX2-66

Caliber ISA 486DX-33

Caliber ISA 486DX-50

Caliber ISA 486DX2-66

Caliber ISA 486SX-33

Caliber VESA 486DX-33

Caliber VESA 486DX-33F

Caliber VESA 486DX-50

Caliber VESA 486DX-50F

Caliber VESA 486DX2-66

Caliber VESA 486DX2-66F

Caliber VESA 486SX-33
Caliber VESA 486SX-33F
Celem 486DX/33 VL
Celem 486DX/33C
Celem 486DX/50 MC
Celem 486DX/50 VL
Chicony Electronics 486 33P
Clone 9433
Commodore 486DX-33C
Commodore 486SLC-25
Commodore 486SX-25
Commodore DT 486SX-20
Commodore LB 486DX-33C
Commodore LB 486DX2-66C
Commodore LB 486SX-33C
Commodore LB T486DX2-66C
Commodore T486DX-50C
COMPAQ Contura 4/25C
COMPAQ Deskpro 386/20e®
COMPAQ Deskpro 386/25®
COMPAQ® Deskpro® 386/25e
COMPAQ Deskpro 386/33®
COMPAQ Deskpro 386/33L
COMPAQ Deskpro 386s®/20
COMPAQ Deskpro 4/66i
COMPAQ Deskpro 486/25
COMPAQ Deskpro 486/25i
COMPAQ Deskpro 486/33i
COMPAQ Deskpro 486/33L
COMPAQ Deskpro 486/33M
COMPAQ Deskpro 486/50L
COMPAQ Deskpro 486/50M
COMPAQ Deskpro 5/60M
COMPAQ Deskpro 5/66M
COMPAQ Deskpro 66M
COMPAQ LTE Lite 4/25
COMPAQ LTE Lite 4/25C
COMPAQ LTE Lite 4/33C
COMPAQ Portable 486c
COMPAQ Portable 486C/66
COMPAQ ProLinea 3/25s
COMPAQ ProLinea 4/50
COMPAQ ProLinea 4/66

COMPAQ ProSignia 486DX/33
COMPAQ ProSignia 486DX2/66
COMPAQ ProSignia 5/60
COMPAQ Systempro®/LT 386/25
COMPAQ Systempro/LT 486/33
COMPAQ Systempro/LT 486DX2/50
COMPAQ Systempro/LT 486DX2/66
COMPAQ Systempro/LT 486SX/25
CompuAdd® 320
CompuAdd 420s
CompuAdd 433
CompuAdd 433 ELB
CompuAdd 433 LB
CompuAdd 433 LP
CompuAdd 433DLC LP
CompuAdd 433E
CompuAdd 450
CompuAdd 450DX2 LP
CompuAdd 466/DX2
CompuAdd 466DX2 LB
CompuAdd 466DX2E LB
CompuAdd MC466EDX2
CompuAdd 486-33DLC
COMPUCON 386DX/40
COMPUCON 486DX/33
COMPUCON 486DX/50
COMPUCON 486DX/50 VL
Compudyne 4DX2/50 EISA16340 DESKTOP
    (incl. MINITOWER and
    SERVERTOWER)
Compudyne 4DX2/50 VLB16340 DESKTOP
    (incl. MINITOWER and
    SERVERTOWER)
Compudyne 4DX2/66 EISA16245 DESKTOP
    (incl. MINITOWER and
    SERVERTOWER)
Compudyne 4DX2/66 Slimnote
Compudyne 4DX2/66 VLB16245 DESKTOP
    (incl. MINITOWER and
    SERVERTOWER)
Compudyne 4DX33 EISA16245 DESKTOP
    (incl. MINITOWER and
    SERVERTOWER)

Compudyne 4DX33 VLB16245 DESKTOP
(incl. MINITOWER and
SERVERTOWER)
Compudyne 4DX50 EISA16340 DESKTOP
(incl. MINITOWER and
SERVERTOWER)
Compudyne 4DX50 VLB16340 DESKTOP
(incl. MINITOWER and
SERVERTOWER)
Computer Extension CESI 486 66
Computer Resources 486DX266 ISA
Computer Resources 486DX33 FULL TOWER
Computer Resources 486DX33 LOCAL BUS
Computer Resources 486DX50 EISA
Computer Sales Prof. 486DX/33 VL
Computer Sales Prof. 486DX2/50 VL
Computer Sales Prof. 486DX2/66 VL
Computer Sales Prof. 486SX/25 VL
Computrend PREMIO 486DX-33
Computrend PREMIO 486DX-50
Computrend PREMIO 486DX2-66
CSS Labs MaxSys 433MTA
CSS Labs MaxSys 433MTMGE
CSS Labs MaxSys 433TA
CSS Labs MaxSys 433TMGE
CSS Labs MaxSys 450MTMGE
CSS Labs MaxSys 450TMGE
CSS Labs MaxSys 452MTMGE
CSS Labs MaxSys 452TMGE
CSS Labs MaxSys 462MTA
CSS Labs MaxSys 462MTE
CSS Labs MaxSys 462MTMGE
CSS Labs MaxSys 462TA
CSS Labs MaxSys 462TE
CSS Labs MaxSys 462TMGE
CSS Labs Preferred 433GA
CSS Labs Preferred 433GE
CSS Labs Preferred 433MGE
CSS Labs Preferred 450MGE
CSS Labs Preferred 452MGE
CSS Labs Preferred 462GA
CSS Labs Preferred 462GE
CSS Labs Preferred 462MGE

Cube 340 ATX
Cube 433 ATX
Cube 450 ATX
Cube 466 ATX
Cube 466 ATX Local Bus
Cube 486/40
Daewoo Modular Desktop/2300
Daewoo Modular Mini Tower/2400
DAN for Windows 25
DAN for Windows 33
DAN for Windows 50
DAN for Windows 66
DAN Vantage/25
DAN Vantage/33
DAN Vantage/50
DAN Vantage/66
Danjen 486DLC 33 MHz
Danjen 486DX 33 MHz Local Bus
Danjen 486DX 50 MHz EISA
Danjen 486DX 50 MHz ISA
Dassault AT CUSTOMER ACTIVATED
TERMINAL D633
Data Stor 386-33DX Desktop/Tower
Data Stor 386-33SX Desktop/Tower
Data Stor 486-25SX Desktop/Tower
Data Stor 486-33DX Desktop/Tower
Data Stor 486-33SX Desktop/Tower
Data Stor 486-50DX Desktop/Tower
Data Stor 486-66DX2 Desktop/Tower
Data Stor 486-66DX2E Desktop/Tower
DATAFILEN PROFF 386DX-40
DATAFILEN PROFF 486DX-33 VL
DATAFILEN PROFF 486DX2-66 VL
Datavarehuset BRICK 486 DX2-50 LocalBus
Datavarehuset BRICK 486DX-33 EISA
Datavarehuset BRICK 486DX2-66 LocalBus
DDK Soft DDK-4066/2LV
Debis DCS Minitower 486 EISA
Debis DCS Tower 486 MC
Debis DCS Tower 486 MP EISA
Deico 486DLC
DELL 325 N Notebook
DELL 325 NC Notebook

DELL 4/50M

DELL® 4033/XE

DELL 4050/XE

DELL 4066/XLE

DELL 425s/L

DELL 433/L

DELL 433/M

DELL 433/ME

DELL 433/T

DELL 450s/L

DELL 466/M

DELL 466/ME

DELL Dimension 466/T

DELL Dimension 486DX/33

DELL Dimension 486DX/50

DELL Dimension 486DX2/50s

DELL Dimension 486SX/25

DELL PowerLine 466DE

DELL PowerLine 466SE

DELL PowerLine System 325

DELL PowerLine System 433DE

DELL PowerLine System 433E

DELL PowerLine System 433SE

DELL PowerLine System 450/T

DELL PowerLine System 450DE

DELL PowerLine System 450DE/2 DGX

DELL PowerLine System 450SE

DELL PowerLine System 486D/33

DELL PowerLine System 486D/50

DELL PowerLine System 486P/25

DELL PowerLine System 486P/33

Delta Micro System GL 4D33V

DFI CCV 486-25SX

DFI CCV 486-DX2-50

DFI CCV 486DX-33-128

DFI CCV 486DX2-66

DFI TN 486DX-33-256

DFI TN 486DX2-50-256

DFI TN 486DX2-66-256

DFI TN 486SX-25-256

DFI UCE 486 DX-33

DFI UCE 486-DX2-66

DFI UCE 486DX-50

DFI UCE 486DX2-50

DFI UCE 486SX-25-128

DFI UCF 486 DX2-66-128

DFI UCF 486DX-33-128

DFI UCF 486DX-50-128

DFI UCF 486DX2-50-128

DFI UCF 486SX-25

Digital Equipment applicationDEC® 400xP

Digital Equipment DECpc 333

Digital Equipment DECpc 425

Digital Equipment DECpc 425 ST

Digital Equipment DECpc 425i

Digital Equipment DECpc 425i DX2

Digital Equipment DECpc 433

Digital Equipment DECpc 433 ST

Digital Equipment DECpc 433 Workstation

Digital Equipment DECpc 433dx DT

Digital Equipment DECpc 433dx LP

Digital Equipment DECpc 433dx MT

Digital Equipment DECpc 433dx MTE

Digital Equipment DECpc 433sx DT

Digital Equipment DECpc 433T

Digital Equipment DECpc 450 ST

Digital Equipment DECpc 450d2 LP

Digital Equipment DECpc 450d2 MT

Digital Equipment DECpc 452 ST

Digital Equipment DECpc 466 ST

Digital Equipment DECpc 466d2 DT

Digital Equipment DECpc 466d2 LP

Digital Equipment DECpc 466d2 MT

Digital Equipment DECpc 466d2 MTE

Digital Equipment DECpc 560 ST

Digital Equipment DECstation® 425c

Dolch C.P.A.C. 486-33C

Dolch C.P.A.C. 486-33E

Dolch C.P.A.C. 486-50 EISA

Dolch C.P.A.C. 486-66C

Dolch C.P.A.C. 486-66E

Dolch M.A.C.H. 486-33

Dolch M.A.C.H. 486-66

Dolch V.P.A.C. 486-33C

Dolch V.P.A.C. 486-33E

Dolch V.P.A.C. 486-66C

Dolch V.P.A.C. 486-66E

DTK 486VL

DTK FEAT01-D33

DTK FEAT01-D50

DTK FEAT01-T66

DTK FEAT03-D50

DTK FEAT31-D33

DTK FEAT31-D50

DTK FEAT31-T66

DTK FEAT33-D50

DTK FEAT34-D50

DTK Grafika 4A

DTK Grafika 4C

DTK Grafika 4D

DTK Grafika 4F

DTK Grafika 4I

DTK Grafika 4J

Dynamic Decisions DYNEX EXEC-50 EISA

Elite Industries MB-1433AEA-V 486/33

Elite Industries MB-1433AEA-V 486/50

Elite Industries MB-1433AEA-V 486DX2/66

Elonex PC-400 Series Computer

Epson® Endeavor WG 4DX2/50

Epson Endeavor WG 4DX2/66

Epson Endeavor WG 4SX33

Epson Equity 4DX/33

Epson Equity 4DX2/50

Epson Equity 4SX/25

Epson PowerSpan 486DX2/66

Epson Progression 486DX/33

Epson Progression 486DX2/66

Epson Progression 486SX/25

Epson Progression 4DX2/50

Epson Progression 4SX/33

Ergo Ultra Moby Brick 486/66

Everex Cube DX/33

Everex™ Step 486-33 ISA

Everex Step DP

Everex Step VL EISA 486DX2-50

Everex Step VL EISA 486DX2-66

Everex Step VL ISA 486DX2-50

Everex Step VL ISA 486DX2-66

Everex Tempo 486/33

Everex Tempo 486/33E

Everex Tempo 486DX2/50

Everex Tempo 486SX/25

Expo-Tech 386 Ultra Slim

Expo-Tech 486DX/3 Desktop

Expo-Tech 486DX/3 Desktop (w/LBVGA)

Expo-Tech 486DX/3 Desktop (w/VLBUS)

Expo-Tech 486DX/3 Tower

Expo-Tech 486DX/3 Tower (w/VLBUS)

Expo-Tech 486DX2/4 Desktop

Expo-Tech 486DX2/4 Desktop (w/LBVGA)

Expo-Tech 486DX2/4 Desktop (w/VLBUS)

Expo-Tech 486DX2/4 Tower

Expo-Tech 486DX2/4 Tower (w/VLBUS)

Expo-Tech 486DX2/6 Desktop

Expo-Tech 486DX2/6 Desktop (w/LBVGA)

Expo-Tech 486DX2/6 Desktop (w/VLBUS)

Expo-Tech 486DX2/6 Tower

Expo-Tech 486DX2/6 Tower (w/VLBUS)

Expo-Tech 486SX/3 Desktop

Expo-Tech 486SX/3 Desktop (w/LBVGA)

Expo-Tech 486SX/3 Tower

Expo-Tech 486SX/3 Ultra Slim

Expo-Tech 486SX/3 Ultra Slim (w/LBVGA)

Expo-Tech 486SX/4 Desktop

Expo-Tech 486SX/4 Desktop (w/LBVGA)

Expo-Tech 486SX/4 Desktop (w/VLBUS)

Expo-Tech 486SX/4 Tower

Expo-Tech 486SX/4 Ultra Slim

Expo-Tech 486SX/4 Ultra Slim (w/LBVGA)

Expo-Tech LT322 Notebook

Expo-Tech LT421 Notebook

Fast 486DY66S520

First Jupiter 486DX66 All In One ISA Bus

First Krypton 486DX50 VL-Bus

First LEO 4386VCV DX33

First LEO 486DX66-VL

First LEO 486VC DX/50

First LEO 486VC DX2/66

First LEO DESKTOP 486/33

First LEO DESKTOP 486/50

First LEO DESKTOP 486/66

First LEO MINITOWER 486/33

First LEO MINITOWER 486/50

First LEO MINITOWER 486/66

First Venus 486DX2/66 EISA and VL-Bus

First Venus 486DX2/66 VL-Bus

Fountain Technology 486DX/33 VL

Fountain Technology 486DX2/50 VL

Fountain Technology 486DX2/66 VL

Fountain Technology 486SX/25 VL

Gain TITON WORKSTATION

Gateway 2000 386/33

Gateway 2000 386SX/20C

Gateway 2000 486/33C

Gateway 2000 486/33E

Gateway 2000 486DX2/50

Gateway 2000 486DX2/50E

Gateway 2000 486dx2/66V

Gateway 2000 4DX-33

Gateway 2000 4DX2/66E

Gateway 2000 4SX-25

Gateway 2000 4SX-33V

Gateway 2000 Nomad 425DXL[1]

Gateway 2000 Nomad 450DXL[1]

GCH AEGIS 433

GCH AEGIS 466

GCH EasyData 433HI

GCH EasyData 466HI

GCH EasyDate 466HI VL

GCH EiSYS Ei433DX

GCH EiSYS Ei466DX

Genitech Capricorn JF/33

Genitech Capricorn JF2/66

GES DATAMINI MF 486DX-33

GES DATAMINI MF 486DX2-66

GES DATAMINI MF 486SX-25

GRiD® 486ei-33

GRiD 486EI25 SVR

GRiD APT/425se

GRiD APT/450e

GRiD MFP 425s+

GRiD MFP 433+

GRiD MFP 433s+

GRiD MFP 450+

GRiD MFP 466+

GRiD MFP/420s

GRiD MFP/425s

GRiD MFP/450

GRiD MFP/540

Hacker 486 for NT®

Hancke & Peter 386w Professional

Hancke & Peter 486/33w Professional

Hancke & Peter 486/50w Professional

Hancke & Peter 486/66w Professional

Hancke & Peter 486w EISA Professional

Harris Epoch 486/33 VESA

Harris Epoch 486/50 EISA

Harris Epoch 486/50 ISA

Hauppauge 4860 EISA DX2-66

Hauppauge 486M Local Bus DX2-66

Hertz 486/D50e

Hertz 486/D50Ee

Hertz 486/D66X2e

Hertz 486/D66X2Ee

Hewlett-Packard® NetServer 4/33 LE

Hewlett-Packard NetServer 4/33 LM

Hewlett-Packard NetServer 4d/66 LE

Hewlett-Packard NetServer 4d/66 LM

Hewlett-Packard NetServer 4s/33 LE

Hewlett-Packard NetServer 5/60 LM

Hewlett-Packard Vectra 386/25

Hewlett-Packard Vectra® 486/25T

Hewlett-Packard Vectra 486/25U

Hewlett-Packard Vectra 486/33N

Hewlett-Packard Vectra 486/33ST

Hewlett-Packard Vectra 486/33T

Hewlett-Packard Vectra 486/33U

Hewlett-Packard Vectra 486/50U

Hewlett-Packard Vectra 486/66 XM

Hewlett-Packard Vectra 486/66ST

Hewlett-Packard Vectra 486/66U

Hewlett-Packard Vectra 486S/20

Hewlett-Packard Vectra 486s/25 MI

Hewlett-Packard Vectra EtherLite 386

Hewlett-Packard Vectra EtherLite 486

Hewlett-Packard Vectra RS/25C

HM Systems Minstrel Xpresso 486

Hyundai 425s

Hyundai 466d2

Hyundai Prestige 433d

IBM® PS/1® 2133-xxx 486SX/25

IBM PS/1 2133-xxx 486SX/33

IBM PS/1 2155-xxx 486DX/33

IBM PS/1 2155-xxx 486DX2/50

IBM PS/1 2155-xxx 486DX2/66

IBM PS/1 2155-xxx 486SX/25

IBM PS/1 2155-xxx 486SX/33

IBM PS/1 2168-xxx 486DX/33

IBM PS/1 2168-xxx 486DX2/50

IBM PS/1 2168-xxx 486DX2/66

IBM PS/1 2168-xxx 486SX/25

IBM PS/1 2168-xxx 486SX/33

IBM PS/2® Model 50/50Z System Board
   Upgrade 486SLC2/50

IBM PS/2 Model 55/55SX System Board
   Upgrade 486SX/25

IBM PS/2 Model 55SX

IBM PS/2 Model 56 8556-xxx 486SLC/20

IBM PS/2 Model 56 9556-xxx 486SLC2/50

IBM PS/2 Model 57 8557-xxx 486SLC/20

IBM PS/2 Model 57 9557-xxx 486SLC2/50

IBM PS/2 Model 60/80 System Board Upgrade
   486DX/33

IBM PS/2 Model 70 8570-xxx 386DX/20

IBM PS/2 Model 70 8570-xxx 386DX/25

IBM PS/2 Model 70 8570-xxx 486DX/25

IBM PS/2 Model 70 System Board Upgrade
   486DX/33

IBM PS/2 Model 76 9576-xxx 486DX2/66

IBM PS/2 Model 76 9576-xxx 486SX/33

IBM PS/2 Model 77 9577-xxx 486DX2/66

IBM PS/2 Model 77 9577-xxx 486SX/33

IBM PS/2 Model 80 8580-xxx 386DX/16

IBM PS/2 Model 80 8580-xxx 386DX/20

IBM PS/2 Model 80 8580-xxx 386DX/25

IBM PS/2 Model 90 XP 486 8590-0H*
   486SX/25

IBM PS/2 Model 90 XP 486 8590-0J*
   486DX/25

IBM PS/2 Model 90 XP 486 8590-0K*
   486DX/33

IBM PS/2 Model 90 XP 486 8590-0L*
   486DX2/50

IBM PS/2 Model 90 XP 486 8590-xxx
   with 486DX2/66 processor upgrade

IBM PS/2 Model 90 XP 486 8590-xxx
   with 486DX/50 processor upgrade

IBM PS/2 Model 90 XP 486 9590-0L*
   486DX2/50

IBM PS/2 Model 90 XP 486 9590-xxx
   with 486DX/50 processor upgrade

IBM PS/2 Model 90 XP 486 9590-xxx
   with 486DX2/66 processor upgrade

IBM PS/2 Model 95 XP 486 8595-0H*
   486SX/25

IBM PS/2 Model 95 XP 486 8595-0J*
   486DX/25

IBM PS/2 Model 95 XP 486 8595-0K*
   486DX/33

IBM PS/2 Model 95 XP 486 8595-0L*
   486DX2/50

IBM PS/2 Model 95 XP 486 8595-0M*
   486DX/50

IBM PS/2 Model 95 XP 486 8595-xxx
   with 486DX2/66 processor upgrade

IBM PS/2 Model 95 XP 486 9595-0L*
   486DX2/50

IBM PS/2 Model 95 XP 486 9595-0M*
   486DX/50

IBM PS/2 Model 95 XP 486 9595-xxx
   with 486DX2/66 processor upgrade

IBM PS/2 Model P70 8573-xxx 386DX/20

IBM PS/2 Model P75 8573-xxx 486DX/33

IBM PS/2 Server 85 9585-0X* 486SX/33

IBM PS/2 Server 85 9585-0X* with 486DX2/66
   processor upgrade

IBM PS/2 Ultimedia DV M57 9557-xxx
   486SLC2/50[1]

IBM PS/2 Ultimedia M57 8557-xxx
   386SLC/20[1]

IBM PS/2 Ultimedia M57 9557-xxx
   486SLC2/50[1]

IBM PS/2 Ultimedia M77 9577-xxx 486DX2/66

IBM PS/2 Ultimedia M77 9577-xxx 486SX/33

IBM PS/ValuePoint 425SX/D 6384-Fxx

IBM PS/ValuePoint 425SX/S 6382-Fxx

IBM PS/ValuePoint 433DX/D 6384-Mxx

IBM PS/ValuePoint 433DX/S 6382-Mxx

IBM PS/ValuePoint 433DX/T 6387-Mxx

IBM PS/ValuePoint 433SX/D 6384-Kxx

IBM PS/ValuePoint 433SX/S 6382-Kxx

IBM PS/ValuePoint 466DX2/D 6384-Wxx

IBM PS/ValuePoint 466DX2/T 6387-Wxx

IBM ThinkPad 300

IBM ThinkPad 700C[1]

IBM ThinkPad 720C[1]

ICL Alfaskop DS 458 Eisa

ICL ErgoPRO C4/33

ICL ErgoPRO D4/25

ICL ErgoPRO D4/33d

ICL System Platform CXe486/66

ICL System Platform CXe486i

ICL System Platform CXe486s

ICL System Platform FX486/33

ICL System Platform FX486/66

Image 486DX2/66 VESA

Image 486DX/50 EISA

Index INDEXPORT 486 OVD 66 LOCAL
    BUS CACHE

Index INDEXPORT 486-33 VL VESA CACHE

Index INDEXPORT 486/33

Index INDEXPORT 486/50 I CACHE

Index INDEXPORT 486/50 VL VESA CACHE

Inelco INTEL XPRESS 50MHZ

Insight EISA/VESA 486DX2/66

Insight ISA/VESA 486DX2/66

Intel® Classic R-Series

Intel Express 486

Intel L486 Series Professional Workstation

Intel L486-Series/Professional GX

Intel X486/50E

INTERCOMP Digit 486SLC/25

INTERCOMP Planet 486/50 EISA

INTERCOMP Target 486/33

Intergraph Technical Desktop 1220

Investronica INVES BS-486

Investronica INVES IFS-486

Investronica INVES MP-900 XM UniProcessor

Investronica INVES WS 900 VL

IPC DYNASTY HE 486DX-33C

IPC DYNASTY HE 486DX2- 66C

IPC DYNASTY HE 486DX2-50C

IPC DYNASTY HE 486SX-25C

IPC DYNASTY LE 486DX-33 (incl. 33C)

IPC DYNASTY LE 486DX2-50 (incl. 50C)

IPC DYNASTY LE 486DX2-66 (incl. 66C)

IPC DYNASTY LE 486SX-25 (incl. 25C)

IPC DYNASTY SE 486DX2-50C

IPC DYNASTY SE 486DX2-66C

IPC DYNASTY SE 486SX-25C

Ipex 486DX2-66 Centra 1000

Ipex 486DX2-66 Centra 1000 EISA

Ipex 486DX2-66 Centra 1000 EISA
    (Entry Level)

Ipex 486DX2-66 Centra 1000 EISA/VL-BUS

Ipex 486DX2-66 Centra 1000 VESA

Ipex 486DX2-66 Centra 2000

Ipex 486DX2-66 Centra 2000 EISA

Ipex 486DX2-66 Centra 2000 EISA
    (Entry Level)

Ipex 486DX2-66 Centra 2000 EISA/VL-BUS

Ipex 486DX2-66 Centra 2000 VESA

Ipex 486DX2-66 Desktop

Ipex 486DX2-66 Desktop (EISA)

Ipex 486DX2-66 Desktop EISA (Entry Level)

Ipex 486DX2-66 Desktop EISA/VL-BUS

Ipex 486DX2-66 Desktop VESA

Ipex 486DX2-66 Mini Tower

Ipex 486DX2-66 Mini Tower EISA

Ipex 486DX2-66 Mini Tower EISA
    (Entry Level)

Ipex 486DX2-66 Mini Tower EISA/VL-BUS

Ipex 486DX2-66 Mini-Tower VESA

Ipex 486DX2-66 Slimline

Ipex 486DX2-66 Slimline (WD Form Factor)

Ipex 486DX33 Centra 1000

Ipex 486DX33 Centra 1000 EISA

Ipex 486DX33 Centra 1000 EISA (Entry Level)

Ipex 486DX33 Centra 1000 EISA/VL-BUS

Ipex 486DX33 Centra 1000 VESA

Ipex 486DX33 Centra 2000

Ipex 486DX33 Centra 2000 EISA

Ipex 486DX33 Centra 2000 EISA (Entry Level)

Ipex 486DX33 Centra 2000 EISA/VL-BUS

Ipex 486DX33 Centra 2000 VESA

Ipex 486DX33 Desktop

Ipex 486DX33 Desktop EISA

Ipex 486DX33 Desktop EISA (Entry Level)

Ipex 486DX33 Desktop EISA/VL-BUS

Ipex 486DX33 Desktop VESA

Ipex 486DX33 Mini Tower

Ipex 486DX33 Mini Tower EISA

Ipex 486DX33 Mini Tower EISA (Entry Level)

Ipex 486DX33 Mini Tower VESA

Ipex 486DX33 Mini-Tower EISA/VL-BUS

Ipex 486DX33 Slimline

Ipex 486DX33 Slimline (WD Form Factor)

Ipex 486DX50 Centra 1000

Ipex 486DX50 Centra 1000 EISA

Ipex 486DX50 Centra 1000 EISA (Entry Level)

Ipex 486DX50 Centra 1000 EISA/VL-BUS

Ipex 486DX50 Centra 1000 VESA

Ipex 486DX50 Centra 2000

Ipex 486DX50 Centra 2000 EISA

Ipex 486DX50 Centra 2000 EISA (Entry Level)

Ipex 486DX50 Centra 2000 EISA/VL-BUS

Ipex 486DX50 Centra 2000 VESA

Ipex 486DX50 Desktop

Ipex 486DX50 Desktop EISA

Ipex 486DX50 Desktop EISA (Entry Level)

Ipex 486DX50 Desktop EISA/VL-BUS

Ipex 486DX50 Desktop VESA

Ipex 486DX50 Mini Tower

Ipex 486DX50 Mini Tower EISA

Ipex 486DX50 Mini Tower EISA (Entry Level)

Ipex 486DX50 Mini Tower VESA

Ipex 486DX50 Mini-Tower EISA/VL-BUS

Ipex 486DX50 Slimline

Ipex 486DX50 Slimline (WD Form Factor)

Ipex 486SX25 Centra 1000

Ipex 486SX25 Centra 1000 EISA

Ipex 486SX25 Centra 1000 EISA (Entry Level)

Ipex 486SX25 Centra 1000 EISA/VL-BUS

Ipex 486SX25 Centra 1000 VESA

Ipex 486SX25 Centra 2000

Ipex 486SX25 Centra 2000 EISA

Ipex 486SX25 Centra 2000 EISA (Entry Level)

Ipex 486SX25 Centra 2000 EISA/VL-BUS

Ipex 486SX25 Centra 2000 VESA

Ipex 486SX25 Desktop

Ipex 486SX25 Desktop EISA

Ipex 486SX25 Desktop EISA (Entry Level)

Ipex 486SX25 Desktop EISA/VL-BUS

Ipex 486SX25 Desktop VESA

Ipex 486SX25 Mini Tower

Ipex 486SX25 Mini Tower (EISA)

Ipex 486SX25 Mini Tower EISA (Entry Level)

Ipex 486SX25 Mini Tower VESA

Ipex 486SX25 Mini-Tower EISA/VL-BUS

Ipex 486SX25 Slimline

Ipex 486SX25 Slimline (WD Form Factor)

Ipex 486SX33 Centra 1000 EISA

Ipex 486SX33 Centra 1000 EISA (Entry Level)

Ipex 486SX33 Centra 1000 EISA/VL-BUS

Ipex 486SX33 Centra 1000 ISA

Ipex 486SX33 Centra 1000 VESA

Ipex 486SX33 Centra 2000 EISA

Ipex 486SX33 Centra 2000 EISA (Entry Level)

Ipex 486SX33 Centra 2000 EISA/VL-BUS

Ipex 486SX33 Centra 2000 ISA

Ipex 486SX33 Centra 2000 VESA

Ipex 486SX33 Desktop

Ipex 486SX33 Desktop EISA

Ipex 486SX33 Desktop EISA (Entry Level)

Ipex 486SX33 Desktop EISA/VL-BUS

Ipex 486SX33 Desktop VESA

Ipex 486SX33 Mini Tower EISA

Ipex 486SX33 Mini Tower EISA (Entry Level)

Ipex 486SX33 Mini Tower ISA

Ipex 486SX33 Mini Tower VESA

Ipex 486SX33 Mini-Tower EISA/VL-BUS

Ipex 486SX33 Slimline

Ipex 486SX33 Slimline (WD Form Factor)

KT Technology KT 386DX-33

KT Technology KT386DX40

KT Technology KT486DX2-50 VESA

KT Technology KT486DX2-66VESA LB

KT Technology KT486DX33

KT Technology KT486DX50

L.E.M. Technologies Sys38640/M

Leading Edge® D4/DX-33 Plus DeskTop

Leading Edge D4/DX-50 Plus DeskTop

Leading Edge D4/DX2-50 Plus DeskTop

Leading Edge D4/MTDX-33 MiniTower

Leading Edge D4/MTDX-50 MiniTower

Leading Edge D4/MTDX2-50 MiniTower

Leading Edge D4/MTSX-25 MiniTower

Leading Edge D4/MTSX-33 MiniTower

Leading Edge D4/SX-25 Plus DeskTop

Leading Edge D4/SX-33 Plus DeskTop

Leading Edge WinPro 486/SX-25

Leading Edge WinPro 486e/DX-33

Leading Edge WinPro 486e/DX-50

Leading Edge WinPro 486e/DX2-50

Leading Edge WinPro 486e/SX-25

Leading Edge WinPro 486e/SX-33

Legacy 486DLC-33 System

Legacy VLB 486DX-33

Lundin 400 Series 486 EISA w/ 486DX/50

Lundin 400 Series 486 ISA w/ 486DX/33

Lundin 400 Series 486 VESA w/ 486DX/33

Master Cascade 386-40 Small Desktop

Master Cascade 486-33 Mini-Tower

Maximus 486-50MHz Maxi-CAD

Maximus Cyrix 486/40 VESA Local Bus

MetaTech 486DX/33 ISA

MetaTech 486DX/33 VESA

MetaTech 486DX/50 EISA

Micron 486VL Magnum 433 DX

Micron 486VL Magnum 433 SX

Micron 486VL Magnum 450 DX2

Micron 486VL Magnum 466 DX2

Micron 486VL MagServer 433 DX

Micron 486VL MagServer 450 DX2

Micron 486VL MagServer 466 DX2

Micron 486VL PowerStation 433 DX

Micron 486VL PowerStation 433 SX

Micron 486VL PowerStation 450 DX2

Micron 486VL PowerStation 466 DX2

Micron 486VL ValueLine 466 DX2

Micron 486VL WinServer 433 DX

Micron 486VL WinServer 450 DX2

Micron 486VL WinServer 466 DX2

Micron 486VL WinStation 433 DX

Micron 486VL WinStation 433 SX

Micron 486VL WinStation 450 DX2

Micron 486VL WinStation 466 DX2

Midwest Micro 486DX2/50 VESA/ISA

MIKROLOG OY Osborne 4280G-66

MIKROLOG OY Osborne LP4D-33CLB

MIKROLOG OY Osborne LP4D-33N

MIKROLOG OY Osborne LP4D-50C

MIKROLOG OY Osborne LP4D-50CLB

MIKROLOG OY Osborne LP4D-50N

MIKROLOG OY Osborne LP4D-66CLB

MIKROLOG OY Osborne LP4D-66N

MIKROLOG OY Osborne LP4S-25N

MIKROLOG OY Osborne LP4S-33CLB

MIKROLOG OY Osborne LP4S-33N

MIKROLOG OY Osborne MT4D-33CLB

MIKROLOG OY Osborne MT4D-33N

MIKROLOG OY Osborne MT4D-50CLB

MIKROLOG OY Osborne MT4D-50N

MIKROLOG OY Osborne MT4D-66CLB

MIKROLOG OY Osborne MT4D-66N

MIKROLOG OY Osborne MT4S-25N

MIKROLOG OY Osborne MT4S-33CLB

MIKROLOG OY Osborne MT4S-33N

MIND 386DX/33 ISA

MIND 486 DX2/66 ISA

MIND 486DX/33 EISA

MIND 486DX/33 ISA

MIND 486DX/50 EISA

MIND 486DX/50 ISA

MIND 486DX2/50 EISA

MIND 486DX2/50 ISA

MIND 486DX2/66 EISA

MIND 486SX/25 EISA

MIND 486SX/25 ISA

MIND 486SX/33 EISA

MIND 486SX/33 ISA

MiTAC DM4066

Modular MST/200

National Instruments® VXIpc-486 Model 200

National Instruments VXIpc-486 Model 500

NCR StarStation

NCR System 3000 Model 3307

NCR System 3000 Model 3314

NCR System 3000 Model 3320

NCR System 3000 Model 3335

NCR System 3000 Model 3345

NCR System 3000 Model 3350

NCR System 3000 Model 3355

NCR System 3000 Model 3445

NCR System 3000 Model 3447

NEC® Image 425

NEC Image 433

NEC Image 466

NEC PowerMate 386/25S

NEC PowerMate 425

NEC PowerMate 433

NEC PowerMate 466

NEC PowerMate 486/33e

NEC PowerMate 486/33i

NEC PowerMate 486/50e

NEC PowerMate 486/50i

NEC PowerMate 486sx/25e

NEC PowerMate DX2/66e

NEC UltraLite® Versa

Netis Ultra N433VL

Netis Ultra N450VL

Network Connection M2

Network Connection T-3000

Network Connection T-4000

Network Connection TNX

Network Connection Triumph T.R.A.C.

Network Connection Triumph T.S.C.V

Nimrod DESKTOP 486DX2/66 ISA

Nimrod LC-DESKTOP 486DX2/66 ISA

Nimrod MINI-TOWER 486DX2/66 ISA

Nimrod TOWER 486DX2/66 ISA

NORTH-EAST NE Micro 433LV

NORTH-EAST NE Micro 450LV

NORTH-EAST NE Micro 466LV

Northgate® 386

Northgate 486/33

Northgate 486/33 Slimline ZXP

Northgate 486/33 VESA ISA

Northgate 486/33e Baby AT

Northgate Elegance 333

Northgate Elegance 425i

Northgate Elegance 433e

Northgate Elegance 433i

Northgate Elegance SP 386/33

Northgate Elegance SP 433

Northgate Elegance ZXP

Northwest Micro Signature I 4/33

Northwest Micro Signature II 4/33 VLB

Oki® if486VX550D

Olivetti® LSX5010

Olivetti LSX5015

Olivetti LSX5020

Olivetti LSX5025

Olivetti LSX5030

Olivetti M300-28

Olivetti M300-30

Olivetti M300-30P

Olivetti M380-40

Olivetti M400-10

Olivetti M400-40

Olivetti M400-60

Olivetti M480-10

Olivetti M480-20

Olivetti M480-40

Olivetti M6-420

Olivetti M6-440

Olivetti M6-460

Olympia Olystar 300D-33

Olympia Olystar 400D-33

Olympia Olystar 400D-66 EISA

Olympia Olystar 400S-25

Optima 486DX2/66vl

Optimus 486DX/50 EISA

Optimus 486DX/50 LocalBus

Optimus 486DX2/50 VL

Optimus 486DX2/66

Optimus 486SX/25 VL

Osborne EISA 486DX50 Fileserver

Osborne Mpower 486DX2-66
Osicom 4133L 486/DX266 VESA LB
Osicom 4133L 486/DX33 VESA LB
Packard Bell 1110
Packard Bell 1120
Packard Bell 1150
Packard Bell 2050
Packard Bell 400T
Packard Bell 470
Packard Bell 485
Packard Bell 486CDM
Packard Bell 486DX/33
Packard Bell 486SX/25
Packard Bell 495
Packard Bell 515E
Packard Bell 525E
Packard Bell 545E
Packard Bell 550
Packard Bell 560
Packard Bell 565E
Packard Bell AXCEL 1033
Packard Bell AXCEL 105
Packard Bell AXCEL 1066
Packard Bell AXCEL 130
Packard Bell AXCEL 2005
Packard Bell AXCEL 2015
Packard Bell AXCEL 2033
Packard Bell AXCEL 205
Packard Bell AXCEL 2066 MINITOWER
Packard Bell AXCEL 230
Packard Bell AXCEL 405 (incl. H model)
Packard Bell AXCEL 410
Packard Bell AXCEL 410E
     (incl. H, F and W G models)
Packard Bell AXCEL 420
Packard Bell AXCEL 450
Packard Bell AXCEL 450G
     (incl. H, J and TJ models)
Packard Bell AXCEL 460
Packard Bell AXCEL 460H (incl. TJ model)
Packard Bell AXCEL 486/33
Packard Bell AXCEL 486A66
Packard Bell AXCEL 486SX

Packard Bell AXCEL 530
Packard Bell AXCEL 533H
     (incl. J and TJ models)
Packard Bell AXCEL 533STJ
Packard Bell AXCEL 550
Packard Bell AXCEL 550MT/J
Packard Bell AXCEL 570
Packard Bell AXCEL 630 MINITOWER
Packard Bell AXCEL 666J
     (incl. TJ and TL models)
Packard Bell AXCEL 850
Packard Bell EXECUTIVE 486/33
     (incl. ELITE model)
Packard Bell EXECUTIVE 486/33 G
     (incl. J model)
Packard Bell EXECUTIVE 486DX2/JW
     (incl. TY model)
Packard Bell EXECUTIVE 486SX
     (incl. -2F and -G models)
Packard Bell EXECUTIVE 486SX ELITE
     (incl. SERIES SI model)
Packard Bell EXECUTIVE 486SX-4G
Packard Bell EXECUTIVE 486SX/FW
     (incl. /HW model)
Packard Bell EXECUTIVE 486SX250
Packard Bell EXECUTIVE 486XE
     (incl. C and S models)
Packard Bell EXECUTIVE Elite Series
     486SXCC
Packard Bell FORCE 1066
Packard Bell FORCE 107
Packard Bell FORCE 110
Packard Bell FORCE 1135
Packard Bell FORCE 1137
Packard Bell FORCE 117
Packard Bell FORCE 200
Packard Bell FORCE 2010
Packard Bell FORCE 2020
Packard Bell FORCE 2040 MINITOWER
Packard Bell FORCE 2233 MINITOWER
Packard Bell FORCE 2376 (incl. F model)
Packard Bell FORCE 2386 MINITOWER
Packard Bell FORCE 250

Packard Bell FORCE 405

Packard Bell FORCE 425

Packard Bell FORCE 486 SX
(incl. E, -M1, and -M130 models)

Packard Bell FORCE 486/25

Packard Bell FORCE 486/33
(incl. +, E, -M1, and -M210 models)

Packard Bell FORCE 486/33G
(incl. J, JW, and PLUS models)

Packard Bell FORCE 48625 (incl. EX model)

Packard Bell FORCE 486CDM-1/TV

Packard Bell FORCE 486DX/DJ-W
(incl. G-W, H, H2, J and JT-W models)

Packard Bell FORCE 486DX2 -WG

Packard Bell FORCE 486DX2/EJT
(incl. W model)

Packard Bell FORCE 486DX2/F JT
(incl. JT-W, J-W and LT-W models)

Packard Bell FORCE 486DX2/G-W

Packard Bell FORCE 486MT50J

Packard Bell FORCE 486SX (incl. /20, /20G, E,
M1, and M130 models)

Packard Bell FORCE 486SX-WG

Packard Bell FORCE 486SX/25
(incl. G and W models)

Packard Bell FORCE 486SX/BE
(incl. FW, FW-2, M, MM and H2 models)

Packard Bell FORCE 486SX/OH-W

Packard Bell FORCE 515

Packard Bell FORCE 515S (incl. PLUS model)

Packard Bell FORCE 525 (incl. B and S
models)

Packard Bell FORCE 545 (incl. B and S
models)

Packard Bell FORCE 565 (incl. S model)

Packard Bell FORCE 600 (incl. B and S
models)

Packard Bell FORCE 715 MINITOWER

Packard Bell FORCE T66

Packard Bell LEGEND 102H
(incl. ELITE model)

Packard Bell LEGEND 1066 WG ELITE

Packard Bell LEGEND 1133

Packard Bell LEGEND 1134 ELITE

Packard Bell LEGEND 1135

Packard Bell LEGEND 1136

Packard Bell LEGEND 115

Packard Bell LEGEND 1166

Packard Bell LEGEND 1176

Packard Bell LEGEND 120

Packard Bell LEGEND 125

Packard Bell LEGEND 126 ELITE

Packard Bell LEGEND 127

Packard Bell LEGEND 128

Packard Bell LEGEND 135 (incl. H model)

Packard Bell LEGEND 140

Packard Bell LEGEND 1900

Packard Bell LEGEND 1910

Packard Bell LEGEND 2000

Packard Bell LEGEND 2001

Packard Bell LEGEND 2002 ELITE

Packard Bell LEGEND 2011 SUPREME

Packard Bell LEGEND 2025

Packard Bell LEGEND 207

Packard Bell LEGEND 2133 MINITOWER

Packard Bell LEGEND 2135 MINITOWER

Packard Bell LEGEND 2176 ELITE MT

Packard Bell LEGEND 2266 MINITOWER

Packard Bell LEGEND 2270 MINITOWER

Packard Bell LEGEND 2276 MINITOWER

Packard Bell LEGEND 2300 MINITOWER

Packard Bell LEGEND 233

Packard Bell LEGEND 234 ELITE

Packard Bell LEGEND 245

Packard Bell LEGEND 33T SUPREME

Packard Bell LEGEND 33T SUPREME
MINITOWER

Packard Bell LEGEND 430 G
(incl. WG and F models)

Packard Bell LEGEND 430 W G ELITE

Packard Bell LEGEND 430E
(incl E2 and EL models)

Packard Bell LEGEND 435E ELITE
(incl. 2 ELITE model)

Packard Bell LEGEND 440G

Packard Bell LEGEND 445 G ELITE
    (incl. G 2 ELITE model)
Packard Bell LEGEND 486CDM-1/TV
Packard Bell LEGEND 486T/50
Packard Bell LEGEND 510H
Packard Bell LEGEND 605H ELITE
Packard Bell LEGEND 625
Packard Bell LEGEND 635J
Packard Bell LEGEND 635TJ ELITE
Packard Bell LEGEND 660
    (incl. ELITE and H models)
Packard Bell LEGEND 660H
Packard Bell LEGEND 660TJ (incl. H model)
Packard Bell LEGEND 66D SUPREME
Packard Bell LEGEND 66T SUPREME
Packard Bell LEGEND 670
Packard Bell LEGEND 695 SUPREME
Packard Bell LEGEND 700 (incl. ELITE model)
Packard Bell LEGEND 740
Packard Bell LEGEND 747 MINITOWER
Packard Bell LEGEND 750 SUPREME
Packard Bell LEGEND 760 SUPREME
Packard Bell LEGEND 770 (incl. ELITE model)
Packard Bell LEGEND 780
Packard Bell LEGEND 780 SUPREME
Packard Bell LEGEND 790
Packard Bell LEGEND 800 SUPREME
    (incl. 800+)
Packard Bell LEGEND 800 SUPREME/50
Packard Bell LEGEND 840 MINITOWER
Packard Bell LEGEND 845 MINITOWER
Packard Bell LEGEND 848 MINITOWER
Packard Bell LEGEND 900 F
    (incl. F-ELITE, and G models)
Packard Bell LEGEND 920SX SUPREME
Packard Bell LEGEND 925 G
    (incl. G ELITE and J model)
Packard Bell LEGEND 933 G
    (incl. G ELITE, J, J ELITE and J+ models)
Packard Bell LEGEND 950
    (incl. ELITE and J ELITE models)
Packard Bell LEGEND 960TJ

Packard Bell LEGEND 966J
    (incl. ELITE model)
Packard Bell LEGEND 966TJ
    (incl. TJ ELITE, TJ2 ELITE, TJ-W
    ELITE, WG and TZ models)
Packard Bell LEGEND M950
Packard Bell LEGEND MT950 (incl. J model)
Packard Bell LEGEND T66
Packard Bell PACKMATE 486/33
    (incl. J and G model)
Packard Bell PACKMATE 486/50
Packard Bell PACKMATE 486/E
Packard Bell PACKMATE 48625
Packard Bell PACKMATE 486DX/33 Y
    (incl. Y-W and X models)
Packard Bell PACKMATE 486DX2/50TY
    (incl TY-W model)
Packard Bell PACKMATE 486DX2/T Z -W
    (incl. Y model)
Packard Bell PACKMATE 486DX33/T Y
    (incl. /TY-W model)
Packard Bell PACKMATE 486SX
Packard Bell PACKMATE 486SX/20 E
    (incl. F, and G models)
Packard Bell PACKMATE 486SX/25G
Packard Bell PACKMATE 486SX/25W
    (incl. TG model)
Packard Bell PACKMATE 486SX/33X
    (incl. X2 and TM models)
Packard Bell PACKMATE 486SX25U
    (incl. U2 and X models)
Packard Bell PACKMATE 733 C MT
Packard Bell PACKMATE X225
Packard Bell PACKMATE X230
Packard Bell PACKMATE X233
Packard Bell PACKMATE X240
Packard Bell PACKMATE X250
    (incl. Y model)
Packard Bell PACKMATE XT266
PC-Brand Leader 486dx/33 Cache
PC-Brand Leader 486dx2/66 Cache
PC-Brand NB 486slc
PC Tech Zeos Upgradable

Peacock 486DX 50

Pionex 486DX/33 VL

Pionex 486DX2/50 VL

Pionex 486DX2/66 VL

Pionex 486SX/25 VL

Poly 486-33VZ

Poly 486-50E

Poly 486-66E

Poly 486-66EV

Poly 486-66VI

Poly 486-66VL

Poly 486SX-25Y

Poly 486SX-33VL

Porchester SKAI 486DX/50VL

Porchester SKAI 486DX2/66EVL

Positive by Tandon 486dx/33

Positive by Tandon 486dx2/66

Precision 486/50 EISA

Precision 486/50F

Precision 486/66 EISA VL-Bus

Precision 486/66 VL-Bus

Precision 486/66E

Primax 486/33E

Primax 486/66E

Professional Concepts Beeker 4-33/VL2

Professional Concepts Beeker 4-50/VL2

Professional Concepts Beeker 4-66/VL2

Professional Concepts Beeker 6900

Professional Concepts Quinn 4-33/VLE

Professional Concepts Quinn 4-50/VLE

Professional Concepts Quinn 4-66/VLE

Professional Concepts Saavij 4-33/VL3

Professional Concepts Saavij 4-50/VL3

Professional Concepts Saavij 4-66/VL3

PROTECH 486-66 MHz EISA

PROTECH 486-66 MHz ISA

QNIX OMNI486DX2/66

Quadrant 486DX/33 VESA LOCAL BUS

Quadrant 486DX/50 VESA LOCAL BUS

Quadrant 486DX2/66 VESA LOCAL BUS

Quadrant 486SX/25 VESA LOCAL BUS

Quadrant 486SX/33 VESA LOCAL BUS

Quantex 486DX/33 VL

Quantex 486DX2/50 VL

Quantex 486DX2/66 VL

Quantex 486SX/25 VL

Radisys EPC-23

Radisys EPC-4

Radisys EPC-5

Radisys EPC-7

Rask REC 486-50F

RDIpc i486DX2/66c Eisa

RDIpc i486DX2/66c Isa

RDIpc i486DX2/66c VL Bus

Repco Data Inc R33B486

Reply Model 32

Reply PS/2 Model 50/50Z System Board
    Upgrade 486SLC2/50

Reply PS/2 Model 55/55SX System Board
    Upgrade 486/25

Reply PS/2 Model 60/80 System Board
    Upgrade 486/33

Reply PS/2 Model 70 System Board
    Upgrade 486/33

Research Machines RM E Series QE-486/33

Research Machines RM S Series PC-486/25SX

Research Machines RM SystemBase 486/33

Research Machines RM V Series V466

Rolta ROLTASTATION 433E

Rose Computer Cidex 386DX-40 ISA(AMD)

Rose Computer Cidex 486-40DX ISA

Samsung DeskMaster 486/33P

Samsung DeskMaster 486D2/66E

Samsung DeskMaster 486S/25N

SCA Professional 3486DX2/66 VLB

SCA Professional 486DX 50 VLB

SCA Professional 486DX2/66 VLB

Seanix ASI 948633VM

Seanix ASI 9DX266VM

Shuttle 486VL 50

Sidus Formula 486/33i

Sidus Formula 486/50e

Siemens-Nixdorf PCD-3M/25

Siemens-Nixdorf PCD-3T/33

Siemens-Nixdorf PCD-4G/33

Siemens-Nixdorf PCD-4G/66

Siemens-Nixdorf PCD-4GSX/25

Siemens-Nixdorf PCD-4H/66

Siemens-Nixdorf PCD-4HSX

Siemens-Nixdorf PCD-4LSL

Siemens-Nixdorf PCD-4LSX

Siemens-Nixdorf PCD-4T/33

Siemens-Nixdorf PCD-4T/66

Siemens-Nixdorf PCE-4C/DX2-66

Siemens-Nixdorf PCE-4C/SX25

Siemens-Nixdorf PCE-4R/33

Siemens-Nixdorf PCE-4RSX/25

Siemens-Nixdorf PCE-4T/66

Siemens-Nixdorf PCE-5S/60

Sirex Eaton 486DX-33 EISA/LocalBus

Sirex PowerMaster486DX2-66 LocalBus

Sirex SpeedMaster 486DX-50 ISA

Softworks Citus MDC 386-33

Softworks Citus MDC 486DX-33

Softworks Citus MDC 486DX-50

Softworks Citus MDC 486DX2-50

Softworks Citus MDC 486DX2-66

Softworks Citus MDC X 486 50

SRC Systems 486DX2/66 VESA LOCAL BUS

SRC Systems GRAPHICSTATION

Standard Computronics HIPPO-VL 486DX2-66
  VESA LOCAL BUS

SuperCom Touch TI433

SuperCom Touch TI450

SuperCom Touch TI466

Swan 486/33DB

Swan 486/33V

Swan 486/50ES

Swan 486/66ES

Swan 486DX/33 EISA-DB

Swan 486DX2-50DB

Swan 486DX2/66 EISA-DB

Swan 486DX2/66DB

Swan 486SX/25DB

Swan 486SX/25V

Syncomp Mega+386i 40 PC

Syncomp Mega+486DX2/50e PC

Syncomp Mega+486DX2/50i PC

Syncomp Mega+486DX2/66e PC

Syncomp Mega+486DX2/66i PC

Syncomp Mega+486e-33 PC

Syncomp Mega+486e-50 PC

Syncomp Mega+486i-33 PC

Syncomp Mega+486i-50 PC

Syncomp Mega+486SXe-25 PC

Syncomp Mega+486SXi 33 PC

Syncomp Mega+486SXi-25 PC

Syncomp Micro 486DX2/50i PC

Syncomp Micro 486i-33 PC

Syncomp Micro 486i-50 PC

Syncomp Micro 486SXi-25 PC

Syncomp Micro386i 40 PC

Syncomp Mini 386i 40PC

Syncomp Mini 486-50i PC

Syncomp Mini 486DX2/50e PC

Syncomp Mini 486DX2/50i PC

Syncomp Mini 486DX2/66e PC

Syncomp Mini 486DX2/66i PC

Syncomp Mini 486e-33 PC

Syncomp Mini 486e-50 PC

Syncomp Mini 486i-33 PC

Syncomp Mini 486SXe-25 PC

Syncomp Mini 486SXi 33 PC

Syncomp Mini 486SXi-25 PC

Syncomp Mini+386i 40 PC

Syncomp Mini+486DX2/50e PC

Syncomp Mini+486DX2/50i PC

Syncomp Mini+486DX2/66e PC

Syncomp Mini+486DX2/66i PC

Syncomp Mini+486e-33 PC

Syncomp Mini+486e-50 PC

Syncomp Mini+486i-33 PC

Syncomp Mini+486i-50 PC

Syncomp Mini+486SXe-25 PC

Syncomp Mini+486SXi 33 PC

Syncomp Mini+486SXi-25 PC

T-DATA LIN 486-33 DX

T-DATA LIN 486-50 DX

Tandon 486dx/33

Tandon 486dx2/66

Tandon MCSII 486dx/33

Tandon MCSII 486dx/33c

Tandon MCSII 486dx2/66c

Tandon NII 486dx/33

Tandon PACII plus 486dx2/66

Tandon PCAII 486dx2/66

Tandon PCAII 486sx/25

Tandon Profile 486dx/33

Tandon TargetII 486dx2/66

Tandon TargetII 486sx/25

Tandon Tower 486dx/66e

Tandon TowerII 486dx2/66

Tandy® 425 SX

Tandy 433 DX

Tandy 433 SX

Tandy 450 DX2

Tandy 466 DX2

Tandy 4820 SX/T

Tandy 4825 SX

Tandy 4833 LX/T

Tandy 4850 EP

Tandy 4866 LX/T

Tangent 486DX/33 EISA

Tangent 486DX/33 ISA

Tatung TCS-8460S 386SX/25

Tatung TCS-9300T 486DX2/66

Tatung TCS-9360T 486DX/33

Tatung TCS-9370T 486DX2/66

Tatung TCS-9620E 486DX2/66

Tatung TCS-9650E 486DX2/66

Tatung TCS-9700 486DLC/40

Tatung TCS-9910S 486SLC/33

Techway Endeavour E62

Techway Endeavour E62VL

Techway Endeavour E77

Techway Endeavour E77VL

Techway Endeavour E84

Techway Endeavour E84VL

TELEMECANIQUE FTX507-6B

Texas Instruments TravelMate™ 4000
   Color Series[1]

Texas Instruments TravelMate 4000 Series[1]

Texas Instruments TravelMate 4000 WinDX2[1]

TFE Atlantic 486 DX 50MHz

Tiki-Data PC UNIVERSAL

Toshiba® T4400SX

Toshiba T4500

Toshiba T6400SX

Tri-Star TriCAD 486/66

Tri-Star Tri-Win Station

TriGem 486/33MM
   (incl. 486 /P (Type 30) model)

TriGem 486/50F

TriGem 486/66F

TriGem 486/66VC

TriGem 486DX2/50MM (incl. 486 /P (Type 40)

TriGem 486DX2/66MM
   (incl. 486 /P (Type 50) model)

TriGem 486VC

TriGem 4DX/33ME

TriGem 4DX2/50ME

TriGem 4DX2/66ME

TriGem 4SX/25ME

TriGem 4SX/33ME

TriGem SX486/25C

TriGem SX486/25MM
   (incl. 486 /P (Type 10 and 12) models)

TriGem SX486/33MM
   (incl. 486 /P (Type 20) model)

Tulip® Vision Line DT/DC 486DX-33i

Tulip Vision Line DT/DC 486DX-50i

Tulip Vision Line DT/DC 486DX-66i

Tulip Vision Line series 486DX-33i

Tulip Vision Line series 486DX-50i

Tulip Vision Line series 486DX-66e

Tulip Vision Line Series 486DX-66i

TWINHEAD Superset 700

U.S. Micro Jet 386-33

U.S. Micro Jet 386-40

U.S. Micro Jet 486-33

U.S. Micro Jet 486-50

U.S. Micro Jet 486DLC-33

U.S. Micro Jet 486DX2-50

U.S. Micro Jet 486DX2-66

U.S. Micro Jet 486SX-25

U.S. Micro Jet EISA 486-33

U.S. Micro Jet EISA 486-50

U.S. Micro Jet EISA 486DX2-50

U.S. Micro Jet EISA 486DX2-66

U.S. Micro Jet EISA 486SX-25

U.S. Micro Jet VL 486-50

U.S. Micro Jet VL 486DX2-50

U.S. Micro Jet VL 486DX2-66

U.S. Micro Jet VL 486SX-25

U.S. Micro Jet VL486-33

Ultra-Comp 486DX-33

Ultra-Comp 486DX-33 EISA VLB

Ultra-Comp 486DX-33 VLB

Ultra-Comp 486DX-50

Ultra-Comp 486DX-50 EISA VLB

Ultra-Comp 486DX-50 VLB

Ultra-Comp 486DX2-66

Ultra-Comp 486DX2-66 EISA VLB

Ultra-Comp 486DX2-66 VLB

Unidata 486 66 MHz ISA

Unisys® PW^2 3336

Unisys PW^2 Advantage 3256

Unisys PW^2 Advantage 3336

Unisys PW^2 Advantage 4163

Unisys PW^2 Advantage 4253

Unisys PW^2 Advantage 4256

Unisys PW^2 Advantage 4336

Unisys PW^2 Advantage 4506

Unisys PW^2 Advantage Plus 4668

Unisys PW^2 Advantage Plus 5606

Unisys PW^2 Advantage Plus 5608

Victor DX/50

Victor 400 DX/50

Victor 400 SX/25

Victor 486 DX/66

Victor 486DX/33

Victor V486DSX/25

Viglen Contender 4DX33

Viglen EX-Series

Viglen Genie 4DX66

Vobis 486 VC-HD 33

Vobis 486 VC-HD 50

Vobis 486 VIO 66

Vobis 486 VIO SX25

Vtech LASER 386 Ultra Slim

Vtech LASER 486DX/3 Desktop

Vtech LASER 486DX/3 Desktop (w/LBVGA)

Vtech LASER 486DX/3 Desktop (w/VLBUS)

Vtech LASER 486DX/3 Tower

Vtech LASER 486DX/3 Tower (w/VLBUS)

Vtech LASER 486DX2/4 Desktop

Vtech LASER 486DX2/4 Desktop (w/LBVGA)

Vtech LASER 486DX2/4 Desktop (w/VLBUS)

Vtech LASER 486DX2/4 Tower

Vtech LASER 486DX2/4 Tower (w/VLBUS)

Vtech LASER 486DX2/6 Desktop

Vtech LASER 486DX2/6 Desktop (w/LBVGA)

Vtech LASER 486DX2/6 Desktop (w/VLBUS)

Vtech LASER 486DX2/6 Tower

Vtech LASER 486DX2/6 Tower (w/VLBUS)

Vtech LASER 486SX/3 Desktop

Vtech LASER 486SX/3 Desktop (w/LBVGA)

Vtech LASER 486SX/3 Tower

Vtech LASER 486SX/3 Ultra Slim

Vtech LASER 486SX/3 Ultra Slim (w/LBVGA)

Vtech LASER 486SX/4 Desktop

Vtech LASER 486SX/4 Desktop (w/LBVGA)

Vtech LASER 486SX/4 Desktop (w/VLBUS)

Vtech LASER 486SX/4 Tower

Vtech LASER 486SX/4 Ultra Slim

Vtech LASER 486SX/4 Ultra Slim (w/LBVGA)

Vtech LASER LT322 Notebook

Vtech LASER LT421 Notebook

Vtech Platinum SMP

Wang Microsystems ASI-CPU-E266

Wang Microsystems DTE-33

Wang Microsystems PC 350/40C

Western 486V25SX VESA LOCAL BUS

Western 486V33 DX EISA

Western 486V33 DX ISA

Western 486V50 DX EISA

Western 486V50 DX ISA

Western 486V50 DX2 ISA

Western 486V66 DX2 EISA

Western 486V66 DX2 ISA

Wyle Laboratories Intel Xpress Deskside
       w/486DX-50MHz

Wyle Laboratories Intel Xpress DeskTop
       w/486DX2-66MHz

Wyle Laboratories Intel Xpress DeskTop
   w/486DX-50MHz
Wyse® Decision 386/40
Wyse Decision 386SX/25C
Wyse Decision 486/25
Wyse Decision 486/33
Wyse Decision 486/33E
Wyse Decision 486/33T
Wyse Decision 486DX2/50
Wyse Decision 486se-25SX
Wyse Decision 486se-33DX
Wyse Decision 486se-33SX
Wyse Decision 486se-50DX2
Wyse Decision 486se-66DX2
Wyse Decision 486si-25SX
Wyse Decision 486si-33DX
Wyse Decision 486si-33SX
Wyse Decision 486si-50DX2
Wyse Decision 486si-66DX2
Wyse Decison 386/25
Wyse Series 6000i Model 640
Wyse Series 6000i Model 645
Wyse Series 7000i Model 740
Zenith Data Systems Z-386/25
Zenith Data Systems Z-386/33E
Zenith Data Systems Z-386SX/20
Zenith Data Systems Z-425/SX
Zenith Data Systems Z-425S+
Zenith Data Systems Z-433/DX
Zenith Data Systems Z-450X+
Zenith Data Systems Z-486/33ET
Zenith Data Systems Z-486SX/20
Zenith Data Systems Z-486SX/25E
Zenith Data Systems Z-Note 425Ln
Zenith Data Systems Z-Server 425SE
Zenith Data Systems Z-Server 433DE
Zenith Data Systems Z-Server 450DE
Zenith Data Systems Z-Station 420SEh
Zenith Data Systems Z-Station 420SEn
Zenith Data Systems Z-Station 420Sh
Zenith Data Systems Z-Station 420Sn
Zenith Data Systems Z-Station 425Sh
Zenith Data Systems Z-Station 425Sn

Zenith Data Systems Z-Station 433DEh
Zenith Data Systems Z-Station 433DEn
Zenith Data Systems Z-Station 433Dh
Zenith Data Systems Z-Station 433SEh
Zenith Data Systems Z-Station 450XEh
Zenith Data Systems Z-Station 450Xh
Zenith Data Systems Z-Station 450Xn
Zenith/INTEQ Tempest Workstation/Server
Zenon Z-Dream IIII EISA/VESA 486DX/66
ZEOS® 486DX/33CDT
ZEOS 486DX/33EISA
ZEOS 486DX/33ISA
ZEOS 486DX/50
ZEOS 486SX/20DT
ZEOS Freestyle 386SL 25
ZEOS Upgradable 486 DX/33 Cache
ZEOS Upgradable 486 DX2/66 Cache
ZEOS Upgradable 486 SX/33 Cache
ZEOS Upgradable EISA 486 DX2/66 Cache
ZEOS Upgradable Local Bus DX2-66

x86 Architecture Multiprocessor Computers

The following multiprocessor systems have been tested.

ACER AcerFrame 3000MP 33 (Model 3255)[1]
ACER AcerFrame 3000MP 50 (Model 3257)[1]
ALR POWERPRO DMP 4/50
ALR POWERPRO DMP 4/66d
ALR PROVEISA DMP 4/33
ALR PROVEISA DMP 4/50D
ALR PROVEISA DMP 4/66D
AST Manhattan SMP 486/50
AST Manhattan SMP Pentium
COMPAQ Systempro/XL Dual 486/50
COMPAQ Systempro Dual 386/25
COMPAQ Systempro Dual 486/33
COMPAQ SystemPro Dual 486DX2/66
Corollary Extended C-bus 486DX2/66
ICL System Platform MX486/50
Micronics MPro 2000

NCR System 3000 Model 3360
NCR System 3000 Model 3450[2]
NCR System 3000 Model 3550[2,3]
Olivetti LSX5040
Sequent WinServer 1000[3]
Sequent WinServer 1500[3]
Sequent WinServer 3000[3]
Sequent WinServer 5000[3]
Siemens-Nixdorf PCE-4T/33 Dual
Siemens-Nixdorf PCE-4T/50 Dual
Wyse Series 7000i Model 740MP/33
Wyse Series 7000i Model 740MP/66
Wyse Series 7000i Model 760MP

MIPS® ARC/R4000™ Series Computers

The following RISC systems have been tested.

ACER ARC1
ACER Formula
Carrera R4000™
DESKStation Evolution RISC PC
MIPS ARCSystem Magnum SC-50
MIPS ARCSystem Magnum PC-50
MIPS Millenium SC-50
MIPS Millenium PC-50
Olivetti M700-10
NeTPower RISCpc Series 100

SCSI® Host Adapters

*The following SCSI adapters have been tested
with the following scanner, CD-ROM, tape,
fixed and removable drives (except as noted):
ArchiveST 4000 DAT, CD-Technologies CD
Porta-Drive T-3401, Hewlett-Packard ScanJet
IIc, NEC Intersect CDR-74, Micropolis 1924,
Peripheral Land Infinity 88, Procom
Technology MCD-DS, Syquest 5110, Toshiba
TXM-3401, WangTek 5150es. Adapters listed
with * have been tested for use with both x86
and MIPS platforms.*

Adaptec® AHA-1510
*Adaptec AHA-1520
*Adaptec AHA-1522
*Adaptec AHA-1540B[4]
Adaptec AHA-1540C
*Adaptec AHA-1542B[4]
Adaptec AHA-1542C[5]
Adaptec AHA-1640
Adaptec AHA-1740[6]
Adaptec AHA-1742[6]
*Adaptec AHA-1740A[7]
*Adaptec AHA-1742A[7]
*Adaptec AHA-2740
*Adaptec AHA-2742
Adaptec AIC-6260[8]
Adaptec AIC-7770[9]
Always IN-2000
BusLogic BT-445S
*BusLogic BT-542B
BusLogic BT-545S
BusLogic BT-640A
BusLogic BT-646S
BusLogic BT-742A
*BusLogic BT-747S
COMPAQ Fast SCSI-2 Controller
COMPAQ 6260 SCSI-2 Controller
DPT PM2011b (incl. cache)[10]
DPT PM2012b (incl. cache)[10]
*Data Technology Corp. 3290
Data Technology Corp. 3292[11]
Future Domain MCS-600
Future Domain MCS-700
Future Domain TMC-845[12,13]
*Future Domain TMC-850[12,13]
*Future Domain TMC-850M(ER)[13]
Future Domain TMC-860[12,13]
Future Domain TMC-860M[13]
Future Domain TMC-885[12,13]
Future Domain TMC-885M[13]
*Future Domain TMC-1650
Future Domain TMC-1660
*Future Domain TMC-1670
Future Domain TMC-1680

*Future Domain TMC-7000EX
IBM PS/2 Microchannel SCSI Host Adapter[14]
IBM PS/2 Microchannel SCSI Host Adapter
    (with cache)[14]
Maynard 16-bit SCSI Adapter[15, 16]
MediaVision Pro Audio Spectrum-16
NCR 53C700 SCSI Adapter
NCR 53C710 SCSI Adapter
NCR 53C90 SCSI Controller[17]
*NCR 53C94 SCSI Controller[18]
Olivetti ESC-1
Olivetti ESC-2
Olivetti EFP-2[19, 20]
Trantor T-128[12, 21, 13]
Trantor T-228[12, 13, 15, 22]
Trantor T-130B[12, 21]
++Trantor T-348 MiniSCSI Plus
*UltraStor 14f[23]
*UltraStor 24f[24]
UltraStor 24fa
UltraStor 34f
UltraStor 124f[20]

SCSI CD-ROM Drives

*The following CD-ROM drives have been tested with the following adapters: Adaptec AHA-1510, AHA-1542C, AHA-1640 and AHA-1742A; Future Domain TMC-1670, TMC-850M and MCS-600; IBM PS/2 Microchannel SCSI Host Adapter (with cache); Ultrastor 24fa. Drives listed with * support multimedia audio.*

*CD-Technology CD Porta-Drive T-3301
*CD-Technology CD Porta-Drive T-3401
Chinon 431[25]
*Chinon 535
*COMPAQ DualSpeed CD-ROM Drive
DEC RRD 42-DA
Denon DRD 253[26]
Hitachi® CDR-1750S
*Hitachi CDR-3750S

IBM 3501[25]
*IBM Enhanced Internal CDROM II Drive
    32G2958
*IBM Enhanced External CDROM II Drive
    3510005
*IBM PS/2 CDROM II Drive
*NEC Intersect CDR-73M[27]
*NEC Intersect CDR-83M
*NEC Intersect CDR-74
*NEC Intersect CDR-84
*NEC Intersect CDR-74-1
Panasoni® CR-501B[25]
Philips / Laser Magnetic Storage CM-215[28]
*Pioneer® DRM-600[29]
*Procom Technology MCD-DS
*Sony CDU-541
*Sony CDU-561
*Sony CDU-6211
*Sony CDU-7211
Texel DM-5021[25]
*Texel DM-5024[30]
Toshiba® TXM-3201[25]
*Toshiba TXM-3301
*Toshiba TXM-3401

Other CD-ROM Drives

*The following CD-ROM drives with proprietary interfaces have been tested. Drives listed with * support multimedia audio.*

++Creative Labs Sound Blaster Pro™
++Panasonic CR-521
++Panasonic CR-561
*++Sony® CDU 31a

SCSI Tape Drives

The following SCSI tape drives have been tested with the following adapters using the Windows NT Backup utility: Adaptec AHA-1510, AHA-1542C, AHA-1640 and AHA-1742A; Future Domain TMC-1670, TMC-850M and MCS-600; IBM PS/2 Microchannel SCSI Host Adapter (with cache); Ultrastor 24fa. Drives are listed under their appropriate Setup Tape entry.

4 Millimeter DAT

> ArchiveST 2000DAT
>   (4520NP, EAX4350)[31]
> ArchiveST 4000DAT (4324NP, 4352XP)
> Exabyte 4200[32]
> Exabyte 4200c[33]
> Hewlett-Packard JetStor 2000
> Hewlett-Packard JetStor 5000
> Hewlett-Packard 35470a[31, 34]
> Hewlett-Packard 35480a
> Hewlett-Packard C1503a[31, 34]
> Hewlett-Packard C1504a
> Hewlett-Packard C2224c[31, 34]
> Hewlett-Packard C2225b
> ++IBM 2.0Gb 4mm Tape Drive Option
> Maynard Maynstream 1300DAT
> Maynard 2000 DAT
> Tecmar DataVault 2000
> Tecmar DataVault 4000
> WangDAT Model 1300XL
> WangDAT Model 3100
> WangDAT Model 3200

Archive® 2150S, 2525S, 2750

> Archive 2150/2250[35]
> Archive 2525
> Archive 2750
> Archive 2800

Exabyte 8200 Series (SCSI-1)

> Exabyte EXB-8200[34, 35]
> Exabyte EXB-8200ST[34, 35]
> Exabyte EXB-8205[32]
> Exabyte EXB-8205ST[32]

Exabyte 8500 Series (SCSI-2)

> Exabyte EXB-8500
> Exabyte EXB-8500ST
> Exabyte EXB-8500c[34]
> Exabyte EXB-8500cST[34]
> Exabyte EXB-8505
> Exabyte EXB-8505ST
> IBM 5.0Gb 8mm Tape Drive Option
> IBM 3445 Model 001 5.0Gb 8mm
>   Tape Drive

Tandberg 3660, 3820, 4120, 4220

> IBM 3450 1.2Gb Tape Drive Model 001
> Tandberg 3660
> Tandberg 3820
> Tandberg 4120
> Tandberg 4220

Wangtek 525, 250

> Tecmar QT-525ES
> Wangtek 5150ES
> Wangtek 5525ES
> Wangtek 51000ES

Other Tape Drives

The following tape drives have been tested using the Windows NT Backup utility.

QIC-40/QIC-80 Floppy Tape Drive[36]

Archive 5150Q (SuperHornet)
Archive 5540
Archive 5580
Colorado Memory Systems Jumbo 250
Iomega Tape 250
Summit Express SE120
Summit Express SE250
WangTek 3040
WangTek 3080

SCSI Removable Media

The following removable media (cartridge) drives have been tested with the following adapters: Adaptec AHA-1510, AHA-1542C, AHA-1640 and AHA-1742A; Future Domain TMC-1670, TMC-850M and MCS-600; IBM PS/2 Microchannel SCSI Host Adapter (with cache); Ultrastor 24fa. Media must be mounted when installing Windows NT.

Hewlett-Packard Series 6300 650/C[37]
IBM 0632 Model C2*[34, 37]
Insite 21mb Floptical
Iomega 21mb Floptical
Iomega Bernoulli Transportable 90 Pro
Iomega Bernoulli Transportable 150
Peripheral Land Infinity 40 Turbo
Peripheral Land Infinity 88
Quantum Passport XL 85
Quantum Passport XL 127

Sony SMO-S511A-11[37]
Sony RMO-S350
Syquest® 555 44mb cartridge
Syquest 5110 88mb cartridge

SCSI Scanners

The following scanners have been tested with the following adapters: Adaptec AHA-1510, AHA-1542c, AHA-1640 and AHA-1742A; Future Domain TMC-1670, TMC-850M and MCS-600; IBM PS/2 Microchannel SCSI Host Adapter (with cache); Ultrastor 24fa.

HP ScanJet® IIc
HP ScanJet IIp

Disk Controllers

The following disk controllers have been tested.

COMPAQ Intelligent Drive Array Controller
COMPAQ Intelligent Drive Array Controller-2
COMPAQ SMART Array Controller
DELL Drive Array Controller
DELL SCSI Array Controller[1]
Western Digital® 1003 (ESDI, IDE)

Storage Cabinets

The following peripheral storage cabinets have been tested.

Hewlett-Packard Storage System with
   HP EISA HBA[38]
Hewlett-Packard Storage System with
   HP MCA HBA[38]

Video Display Support

The following display adapters have been tested. Most common scan frequencies are supported. Your video monitor should support the same resolutions and scan frequencies as your display adapter. Please refer to README.WRI for more information on display support.

Display Adapter	Driver	640x480		800x600		1024x768		Other
		x16	x256	x16	x256	x16	x256	
ACTIX GRAPHICS ENGINE	S3		NI		NI		NI	
ACTIX GRAPHICS ENGINE 32 PLUS	S3		NI		NI		NI	
ATI 8514 ULTRA	ATI		NI		NI		NI	
ATI GRAPHICS ULTRA PRO	ATI		NI		NI		NI	2, 3, 4, 5, 6, 7, 11
ATI GRAPHICS ULTRA PRO VLB	ATI		NI		NI		NI	2, 3, 4, 5, 6, 7, 11
ATI GRAPHICS ULTRA PLUS	ATI		NI		NI		NI	2, 3, 4, 5, 6, 7, 11
ATI GRAPHICS ULTRA	ATI		NI		NI		NI	
ATI GRAPHICS VANTAGE	ATI		NI		NI		NI	
COMPAQ AVGA	++AVGA	NI	NI	NI				
COMPAQ QVISION 1024/I	QVISION		NI		NI		NI	
COMPAQ QVISION 1024/E	QVISION		NI		NI		NI	
COMPAQ QVISION 1024/I (ENHANCED)	QVISION		NI		NI		NI	
COMPAQ QVISION 1024/E (ENHANCED)	QVISION		NI		NI		NI	
COMPAQ QVISION 1280/I	QVISION		NI		NI		NI	11
COMPAQ QVISION 1280/E	QVISION	NI	NI	NI	NI		NI	11
DELL DGX	DGX		NI		NI		NI	2, 5, 7, 9, 10, 11
DIAMOND SPEEDSTAR	ET4000	NI	NI	NI	NI	B	B	
DIAMOND SPEEDSTAR 24X	WD	NI	NI	NI	NI	B	B	
DIAMOND SPEEDSTAR PRO & PRO VLB	CIRRUS	NI	NI	NI	NI	NI	NI	
DIAMOND STEALTH 24	S3		NI		NI		NI	
DIAMOND STEALTH 24 VLB	S3		NI		NI		NI	
DIAMOND STEALTH PRO & PRO VLB	S3		NI		NI		NI	
DIAMOND STEALTH VRAM	S3		NI		NI		NI	
ELSA WINNER 1000	S3		NI		NI		NI	
GENOA VLB	CIRRUS	NI	NI	NI	NI	NI	NI	
IBM XGA	XGA		NI				I	
IBM XGA-2	XGA		NI		NI		B	1, 8

Display Adapter	Driver	640x480		800x600		1024x768		Other
		x16	x256	x16	x256	x16	x256	
MEDIAVISION THUNDER & LIGHTNING	CIRRUS	NI	NI	NI	NI	NI	NI	
METHEUS PREMIER 928	S3		NI		NI		NI	
METHEUS PREMIER VL-BUS 928	S3		NI		NI		NI	
MICRONICS VL-BUS	S3		NI		NI		NI	
NCR 77C22	NCR77C22	NI	NI	NI	NI	NI		
NCR 77C22E	NCR77C22	NI	NI	NI	NI	NI	NI	
NUMBER 9 GXE	S3		NI		NI		NI	11
ORCHID FAHRENHEIT 1280	S3		NI		NI		NI	
ORCHID FAHRENHEIT VA	S3		NI		NI		NI	
ORCHID FAHRENHEIT VA/VLB	S3		NI		NI		NI	
ORCHID PRODESIGNER 2	ET4000	NI	NI	NI	NI	B	B	
ORCHID PRODESIGNER IIS	ET4000	NI	NI	NI	NI	B	B	
PARADISE WINDOWS GRAPHICS ACCELERATOR	WD	NI	NI	NI	NI	B	B	
STB POWERGRAPH X-24	S3		NI		NI		NI	
STB POWERGRAPH VL-24	S3		NI		NI		NI	
STB WIND/X HC	S3		NI		NI		NI	
TRIDENT 8900C	TRIDENT	NI	NI	NI	NI	B	B	
TRIDENT 9000	TRIDENT	NI		NI		B		
VIDEO SEVEN® VRAM	VIDEO7	NI	NI	NI		NI		
VIDEO SEVEN VRAM II	VIDEO7	NI	NI	NI	NI	NI	NI	

Common modes in table above

NI   Non-Interlaced only

I   Interlaced only

B   Both Interlaced and Non-Interlaced

Other resolutions

1	640x400x256	5	800x600x65k	9	1152x900x256
2	640x480x65k	6	800x600x16m	10	1152x900x65k
3	640x480x16m	7	1024x768x65k	11	1280x1024x256
4	640x480, true color	8	1040x768x256		

Display adapters not listed above are expected to work if they use the following supported chip sets. Install first as Standard VGA, then select the corresponding driver from the Setup application in Program Manager.

Chip Set	Driver
ATI Mach 8	ATI
ATI Mach 32	ATI
ET4000	ET4000
S3 801, 805, 911, 911A, 924, 928	S3
WD90C30	Western Digital/Paradise
WD90C31	Western Digital/Paradise
VGA	VGA

The following table shows the maximum display and color resolutions available with each video driver using different amounts of video RAM. Most display adapters can use the standard VGA driver for 16-color modes.

Drivers	Video RAM	Colors				
		16	256	65k	16m	True Color
ATI	1Mb		1024x768	640x480	640x480	
	2Mb		1280x1024	1024x768	800x600	640x480
Cirrus	1Mb	1024x768	1024x768			
COMPAQ AVGA	512Kb	800x600	640x480			
COMPAQ Qvision	512Kb		640x480			
	1Mb		1024x768			
	2Mb		1280x1024			
DGX	2Mb		1280x1024	1152x900		
ET4000	512Kb	1024x768	640x480			
	1Mb	1024x768	1024x768			
NCR 77C22	1Mb	1024x768	1024x768			
S3	1Mb		1024x768			
	3Mb		1280x1024			
Trident	512Kb	1024x768				
	1Mb	1024x768	1024x768			
Video7	512Kb	1024x768	640x480			
	1Mb	1024x768	1024x768			
VGA	256Kb	640x480				
	512Kb	800x600				
WD	1Mb	1024x768	1024x768			
XGA	1Mb		1040x768			

Network Adapters

*The following network adapters have been tested. Adapters listed with * have been tested for use with both x86 and MIPS platforms.*

*3Com 3C503 EtherLink II® (Coax & TP)
*3Com 3C503/16 EtherLink II/16 (Coax & TP)
*3Com 3C507 EtherLink® 16 (Coax & TP)
*3Com 3C509 EtherLink III Parallel Tasking
    Adapter - ISA (Coax, TP and Combo)
3Com 3C523 EtherLink/MC (Coax & TP)
3Com 3C529 EtherLink III Parallel Tasking
    Adapter - MCA (Coax & TP)
*3Com 3C579 EtherLink III Parallel Tasking
    Adapter - EISA (Coax & TP)
Advanced Micro Devices Am1500T Ethernet
    Adapter
Advanced Micro Devices Am2100 Ethernet
    Adapter
Advanced Micro Devices PCnet
Advanced Micro Devices PCnet-ISA Single
    Chip Ethernet Controller
*COMPAQ 32-Bit Dualspeed Token Ring
    Controller
COMPAQ 32-Bit Netflex Controller
COMPAQ 32-Bit Netflex Controller with
    Token Ring Module
COMPAQ Ethernet 16TP Controller
COPS LTI ISA
*DEC DE100 EtherWORKS LC
*DEC DE101 EtherWORKS LC/TP
*DEC DE200 EtherWORKS Turbo
*DEC DE201 EtherWORKS Turbo/TP
*DEC DE202 EtherWORKS Turbo TP/BNC
*DEC DE422 EtherWORKS EISA TP/BNC
*IBM Token Ring Adapter 16/4
IBM Token Ring Adapter 16/4 /A
Intel EtherExpress™ 16 MCA PCLA8110
Intel EtherExpress 16 MCA TP PCLA8120
*Intel EtherExpress 16 PCLA8110

*Intel EtherExpress 16C PCLA8100
*Intel EtherExpress 16TP PCLA8120
*Intel EtherExpress FlashC PCLA8105
National Semiconductor DP83932 (SONIC)
    Motherboard Ethernet Controller on
    MIPS ARC/R4000 systems
*Network Peripherals NP-EISA/S FDDI
Network Peripherals NP-MCA/S FDDI
Novell/Eagle Technology NE1000
*Novell/Eagle Technology NE2000
*Novell/Eagle Technology NE3200
*Proteon ProNET-4/16 p1390 ISA Adapter
Proteon ProNET-4/16 p1990 EISA Adapter
*Standard Microsystems 8003EP EtherCard
    PLUS
*Standard Microsystems 8013EBT EtherCard
    PLUS16
*Standard Microsystems 8013EP EtherCard
    PLUS Elite16
Standard Microsystems 8013EP/A EtherCard
    PLUS Elite/A
*Standard Microsystems 8013EPC EtherCard®
    PLUS Elite16
*Standard Microsystems 8013EW EtherCard
    PLUS EliteCombo
*Standard Microsystems 8013EWC EtherCard
    PLUS EliteCombo
*Standard Microsystems 8013W EtherCard
    PLUS Elite16T
*Standard Microsystems 8013WB EtherCard
    PLUS
*Standard Microsystems 8013WC EtherCard
    PLUS Elite16T
Standard Microsystems 8013WP/A EtherCard
    PLUS Elite10T/A
Ungermann-Bass NIUpc
*Ungermann-Bass NIUpc/EOTP
Ungermann-Bass NIUps/EOTP

Multimedia Audio Adapters

The following audio adapters have been tested.

COMPAQ Business Audio
Creative Labs Sound Blaster™ 1.x
Creative Labs Sound Blaster Pro[39]
Media Vision Pro AudioSpectrum-16[40]
Media Vision Pro AudioStudio[40]
Media Vision Thunder Board[39]
Microsoft Windows™ Sound System
Built-in audio adapter on MIPS ARC/R4000
systems.

Modems

*The following modems are supported for use
with Remote Access Services.*

ATI 2400 etc/e
ATI 9600 etc/e
AT&T® 2224 CEO
AT&T Comsphere 3810
AT&T Comsphere 3811
AT&T Comsphere 3820
AT&T Comsphere 3830
AT&T Dataport
AT&T 4024
Bocamodem M1440
Cardinal 2400e
Cardinal 9600
Cardinal 14400
Cardinal 14400 Internal
Codex 2264
Codex 3220
Codex 3260
Codex 3261
Codex 3262
Codex 3263
Codex 3265
Codex 3260 Fast

Codex 3261 Fast
Codex 3262 Fast
Codex 3263 Fast
Codex 3265 Fast
Codex 3220 Plus
CXR Telcom 1445
DataRace RediModem V.32bis[41]
Datatrek 2424AMH
Datatrek Elite 624D[42]
Datatrek V.32[43]
Digicom Scout
Digicom Scout Plus
DSI 9624LE Plus
DSI 9624E
ETech UFOMATE P1496MX
Evercom 24
Evercom 24E
Evercom 24E+
Gateway 2000 Telepath Internal
GVC SM2400
GVC SM96
GVC FM14400
Hayes® Compatible 1200
Hayes Compatible 2400
Hayes Compatible 9600
Hayes Pocket Modem 2400
Hayes Smartmodem™ 2400
Hayes Smartmodem 9600
Hayes Optima 9600
Hayes Optima 14400
Hayes Ultra 9600
Hayes Ultra 14400
Hayes V Series 9600
Intel SatisFaxtion® 100
Intel SatisFaxtion 400e
Intel 9600EX
Intel 14400EX
Macronix Maxlite Fax 9696
Macronix VOMAX 2000
Megahertz P2144 Pocket Faxmodem
Megahertz T3144 for Toshiba
Megahertz Z3144 for Zenith
Megahertz C5144 for COMPAQ LTE

MicroCom QX® 4232bis[42]
MicroComQX 4232HS
MicroGate MG96[41]
MicroGate MG144[41]
MicroPorte 1042
MultiTech MultiModem 224[44]
MultiTech MultiModem MT932
NEC 9635E Plus
Octocom 8324[41]
Octocom 8396
PDI-1000[43]
Practical Peripherals 2400 Pocket
Practical Peripherals 2400SA[43]
Practical Peripherals 2400MNP[42]
Practical Peripherals 9600SA
Practical Peripherals 14400SA
Racal-RMD 2412
Racal-RMD 2412/2[45]
Racal-RMD 3221
Racal-RMD 3222
Racal-RMD 3226
Racal-RMD 3223
Racal-RMD 9632PA
Racal-RMD 9642PA
SupraModem 2400
Supra Fax Modem 9624 Internal
Supra Fax Modem V32
Supra Fax Modem V32bis
Supra Fax Modem Plus
Telebit® QBlazer
Telebit T1000
Telebit T1500[43]
Telebit T1600[42]
Telebit T2000
Telebit T2500
Telebit T3000
Telebit TrailBlazer® Plus
Telebit WorldBlazer
Telebit WorldBlazer-Rackmount
UDS Motorola® V.3225[42]
UDS Motorola V.3227[46]
UDS Motorola V.3229
UDS Motorola FasTalk V.32/42b[46]

US Robotics Courier Dual
US Robotics Courier HST
US Robotics Courier V.32bis
US Robotics Sportster 2400
US Robotics Sportster 9600
US Robotics Sportster 14400
Ven-Tel 9600 Plus II[47]
Ven-Tel Pocket 24 V.42bis FAX
Ven-Tel 14400 Fax
Ven-Tel 14400 Fax Internal
Western Datacom Worldcom V32bis[43]
Zoom AFX
Zoom FX 9624V
Zoom VFX V.32bis
ZyXel U-1496
ZyXel U-1496E

Hardware Security Hosts

The following hardware security hosts have been tested for use with Remote Access Services.

Digital Pathways Defender 1000D
Racal Gaurdata GSM
Security Dynamics ACM400

ISDN Adapters

The following ISDN adapters have been tested for use with Remote Access Services.

DigiBoard PCIMAC ISA Adapter
DigiBoard PCIMAC MC Adapter
DigiBoard PCIMAC/4 Adapter

Multi-port Serial Adapters

The following multi-port adapters have been tested for use with Remote Access Services. Adapters listed with * have been tested as standard serial ports only.

*Comtrol Hostess 550
DigiBoard 2Port
DigiBoard 4Port
DigiBoard 8Port
DigiBoard CX Adapter
*DigiBoard DigiCHANNEL PC/X Host
      Adapter for ISA bus
DigiBoard PC/4e Adapter
DigiBoard PC/8e Adapter
DigiBoard PC/8i Adapter
DigiBoard PC/Xem Adapter
*Stargate Technologies Plus 8

Uninterruptable Power Supplies

The following uninterruptable power supplies have been tested

American Power Conversion Back-UPS
American Power Conversion Smart-UPS
Para Systems MinuteMan
Tripp Lite BC800LAN[48]
Unison (Tripp Lite) UNIPower PS

Keyboards

Any keyboard 100% compatible with those listed below.

101/102-key
IBM AT® (84-key)

Pointing Devices

The following pointing devices have been tested.

A4 Tech Serial Mouse
Acer M-SG14
AT&T 320 Mouse CA-93-6MD
CompuAdd Serial Mouse
Dexxa MF21-9F
Digital Equipment PCXAS-AA
Hewlett-Packard C1413A
Honeywell 2HW53-3E
IBM 33G3835
IBM 33G5430
ICL M-SF14-6MD
Kensington Expert Mouse Ver. 2.0
Key Tronic Trak101
Logitech® CA-93-6MD
Logitech M-MD14-2
Logitech M-MD14-9F
Logitech M-MD15L
Logitech M-SF14-6MD
Logitech M-SF15-6MD
Logitech Mouseman, Bus
Logitech Mouseman, Cordless
Logitech Mouseman, Serial
Logitech PA-82-9MI
Logitech Series 9 CC-93-9F
Logitech Trackman Mouse
Logitech Trackman Portable Mouse
Logitech Trackman Stationary Mouse
Microsoft Bus Mouse
      (Original - Green Buttons)
Microsoft Mouse, BallPoint®
Microsoft Mouse, Inport
Microsoft Mouse, PS/2 Compatible
Microsoft Mouse, Serial
Microsoft Mouse, Serial / PS/2
Microsoft Mouse 2.0, Bus
Microsoft Mouse 2.0, MousePort
Microsoft Mouse 2.0, Serial
Microsoft Mouse 2.0, Serial-MousePort

MotorMouse
Olivetti M-SE9-6MD
Sejin Electronics SWB-200
Ultra Mouse 260

Printers

*Drivers are included for the following printers.
Tested models are listed with *.*

Adobe® LaserJet II Cartridge v52.3
Agfa Compugraphic 400PS
Agfa Compugraphic Genics
Agfa Matrix ChromaScript v51.8
Agfa TabScript C500 PostScript Printer v50.3
Agfa-Compugraphic 9400P v49.3
Apple® LaserWriter® II NT v47.0
*Apple LaserWriter II NTX v47.0
Apple LaserWriter II NTX v51.8
Apple LaserWriter II NTX-J v50.5
Apple LaserWriter IIf v2010.113
Apple LaserWriter IIg v2010.113
Apple LaserWriter Plus v38.0
Apple LaserWriter Plus v42.2
Apple LaserWriter v23.0
Apple Personal LaserWriter NTR v2010.129
Apricot Laser
APS-PS PIP with APS-6-108 v49.3 or 52.2
APS-PS PIP with APS-6-80 v49.3 or 52.2
APS-PS PIP with LZR 1200 v49.3 or 52.2
APS-PS PIP with LZR 2600 v49.3 or 52.2
AST TurboLaser-PS v47.0
AT&T 470/475
AT&T 473/478
Brother® HJ-100
Brother HJ-100i
Brother HJ-770
Brother HL-10DV
Brother HL-10V
*Brother HL-4
Brother HL-4V
Brother HL-4Ve

*Brother HL-8
*Brother HL-8D
*Brother HL-8e
Brother HL-8V
Brother M-1309
Brother M-1324
Brother M-1809
Brother M-1818
Brother M-1824L
Brother M-1909
Brother M-1918
Brother M-1924L
*Bull Compuprint PageMaster 1025
Bull Compuprint PageMaster 413
Bull Compuprint PM 201
Canon® Bubble-Jet BJ-10e
Canon Bubble-Jet BJ-10ex
Canon Bubble-Jet BJ-10sx
Canon Bubble-Jet BJ-130
Canon Bubble-Jet BJ-130e
Canon Bubble-Jet BJ-20
Canon Bubble-Jet BJ-200
*Canon Bubble-Jet BJ-230
Canon Bubble-Jet BJ-300
*Canon Bubble-Jet BJ-330
Canon Bubble-Jet BJC-800
Canon LBP-4 PS-2 v51.4
Canon LBP-8III PS-1 v51.4
Canon LBP-8IIIR PS-1 v51.4
Canon LBP-8IIIT PS-1 v51.4
Canon PS-IPU Color Laser Copier v52.3
Canon PS-IPU Kanji Color Laser Copier v52.3
Citizen 120D
Citizen 120D+
Citizen 124D
Citizen 180D
Citizen 200GX
Citizen 200GX/15
Citizen 224
Citizen GSX 240 Scalable Font
Citizen GSX-130
Citizen GSX-140
Citizen GSX-140+

Citizen GSX-145
Citizen GSX-230
Citizen HSP-500
Citizen HSP-550
Citizen PN48
Citizen Prodot 24
Citizen Prodot 9
Citizen Prodot 9x
Citizen PROjet
Citizen Swift 200
Citizen Swift 24
Citizen Swift 240 Scalable Font
Citizen Swift 24e
Citizen Swift 24x
Citizen Swift 9
Citizen Swift 9x
C-Itoh 8510
Colormate PS v51.9
COMPAQ PAGEMARQ 15 v2012.015
COMPAQ PAGEMARQ 20 v2012.015
Dataproducts LZR 1260 v47.0
Dataproducts LZR 1560 v2010.127
Dataproducts LZR 960 v2010.106
Dataproducts LZR-2665 v46.2
Diconix 150 Plus
Digital Colormate PS v51.9
Digital DEClaser 1100 (LJ)
*Digital DEClaser 1100
Digital DEClaser 1150 v51.4
Digital DEClaser 1152 17 fonts
Digital DEClaser 1152 43 fonts
*Digital DEClaser 2100
Digital DEClaser 2100 plus (LJ)
Digital DEClaser 2150 plus v51.4
Digital DEClaser 2150 v51.4
*Digital DEClaser 2200
Digital DEClaser 2200 plus (LJ)
Digital DEClaser 2250 plus v51.4
Digital DEClaser 2250 v51.4
Digital DEClaser 3200 (LJ)
*Digital DEClaser 3200
Digital DEClaser 3250 v47
Digital DECmultiJET 1000

Digital DECmultiJET 2000
Digital DECwriter 95
Digital® LA310
Digital LA324
Digital LA424
Digital LA70
Digital LA75
Digital LA75 Plus
Digital LN03R ScriptPrinter
Digital PrintServer 17 v48.3
Digital PrintServer 20 v48.3
Digital PrintServer 32 v48.3
Digital PrintServer 40 Plus v48.3
Digital turbo PrintServer 20
EPSON® ActionLaser II
EPSON AP-3250 Scalable Font
EPSON AP-5000 Scalable Font
EPSON AP-5500 Scalable Font
EPSON Compatible 24 Pin
EPSON Compatible 9 Pin
EPSON DFX-5000
EPSON DLQ-2000
EPSON EPL-4000
EPSON EPL-4300
EPSON EPL-6000
EPSON EPL-7000
EPSON EPL-7500 v52.3
EPSON EPL-8000
EPSON EPL-8100
EPSON EX-1000
EPSON EX-800
EPSON FX-100
EPSON FX-100+
EPSON FX-1000
EPSON FX-105
EPSON FX-1050
EPSON FX-185
EPSON FX-286
EPSON FX-286e
EPSON FX-80
EPSON FX-80+
EPSON FX-800
*EPSON FX-85

EPSON FX-850

EPSON FX-86e

EPSON GQ-3500

EPSON JX-80

EPSON L-1000

EPSON L-750

EPSON LP-3000PS F2 v52.3

EPSON LP-3000PS F5 v52.3

EPSON LQ-100 Scalable Font

EPSON LQ-1000

EPSON LQ-1010

EPSON LQ-1050

EPSON LQ-1060

EPSON LQ-1070 Scalable Font

EPSON LQ-1170 Scalable Font

EPSON LQ-1500

EPSON LQ-200

*EPSON LQ-2500

*EPSON LQ-2550

EPSON LQ-400

EPSON LQ-450

EPSON LQ-500

*EPSON LQ-510

EPSON LQ-550

EPSON LQ-570 Scalable Font

EPSON LQ-800

EPSON LQ-850

EPSON LQ-850+

EPSON LQ-860

EPSON LQ-870 Scalable Font

EPSON LQ-950

EPSON LX-1050

EPSON LX-400

EPSON LX-80

EPSON LX-800

EPSON LX-810

EPSON LX-850

EPSON LX-850+

EPSON LX-86

EPSON MX-100

EPSON MX-80

EPSON MX-80 F/T

EPSON PostScript CARD v52.5

EPSON RX-100

EPSON RX-100+

EPSON RX-80

EPSON RX-80 F/T

EPSON RX-80 F/T+

EPSON SQ-1170 Scalable Font

EPSON SQ-2000

EPSON SQ-2500

EPSON SQ-2550

EPSON SQ-850

EPSON SQ-870 Scalable Font

EPSON T-750

EPSON T-1000

Fujitsu® Breeze 100

Fujitsu Breeze 200

Fujitsu DL 1100

Fujitsu DL 1100 Colour

Fujitsu DL 1150

Fujitsu DL 1200

Fujitsu DL 1250

Fujitsu DL 2400

Fujitsu DL 2600

Fujitsu DL 3300

Fujitsu DL 3350

Fujitsu DL 3400

Fujitsu DL 3450

Fujitsu DL 3600

Fujitsu DL 4400

Fujitsu DL 4600

Fujitsu DL 5600

Fujitsu DL 900

Fujitsu DX 2100

Fujitsu DX 2200

Fujitsu DX 2300

Fujitsu DX 2400

Fujitsu RX7100PS v50.3

GCC BLP Elite v52.3

GCC BLP II v52.3

GCC BLP IIS v52.3

GCC Business LaserPrinter v49.2

GCC Business LaserPrinter v51.4

Generic IBM Graphics 9pin wide

Generic IBM Graphics 9pin

Gestetner GLP800-Scout v52.3

Hermes H 606 PS (13 Fonts)

Hermes H 606 PS (35 fonts)

*Hermes H 606

HP DeskJet

*HP DeskJet 1200C

*HP DeskJet 500

HP DeskJet 510

HP DeskJet 500C

HP DeskJet 500C (Monochrome)

HP DeskJet 550C

HP DeskJet Plus

HP DeskJet Portable

HP LaserJet

HP LaserJet 2000

*HP LaserJet 4

HP LaserJet 4 PostScript v2011.110

*HP LaserJet 4Si

HP LaserJet 4Si/4Si MX PS

HP LaserJet 500+

HP LaserJet ELI PostScript v52.3

HP LaserJet IID PostScript Cartridge v52.2

*HP LaserJet IID

HP LaserJet III PostScript Cartridge v52.2

HP LaserJet III PostScript Plus v2010.118

*HP LaserJet III

HP LaserJet IIID PostScript Cartridge v52.2

HP LaserJet IIID PostScript Plus v2010.118

*HP LaserJet IIID

*HP LaserJet IIIP PostScript Cartridge v52.2

HP LaserJet IIIP PostScript Plus v2010.118

*HP LaserJet IIIP

*HP LaserJet IIISi PostScript v52.3

*HP LaserJet IIISi

HP LaserJet IIP Plus

*HP LaserJet IIP PostScript Cartridge v52.2

*HP LaserJet IIP

HP LaserJet Plus

*HP LaserJet Series II

*HP PaintJet

*HP PaintJet XL

HP PaintJet XL 300

HP PaintJet XL 300 v2011.112

HP QuietJet

HP QuietJet Plus

HP ThinkJet (2225 C-D)

IBM 4019 LaserPriner PS17

*IBM 4019 LaserPrinter PS39

IBM 4029 LaserPrinter PS17

IBM 4029 LaserPrinter PS39

*IBM 4039 LaserPrinter

IBM 4039 LaserPrinter PS39

IBM 4070 IJ

IBM 4079 Color Jetprinter PS

IBM 4216-020 v47.0

IBM 4216-030 v50.5

IBM ExecJet 4072

IBM Graphics

IBM Personal Page Printer II-31

IBM Personal Printer II 2380

IBM Personal Printer II 2381

IBM Personal Printer II 2390

IBM Personal Printer II 2391

IBM Portable 5183

*IBM Proprinter®

*IBM Proprinter II

IBM Proprinter III

IBM Proprinter X24

IBM Proprinter X24e

*IBM Proprinter XL

IBM Proprinter XL II

IBM Proprinter XL III

IBM Proprinter XL24

IBM Proprinter XL24e

IBM PS/1 2205

*IBM QuickWriter 5204

IBM QuietWriter III

Kodak® EktaPlus 7016

Kyocera® F-1000

Kyocera F-1000A

Kyocera F-1010

Kyocera F-1200S

Kyocera F-1800

Kyocera F-1800A

Kyocera F-2000A

Kyocera F-2010

Kyocera F-2200

Kyocera F-2200S

Kyocera F-3000

Kyocera F-3000A

Kyocera F-3010

Kyocera F-3300

Kyocera F-5000

Kyocera F-800

Kyocera F-800A

Kyocera F-820

Kyocera FS-1500 / FS-1500A

Kyocera FS-3500 / FS-3500A

Kyocera FS-5500 / FS-5500A

Kyocera FS-850 / FS-850A

LaserWriter Personal NT v51.8

Linotronic™ 100 v42.5

Linotronic 200 v47.1

Linotronic 200 v49.3

Linotronic 200/230

Linotronic 300 v47.1

Linotronic 300 v49.3

Linotronic 330 v52.3

Linotronic 330-RIP 30 v52.3

Linotronic 500 v49.3

Linotronic 530 v52.3

Linotronic 530-RIP 30 v52.3

Linotronic 630 v52.3

Mannesmann Tally® MT 130/24

Mannesmann Tally MT 131/24

Mannesmann Tally MT 150/24

Mannesmann Tally MT 151/24

Mannesmann Tally MT 230/24

Mannesmann Tally MT 330

Mannesmann Tally MT 350

Mannesmann Tally MT 360

Mannesmann Tally MT 730/735

Mannesmann Tally MT 82

Mannesmann Tally MT 90

Mannesmann Tally MT 904 Plus

Mannesmann Tally MT 908

Mannesmann Tally MT 91

Mannesmann Tally MT 92

Mannesmann Tally MT 92C

Mannesmann Tally MT 93

Mannesmann Tally MT 94

Mannesmann Tally MT 98/99

Microtek TrueLaser

Minolta SP 3000

Minolta SP 3500

Monotype® ImageMaster 1200 v52.3

Monotype Imagesetter v52.2

NEC Colormate PS/40 v51.9

NEC Colormate PS/80 v51.9

*NEC Jetmate 400

*NEC Jetmate 800

NEC Pinwriter CP6

NEC Pinwriter CP7

NEC Pinwriter P20

NEC Pinwriter P2200

NEC Pinwriter P2plus

NEC Pinwriter P30

NEC Pinwriter P3200

NEC Pinwriter P3300

NEC Pinwriter P5200

*NEC Pinwriter P5300

NEC Pinwriter P5XL

NEC Pinwriter P6

NEC Pinwriter P60

NEC Pinwriter P6200

NEC Pinwriter P6300

NEC Pinwriter P6plus

NEC Pinwriter P7

NEC Pinwriter P70

NEC Pinwriter P7plus

NEC Pinwriter P90

NEC Pinwriter P9300

NEC Pinwriter P9XL

NEC SilentWriter 95 v2010.119

NEC Silentwriter 95 v2011.111

NEC Silentwriter 97 v2011.111

NEC Silentwriter LC 860

NEC Silentwriter LC 860 Plus

NEC Silentwriter LC890 v47.0

NEC Silentwriter LC890XL v50.5

NEC Silentwriter S102

NEC Silentwriter2 290 v52.0

NEC Silentwriter2 90 v52.2

NEC Silentwriter2 990 v52.3

NeXT™ 400 dpi Laser Printer v2000.6

OceColor G5241 PS

OceColor G5242 PostScript Printer v50.3

Oki MICROLINE 801PS+F v52.3

Oki ML 182 Elite (IBM)

Oki ML 192 Elite (IBM)

Oki ML 193 Elite (IBM)

Oki ML 280 Elite (IBM)

Oki ML 320 Elite (IBM)

Oki ML 321 Elite (IBM)

Oki ML 3410 Elite (IBM)

Oki ML 380 Elite

Oki ML 390 Elite

Oki ML 391 Elite

Oki ML 393 Elite

Oki ML 393C Elite

Oki ML 590

Oki ML 591

Oki OL-400

Oki OL-410

Oki OL-800/840

Oki OL-810

Oki OL830-PS v52.5

Oki OL840-PS v51.8

Okidata LaserLine 6

Okidata ML 192

*Okidata ML 192-IBM

Okidata ML 192 Plus

Okidata ML 193

*Okidata ML 193-IBM

Okidata ML 193 Plus

Okidata ML 292

*Okidata ML 292-IBM

Okidata ML 293

*Okidata ML 293-IBM

Okidata ML 320

*Okidata ML 320-IBM

Okidata ML 321

*Okidata ML 321-IBM

Okidata ML 380

Okidata ML 390

Okidata ML 390 Plus

Okidata ML 391

Okidata ML 391 Plus

Okidata ML 393

Okidata ML 393 Plus

Okidata ML 393C

Okidata ML 393C Plus

Okidata ML 92-IBM

Okidata ML 93-IBM

Okidata OL-400

Okidata OL-800

Olivetti DM 109

Olivetti DM 124

Olivetti DM 124 C

Olivetti DM 124 L

Olivetti DM 309

Olivetti DM 309 L

Olivetti DM 309 S

Olivetti DM 309 SL

Olivetti DM 324

Olivetti DM 324 L

Olivetti DM 324 S

Olivetti DM 324 SL

Olivetti DM 600

Olivetti DM 600 S

Olivetti DM 624

Olivetti ETV 5000

Olivetti JP 150

Olivetti JP 350

Olivetti JP 350S

Olivetti PG 108

Olivetti PG 208 M2

Olivetti PG 306

Olivetti PG 306 PS (13 Fonts)

Olivetti PG 306 PS (35 Fonts)

Olivetti PG 308

Olivetti PG 308 HS

Olivetti PG 308 HS PostScript

Olivetti PG 404

Olivetti PG 408

Panasonic KX-P1081

Panasonic KX-P1123

Panasonic KX-P1124

Panasonic KX-P1124i

Panasonic KX-P1180

Panasonic KX-P1624

Panasonic KX-P1695

Panasonic KX-P2123

Panasonic KX-P2124

Panasonic KX-P2180

Panasonic KX-P2624

Panasonic KX-P4410

Panasonic KX-P4420

Panasonic KX-P4430

*Panasonic KX-P4450

Panasonic KX-P4450i

Panasonic KX-P4451

Panasonic KX-P4455 v51.4

QMS® 1725 Print System

QMS 2025 Print System

QMS 3225 Print System

QMS 420 Print System v2011.22 r15

QMS 4525 Print System

QMS 860 Print System v2011.22 r15

*QMS ColorScript™ 100 Model 10 v50.3

QMS ColorScript 100 Model 20 v50.3

QMS ColorScript 100 Model 30 v50.3

QMS ColorScript 100 Model 30si

QMS ColorScript 100 v49.4

QMS ColorScript 210 v2011.22

QMS ColorScript 230 v2011.22

QMS PS® Jet Plus v46.1

QMS PS Jet v46.1

QMS-PS 1700 v52.4

QMS-PS 2000 v52.4

QMS-PS 2200 v51.0 or 52.3

QMS-PS 2210 v51.0 or 52.3

QMS-PS 2220 v51.0 or 52.3

QMS-PS 410 v52.4

QMS-PS 800 Plus v46.1

QMS-PS 800 v46.1

*QMS-PS 810 Turbo v. 51.7

*QMS-PS 810 v47.0

QMS-PS 815 MR v52.4

QMS-PS 815 v52.4

QMS-PS 820 Turbo v51.7

QMS-PS 820 v51.7

QMS-PS 825 MR v52.4

QMS-PS 825 v52.4

QuadLaser I

Qume ScripTEN v47.0

Ricoh LP-1200

Ricoh PC Laser 6000-PS v50.5

*Royal CJP 450

Scantext 2030-51 v49.3 or 52.2

Schlumberger 5232 Color PostScript
    Printer v50.3

Seiko ColorPoint PS Model 04

Seiko ColorPoint PS Model 14

*Seiko Professional ColorPoint 8BPP

Seikosha LT-20

Seikosha SL-80 IP

Seikosha SL-92

Seikosha SL-92 Plus

Seikosha SP-1900

Seikosha SP-1900+

Seikosha SP-2000

Seikosha SP-2400

Seikosha SP-2415

Sharp JX-9300

Sharp JX-9500

Sharp JX-9500E

Sharp JX-9500H

Sharp JX-9600

Sharp JX-9700

Sharp JX-9700E

Shinko Color CHC-746PSJ PostScript
    Printer v52.2

Star FR-10

Star FR-15

Star LaserPrinter 4

Star LaserPrinter 4 III

Star LaserPrinter 5

Star LaserPrinter 5 EX

Star LaserPrinter 8

Star LaserPrinter 8 DB

Star LaserPrinter 8 DX

Star LaserPrinter 8 II

Star LaserPrinter 8 III

Star LC-10

Star LC-10 Colour

Star LC-100 Colour

Star LC-15

Star LC-20

Star LC-200

Star LC24-10

Star LC24-100

Star LC24-15

Star LC24-20

Star LC24-200

Star LC24-200 Colour

Star NB24-10

Star NB24-15

Star NL-10

Star NX-1000

Star NX-1000 Rainbow

Star NX-1001

Star NX-1020 Rainbow

Star NX-1500

Star NX-2400

Star NX-2410

Star NX-2415

Star NX-2420

Star NX-2420 Rainbow

Star NX-2430

Star SJ-48

Star XB-2410

Star XB-2415

Star XB-2420

Star XB-2425

Star XB24-10

Star XB24-15

Star XB24-200

Star XB24-250

Star XR-1000

Star XR-1020

Star XR-1500

Star XR-1520

Star ZA-200

Star ZA-250

Tandy LP-1000

Tegra Genesis

Tektronix® Phaser 200e with 17 fonts
    v2011.108(3)

Tektronix Phaser 200e with 39 fonts
    v2011.108(3)

Tektronix Phaser 200i v2011.108(3)

Tektronix Phaser II PX

Tektronix Phaser II PXe v2010.128 with
    17 fonts

Tektronix Phaser II PXe v2010.128 with
    39 fonts

Tektronix Phaser II PXi v2010.116

Tektronix Phaser II PXi v2011.108

Tektronix Phaser II PXiJ v2011.108

Tektronix Phaser III PXi v2010.116

*Tektronix Phaser III PXi v2011.108

Tektronix Phaser III PXiJ v2011.108

Tektronix Phaser IISD v2011.108

Tektronix Phaser PX

TI 2115 13 fonts v47.0

TI 2115 35 fonts v47.0

TI 850/855

TI microLaser PS17 v.52.1

TI microLaser PS35 v.52.1

TI microLaser XL PS17 v.52.1

TI microLaser XL PS35 v.52.1

TI microLaser16 Turbo v2010.119

TI microLaser6 Turbo v2010.119

TI microLaser9 Turbo v2010.119

TI OmniLaser 2108 v45.0

TI Omnilaser 2115 v47.0

Toshiba GX-400

Toshiba PageLaser12

Triumph Adler SDR 7706

Triumph Adler SDR 7706 PS13

Triumph Adler SDR 7706 PS35

Unisys AP9210

Unisys AP9210 17 Fonts v52.1

Unisys AP9210 39 Fonts v52.1

Unisys AP9415 v47.0

Varityper 4000-L300 v52.3

Varityper 4000-L330 v52.3

Varityper 4000-L500 v52.3

Varityper 4000-L530 v52.3

Varityper 4200B-P v49.3 or 52.2

Varityper 4300P v49.3 or 52.2

Varityper Series 4000-5300 v49.3 or 52.2

Varityper Series 4000-5330 v49.3 or 52.2

Varityper Series 4000-5500 v52.2

Varityper VT-600P

Varityper VT 600P v48.0

Varityper VT 600W v48.0

Varityper VT4_510A v52.3

Varityper VT4990 v52.3

VT4_530A v52.3

VT4_530B v52.3

VT4_530C v52.3

VT4_533B v52.3

VT4_533C v52.3

VT4_53EA v52.3

VT4_53EB v52.3

VT4_550A v52.3

VT4_550B v52.3

VT4_550C v52.3

VT4_551A v52.3

VT4_563A v52.3

VT4_563B v52.3

Wang® LCS15 FontPlus

Wang LCS15

Wang LDP8

Xerox® DocuTech 135 v2010.130

Xerox DocuTech 85 v2010.130

Xerox DocuTech 90 v2010.130

Technical Notes

Items listed with ++ are supported with device drivers available in the Windows NT Driver Library.

1   Refer to SETUP.TXT for information on configuring this machine/device before installation.

2   Only the NCR 53c710 SCSI Host Adapter is supported in this machine.

3   Contact the manufacturer for information on running Windows NT on this machine.

4   Tested with firmware revisions 3.10 and 3.20.

5   This adapter requires an active terminator for proper performance.

6   This adapter must be configured for 5 MB/second asynchronous I/O to work with listed CD-ROM drives from NEC.

7   This adapter must be configured for 5 MB/second asynchronous I/O to work with listed CD-ROM drives from Chinon, Hitachi and NEC.

8   Tested with the Unisys PW^2 Advantage 3256 (Flemington).

9   Tested with the Unisys PW^2 Advantage Plus MPE 4668.

10   Removable media drives are not supported with cache module installed.

11   CD-audio, tape drives and scanners are not supported on this controller.

12   To use this adapter, at least one device on the bus must provide termination power.

13   Refer to SETUP.TXT for information on configuring this adapter.

14   SCSI BIOS dated before 1991 requires PS/2 Reference Diskette version 1.21 or later.

15   This adapter cannot be used for CD Setup. To install Windows NT with this adapter, use the WINNT.EXE Setup method.

16   Scanners are not supported with this adapter.

17   Tested with COMPAQ Portable 486c.

18   Tested with NCR System 3000 Model 3350.

19   This adapter is currently supported in its ESC-1/ESC-2 compatibility mode only.

20   This adapter is a RAID controller which supports hard drives only.

21   This adapter is only supported on IRQ-5.

22   This adapter is only supported for use with scanners and CD-ROM drives.

23   Tested with firmware revision 005.

24   Tested with firmware revision 008.

25   Audio is not supported on this drive.

26   This drive is not supported for use with the Adaptec AHA-1542c.

27   This drive requires double-termination when used with the Adaptec AHA-1742A.

28   This drive is not supported for use with the Future Domain TMC-850M and TMC-1670 adapters.

29   The Adaptec AHA-1640 and Ultrastor 24f support only a single disk when used with this drive. This drive is not supported for use with the Future Domain MCS-600 adapter.

30   Requires firmware revision 1.10C to function properly with Windows NT.

31   This drive is not supported with the Adaptec AHA-1640 adapter.

32   This drive is not supported with the IBM PS/2 Microchannel SCSI Host Adapter (with cache).

33   This drive is not supported with the Future Domain TMC-850M(ER).

34   This drive is not supported with the Adaptec AHA-1742A adapter.

35   This drive is not supported with the UltraStor 24fa adapter.

36   For use with floppy controllers. Separate interface controllers for these types of drives are not supported.

37   Requires that 512-byte sector-sized media be mounted during installation.

38   Tested with HP C2225B tape drive, HP C2229B disk drive and HP C2226A CD-ROM drive.

39   Supported in Sound Blaster 1.x compatibility mode.

40   Not supported in Sound Blaster 1.x compatibility mode.

41   Error control and flow control forced on.

42   Advanced features disabled.

43   Supported as a client modem only.

44   Flow control forced on.

45   Maximum DTE speed set to 2400.

46   Maximum DTE speed set to 9600.

47   Modem compression forced on.

48   In the UPS applet, check the box "Remote UPS Shutdown" and set it to high.

Glossary

A

access control entry (ACE) An entry in an access control list (ACL). The entry contains a security ID (SID) and a set of access rights. A process with a matching security ID is either allowed access rights, denied rights, or allowed rights with auditing. See also *access control list.*

access control list (ACL) The part of a security descriptor that enumerates the protections applied to an object. The owner of an object has discretionary access control of the object and can change the object's ACL to allow or disallow others access to the object. ACLs are made up of *access control entries* (ACEs).

access mask In an ACE, defines all possible actions for a particular object type. Permissions are granted or denied based on this access mask.

access right The permission granted to a process to manipulate a particular object in a particular way (for example, by calling a service). Different object types support different access rights, which are stored in an object's *access control list* (ACL).

account See *user account.*

ACE See a*ccess control entry.*

ACK An acknowledgment signal.

ACL See a*ccess control list.*

address resolution protocol (ARP)
An IP maintenance protocol that supports the IP framework.

administrative alerts Relate to server and resource use; warn about problems in areas such as security and access, user sessions, server shutdown because of power loss (when UPS is available), directory replication, and printing. When a computer generates an administrative alert, a message is sent to a predefined list of users and computers. See also *Alerter service.*

Alerter service A Windows NT Advanced Server service that notifies selected users and computers of administrative alerts that occur on a computer. Used by the Server and other services. Requires the Messenger service. See also *administrative alerts.*

API See *application programming interface.*

application programming interface (API)
A set of routines that an application program uses to request and carry out lower-level services performed by the operating system.

ARC computer See *RISC-based computer.*

ARP A TCP/IP command that allows a user to view and modify the ARP (*address resolution protocol*) table entries on the local computer.

asynchronous I/O A method many of the processes in Windows NT use to optimize their performance. When an application initiates an I/O operation, the I/O Manager accepts the request but doesn't block the application's execution while the I/O operation is being performed. Instead, the application is allowed to continue doing work. Most I/O devices are very slow in comparison to a computer's processor, so an application can do a lot of work while waiting for an I/O operation to complete. See also *synchronous I/O.*

audit policy Defines the type of security events that are logged for a domain or for an individual computer; determines what Windows NT will do when the security log becomes full.

auditing The ability to detect and record security-related events, particularly any attempt to create, access, or delete objects. Windows NT uses *security IDs* (SIDs) to record which process performed the action.

authentication A security step performed by the Remote Access server, before logon validation, to verify that the user had permission for remote access. See also *validation.*

B

banding A process in printing whereby the document is replayed several times to generate the full image.

batch program An ASCII file (unformatted text file) that contains one or more Windows NT commands. A batch program's filename has a .BAT or .CMD extension. When you type the filename at the command prompt, the commands are processed sequentially.

binding A process that establishes the initial communication channel between the protocol driver and the network adapter card driver.

Boot Loader The operating system loader, provided by NTOSKRNL in Windows NT. Defines the information needed for system startup, such as the location for the operating system's files. Windows NT automatically creates the correct configuration and checks this information whenever you start your system.

boot partition The volume, formatted for either an NTFS, FAT, or HPFS file system, that contains the Windows NT operating system and its support files. The boot partition can be (but does not have to be) the same as the *system partition.*

bound application An application that can run under both OS/2 and MS-DOS.

browser service See *Computer Browser service.*

B-tree A tree structure with a root and several nodes. It contains data organized in some logical way so that the whole structure can be quickly traversed.

buffer A reserved portion of memory in which data is temporarily held pending an opportunity to complete its transfer to or from a storage device or another location in memory.

buffering The process of using buffers to hold data that is being transferred, particularly to or from I/O devices such as disk drives and serial ports.

C

character mode A mode of operation in which all information is displayed as text characters. This is the mode in which MS-DOS–based and OS/2 version 1.2 applications are displayed in windows under Windows NT. Also called alphanumeric mode or text mode.

client A computer that accesses shared network resources provided by another computer (called a server). See also *server.*

Computer Browser service Maintains an up-to-date list of computers and provides the list to applications when requested, for example, in the Select Computer and Select Domain dialog boxes. When a user attempts to connect to a resource in the domain, the domain's browser is contacted to provide a list of resources available. The active browser for the domain is elected dynamically through a network election process.

computername A unique name of up to 15 uppercase characters that identifies a computer to the network. The name cannot be the same as any other computer or domain name in the network, and it cannot contain spaces.

Configuration Registry See *Registry.*

connected user A user accessing a computer or a resource across the network.

console A character-mode window managed by the Win32 subsystem in Windows NT. Environment subsystems direct the output of character-mode applications to consoles.

container object An object that logically contains other objects. For example, a directory is a container object that logically contains files and other directories. Files are noncontainer objects.

control set A complete set of parameters for devices and services in the HKEY_LOCAL_MACHINE\SYSTEM key in the Registry.

CPU cycles The smallest unit of time recognized by the central processing unit—typically a few hundred-millionths of a second; it is also used to refer to the time required for the CPU to perform the simplest instruction. Also called a clock tick.

D

data frame Logical, structured packets in which data can be placed. The Data Link layer packages raw bits from the Physical layer into data frames. The exact format of the frame used by the network depends on the topology.

Data Link Control (DLC) A protocol interface device driver in Windows NT, traditionally used to provide connectivity to IBM mainframes and also used to provide connectivity to local-area network printers directly attached to the network.

data type The second of three components that make up a value entry in the Registry. Five data types can be edited in Registry Editor: *REG_BINARY, REG_DWORD, REG_EXPAND_SZ, REG_MULTI_SZ,* and *REG_SZ.*

datagram A packet of information and associated delivery information, such as the destination address, that is routed through a packet-switching network.

DDE See *dynamic data exchange.*

default profile See *system default profile, user default profile.*

default printer The printer that is used if you choose the Print command without first specifying which printer you want to use with an application.

demand paging Refers to a method by which data is moved in pages from physical memory to a temporary paging file on disk. As the data is needed by a process, it is paged back into physical memory.

dependent service A service that requires the support of another service. For example, the Alerter service is dependent on the Messenger service.

device A generic term for a computer subsystem such as a printer, serial port, or disk drive. A device frequently requires its own controlling software called a *device driver.*

device contention The way Windows NT allocates access to peripheral devices, such as a modem or a printer, when more than one application is trying to use the same device.

device driver A software component that allows the computer to transmit and receive information to and from a specific device. For example, a printer driver translates computer data into a form understood by a particular printer. Although a device may be installed on your system, Windows NT cannot recognize the device until you have installed and configured the appropriate driver.

directory replication The copying of a master set of directories from a server (called an export server) to specified servers or workstations (called import computers) in the same or other domains. Replication simplifies the task of maintaining identical sets of directories and files on multiple computers, because only a single master copy of the data must be maintained. Files are replicated when they are added to an exported directory and every time a change is saved to the file. See also *Directory Replicator service.*

Directory Replicator service Replicates directories, and the files in those directories, between computers. See also *directory replication.*

disk caching A method used by a file system to improve performance. Instead of reading and writing directly to the disk, frequently used files are temporarily stored in a cache in memory, and reads and writes to those files are performed in memory. Reading and writing to memory is much faster than reading and writing to disk.

disk duplexing Establishing a mirrored copy on a disk with a different controller.

disk mirroring Maintaining a fully redundant copy of a partition on another disk.

disk striping Writing data in stripes across a volume that has been created from areas of free space on from 2 to 32 disks.

distributed application An application that has two parts—a front-end to run on the client computer and a back-end to run on the server. In distributed computing, the goal is to divide the computing task into two sections. The front-end requires minimal resources and runs on the client's workstation. The back-end requires large amounts of data, number crunching, or specialized hardware and runs on the server.

DLC See *Data Link Control.*

DLL See dynamic-link library.

DMA channel A channel for direct memory access that does not involve the microprocessor, providing data transfer directly between memory and a disk drive.

domain For Windows NT Advanced Server, a networked set of workstations and servers that share a Security Accounts Manager (SAM) database and that can be administered as a group. A user with an account in a particular network domain can log onto and access his or her account from any system in the domain. See also *SAM database*; *workgroup.*

domain controller For a Windows NT Advanced Server domain, the server that authenticates domain logons and maintains the security policy and the master database for a domain. Both servers and domain controllers are capable of validating a user's logon; however, password changes must be made by contacting the domain controller. See also *server.*

domain database See *SAM database.*

domain master browser The domain controller responsible for keeping in sync all the master browsers for its domain in the internet.

domain name The name by which a domain is known to the network.

Domain Name System (DNS) A hierarchical name service for TCP/IP hosts (sometimes referred to as the BIND service in BSD UNIX). The network administrator configures the DNS with a list of *hostnames* and IP addresses, allowing users of workstations configured to query the DNS to specify remote systems by *hostnames* rather than IP addresses. DNS domains should not be confused with Windows NT networking *domains*.

domain synchronization See *synchronize*.

downloaded fonts Fonts that you send to a printer either before or during the printing of a document. When you send a font to a printer, it is stored in printer memory until it is needed.

dynamic data exchange (DDE) A form of interprocess communication (IPC) implemented in the Microsoft Windows family of operating systems. Two or more programs that support dynamic data exchange (DDE) can exchange information and commands.

dynamic-link library (DLL) An application programming interface (API) routine that user-mode applications access through ordinary procedure calls. The code for the API routine is not included in the user's executable image. Instead, the operating system automatically modifies the executable image to point to DLL procedures at run time.

E

environment subsystems User-mode protected servers that run and support programs from different operating systems environments. Examples of these subsystems are the Win32™ subsystem and the OS/2 subsystem. Contrast *integral subsystem.*

environment variable A string consisting of environment information, such as a drive, path, or filename, associated with a symbolic name that can be used by Windows NT. You use the System option in Control Panel or the **set** command from the Windows NT command prompt to define environment variables.

event Any significant occurrence in the system or in an application that requires users to be notified or an entry to be added to a log.

Event Log service Records events in the system, security, and application logs.

Executive module The Kernel-mode module that provides basic operating system services to the environment subsystems. It includes several components; each manages a particular set of system services. One component, the Security Reference Monitor, works together with the protected subsystems to provide a pervasive security model for the system.

export server In directory replication, a server from which a master set of directories is exported to specified servers or workstations (called import computers) in the same or other domains. See also *directory replication.*

extended partition Created from free space on a hard disk, it can be subpartitioned into zero or more logical drives. Only one of the four partitions allowed per physical disk can be an extended partition, and no primary partition needs to be present to create an extended partition.

extensibility Indicates the modular design of Windows NT, which provides for the flexibility of adding future modules at several levels within the operating system.

external command A command that is stored in its own file and loaded from disk when you use the command.

F

FAT file system A file system based on a file allocation table maintained by the operating system to keep track of the status of various segments of disk space used for file storage.

fault tolerance The ability of a computer and an operating system to respond gracefully to catastrophic events such as power outage or hardware failure. Usually, fault tolerance implies the ability to either continue the system's operation without loss of data or to shut the system down and restart it, recovering all processing that was in progress when the fault occurred.

file control block (FCB) A small block of memory temporarily assigned by the operating system to hold information about a file that has been opened for use. An FCB typically contains information such as the file's ID, its location on disk, and a pointer that marks the user's current (or last) position in the file.

File Replication service The Windows NT file replication service allows specified file(s) to be replicated to remote systems ensuring that copies on each system are kept in synchronization. The system that maintains the master copy is called the *exporter*; the systems that receive updates are known as *importers*.

file sharing The ability for a Windows NT workstation or Windows NT Advanced Server to share parts (or all) of its local file system(s) with remote computers. An administrator creates *shares (or sharepoints)* by using either the File Manager or by using the **net share** command from the command line.

file system In an operating system, the overall structure in which files are named, stored, and organized.

Finger A TCP/IP application that allows the user to retrieve system information on remote systems supporting TCP/IP and a Finger service.

Fnodes Each directory points to Fnodes for files contained in that directory. An Fnode is 512 bytes in length and contains a header, the filename (truncated to 15 characters), the file length, extended attributes (EA) and access control list (ACL) information, and the location of the file's data.

font set A collection of font sizes for one font, customized for a particular display and printer. Font sets determine what text looks like on screen and on paper.

frame See *data frame*.

free space An unused and unformatted portion of a hard disk that can be partitioned or subpartitioned. Free space within an extended partition is available for the creation of logical drives. Free space that is not within an extended partition is available for the creation of a partition, with a maximum of four partitions allowed.

FTP service File transfer protocol service, which offers file transfer services to remote systems supporting this protocol. FTP supports a host of commands allowing bidirectional transfer of binary and ASCII files between systems.

Ftpsvc service The FTP Server services, which provides an FTP server for Windows NT. This service is not installed by default but can be installed by choosing the Network icon in Control Panel.

Fully Qualified Domain Name (or FQDN)
In TCP/IP, *hostnames* with their *domain names* appended to them. For example, a host with hostname *rhino* and domain name *microsoft.com* has a FQDN of *rhino.microsoft.com.*

G

global account For Windows NT Advanced Server, a normal user account in a user's home domain. If there are multiple domains in the network, it is best if each user in the network has only one user account, in only one domain, and each user's access to other domains is accomplished through the establishment of domain trust relationships. See also *local account.*

global group For Windows NT Advanced Server, a group that can be used in its own domain, servers and workstations of the domain, and trusting domains. In all these places it can be granted rights and permissions and can become a member of local groups. However, it can contain only user accounts from its own domain. Global groups provide a way to create handy sets of users from inside the domain, available for use both in and out of the domain.

Global groups cannot be created or maintained on Window NT workstations. However, for Windows NT workstations that participate in a domain, domain global groups can be granted rights and permissions at those workstations and can become members of local groups at those workstations. See also *group, local group.*

graphics engine GDI32.DLL, which is the print component that provides WYSIWYG support across devices. This component sits between the GDI and the DDI, and communicates through the GDI to the application and through the DDI to the printer driver.

group In User Manager, an account containing other accounts called members. The permissions and rights granted to a group are also provided to its members, making groups a convenient way to grant common capabilities to collections of user accounts. For Windows NT, groups are managed with User Manager. For Windows NT Advanced Server, groups are managed with User Manager for Domains. See also *global group, local group, user account.*

group memberships The groups to which a user account belongs. Permissions and rights granted to a group are also provided to its members. In most cases, the actions a user can perform in Windows NT are determined by the group memberships of the user account the user is logged on to. See also *group.*

H

handle See *object handle.*

hard links POSIX applications need certain file-system functionality, such as support for case-sensitive filenames and support for files with multiple names, called *hard links*. The Windows NT file system, NTFS, supports these POSIX requirements.

Hardware Abstraction Layer (HAL)
Virtualizes hardware interfaces, making the hardware dependencies transparent to the rest of the operating system. This allows Windows NT to be portable from one hardware platform to another.

hive A discrete body of keys, subkeys, and values that is rooted at the top of the Registry hierarchy. A hive is backed by a single file and a .LOG file. For example, the hive HKEY_USERS\.DEFAULT maps to the physical file *SystemRoot*\SYSTEM32\CONFIG \DEFAULT. Hives were named by a Windows NT developer as an analogy for the cellular structure of a bee hive.

HKEY_CLASSES_ROOT A predefined Registry handle that defines object linking and embedding (OLE) and file-class association data. This key is a symbolic link to a subkey of HKEY_LOCAL_ MACHINE\SOFTWARE.

HKEY_CURRENT_USER A predefined Registry handle that defines the current user's preferences, including environment variables, personal program groups, desktop settings, network connections, printers, and application preferences. This key maps to a subkey of HKEY_USERS.

HKEY_LOCAL_MACHINE A predefined Registry handle that defines the hardware and operating system characteristics such as bus type, system memory, installed device drives, and boot control data.

HKEY_USERS A predefined Registry handle that defines the default user configuration for users on the local computer and configuration data from user profiles stored on the local computer.

home directory A directory that is accessible to the user and contains files and programs for that user. A home directory can be assigned to an individual user or can be shared by many users.

host table The HOSTS or LMHOST file that contains lists of known IP addresses.

hostname A TCP/IP command that returns the local workstation's *hostname* used for authentication by TCP/IP utilities. This value is the workstation's *computername* by default, but it can be changed by using the Network icon in Control Panel.

hot-fixing A technique HPFS uses to handle write errors.

HPFS The high-performance file system designed for OS/2 version 1.2.

I

impersonation A technique by which Windows NT allows one process to take on the security attributes of another.

import computers In directory replication, the servers or workstations that receive copies of the master set of directories from an export server. See also *directory replication*.

import path In directory replication, the path to which imported subdirectories, and the files in those subdirectories, will be stored on an import computer. See also *directory replication*.

.INI files Initialization files used by Windows-based applications to store per-user information that controls application startup. In Windows NT, such information is stored in the Registry, and the correlation between Registry entries and .INI entries is defined under HKEY_LOCAL_ MACHINE\SOFTWARE\Microsoft\Windows NT \CurrentVersion\IniFileMapping.

integral subsystem A subsystem such as the Security subsystem that affects the entire Windows NT operating system. Contrast *environment subsystems*.

interactive logon The user must type information at the keyboard in response to a dialog box the operating system displays on the screen. Windows NT grants or denies access based upon the information provided by the user. Contrast *remote logon.*

internal command Commands that are stored in the file CMD.EXE and that reside in memory at all times.

internet control message protocol (ICMP) An IP maintenance protocol that supports the IP framework.

interrupt An asynchronous operating condition that disrupts normal execution and transfers control to an interrupt handler. Interrupts are usually initiated by I/O devices requiring service from the processor.

interrupt request lines (IRQ) Hardware lines over which devices can send signals to get the attention of the processor when the device is ready to accept or send information. Typically, each device connected to the computer uses a separate IRQ.

I/O device An input/output device, which is a piece of hardware used for providing information to and receiving information from the computer, for example, a disk drive, which transfers information in one of two directions, depending on the situation. Some input devices such as keyboards can be used only for input, and some output devices such as a printer or a monitor can be used only for output. Most of these devices required installation of device drivers.

I/O request packet (IRP) Data structures that drivers use to communicate with each other.

IP router Describes a system connected to multiple physical TCP/IP networks, capable of routing or delivering IP packets between them. Also called a *gateway.*

IRP See *I/O request packet.*

IRQ See *interrupt request lines.*

K

kernel The portion of Windows NT that manages the processor.

kernel driver A driver that accesses hardware.

Kernel module The core of the Windows NT layered architecture that manages the most basic operations of Windows NT. The Kernel is responsible for thread dispatching, multiprocessor synchronization, hardware exception handling, and the implementation of low-level, hardware-dependent functions.

kernel objects Two types of objects used only by the Kernel: Dispatcher objects, which include events, mutants, mutexes, semaphores, threads, and timers. Dispatcher objects have a signal state (signaled or nonsignaled) and control the dispatching and synchronization of system operations; and Control objects, which include asynchronous procedure calls, interrupts, power notifies, power statuses, processes, and profiles. Control objects are used to control the operation of the Kernel but do not affect dispatching or synchronization.

L

LastKnownGood The control set that is a clean copy of the last control set that actually worked while starting the computer.

lazy commit Similar to *lazy write.* Instead of immediately marking a transaction as successfully completed, the committed information is cached and later written to the file system log as a background process.

lazy write The ability to record changes in the file structure cache, which is quicker than recording them on disk; later, when demand on the computer's CPU is low, the Cache Manager writes the changes to the disk. See also *lazy commit.*

link A connection at the LLC layer that is uniquely defined by the adapter's address and the destination service access point (DSAP).

LLC Logical link control, in the Data Link layer of the networking model.

local account For Windows NT Advanced Server, a user account provided in a domain for a user whose global account is not in a trusted domain. Not required where trust relationships exist between domains. See also *global account, user account.*

local group 1. For Windows NT, a group that can be granted permissions and rights only for its own workstation. 2. For Windows NT Advanced Server, a group that can be granted permissions and rights only for the servers of its own domain. See also *global group, group.*

local printer A printer that is directly connected to one of the ports on your computer.

Local Security Authority (LSA) Creates a security access token for each user accessing the system.

locale The national and cultural environment in which a system or program is running. The locale determines the language used for messages and menus, the sorting order of strings, the keyboard layout, and data and time formatting conventions.

logical drive A subpartition of an extended partition on a hard disk.

logon authentication Refers to the validation of a user either locally or in a domain. At logon time, the user specifies his or her name, password, and the intended logon domain. The workstation then contacts the *domain controllers* for the domain, which verify the user's logon credentials.

LSA See *Local Security Authority.*

M

MAC Media access control. A layer in the network architecture.

management information base (MIB) The entire set of objects that any service or protocol uses in SNMP. Because different network-management services are used for different types of devices or for different network-management protocols, each service has its own set of objects.

mandatory user profile For Windows NT Advanced Server, a user profile created by an administrator and assigned to one or more users. A mandatory user profile cannot be changed by the user and remains the same from one logon session to the next. See also *personal user profile, user profile.*

map To translate one value into another.

MAPI See *Messaging Application Program Interface.*

Messaging Application Program Interface (MAPI) A set of calls used to add mail-enabled features to other Windows-based applications.

Messenger service Sends and receives messages sent by administrators or by the Alerter service. Examples of the Messenger service include print job notification or a message from an administrator that a server will be going down for service shortly.

MIB See *management information base.*

MS-DOS–based application An application that is designed to run with MS-DOS and which therefore may not be able to take full advantage of all Windows NT features.

multihomed workstation A system that has multiple network adapters.

N

named pipe An interprocess communication mechanism that allows one process to send data to another local or remote process.

NBF transport protocol NetBEUI Frame protocol. A descendant of the NetBEUI protocol, which is a Transport layer protocol, not the programming interface NetBIOS.

NDIS See *Network driver interface specification.*

NetBEUI transport NetBIOS (Network Basic Input/Output System) Extended User Interface. The primary local area network transport protocol in Windows NT. See also *NetBIOS interface.*

NetBIOS interface A programming interface that allows I/O requests to be sent to and received from a remote computer. It hides networking hardware from applications.

Netlogon service For Windows NT Advanced Server, performs authentication of domain logons and keeps the domain's database synchronized between the domain controller and the other Windows NT Advanced Servers of the domain.

Network DDE service The Network DDE (dynamic data exchange) service provides a network transport and security for DDE conversations. The Network DDE DSDM (DDE share database manager) service manages shared DDE conversations.

network device driver Software that coordinates communication between the network adapter card and the computer's hardware and other software, controlling the physical function of the network adapter cards.

network directory See *shared directory.*

network driver interface specification (NDIS) A Windows NT interface for network card drivers that provides transport independence, because all transport drivers call the NDIS interface to access network cards.

network-interface printers Printers with built-in network cards. Network-interface printers need not be adjacent to a print server since they are directly connected to the network.

non-Windows NT application Refers to an application that is designed to run with Windows 3.*x*, MS-DOS, OS/2, or POSIX, but not specifically with Windows NT and that may not be able to take full advantage of all Windows NT features (such as memory management).

nonpaged pool The portion of system memory that cannot be paged to disk. Compare *paged pool.*

NTDETECT.COM The Windows NT Hardware Recognizer program for *x*86-based computers.

NTFS The Windows NT file system.

NTFS (Windows NT file system) An advanced file system designed for use specifically with the Windows NT operating system. NTFS supports file system recovery and extremely large storage media, in addition to other advantages. It also supports object-oriented applications by treating all files as objects with user-defined and system-defined attributes.

O

object 1. A single run-time instance of a Windows NT object type that contains data that can be manipulated only by using a set of services provided for objects of its type. 2. Any piece of information, created by using a Windows-based application with object linking and embedding capabilities, that can be linked or embedded into another document.

object handle Includes access control information and a pointer to the object itself. Before a process can manipulate a Windows NT object, it must first acquire a handle to the object through Object Manager.

object linking and embedding (OLE)
A way to transfer and share information between applications.

object type Includes a system-defined data type, a list of operations that can be performed upon it (such as wait, create, or cancel), and a set of object attributes. Object Manager is the part of the Windows NT Executive that provides uniform rules for retention, naming, and security of objects.

OLE See *object linking and embedding.*

orphan A member of a mirror set or a stripe set with parity that has failed in a severe manner, such as a loss of power or a complete head crash.

P

packet A unit of information transmitted as a whole from one device to another on a network.

page 1. In ClipBook, one complete entry that has been pasted in. 2. In memory, a fixed-size block.

paged pool The portion of system memory that can be paged to disk. Compare *nonpaged pool.*

paging file A system file that contains the contents of virtual pages that have been paged out of memory by the Virtual Memory Manager. Sometimes called a *swap file.*

partition A portion of a physical disk that functions as though it were a physically separate unit. See also *system partition.*

password A unique string of characters that must be provided before a logon or an access is authorized as a security measure used to restrict logons to user accounts and access to computer systems and resources.

permission A rule associated with an object (usually a directory, file, or printer) in order to regulate which users can have access to the object and in what manner. See also *right.*

personal user profile For Windows NT Advanced Server, a user profile created by an administrator and assigned to one user. A personal user profile retains changes the user makes to the per-user settings of the Windows NT environment and reimplements the newest settings each time that user logs on at any Windows NT workstation. See also *mandatory user profile, user profile.*

port A connection or socket used to connect a device to a computer, such as a printer, monitor, or modem. Information is sent from the computer to the device through a cable.

portability Windows NT runs on both CISC and RISC processors. CISC includes computers running with Intel 80386 or higher processors. RISC includes computers with MIPS R4000 or DEC Alpha processors.

POSIX Portable Operating System Interface for Computing Environments. A set of standards being drafted by the Institute of Electrical and Electronic Engineers (IEEE) that define various aspects of an operating system, including topics such as programming interface, security, networking, and graphical interface.

postoffice A temporary message store, holding the message until the recipient's workstation retrieves it. The postoffice exists as a directory structure on a server and has no programmatic components.

primary partition A portion of a physical disk that can be marked for use by an operating system. There can be up to four primary partitions (or up to three, if there is an extended partition) per physical disk. A primary partition cannot be subpartitioned.

print device Refers to the actual hardware device that produces printed output. See also *printer*.

printer In Windows NT, refers to the software interface between the application and print device. See also *print device*.

printer driver A program that controls how your computer and printer interact.

printer fonts Fonts that are built into your printer. These fonts are usually located in the printer's read-only memory (ROM).

print monitor Keeps track of printers and print devices. It is the component that receives information from the printer driver via the spooler and sends it on to the printer or destination file. The print monitor tracks physical devices so the spooler doesn't have to.

print processor A dynamic link library that interprets data types. It receives information from the spooler and sends the interpreted information to the graphics engine.

print provider A software component that allows the client to print to the print server's device.

protocol A set of rules and conventions by which two computers pass messages across a network. Networking software usually implements multiple levels of protocols layered one on top of another. Windows NT includes NBT, TCP/IP, DLC, and NWLink protocols. Windows NT Advanced Server also includes AppleTalk.

provider The component that allows a Windows NT computer to communicate with the network. Windows NT includes a provider for the Windows NT network; other provider DLLs are supplied by the alternate networks' vendors.

R

redirector Networking software that accepts I/O requests for remote files, named pipes, or mailslots and then sends (*redirects*) them to a network service on another computer. Redirectors are implemented as file system drivers in Windows NT.

REG_BINARY A data type for Registry value entries that designates binary data.

REG_DWORD A data type for Registry value entries that designates data represented by a number that is 4 bytes long.

REG_EXPAND_SZ A data type for Registry value entries that designates an expandable string. For example, in the entry *%SystemRoot%\file*.**exe**, the string *%SystemRoot%* will be replaced by the actual location of the directory containing Windows NT system files.

REG_MULTI_SZ A data type for Registry value entries that designates a multiple string.

REG_SZ A data type for Registry value entries that designates a data string that usually represents human readable text.

Registry In Windows NT, the database repository for information about the computer's configuration, including the hardware, installed software, environment settings, and other information.

Registry Editor An application provided with Windows NT that allows users to view and edit entries in the Registry.

remote administration Administration of one computer by an administrator located at another computer and connected to the first computer across the network.

remote logon When a user establishes a connection from a remote computer, the access validation performed by a server on which no security access token currently exists for the user. (Security access tokens are otherwise created during interactive logon.) Contrast *interactive logon.*

A process invisible to the user where The user must type information at the keyboard in response to a dialog box the operating system displays on the screen. Windows NT grants or denies access based upon the information provided by the user. Contrast *remote logon.*

Remote Procedure Call (RPC) A message-passing facility that allows a distributed application to call services available on various computers in a network. Used during remote administration of computers. RPC provides a procedural view, rather than a transport-centered view, of networked operations. The RPC subsystem includes the endpoint mapper and other miscellaneous RPC services. See also *RPC Locator Service.*

replication See *directory replication.*

Replicator service See *Directory Replicator service.*

resource Any part of a computer system or a network, such as a disk drive, printer, or memory, that can be allotted to a program or a process while it is running.

right Authorizes a user to perform certain actions on the system. Rights apply to the system as a whole and are different from *permissions*, which apply to specific objects. (Sometimes called a *privilege.*)

RISC-based computer A computer based on a RISC (reduced instruction set) microprocessor, such as a Digital Alpha AXP, MIPS R4000 or Atlas computer. Compare with the *x86-based computer.*

router 1. The printing model component that locates the requested printer and sends information from the workstation spooler to the print server's spooler. 2. TCP/IP gateways—computers with two or more network adapters that are running some type of IP routing software; each adapter is connected to a different physical network.

RPC Remote procedure call. For TCP/IP, RPC provides a mechanism to copy files between two systems unidirectionally.

RPC Locator service The Remote Procedure Call Locator service allows distributed applications to use the RPC Name service. The RPC Locator service manages the RPC Name service database.

The server side of a distributed application registers its availability with the RPC Locator service. The client side of a distributed application queries the RPC Locator service to find available compatible server applications.

RPC transport provider interface A DLL that acts as an interface between the RPC facility and network transport software, allowing RPCs to be sent over various transports.

rules Printable rectangles extracted from the bitmap and sent to the printer as a separate command as supported by Hewlett-Packard LaserJet and compatible printers.

S

SAM See *Security Accounts Manager.*

SAM database The database of security information that includes user account names and passwords and the settings of the security policies. For a Windows NT workstation, it is managed with User Manager. For a Windows NT Advanced Server domain, it is managed with User Manager For Domains.

scalability Windows NT is not bound to single-processor architectures but takes full advantage of symmetric multiprocessing hardware.

Schedule service Supports and is required for use of the **at** command, which can schedule commands and programs to run on a computer at a specified time and date.

screen fonts Fonts displayed on your screen. Soft-font manufacturers often provide screen fonts that closely match the soft fonts for your printer. This ensures that your documents look the same on the screen as they do when printed.

security access token Includes a security ID for the user, other security IDs for the groups to which the user belongs, plus other information such as the user's name and the groups to which that user belongs. In addition, every process that runs on behalf of this user will have a copy of his or her access token.

Security Accounts Manager (SAM)
A Windows NT protected subsystem that maintains the SAM database and provokes an API for accessing the database.

security context Controls what access the *subject* has to *objects* or system services. When a program or process runs on the user's behalf, it is said to be running in the security context of that user.

security database See *SAM database.*

security descriptor The security attributes for an object, which include an owner *security ID*, a group security ID, a discretionary *access control list* (ACL), and a system ACL.

security ID (SID) A unique name that identifies a logged-on user to the Windows NT security system. A security ID can identify either an individual user or a group of users.

send window The number of frames that the sender is allowed to send before it must wait for an ACK.

server 1. For a LAN, a computer running administrative software that controls access to all or part of the network and its resources. A computer acting as a server makes resources available to computers acting as workstations on the network. 2. For Windows NT, refers to a computer that provides shared resources to network users. See also *client.* 3. For Windows NT Advanced Server domains, refers to a computer that receives a copy of the domain's security policy and domain database, and authenticates network logons. See also *domain controller.*

Server service A Windows NT service that supplies an API for managing the Windows NT network software. Provides RPC (remote procedure call) support, and file, print, and named pipe sharing.

service A process that performs a specific system function and often provides an application programming interface (API) for other processes to call. Windows NT services are RPC-enabled, meaning that their API routines can be called from remote computers.

service controller The networking component that loads and starts Windows NT services and also loads and unloads many drivers, including device drivers and network transport drivers.

session A connection that two applications on different computers establish, use, and end. The Session layer performs name recognition and the functions needed to allow two applications to communicate over the network.

share To make resources, such as directories, printers, and ClipBook pages, available to network users.

share name The name of a shared resource.

shared directory A directory that network users can connect to.

shared resource Any device, data, or program that is used by more than one other device or program. For Windows NT, shared resources refer to any resource that is made available to network users, such as directories, files, printers, and named pipes.

SID See *Security ID*.

SMB Server message block.

socket Provides an end point to a connection; two sockets form a complete path. A socket works as a bidirectional pipe for incoming and outgoing data between networked computers. The Windows Sockets API is a networking API tailored for use by programmers using the Microsoft Windows family of products.

source directory The directory that contains the file or files you intend to copy or move.

spooler A scheduler for the printing process. It coordinates activity among other components of the print model and schedules all print jobs arriving at the print server.

string A data structure composed of a sequence of characters, usually representing human-readable text.

stubs Nonexecutable placeholders used by calls from the server environment.

subject The combination of the user's access token plus the program acting on the user's behalf. Windows NT uses subjects to track and manage permissions for the programs each user runs. A *simple subject* is a process that was assigned a security context when the corresponding user logged on. A *server subject* is a process implemented as a protected server (such as the Win32 subsystem) and does have other subjects as clients.

Subnet masks Under TCP/IP, 32-bit values that allow the recipient of IP packets to distinguish the network ID portion of the IP address from the host ID.

swap file See *paging file*.

synchronize To replicate the domain database from the domain controller to one server of the domain or to all the servers of a domain. This is usually performed automatically by the system, but can also be invoked manually by an administrator.

synchronous I/O The simplest way to perform I/O, by synchronizing the execution of applications with completion of the I/O operations that they request. When an application performs an I/O operation, the application's processing is blocked. When the I/O operation is complete, the application is allowed to continue processing. See also *asynchronous I/O*.

syntax The order in which you must type a command and the elements that follow the command. Windows NT commands have up to four elements: command name, parameters, switches, and values.

system default profile
For Windows NT Advanced Server, the user profile that is loaded when Windows NT is running and no user is logged on. When the Welcome dialog box is visible, the system default profile is loaded. See also *user default profile, user profile*.

system partition The volume that contains the hardware-specific files needed to load Windows NT. See also *partition*.

T

TCP/IP transport Transmission Control Protocol/Internet Protocol. The primary wide area network (WAN) transport protocol used by Windows NT to communicate with systems on TCP/IP networks and to participate in UNIX-based bulletin boards and electronic mail services.

TDI See *Transport Driver Interface*.

Telnet service The service that provides basic terminal emulation to remote systems supporting the Telnet protocol over TCP/IP.

text file A file containing only letters, numbers, and symbols. A text file contains no formatting information, except possibly linefeeds and carriage returns. A text file is an ASCII file.

thread An executable entity that belongs to a single process, comprising a program counter, a user-mode stack, a kernel-mode stack, and a set of register values. All threads in a process have equal access to the processor's address space, object handles, and other resources. In Windows NT, threads are implemented as objects.

thunking The transformation between 16-bit and 32-bit formats, which is carried out by a separate layer in the VDM.

Ti The inactivity timer in a transport protocol.

time-out If a device is not performing a task, the amount of time the computer should wait before detecting it as an error.

time slice The amount of processor time allocated to an application, usually measured in milliseconds.

Transport Driver Interface (TDI) In the networking model, a common interface for network components that communicate at the Session layer.

transport protocol Defines how data should be presented to the next receiving layer in the networking model and packages the data accordingly. It passes data to the network adapter card driver through the *NDIS* Interface, and to the *redirector* through the *Transport Driver Interface*.

trust relationship Trust relationships are links between domains that enable pass-through authentication, in which a user has only one user account in one domain, yet can access the entire network. A trusting domain honors the logon authentications of a trusted domain.

U

UDP See *user datagram protocol.*

UI frames Used by the NBF protocol to establish connections and for connectionless services such as datagrams.

UNC See *uniform naming convention names.*

Unicode A fixed-width, 16-bit character encoding standard capable of representing all of the world's scripts.

uniform naming convention (UNC) names
Filenames or other resource names that begin with the string \\, indicating that they exist on a remote computer.

user account Consists of all the information that defines a user to Windows NT. This includes the user name and password required for the user to log on, the groups in which the user account has membership, and the rights and permissions the user has for using the system and accessing its resources. See also *group.*

user datagram protocol (UDP) A TCP complement that offers a connectionless datagram service that guarantees neither delivery nor correct sequencing of delivered packets (much like IP).

user default profile For Windows NT Advanced Server, the user profile that is loaded by a server when a user's assigned profile cannot be accessed for any reason, when a user without an assigned profile logs on to the computer for the first time, or when a user logs on to the Guest account. See also *system default profile, user profile.*

user mode A nonprivileged processor mode in which application code runs.

user profile Configuration information retained on a user-by-user basis. The information includes all the per-user settings of the Windows NT environment, such as the desktop arrangement, personal program groups and the program items in those groups, screen colors, screen savers, network connections, printer connections, mouse settings, window size and position, and more. When a user logs on, the user's profile is loaded, and the user's Windows NT environment is configured according to that profile.

user right See *right.*

username A unique name identifying a user account to Windows NT. An account's username cannot be identical to any other group name or username of its own domain or workstation. See also *user account.*

V

validation Authorization check of a user's logon information. When a user logs on to an account on a Windows NT workstation, the authentication is performed by that workstation. When a user logs on to an account on a Windows NT Advanced Server domain, that authentication may be performed by any server of that domain. See also *trust relationship.*

value entry A parameter under a key or subkey in the Registry. A value entry appears as a string with three components: a name, a type, and the value.

value name The first of three components that make up a Registry value entry.

VDM See *virtual DOS machine.*

virtual DOS machine (VDM) A Windows NT-protected subsystem that supplies a complete MS-DOS environment and a console in which to run an MS-DOS–based application or Windows 16-bit applications. A VDM is a Win32 application that establishes a complete virtual *x*86 (that is, 80386 or higher) computer running MS-DOS. Any number of VDMs can run simultaneously. See also *console*.

virtual memory Space on a hard disk that Windows NT uses as if it were actually memory. Windows NT does this through the use of paging files. The benefit of using virtual memory is that you can run more applications at onc time than your system's physical memory would otherwise allow. The drawbacks are the disk space required for the virtual-memory paging file and the decreased execution speed when swapping is required.

virtual printer memory In a PostScript printer, a part of memory that stores font information. The memory in PostScript printers is divided into banded memory and virtual memory. The banded memory contains graphics and page-layout information needed to print your documents. The virtual memory contains any font information that is sent to your printer either when you print a document or when you download fonts.

volume A partition or collection of partitions that have been formatted for use by a file system.

W

wildcard A character that represents one or more characters. The question mark (?) wildcard can be used to represent any single character, and the asterisk (*) wildcard can be used to represent any character or group of characters that might match that position in other filenames.

Win32 API A 32-bit application programming interface for both Windows for MS-DOS and Windows NT. It updates earlier versions of the Windows API with sophisticated operating system capabilities, security, and API routines for displaying text-based applications in a window.

Windows NT The portable, secure, 32-bit, preemptive multitasking member of the Microsoft Windows operating system family.

Windows NT Advanced Server A superset of Windows NT, Windows NT Advanced Server provides centralized management and security, advanced fault tolerance, and additional connectivity.

Windows on Win32 (WOW) A Windows NT-protected subsystem that runs within a virtual DOS machine (VDM) process. It provides a 16-bit Windows environment capable of running any number of 16-bit Windows applications under Windows NT.

workgroup For Windows NT, a workgroup is a collection of computers running Windows NT and/or Windows for Workgroups that are grouped for browsing and sharing purposes. Each workgroup is identified by a unique name. User accounts maintained on workgroup servers are local to the servers themselves, that is, each server maintains all accounts for users wanting to share its resources. See also *domain*.

workstation In general, a powerful computer having considerable calculating and graphics capability. For Windows NT, computers running the Windows NT operating system are called workstations, as distinguished from computers running Windows NT Advanced Server, which are called servers. See also *server, domain controller*.

Workstation service A Windows NT service that supplies user-mode API routines to manage the Windows NT redirector. Provides network connections and communications.

WOW The subsystem for running Windows for MS-DOS under Windows NT; sometimes also called Win16 on Win32.

x86-based computer A computer using a microprocessor equivalent to an Intel® 80386 or higher chip. Compare with a *RISC-based computer.*

Index

X

The following list of trademarks and trademark owners is continued from page ii.

Ungermann-Bass is a registered trademark of Ungermann-Bass, Inc. Unicode is a trademark of Unicode, Inc. UNIX is a registered trademark of UNIX Systems Laboratories. Unisys is a registered trademark of Unisys Corp. Video Seven is a trademark of Headland Technology, Inc. VMS and DEC are registered trademarks and Alpha AXP, Pathworks, VT-100, and DECnet are trademarks of Digital Equipment Corp. Western Digital is a trademark of Western Digital Corp. WYSIfonts is a registered trademark of Softcraft, Inc. Wyse is a registered trademark of Wyse Technology. Xerox, SmallTalk, and XNS are registered trademarks of Xerox Corp.

Microsoft® Win32™ Programmer's References

This is the official documentation for the Microsoft Win32 Software Development Kit (SDK).
It's the resource material that you'll need to turn to during the design and development of a
Win32-based application. The *Programmer's References* contain overview material on systems, services,
Window management, and the Graphics Device Interface, as well as the alphabetical Application
Programming Interface (API) references and information about messages, structures, and data types.

Microsoft® Win32™ Programmer's Reference, Vol. 1
Window Management and Graphics Device Interface
896 pages, softcover $20.00 ($26.95 Canada) ISBN 1-55615-515-8

Microsoft® Win32™ Programmer's Reference, Vol. 2
System Services, Multimedia, Extensions, and Application Notes
1040 pages, softcover $20.00 ($26.95 Canada) ISBN 1-55615-516-6

Microsoft® Win32™ Programmer's Reference, Vol. 3
Functions (A-G)
768 pages, softcover $20.00 ($26.95 Canada) ISBN 1-55615-517-4

Microsoft® Win32™ Programmer's Reference, Vol. 4
Functions (H-Z)
800 pages, softcover $20.00 ($26.95 Canada) ISBN 1-55615-518-2

Microsoft® Win32™ Programmer's Reference, Vol. 5
Messages, Structures, and Macros
704 pages, softcover $20.00 ($26.95 Canada) ISBN 1-55615-519-0

Essential Resources from Microsoft Press

Solid Programming Advice

Code Complete

Steve McConnell

This practical handbook of software construction covers the art and science of the entire development process, from design to testing. Examples are provided in C, Pascal, Basic, Fortran, and Ada—but the focus is on programming techniques. Topics includ upfront planning, applying good design techniques to construction, using data effectively, reviewing for errors, managing construction activities, and relating personal character to superior software.

880 pages, softcover $35.00 ($44.95 Canada)   ISBN 1-55615-484-4

Writing Solid Code
Microsoft Techniques for Developing Bug-Free C Programs

Steve Maguire

Foreword by Dave Moore, Director of Development, Microsoft Corporation

Written by a former Microsoft developer and troubleshooter, this book is an insider's view of the most important aspect of the development process: preventing and detecting bugs. Maguire identifies the places developers typically make mistakes and offers practical advice for detecting costly mistakes. Includes proven programming techniques for producing clean code.

228 pages, softcover $24.95 ($32.95 Canada)   ISBN 1-55615-551-4

Programming Windows™ 3.1, 3rd ed.

Charles Petzold

"If you're going to program for Windows, buy this book. It will pay for itself in a matter of hours."   **Computer Language**

The programming classic for both new Windows 3.1 programmers and owners of previous editions. It's packed with indispensable reference data, tested programming advice, keen insight, and page after page of sample programs. This edition includes two disks that contain the source code and associated files from the book.

1008 pages, softcover with one 1.44-MB 3.5-inch disk
$49.95 ($67.95 Canada)   ISBN 1-55615-395-3

Microsoft Press books are available wherever quality computer books are sold and through CompuServe's Electronic Mall—GO MSP.
Or call 1-800-MSPRESS for ordering information or for placing credit card orders.*
Please refer to BBK when placing your order. Prices subject to change.

*In Canada, contact Macmillan Canada, Attn: Microsoft Press Dept., 164 Commander Blvd., Agincourt, Ontario, Canada M1S 3C7, or call (416) 293-8141.
In the U.K., contact Microsoft Press, 27 Wrights Lane, London W8 5TZ. All other international orders will be forwarded to the appropriate distributor.

IMPORTANT — READ CAREFULLY BEFORE OPENING SOFTWARE PACKET(S).
By opening the sealed packet(s) containing the software, you indicate your acceptance
of the following Microsoft License Agreement.

Microsoft License Agreement

MICROSOFT LICENSE AGREEMENT
(Resource Kit Companion Disks)

This is a legal agreement between you (either an individual or an entity) and Microsoft Corporation. By opening the sealed software packet(s) you are agreeing to be bound by the terms of this agreement. If you do not agree to the terms of this agreement, promptly return the unopened software packet(s) and any accompanying written materials to the place you obtained them for a full refund.

MICROSOFT SOFTWARE LICENSE

1. GRANT OF LICENSE. Microsoft grants to you the right to make and use copies of the Microsoft software program included with this book (the "SOFTWARE") for your internal use. The SOFTWARE is in "use" on a computer when it is loaded into temporary memory (i.e.. RAM) or installed into permanent memory (e.g., hard disk, CD-ROM, or other storage device) of that computer.

2. COPYRIGHT. The SOFTWARE is owned by Microsoft or its suppliers and is protected by United States copyright laws and international treaty provisions. Therefore, you must treat the SOFTWARE like any other copyrighted material (e.g., a book or musical recording). You may not copy the written materials accompanying the SOFTWARE.

3. OTHER RESTRICTIONS. You may not rent or lease the SOFTWARE, but you may transfer the SOFTWARE and accompanying written materials on a permanent basis provided you retain no copies and the recipient agrees to the terms of this Agreement. You may not reverse engineer, decompile, or disassemble the SOFTWARE. If the SOFTWARE is an update or has been updated, any transfer must include the most recent update and all prior versions.

DISCLAIMER OF WARRANTY

The SOFTWARE (including instructions for its use) is provided "AS IS" WITHOUT WARRANTY OF ANY KIND. MICROSOFT FURTHER DISCLAIMS ALL IMPLIED WARRANTIES INCLUDING WITHOUT LIMITATION ANY IMPLIED WARRANTIES OF MERCHANTABILITY OR OF FITNESS FOR A PARTICULAR PURPOSE OR AGAINST INFRINGE-MENT. THE ENTIRE RISK ARISING OUT OF THE USE OR PERFORMANCE OF THE SOFTWARE AND DOCUMENTA-TION REMAINS WITH YOU.

IN NO EVENT SHALL MICROSOFT, ITS AUTHORS, OR ANYONE ELSE INVOLVED IN THE CREATION, PRODUCTION, OR DELIVERY OF THE SOFTWARE BE LIABLE FOR ANY DAMAGES WHATSOEVER (INCLUDING, WITHOUT LIMITATION, DAMAGES FOR LOSS OF BUSINESS PROFITS, BUSINESS INTERRUPTION, LOSS OF BUSI-NESS INFORMATION, OR OTHER PECUNIARY LOSS) ARISING OUT OF THE USE OF OR INABILITY TO USE THE SOFTWARE OR DOCUMENTATION, EVEN IF MICROSOFT HAS BEEN ADVISED OF THE POSSIBILITY OF SUCH DAMAGES. BECAUSE SOME STATES/COUNTRIES DO NOT ALLOW THE EXCLUSION OR LIMITATION OF LIABILITY FOR CONSEQUENTIAL OR INCIDENTAL DAMAGES, THE ABOVE LIMITATION MAY NOT APPLY TO YOU.

U.S. GOVERNMENT RESTRICTED RIGHTS

The SOFTWARE and documentation are provided with RESTRICTED RIGHTS. Use, duplication, or disclosure by the Government is subject to restrictions as set forth in subparagraph (c)(1)(ii) of The Rights in Technical Data and Computer Software clause at DFARS 252.227-7013 or subparagraphs (c)(1) and (2) of the Commercial Computer Software — Restricted Rights 48 CFR 52.227-19, as applicable. Manufacturer is Microsoft Corporation/One Microsoft Way/Redmond, WA 98052-6399.

If you acquired this product in the United States, this Agreement is governed by the laws of the State of Washington.

Should you have any questions concerning this Agreement, or if you desire to contact Microsoft Press for any reason, please write: Microsoft Press/One Microsoft Way/Redmond, WA 98052-6399.

08/03/93   32100017.DOC